STENDHAL
The education of a novelist

COMPANION STUDIES

Odette de Mourgues: *Racine: or, The Triumph of Relevance*
Ronald Gray: *Goethe, a Critical Introduction*
R. F. Christian: *Tolstoy, a Critical Introduction*
C. B. Morris: *A Generation of Spanish Poets, 1920–1936*
Richard Peace: *Dostoyevsky, an Examination of the Major Novels*
John Bayley: *Pushkin, a Comparative Commentary*
Dorothy Gabe Coleman: *Rabelais: a Critical Study in Prose Fiction*
W. E. Yates: *Grillparzer, a Critical Introduction*
John Northam: *Ibsen, a Critical Study*
Ronald Gray: *Franz Kafka*

Other volumes in preparation

STENDHAL

The education of a novelist

GEOFFREY STRICKLAND

Lecturer in French, University of Reading

CAMBRIDGE UNIVERSITY PRESS

Published by the Syndics of the Cambridge University Press
Bentley House, 200 Euston Road, London NW1 2DB
American Branch: 32 East 57th Street, New York, N.Y.10022

Library of Congress Catalogue Card Number: 73-91619

ISBNS:
0 521 20385 6 Hard covers
0 521 09837 8 Paperback

First published 1974

Printed in Great Britain
at the University Printing House, Cambridge
(Brooke Crutchley, University Printer)

In memory of my father
Reginald Bertram Strickland (1887-1965)
Royal Engineers

Contents

Acknowledgments ix

A note on the quotations and references xi

1 The life and times of Henri Beyle
Introduction   1
An age of cant   8
The childhood of Henri Beyle   18
Coming of age in post-Revolutionary France   21

2 Le Beylisme
Beylisme and 'de-Rousseauisation'   27
Beylisme and Utilitarianism   33
De l'amour and *D'un nouveau complot contre les industriels*   44

3 Beyle the critic
Beyle and heroic drama   52
'Le style est ceci'   63
The discovery of a 'natural' style   72
'Le plus grand plaisir possible'   79
'Le beau idéal' in painting   89
'Le beau idéal' in music   94

4 The chronicler and historian
Beyle and Napoleon   99
Italy and the eruption of energy   107
The chronicler of contemporary France   114
History and truth   121

5 *Le rouge et le noir*
The problem of form 126
'Apprendre à vouloir' 135
'Scènes probantes' and the historical revelation 145
The mind of the assassin and the language of the author 149
Two kinds of heroism 156

6 *Lucien Leuwen* and autobiography
Souvenirs d'égotisme 165
Lucien Leuwen, part one 171
Lucien Leuwen, part two 190
Lucien Leuwen and the critic 208
La vie de Henry Brulard 212

7 *La chartreuse de Parme*
Le rose et le vert and *Les chroniques italiennes* 220
Fabrice and Clélia 224
Mosca and Gina 237
Lamiel and *Suora Scolastica* 254

8 Some conclusions 259

Notes to the text 267

Chronological table 288

Index 293

Acknowledgments

I originally planned to write an account of the relation between Beyle's novels and his criticism as a doctorate thesis for the University of Paris. The fact that I never completed it is not entirely due to my indolence – the more I came to enjoy his poise and intelligence, the more daunting my chosen subject came to seem; nor can I pretend I was not encouraged. Mr H. A. Mason, my supervisor at Cambridge, communicated to me some of his own enthusiasm and gave me my first copy of *La vie de Henry Brulard* and his own notes on Beyle and his contemporaries. Professor Vittorio del Litto, the late Pierre Moreau and Professor Robert Escarpit gave me their valuable time and attention and both the Office des Universités in 1954 and the Centre National de Recherche Scientifique in 1964 gave me generous grants enabling me to spend two periods of uninterrupted study in the Bibliothèque Nationale in Paris and the Bibliothèque Municipale in Grenoble. I have also been helped considerably by the students with whom I have discussed Beyle's work in the University of Reading, in Scripps College, California and the University of California at Los Angeles and by the comments on what I have written by various colleagues and friends. I should like to mention especially Mrs Marie-Pierrette Allum, Mme Gaynor Bartagnan, Mr Michael Black, Dr Margaret Davies, Mr Norman Henfrey, Professor B. C. J. G. Knight, Professor Haydn Mason, Dr Walter Redfern, Mr Ian Robinson, Mr Morris Shapira, Professor Colin Smith, my brother Edward Gale Strickland and Professor Stephen Werner. I wish to acknowledge my debt to all those who have helped me and not least of all to Philothei for her encouragement, advice and patience.

Part of chapter 3 appeared originally in *The Human World* and I should like to thank the editors for permission to reproduce it here.

GEOFFREY STRICKLAND

Department of French Studies
University of Reading
April 1973

x

A note on the quotations and references

There is no standard edition of Stendhal's writings. The most reliable and the most carefully annotated – also the most sumptuously bound and most expensive – is that published in Geneva by the Cercle du Bibliophile under the direction of Vittorio del Litto and Ernest Abravanel. Many of the volumes in this collection, I gather, are to be reprinted in the Gallimard Pléïade series, while a new edition of *Lucien Leuwen* is being prepared by Professor del Litto for the Gallimard Livres de poche. This may also be the appropriate place in which to recommend the very inexpensive edition of *Racine et Shakspeare* published by J.-J. Pauvert in their admirable 'Libertés' collection and the edition of *D'un nouveau complot contre les industriels*, presented with an accompanying 'dossier' by P. Chartier and published by Flammarion.

Not all libraries can afford to keep up to date with new editions and not even collectors of Stendhal own all those that have appeared in the last fifty years. I have therefore decided to refer wherever possible to chapters of works by Stendhal and to the dates of letters and entries in his diaries and travel books. I refer to specific editions, usually Martineau's Divan or Pléïade editions, only where this is unavoidable.

All quotations are given in English, or in French, followed by a translation, in places where a tolerably adequate translation is impossible or where I wish to draw attention specifically to the language of the original. The translations are my own.

I

The life and times of Henri Beyle

Introduction

The reader of Stendhal who feels curious to know about his life and personality will find that there is no lack of easily available information. Few men have left a more minute record of their thoughts and sensations from one day to another and few lives have been studied with closer scholarly attention. Much of what he committed to paper over the years in letters, diaries, notebooks and in the margins of books, as well as in his unfinished autobiographies, has survived and can now be read in the carefully annotated editions of the late Henri Martineau and Professor Vittorio del Litto. Many of the enigmas with which biographers have been confronted have now been solved, though fresh information concerning Stendhal himself and the influences on his work still continues to be published regularly in *Stendhal Club,* the journal edited by Professor del Litto in Grenoble, Stendhal's birthplace.

My purpose in writing this book has been not to provide a summary of all that is now known about Stendhal the writer and Henri Beyle the man, or to add to this any new information, but to consider one particular aspect of his life and literary career. My subject, briefly, is the education of Stendhal: not merely the schooling which he underwent during his early years in Grenoble but the education which ended only with his sudden death in 1842. My argument is that the education took place and that Stendhal's writings, particularly in his later years, are those of a genuinely educated man. The phenomenon is not a common one and it is for this reason, I wish to argue, that

Stendhal's life and writings are of general interest. They illustrate what education can mean.

One of my reasons for saying this is that Beyle – as it may be more appropriate from now on to call him – seems to have belonged to the class of human beings for whom an education is never complete. Nietzsche, who was to describe himself as Beyle's 'posthumous son', has talked of those writers who are 'seekers' and of the irony of their being transformed into 'classics':

But how has our Philistine culture judged these seekers? As if they had found what they were looking for. It forgets that they never thought of themselves as anything other than seekers. 'We have a culture of our own', we then hear, 'because we have our classics. And not only have we the foundations of a culture. We have also the edifice and *we* are the edifice.' On which the Philistine proudly taps his forehead.[1]

One may be reminded here of what Beyle himself said towards the end of his life of his own literary talents: 'If there's another world, I shall certainly go and see Montesquieu. He may say: "My dear fellow, you had no talent at all." I shall be vexed if he does but not at all surprised. This is something I often feel: what eye can see itself?'[2] and of his letter to Balzac thanking him for his article on *La chartreuse de Parme* and replying to the criticism that the novel suffered from certain faults of con-struction: 'I see only one rule: *to be clear*. If I am not clear, *my whole world* is annihilated.'[3] These two quotations provide, I believe, one of the essential clues to Beyle's genius and to his art as a novelist.

Since the days of Nietzsche, Beyle too of course has become a 'classic'. (Nietzsche had found that few of his fellow academics were capable even of spelling Beyle's name.) Much of what has been written about him during the present century corre-sponds perfectly to what Nietzsche has said of the homage and attentions of the Philistine. The twentieth-century Stendhalian scholars differ in this respect from the nineteenth-century 'Beylistes' who established his present reputation, acknowledged gratefully what they had learned from him as men and who spoke of how he had opened their eyes to the world around them and its past. They differ, that is to say, from Taine, who spoke of Beyle as a *maître à penser* and a pioneer in the study of art and society, from those who saw in him the exponent of a way of life based on a revolutionary moral code, and above all from Nietzsche himself. No French critic that I know of has said more, for example, to suggest why Beyle should be thought of as an educated man. I quote from one of Nietzsche's few passing allusions to Beyle, allusions which have a Stendhalian quality in that they are tantalisingly brief and yet go straight to the point:

> In contrast to the German lack of experience and the German innocence *in voluptate psychologica*...and as the most perfect expression of a truly French curiosity and inventiveness in the domain of delicate sensations and emotions, there is Henri Beyle, that remarkable precursor and pioneer who, with Napoleonic impetuosity, made his way through *his own* Europe, through several centuries of the European spirit, exploring this spirit and submitting it to his scrutiny; it has taken us two generations to catch up with him, to become aware of some of the enigmas which tormented and thrilled this strange inquisitive Epicurean, who was the last of the great French psychologists.[4]

I have set out in writing this study to follow some of the implications of this passage.

The evidence on which my argument is based is to be found principally in the writings by which he is now best known, in *Le rouge et le noir*, in *La chartreuse de Parme* and in the unfinished *Lucien Leuwen*. It is to be found also, however, in the copious letters and notebooks published since his death, and in the journalism, criticism and popular travel books published during his own lifetime. These are practically the only documents from which a biographer can hope to draw any conclusions about his mind and character. Among his acquaintances there was no Boswell or Eckermann, and the French custom of publishing the table talk of famous men had gone out of fashion before he was born. Consequently there are no accounts of his conversation anywhere near as detailed as those that survive of Boileau's, Dr Johnson's or Goethe's. Even Mérimée's little memoir, *H.B.* tells us disappointingly little of Beyle the talker and what we are told is related in a tone of amused if affectionate superiority which may have dictated the choice of reminiscence. The main impression one gathers from Mérimée's anecdotes and from those of others who know him is that Beyle's conversation was witty and outrageous, though Lamartine also tells us that it was learned and instructive whereas he was expecting it to be blasphemous.[5] From Beyle's earliest years, the education he acquired was one that he saw as serving one particular end. 'Few men have prepared themselves to write with so much effort and conscientiousness as the young Beyle', wrote Jean Prévost.[6] Beyle's literary ambitions date apparently from the age of twelve or thirteen when he began the habit of voracious reading which was to last throughout his life and wrote a comedy based on the *Nouvelles* of Florian. The comedy was never performed and none of the plays which he planned and worked on for the next twenty-five years was ever completed, even though the manuscript of one of them, *Letellier*, which was to have been a satirical drama of the intellectual world under the despotism of Napoleon, accompanied him on his many travels through Europe and even on the retreat from Moscow. In 1826, at the age of forty-three, he began work on his first novel, to console himself, he writes, for the separation from his mistress, the comtesse Curial. The novel, *Armance*, was completed and published in a few months, and from then on he wrote quickly, and without any of the inhibitions he had known as a dramatist, the stories and novels for which he has since become famous. Beyle's long 'apprenticeship', as Prévost calls it, was continued under conditions and over a period of time that would have discouraged almost any other man. Even when he finally found himself as a writer, he enjoyed little popular success except as an amusingly outrageous pamphleteer and he was forced to console himself with the thought that his novels would perhaps be read in 1935. Most of his comments on his lack of success are made, however, with stoical cheerfulness and he appears to have suffered far more from the miseries and frustrations he experienced as a lover than from those of disappointed ambition. For one thing, his ambition involved far more than merely 'being a writer' and enjoying the prestige which goes with the rôle. Nor is it easy to think of him as a martyr to his art. The patience and stubbornness with which he pursued his apprenticeship were not those of a dedicated craftsman wrestling with an intractable subject or medium. In this respect, as in many others, he was very different from

Gustave Flaubert. 'What is my aim?', Beyle wrote at the age of twenty. 'To be the greatest poet possible.' (With characteristic precision and realism even when writing in a mood of exaltation, he does not say, for example, 'the greatest poet of my time'.) 'For this I must know man perfectly. In poetry style is of secondary importance.'[7]

Beyle's single-mindedness lay principally in the way he set out to realise the second of these ambitions, 'to know man perfectly'. The oddity of the phrase to the modern reader is a reminder of how much he was influenced by the fashionable psychology and philosophy of his early years. ('What is general grammar? What is its purpose? What is man?' were questions to which the boys were expected to find an answer in one of the newly-created Ecoles Centrales in 1799.[8]) Beyle outgrew the optimistic belief that he would ever understand human nature 'perfectly', but the ambition to understand it as well as it was humanly possible never left him. Nor did his preoccupation with a small number of 'principal ideas'. 'By instinct', he wrote towards the end of his life in *La vie de Henry Brulard*, 'my whole moral existence has been spent in considering attentively five or six principal ideas and in trying to understand in what ways they are true.'[9] And again:

Madame Le Brun, today marquise de la Grave, told me that all those who attended her little salon were astonished by my complete silence. I was silent by instinct, I felt that no one would understand me...It was the only way in which I could maintain a little personal dignity. If ever I see that very wise woman again, I must question her closely to find out what I was like in those days. I myself haven't the least idea. I can only tell the degree of happiness which my organism experiences. As I have gone on ever since penetrating deeper into the same ideas, how can I tell what stage I had reached then? The shaft was only ten feet deep, each year I have added another five. Now that it is a hundred and ninety feet deep, how can I have any conception of what it seemed like in 1800 when it was only ten?[10]

Beyle's writings over the years confirm this impression. So too do the concentration and ease of his major novels written in a prose which, as Prévost puts it, 'conveys in a few hastily thrown off pages the long progressive refinement of his mind'.[11] It is easy, however, to mistake the originality and independence of Beyle's mind for an imperviousness to external influences, to think of him as habitually unobservant, self-preoccupied and given to introspective reveries. This has been the tendency of many of Beyle's modern critics. It is even implied by Prévost, though perhaps unintentionally, for his book on Stendhal was finished hastily during the Second World War shortly before his death in action and, by a tragic coincidence, fighting with the Resistance in the mountains above Grenoble. Beyle, as he points out, was essentially a critic, though he leaves us with little idea how fine a critic. Because of this Beyle was not only able to see through or ignore what was merely fashionable. He was also able to respond whole-heartedly to all that appealed to his finer instinct, to follow his instinct without misgiving, and to learn in this way from the experience of others. There is a passage from a review by the young Henry James of A. A. Paton's life of Beyle which puts what I am trying to say far better than I am able to myself:

In repudiating Mr Paton's assumption that he is a light writer, we would fain express that singular something which is fairly described neither as serious nor solemn – a kind of painful tension of feeling under the disguise of the coolest and easiest style. It is the tension in part of conceit – the conceit which leads him with every tenth phrase to prophesy in the most trenchant manner the pass to which 'les sots' will have brought things within such and such a period – and in part of aspiration, of deep enjoyment of some bold touch of nature or some fine stroke of art. This bespeaks the restlessness of a superior mind, and makes our total feeling for Beyle a kindly one. We recommend his books to persons of 'sensibility' whose moral convictions have somewhat solidified. [12]

Prévost's study gives us little idea of Beyle's capacity to learn and enjoy and it tells us little of the influences by which he was formed. It is true that these influences have been much exaggerated and that scholars who dwell on them rarely show us the ways in which other men's ideas became his own. The task of deciding what Beyle learned, whether or not he was conscious of learning, is extremely delicate. But it is also indispensable if we are to understand more than a little of what he wrote and became. T. S. Eliot's well-known remarks on 'tradition' are made with specific reference to poetry but their relevance here will, I hope, seem obvious:

We dwell with satisfaction upon the poet's difference from his predecessors, especially his immediate predecessors; we endeavour to find something that can be isolated in order to be enjoyed. Whereas if we approach a poet without this prejudice we shall often find that not only the best, but the most individual parts of his work may be those in which the dead poets, his ancestors, assert their immortality most vigorously. And I do not mean the impressionable period of adolescence, but the period of full maturity.

Yet if the only form of tradition, of handing down, consisted in following the ways of the immediate generation before us in a blind or timid adherence to its successes, 'tradition' should positively be discouraged. We have seen many such simple currents soon lost in the sand; and novelty is better than repetition. Tradition is a matter of much wider significance. It cannot be inherited and if you want it you must obtain it by great labour. It involves, in the first place, the historical sense, which we may call nearly indispensable to anyone who would continue to be a poet beyond his twenty-fifth year...This historical sense, which is a sense of the timeless as well as the temporal, is what makes a writer traditional. And it is at the same time what makes a writer most acutely conscious of his place in time, of his own contemporaneity.[13]

Nietzsche has described the nature of Beyle's 'historical sense' in a passage which I have quoted already. I wish to show in the following chapters some of the ways in which Beyle acquired it and at the same time became aware of his 'place in time, of his own contemporaneity'.

In order to do this it is necessary to distinguish between the various influences which Beyle underwent and resisted. And it would be absurd to argue as if these were merely philosophical or literary. Beyle was very much a man of the world, a role he cultivated conscientiously despite his liability to attacks of shyness. Few men have observed more attentively the customs and beliefs of the society they lived in, and few men have been more affected by these beliefs, more acutely aware of the ways in which they resembled or differed from their own. He was born in 1783, during the last years of the *ancien régime*, the son of a lawyer and landowner of royalist convictions, served under Napoleon as a civil servant travelling with the Imperial armies and died under the 'bourgeois' monarchy of Louis Philippe, whom he represented as consul in the port of Civita Vecchia. The 'ideas' he talks about in *La vie de Henry Brulard* and which occupied his thoughts throughout most of his life owe much to the influences of his boyhood and youth. It is partly because of this that in later years his writings had little popular success, while he himself was famous chiefly as an eccentric. The profound political and social changes which Beyle witnessed went with an inevitable transformation in customs and beliefs of the most ordinary-seeming kind. Beyle refused, or was perhaps unable, to change with his contemporaries, to conform merely for the sake of conforming to new moral and religious codes or to follow new fashions in philosophy. In order therefore to understand his evolution, it is necessary to consider, if only briefly, certain of the widespread popular beliefs of his boyhood and youth. These beliefs may have influenced his mind far more profoundly and permanently than much of the literature and philosophy he read. Often in fact they help us to understand why he read with enthusiasm writers whom today it is difficult to imagine being read even with sustained attention. The beliefs are in themselves simple enough and easy to summarise, so much so that it may be difficult to understand why they were held by men who, like Beyle himself, were far from simple-minded. Their strength and, despite this, their rapid widespread decline can easily be traced though far less easily explained. We may succeed in understanding them more clearly perhaps if we take them in the right order and consider first among the changes between the France of Beyle's childhood and that of his later years the changes in the function of the Catholic Church and in the attitude of wealthy citizens to organised religion and to the traditional Christian virtues.

An age of cant

'...all our words, manners, religion, morals, and our whole mind and existence in modern Europe, turn upon one single hinge, which the English in one expressive word call cant.'

(Byron in a letter to the Rev. C. Bowles quoted by Beyle in an article in *The London Magazine* for October 1826.)

Beyle was a child of six when the newly constituted National Assembly ordered the seizure of the enormous properties belonging to the Catholic Church in France and placed them 'at the disposal of the nation'. In the following year the Civil Constitution of the Clergy was approved, according to which bishops and parish priests should henceforth he appointed by the elective assemblies of each department and paid according to a fixed salary by the state. The Reign of Terror, which followed the invasion of France by the armies of the Duke of Brunswick and the royalist revolts in the south and west, was directed partly against the Church, which in 1793 was virtually disestablished, though many of its priests had refused in any case to accept their new role as elected functionaries. Grenoble remained calm during the Civil War and the Terror but Beyle's father was a royalist and devoutly catholic and Beyle recalls how during this period there would always be a priest or two living in hiding in their home. One of them revolted him by the bolt-eyed way in which he would wolf his food.

The Terror ended throughout the country after a series of military victories had ensured the survival of the new régime. Yet the régime, as we know, was to undergo what may have seemed like a wholly unexpected transformation. The decisive victories of Desaix in Italy and of Moreau at Hohenlinden and the conclusion of the Revolutionary Wars might have been expected to lead to a consolidation of what had been achieved ten years earlier: the creation of certain democratic institutions and the abolition of hereditary privileges or of the special privileges of any one religious sect; to the establishment, that is, of a social order like that which exists in France today. Instead of this, Napoleon was created Emperor of the French 'by the grace of God', the ceremony taking place in Notre Dame only ten years after the ceremonies in the same cathedral in honour of the goddess Reason. Priests were once again paid from the public exchequer (as well, it is true, as Protestant ministers) and Roman Catholicism recognised as the religion, if not of the state, 'of the majority of French citizens'. Napoleon's own relations with the Vatican were clearly not always of the most amicable. Yet in a decree of 1808 he stipulated that the 'basic principles of education' in the Empire should be 'firstly the precepts of the Catholic religion and the maxims on which are founded the organic laws of different creeds; secondly, fidelity to the Emperor, to the Imperial monarchy, guarantor of the people's welfare...; thirdly, obedience to the statutes of the teaching profession', etc. The Church honoured the new *entente* in its own way; in its catechisms, for example, in which fidelity to the Emperor and the Imperial dynasty was included among the duties of the Christian, failure to comply with which might lead to eternal punishment.[14] The fall of Napoleon and of Charles X were not, in either case, accompanied by fundamental changes in the relationship between Church and State and the Church continued to enjoy most of the privileges granted to it under Napoleon until its final disestablishment in 1904.

The religious and educational policies of Napoleon and his successors received the support of large sections of the middle and upper classes including many whose support had rendered possible the anti-ecclesiastical policies of the various Revolutionary governments. The rationalistic and deistic anti-clericalism which had inspired these policies survived, but generally in a more subdued and conciliatory form. Voltaire, Diderot and Helvétius continued to be read but their influence was counteracted by that of the most powerfully influential work of the first half of the nineteenth century, Chateaubriand's *Génie du christianisme*, published two years before the coronation of the Emperor. Chateaubriand had been an officer in the émigré armies which fought against the Republic, and though *Le génie du christianisme* is couched in terms that will appeal to the religious sceptic whose main concern is not with dogma but with the state of 'civilisation', it is an apology for orthodox Catholicism and an attack on the 'sophistry' of the eighteenth century. Voltaire, he writes, 'had the fatal talent, writing as he did for an amiable and capricious nation, which enabled him to render fashionable incredulity in matters of religion...His destructive system spread throughout France. It became established in the provincial academies, which became so many sources of faction and bad taste. Fashionable ladies and grave philosophers occupied chairs of scepticism.' His own intention was to prove that 'of all the religions which have existed, the Christian religion is the most poetic, the most human, the most favourable to liberty, to the arts and to literature; that the modern world owes to Christianity everything from agriculture to the abstract sciences, from the shelters and almshouses for the poor and indigent to the temples built by Michaelangelo and adorned by Raphael'.[15]

No work did more to determine the form taken by French Romanticism during the first three decades of the century.

Lamartine and the young Vigny, Victor Hugo and Sainte Beuve often seem like versifiers of Chateaubriand's noble declamatory prose. Yet the reasons for Chateaubriand's success and influence were almost certainly far more fundamental than his own obvious genius and Celtic powers of persuasion. And to understand Beyle's career and his general dislike for Chateaubriand's prose and for French – as opposed to either English or Italian – Romanticism, it is necessary to consider what these reasons may have been.

One reason for the decline of anti-clerical feeling after the Revolution is offered by Professor Charles Morazé in his sketch for a study of the French middle classes. The widespread popularity, Morazé argues, of anti-religious ideas in the eighteenth century and of an idealistic secular humanism, can be explained partly in economic terms. For the middle-class merchants and their dependents, the Church and the monastic orders, because of their enormous wealth and their commercial and fiscal privileges, were an obstacle to their own enrichment. If Voltaire and the Encyclopédistes were read with enthusiasm, it was because '...a century of philosophy had gilded the aspirations of the productive classes with a number of doctrines'.[16] If the same classes after 1804 tolerated the revival of the Church, it was again because this was, to say the very least, in no way against their own interests. After the seizure and sale of Church property and the abolition of its commercial privileges, the Church ceased to function as a major economic rival. And in agreeing to the terms of the Concordat with Bonaparte, the Vatican had wisely refrained from pressing for a restitution of either. There is no reason to believe then that the Catholic revival coincided with a revival of genuine faith. On the contrary. Under the Empire and the Bourbon Restoration '...the church and the temple are forsaken and if they are attended at all, it is for the sake of fashion or good form and as a result of the influence of the old nobility whose prestige in matters of everyday behaviour is all the greater since it has become harmless. Fundamentally, however, Christianity is no more now than a form of art. It is no longer a faith.'[17] Morazé's analysis of the conventional religiosity of the early nineteenth century is corroborated by some of the more perceptive writers of the day, by Gérard de Nerval, for example, who is not usually credited with insight of this kind, a comment perhaps on the survival until recently of the nineteenth century's own conventional view of itself:

There is certainly something more terrifying in history than the fall of empires; the death of religions. Volney himself experienced this sentiment when visiting the ruins of edifices which had once been sacred. This impression is perhaps unknown to the true believer, but a man who shares the scepticism of our times shudders occasionally when he sees so many sombre doors opening on the void.

There is one door which still seems to lead somewhere – the pointed doorway whose Gothic ribs and broken and defaced statuettes have been piously restored and through which can still be seen the elegant nave lit by the magical stained glass of the rose-windows. The faithful surge forward over the marble flags and past the whitened columns on which can be seen the coloured reflections of saints and angels. The incense burns, the voices resound, the Latin hymn and its accompaniment are raised high to the vaulted ceiling. But beware of the unhealthy breath rising from the feudal tombs where so many kings are heaped together! They have been disturbed from their eternal rest by the irreligion of the last century and piously re-interred by our own.

Why should one care about the shattered tombs and desecrated bones of Saint-Denis? The hatred of the desecrators was a kind of homage; their restoration today is the work of indifference. They have been restored out of a love of symmetry, as if they were mummies in an Egyptian museum.

However, what creed is there which when it has triumphed over the forces of impiety has not more to fear from simple indifference? What Catholic would not prefer to think of the crazy orgies of Newstead Abbey and of the drinking companions of Noel Byron setting drinking songs to parodies of plain chant, dressed as monks and drinking claret out of skulls, rather than see the ancient abbey turned into a museum? There is true religious feeling in the wild laughter of Byron and in the materialistic impiety of Shelley. But today who would deign even to be impious? One wouldn't dream of such a thing.[18]

The pervasiveness of the conventions which were to identify poetic feeling and moral decency with religious observance and belief can be seen in the work of those who in everyday life were to confess their own religious scepticism. It is seen, for example, in Vigny's extraordinary and in its own time popular allegory, *Eloa*, the story of a tear shed by Christ, transformed

into an angel and at the end of the poem seduced by Satan. Of
Eloa's influence on the terrestrial sphere as she passes through
its orbit, Vigny tells us:

> Tous les poignards tombaient oubliés par la haine;
> Le captif souriant marchait seul et sans chaîne;
> Le criminel rentrait au temple de la loi;
> Le proscrit's s'asseyait au palais de son roi...

[All daggers dropped, forgotten by hatred; the smiling captive
walked alone and without chains; the criminal returned to the
temple of the law; the condemned man sat down in his king's
palace.]
The modern reader may be reminded here of the ethos of
Dr Frank ('Love thy Boss') Buchman, as the *Daily Worker* used
to call him, the founder of Moral Rearmament. *Eloa* is a fairly
extreme example.[19] Reviewing it in *The New Monthly Magazine*
for December 1824, Beyle had to assure his English readers that
the author of 'this strange quintessence of absurdity' was 'not
actually mad; for a great portion of his verses are well turned
and most elaborately polished, so much so as to render obvious
the great art and labour employed upon them'. Furthermore,
'this incredible amalgam of absurdity and profaneness is most
enthusiastically admired by a great city containing 80,000 inhabitants and called the Faubourg St. Germain...'. He might
have added that the young Victor Hugo had praised *Eloa* in
the most extravagant terms in May of the same year in a review
in *La muse française*.

The widespread religious scepticism of the first half of the
nineteenth century and, going with this, the popular cult of
religious sentiment as opposed to religious belief, may explain
why Beyle was to write in one of his unfinished lives of Napoleon
of the 'formidable progress' made 'in the art of lying'.[20] And
seven years earlier: 'Today in 1822 men nearly always lie when
they speak of the true motives of their actions.'[21] It may explain
too why Nietzsche was to admire in him 'a sincere atheism rarely
to be found in France'.[22]

The question of Beyle's 'atheism' is one to which it will be
necessary to return. For Beyle can disconcert us by the respect
with which he writes of the honest Christian. His judgment in
ethical matters may equally strike us as enigmatic unless, like

his beliefs concerning religion, they are seen as a response to the real and feigned beliefs of his own contemporaries.

Beyle habitually addresses his readers, and it is one of the most striking singularities of his prose, as if he were perfectly aware that we may or may not share his own feelings of admiration or disgust. It was this that struck Bussière, the author of his obituary in *La revue des deux mondes* for January 1843:

M. de Stendhal does not seek to establish his success on the kind of embellishment which is achieved when the reader is taken unawares and his good faith abused. He is so little concerned to earn this strange distinction that rather than that the latter's vigilance should grow dull, he takes care himself to hold it in suspense and constantly maintains him on his guard. He makes few assertions which are not followed by a warning which he repeats in every conceivable form: 'I invite the reader to mistrust everyone, even myself...Only ever believe what you have seen, only admire what has given you pleasure and assume that the neighbour who addresses you is a man paid to lie.'

In this he differs from those of his contemporaries who, like Vigny in *Eloa* – despite the thrilling and conveniently vague implications of the ending of the poem – write of virtue and vice as a simple matter involving few problems of identification. Balzac is in the habit of referring to the fallen women, of whom many varieties appear in his novels, as *cette sorte de femme* or *ces créatures*. ('Monarchist and catholic', his friend Gautier wrote of him, 'he defends authority, exalts religion, preaches duty, lectures against passion and denies the possibility of happiness outside marriage and outside the family.'[23]) And Musset's Count uses the same expression at the end of *Il faut qu'une porte soit ouverte ou fermée*, when clearing up the misunderstanding between himself and the young widow on whom he has called (Musset, unlike Beyle, succeeded in writing successful stage comedies):

La Marquise. What? Really, I'm losing patience. Do you imagine that I'm going to be your mistress or another of your women in rose-coloured hats? I warn you: not only do I dislike the idea, I find it repulsive.
Le Comte. By all that is mighty, if I could, I would lay down all that I have and all that I shall ever be at your feet. I would give you my name, my possessions and even my honour. Do you think that I would dream of comparing you for a single instant with those creatures whom you mention only in order to wound my feelings – or for that

matter, with any woman in the world? You must think I am out of my mind!...You told me just now that you don't altogether dislike my company and that you even perhaps feel a certain affection towards me. I believe that is what you said, Marquise. Do you imagine that a man who had been worthy of such a precious, such a heavenly favour would ever be capable of disrespect? Do you think I am blind or mad? You my mistress? No, my wife.

La Marquise. Ah! Well, if you'd said that when you came, there'd have been no need to argue.

Musset, of course, was himself a confessed sinner. The 'confession' – and the word is entirely appropriate – is elaborated in *Les confessions d'un enfant du siècle* in which the sins receive appropriate psychological retribution. They resemble, in this respect, those alluded to in a contemporary best-seller, Byron's *Childe Harold*. Childe Harold too sins and suffers and it is for this reason possibly that his adventures were regarded both in France and England as morally edifying, certainly more edifying, in any case, than those of his unrepentant Don Juan, a spiritual descendant of Fielding's Tom Jones, in the poem which Beyle himself considered to be Byron's masterpiece. However, as far as questions of morality were concerned, Beyle was not, according to another contemporary, Sainte-Beuve, the most reliable of guides: '...he lacked in writing our own sense of moderation in moral matters; he saw hypocrisy where there is only a sentiment of legitimate conventionality and a reasonable and honest observation of nature, such as we wish to find even in the midst of passion'.[24]

The reader of the present study may find, of course, that he agrees with Sainte-Beuve. Yet he will also agree, I hope, that there are certain periods of history in which the moral sentiments to which Sainte-Beuve refers will seem familiar to a majority of those who regard themselves as reasonably civilised and other periods in which this will not be so. It is doubtful, moreover, whether, holding the views he expresses, Sainte-Beuve would have felt the same moral solidarity between himself and his readers during the eighteenth century. The common meaning of a word like *virtue* seems to have changed during the intervening years and to have been associated less with service to one's country or a dedication to the betterment of mankind that with the cultivation of a blameless private life, the kind of life evoked by Sainte-Beuve himself in *Les Consolations* or led by Balzac's virtuous heroines. It seems to have been thought of, in other words, as Christian virtue rather than the *virtus* of Republican Rome.

The change in conventional ideas of morality is described by De Tocqueville, among others, in *L'ancien régime* written in the 1850s:

> The men of the eighteenth century were on the whole unfamiliar with that passion for well-being, if one can describe it in this way, which engenders servitude, which is feeble and yet tenacious, which readily mingles and becomes, so to speak, inextricably confused with the private virtues: with the love of one's family, with moderation of behaviour, with respect for religious beliefs and even with the lukewarm but assiduous practice of the established religion; which allows respectability but prohibits heroism, which excels in forming men of regular habits and at the same time cowardly citizens. They were better than that and also worse.
>
> The French in those days loved gaiety and adored pleasure. They were perhaps wilder and more undisciplined in their passions and ideas than we are, but they knew nothing of that well-tempered and seemly sensuality that we witness today. In the upper classes it was considered important to render one's life distinguished rather than comfortable and to gain merit rather than riches. Even in the middle classes life was never absorbed entirely in the pursuit of well-being; this was often abandoned for that of higher and more delicate pleasures; there was no class in which money was considered to be the only desirable end...[25]

> If the Frenchmen who made the Revolution were more prone to incredulity than we are in matters of religion, they possessed one admirable belief which we lack: they believed in themselves. They had no doubt of the perfectibility and power of man, they had faith in his virtue. They had proud confidence in their own powers of the kind which often leads to error, but without which a nation is only capable of servility; they had no doubt whatever that they had been called upon to transform society and regenerate our species...[26]

This account is corroborated in an undeservedly little known essay by a young critic who was to become one of Louis Philippe's ministers, Charles de Rémusat's *Des moeurs du temps*.[27] Ideas of virtue in the nineteenth century can be summed up, according to Rémusat, by the single phrase: *Je suis bon père.*

These quotations inevitably simplify what happened over a period of half a century. And to quote De Tocqueville out of context is to give a very incomplete notion of his awareness of the complexity of social change, since his characteristic method of writing history is to advance a series of bold clear generalisations, all of which in effect qualify one another and together leave us with an impression of the many-faceted nature of the society he describes; meanwhile, and this is one of the many virtues of the method, each generalisation corresponds to the way in which we actually think of a society, which is usually in simple terms and as a result of mood, circumstances or the particular facts on which we are concentrating and which determine our view of the society as a whole. It is obvious that eighteenth-century ideas of such matters as religion and virtue varied to a considerable extent from one man and one moment to another, as did those of the Empire and Restoration. It is also obvious that the two contrasting *codes*, for want of a better term, were not altogether peculiar to any one phase of history. Most of the ideals of the French Revolution have survived throughout the nineteenth century and into our own time. (Flaubert's Homais, the apothecary in *Madame Bovary*, voices them parrot-fashion.) So too has the tendency, described by De Tocqueville and Rémusat, to confuse private and domestic morality with public and even political morality. After the dissolution by the National Assembly of the Third Republic in 1940, the Republican motto, *Liberté, Egalité, Fraternité* ceased to appear on coins and official documents and was replaced, in what may seem a significant order of priority, by the words, *Travail, Famille, Patrie*.

However, when all these necessary qualifications have been made, Beyle's sense of isolation from his contemporaries is no less comprehensible. Nor is his tendency to see the changes described by De Tocqueville in what to many of his critics have seemed like exaggerated and perversely simple terms, his tendency to sound like a nineteenth century version of Molière's misanthropic Alceste, one of his numerous *noms de plume*. However, in order to understand it, it is necessary that we should know how discerning or how obtuse a critic he was of his own contemporaries; how often, in other words, he was right. It is also necessary to appreciate the extent to which he was himself a man of the eighteenth century, and the extent to which he was formed by the same ideals and the same influences which made the Revolution possible.

The childhood of Henri Beyle

The origin of Beyle's attachment to these ideals is described in *La Vie de Henry Brulard*; and so are the circumstances which made him a precocious rebel and which turned his childhood into a 'constant period of misery, hatred and perpetual impotent desire for vengeance'.[28] His mother, with whom he tells us he was 'in love' and whom he would sometimes kiss so passionately that she was forced to leave him, died in childbirth when he was seven years old. His mother's elder unmarried sister, Séraphie, who took her sister's place in the home and whom he could never recall in later years without intense loathing, reproached him after the funeral for not having shed enough tears. The influence which she and his father exerted on him for the rest of his childhood explain to a great extent the hatred he felt throughout his life for false piety and false sentiment of every kind as well as for the compulsory pleasures on which the puritanical mind insists. He was never to forget the long walks on which he was taken by his well-meaning aunt and father 'for a treat'. His Jacobinism, he admits frankly, was partly inspired by their own devout royalism, as was his joy when the news came of the execution of Louis XVI:

The house shook as the mail-coach from Lyon and Paris drew up outside. My father rose to his feet: 'I must go and find out what those monsters have done.'

I thought to myself: 'I hope the traitor will be executed'. Then I began to reflect on the extreme difference between my own feelings and those of my father. I felt a tender love for our regiments which I would watch from my grandfather's window on their way through the Place Grenette. I imagined that the king wanted the Austrians to beat them. (As you will notice, although barely ten years old, I was not far from the truth.) But I must confess that the concern for the king's fate shown by the vicar-general Rey and the other priests who were friends of the family, would have been enough to make me wish for his death. I considered at the time, on the strength mainly of the verses of a song which I would sing to myself when there was no danger of being heard by my father or Aunt Séraphie, that it was one's *strict duty* to die for one's country when this was necessary.

What did I care for the life of a traitor who, by means of a secret letter, could slaughter one of the fine regiments I saw go through the Place Grenette? I was passing judgment on my family and myself when my father returned. I still see him in his white flannel frock-coat, which he had not bothered to take off, as the mail office was only a few yards away.

'It's all over', he said with a deep sigh. 'They've murdered him.'

I experienced one of the most intense moments of joy I have ever known in my life. The reader will perhaps think I am cruel, but I am still the same at the age of fifty-two as I was at the age of ten... I could fill ten pages describing that evening, but if the readers of 1880 are as feeble-hearted as the fashionable circles of 1835, both the scene and the hero will fill them with deep aversion and even horror, as those *papier mâché* souls would say. As for myself, I would always feel a great deal more pity for a man condemned to death for murder without entirely conclusive proof than for a king who found himself in the same position. The death of a guilty king is always useful *in terrorem* to prevent the strange abuses into which such people are driven by the *extreme folly* produced by absolute power.[29]

Beyle's precocious Jacobinism was accompanied by an appropriate veneration for the heroes of Roman antiquity:

One cold evening as the sun was setting, I had the audacity to escape on the pretext of joining my Aunt Elizabeth at the house of Mme. Colomb and I plucked up the courage to go to a meeting of the Jacobin Club, which held its meetings in the church of St. André. My mind was full of the heroes of Roman history and I thought of myself sometimes as a Camillus, sometimes a Cincinnatus and sometimes both at the same time. Heaven alone knows what will happen to me, I thought, if one of Séraphie's *spies* (this is how I thought at the time) should see me here.[30]

He was disconcerted by the disorder which reigned throughout the meeting and by the vulgarity of his fellow Jacobins, and found himself experiencing one of the contradictions of his later years. He 'loved' the common people, he tells us, and hated their oppressors – but would do anything rather than have to live with them.

The young Beyle's ideas of nobility, and particularly nobility inspired by Roman models, were shared by many older and more active revolutionaries throughout the country. The 'classical' inspiration is seen in the speeches of the period and in the noble theatrical gestures of the revolutionary politicians in the paintings by Louis David, the same nobility and often the same gestures as in his paintings of conventional classical subjects. It is even seen in the Greek and Roman names given to children born during the Revolution, which Edmond Schérer has compared with the Old Testament names given to English children during the English Civil War.[31] Beyle, like many of his contemporaries, read Plutarch's *Lives of Illustrious Men* (probably in the sixteenth-century translation by Amyot) and in his letters to his younger sister Pauline, written from Paris before joining the Republican armies in Italy, he recommends Plutarch enthusiastically and scolds her for not having followed his advice. His taste for Plutarch and for Roman virtue explains too his early enthusiasm for the tragedies of Corneille and Alfieri.

Beyle's brief period of formal schooling, from 1796 until 1799, confirmed these heroic and patriotic influences, while at the same time awakening his interest in philosophy and painting and his liking and respect for mathematics. The twelve-year-old Henri was a willing pupil, for school meant release from home and from the tyranny of the priest who was his private tutor. The subject matter of the lessons, moreover, and the way they were taught seem to have suited his mind and his temperament. The Ecole Centrale in Grenoble, which Beyle attended on the day it opened, was the creation of the law of 1795[32] which established similar institutions throughout the country and sought to apply the educational theories which had been debated over the past five years by men such as Condorcet, Talleyrand, Siéyès and a thinker to whom Beyle was to owe a great deal, the former Count Destutt de Tracy. The innovations of the Ecoles Centrales included, partly on Talleyrand's insistence, an extremely flexible system of optional courses, as opposed to the rigid identical syllabuses of the old Jesuit college and the future lycée. They included also instruction in the natural sciences, painting and drawing – Beyle's first duel was fought with another pupil who had obstructed his view of the model– and, perhaps most important of all, the philosophy or 'general grammar', as it was called, which it was hoped would provide the future citizens with the same basic, rational and non-metaphysical notions of the nature of man. Destutt de Tracy's own major philosophical work, the *Eléments d'Idéologie*, was conceived as having a pedagogical function and it was as a result of his own optimistic influence on the Committee for Public Instruction that schoolboys throughout France were expected to answer such questions as ' What is general grammar? What is its purpose? What is man?' With other pupils, Beyle read Condillac's *Logic* and was thus initiated into the philosophical tradition running from Locke to Tracy himself. Literature and the study of French and Latin occupied a relatively unimportant place in the syllabus, which may account for his notorious departures in later life from normal grammar, usage and even spelling, though he was fortunate in having in Citizen Dubois-Fontenelle, author of the tragedy of *Ericie ou la Vestale*, a master of *belles-lettres* who taught his pupils to look out for and despise pedantry, to look to other countries, including England, for inspiration in the theatre, and to appreciate the relevance of the thought of Locke and Condillac to the study and practice of literature itself.[33] The implications of these lessons, which for Beyle were very far-reaching indeed, are something to which we shall have to return.

The Ecoles Centrales were abolished by order of the First Consul in 1803 and replaced by the more highly organised lycées, with their quasi-military discipline and rigid syllabuses as we have known them up to the present day. (It is questionable whether Beyle would have been so apt a pupil had he been born ten years later.) Destutt de Tracy, who had helped prepare the coup d'état by which Bonaparte seized power, was dismissed from his post on the Committee of Public Instruction and the philosophy syllabus in schools altered to exclude the thinkers whom Tracy favoured. Beyle, whose admiration for Napoleon was never, even in later life, to remain unqualified, always deplored these two decisions. In this respect and on account of the terms of the Concordat, he was to regard the Revolution as having been betrayed.

Coming of age in post-Revolutionary France

The story of Beyle's education from the time he left Grenoble a few days before Bonaparte's coup d'état, can be traced more easily than during his childhood and youth, for it is a matter simply of reading the copious diaries, letters and notebooks that have survived. The story belongs to the following chapters of this study which are concerned with these and his other writings. This study will, needless to say, exclude much that is crucial to an understanding both of Beyle and the age he lived in and this is due not only to its brevity but to the nature of the subject itself. 'I wrote biographies in my youth', he was to note in the margins of a copy of *Le rouge et le noir*, 'which are a kind of history, lives of Mozart and Michelangelo.[34] I regret it now. With the biggest just as much as with the smallest things, it seems to me impossible to get to what is true, at least to what is true in *some detail*.'[35] Many of the details that would enable us to understand the important truths about the life of Beyle and the facts of his everyday existence are missing from this study and many more, of course, are lost irretrievably.

I have chosen so far to stress the early influences which helped to determine Beyle's feelings towards the world he knew as an adult and in doing so to offer one of a number of possible explanations of his development. Yet I do not wish to argue, even if I may seem to imply, that Beyle virtually never grew up or that he closed his mind – which would be the same thing – to anything other than the remembered influences of his childhood and adolescence. Unfortunately, this is what certain of Beyle's finest critics have not only suggested but seemingly believed, among them the young Léon Blum in the book in which, during the first years of the present century, he tried to rescue Beyle from his more cynical admirers and portray him as a human being:

> Beyle's early character remained intact beneath his borrowed manners and deliberate attitudes. It remained, one might say, like something fresh and subterranean in his inner life and gushed out freely in his written work. Chronologically his books are those of a mature man; psychologically they belong to his youth, in so far as they are governed by his early ideas and nourished by his first impressions...[36]

Blum continues, in a passage which may tempt us to ponder the significance of the fact that this was written at the same time as *A la recherche du temps perdu*:

> A poet has defined happiness as the realisation in the years of manhood of the dreams of youth. For Stendhal these dreams, with their con-

comitant disappointments and interrupted aspirations, continued throughout his entire life and never came true. His inner life is one of a constant youthfulness expressed or rather confessed to in his writings with a clarity of insight which owes almost nothing to experience and age. M. Paul Bourget expresses this admirably: 'After his eighteenth year he acquired nothing other than an amplification of his early tendencies.' He acquired nothing and, what is more significant and rare, he lost nothing. When we try and envisage Stendhal, or when we imagine Julien Sorel, a process which is not very different, we should take care not to give too much thought to the fact that the novel appeared in the Paris of 1830.[37]

(Beyle himself had something to say about this kind of extrapolation. 'The resource of envy', he wrote to Mme Alberthe de Rubempré, who had found the same familiar traits in Julien Sorel, 'is to say, when the author depicts an energetic and hence somewhat scoundrelly character: "The author has portrayed himself!" What can one possibly say to that? A man sees himself only from the inside, as one sees the Georama in the Rue de la Paix.'[38]) As Blum points out, there is a remarkable similarity between the prose of Beyle's youth and that of his mature years. The early prose is often startlingly fine. But there is a simple test to which Blum's further claims should be submitted and this is to compare Beyle's letters to his sister Pauline written during his early twenties and his letters of twenty-five or more years later. The following extract is fairly typical of the former:

What the devil are you up to? Are you in love? So much the worse for you if you are. Take care not to marry a man you love; unless you marry a man who is very intelligent, you will be unhappy. If I were you, I should choose some decent fellow with plenty of money who is not as clever as you are.[39]

So too is the letter of three weeks later when Beyle realises to his alarm that Pauline may have been responding to years of his highly unorthodox advice and is thinking seriously of running away from home:

Remember this. Who would ever want to marry a girl, even if he were in love with her, if she had run away from her parents? I can think of no one with fewer prejudices than I have and I assure you that even I wouldn't marry such a girl. If I were in love with her, I would *debauch* her and then have nothing else to do with her.[40]

The Beyle who wrote these letters has certainly something in common with Julien Sorel and, as in Julien, there is something both comic and frightening in his fierce affectation of wordly wisdom. They would seem more amusing still if we could be sure that Pauline was capable of taking them light-heartedly herself. Unfortunately, it seems that she took her brother very seriously and that this did not contribute to the future happiness of her life.[41]

These extracts may be compared with a letter written in March 1830, when Beyle was still working on *Le rouge et le noir*, to the young Sainte-Beuve, who had just expressed his own views on domestic virtue and happiness in his collection of poems *Les consolations*. Beyle had just gone through them at a single reading:

If there were a God, I should be delighted, for he would pay me for being the gentleman I am by sending me to his Paradise.

Thus I would not change my conduct in the least and I should be rewarded for doing exactly what I do now.

One thing, however, would diminish the pleasure I feel whenever I think of the warm tears which a fine deed brings to the eyes: the idea of being *paid* by a reward, a paradise.

This, Sir, is what I would tell you in verse if I could write verse as well as you. I am shocked that those of you who *believe in God* imagine that to be *in despair* for three years because a mistress has left you, you have first to believe in God. In the same way, a Montmorency imagines that to be brave on the battlefield you have to be called Montmorency.

I believe, Sir, that you are destined for the greatest of literary careers; but I still find a little affectation in your verse. I wish it were more like La Fontaine's. You talk too much of glory...La Fontaine once said to La Champmeslé, 'We shall both achieve glory, I for writing, you for reciting.' He had guessed the truth. But why talk of such things? Passion has its own modesty. [*La passion a sa pudeur.*] Why reveal these intimate details? It looks like sharp practice, a kind of *puff*.

These, Sir, are my thoughts and all my thoughts. I think you will still be spoken of in 1890. But you will do better than the *Consolations*, something stronger and purer.

Les consolations were written in Sainte-Beuve's earlier, more conventional manner, in which the combined influences of Chateaubriand and Lamartine were predominant:

Mais comme au lac profond et sous son limon noir
Le ciel se réfléchit, vaste et charmant á voir
Et déroulant d'en haut la splendeur de ses voiles,
Pour décorer l'abîme y sème les étoiles,
Tel dans ce fond obscur de notre humble destin
Se révèle l'espoir de l'éternel matin;
Et quand sous l'oeil de Dieu l'on s'est mis de bonne heure;
Quand on s'est fait une âme où la vertu demeure,
Quand, morts entre nos bras, les parents révérés
Tout bas nous ont bénis avec des mots sacrés;
Quand nos enfants, nourris d'une douceur austère,
Continueront le bien après nous sur la terre;
Quand un chaste devoir a réglé tous nos pas,
Alors on peut encore être heureux ici-bas...

[But just as the vast sky, which is so delightful to contemplate, is mirrored in the deep lake and beneath its black slime, just as it draws aside the splendour of its veils to adorn the abyss by sowing it with stars, so is the hope of eternal morning revealed to us here below in this dark place of our humble destiny; and when one has placed oneself early on in the sight of God, when one has formed a soul in which virtue can dwell, when our revered parents dying in our arms have blessed us with quiet holy words, when we know that our children nourished in austere sweetness will continue to live worthily after us on earth, when a chaste duty has commanded our every step, then we can still live happily down here...]

Sainte-Beuve grew out of it, as Beyle hoped that he would, but the latter's comments may explain why in later life Sainte-Beuve was to write that Beyle was a poor judge of style and poetry.[42]

If we consider only Beyle's deeper formative and dynamic beliefs, it is true that, as Blum says, he changed very little. Yet 'psychologically' there is a world of difference between his adolescence and his mature years. One thing that has happened is that Beyle has learned to live, if not happily at least without 'impotent hatred', in a world which is not of his own choosing, a world in which the language of *Les consolations*, for example, is what passes for the language of poetry and ethics. And the effect on his character of events obviously explains to some extent why he evolved in this way: the effect of the years spent as a high-ranking public servant travelling with the Imperial armies and then as a *dilettante* subsisting by means of a small pension on the fringes of distinguished society; the effect too of a lifetime spent in the way he describes in *La vie de Henry Brulard*:

I see that I have been constantly occupied with unhappy love affairs... And what is strange and unfortunate, I was thinking this morning, is that my *victories* (as I used to call them with my head full of military ideas) never procured me a pleasure half as great as the profound chagrin caused by my defeats.[43]

A longer study than this would have room to describe the various adventures into which Beyle plunged, according to his own account all too eagerly, in the course of his protracted bachelor life, as well as the joy and liberation he experienced on discovering Mozart, Cimarosa, the southern slopes and valleys of the Alps and the social amenities of the city of Milan, of which he wished on his tomb to be remembered as a citizen. If Beyle evolved as he did, it was partly because of such accidents of good fortune. It was not, however, I should like to suggest, due only to these or to a natural 'mellowing' of character. Characters do not usually mellow naturally, even when their owners are lucky enough not to be plagued, as Beyle was, by poor health, an unattractive physique and repeated humiliating disappointments. The charm, frankness, urbanity and wit of Beyle's later writings may seem 'natural' in the sense of seeming unaffected. But this does not mean that they are the product of circumstances over which he himself had no control. The character and style of the mature Beyle were the result in part of years of self-interrogation and self-discipline and of the cultivation of a personal philosophy – one could also describe it as an art of living – of which the art of his novels was perhaps the most perfect expression. It is this personal philosophy, to which Beyle himself gave the name of 'Beylisme', that I wish to consider now.

2

Le Beylisme

Beylisme and 'de-Rousseauisation'

To describe Beyle as a man of the eighteenth century is, of course, all very well. The eighteenth century speaks to us with many discordant voices. We may understand 'Beylisme' a little better if we consider how he responded to them at various times in his career and why he found some more congenial than others.

'I have never enjoyed the writings of Voltaire', he recalls, looking back to his childhood. 'At the time they seemed to me childish only. I think I can say that nothing by that great man has ever given me any pleasure. [When I was a boy] I was unable to see that he was the legislator and apostle of France, our Martin Luther.'[1] And in the *Racine et Shakspeare* of 1823: 'Foreign critics have noticed that there is always something *malevolent* behind the gayest of the jokes in *Candide* and *Zadig*. The rich Voltaire amuses himself by directing our gaze on the inevitable misfortunates of poor human nature.'[2] We tend to forget that during Voltaire's lifetime and for years after his death, he was thought of not only as a satirist and philosopher but as the brilliant successor in the theatre to Corneille and Racine. Beyle, however, even in his early twenties, considered him to be an inferior dramatist and incapable of a true understanding of the heroic.

I feel that, as he had never conceived the idea of a great republican, he knew almost nothing of those whose lives have reflected honour on the human species; he judged mankind by the kings and courtiers he had frequented. He knew nothing of true greatness, he often talks

27

about it but he doesn't feel it, he doesn't talk about it well. He lacked *the comprehensive soul*, [in English in the text] a quality necessary in any poet. This is why all his characters resemble one another.[3]

He admired Voltaire's use in his prose works of what in the eighteenth century is known as *le style coupé*, the equivalent in writing of conversation between witty and intelligent equals, but he found him, none the less, inferior to Montesquieu. Voltaire 'flatters the reader's self-esteem by leaving him to guess a great many things; but in Montesquieu the veil is less thin'.[4]

Montesquieu receives warmer and more consistent praise from Beyle than almost any other French writer and it is obvious that his interest in the ways in which notions of the good, the true and the beautiful can *vary* from one culture to another accounts to some extent for his appeal. Yet his appeal for Beyle seems to have been not so much that of his ideas as such, but rather that of a congenial temperament and of a refined generous civilisation which speaks to us in the very rhythms of his prose. After the fall of Napoleon and during the years when Beyle, despite his earlier Republicanism, was ready to express what seems to have been a sincere allegiance to the new constitution imported from England,[5] he read Tracy's *Commentary* on *L'esprit des lois* and agreed completely with Tracy's strictures on Montesquieu's excessive Anglophilism and failure to understand the need for practical safeguards to protect individual liberties.[6] The science of politics, Beyle concluded, had advanced considerably since Montesquieu's day. Again, if he learned something from Montesquieu's study of the moral and cultural differences between nations, he learned even more from Mme de Staël,[7] though he never admired Mme de Staël's prose and never wished to imitate it.[8] Yet something remarkably like Montesquieu's formal, though often quietly mischievous decorum is evident in Beyle's mature writing, together with the rhythms of his prose. Compare, for instance, the two following passages from *L'esprit des lois* and *De l'amour*:

Avec cette délicatesse d'organes que l'on a dans les pays chauds, l'âme est souverainement émue par tout ce qui a du rapport à l'union des deux sexes: tout conduit à cet objet.

Dans les climats du nord, à peine le physique de l'amour a-t-il la force de se rendre bien sensible; dans les climats tempérés, l'amour accompagné de mille accessoires, se rend agréable par des choses qui d'abord semblent être lui-même, et ne sont pas encore lui; dans les climats plus chauds, on aime l'amour pour lui-même; il est la cause unique du bonheur; il est la vie.

Dans les pays du midi, une machine délicate, faible, mais sensible, se livre à un amour qui, dans un sérail, naît et se calme sans cesse; ou bien à un amour qui, laissant les femmes dans une plus grande indépendance, est exposé à mille troubles.[9] [Because of the delicacy of the human organs in hot countries, the soul is moved, above all, by everything related to the uniting of the two sexes: everything leads to this end.

In northern climates the physical concomitants of love have hardly the strength to make themselves felt; in the temperate climates, love, accompanied by a thousand accessories, is rendered agreeable by circumstances which at first seem to be, but are not yet love itself; in the hotter climates love is loved for its own sake; it is the sole cause of happiness; it is life.

In the countries of the south, a delicate, fragile but sensitive organism abandons itself to love which, in a seraglio, is ceaselessly aroused and calmed; or else to love which, when women are left in greater independence, is exposed to a thousand torments.]

Voici ce qui se passe dans l'âme:
1. L'admiration.
2. On se dit: Quel plaisir de lui donner des baisers, d'en recevoir, etc.!
3. L'espérance.

On étudie les perfections; c'est à ce moment qu'une femme devrait se rendre pour le plus grand plaisir physique possible. Même chez les femmes les plus réservées, les yeux rougissent au moment de l'espérance; la passion est si forte, le plaisir si vif qu'il se trahit par des signes frappants.
4. L'amour est né.[10]

[This is what takes place within the soul:
1. Admiration.
2. One thinks to oneself: how very delightful it would be to kiss her, for her to kiss me, etc.!
3. Hope.

One studies the perfections of the person one loves; this is when a woman should surrender to the advances of her lover in order to enjoy the greatest possible physical pleasure. Even the eyes of the most reserved women are red during the moment of hope; the passion they feel is so strong and the pleasure so intense that it is betrayed in the most strikingly obvious ways.

4. Love is born.]

The stylistic resemblance may seem even more obvious if one compares these accounts of the sexual love experienced both by men and women with the following passage from Rousseau's *Emile*:

L'Etre suprême a voulu faire en tout honneur à l'espèce humaine: en donnant à l'homme des penchants sans mesure, il lui donne en même temps la loi qui les règle, afin qu'il soit libre et se commande à lui-même; en le livrant à des passions immodérées, il joint à ces passions la raison pour les gouverner; en livrant la femme à des désirs illimités, il joint à ces désirs la pudeur pour les contenir. Pour surcroît, il ajoute encore une récompense actuelle au bon usage de ses facultés, savoir le goût qu'on prend aux choses honnêtes lorsqu'on en fait la règle de ses actions. Tout cela vaut bien, ce me semble, l'instinct des bêtes.[11]

[The Supreme Being has chosen to treat the human species honourably: while giving the man leanings without limit or measure, he has at the same time given him the law which regulates them, so that he may be free and his own master; while abandoning him to immoderate passions, he has combined with these passions the reason which governs them; while abandoning the woman to limitless desires, he has combined with these desires the modesty which contains them. Over and above this, he has added one more immediate recompense for the good use of our faculties, that is the pleasure one takes in worthy considerations when one allows them to regulate one's acts. All this, it seems to me, has at least as much to be said for it as the instinct of the beasts.]

The differences in sensibility, in vital rhythm and in the implicit assumptions of the prose are so obvious as to require no comment.

Rousseau's influence, none the less, on Beyle and on most of Beyle's older and younger contemporaries can be seen as powerful and pervasive. His way of thinking and feeling, with its startling paradoxes and *voltes-face*, is in fact common to many of those who made not only the Revolution possible but also the Concordat, the Empire and the constitutional monarchy of the Restoration, men whose minds were far simpler than that of Rousseau and who were fired by one or other of the many contradictory-seeming arguments he so passionately expounded. Both Robespierre and the royalist Romantics of the Restoration were in varying ways and degrees Rousseau's disciples. The full extent of his influence on Beyle is difficult to estimate, for after worshipping Rousseau

*S.'s
aun philosophy*

as a boy and a young man, he embarked in his early twenties
on what he was to describe as a process of 'de-Rousseauisation'.
It is clear when one compares the three passages I have quoted
that the cure was conducted with some success. Yet in the very
process of reacting against Rousseau, he was defining, in a way
that might not otherwise have been possible, what it was he
wanted to be. He was working out what he begins to refer to,
with mock pomposity, in his diaries and letters, as the philosophy
of 'Beylisme'.

The Rousseau he admired as a boy was the Rousseau of *The
Confessions* and *La nouvelle Héloïse*, and in *Henry Brulard* he recalls
his impressions in the spring of 1800 on his first journey to
Italy when he passed through the landscape described in the
letters of Rousseau's Saint-Preux and Julie d'Etange:

...drunk with joy at having read *La nouvelle Héloïse* and at the thought
of being about to pass through Vevey – I may have mistaken Rolle
for Vevey – I suddenly heard the majestic peal of the bells of a church
on the hill a quarter of a league above Rolle, or Nyon, and climbed
towards it. The lake stretched out before my gaze, the peal of bells
accompanied my thoughts with their ravishing music and gave to
them a sublime physiognomy.

This, I would say, is the nearest I have ever come to a state of
perfect happiness.[12]

However, in reliving the past Beyle forgets, characteristically,
the superlative in the last sentence. A few days later in the
opera house in Ivrea he heard the music of Cimarosa for the
first time:

Straight away, the thought of my two great exploits: firstly, having
crossed the Saint-Bernard Pass; secondly, having been under fire,
became as nothing and seemed merely common and vulgar. What
I experienced was something like my enthusiasm by the church above
Rolle, but an enthusiasm which was far purer and more intense. The
pedantry of Julie d'Etange made me uncomfortable, whereas everything in Cimarosa was divine.[13]

Beyle often confesses in his letters and diaries how much he had
been formed by Rousseau and how much Rousseau had influenced
his ideas of what it would be like to fall in love or meet noble
and virtuous men and women; how much Rousseau had also
prepared him for the inevitable disappointments by his romanti-

31

cising of self-pity and of a noble self-pitying aloofness from the world.[14] It was for this reason that he began to 'de-Rousseauise' himself. In the little treatise which he sketched out in 1812 with his friend Louis Crozet and to which they gave the title *Du style*, he takes the process further by analysing the tendency in Rousseau to dominate the reader-and tell him exactly what he should think and feel:

We think that the style of Fénelon (the *Dialogue des morts* and the *Contes pour le duc de Bourgogne*) is far superior to that of Rousseau, in that it holds up a faithful mirror to nature and leaves it with its *infinite variety*; whereas the style of Jean-Jacques gives everything a certain colour.

In Jean-Jacques, a cool grove of trees is a lesson in virtue; in Fénelon it leads one only to feel a certain voluptuous delight, which is its natural effect in hot countries.

Since the style of Fénelon is perfectly natural, it allows both for comic and tragic effects and for everything else in nature. Rousseau's has a certain dose of exaggerated tragic affectation and hence cannot be employed humorously... [15]

While conforming entirely to the style of Fénelon, one can describe the feelings of the heart as successfully as Jean-Jacques; but one can't say what the reader is to think of them; one can't produce his feelings for him, one can only leave him to himself. Rousseau tells us what we are to think of everything he describes.

Not only does Rousseau expose himself to the ridicule of having his assertions denied, often he provokes his readers by abusing those who might be merely tempted to deny them. For example: 'This state of mind [i.e. the refusal to take anything on trust recommended by Descartes at the beginning of the *Discours de la méthode*] is scarcely made to last; it is disturbing and painful; it is in the interests of vice alone and spiritual sloth that we should be left in such a state.'[16]

To begin with, we know first-hand examples which strike us as evidence that the state of mind in question is neither disturbing nor painful. Also, insults put us in a bad mood. This passage is as unlike Fénelon as it is possible to imagine.

Rousseau would have upset no one and would not have departed from the style of Fénelon had he said: 'This state of mind, it seems to me, is scarcely made to last; I found it disturbing and painful and I have always noticed that vice and spiritual sloth alone rendered it tolerable.'[17]

In Moscow, after his arrival in the city in the early autumn of 1812, Beyle re-read Rousseau's *Confessions* in the intervals of working on his *History of Painting in Italy* and gave the following impressions of them in a letter to Félix Faure:

I was reading Rousseau's *Confessions* a week ago. It is only for want of three or four of the principles of *Beylisme* that he was so miserably unhappy. His mania for seeing duties and virtues everywhere made his style pedantic and his life wretched. He gets to know a man for a few weeks and then, before you know where you are, he's talking about the *duties of friendship*, etc. *Beylisme* would have told him that two bodies approach one another, that this produces a certain heat and fermentation, but that all phenomena of this kind are ephemeral, that it's a flower to be enjoyed voluptuously, etc. Do you follow what I mean? The finest things in Rousseau, for me, have something over-heated about them. They lack the Correggio-like grace which the least shade of pedantry will destroy.[18]

The differences of outlook were by now fundamental. The implications of the error he ascribes to Rousseau are profound and tragic. The differences are inevitable, moreover, if one considers the eighteenth-century philosophy he did admire and the principles to which, throughout the rest of his life, he was able to give his entire allegiance.

Beylisme and Utilitarianism

At the age of nineteen, Beyle began to study intensively the writings of Claude-Adrien Helvétius, the farmer-general, philanthropic reformer and author of *De l'esprit* and *De l'homme,* together with the philosophers who acknowledged his influence, the *idéologistes* or *idéologues*, the term used disparagingly by Chateaubriand and Napoleon and which has since passed into general usage. This was after Beyle had resigned his commission as a lieutenant of dragoons and settled in Paris on a small private income provided by his father who, as a devout royalist, preferred that his son should remain unemployed rather than serve in the armies of a Republic. It was the moment too at which this school of philosophy began to fall into general disfavour and to undergo the effects of the eloquent criticisms made by Chateaubriand and Mme de Staël,[19] though Beyle seems to have been undeterred by the new official and fashionable views. In settling down to study the *idéologues,* he planned to further his ambition to 'know man perfectly' and hence to become a great dramatic poet. He was encouraged in this by the example of 'the divine Alfieri' who had proved to him that 'a man whose mind is full of Helvétius can be a sublime poet'.[20]

A man whose mind was full of Helvétius could not very well find room for Rousseau as well, at least not for the Rousseau of *Emile* or *The Social Contract*. In 1837 Beyle was to remark that the principal merit of the latter work lay in its title,[21] and it is obvious that, despite his lifelong interest in the *Confessions* and his sympathy for the persecuted Rousseau, he gained little from Rousseau's ideas. Beyle took sides early in life, as we can see from his notebooks and letters, in one of the main philosophical controversies of his day, one in which few, if any European thinkers remained altogether uninvolved. The main issue and some of those related to it may be familiar to students of the history of ideas, for they involve perennial philosophical problems, but the late eighteenth and early nineteenth centuries were a period in which their practical implications were widely recognised and discussed. Broadly speaking, the issues were whether the mind and its experiences were to be thought of as the adventures of a specially constituted body in the world or as subject to other than material laws; whether there is a known or knowable human nature; and whether any man is capable of behaving in a purely disinterested way – that is, of seeking and gaining gratification of something other than his own desires. Helvétius, like Condillac and Locke, accepted a physiological explanation of the mind's experiences. (*Esprit*, of course, means not only 'mind' but 'soul'; Condillac, as a priest of the Church, had overcome one obvious disadvantage of this explanation by distinguishing between the immortal *esprit* and the *esprit* that thinks, remembers and wills.) Helvétius accepted this explanation as alone constituting limitations on the nature of man, for the mind of any man, he maintained, is liable to the same degree to degradation or perfection according to whatever influences he will have undergone in the world; and he asserted categorically – the assertion for which Beyle was always to express particular gratitude, though Helvétius was by no means the first to say it – that all living creatures in all their actions, and by the mere fact of being alive, are seeking their own interest, whatever this may be, even if it is often with a mistaken idea of where their true interest lies.

34

Helvétius's influence in France has been traced by Picavet in *Les idéologues*, which, though it was written at the end of the last century, is almost the only study of its kind, for the *idéologues* have never come back into fashion. Helvétius's influence in England has been traced by Elie Halévy in *The Growth of Philosophic Radicalism*. (I quote the title of the English translation, as the original French text is also out of print.) Helvétius influenced Bentham directly and through Bentham the English Utilitarian school. In France, during his own lifetime, however, Helvétius was condemned not only by the Parlement de Paris, which in 1757 ordered the public burning of his second major treatise *De l'homme*, but by Rousseau himself in that section of *Emile* which is entitled *La profession de foi du vicaire savoyard*, though it can easily be taken and usually has been for Rousseau's own personal credo. The allusions to Helvétius are clear, even though he is not mentioned by name, for when Rousseau heard of the persecution of Helvétius he burned his own explicit refutation in order not to join in the general hue and cry.[22]

For Rousseau there emphatically *is* a soul, immaterial in its origin and perceptions, which makes itself heard through the voice of 'conscience' and exercises itself through 'will', the most difficult human attribute to explain if consciousness is seen in simple Lockean terms as the combined effect of passively experienced sensations. Where Helvétius had written, at the opening of *De l'esprit*, that 'to judge is to feel', the vicaire savoyard asserts: 'To perceive is to feel; to compare is to judge; to judge and to feel are not the same thing.' And where Helvétius had insisted that judgment of value is judgment of where one's true interest lies, Rousseau's country priest speaks as follows:

Conscience! conscience! divine instinct, immortal and celestial voice, the sure guide of one who is ignorant and limited but intelligent and free; the infallible judge of good and evil rendering man akin to God, it is to you that the excellence of man's nature and the righteousness of all his acts is due; if it were not for you, I would feel nothing within me to raise me above the level of the beasts, nothing but the wretched privilege of wandering from error to error with the aid of an understanding that knows no rules and a reason that knows no principles.

We have been delivered, thank Heaven, from the clutches of philosophy: we can be men without being learned; we have been spared from having to sacrifice our entire lives to the study of morality, and we have a less expensive and more certain guide to lead us through the labyrinth of human opinions. Yet it is not enough that this guide should exist, we need to know how to recognise and follow it. How is it that so few understand it, if it is true that it speaks to every heart? Because it speaks to us in the language of nature which everything has conspired to make us forget. Conscience is timid, she loves solitude and peace; the noises of the world appal her: prejudices, from which men claim she is born, are her cruellest enemies and she flees or is silent before them; their noisy voices drown her own and prevent her from making herself heard; fanaticism has the audacity to borrow her garb and to dictate crime in her name. In the end, she is disheartened as the result of so many rebuffs; she speaks to us no longer, she no longer replies and after despising her so long, it costs as much to recall her as it once cost to banish her.

Belief in this natural goodness, expressing itself in 'natural religion' and a 'natural law' is indispensable to Rousseau's ethical, pedagogical and political systems. 'The general will' of society in which sovereignty alone can be found, a concept which has mystified generations of students of *The Social Contract*, is explicable perhaps only if we see it as an expression of natural goodness, for like 'conscience' the 'general will' can never be wrong.

Beyle's rejection of Rousseau's main premises and their implications seems to have been conscious and over the years consistent. It is significant, for example, that if he showed little interest in Rousseau's ideas, he was unimpressed also by Descartes, whose theory of clear, distinct and infallible ideas, non-material and ultimately divine in origin, has obvious affinities with Rousseau's notions of conscience and consciousness. Beyle recognised Descartes' historical importance and in particular because he led to Pascal,[23] but on one of the few occasions when he mentions him at all, he describes him, together with Plato, Aristotle, Leibnitz and Spinoza, as a 'great genius' who wrote 'boring poems'.[24] The word Cartesian has been somewhat overused in accounts of French intellectual history and it would be wrong to assume that when Beyle insists, as he so often does, on the virtues of 'clarity', he is using this word in the Cartesian sense.[25] As for the Kant whose daily walk through Königsberg was delayed, according to legend, because he had started to read *Emile* and was unable to put it down and whose ideas of ethical judgment were strongly influenced by Rousseau's own, Beyle professed to find him unreadable.[26] For that matter, despite his choice of a German pseudonym, his knowledge of the language was never more than rudimentary, while German philosophy in general remained for him literally a closed book.

In politics too, for all his revolutionary sympathies, it would be difficult to think of him as a Rousseauist or as a fervent admirer of the Robespierre and Saint-Just who regarded themselves as Rousseau's heirs and who, as well as resisting the enemies of the Republic outside and within her frontiers, followed the teachings of *The Social Contract* by endeavouring to suppress any institution or faction which was independent of the central authority of the state. His political thinking was far closer to that of Helvétius himself and Helvétius's friend and admirer Montesquieu, if only because of their readiness to admit the diversity of human needs and their freedom from any over-riding preoccupation such as Rousseau's with the possibilities of a natural law springing from natural human goodness. At the age of twenty-two, Beyle also read the essay *On Human Nature* by Thomas Hobbes, which he described anachronistically as 'an edifice built on the foundations of Helvétius'.[27] And though he did not go on to draw the conclusions of *The Leviathan*, there is no reason to think that he disagreed with Hobbes in regarding natural law as 'the natural law of the power of the strong over the weak'.[28] 'There is no natural law', Julien Sorel reflects in the penultimate chapter of *Le rouge et le noir*. 'The word is only an antiquated piece of humbug worthy of the advocate general who hunted me down the other day and whose ancestor was enriched by property confiscated by Louis XIV. There is only *law* when a man is prevented from doing something by fear of punishment. Before the *law* exists, there is nothing *natural* at all except the strength of the lion or the need of any cold or hungry creature...' Beyle goes on to question the conclusions that Julien draws from this belief. He says nothing to suggest that the belief is mistaken.

Beyle's debt to Helvétius must not be exaggerated, for there were large areas of contemporary intellectual discussion in which his attitude seems to have been one of indifference or the philosophical equivalent of agnosticism. He did not seriously question, for example, as William Blake had in England, the epistemology that Helvétius derived from Locke. Nor, however, did he seriously attempt to defend it. It was Helvétius's version of the basic Utilitarian premiss that particularly won his admiration and this was a principle he could easily have found stated elsewhere. 'Every man regards the actions of another as *virtuous, vicious* or *tolerable* according to whether they are *useful* to him, *harmful* or *indifferent...*', he wrote to Pauline in 1803. 'You will be able to see as a consequence of this luminous principle that men have described as *great* someone who has rendered them an important service or who has given them much entertainment. Henri IV is known as Henry the Great because Frenchmen hope, by paying him homage, to encourage other kings to follow his example.'[29] What is striking and curious is that, from this time onward, Beyle should have attached such importance to the principle in question and that he should not, in any of his surviving writings at least, have considered the obvious objection that when problems of value and ethics are reduced to such simple terms they merely become easily solved problems of definition. Everything depends simply on what one happens to mean by interest or pleasure.

One of the advantages of using such language, however, and one of its attractions possibly for Beyle, is that it disposes of certain problems which to those in whom conscience has been carefully nurtured may seem insoluble and inescapable. It is no longer necessary to ask oneself: *what right* have I to do this or that or to judge others or myself in a certain way? To judge is simply, from the point of view of Helvétius, to observe one's own and other people's behaviour and to find out that they are acting in a way which gives some degree of satisfaction or is harmful or offensive to oneself or to them; to judge behaviour, in other words, in a way which is unavoidable, whether or not it can be justified in other ways. In his article on Helvétius in *The Paris Monthly Review* for April 1822,[30] Beyle illustrates the attractive and frightening simplicity of the philosophy he is defending by quoting from Book II of Virgil's *Eclogues*:

> Torva laena sequitur; lupus ipse capellam;
> Florentem cytisum sequitur lasciva capella;
> ...trahit sua quemque voluptas.

[The lioness with the bloodshot eyes pursues the wolf; the wolf the goat; the goat seeks out fresh clover...each one is drawn by his desire.]

Another of the attractions of the 'luminous principle' described in the letters to Pauline was almost certainly that it reconciled two apparently contradictory tendencies in Beyle's own nature: his hatred of false sentiment and of the dutiful affectation of certain feelings – such as those he was scolded for not exhibiting at his mother's funeral – and his own extreme emotional susceptibility, shown in what he tells us of his passionate adoration of his mother, his loathing of his father and Aunt Séraphie and his correspondingly ardent 'Roman' patriotism. It is natural, if one considers the implications of the principle, for men to admire actions they regard as conducive to the general good, which includes their own. In the same way, the desire to serve the interests of others can be seen either as a wish to be admired or a desire to improve or safeguard one's own interests, that is, to improve or safeguard the world one lives in. Saying this in no way obliges us to use words like 'materialistic'. The world will seem a better place to live in, arguably to anyone, if certain things have been said or done in it. The Helvetian standpoint, in other words, enables us to distinguish in principle between moral feelings which are simulated in a desire to persuade oneself or others of one's own respectability and moral feelings which are unfeigned.

For the pursuit of one's own interest and pleasure is seen even in the most heroic deeds. In one of the illustrations of this theory which Beyle borrowed from Helvétius himself, we are asked to consider the motives of Regulus, who, after his capture by the Carthaginians, was sent back to Rome to convey terms of peace, having sworn on his honour to return if he failed, though this would mean, as he knew, certain torture and death:

A man of ordinary character and intelligence, such as Prince Eugene of Savoy, if placed in the same position as Regulus on his return from Carthage, would have calmly remained in Rome and laughed at the credulous simplicity of the Carthaginian Senate. Prince Eugene would have been following the dictates of his own *interest* in remaining and in the same way Regulus was following his by returning to be tortured.

In almost all the circumstances of life, a generous mind will perceive the possibility of certain actions, the idea of which a commonplace mind is incapable of understanding. The moment that the possibility of accomplishing these actions becomes apparent to a man of generous instincts, it is immediately in his own interest that he should carry them out. If he fails to, he feels the sting of self-abasement and as a result becomes unhappy.[31]

In distinguishing between the conceptions of honour of a 'generous' and a 'commonplace' mind, Beyle touches on a further principle which he had found in Helvétius: the simple axiom according to which ideas of the public and general good vary from one man to another. It was for this reason that Helvétius insisted that 'In matters of integrity one should only consult and have faith in the public interest, not in the men among whom we live, who are too often deluded by personal interest.'[32] The truth of this axiom had almost certainly been brought home to followers of Helvétius such as Destutt de Tracy during the Revolution and the Reign of Terror. (Tracy, one of the most active legislators both of the early years of the Revolution and later of the Directory, who, at the age of seventy-six, wearing his green eye-shade and carrying a long staff, joined the insurgents of 1830 on the barricades, had been imprisoned and condemned to death for treason during the rule of Robespierre's Committee of Public Safety and saved only by the execution of Robespierre himself.) It was an axiom for which Beyle too was to be permanently grateful and which helped him to tolerate in later life his own lack of success as a writer and the unpopularity of most of what he believed in. Characteristically, he refers on a number of occasions to literary success as a prize in a lottery and to his own books as lottery tickets. 'What distinguishes me', he writes in *Henry Brulard*, 'from the conceited fools...*who hold up their heads like a holy sacrament* is that I have never believed that society owes me a single thing. I have been saved from such immense foolishness thanks to Helvétius. *Society rewards the services it sees.*'[33] These remarks should be read together with those on Rousseau in the letter from Moscow to Félix Faure (quoted on page 33). They explain as clearly as is at all possible what Beyle himself meant by Beylisme.

An American admirer of Beyle has defined Beylisme in the following terms:

Livy tells us how the ideal of behaving in a manner worthy of the name of Fabius inspired the Fabii to tremendous exertions; and Shakespeare's Romans are particularly eloquent on the subject. Antony will do nothing unworthy of Antony; Caesar must live up to a public idea of Caesar which he has himself created. Perhaps it was this notion, that a man owes a duty to his own definition of himself, which furnished to Stendhal the seed for his concept of Beylism; a 'philosophy' which actually provides not only obligations and guidance but immunities and liberty, based upon one's consciously defined relation to a self one is in effect creating.[34]

This is not only less clear than Beyle's own explanations. It also introduces abstract considerations which are, I would suggest, unhelpful if we are to understand either his behaviour or his philosophy. Beyle may not have read the passage in the *Treatise of Human Nature* in which Hume confesses his inability to find anything in his perceptions or feelings that corresponds to the notion of 'self' and that is thus 'constant and invariable'.[35] (He seems to have known and admired Hume only as the author of *The History of England*.) It is unlikely, however, that he would have thought that Hume was talking nonsense. He speaks with scorn, for example, when writing as a journalist for the English reviews, of the contemporary French philosophers who claimed to have succeeded in an operation similar to the one in which Hume had failed:

They assert that 'consciousness is a feeling in itself, and is not felt through the senses'. They pretend that to hear the revelations of consciousness, it is necessary to wrap oneself in silence and obscurity, so as to be free from the operations of the senses. In a word, one must 'hear oneself think'. The philosophers of this new school allege that, after being long accustomed to these reveries, they discern an immeasurable perspective extending from man to God.[36]

The 'self', whether it is to be thought of as consciousness or a sense of identity, is not something in which he seems to have been greatly interested *as an idea*, though it is true that he was concerned to more than a normal degree with the impression he himself produced on others and that he was far more than usually introspective. The Helvetian idea of the perfectibility of each individual, given the right education and environment and provided that the individual wishes to be perfect, also aroused his enthusiasm for a time and it encouraged him in the course of self-training and self-observation which he underwent as an aspiring successor to Molière. In this respect, furthermore, he shared the enthusiasms of many of his older contemporaries.

41

For the eighteenth-century belief, as De Tocqueville puts it, in 'the perfectibility and power of man' and their assurance that 'they had been called upon to transform society and regenerate our species'[37] can be seen in the discipline and education which certain of them imposed on themselves. Tracy's close friend and collaborator the physician Canabis met, in the salon of Helvétius's widow, Benjamin Franklin, who presented him when he returned to America, together with his sword and the stick he had used in his experiments on calming waves, his own meticulously kept journal. In it, as Cabanis wrote in his essay on Franklin, the reader could follow 'the chronological history of Franklin's mind and character'. He could see 'how both had developed, strengthened and been adapted to all the acts in which their perfection consists'. What the journal offered was an example of 'the art of life and the art of virtue, learned as one learns to play an instrument or to fashion weapons'.[38] Beyle's own intimate journal, which he kept regularly for fourteen years, had a similar purpose, one that is apparent as well in other intimate diaries of the day:[39] 'If an indiscreet reader should find this journal, I wish to deprive him of the pleasure of laughing at the author by pointing out that what he sees can be nothing other than a mathematical and inflexible report on what I have been. I neither flatter nor slander, but state purely and severely what I believe to have been the truth. It is written with the intention of curing me of all that is ridiculous in my character when I read it in 1820...the best moments I have known, what I felt when listening to the music of Mozart, when reading Tasso, when waking to the sound of a street organ or offering my arm to my mistress, are not mentioned.'[40] Beyle's abandonment of his journal may correspond to an outgrowing of his original belief in his own or anyone else's perfectibility[41] and, as he grew older, in the possibility even of self-knowledge in the sense of seeing oneself as others see us.[42] 'With the exception of his *omnia possunt omnes*', he wrote in the May of 1818 to his friend Mareste, 'everything in Helvétius is divine.'

Helvétius may well be divine and the greatest philosopher of whom the French can boast, as Beyle describes him in *The Paris Monthly Review*. It is disconcerting, none the less, how little Beyle ever wrote to substantiate such a claim. According to Mérimée, though he was always recommending Helvétius's writings to his friends, he could never be persuaded to re-read them himself. This could be taken as one of his many notorious inconsistencies, though there are two good reasons at least for thinking that, as far as Helvétius was concerned, he was perfectly serious. For the discredit into which Helvétius had fallen was not merely one of the periodic wanings of the reputation of an honest and intelligent man. There is every reason to believe that the simple truth of his teaching was unwelcome in the society that succeeded the Revolution, a society which often preferred not to say or know where its own true interests lay. The young Karl Marx, while seeing in the theory of economic exploitation sketched by Helvétius a poorer version of the middle-class ideology of the English Utilitarians,[43] admired Helvétius's contribution to the development of materialist thinking and saw him as a forerunner of socialism.[44] And it is significant that during the first decades of the nineteenth century, Helvétius was not so much forgotten as periodically resurrected for the purposes of vehement refutation. 'There is no means of proving', Mme de Staël writes, 'that virtue is always in accordance with interest, unless one comes back to thinking of man's happiness as lying in the repose of his conscience.'[45] According to Benjamin Constant, 'The natural effect of this system of philosophy is to make every individual his own centre. Now when everyone is his own centre, all are isolated. When the storm comes, the dust is turned to mud.'[46] And the most influential academic philosopher of the 1820s in France, Nerval's examiner in the *baccalauréat*, insists that 'the human race' is unable to believe when it thinks of Regulus 'voluntarily encased in a coffin sprouting with upturned spikes', that he chose this fate 'from a love of pleasure'.[47]

It was partly because of the dangerous mystifications that can arise when the propositions enunciated by Helvétius are denied – as opposed to being dismissed on certain occasions as of little relevance or use – that Beyle chose to remain their champion. It was almost certainly too because they provided the starting point for what was to become a lifelong preoccupation. In his letter to Balzac thanking him for his review of *La chartreuse de Parme* and telling him how the novel was written, he uses a phrase which has become notorious – unfortunately, since it is usually taken out of context:

I first take someone I know very well; I let him keep all the habits he has formed in the art of setting out every morning on the pursuit of happiness (*la chasse du bonheur*); and then I make him more intelligent.[48]

It has often been assumed that Beyle is writing here as a mere hedonist and advocating or stating his interest in one particular kind of happiness, rather than describing the pursuit in which, as in Virgil's *Eclogues*, every living creature is engaged. What do men 'find to live *for* – what kinds of motive force or radical attitude can give life meaning, direction, coherence?' Our most distinguished living critic sees this question as one to which each of the main characters in Conrad's *Nostromo* 'enacts a particular answer...'[49] And it is a question that is by no means irrelevant to *La chartreuse de Parme* itself. How is it, to use Beyle's own language, that men so often 'lose their way on the road to happiness?' We may be disconcerted by the deliberate simplicity or nakedness of Beyle's language in the letter to Balzac, in an early essay entitled, significantly, *Si la comédie est utile* or in his early notebooks where he will formulate for his own guidance working principles such as the following:

> Since every comedy is an indictment of something harmful, it ceases to have any interest for us as soon as whatever this is is regarded as harmful and ridiculous and, as such, is banished from society.[50]

If the principles he enunciates appear simple, however, he was too intelligent not to realise the difficulties and improbability of their being successfully applied. He failed ever to write the comedies on which he brooded in vain for so many years and his writings on literature reveal as he grows older a growing refinement and subtlety in the expression of what remains, none the less, a very conscious Utilitarianism.[51]

De l'amour and *D'un nouveau complot contre les industriels*

What is positive and original in Beylisme, or rather in the thought and outlook implicit in his writings, is particularly apparent in his critical notes and essays and even more so in his three major novels. It can be seen also in *De l'amour* of 1822 and in his polemic of three years later directed against the new Saint-Simonian doctrines, works which belong to one of the most wretchedly unhappy and yet spiritually formative and intellectually fruitful periods of his entire career. In the summer of 1821 Beyle had left his beloved Milan, partly because of his fears of the Austrian police who may have suspected him of Liberal and *carbonaristo* sympathies but also because of the hopeless state of his passion for Mathilde Dembowski, the Milanese wife of a Polish-born general, whose portrait we may be glimpsing at times in all three of Beyle's major novels. This proud, idealistic and beautiful woman, who had been loved also by the poet Foscolo, found Beyle's attentions increasingly importunate. Beyle contemplated suicide and then returned to France taking with him the unfinished manuscripts of the book in which he was attempting to analyse and universalise his own experiences of love.

De l'amour, the first of his books not to be published at his own expense, enjoyed a certain notoriety during Beyle's lifetime. It is still a work that needs little introduction. In any case, it almost defies introduction. One can point out that in it Beyle categorises and illustrates four of the varieties of sexual love: *passionate love, love arising from enjoyment and the satisfaction of taste* (*l'amour goût*), *physical love* and *the love inspired by vanity*. One can point out also that in defining love, Beyle introduced into the European languages a new term: *crystallisation*, corresponding to a slightly less original concept, that of the emergence of real or apparent facts as the result of unacknowledged hopes or fears. It is impossible, however, to suggest the actual scope of Beyle's thinking in this work except by quoting it more lengthily than there is space for here.

One of the problems which Beyle tried to overcome in writing it is suggested in the ninth chapter, which consists of the following three sentences:

I make every possible effort to write *drily*. I wish to impose silence on my heart, which has a great deal, it believes, to say. I am always trembling at the thought that I may have only written a sigh, when I believe that I have noted down a truth.

Beyle wrote *De l'amour* partly as a contribution to the pursuit of truth as envisaged by the *idéologues* and partly too in the spirit in which Petrarch had composed the poems addressed to and inspired by Laura:

Ove sia chi per prova intenda amore,
Spero trovar pietà, non che perdono.
Sonnetti e canzoni, I.

[Wherever there may be someone who understands love from experience, I hope to find pity and not just pardon.]

The two forms of inspiration were not incompatible, for in describing such directly personal experience and in telling the reader that he would be able to understand him only if his experience of love were similar, Beyle was simply taking the methods of proof and description that had been adapted by the followers of Locke a step further towards true precision. It has often been said that the psychological theories and the epistemology of Locke and the French *idéologues* depend on large unproven assumptions concerning the nature of our senses and the external world and on evidence that can be revealed and corroborated only by introspection. And a modern critic of Locke (whose thought in this respect and in a number of others is akin to Beyle's) has seen the way forward from this position in two alternative kinds of psychology:

One unobjectionable sort of psychology is biological, and studies life from the outside. The other sort, relying on memory and dramatic imagination, reproduces life from the inside, and is literary. If the literary psychologist is a man of genius, by the clearness and range of his memory, by quickness of sympathy and power of suggestion, he may come very near to the truth of experience, as it has been or might be unrolled in a human being.[52]

De l'amour has no pretentions to being anything other than psychology of the second kind and it is perhaps for this reason that Destutt de Tracy was unable to believe that it was meant to be taken seriously.[53] It consists almost entirely of fictitious anecdotes and Beyle's own painfully recent memories, while its characteristic form of argument is by analogy rather than deduction from general principles. The precision that Beyle achieved in writing it is that of the minutely noted fact or *le petit fait vrai*, a term that appears repeatedly in his writings. The test of the truth of each fact lies in its compatibility both with the reader's own experience and with facts observed in different moods and circumstances. The passionate lover, for example, may, during his first conversations with the woman he loves:

let slip any number of things having no meaning or meaning the opposite of what he feels; or, what is even more agonizing, he may exaggerate his feelings, so that they become ridiculous in her eyes. As one is vaguely aware that she is not paying sufficient attention to what one says, an automatic impulse leads one to address her in carefully formed, heavy, declamatory phrases...During the first moments of love I ever knew, this peculiarity that I felt within me made me wonder whether I was really in love after all.

I understand now how a man can be a coward and why it is that conscripts try to overcome their fear by throwing themselves recklessly into the line of fire.[54]

De l'amour is not a novel, though it is obviously the work of a novelist of unusual inventive powers, for the illustrations which well up on every page contain the essential material for much longer stories. Nor is it, obviously, a poem in any ordinary sense of the word, though the disconcerting form of many chapters has something akin to a poetic structure. It is a work that makes its own shape – understandably, since, as in genuine poetry, the effort to understand and identify an experience has arisen from and is part of the experience itself, rather than an interpretation made in terms of a dominant preconceived idea. The prose of *De l'amour*, as in genuine poetry, conveys the swiftness and sudden reflective pauses of actual thought animated by a developing and hence constantly changing mood. Beyle will even momentarily on occasions (as in chapters 3 and 5) fall into a kind of free verse.[55] However, it would be wrong to conclude from this that *De l'amour* is a 'lyrical rapture' in which Beyle 'ventured far down the path of imaginative sensibility towards a world of private values...', to quote one fairly common view.[56] Mme Simone de Beauvoir has found in Stendhal's work in general and in *De l'amour* in particular one of the most humane and realistic accounts in literature of women's character, intelligence and needs and, like George Eliot(whose praise is admittedly more qualified[57]) admires him for seeing in female frivolity or stupidity the effects not of an inherent biological weakness but of particular social conventions and rules and particular forms of female education.[58] Beyle advocates in *De l'amour* opportunities and an education which, as far as possible, will be the same for men as for women and he replies to the objection that women would then become the rivals and not the companions of men:

Yes, they would, and as soon as love had been banished by decree. Until such a law is passed, the delights and transports of love will be redoubled and that is all. The foundation on which crystallisation takes place will grow even wider than before; the man will be able to enjoy all his thoughts together with the woman he loves, the whole of nature will take on new charms in their eyes and, as ideas always reflect certain shades of character, they will know each other better and commit fewer acts of imprudence; their love will be less blind and produce fewer misfortunes.[59]

He is, needless to say, an advocate too of matrimony as a result of love and free choice, rather than the usual business arrangement of the times and, like Helvétius, of divorce in the case of obvious incompatibility. *De l'amour* is inspired not only by the desire to note down certain 'truths' and to enjoy the luxury of addressing unknown kindred spirits but by the passion for social reform which makes him an authentic as well as a professed Utilitarian.

It is as a Utilitarian also, believing in what is 'useful to the greatest number' that he appears in his pamphlet of three years later, *D'un nouveau complot contre les industriels*, though the term has also been used to describe the doctrine against which it is aimed, and Beyle himself in using it points out the obvious truth that the greatest good of the greatest number can be envisaged in many different and conflicting ways. The issues with which Beyle is concerned in the pamphlet are both political and economic, which may explain partly why it has been so long neglected, for it is only in fairly recent years that his wide reading and insight as an amateur economist have been noticed by readers capable of appreciating them, notably M. Fernand Rude in his *Stendhal et la pensée sociale de son temps* and M. Lucien Jansse in an article in which Beyle is depicted as a forerunner of Keynes.[60] Between the ages of twenty and thirty, Beyle studied carefully and pen in hand Jean Baptiste Say's *Traité d'économie politique*, Adam Smith's *Wealth of Nations* and Malthus's *Essay on Population*. After 1814, he seems to have read also, soon after they appeared, the works of Ricardo, James Mill, the French statistician Baron Charles Dupin[61] and Count Henri de Saint-Simon together with the members of the school which was to bear his name. It is against these latter that the pamphlet of 1825 was directed.

The theories of Saint-Simon have often been confused with those of his self-professed disciples and with those of modern socialism. Yet Beyle's polemic may be all the easier to follow when we recall that the Utopia envisaged by Saint-Simon himself in works such as the *Système industriel*, *Le catéchisme des industriels* and *Le nouveau christianisme* is authoritarian and hierarchical. Saint-Simon, like Joseph de Maistre, whom he and his younger collaborator Auguste Comte both admired, looked on the French Revolution as merely destructive and deplored Jacobin egalitarianism. What Saint-Simon advocated was 'industrial inequality' in which the 'captains of industry' (to use Carlyle's consciously Saint-Simon phrase) would assume the rôle and functions of the old priesthood and feudal aristocracy. What is new and may seem socialistic in Saint-Simon's works and in the writings of the contributors to the Saint-Simonian journals is the condemnation as merely parasitic of all but the productive members of society, that is the *industriels*, and the belief that the latter should exercise supreme authority. The highest degree of productivity, according to Saint-Simon himself, was that which was apparent in capital investment, and the natural leaders of society therefore necessarily included the bankers.

Elie Halévy has pointed out how much of Saint-Simonianism survives in the ethos and practice of modern capitalism, in the fascist corporate state and in modern Marxian socialism.[62] Napoleon III himself, who in 1838 had produced his Saint-Simonian pamphlet, *Idées napoléoniennes,* was to think of himself after his seizure of power as a Saint-Simonian on the throne. Beyle's own pamphlet does not prophesy these developments, but the prophetic insights that it does contain may be appreciated if one reads it together with Halévy's analysis of Saint-Simonian economic doctrine. For the assumptions that the pamphlet exposes with deadly accuracy of aim and yet apparent flippancy have been current for many years along the whole range of the political spectrum.

The text on which Beyle's pamphlet is a commentary is taken from *Le catéchisme des industriels*:

It is industrial capacity that has to take the first place and adjudicate between the value of all other capacities, while making them all work for its own greater advantage.

The modern cult of productivity, the orders of nobility conferred on the directors of chain stores, and the exaltation of labour in

Soviet art, are all foreshadowed in this unusually candid affirmation of belief. What Beyle questions is the equation between a man's productive capacities and his claims on our admiration or his claims to be an infallible judge of what is admirable:

I am willing to believe that a thousand *industriels* who, with no sacrifice of probity, each gain a thousand écus, add to the strength of France; but these gentlemen have contributed to the general good *only after* contributing to their own. They are all fine honest men, whom I honour and whom I should be pleased to see elected as mayors or deputies; for the fear of bankruptcy has led them to acquire habits of suspicion and, what is more, they can count. But what I look for in vain is what is *admirable* in their conduct. Why should I admire them more than the doctor, the lawyer or the architect?...

The *industriels* lend money to those who govern and often oblige them to make a reasonable budget and not to waste the taxes. That probably is all one can say of their *usefulness* to the public at large; for they care little whether with the money they lend, help is sent to the Turks or the Greeks...

Industrialism, which is a not too distant relative of charlatanism, pays for the newspapers and, without even being asked to, assumes the responsibility for the defence of the cause of industry; moreover, it allows itself a little error of logic: it proclaims that industry is the cause of *all* the happiness enjoyed by the brave new world of America. If it will allow me to say so, industry has merely profited in America from excellent laws and the advantages of not having frontiers that can be attacked. The *industriels*, by means of the money they lend to a government, that is *after they have guaranteed themselves against loss*, momentarily add to the *strength* of that government; but they care little about the actual direction in which the strength is exerted...

The relevance of these observations to the contemporary world calls for no comment. It is by the standards of a truly general usefulness that Beyle condemns mere productivity.

Already in 1810, before Sismondi and Fourier[63] and before the first of the great industrial slumps in England, Beyle had questioned in the notes for an unwritten treatise on 'wealth, population and happiness', the widely accepted theory of Jean-Baptiste Say, according to which under normal conditions, each product will naturally find its own market. The only justification of productivity, Beyle argues, lies in the enjoyment of what is produced and it is because of the variation in men's capacity for various kinds of enjoyment that markets are so often saturated or unexploited. How then can the general good be either measured or foreseen? To begin with, at least, he argues in *D'un nouveau complot*, by not confusing fundamental issues. We should, for example, distinguish between the good which is done as an indirect consequence of some other aim and the good that is directly intended. We should remember too – and here certainly take a lesson from Saint-Simon – from what point of view and with what interests in mind the arbiter of the general good speaks for us. Beyle himself speaks as a member of the class of those who possess a private income of 6,000 livres:

They alone have the *leisure* to form an opinion which is their own and not that of the newspaper they read. To think is the least costly of pleasures...

The thinking class accords its consideration to whatever is *useful to the greatest number*. It recompenses by its esteem and sometimes with glory the William Tells, the Porliers, the Riegos, the Codrus, those, in other words, who risk a great deal in order to obtain what, rightly or wrongly, they believe to be useful to the public...

For to deserve a high esteem, it is on the whole necessary that there should be a *sacrifice* of interest to some noble end.[64] What sacrifices have Zamet, Samuel Bernard, Crozat, Bouret, etc. ever made, that is the richest *industriels* whose memory is preserved by history? God forbid that I should conclude from this merely historical observation that the *industriels* are without honour. All I mean to say is that they are not heroic...

What is heroism? Is it possible in the modern world? Beyle's experience of armed encounter, gunfire and perilous adventure was limited – possibly even more so than he wished posterity to believe.[65] It is in his own novels and his comments on the poets and dramatists he admired that we can best hope to find an answer to these questions.

3

Beyle the critic

Beyle and heroic drama

During his own lifetime, Beyle seems to have been best known as the habitué of various salons, as a pamphleteer writing under a somewhat absurd German aristocratic pseudonym and as a connoisseur of music and the arts. After the publication in 1823 and 1825 of his two brochures on *Racine et Shakspeare*, he also achieved notoriety for a time as a literary critic given to amusing polemic, and a defender in theory of the new Romanticism. With the discovery since his death by the general public of his three major novels, his critical writings have been neglected, for they have long since lost their *actualité* and their claims to permanent interest have still to be recognised. I myself have been taken to task by a well-known authority on French literature[1] for suggesting, what I wish to argue here, that if Beyle's work as a whole were better known he would be recognised as one of the great French critics.

Beyle's critical writings – those that he himself published and those that survive in letters, notebooks and diaries – are, to use T. S. Eliot's term, those of a 'practitioner', an aspiring dramatist who, after the age of forty, resigned himself to the rôle of a not very fashionable novelist writing mainly for posterity. His interest in literature was in no sense academic. In reading he was guided by his deep and volatile enthusiasms, by his need to understand human nature and history and by his desire to learn from writers of the past how to speak to a contemporary audience. Beyle's 'interest' in writing criticism is plain – if we use 'interest' in its Helvetian sense – and it is this which accounts for its unusual clarity and its freedom from such affectations as those of academic impartiality. If Beyle so often hit on the actual truth about those he read, it was precisely because of this all-embracing need to learn from his predecessors rather than judge them.

Beyle's critical writings give us the principal clue to what Prévost has described as his apprenticeship (see pages 5–6 above) and one can trace in his comments on what he read over the years certain major preoccupations which presumably correspond to the 'five or six principal ideas' he had spent his life 'considering attentively', preoccupations which are apparent also in the subject matter and technique of his novels. To avoid confusion, it may be necessary to consider these singly and therefore once again, while considering the history of Beyle's education, to avoid an exact chronological sequence.

Beyle's preoccupation with the heroic and the possibilities of heroic action in the modern world dates, not surprisingly, from his early childhood. It is of course normal for any small boy to dream of acts of heroic daring and sacrifice and to grow up realising that these were nothing but dreams. But Beyle was unusual in that he grew to consciousness during the great adventure of the Revolution and the Revolutionary wars when many responsible-seeming adults spoke of themselves as re-living the annals of the Roman Republic. He would exult in secret not over the exploits of warriors remote in time but over the heroes of the daily news, and the thought that men might actually live through such days again was never to leave him. The 'tender love' he felt at the age of nine for the regiments he would watch from his grandfather's window riding through the Place Grenette in Grenoble was to remain with him throughout his life and survive the disillusionment of his serving as an officer in the very same army only seven years later. The same regiments were to appear, if only briefly, in his novels as the embodiment of some supreme unfulfilled possibility.

Epic and heroic drama understandably exerted an enormous appeal over Beyle's imagination as a youth and, for that matter, throughout his life. Ariosto's *Orlando Furioso*, Tasso's *Gerusalemme Liberata* (and *Don Quixote*) were to remain lifelong favourites, though in middle age, he decided regretfully that Ariosto's heroes had too much of the 'ostler'[2] about them and that it was Tasso who was the superior genius of the two. The heroic drama of Corneille seemed to him for several years the most sublime achievement of the theatre and undervalued only because there were so few capable of understanding the character and behaviour of Corneille's heroes. 'Since the eyes of petty men are too weak to bear the light of true greatness', he wrote in an early notebook,[3] 'they prefer Racine to Corneille and Virgil to Homer.' And again: 'It is in his depiction of character that a poet has always been great; this is why Homer, Corneille and Molière are superior to Virgil, Racine, etc.'[4] In his admiration for Corneille, moreover, he was encouraged by Helvétius, who, in *De l'esprit*, defines the hypocrite as 'someone who, not being sustained in his own study of moral qualities by a desire for the happiness of humanity, is too much absorbed in himself...' and who recommends Corneille for his 'depiction of great heroes and statesmen'.[5] Not surprisingly, the hero of his own unwritten comedy *Les deux hommes* was to have received a proper philosophic education, unlike his decadent and affected rival, and the effects of his education were to have been apparent in his generosity, integrity and realism. Beyle's admiration for Corneille and, after his first stay in Italy, of the plays of Vittorio Alfieri, seems to have waned only after his discovery of Shakespeare.

Beyle's comments on Corneille and Alfieri, like those on Rousseau, are of interest not only for what they tell us of these authors themselves but as an indication of the kind of man he became in the process of growing older. For his various comments over the years on the pride and honour which Corneille and Alfieri exalt in their plays remind one of what he wrote both about his own precocious Roman Republicanism and about the influence on his character of his beloved great-aunt Elizabeth Gagnon. Mlle. Gagnon, when he knew her as a boy, was a tall thin elderly lady with a dignity which had something Spanish about it in its refinement and scrupulosity: 'In this respect, she formed my character and it is to my Aunt Elizabeth that I owe the absurd would-be Spanish dignity of which I was the dupe and victim for the first thirty years of my life.'[6]

One has only to read one of the few works by Alfieri which can still be read as living literature, his superb autobiography, to realise why Beyle found him congenial as a young man and in later life a somewhat dangerous influence. The description of Alfieri's lonely childhood, in the Piedmont of the 1750s, during which he rarely saw his own family and was left to the care of servants and priests, resembles Beyle's in the impression it leaves of an acute spiritual malnutrition, though the deprivations from which Alfieri suffered were probably more cruel than those of Beyle after the death of his mother. It is impossible to tell whether Beyle exaggerated the miseries of his own childhood in *La vie de Henry Brulard* but if he did, it is arguable that he was influenced unknowingly by the *Life* of Alfieri. Brought up as he was, Alfieri developed the fierce proud independence of character which is seen in his account of the duels he fought, in his passion for hard dangerous horse-riding, in the terseness of his prose and verse, and in his hatred of political tyranny and admiration for Plutarch's *Lives*. It is also seen in the determination with which he set out to learn the Italian of Florence (which, for a Piedmontese educated in Turin, was almost a foreign language) and to become the author of tragic masterpieces written in the Italian of Dante. His conception of tragedy is also what one would expect from what he tells us of his life. Despite his Republicanism, his admiration for England and his contempt for France; despite also his dislike of the French classical alexandrine and of the classical convention of the *confident*, his conception of tragedy is essentially close to Corneille's. 'When Alfieri wrote one of his immortal tragedies', Beyle wrote in a letter to Pauline, 'who could afterwards rob him of the infinite satisfaction he had found in giving utterance to the minds of those men who have come closer to being divine than any others before him or since, to men like Brutus, Timoleon, etc.?'[7]

Feeling or at least imagining he felt a close kinship with Alfieri, Beyle became increasingly conscious as he grew older of the penalties of the proud independence which is achieved at the expense of an awareness of different ways of thinking and feeling and which is hence fatal in a dramatist. He became aware also of a curious emptiness behind Alfieri's terse magniloquence. In December 1804, after seeing Talma act in a version of *Macbeth* by Jean-François Ducis, he noted in his diary that 'there is no sensibility *without detail* [my italics]. Their failure to remember this is one of the principal failings of French dramatists. I felt this too when reading the other day Alfieri's *Oreste* in which I found the same defect...Shakespeare is much closer to the kind of tragedy I have in mind but shall probably never write.'

And seven years later, after seeing *Oreste* performed in Florence, he noted: 'Full of rapidity, vengeance; but completely without interest. It seems to me too sublime...there is not enough of the *human* to make sympathy possible.'[8]

A similar evolution is seen in Beyle's attitude to Alfieri's politics. On the day of Napoleon's coronation, in the year following Alfieri's death, after seeing 'religion come to sanctify tyranny and all this in the name of human happiness', he had read some of Alfieri's prose in order, he writes, 'to rinse out my mouth'.[9] His admiration for Alfieri's Republicanism waned, however, after he had read the latter's denunciation of all that had happened in France since 1789. He found himself wondering in what sense, if any, Alfieri had ever cared about human liberty.

Beyle's early enthusiasm for Alfieri and his subsequent misgivings explain perhaps why, after he had discovered *The Edinburgh Review*, a journal he was to describe as a revelation,[10] he paid special attention to an article by Francis Jeffrey on Alfieri's life and writings which appeared in January 1810. Long passages from this essay are translated and introduced into *Rome, Naples et Florence en 1817* and the extracts are attributed to the fictitious Count Neri of Bologna. (Where Beyle has translated directly from Jeffrey the text here is in italics.)

Though professedly a Republican, it is easy to see that the republic he wanted was one on the Roman model – where there were Patricians as well as Plebeians, and where a man of great talents had even a good chance of being one day appointed Dictator...Boredom, together with a hatred for those who are happy, was the dominant feature of his existence and on the throne he would have been a Nero.

As it is the great excellence, so it is occasionally the chief fault of Alfieri's dialogue, that every word is honestly employed to help forward the action of the play, by serious argument, necessary narrative or the direct expression of natural emotion. There are no excursions or digressions – no episodical conversations,– and none but the most brief moralizings. This gives a certain air of solidity to the whole piece, that is apt to prove oppressive to the ordinary reader and reduces the entire drama to too great uniformity. The intelligent reader anticipates far too easily what is going to be said. There is nothing striking, nothing stirring; when one has read three or four of his tragedies, the others leave no surprises. One reads him as one reads Milton out of a sense of duty and leaves off without regret.

I say this speaking as a learned man of letters; as for my own particular feelings, *I believe that those who are duly sensible of the merit of*

Shakespeare will never be much struck with any other dramatical compositions. In these respects he disdains all comparison with Alfieri or with any other poet. Alfieri, Corneille and all the others consider a tragedy as a poem; Shakespeare saw it as a presentation of the character and passions of men, which, if it is to move the spectator must do so by arousing his sympathy and not because of a vain admiration on his part for the poet's talents . . .

Alfieri was incapable of seeing things from this point of view and of distinguishing between the actions of men and the different ways of portraying them which have given rise to the various dramatic schools. He took as his guide the French school, the only one he knew. He mistook his memories for the result of his observations. With a little more intelligence, he would have recognised that he had never really observed anything . . . [11]

The change in Beyle's attitude to Alfieri coincided, as the above extract suggests, with a reassessment of Corneille. 'Racine is often perfect in his depiction of love . . .', he had written in his early twenties. 'His style is nearly always perfect. What is perfect in Corneille is often the thought rather than the style. From which it follows that Corneille will be enjoyed by those who look for the substance rather than the shadow and enjoyed far less by the common herd.'[12] The latter judgment was one which he had come to modify as time went on and as he came to realise how baffling the thought of Corneille can be, despite the superficial clarity of his style.

During Beyle's periods of leave from 1811 to 1813, he had sketched out with his former school friend, the engineer Louis Crozet, character-studies of mutual acquaintances and notes on the books they read together. Their notes on Corneille's *Cinna*, which survive in the handwriting of Beyle and Crozet, were never intended for publication, though they constitute perhaps one of the finest commentaries on classical drama to have found its way into print. The notes are an analysis of the first act of *Cinna*, beginning with Emilie's opening tirade, in which she tells us of her 'impatient desire' to avenge her father condemned to death by her own protector, the Emperor Augustus:

> Impatients désirs d'une illustre vengeance
> Dont la mort de mon père a formé la naissance,
> Enfants impétueux de mon ressentiment

Que ma douleur séduite embrasse aveuglément,
Vous prenez sur mon âme un trop puissant empire...
[Impatient desires of an illustrious vengeance, engendered by the death of my father, impetuous children of my resentment that my seduced grief blindly embraces, you hold too powerful a sway over my soul...]

Beyle and Crozet comment on these lines:

The main fault of this monologue is that Emilie talks to herself with all the clarity and eloquence of a woman addressing a stranger. We feel that Shakespeare would have made this scene altogether more natural by giving Emilie the simple authentic language of a troubled soul. He would have shown her, for example, at two o'clock in the morning leaving her bed and walking agitatedly up and down in her room to the great astonishment of one of her maidservants. What a difference it would have made to the interest of the drama if Cinna were to enter her room at two o'clock in order to talk to her of the conspiracy! Otherwise, if the risk were too great, Emilie could have been made to form some decision of which she informed Cinna the following day in the course of a hunt.

The style is not suited to Emilie's character, but if we assume for a moment that it is, we find that it is noble and passionate (or tragic); it is clear, and it has the terseness which is that of a mighty soul. To prove this, one has only to imagine the four lines ('Vous prenez sur mon âme', etc.) spoken by a character like Voltaire's Amenaïde and the disconcerting effect they would produce.

Imagine that the dialogue is a portrait. Imagine, that is, that the poet claimed to be repeating what Emilie herself had said in his hearing. If this were the case, we should blame the poet for everything that struck us as contrary to nature...The problem we wish to raise is the following: what would our conception of Emilie be after we had heard this monologue? We would imagine her as a woman of firm character, lacking consequently in grace (in the charms of weakness), a little in love with Cinna and unable to distinguish between her vengeance and her love. It is difficult to imagine (still with reference to this one monologue) one of these two passions, love and vengeance, completely overcoming the other; or, in other words, which is the stronger of the two.[13]

The speeches of Cinna himself are also disconcertingly out of character and give no hint of his subsequent eager gratitude to the forgiving Augustus. Beyle and Crozet analyse his account of the propaganda of the conspirators preparing to overthrow Augustus and his henchmen:

> Je les peins dans le meurtre à l'envi triomphants,
> Rome entière noyée au sang de ses enfants:
> Les uns assassinés dans les places publiques,
> Les autres dans le sein de leurs dieux domestiques;
> Le méchant par le prix au crime encouragé;
> Le mari par sa femme en son lit égorgé...
> (act I, scene iii, lines 195–200)

[I depict them striving to outdo each other and triumphant in murder, the whole of Rome drowned in its children's blood; some assassinated in the public places, others in the bosom of their household gods; the evil man enticed to crime by gold; the husband's throat cut by his wife as he lies in bed...]

This is a perfect model of the tragic style. There is a certain seeking after effect, but this is in no way cold or vulgar...nor, we may add, is there any hint that the speaker is a man without character, momentarily exalted.

The ending,

> Demain j'attends la fin, etc.,

announces a mighty character and induces in the reader the quivering of a proud smile; the reader admires himself and imagines himself to be capable of sentiments as elevated as these.[14]

What in fact is the play about? Beyle and Crozet admit their bafflement:

In general, in what we have seen of the play, we do not acquire an *intimate knowledge* of the characters. Basing our judgment merely on what they say, we are able to form three or four totally distinct impressions of their character.

Is Emilie moved by the sheer love of liberty, by filial piety or by a proud desire not to remain unavenged?

After five minutes, we see at once what sort of a woman Lady Macbeth is or Desdemona...[15]

This analysis of Corneille resembles in more than one respect Beyle's and Jeffrey's analysis of Alfieri. In the writings of both poets, we are shown the inhibiting effect of the desire to 'appear noble'. To quote once again from the fictitious Count Neri:

...the correct gravity of the sentiments expressed in these tragedies, the perfect propriety and the wise moderation with which the author depicts passion are exactly the opposite of what might have been expected from his fiery and independent character...Not even the most inattentive reader can fail to notice the immense labour he devoted to his style. Faithful to his patrician character, Alfieri imagined that by writing in this way he would be *more respected*. He would have been much greater and certainly more original if he had been himself.[16]

One of the advantages of this approach to Alfieri and, in so far as he resembles him, to Corneille as well, is that it explains not only why their plays can seem so baffling and unsatisfactory but also why they can seem the opposite; why it is, for example, that *Cinna*, despite what Beyle and Crozet say, has gone on appealing over the centuries to readers and playgoers. The spectator or playgoer to whom the play appeals responds presumably to the pride and joy in living of Corneille's characters, to their passionate even if simple sense of justice and to the serene courage with which they are able to confront inevitable and appalling dangers. To quote Beyle and Crozet once again:

> The ending,
>> *Demain j'attends la fin*, etc.
> announces a mighty character and induces in the reader the quivering of a proud smile...

Yet it is possible for the reader or spectator who finds the play inspiring in this way to allow such moments as those to dominate his impression of the play as a whole and not to notice how much he is seeing in it only what he wishes to see. What Beyle and Crozet criticise in *Cinna* is not the fact that it arouses a response of this kind, but that because of something inhibited in Corneille, it fails to satisfy it, all the more so if one wishes to learn from the play and find in it something more than a reflection of what one knows, feels and believes already. The conclusions they reach are all the more eloquent in that they confine their comments to the first act, saying nothing of the capitulation of the proud Emilie and the intrepid Cinna when their conspiracy is discovered or of their effusive thanks when the Emperor Augustus decides to forgive them.

As Beyle himself makes perfectly clear, the fact that he became increasingly demanding in his reading of Corneille and Alfieri is explained to a great extent by his discovery of Shakespeare, whom he read both in English and in the translation of Le Tourneur. 'He is like a flowing river', he wrote in 1805 after re-reading *Othello*, 'a river which sweeps over everything and carries everything with it. His sheer vitality is like a river. He is nature itself...'[17] And a few days before this, in the mixture of languages of which he had already grown fond: '*O divin Shakespeare*, oui thou art the greatest Bard in world!'[18]

The Shakespeare of whom he speaks most often and with most enthusiasm is not, however, the Shakespeare who was able to show heroic idealism in the most bleakly cynical and withering light. If he soon came to prefer him to Corneille, it was not because he had come to hold the views of Thersites or Falstaff on 'honour'. Beyle's ideas of honour and heroism changed over the years, it is obvious. They ceased to be of the kind one associates with adolescent hero-worship. One could say perhaps that he came to be more imaginative and perceptive and hence more prone to scepticism in his thoughts concerning the kind of life in which survival is only tolerable when consistent with self-respect and the demands of principle. Beyle's increasing proneness to scepticism, however, went with a deepening of his admiration for what he saw as acts of genuine rather than merely self-dramatising honour and heroism. ('For to deserve a high esteem, it is on the whole necessary that there should be a *sacrifice* of interest to some noble end.'[19]) In this respect, as in many others, there is a continuity of feeling between the mature and the adolescent Beyle.

Much of what he has written on Shakespeare suggests that he found in his plays a satisfaction not unlike that which he had formerly derived from those of Corneille and Alfieri. There is little sign that he recognised that it is also far less obviously heroic. His commentary on *Julius Caesar*, which he wrote with Crozet at the same time as the notes on *Cinna* is in this respect very revealing. The commentary tells us virtually nothing of the ferocious irony of the play, the irony, that is, on Shakespeare's part, of such lines as the following:

> Stoop, Romans, stoop,
> And let us bathe our hands in Caesar's blood
> Up to the elbows and besmear our swords:
> Then walk we forth, even to the market place,
> And waving our red weapons o'er our heads,
> Let's all cry, 'Peace, freedom and liberty!'
>
> (act III, scene i.)

The subtle hypocrisy of Shakespeare's Brutus (what Mr Morris

Shapira has described in a lecture as 'the leak in his nobility') is something also of which they say nothing:

> What we are shown very vividly is the purity of Brutus's character: the character of a sensitive and affectionate man who loves Caesar and who realises that it is necessary to kill him. He says
> We shall be call'd purgers, not murderers...[20]

What they criticise in Brutus and Cassius is that they are too magnanimous and too much addicted to philosophising:

> They should never have hesitated to sacrifice Mark Antony. Instead of this, when Caesar is dead, they amuse themselves by giving lectures in philosophy...Moreover, if these two Romans were to come back to life and read Plutarch themselves, I think they would have been annoyed with him and amused at us for seeing in a conspiracy only what an old sweet-tempered philologist had imagined...[21]

These comments were made in 1811. Beyle's tendency, however, to attribute to Shakespeare's heroes motives of an unequivocally noble and virtuous kind is seen twelve years later in his comments on *Othello*, one of the plays which he seems always to have considered among the finest. In *La vie de Rossini* of 1823, he criticises Rossini's Othello who, from the moment of his first triumphant entry, is made to seem far too proud: 'For pride is the one thing in Othello one should avoid suggesting.' Rossini's Othello lacks also 'the tenderness which would have made it clear to me that it is not vanity which places the dagger in Othello's hand'. In Shakespeare's Othello, the love we are shown is a love like Werther's, 'a love which can be sanctified by suicide'.[22] One is tempted to add: a love like that of Julien Sorel in *Le rouge et le noir* for Mme de Rênal.

The temptation is one which it is better to resist, however. It is quite likely that the inspiration for Julien's attempted murder of his former mistress came from the tragedy Beyle most admired as well as from the newspaper account of the shooting by Antoine Berthet of Mme Michoud in 1827. Julien's motivation is complex, however, and is shown as such, far more than that attributed by Beyle to Othello. It is possible too that the subtlety of insight which we find in *Le rouge et le noir* is a consequence of his reading of Shakespeare even though his comments on the psychology of Shakespeare's characters may sometimes disappoint us by their simple-mindedness. What is certain is that his notions of the heroic were no longer as simple as when he sat down at the age of twenty with the intention of becoming 'the greatest poet possible'.

'Le style est ceci'

There is one other conclusion which can be drawn from Beyle's comments on Corneille and Alfieri: his interest in these writers is invariably, as in his comments on the prose of Rousseau, an interest in the language they use. The point of view from which he writes is always that of the literary critic, whatever else this point of view may involve.

Since ideas both of the function of language and of the nature of criticism are always changing, it is necessary, however, to be more specific. I should like therefore to quote two rather disparaging accounts of Beyle's qualifications as a literary critic and then to explain why I find them unjust.

The first is taken from Sainte-Beuve's essay on Beyle in *Portraits contemporains*:

It is to be noticed that, as far as style is concerned, through wishing it to be limpid and natural, Beyle seemed to exclude from it the poetry, the colour, the images and those expressions of genius which clothe the passions and enhance the language of dramatic personages, even in Shakespeare – and I would say, above all in Shakespeare.[23]

This judgment has been echoed by most of Beyle's critics ever since and I feel a certain temerity in describing it as nonsense. It is echoed, for example, by M. Georges Blin in his recent study of *Stendhal et les problèmes du roman*. In the second of the two passages which I wish to consider, M. Blin talks of the contradiction or 'tension' between Beyle's insistence on truth and realism in drama and the novel and his interest in the various kinds of sheer beauty to be found in painting and in sculpture:

The tension is such between the realistic end which he ascribes to all works of literature and the criteria of which he approves as an aesthetician, that one wonders whether he thought of literature as art at all, as something, that is, corresponding to the same conditions and liable to the same kind of judgment. One's doubts are all the more legitimate since he tended to expel from the realm of letters all poetry, that is to say, the form of literature which achieves the highest degree of insubordination to any meaning.[24]

Neither Sainte-Beuve nor M. Blin explain why if Beyle wishes to exclude from literature all poetry, he should have found in the poetry of Dante and Shakespeare the qualities he had looked for in vain in Corneille and Alfieri. ('No man has ever been *more himself*', he writes than Dante. 'Alfieri was not himself in his language and much less than he thought in his ideas.')[25]

However, it is Beyle's conception of poetry and style in general to which Sainte-Beuve and M. Blin take exception and in taking exception, they each invoke an alternative view of how language works. Sainte-Beuve's analogy with clothing is a familiar one. It is used, for example, by Alfieri himself when talking of his first attempts to write verse in the Italian of Florence while thinking still in the half-French dialect of his native Piedmont. The substance of his *Cleopatra*, he writes, when given expression in French was altogether excellent. Rewritten in Italian verse, it was worse than mediocre: 'So true is it that in all poetry the clothing is half the body, while in some kinds of poetry, in the lyric, for example, the clothing is everything.'[26]

The comparison between clothing and literary style is as familiar in English as in French or Italian and because of this it is very easy to believe that one understands it. Yet the distinction that Sainte-Beuve and Alfieri have in mind is not between the words themselves and what they stand for; between what contemporary linguisticians describe, that is, as *le signifiant* and *le signifié*. If it were, they would be referring presumably to all forms of language, even that used in railway timetables. It is by no means certain what they mean but it is likely, none the less, that they are distinguishing between what can be understood and adequately conveyed in different words when one is reading poetry (or prose that has a poetic quality) and what is conveyed to the reader without his understanding what he is experiencing or why. They may have in mind, that is to say, what we mean when we talk of the 'magic' of someone's style or what critics such as the Abbé Bouhours in the seventeenth century described more clearly and unpretentiously as the *je ne sais quoi*, a phrase which has unfortunately become trivialised beyond redemption.

The analogy between style and clothing is one which Beyle himself, as far as I know, never used. The one comparison which resembles it and which he did use on a number of occasions is a comparison with varnish. 'Style ought to be like a transparent varnish: it must not alter the colours or the facts and thoughts on which it is placed', he and Crozet remark when writing of the style of Rousseau.[27] However, in his more rigorously precise definitions of style, he avoids altogether simile and metaphor. In the same notebook he and Crozet assert roundly:

Le style est ceci: 'ajouter à une pensée donnée toutes les circonstances, propres à produire tout l'effet que doit produire cette pensée.[28]
[Style is this: to add to a given thought all the circumstances liable to produce the total effect which this thought must produce.]

'Thought' here, as in general in Beyle's vocabulary and that of the idéologues, is a term which covers not only 'ideas' and 'memories' but also 'sensations' and 'emotions'.[29] 'A given thought' is here a deliberately comprehensive phrase, as is also 'circumstances'. The attention given to style when reading is, according to this view, nothing more than the detailed attention to what is implied or betrayed by the use of words. Style is seen as a function of meaning. The definition is, in other words, perfectly consistent with one's experience of the *je ne sais quoi* and with the view that there are forms of literature which, in the words of M. Blin, achieve a 'high degree of insubordination to any meaning.'

There is a difference, however, between the insubordination to meaning which appears to be a consequence of what is unfamiliar or mysterious in what is communicated (in certain passages of Shakespeare, for example) and the meaninglessness which is merely the result of self-deception, obscurity and incoherence on the part of the author. According to Beyle, the poetry of Alfieri is of the latter kind and he reproaches him, together with other Italian poets born and educated outside Tuscany, for forcing himself to write in the Italian of Florence rather than in his native dialect: 'You will acknowledge, I think, that a man can be a poet in that language alone in which he talks to his mistress and his rivals.'[30] There is an analogy, in this respect, between the Tuscan of Alfieri and the conventional *style noble* used by Chateaubriand in his novels. Speaking, for example, of the latter's *Le dernier des Abencérages* in the *New Monthly Magazine* for September 1826, Beyle writes: ... 'The author has not observed that extreme loftiness is only attainable in French by the rejection of words degraded by common use. Now this rejection casts at once a *veil of obscurity* [my italics] over the language, which is a deadly fault in a novel.'[31]

These two quotations may not invalidate the point M. Blin is making but the injustice of his argument is apparent when one reads other general pronouncements by Beyle on the nature of language, style and poetry. By 'high degree of insubordination to any meaning' one may assume that he is referring to what Sainte-Beuve and Alfieri presumably have in mind when they talk of the 'clothing of style', to what in genuine poetry, that is to say, defies paraphrase or translation. And to say that Beyle was blind to poetry in this sense of the term is to ignore his comments over a period of forty years on the poets he most admired.

His preoccupation with what is unique and irreducible to other terms in genuine poetry is seen in the importance he attaches to *detail*:

...there is no sensibility without detail. Their failure to remember this is one of the principal failings of French dramatists. I felt this the other day when reading Alfieri's *Oreste*...[32] Surely a poet would benefit greatly by particularising far more his comparisons; 'I go up a majestic river'. Why not name either the Rhine or the Rhône? It seems to me that this is Ariosto's way of writing.[33]

'Detail' or 'the little true fact' is a term which recurs constantly in Beyle's writing throughout his career. (One is reminded of Blake's dictum that 'Truth lies in minute particulars.') For Beyle, as also for Destutt de Tracy, it is that which precedes all thought, or rather on which thought, reflection and memory depend. According to Tracy, it is our general ideas which are incorporated in particular perceptions and memories rather than the other way round.[34]

If Beyle learned from Tracy in this respect, he learned also from the poetry he admired. The actual detail and observation which he found in Shakespeare he found also in La Fontaine, the only poet, he once wrote, 'who touched his heart in the same spot as Shakespeare'.[35] And what he also noted and admired was the tact and delicacy of their appeal to the reader's imagination. I quote from the entries in his diary for 23 August 1804 and for 5 February of the following year:

The poet is someone who arouses the emotions of his reader; there are two ways in which this can be done.

One can depict perfectly things capable of giving a very small quantity of emotion. By this means, one can make them convey the whole of this emotion:

La Fontaine, for example, when he portrays the weasel trying to get out of the granary [see Fables, Book 3, Fable 17].

Or one can depict more or less successfully something capable of arousing a great deal of emotion:

As Voltaire does when he shows us the situation in which Mérope finds herself and what she does in the tragedy of that name.

I believe that if I were to read attentively (and with a well practiced feeling for what is bad and false in feeling, if I were to read as a poet would) *Mérope* and then the fable of the poor woodcutter burdened with faggots, the first fifteen lines of the fable [book 1, fable 16] would move me far more than the entire tragedy.

One way of moving the reader is to show the *facts, the things themselves*, while saying nothing of the effect they produce. This method can be employed by a person of sensibility who is not a philosopher...It is a method which Mme de Staël seems completely unable to use herself. Her book *Delphine* is wholly lacking in moments of repose like those which the great Shakespeare offers the reader in his tragedy of *Macbeth*. In this play, in which terror is carried to the utmost pitch, one of the gentlemen who is accompanying Duncan as he enters the castle of Macbeth points out, at a moment which is terrifying for the spectator and perfectly ordinary for him and his companions, the sweet pure beauty of the site of the castle where the 'temple-haunting martlet...Hath made his pendant bed and procreant cradle.' It is one of the most divine strokes of this great man and one which I feel is more profound that the 'Qu'il mourût' of Corneille[36] and the 'Qui te l'a dit?' of Racine.[37]

The conscious delicacy with which Beyle notes the precise degree and kind of enjoyment he experiences when reading La Fontaine and Shakespeare reminds one of how much he shared the preoccupation with 'taste' and 'sensibility' of a number of contemporary French and, more particularly English philosophers and critics, especially those who had found in David Hartley's theory of the Association of Ideas the foundation of an aesthetic theory justified both by common sense and by what was revealed in flights of imagination. Beyle read and admired not only the *Discourses* of Sir Joshua Reynolds[38] but also the far more interesting and now undeservedly forgotten *Analytical inquiry into the principles of taste* of Richard Payne Knight. [39] His interest in the *effect* of poetry is an interest in what John Stuart Mill has described as 'not an illusion but a fact' and his writings from his earliest years make it seem more than likely that he would have endorsed Mill's arguments in favour of 'the cultivation of the feelings' through the imagination. Mill describes in his *Autobiography* his defence of Wordsworth in a debate with his friend J. A. Roebuck, a man 'of very quick and strong sensibilities', though 'like most Englishmen who have feelings, he found his feelings stand very much in the way'.

It was in vain that I urged on him that the imaginative emotion which an idea, when vividly conceived, excites in us, is not an illusion but a fact, as real as any of the other qualities of objects; and far from implying anything erroneous and delusive in our mental apprehension of the object, is quite consistent with the most accurate knowledge and most perfect recognition of all its physical and intellectual laws and relations. The intensest feeling of the beauty of a cloud lighted by the setting sun, is no hindrance to my knowing that the cloud is vapour of water, subject to all the laws of vapours in a state of suspension... [40]

There is some significance in the fact that Mill, like Beyle, was formed to some extent by the reading of Helvétius.

Beyle's debt to Helvétius is considerable and a study of Helvétius himself and the other philosophers and critics by whom he was influenced can help the reader to appreciate, more readily than he might have otherwise, the kind of thinking that lies behind Beyle's often misleadingly laconic remarks on the style of other writers. [41] Beyle was fortunate in being able to read some of the best eighteenth-century philosophy and criticism and differed from his contemporaries mainly in the quickness with which he came to realise the truth of its finer insights and the whole-heartedness and pertinacity with which he continued to learn from them. In making these insights his own he was, of course, following not only the spirit but the letter of a philosophy for which personal experience and judgment are the beginning and the end of knowledge. As Helvétius wrote in a passage which Beyle copied and commented on in his early notebooks:

In every *genre* and in particular in those which seek to give pleasure, the beauty of a work varies according to the sensation it arouses in us. The more clear and distinct this sensation is, the keener the beauty. [42]

What is true of 'the beauty of a work' is true equally of the feelings and experiences of a fictitious character. The following is another of the principles which Beyle noted as a young man and which helped to form his idea of literature:

...one can never depict the passions and feelings convincingly unless one is capable of experiencing them oneself. Suppose that a character is placed in circumstances which are liable to set in motion the entire activity of the passions within him. In order to depict them in an authentic way, it is necessary that one should first be susceptible to the feelings whose effects one has set out to show. One's model must be within oneself... [43]

Yet Helvétius's comments on language and style, or at least language and style considered as such, are more cursory and less original than those of Condillac or Destutt de Tracy. They are interesting partly because of what he fails to say – because of his freedom, that is, from many of the beliefs and preoccupations of his own contemporaries, and in particular from those which we associate with the name of Voltaire.

Chief among these is a belief not only in the desirability but the feasibility of what amounts to a perfect language, in other words of a language capable of expressing all that we ever need to say and of conveying this, without loss or distortion, to any normally intelligent educated adult. Expressing oneself with perfect accuracy, according to this belief, should be merely a matter of knowing and finding *le mot juste*.[44] A perfect language for Voltaire is also one in which the meaning of words has been established for all time. He speaks of the period when English poets learned to write 'correctly'[45] and when criticising a turn of phrase used by Corneille, he objects to it on the simple grounds that it is no longer in use. 'It is shameful for the human spirit', he writes, 'that the same expression should be found good at one period of history and bad at another.'[46]

A 'perfect' language for Destutt de Tracy is an impossibility, '...for we have seen', he writes in his *Grammaire*, 'that the uncertainty of the value of the signs of our ideas is inherent, not in the nature of the signs but in our intellectual faculties. It is impossible for the same sign to have exactly the same value for all those who employ it or even for the individual who employs it on different occasions.'[47] The conventions of a language are established by habit and it is only by habitually using it that one can hope to master its resources. Hence the importance for Tracy of the spoken language of the people and his insistence on the rôle it can play not only in the expression but also the formation of the most sophisticated and subtle ideas:

> ...according to the theory of the formation of ideas and of the influence of habit, even unusually gifted men have a great deal to lose when they study and write in a language which is not their natural language and which is not associated intimately and completely with their most deeply rooted habits. Although the truth of this last consideration is rarely acknowledged, it is of extreme importance, for it follows from this that those men who write as scholars and philosophers in the language in which they normally converse enjoy an incontestable advantage...[48]

One might add: not only scholars and philosophers. There is an obvious analogy between these arguments and Beyle's often repeated assertion that the poet should write in the language in which he speaks to his mistress and his rivals.

The same view of the importance of the vernacular is expressed by the now forgotten critic and poet Jean-Marie Clément in his *Lettres à M. de Voltaire*, which Beyle studied closely and admired, and which are a refutation, among other things, of Voltaire's belief in the possibility of a 'fixed' literary idiom which lends itself with perfect ease to translation into another language. The greatest writers, Clément argues, are often those who, like La Fontaine, are the most difficult of all to translate.[49] For Clément, as for Tracy, the use of the vernacular is a means of achieving 'precision'. No writer, he maintains, was ever more 'precise' than Montaigne, and Montaigne wrote at a time when the language of men of letters resembled closely that used in ordinary familiar conversation.[50]

Clément talks of the 'boldness' of the popular idiom and deplores the fact that the language used by the French upper classes and in works of literature has lost its former freedom and strength and become as a consequence 'sterile for poetry'.[51] Even the style of Racine, he argues, is closer to the popular idiom than that of the eighteenth century and in this respect has much in common with that of the Bible and Montaigne.[52] The 'boldness' and 'strength' of which Clément speaks are, needless to say, more than merely stylistic qualities. When Clément uses these terms one is reminded of what one of Beyle's other *maîtres à penser*, Thomas Hobbes, refers to as that quick ranging' of the mind 'from which proceed those grateful similes, metaphors and other tropes, by which both *poets* and *orators* have it in their power to make things both please and displease, and show well or ill to others, as they like themselves; or else in discerning suddenly dissimilitude in things that otherwise appear the same'.[53]

One could go on giving instances of how the philosophers and critics whom Beyle read as a young man may have helped to form his ideas of the nature of style; how also they may have helped him to understand the use of language of Shakespeare and La Fontaine. One thing, however, I hope, emerges from those instances 1 have already given: Beyle's education would not have *blinded* him to the ways in which a poet uses words. It would not have closed his mind, that is, to the use of language of those writers for whom words are the servant of the imagination, those, who, as Clément puts it, 'force their language... to express what they feel'[54] and for whom precision lies in the accuracy and vividness with which they convey perception and feeling rather than in the conformity of the words they use with conventional usage. The principles which underlie his criticism are on the whole simple and are confined deliberately, when he formulates them himself, to the maximum degree of generality. They resemble what is best in the thought of Helvétius and Tracy in the extent to which they allow for what is unpredictable in the expression of thought and feeling and in their freedom from anything at all resembling the deliberate conventionality of Voltaire. The principles that are implicit in Beyle's criticism, his conception of 'style', 'poetry', 'precision' and 'clarity', are implicit equally in the art of his novels. Sainte-Beuve recognised this when talking of their inadequacy. 'Beyle's failing as a novelist', he wrote in the essay from which I have already quoted, 'is that he came to this form of composition by way of criticism and by conforming to certain preconceived ideas.' While not agreeing in the least that this was a 'failing', I should like now to consider some of the other ways in which the development that Sainte-Beuve refers to took place.

The discovery of a 'natural' style

Léon Blum in his study of *Stendhal et le Beylisme* speaks of the precocity of the young Henri Beyle and of the speed with which he found himself as a writer. 'There is perhaps no other example of a formation so complete at the same age and involving so many aspects of the mind, of a self-awareness so lucid or of a personality so unique and carefully preserved.'[55] In saying this Blum is referring to Beyle's early letters and diaries and not to his unsuccessful attempts at drama or the alexandrines which he hammered out in order to train himself to write dramatic verse. If Beyle found himself so soon as a writer and took so long to find himself as an artist, it is partly because it took years for him to realise that what was true of writers such as Alfieri was also true of himself. It was impossible for him to write in a way which was lively, clear and dramatic unless he had the courage to 'be himself' and write in his own natural idiom.

What, however, do we mean when we talk about the 'natural idiom' of Beyle or, for that matter, anyone else? One answer is given in Tracy's *Grammaire*: it is the language which one commonly hears and speaks and which is 'associated intimately and completely' with one's most 'deeply rooted habits', the language in which one 'thinks immediately'.[56] This is no less true of the intellectual élite than of the people as a whole. For

the mass of the public reacts so powerfully on those who instruct it, by judging them, by offering them subjects of observation, by suggesting to them different points of view;...in short, it is so difficult to be to any great degree above the level of those with whom one lives and one is so strongly influenced by the state of enlightenment of one's country, that the very men who are made to surpass their compatriots have much to lose from anything that holds their compatriots back in a state inferior to that which they might have reached.[57]

To talk therefore of the natural idiom of any writer is to talk at the same time about the kind of audience he is addressing.

Beyle appears, as he grew older, to have to come to regard the latter assumption as axiomatic and it is partly for this reason that in later years when advocating a 'natural' style, he spoke several times of the intimate letter as one of the models that a writer should follow and which he himself preferred to any other. He tells us, for example, at the beginning of *Henry Brulard* that 'Since I seem to be good for nothing and not even able to write official letters to earn my living, I have had the fire lit and I am writing this without lying, I hope, and without deluding myself, for my own enjoyment as when writing to a friend. What will this friend's ideas be like in 1880? How different from my own?'[58] A year before, in a letter to Mme Jules Gaulthier, when criticising her attempts to write a romantic novel, he advised her to tell the story 'as if you were writing to me' and recommended as a model Marivaux's novel *La vie de Marianne*.[59]

Beyle's choice of the epistolary style as a model for the novelist appears to have been the consequence of many years of thought devoted to the whole problem of style. (The epistolary style, as Beyle understood it, is something quite different from the style of such epistolary novels as *La nouvelle Héloïse*.) It is obvious, and was obvious to Beyle, that the style of the intimate letter is only one of the virtually unlimited range of conventions to which the word 'natural' can be applied. The tone and idiom of a politician's speech, of verse written to a formal measure or of prose or verse recited from a stage can themselves be entirely appropriate to a given situation and 'be associated intimately and completely' with certain habits which the speaker and his audience share. It is possible to regard the style of Molière and even of Racine as natural in this way. Racine, according to the definition of Romanticism given in the *Racine et Shakspeare*, was in his own time himself a Romantic:

Romanticism is the art of presenting to a people the literary works which, given their habits and beliefs at the time, are capable of giving them the greatest possible pleasure.

Classicism, on the other hand, confronts them with the literature which gave the greatest possible pleasure to their great-grandparents...

I do not hesitate to affirm that Racine was a Romantic; he gave to the aristocrats of the court of Louis XIV a painting of the passions tempered by *the extreme dignity* which was then the fashion and which was such that a duke in 1670, even in the most tender effusions of paternal love, never failed to address his son as *Monsieur*.

This is why Pylade in *Andromaque* always addresses Oreste as *Seigneur*; and yet what greater friendship could there be between them!

The same dignity is nowhere to be found in the Greeks and it is because of this *dignity*, which chills us today, that Racine was a Romantic...[60]

One needs courage to be a Romantic for one has to *take chances*... It seems to me that the writer needs almost as much courage as the warrior; the one must no more think about the journalists than the other does about the hospital.[61]

The conventions to which the plays of the great seventeenth-century dramatists conform are at the same time literary and social. Moreover, they are not merely arbitrarily chosen and consciously held at the forefront of consciousness but resemble more the tacit assumptions on which intimate conversation depends.

For it to be possible for a dramatist to write for his audience in a natural-seeming way, it is necessary that there should exist already a certain understanding between them, an understanding such as that which there had been, so Beyle argued, in the time of Molière. Such an understanding, he came to believe in later life, was no longer possible and this was an inevitable consequence of the radical changes in French society brought about by the French Revolution. His own decision to become a novelist and to abandon his former ambition to be a dramatist was influenced, as he himself admits, by realising how far-reaching in their consequences these changes were. As he wrote in the title of an article of 1836 (intended originally as a preface to a new edition of the *Lettres* of the Président de Brosses), *La comédie est impossible*. The language used in the theatre, he argued here, was bound to be affected by the state of mind in which the new kind of audience came to the theatre:

The Faubourg Saint-Germain [that is the old aristocracy] is afraid and has formed an alliance with the Church...As for the Third Estate, which is now so wealthy with its fine carriages and mansions in the Chaussée d'Antin, it is still accustomed to seeing courage only under a fine moustache. Unless one tells it at the top of one's voice: 'Listen, I am going to be witty', it fails to notice a single thing and it is capable of regarding a style which is simple as an insult to its dignity.

Hence the impossibility of comedy in the present century.[62]

The boredom and enforced idleness of the courtiers of Louis XIV had at least, he argues, forced them to cultivate the art of conversation and had generally undermined their resistance to humour:

cette société avait été portée au même point de *détente pour le comique*, si j'ose m'exprimer ainsi...

(this society had been brought to the point at which its members were able *to feel at ease together and therefore laugh at the same things*, if I may put it this way)... [63]

Beyle's own contemporaries were far too preoccupied by class resentment, mutual rivalries and the preoccupations of business and politics, and literature had lost as a result 'the admirable effects of reciprocal sympathy in an extensive audience moved by the same emotion', as R. G. Collingwood has put it. [64] It could be objected perhaps that Beyle here lays too much emphasis on the part played by the courtiers of Versailles in the development of seventeenth-century taste, and underestimates the importance of the commercial and professional classes for whom Molière and Racine wrote most of their plays [65] and in which they themselves had been born. The general comparison he makes, however, between the theatre public of his own day and that of the *ancien régime* is, to say the very least, plausible, and whenever one thinks of the kind of entertainment provided in the best plays of each period, the comparison seems to be true. It helps us to explain, for example, why the wit of Musset's *Fantasio* or *Il faut qu'une porte soit ouverte ou fermée* is so different from that of the dramatist from whom one is often told he derives, the Marivaux of *La seconde surprise de l'amour* and *Le jeu de l'amour et du hasard*; why it is that Musset's characters seem to say: 'Listen, I am now being serious' and 'Now I am being witty.' The serious implication of what Marivaux offers as the lightest of entertainment is something that the audience is left to infer. Adultery, for example, is neither condemned nor condoned in his plays and both its comic and tragic possibilities as a theme are deliberately left unexploited.

The interest of *La comédie est impossible* does not, however, lie only in the truth – or likely truth – of the comparison Beyle makes between the theatre audiences of his own day and those of the eighteenth and seventeenth centuries. It lies also in the necessary relationship that he discerns between a way of writing and the kind of public the author addresses. [66] Beyle resembles Molière and the major writers of the seventeenth century in the importance he attaches to the social virtues, to literature seen as a social activity and to the possibilities of 'the art of pleasing'.

He is also free in this respect from the characteristically Romantic tendency to ignore or despise such considerations and to cultivate a non-conformity in keeping with a devotion to Nature with a capital N, with an intensive interest in the life of societies remote from one's own in space or time and with the dictates of artistic 'genius'. ('I am so tired of genius', the old-fashioned lady complains, in a play by Eugène Scribe.[67] 'I should so much like a little wit.')

Yet the paradox remains that in his own novels and in his conversation, from what we are told of it, Beyle was thought of by his own contemporaries as an eccentric, a blasphemer and a violator of most of the principles of good taste. The writer who had devoted so much thought to the ways of charming the public of his own day began to enjoy popularity more than half a century after he died. The paradox does not lie in his lack of success during his own lifetime. Beyle realised that any popular success he enjoyed would be in years to come, and his decision to write for a small number of unknown, isolated and sympathetic individuals – the 'Happy Few' to whom many of his books are dedicated – was a conscious decision made *en connaissance de cause*. 'I imagine that I may have a little success in 1860 or 1880', he wrote in his letter to Balzac two years before he died. The paradox lies rather in the simultaneous desire to win over an audience and play the rôle of public entertainer and his inability to do this except on his own terms. Beyle believed in the social virtues – or at least, in the degree of conformity necessary for strangers to communicate – but there is no evidence that he ever thought that they should take precedence over every other kind of virtue. He is never in his comments on *Le Misanthrope* an apologist for Philinte, the 'reasonable' conformist. In his *Racine et Shakspeare* furthermore, the seventeenth century's extreme preoccupation with the social virtues is something he positively deplores:

> All the subjects of Louis XIV prided themselves on imitating a certain model of elegance and good taste and Louis XIV was himself the god of this religion. There was *bitter laughter* when a man was seen to have made a mistake in his imitation of the model. The gaiety of the letters of Mme de Sévigné is nothing more in fact than this. In 1670 a man who allowed his imagination to run away with him would have been thought of not as amusing but mad.

Molière, a genius if ever there was one, was unfortunate enough to work for this society.

Aristophanes, on the other hand, undertook to entertain a society of amiable and happy-go-lucky people who sought their happiness *by every means*. Alcibiades, I have the impression, gave little thought to imitating anyone; he believed he was happy when he laughed and not when his pride was flattered by the thought that he had a great deal in common with someone like Lauzun, d'Antin, Villeroy or another of Louis XIV's favourite courtiers... [68]

Beyle's opinion of 'the contemporaries of Mme de Sévigné' is clearly very different in *La comédie est impossible*. Yet it is his judgment of this society, rather than the feelings and beliefs which had inspired the judgment, which have changed. At least, there is no glaring inconsistency between the views expressed in the above quotation and those that he develops here. 'The contemporaries of Mme de Sévigné', he writes, were not only able to 'laugh at the same things', and this whatever their social origin. They also 'shared a certain understanding of literary matters and in this respect had received the same education'. [69] The education they had received was one which gave them the immense advantage of not taking literature *too seriously*:

True comedy, for our sins, is even less conceivable than before, now that we have political parties. We no longer think of literature as something to be taken lightly and enjoyed like a joke. It is now regarded with such esteem that the parties are longing to take it over; even the Government is meddling with it in the hope that we will return to the prudent moderate literature of the Empire.

One could have hoped for something better from the descendants of the friends of Mme de Sévigné; but imagine what would happen if these gentlemen went to the theatre and saw for the first time, in a comedy which had just been written, the well-bred Dorante of *Le bourgeois gentilhomme*. They would think of it as an atrocious insult, an insult to be wiped out in blood.

And it would be a waste of time for the poor dramatist to protest: 'But gentlemen, all I'm asking you is whether this character is true to life and whether or not you find him funny.' [70]

What Beyle had come to admire in the societies of the seventeenth and early eighteenth centuries was their freedom from the cares of personal ambition and, as a consequence of this, from the class hatreds of modern times. A man's career, in most classes of society, had been pre-determined at the time of his birth. There was little point in resenting the greater wealth or power of one's fellow-countrymen since there was little one could hope to change and little, consequently, for the powerful and wealthy to fear from those less fortunate than themselves. The upper classes of 1836 lived, by contrast, in constant fear of another Jacobin Terror. Personal ambition, the spirit of party and class resentment, Beyle argues, made it impossible for the theatre public to enjoy humour at its own expense.

Beyle's conclusions are optimistic. He believes that now that the 'atrocious abuses' of the old order have been swept away, French society will be the first to recover its former frankness and gaiety. The essay ends, however, with an appeal to the contemporary reader:

> Meanwhile, kind reader, as the angry waves grow calmer, try to hate as little as possible and try not to be a hypocrite. I can understand why a poor devil who is the fifth son of the weaver of my village prefers any job to that of tilling the soil. To lie all day long is certainly less painful. Not only that, the lies he tells don't react on his heart, don't corrode it as they corrode yours. What the rascal utters aren't really lies but only words that he doesn't understand: he doesn't realise that he is robbing the man to whom he is speaking and that he deserves his contempt; but you, kind reader, who have enjoyed Voltaire's poem and Courier's pamphlets, you who have three horses in your stable, how can you possibly agree to render your life dismal through foul hypocrisy?

It will only be when the reign of hatred and hypocrisy has come to an end that comedy will once again 'be possible'.

What is defined in *La comédie est impossible* are certain conditions on which a human community depends, one could almost say, for its existence as such. The community is one which Beyle sees as having existed among the French upper classes of the old régime and to whose return under a new dispensation he looks forward in years to come. No explicit reference is made to Beyle's own novels in the essay. Yet it describes also, I should like to suggest, the kind of reader for whom they are written.[71] Reading the essay can help us to understand the characteristic tone of the novels, the attitude to the reader, that is, which determines the nature of his style. It indicates the kind of audience with which he was able to 'be himself' and write in a 'natural'-

seeming way. It indicates too why Beyle should have attached so much importance to positive enjoyment as a criterion of literary value.

Le plus grand plaisir possible

Few of Beyle's readers can have failed to notice how often he talks of the enjoyment to be derived from literature, music and painting and it has even been objected that he talks about it far too much. Rémy de Gourmont, for example, maintained that it was this preoccupation with *le plaisir* which prevented him from being a serious literary critic:

There was no principle...to which Stendhal was more faithful than that of the greatest possible pleasure; it is also unfortunately the principle on which it is most difficult to found a literary doctrine which possesses the merits of good sense. Moreover, the idea of such a doctrine scarcely ever occurred to him; [in the *Racine et Shakspeare*] he merely sets out the purely personal reflections inspired by his impressions of the theatre.[72]

Stendhal has many more admirers today than when these remarks were written and much of his criticism which Gourmont could not have seen is now collected and in print. Yet the remarks which I have quoted have never, as far as I know, been challenged and few critics have commented on the fact that he usually tries to be clear about why and in what sense he is stressing enjoyment. We find this even when he is writing as a professional reviewer of work which has little interest for him and when he is explaining why it bores or repels him. Take, for instance, these comments in *The London Magazine* for February 1825 on *Monsieu le Préfet*, a political satire by the former prefect Baron Lamothe-Langon (I quote from the English translation of the time, the French original having been lost):

We cannot deny the author the merit of resemblance; but this resemblance is hideous. On reading *M. le Préfet* I experienced the disagreeable feeling of a profound but *impotent hatred*. Now impotent hatred destroys in an instant all literary pleasure. For this reason I suppose it is that a mixture of politics is in France fatal to a work of literature. If the author of this romance, which I beg of you to read, had had the least dramatic genius, he would have perceived the necessity of *softening* the abject servility of his characters.

Even in Byron's *Beppo* and *Don Juan*, which he warmly admired, Beyle was disturbed by what he saw as an implicit appeal to the reader's feelings of 'hatred and misery':

Lord Byron's humour is bitter in Childe Harold; it is the anger of youth; it is scarcely more than ironical in *Beppo* and *Don Juan*. But this humour does not bear too close an examination; instead of gaiety and light-heartedness, hatred and misery lie beneath.[73]

One answer to Gourmont would be to say that the enjoyment Beyle sought in literature was, as it happens, of the deepest kind and that he was unusually aware of the temptations to bitterness and despair which can make the sympathetic reading of a novel or poem intolerable.

Both of these passages were written between 1823 and 1830, a period immediately following the emotional crisis described in the *Souvenirs d'égotisme*, after Beyle had left or rather wrenched himself away from Milan and the house of Mathilde Dembowski. The preoccupation which is common to these passages is one, however, which had been with him from late adolescence at least. It scarcely need be added that if these reflections are those of a literary critic, they are in no way exclusively literary. As so often in Beyle's criticism, the literary judgments are all the more telling for being at the same time those of a man reflecting on his own experience.

A proneness to feelings of hatred and misery is one of the most obvious characteristics of the young Henri Beyle and was to remain one of his most vivid memories of his childhood and early youth. 'At one time', he writes in *Henry Brulard*,

when I used to hear of the innocent joys and follies of childhood or the happiness of early youth, which, one is told, is the only genuine happiness a man ever knows, my heart would contract. This is something I never experienced; and what is more, this period of my life was one of constant misery and hatred, of a constant and always impotent desire for vengeance. The reasons for my misery can be summed in a few words: I was never allowed to play with a child of my own age. And my relatives, bored by their social isolation, honoured me with their constant attention.[74]

Beyle's disposition does not seem to have changed after he had escaped from the claustrophobic atmosphere of his home in Grenoble. The one member of the family circle whom Beyle was later to remember with affection, his maternal grandfather Henri Gagnon, wrote to him when he was twenty-two and engaged in a business enterprise in Marseille: 'The contact you have had with one or two men has inspired in you a contempt and disrespect which are far too general. Normally one is pleased to come across honest men who can behave generously; but I feel that you, my dear boy, like nothing better than to discover an act of treachery or some other horror.'[75] The pleasure he derived from such discoveries was bound to be of an equivocal kind and he himself noted in his diary a few years later how much he was the victim of this habit. 'How is it', he asks, 'that I may not give a damn for a sum of twenty-five louis that I've lent and yet my heart is shaken with anger and I'm in a rage if someone tries to outwit me and get out of paying me back? And yet no one proves better than I do that the man who is in a rage is the first to be punished.'[76] One can only assume that it was because of the circumstances of his early life and the fine and easily exasperated sensibility, which was due as much to physiological as to other causes, that the temperament revealed in his writings resembles less that of his beloved Montesquieu than that of his younger contemporary, Flaubert. I say temperament, for Beyle's character and intelligence – what he made of his temperament – were clearly very different.

It is interesting to recall that to Rémy de Gourmont it was Flaubert who seemed the superior artist and whose art seemed the incarnation of a superior wisdom, much though he admired the intelligence he found in Beyle's writings as a whole. 'Stendhal', he writes, while 'more personal' is somehow 'less complete' than Flaubert. 'He gives little satisfaction which is not a satisfaction of the mind, whereas Flaubert delights both our intelligence and our sensibility for the plastic beauty of his style matches the spiritual beauty of his thought.'[77] It is also significant that the Flaubert he admired was the Flaubert of the later novels and for the reasons given in his essay entitled *Flaubert et la bêtise humaine*: '*Bouvard et Pécuchet* amuses us (and I am using the word in its deepest sense) as much as *Don Quixote* amused our ancestors and still amuses many of our contemporaries. It is perhaps the book of books, the book for the strong, for it contains much bitterness and the taste of nothingness which it leaves (*son goût de néant*) goes straight to the heart.'[78] The standards by which

Beyle is found wanting are presumably therefore those set by Flaubert's narrative of the comic adventures of his two indefatigable autodidacts engaged in a quest for knowledge which is doomed from the very outset. The vision of life which Gourmont offers as the most bracing and realistic is one which springs from a belief in the sheer futility of most if not all of human endeavour.[79] It is true that both the vision and the belief correspond to a mood with which few people with good memories could honestly say they were unfamiliar. Yet as the expression of a consistently held or consistently tenable philosophy of life, *Bouvard et Pécuchet* doesn't exist, for all its magnificent slapstick humour and despite the wonderful plastic beauty of its style. If all endeavour is futile and all knowledge unattainable, how can we know even this and what is the point of making this clear with such meticulous and pondered art? It is this which may lead one to conclude that Gourmont's idea of 'strength' and 'bitterness' was a poor idea, an idea which he himself was incapable of taking with complete seriousness. Despite its truculence and the momentary conviction with which Gourmont, like Flaubert, is able to express it, it is something very different from the 'strong pessimism' which Nietzsche, Beyle's self-proclaimed 'posthumous son', looked for in Greek tragedy: 'A penchant of the mind for what is hard, terrible, evil, dubious in existence, arising from a plethora of health, plenitude of being...Could it be, perhaps, that the very feeling of superabundance created its own kind of suffering: a temerity of penetration, hankering for the enemy (the worth-while enemy) so as to prove its strength, to experience at last what it means to fear something?'[80]

To return to what Beyle himself was looking for when he spoke of the enjoyment which art can give and of the '*impotent hatred*' which can destroy in an instant all literary pleasure', one can find no better illustration of what he meant or, at least, of what he was able to imagine, than the art of his own novels. It may be useful here to anticipate what should properly fall into the argument of a later chapter and consider for a moment the penultimate chapter of *Le rouge et le noir*, in which we are told of Julien Sorel's meditations as he waits for death in the condemned cell having been accused 'justly', he confesses, of an 'atrocious crime'. The chapter provides ample evidence of Beyle's ability to understand the feelings of misery and impotent hatred of which he so often speaks in other writers. Julien admits that he has been justly condemned, but asks himself whether the word justice can ever have any other than a conventional meaning:

'There is no such thing as *natural law*: the word is only an antiquated piece of humbug worthy of the advocate general who hunted me down the other day and whose ancestors were enriched by property confiscated by Louis XIV. There is only *law* when a man is prevented from doing something by fear of punishment. Before the *law* exists, there is nothing *natural* at all except the strength of the lion or the need of any cold or hungry creature. There is only *need* in fact...No, the men one honours are only scoundrels who have had the good fortune not to be caught in the act. The prosecutor whom society sets on to me was enriched by a crime...I have committed a murder and am justly condemned, but apart from this, a man like Valenod who found me guilty is a hundred times more harmful to society.'

'Despite his avarice then', Julien added sadly but without anger, 'my father is no worse than any of them. He has never loved me and now I have added the final touch to his displeasure by dishonouring him. To think of his only son condemned to a humiliating death! His fear of being without money, his exaggerated belief in human malevolence, which is really what we mean when we talk of avarice, shows him one prodigious source of consolation and security: a sum of three or four hundred louis which I shall be able to leave him. One Sunday after dinner he will show his gold to all those who envy him in Verrières. "At the price", his look will say, "which of you would not be delighted to have a son sent to the guillotine?"'

This passage has been taken by one of Beyle's most gifted critics, and one of the first in France to champion his reputation, as an expression of Beyle's philosophy of life and a striking instance of his own intelligence:

Julien's intelligence is of the first order; it is quite simply that of Stendhal himself: penetrating and tormented, lucid as an algebraic theorem and as biting and acid as a formal indictment.[81]

'Penetrating', 'tormented' and 'lucid' describe it well and it is true that Beyle never pretends that Valenod or Julien's father are any different from what Julien sees them as being. Nor does he ever appear to have thought of 'natural law' as anything other than the Hobbesian kind of which Julien speaks. Yet is this an example of 'intelligence'? Did Beyle himself think of it as such? If these facts and beliefs were to correspond to the *whole* of truth about human life, a thoughtful and generous mind would have either to turn his back on the truth or bring his life to an end in despair. The 'philosophy', Beyle goes on to say, to which Julien's life and circumstances have led him is not just pessimistic but suicidal:

> This philosophy might have been true, but it was such as to make one long for death. Five long days went by in this way. He was polite and gentle towards Mathilde, whom he could see was tormented by the keenest jealousy. One evening he thought seriously of taking his own life. His spirits were oppressed by the profound unhappiness into which he had been thrown by the departure of Mme de Rênal. Nothing gave him pleasure, whether in the real world or the world of the imagination. The lack of exercise began to impair his health and to give him the weak overwrought character of a young German student. He lost that masculine self-respect which is able to dispel with a vigorous oath certain uncongenial thoughts by which the minds of the unhappy are assailed.

Julien's meditations bring home to us the full extent of what he has to endure as he waits for death in a damp cell visited every day by a woman he no longer loves. His mortification and despair are unendurable, though *how* unendurable we are made to understand by his efforts to overcome them or rather to understand their true cause and what it is he is deprived of and needs:

> 'To live in isolation! What torment!'
> 'I am becoming insane and unjust', thought Julien striking his brow. 'I am isolated in this cell; but I have not lived in *isolation* on this earth; the thought of duty has always given me strength. The duty which, rightly or wrongly, I have always forced myself to accept has been like the trunk of a solid tree against which I leaned during the storm; I wavered, I was shaken. After all, I was only a man...but I wasn't swept away.
> It must be the damp air of this cell which makes me think of isolation.'

This consolation, though real (for Julien's self-imposed challenges have obviously been real as well) is less effective than the consolation which comes from realising what has given him most happiness, what it is of which he is now deprived and what it really is therefore that he now has to endure and suffer:

'And why curse hypocrisy and be still more hypocritical? I'm not feeling like this because of death or this cell but because Mme de Rênal isn't here. If I had to live for weeks on end hidden in the cellars of her house in Verrières in order to see her, would I complain?'

It is at this point that the mood changes and that we realise how in longing passionately to go on living, Julien has been released not only from despair and self-loathing but from the horror which the prospect of death had come to hold for him:

'So I am going to die at the age of twenty-three. Give me five more years to live with Mme de Rênal...

This is what makes me feel isolated and not the absence of a just, good, all-powerful God without malevolence or the thirst for vengeance.

Ah! if he existed... Alas, I would fall at his feet. "Death is what I have deserved", I would say, "but God in your greatness, goodness, indulgence, give me back the woman I love."'

By this time it was late at night. After an hour or two of peaceful sleep, Fouqué arrived.

Julien felt strong and resolute like a man who sees clearly into his own mind.

It is stating the obvious to say that the note on which the chapter and the novel end is not one of misery or hatred. Nor has it anything in common with the mood of *Bouvard et Pécuchet*. If the reader experiences when he finishes the novel a sense of enjoyment and invigoration, it is an enjoyment different from the grim 'amusement' which Gourmont derived from the latter novel. It has in fact far more in common with Nietzsche's 'strong pessimism'. The novelist and the reader follow the hero into an appalling trap in which he is unable to escape from brutally disconcerting truths and at the same time deprived of what he most wants and needs as a man. Julien is shaken to the point at which a self-respecting bracing of the nerves and a manly oath are no longer enough to keep away the horror and despair he has come to feel. Yet the point of the exercise for the novelist and the reader is not simply to enjoy the thrills of a nightmare vision. It is to think about the ways in which horror and despair might be confronted, tracked down and overcome in the one place in which they can be fought and on the only terms on which the fight is possible: namely in the imagination and with the weapons of the imagination. For a man whose intelligence and imagination were less quick and resilient than Julien's would probably have been incapable of the victory he wins over himself. This is something on the novelist's part – though not, of course, on Julien's – akin to Nietzsche's 'temerity of penetration, hankering for the enemy (the worth-while enemy)' and it is something alien to Flaubert's and Gourmont's would-be candid and defiant, though necessarily incomplete or insincere, surrender to horror and despair.

It is unlikely that Beyle's remarks on the kind of enjoyment which art and literature can offer will make much sense to the casual reader unless he appreciates how clear Beyle was in his own mind from an early age about the *usefulness* of art. However much he may have been bored and irritated by the moralising cant of his own contemporaries, he never in reaction took up the understandably extreme stance adopted by those who, later in the century, were to proclaim that art is by its very nature *useless*, existing in a world of its own, and that this is its principal justification. *Si la comédie est utile* is the characteristic title of an essay on Molière's *L'école des femmes* written in 1811 and in it the aim of comedy is described explicitly as 'showing up for the benefit of each society what is ridiculous in the bad habits which prevent them from achieving happiness'.[82] *Le bonheur*, the full uninhibited enjoyment of life is the end which, for Beyle, art must serve and the function of comedy as such is to laugh us out of whatever it is which holds us back from such enjoyment:

It requires a certain strength of mind in a man for him to be able to understand what impedes or advances his happiness and not to have tears brought to his eyes by the thought of the extreme importance that this has for him, tears which can blur his vision. It often happens that when one is talking to a woman about what goes to make up her happiness, she begins by not understanding you and then, when she has, she will burst into tears simply because she has at last understood that she too could be unhappy. Thus you find that you have been unable to hold her attention; at first, she was unable to understand what you were saying and then, when she did, she was too overcome to be able to reason or judge.

Moreover, in order to persuade the bourgeois from Auxerre whom I mentioned earlier that such and such a thing is contrary to his happiness, it would be necessary to present a *tableau* of the plight into which habits similar to his own have led the hero of one's comedy. This spectacle will certainly not delight his heart; he will not want to come back to it and he will simply dismiss it from his mind like a bad memory.

I conclude then that this method will have to be left to the writers of sermons, if there are any who are good enough to carry it off with the necessary degree of conviction.

It remains then *to show up for the benefit of each society what is ridiculous in the bad habits which prevent them from achieving happiness.*

Arnolphe [in *L'école des femmes*] could have been happy. He is wealthy and he is certainly no fool. During his youth he has cuckolded many men and he has always laughed at all the absurdities he has come across. He is now forty-five years old but he still has plenty of sap. Five or six paths might have led him to happiness, but he stubbornly insists on carrying out his pet scheme of marrying and yet *never being deceived.*

Molière could, if he liked, have shown to the Arnolphes in real life all the miseries that the pursuit of this chimera are likely to entail. He could have shown us Arnolphe dishonoured or even an Arnolphe led to the scaffold or blowing out his brains.

What he did was to make Arnolphe ridiculous and to allow us only a glimpse of his unhappiness.

The same is true of Orgon [in *Tartuffe*] whom he shows as ridiculous and not unhappy.

Beyle is perhaps the most acute and penetrating critic of Molière who has ever written, though it is unfortunate for his own reputation that his best remarks were made in the notebooks in which he developed his ideas rather than in the *Racine et Shakspeare*, by which his work as a critic is principally known and in which we are often merely given the conclusions which he had reached by the age of forty. He is aware, as for example, Bergson seems not to be, in his own study of *Le rire,* of the *tact* which is an essential feature of Molière's humour and which normally prevents it from being of the merely satirical, crudely punitive kind to which all humour, if we are to believe Bergson, somehow conforms by its very nature. He is also a remarkably perceptive critic of Molière's failings as a comic dramatist, particularly in his notes written two years before *Si la comédie est utile,* on Molière's strange and uncharacteristic *Georges Dandin* – a play, incidentally, whose humour Bergson analyses as if it were of the same kind as the rest of Molière's dramatic *oeuvre.* Beyle notes how little the audience is left to learn, after the first few scenes, of Dandin's, the deceived husband's plight and how much the play is taken up with the prolonged spectacle of Dandin's ordeal. Dandin, the simple-minded but wealthy peasant, has married the daughter of a poor nobleman and is alternatively deceived by his wife and snubbed, patronised and reprimanded by his wife's doting snobbish parents. What, Beyle asks, could have led Dandin to contract such an impossible marriage? Vanity? Perhaps, but poor Dandin, when the play begins, has no vanity left:

> Molière, in short, for reasons best known to him and which I am unable to discuss, shows us:
> 1. Dandin when he is already repentant.
> 2. Dandin with no escape holes left (*les trous bouchés*). He thus deprives himself of a host of what might have been comic situations.[83]

Beyle, of course, might have added that often the audience, or at least part of the audience, does in fact go on laughing right through to the end of the play, though not presumably if it is looking at Dandin with any degree of fellow-feeling.

Beyle's observations on comedy and on the feelings of misery and hatred which can make any deep or sustained enjoyment of literature impossible are an obvious expression of the beliefs and outlook which he himself described as *Beylisme*, and to say this brings us back to the problems touched on earlier in the present study. Is it true to say that pleasure is always what men pursue, not only by choice but by definition in that whatever we desire is always, as far as we are concerned, desirable, irrespective of whether it may prove to be satisfying? Is pleasure the only possible measure of goodness or the good? The English reader will probably be familiar with the objections raised against both of these beliefs by G. E. Moore in the *Principia Ethica*, objections which perhaps deserve more serious attention than those of Beyle's own French contemporaries. Moore rejects both the 'naturalistic fallacy' which identifies the simple predicate 'good' with something different, such as happiness or whatever is regarded as 'desirable' (as in the system of Bentham and John Stuart Mill) and 'metaphysical ethics' which, similarly, assume that good actually means something else: namely, in the system of Kant for example, compatibility with ultimate realities and with obligations imposed on us by universal authority. It is impossible in a study of this length to do justice either to the beliefs which Moore regards as fallacious or to the objections he and others have raised against them. But it may be enough in this context to point out that Beyle was not himself a systematic thinker or rather did not have a system to offer – which is different from saying that his thought was lacking in coherence, depth or consistency – and that Moore's objections do not necessarily apply to anything that he actually wrote. It can be brought against him that his admiration for the thought of Locke, Helvétius, Bentham and Tracy was, on the whole, uncritical, or, at least, that what he says in their favour does not begin to answer the more serious kind of objection that has been brought against them. Yet he took from them what he needed and did not, at least in any of his writings which survive, place himself in a position where he needed to believe or pretend that 'good' or 'desirable' or any of its synonyms are merely different words meaning exactly the same thing. Nor, since Moore mentions this fallacy too,[84] did he identify pleasure and the objects of pleasure, or the experience that is anticipated or enjoyed and the enjoyable feelings which may be indistinguishable from but are only part of that experience.[85] This, however, is merely to defend Beyle's thought, as it evolved, against possible objections and there are more positive reasons for hoping that what he wrote about art and ethics may one day be recognised as of interest even to philosophers as such.

'Le beau idéal' in painting

'Beauty is merely the promise of happiness', Beyle wrote in his *History of Painting in Italy* of 1817. The definition is one which Nietzsche compares in chapter 6 of his *Genealogy of Morals* with Kant's argument that what is beautiful is what gives us 'disinterested pleasure':

Disinterested! Compare with this definition that other one, framed by a real spectator and artist, Stendhal...Here we find the very thing which Kant stresses exclusively in the aesthetic condition rejected and cancelled. Which is right, Kant or Stendhal? – When our aestheticians tirelessly rehearse, in support of Kant's view, that the spell of beauty enables us to view even *nude* females 'disinterestedly' we may be allowed to laugh a little at their expense. The experiences of artists in this delicate matter are rather more 'interesting'; certainly Pygmalion was not entirely devoid of aesthetic feeling. Let us honour

our aestheticians all the more for the innocence reflected in such arguments – Kant, for example, when he descants on the peculiar character of the sense of touch with the ingenuousness of a country parson...

I do not myself feel competent to judge whether Beyle's writings on art have received the recognition from writers on aesthetics they deserve. But I suspect that they have not and that once again his friend Mérimée's judgment of his competence in these matters is the one that has on the whole prevailed:

He appreciates the great masters from a French outlook, that is from a literary point of view. He examines the paintings of the Italian school as if they were dramas. This is still the way we judge in France where we have neither the sentiment of form nor an innate taste for colour. To love and understand form and colour calls for a particular type of sensibility and prolonged practice...[86]

Another acquaintance, nevertheless, Eugène Delacroix, though on the whole he despised the amateurish opinions on painting of men of letters, copied out in his notebooks extracts from the *History of Painting in Italy* and in an article on Michelangelo,[87] described Beyle's description of the *Last Judgment* as among the most striking and poetic he knew. He also recommended warmly Beyle's chapter on Leonardo's *Last Supper*.[88]

My purpose here is not, however, to consider Beyle's past or possible future influence on others but the growth and nourishment of the sensibility and intelligence which are manifest in the art of his novels. Beyle's writings on the other creative arts have no immediately obvious relevance to his education as a novelist. And if we say that it has, this may sound as if we are agreeing with Mérimée that what he saw in the paintings by which he was moved and fascinated was not colour and form but only stories and poems. My own contention is that Nietzsche and Delacroix were right to attribute to Beyle a truly professional eye, that of what Nietzsche calls a 'real spectator and artist', and that this is apparent particularly in what he says of *technique*.

'No one loved Virgil more than Dante and nothing resembles the *Aeneid* less than the *Inferno*. Michelangelo was deeply struck by the art of antiquity and nothing is more opposed to it than what he created himself.'[89] It has been said that the highest tribute that one true artist can pay to another is to admire or even worship and then do otherwise. This could certainly be said of Beyle. In any case, if he learned from the technique of Correggio, it was not by including in his novels descriptions of heads or poses which would sound like detailed descriptions of one of Correggio's paintings. (There is only one detail specified, for example, in the remark in *La chartreuse de Parme* concerning Fabrice's 'Correggio-like physique':[90] he has 'a certain expression in his eyes of tender voluptuousness'. A novelist like Zola is far closer to painting in this sense and the description, for example, in *La curée* of carriages on a showery sunny day driving through the Bois de Boulougne reads like a sketch for an Impressionist painting.) Beyle's understanding of technique is apparent in what he says of it as a means to a particular end:

> Everyone realises that when a woman is waiting to see her lover she will not wear the same hat as when she sees her confessor.
> Each great painter has looked for those devices which would convey to the soul that *particular impression* which was for him the one main purpose of painting.
> It would be absurd to ask the connoisseurs to point out the end which any painter seeks to achieve [*le but moral*]. But, to make up for this, they excel at distinguishing the hard abrupt strokes of a Bassano from the melting colours of Correggio. They have learned that Bassano can be recognised by the brilliance of his greens, that he can't draw feet and throughout his life repeated a dozen of the same familiar subjects; that Correggio goes in for graceful foreshortening effects, that his faces are never in the least severe or forbidding, while his eyes have a celestial voluptuousness and that his paintings look as if they are covered by six inches of crystal...
> The draughtsmanship or the contours of the muscles, the shadows and the draperies, the imitation of light and of local colours have all a particular tonality in the *style* of each painter, that is if he has a *style*. In the work of the true artist, a tree will have one kind of green if it throws a shadow over the pool in which Leda is playing with the swan and another if robbers are taking advantage of the obscurity of the forest in order to cut a traveller's throat.[91]

Technique, style and convention are seen as appropriate also to the spirit of the age, in so far as this is determined by the state of existing knowledge and belief, the ways in which an individual or a community are in the habit of defending themselves and the existing political dispensation. *The History of Painting in Italy* has been described as the first of his Romantic manifestos and it is because of the closely argued development of the idea of the relativity of style and taste that it has an imoprtant place in the history of ideas. Taste and style are not, however, the only terms that Stendhal uses. The key term in the development of his main argument is *'le beau idéal'* or 'ideal beauty', as it has somewhat inadequately to be rendered in English, and Books 5 and 6 of the *History* are devoted to a comparison between ideal beauty in antiquity and today. The imitation of antiquity, with its veneration for athletic prowess and the visible virtues of the warrior or wise counsellor, is seen as inappropriate in an age when women are no longer the mere servants of their husbands and when elegance and amiability have taken precedence over every other human quality. As Beyle was to put it in his *Salon* of 1827: 'Beauty in each century is simply then *the expression of the qualities which are useful at the time*...'[92] He is saying to the contemporary painter, in other words, what he was to say also to the contemporary dramatist in the *Racine et Shakspeare*: it is absurd to imitate the art that satisfied the different needs of a different generation or epoch. Ideal beauty today is bound to take another form.

In the section on the *History of Painting in Italy* in his *Stendhal romancier*, M. Maurice Bardèche has suggested that what Stendhal is saying in effect is that, given the complexity of the character and social habits of modern man, painting and sculpture can no longer express them in either their real or their ideal forms[93] and that the *History* is addressed not so much to the contemporary painter as to the contemporary novelist. Certainly, no contemporary painter or sculptor is hailed as an evident genius comparable to Michelangelo or Leonardo, and among his older and younger contemporaries only Ingres, David and Delacroix seem momentarily to have fired his enthusiasm,[94] David, interestingly enough because of his rejection after 1780 of the *niais* style of Boucher and Fragonard and his bold return to the imitation of antiquity. The historical appropriateness of this 'revolution' in style is something that the present study has already touched on.[95]

M. Bardèche argues that the 'amiable man' of modern civilisation, as Beyle saw him in the memoirs of Bezenval or the Prince de Ligne, was *the* hero not only of modern times but for Beyle personally and without reservations – at least, M. Bardèche doesn't mention any. For Beyle he was also, we are told, an ideal representation of himself. It is this interpretation that we may find more difficult to accept, particularly when it leads M. Bardèche to analyse what he sees as profound contradictions in Beyle between the idealist and the realist painting his contemporaries as they really were and at the same time knowing that passion can transform a man utterly and give him 'a new goal in life, a new way of going after happiness which will make him forget any others and make him forget any habit he has formed'.[96] Beyle is certainly aware of how much the life within us can astonish us and make nonsense of our ideals and it is not he, surely, but M. Bardèche who has made the ideal of the modern amiable man seem somehow final and supreme. It is obviously an ideal to which the heroes of his novels conform on occasion only and they are capable when under pressure of acting with animal-like ferocity and decisiveness. In the *History of Painting* itself, moreover, the ideal is described, on the whole, neutrally, or rather with a half-serious, half-amused respect;[97]

If ever we meet Socrates or Epictetus in the Elysian fields, we will tell them something that will shock them considerably: that a great character for us is not what makes the happiness of private life.

Leonidas, who is so great when he traces the inscription: 'Traveller, go and say to Sparta', etc. could have been and I shall go further and say certainly was an insipid lover, husband and friend.[98]

The subject of Beyle's *History*, however, is painting in Italy during a period far closer to that of modern times and with far more obvious resemblances, particularly as far as Italy itself is concerned. And it is clear that Beyle is capable of seeing the great painters of the Renaissance and wrote as if his contemporaries might see them too as being, like Shakespeare, still very much alive. To write or paint in a way which satisfies modern needs by no means excludes an ability to respond to and learn from the art and literature of the past, and in the last chapter of the *History*, Beyle predicts that now that the age of mere elegant mockery is over – that is the age of Pope and Voltaire – men will learn to treat gay things with gaiety, serious things seriously and a great man as truly great. It is then that Michelangelo will come back into his own.

It is in the portrait of the lonely, embittered Abbé Pirard in

Le rouge et le noir, passionately austere and devout and yet help-
lessly drawn to the young Julien Sorel, and in the chapters
describing Julien's own confrontation with the realities of death
in the condemned cell that we may be reminded of what Beyle
had written both on the overwhelming effect and the technique
of Michelangelo's *Last Judgment* as he stood looking up at it in
the Sistine Chapel noting down his immediate impressions.[99]
After a detailed description of each of the figures he concludes:

> In Michelangelo, as in Dante, one's soul is chilled by the excess of
> seriousness. The absence of any rhetorical device adds considerably
> to this impression. We see the face of a man who has just seen
> something which has struck him with horror.
> Dante tries to arouse the interest of men whom he assumes to be
> unhappy. He does not, like the French poets, describe external
> objects. His one device is to excite sympathy for the emotions by
> which he is possessed. It is never the object he shows us but the
> impression it produces on his heart.
> Possessed by divine fury like that of a prophet in the Old Testament,
> the pride of Michelangelo rejects all sympathy. He is saying to
> mankind: 'Think of your own interest. Here is the God of Israel
> come to you in all his vengeance.'[100]

It is in the portraits of Stendhal's heroines and young men that
we may be reminded of what he has written of Correggio. Yet
between Michelangelo, Veronese and Correggio there is 'nothing
in common'.[101] M. Bardèche talks of the contradictions in
Beyle's aesthetic principles and practice as a novelist. I would
suggest as an alternative to this view that the range and flexibility
of imaginative response for which the novels are remarkable
corresponds to that which we find in *The History of Painting in
Italy*.

'Le beau idéal' in music

That Beyle borrowed directly in *The History of Painting*, and
without acknowledgement, from a number of sources, principally
Luigi Lanzi's *Storia pittoresca dell'Italia* of 1792 and Vasari's *Lives
of the Painters*, is well known. So too is the fact that his first
published work, the *Lives of Haydn, Mozart and Metastasio*, is, for
the most part, a word-for-word translation from Giuseppe
Carpani's *Letters on Haydn*. Beyle chose to describe himself as
a 'dilettante' where music and art were concerned, and his

outrageous plagiarism and preposterous choice of pseudonyms have discouraged those who look no further than a man's professed valuation of himself from taking either his art criticism or his music criticism seriously. Yet even Hector Berlioz, who, in many ways, reminds one almost uncannily of his fellow-Dauphinois – both passionately loved Shakespeare, reacted contemptuously against the academicism and provincialism of Paris and preferred to make utter fools of themselves rather than timidly following a prescribed model – even Berlioz regarded Beyle as an impostor. In chapter 35 of his *Memoirs* we are given a glimpse of the Consul from Civita Vecchia driving through a Roman carnival, 'a little man with a round stomach and a mischievous smile trying to look serious' and Berlioz adds in a footnote that this is 'M. Beile, or Beyle or Baile, who has written a *Life of Rossini* under the pseudonym of Stendhal and the most irritating stupidities on music for which he believed that he had some sort of feeling.'

As a music critic certainly, Beyle was less influential than in his *History of Painting in Italy* and none of his lives of the composers, not even the *Life of Rossini* of 1824, brought recognition to neglected masterpieces. The success of the latter volume was due almost certainly to that of Rossini himself and those composers who badly needed recognition in France – Beethoven notably and the young Berlioz – had little or nothing to thank him for. Berlioz's extreme irritation at Beyle could possibly be due to this latter circumstance more than any other, for despite Beyle's qualified admiration for Rossini,[102] he could easily be taken for one of the 'dilettanti' whose lionizing of Rossini in the 1820s prevented far better music from being heard and whom Berlioz dreamed of running through with a red-hot poker or blowing sky high by means of a well-placed mine during a performance of Rossini in the *Théâtre Italien*.[103]

Beyle's first-hand experience of music was more limited than we might imagine from reading his music criticism, and Professor Coe has pointed out, for example, that while warmly recommending *The Magic Flute* and insisting that it should be heard in the original version and not in the travesty of it performed in France, he had almost certainly never heard the original version himself.[104] Yet the experience of listening to Cimarosa and Mozart – above all perhaps the Mozart of *Le Nozze di Figaro* –

seems to have been among the happiest and most moving memories of his life and there is no reason to assume that he was not perfectly candid when he asked for his love of Mozart, Cimarosa and Shakespeare to be commemorated on his tomb. Rossini, however much Beyle may have enjoyed his music and however fascinating he may have found him as the perfect living example of the Italian *maestro*, formed by the most individualistic, least impartial and most attentive music lovers in the world, is repeatedly shown to be inferior to Mozart, both in the *Life of Rossini* and in the reviews of productions of his work that Beyle wrote during the 1820s for the *Journal de Paris*. And in the various tributes that he pays to Mozart, we can perhaps, as in what he has said of Michelangelo and Correggio, find the clue to certain effects of his novels.

Both in *Le rouge et le noir* and *La chartreuse de Parme*, Beyle apologises for interrupting the story with the details of political intrigue. His apology in both novels is couched in almost identical terms:

Politics...are a stone tied round the neck of literature which drown it in less than six months. Politics, amidst the interests of the imagination, are like a pistol shot in the middle of a concert. This noise is ear-rending without being energetic. It clashes with every other instrument...

(*Le rouge et le noir*, book 2, ch. 23)

Beyle might have written: 'in the middle of an opera'. As an epigraph to chapter 6 of book 1, in which Mme de Rênal and the youthful Julien Sorel begin unconsciously to fall in love with one another, we are given two lines from an aria by the passionate little Cherubino in *Le Nozze di Figaro*. The epigraph is plainly only a hint and one of the great, if obvious, lessons that Beyle learned from Mozart was that music is capable of saying far more than the written or spoken word:

One's first reflection on hearing *Figaro* is that the composer, dominated by his sensibility, has transformed into veritable passions the somewhat light predilections which in Beaumarchais occupy the amiable inhabitants of the Chateau d'Aguas-Frescas. Beaumarchais's Count Almaviva desires Suzanne and nothing more. He is far from feeling the passions which breathe in

> Vedrò mentr'io sospiro
> Felice un seno mio!

and in the duet

> Crudel! perchè finora?

...In the play, one feels that the attraction of the little page for Rosina could become more serious. But her state of mind, her sweet melancholy and her reflections on the share of happiness which destiny affords us; in other words, all the agitation which precedes the birth of great passions, are brought out infinitely more by Mozart than by the French dramatist. There are almost no words to express this state of mind and it is perhaps one which music can render far better than words.[105]

The deliberately prosaic style of the novels, the lack of declamation or of what Beyle called *emphase* are like a constant implicit acknowledgement of the limitations of prose as a medium. The lesson of Mozart in this respect was the same as that of the great Italian painters.

And yet, paradoxically, a novelist's prose can hint at and evoke what it is unable to present directly or explicitly, and this more successfully than prose or verse in the theatre where there is so much to impede the imagination and confine it to the visible realities of the stage. Perhaps the most interesting remark of all that Beyle makes concerning the nature of music in general is the one which also helps us to understand why he should have eventually chosen the novel as the only possible medium for what he had to convey:

Why is music so consoling to misery? Because, in an obscure fashion and one which in no way offends our amour-propre, it induces us to believe in tender pity. This art can change the sterile grief of the sufferer into the grief which is that of regret; it depicts men as being less hard, it brings tears to the eyes, it brings back the happiness of the past in a way that the sufferer might have thought impossible.

The main disadvantage of comedy is that the characters who make us laugh seem far too dry and lacking in emotion to sadden the more tender side of our nature. The spectacle of suffering would make us forget to think of our superiority to those at whom we laugh; this explains the charm for some people of a good comic opera and why it is superior to a good comedy: a good comic opera is the most astonishing combination of pleasures. Imagination and tenderness are engaged at the same time as the wildest laughter.[106]

As a footnote to this footnote in *The History of Painting in Italy*, Beyle gives as an instance of this kind of opera Cimarosa's *I nemici generosi*.

Music can make us believe in 'tender pity' without offending our amour-propre. And in *The Life of Rossini*, developing an idea of Richard Payne Knight's,[107] he reminds the reader of how sometimes the power of Mozart's music is such that 'the image it presents to the imagination is extremely indistinct and, as a result, one feels suddenly as if one had been invaded and inundated by melancholy'.[108] This is a development of the earlier idea that, unlike painting, music 'carries us away, we do not judge it', whereas 'pleasure in painting is always preceded by a judgment'.[109] Beyle no doubt stresses too much the melancholy of Mozart's music. He claims, rather surprisingly, that Mozart was only ever gay twice during his whole musical career: in *Così fan tutte* and when Leporello in *Don Giovanni* delivers his message to the Commendatore.[110] What he says, none the less, of the shared feelings and freedom from the inhibiting distractions of vanity of any public to whom Mozart and Cimarosa appeal is similar, in one respect at least, to what he was to write in *La comédie est impossible* of the seventeenth century public of men and women who were able 'to feel at ease together' and 'laugh at the same things.' The modern would-be dramatist, Beyle argued, could hope to find such an audience again among the isolated individuals for whom he would have to write novels. It would not, I think, be misrepresenting him to say that if Molière, in this respect, was among the formative influences on his own art as a novelist, so too were Mozart and Cimarosa. To say that this is evident from the novels themselves would, in any case, have been for Beyle among the highest compliments one could have paid him.

4

The chronicler and historian

Beyle and Napoleon

It is for a historian to assess the value of Beyle's contribution to our knowledge of the past. This book is concerned with the ways in which, rightly or wrongly, he came to think of 'his place in time, his own contemporaneity'[1] and of the thinking and exploration that, without his knowing it, was to lead to the writing of his three major novels.

Unfortunately, historians have not always taken him sufficiently seriously even to examine what he tells us of his own age[2] – at least until recently. The best work on Beyle as a chronicler of the France and Italy of his day is M. Fernand Rude's *Stendhal et le pensée sociale de son temps* and M. H. F. Imbert's *Les métamorphoses de la liberté*, both of which appeared in 1967. Thanks to these and to the articles by M. Lucien Jansse on Beyle as an economist and political scientist,[3] we now know more than earlier admirers about the opinions he held, in so far as we know more exactly how they resembled and differed from those of his own contemporaries. We may be less inclined as a consequence to congratulate him merely on having anticipated our own opinions and we are in a better position to judge the truth of his insights and the nature and interest of his idea of history.

It is still probably common, none the less, to assimilate Beyle to Tolstoy in this respect and to attribute to the former a scepticism with regard to historical truth as such similar to that which is expressed and exemplified in *War and Peace*. Professor Henri Marrou, for example, has described the affinity between them in the following terms:

... when it was the present, the past was like the present that we are living at this very moment, lacking cohesion, confused, multiform unintelligible, a dense network of causes and effects, a field of forces infinitely complex that the consciousness of man, whether he be actor or witness, is unable to grasp in its authentic reality (there is no privileged observation point, at least not on this earth). We have to go back here to the example which has been the classical one ever since... Stendhal's Waterloo in *La chartreuse de Parme*, or even better (for Napoleon himself, according to Tolstoy, is as lost as Prince Andrei or Pierre Bezuhov), the Austerlitz and Borodino of *War and Peace*.[4]

Professor Marrou describes graphically what may seem at times like the impossible conditions in which the historian seeks to understand the truth. But neither Beyle nor Tolstoy leave the problem there. And despite Beyle's influence on Tolstoy,[5] their approach to history, and specifically the history through which Beyle lived as a public servant under Napoleon, is as divergent as their whole philosophy of life.

This is most obviously the case if we compare the ways in which each looked on the dominant figure of the age, 'the greatest figure the world has seen since Caesar',[6] as Beyle put it, and whom Tolstoy tells us was as unimportant as all so-called dominant men. For Tolstoy, there is a law according to which 'men concerned to take common action combine in such relations that the more directly they participate in performing the action, the less they can command and the more numerous they are, while the less they take any direct part in the work itself the more they command and the fewer they are in number'.[7] And the folly of Napoleon lay in his failing to understand this law; unlike his Russian adversary Kutuzov, who recognised his own inability, as a general, to influence events in any decisive way or even to know what was happening while a battle was being waged.

For Beyle, the difficulties of understanding events while they are unfolding and of influencing them decisively are not insuperable, and genius lies in realising this more quickly than other men. He nowhere suggests, for example, in the famous example of his Waterloo in *La chartreuse*, that Napoleon or Wellington were as unaware of what was happening on the battlefield as a whole as his innocent novice in the art of war,

Fabrice. Take this account, moreover, of Bonaparte's Italian campaign written in the same year as *La chartreuse*:

The principle on which a commander-in-chief works is absolutely the same as that of the thieves who, on a street corner, ensure that they will be three against one and a hundred yards away from a patrol of ten men. What does the patrol matter if it will take three minutes for it to reach the hapless victim of the theft?

Every time Napoleon cut a wing of the enemy army, he merely put himself in the position of being two against one...

Any other general of the day would have thought himself lost in Napoleon's position [in July 1796 after the retreat of Masséna from the Adige]; he, however, saw that the enemy by dividing, gave him a chance to throw himself between the two wings of the Austrian army and to attack them separately.

But he had to make an immediate decision; and if one can't do this, one isn't a general.

It is obvious, incidentally, why it is so easy to write in a perfectly reasonable way about war and to indicate the decisions that should have been taken, with the wisdom of hindsight.

It was necessary to avoid at any price allowing Wurmser to join up his forces at Quasdanowich on the Mincio, for then he would have been irresistible. Napoleon had the courage to raise the siege of Mantua and abandon 140 pieces of heavy artillery in the trenches, the only heavy cannon the army possessed.

He had the courage to reason as follows and to believe in his own argument: 'If I'm beaten, what use will my siege equipment be to me anyway? I shall have to abandon it at once. If I succeed in beating the enemy, I shall go back to Mantua and find my cannon waiting for me...'[8]

And compare this with Tolstoy on the same campaign:

The incompetence of his colleagues, the weakness and inanity of his rivals, the frankness of his falsehoods and his brilliant and self-confident mediocrity raise him to the head of the army. The brilliant quality of the soldiers of the army sent to Italy, his opponents' reluctance to fight and his own childish insolence and conceit secure him military glory...[9]

Beyle may be charged with giving in to a naïve mystique of the great leader in his writings on Napoleon, 'the only man he respected', as he wrote in a note for his own epitaph in the year of the Emperor's death. Yet the alternative to such a mystique may easily be merely another form of irrationalism such as that which led Tolstoy to attribute all the events of Napoleon's career to something other than Napoleon's powers of judgment. It is true that there is much in Beyle's two attempted lives of Napoleon which is unconvincing, if only because of the adoring hearsay on which it seems based; though we should remember, when saying this, that it was not he himself who was responsible for publishing them as they stand.[10] We should perhaps remember too that, though he was anything but blind to Napoleon's many disastrous errors, he was also, as in his writings on literature, conscious of the timeliness or, in the Nietzschian sense, 'untimeliness' of the effect of any judgment he made on his immediate public in France.

The first attempted life of Napoleon was written, as he says in the opening words of the manuscript, 'in reply to a libel... launched by the outstanding talent of the century against a man who for four years has been a target for the vengeance of the mightiest powers on earth'. The defence of the exile in St Helena begun in Milan in 1817 has something of the noble eloquence of Mme de Staël to whose account of Napoleon (in the *Considérations sur la Révolution Française*) his own biography was to have been a reply. And it is in contrast with the tone of all Beyle's surviving comments on Napoleon during the Consulate and Empire. Under the Consulate, he had sympathised strongly with Bonaparte's political adversary General Moreau, and he claimed afterwards that he had taken part in the conspiracy for which Moreau was tried and exiled.[11] As a republican, he had deplored the crowning of the Emperor; 'religion come to sanctify tyranny and all this in the name of the happiness of men'[12] and though his comments on Napoleon are more loyal in the letters written after he had himself entered the Imperial service, he had sought employment under the first Bourbon restoration, welcomed the Restoration in his first published writings[13] and even spoken of Wellington as the 'liberator' of Portugal in his *Lives of Haydn, Mozart and Metastasio* in 1814.[14]

The conversion to a passionate Bonapartism seems to have been partly due to Beyle's horror at the reprisals following the Hundred Days, the treatment of his former fellow administrators who had remained at their posts and the barbaric execution of Marshal Ney. Also to a realisation that, even if Napoleon were no longer appreciated in France (where Beyle hoped his former treacherous subjects would be 'well vexed' by the Prussians billeted in their homes)[15] he was deeply respected and seen as a liberator in the enlightened circles of Italy and even of England itself. In the circle of Ludovico de Brême, a former chaplain to Napoleon, Beyle met and conversed with Silvio Pellico, Vincenzo Monti, John Cam Hobhouse and Byron during the latter's visit to Milan in 1816 and passed himself off as a former secretary to the Emperor and subsequently to Murat, during the retreat from Moscow, retailing anecdotes about what he had seen and heard in this capacity which Hobhouse eagerly noted down.[16] The extravagance of these fantasies suggests that Beyle may have regretted not being more fully and loyally identified with the Napoleonic epic while the epic was taking place; though his letters of the period, particularly those from Moscow and Smolensk for 4 October and 7 November 1812, are masterpieces of first hand *reportage*, historical documents in their own right and bear ample witness to how much he had seen. The heroes of his major novels, however, will all regret not having lived through the epic themselves, and in the case of Fabrice regret not knowing whether the fighting he joined in was the Battle of Waterloo or not; while Beyle himself saw the final overthrow of Napoleon as bringing an end to an age of immense opportunities. 'Everything that will happen in France from now on', he wrote in his diary during a trip to Venice in the July of 1815, 'will bear the epigraph "under the extinguisher"' and the words, as often at moments of emotional stress, are accompanied by a sardonically meticulous sketch.

How adequately though, we may ask, does Chateaubriand's account of the Bonapartism which became increasingly popular in France during the next thirty years describe that of Beyle himself:

It is a matter of daily observation that the Frenchman's instinct is to strive after power; he cares not for liberty; equality is his idol. Now there is a hidden connection between equality and despotism. In both these respects, Napoleon had a pull over the hearts of the French, who have a military liking for power and are democratically fond of seeing everything levelled. When he mounted the throne, he took the people with him. A proletarian king, he humiliated kings and noblemen in his anti-rooms. He levelled the ranks not down but up...Another cause of Napoleon's popularity is the affliction of his latter days. After his death, as his sufferings on St. Helena became better known, people's hearts began to soften; his tyranny was forgotten...His misfortunes have revived his name among us, his glory has fed on his wretchedness.

The miracles wrought by his arms have bewitched our youth, and have taught us to worship brute force. The most insolent ambition is spurred on by his unique career to aspire to the heights which he attained.[17]

A superficial reading of Beyle may leave us with the impression that his 'respect' for the Emperor amounted to no more than this, that it was indistinguishable, in other words, from that of Julien Sorel. Yet it is as a self-professed lover of liberty that he praises and condemns Napoleon. And there is no fundamental difference in this respect between the angry young republican walking back to his lodgings on the day of Napoleon's coronation to read Alfieri and the Bonapartist of later years. In the ringing dedication to Napoleon in the *History of Painting in Italy* published in 1817, Beyle claims that posterity will see his overthrow as a disastrous setback for *'les idées libérales'*, and in the eloquent Roman simplicity of the prose, the word *'libérales'* is given the full weight of its original connotations; while in the first attempted *Life of Napoleon* begun in the same year, he regrets that, none the less, he did not do more to create liberal institutions. Beyle's idea of the form such institutions might take seems, incidentally, to have varied little over the years. Two chambers, he argues in 1817, might have saved the Republic before Bonaparte seized power. And the Directory fell 'not because a Republic is impossible in France' but 'because there was no conservative Senate to maintain the equilibrium between a House of Commons and the Directory...' (chapter 17). It is this form of government that Beyle outlines in detail in his notes of 1810 on 'the constitution desired by the people in 1789' and his allegiance in later years if not to the governments, at least to the constitutions of the Restoration and the July monarchy is clearly due to the extent to which they both conform to this model.

Beyle's fascination with the form and effect of constitutional arrangements, of which his notebooks offer ample evidence, corresponds frequently to a lack of faith in any collective genius or will. The Republic, given the right institutions, might have been saved in France but, in terms almost identical with those of Chateaubriand, he blames not only Bonaparte but the French themselves for the tyranny he created after 1799:

> ...Bonaparte didn't want institutions to be rooted in public opinion. It was necessary, he considered, for an acutely intelligent people to hear constant solemn reminders of the need for *stability* and safeguards for the interests of *posterity* and to feel that nothing was stable but his power alone and nothing progressive but his authority. 'The French', he said round about this time, 'are indifferent to liberty: they neither understand nor love it; vanity is their sole passion and political equality, which gives to all the hope of arriving at any place in society one wishes, is the only political right they regard as worth having.'
>
> Nothing truer has ever been said...   (*Vie de Napoléon*, ch. 23)

Napoleon's dynastic ambitions, his Concordat with Rome, his encouragement of mediocrity and flattery and his inability to act as an efficient commander-in-chief while weighed down with the responsibilities of a head of state are consistently deplored in all that Beyle wrote on Napoleon over a period of thirty years. He reveres him, and in the manuscript of 1837 in which he identifies himself with the veterans of the Revolutionary wars, claims always to have revered him for his 'usefulness' to the nation at a particular moment in time,[18] for having in fact saved the Revolution and in doing so, saved humanity itself. Had it not been for the reorganisation of France after Bonaparte had become the virtual dictator of France,

> ...the conquering kings would have divided France among themselves. It would have been found prudent to destroy this source of Jacobinism. The Duke of Brunswick's manifesto would have been applied to the letter and all the noble writers who adorn the academies would have proclaimed the impossibility of liberty. Never since 1793 had the new ideas been in such danger. The civilisation of the world was on the point of being set back by several hundred years. The wretched Peruvian would still have groaned under the iron yoke of Spain and the conquering kings of Europe would have abandoned themselves to the delights of cruelty, as [after the fall of the Empire] in Naples...   (*Vie de Napoléon*, ch. 16)

And after France had been saved from the fate of Poland, Bonaparte rendered to the rest of the world his most inestimable service:

For the last century, it has not been exactly good intentions that Europe has lacked but the energy necessary to shake the enormous mass of contracted habits. Any profound movement now can only be morally advantageous, that is conducive to the happiness of men...

(*Vie de Napoléon*, ch. 23)

The reorganisation of the former states of the Empire after Waterloo showed the beneficial effects of the shock produced by Napoleon and corresponded, he adds, to a more 'true equilibrium' than the habits and institutions of the old order.

Beyle is very different from Tolstoy in his belief in the influence that an individual can exert on a nation, different, that is, from the Tolstoy who wrote the epilogue to *War and Peace*. (The utterances and thoughts of Pierre Bezuhov in the same novel show that even Tolstoy felt the power of the Napoleonic charisma.) Beyle is closer in his account of Napoleon to D. H. Lawrence:

Peter the Great, Frederick the Great, and Napoleon... They established a *new* connection between mankind and the universe, and the result was a vast release of energy... [19]

though his interest in the actual mechanism of society is very un-Lawrencian and much closer to the spirit of the eighteenth-century enlightenment. One of Napoleon's greatest achievements, he believed, was his establishment of a rational code of law; while his analysis of the various kinds of liberty that existed under Napoleon is reminiscent of Montesquieu in its epigrammatically succinct and consciously paradoxical account of the ways in which institutions make themselves felt by the mass of ordinary citizens.[20] It is reminiscent also of the manner and arguments of Mme de Staël and Chateaubriand, to whose accounts of Napoleon his own were intended as a reply. It would be wrong certainly to say that he goes in for that 'naïve method of interpreting history merely as the story of great tyrants and great generals' against which Sir Karl Popper tells us Tolstoy rightly reacted.[21] Beyle's firm insistence on the *usefulness* of Napoleon is itself an evident refusal to surrender to any such cult of the personality. Yet there is more obviously to Napoleon for Beyle than any political argument could adequately explain. And in the *Mémoires sur Napoléon*, which was written a year before *La chartreuse de Parme*, far more wonder and joy are associated with the arrival of Bonaparte's army in

Italy than can be expressed in conventional historical terms. There is probably, in other words, more significance than critics and admirers of the lives of Napoleon have seen in the fact that Beyle never tried to publish them and that it is in the unsophisticated minds of the heroes of his novels that he was to make the Napoleonic legend appear most real and at the same time most clearly comprehensible.

Italy and the eruption of energy

I have argued in an earlier chapter that Beyle's conscious utilitarianism and his belief in the heroic follow from one another and that to understand one we must take into account the other. In his anti-Saint-Simonian pamphlet of 1825, he had claimed that the citizens most worthy of public esteem were those who 'risk a great deal in order to obtain what, rightly or wrongly, they believe to be useful to the public' and not those whose own pursuit of wealth is of only incidental benefit to society as a whole. The qualification, 'rightly or wrongly' is crucial to Beyle's argument about those who seek the public good, for though the public good is something real and desirable, there is no certain way of knowing what this is.

Beyle was the last person to denigrate the benefits of prosperity, but he seems to have regarded this always as one means only, and this one by no means indispensable, to the realisation of happiness. The good society, as he conceived it, was not merely one in which prosperity and the opportunities for social advancement would be universal; though, in the late 1830s in the *Mémoires sur Napoléon* and the *Mémoires d'un touriste*, he looks forward to a continuation of progress in this direction. It would be one which would encourage the greatest possible release of human 'energy', one of his most frequently used terms, though to understand what he meant by it, we have to read what he said about the society he most admired, that of Italy from the age of Dante to the end of the sixteenth century.

Despite his early republicanism and his fondness for Plutarch and Livy, Beyle did not become a classical historian or an active member of the Jacobin opposition to Napoleon, and the period of political disillusion followed by professional conformity as a civil servant after the crowning of Napoleon was the period in which he discovered the past of Italy and became increasingly absorbed in its way of life and its art. The pages of Alfieri with which he had 'rinsed out his mouth' on the day of Napoleon's coronation may have been from *Del Principe e delle lettere* in which he would have read that 'the fearful and sublime crimes' committed even in the depths of Italy's moral degradation, are a proof of the hot and ferocious spirits that abound within her more than anywhere else in Europe...'.[22] And in Sismondi's *History of the Italian Republics*, which he had bought in 1808, he would have read that 'political passions', such as those the republican spirit inspires, 'make more heroes than individual passions and though the connection may not be obvious, more artists, poets, scholars and seers...'.[23] A return visit to Milan in 1811, followed by a tour of the peninsula, had confirmed him in his lifelong attachment to Italy and much of his career as a writer from then on was to be spent describing and explaining the innate superiority of the Italian people as a whole.

This did not lie merely in the republican spirit. According to Professor Carlo Cordiè, 'the Renaissance with its tyrants and city states...represents for him an aesthetic ideal...'.[24] And in the introduction to the *History of painting in Italy*, written between 1811 and 1818, Beyle tells us how 'after three centuries of misfortune, and what misfortune – the most fearful, that which renders men vile – there is nowhere one hears pronounced as in Italy the words "O Dio, com' è bello"'. Beyle's 'aestheticism', if this is the right word, is certainly not the exclusive variety associated with the belief in art for art's sake. (And the word *bello* has a less restricted application than 'beautiful' or even '*beau*'.) It is rather a deep interest in life lived with a fulness of energy and a vulnerability and sensitiveness which are manifest *both* in art and in life. Freedom is essential to such energy and one of the merits of the *History of painting* is its reminder that liberty can exist without liberal institutions to protect it and that the latter can exist in a society in which the spirit of liberty itself is dead:

Let me say to the modern princes, so proud of their virtues and who so despise the little tyrants of the middle ages: 'These virtues on which you pride yourselves are only private virtues. As a king, you are nothing. Whereas the tyrants of Italy had private vices and public virtues...

Florence, a republic without a constitution, but in which the horror of tyranny enflamed every heart, knew that stormy liberty which is the mother of great characters...It was constantly necessary to resort to arms against the nobles; but it is degradation and not danger which kills a people's spirit... [25]

(Introduction)

It is natural for Beyle to approach each of the painters in his history as a biographer, so much so that even his admirer Taine agreed with Mérimée that he was not sufficiently interested in painting in its own right. And the anecdotes which make up the biographies illustrate, among other things, the general truth that he will state twenty years later in *L'Abbesse de Castro*:

Melodrama has so often shown us the Italian brigands of the sixteenth century and so many people have spoken of them in ignorance, that we now have the most false ideas concerning them. In general, one can say that these brigands formed the *opposition* against the atrocious governments which, in Italy, succeeded the Republics of the middle ages. The new tyrant was usually the wealthiest citizen of the defunct Republic and in order to win over the people, he would adorn the city with magnificent churches and fine paintings. Such were the Polentini of Ravenna, the Manfredi of Faenza, the Riarios of Imola, the Bentivoglios of Bologna, the Viscontis of Milan and, the most bellicose and hypocritical of all, the Medici of Florence. Among the historians of these little states, none has dared to recount the poisonings and assassinations without number commanded by the fear which tormented these little tyrants; the grave historians were in their pay. Consider that each of these tyrants knew personally each of the republicans by whom he knew he was loathed, that several of these tyrants were assassinated and you will then understand the profound hatreds and eternal suspicions that gave so much intelligence and courage to the Italians of the sixteenth century and so much genius to their artists. You will see how these profound passions prevented the birth of the ridiculous prejudice that went by the name of *honour* in the days of Mme de Sévigné and which consists essentially in sacrificing one's life for the master to whom one is subject by birth or in order to impress a lady...In Italy, a man distinguished himself by merit *of every kind*, by wielding a sword or discovering ancient manuscripts: think of Petrarch, the idol of his age. A woman in the sixteenth century would love a scholar of Greek as much as, if not more than a man celebrated for his military prowess and valour. It was then that one saw passions and not the habit of *galanterie*. This is the great difference between Italy and France and why Italy saw the birth of the Raphaels, Giorgiones, Titians and Correggios, while France produced all those brave captains of the sixteenth century, so little known today and each one of whom killed such an impressive number of enemies... (ch. 1)

In his earlier writings on Italy, *Rome, Naples et Florence en 1817*, and his most serious attempt at a conventional guide book, the *Promenades dans Rome* of 1829, it is the miraculous survival of the old Italian spirit, despite centuries of oppression, he records; though painting

...is now dead and buried. Canova has burst through to the light by chance, by dint of the vegetative force with which the soul of man is endowed in this lovely climate: but like Alfieri, he's a monster; there is nothing else like him, nothing that even approaches him, and sculpture otherwise is as dead in Italy as the art of Correggio... Music alone remains alive, and in this beautiful country, the only other thing to do is to make love; the other pleasures of the soul encounter obstacles and constraints; in so far as one feels one is a citizen of the country, one will die poisoned by melancholy...

(*Rome, Naples et Florence en 1817*, 17.11.1816)

The implications of this comment are pursued in detail in each of the travel books, in *The life of Rossini* and, as far as 'love' is concerned, in the story of Fabrice del Dongo in *La chartreuse de Parme*. And it expresses Beyle's simultaneous reverence for the irrepressible Italian spirit and his conviction that Italy has become ungovernable except through a naked assertion of power. The rulers and statesmen of the Italy of his own day that he admires are autocrats like Napoleon, whom he pardons for having suppressed the Republic of Venice – a republic only in name and one which was especially mourned, as he points out, by English aristocrats[26] – or like the Austrian governors themselves whose rule of Lombardy he deplores while recognising the fairness with which they apply their laws, their success in restraining the fanaticism of the Church and their encouragement during the eighteenth century of the work of Beccaria and consequent services to the cause of Utilitarianism.[27] Rome itself also fascinated Beyle and in his travel books he devotes many pages to its ceremonies, to the history of Papal intrigues and to its primitive constitution, for which he sketches a number of reforms. He admired particularly 'the military talents and force of will' of Michelangelo's patron Julius II, and among his own contemporaries the administrative genius of the reforming minister Cardinal Consalvi; while in the letters he wrote as Consul in Civita Vecchia to the Minister of Foreign Affairs in Paris and which are among the best things he wrote about the Italy of his day, we learn of the 'active intelligent' Minister of Police in Rome, Mgr Ciachi, a former officer of dragoons, who is 'adored by his subordinates because the only harm he has done is that which is useful to himself...' (8.4.1835). In all these figures and especially the last, Beyle's reforming minister, Count Mosca della Rovere in *La chartreuse de Parme* is foreshadowed, together with the despotic rule he successfully wields. There is even perhaps an intended significance in the fact that Julius II and Mosca share the same family name.

Beyle's conviction that Italy since the sixteenth century has needed the strong enlightened rule of individuals, given the absence of what sociologists since Hegel have often referred to as 'civil society', consorts naturally with his frequent admiration for the anarchic and even criminal ways in which Italian energy is displayed. Beyle shared and was one of the first to express the common nineteenth-century interest in the psychology of crime, and *Promenades dans Rome* in particular is full of anecdotes concerning the use of poison in Italy and the refinements of cruelty invented by the country's many assassins. The *Promenades* contains also Beyle's eulogy of the common people of Rome, whose long history of submission to the caprice of the Popes and the consequent need to *'inventer et vouloir'* [28] have made them more courageous than the people of London or Paris. It is an animal freedom that Beyle is celebrating, however, under the name of energy, and he reminds us consequently of its atrocious as well as its more attractive forms. Between 1775 and 1800, for example, there were '18,000 assassinations in Rome, that is two a day'.

The atrociousness of Napoleon's laws, to employ the manner of speaking of Cardinal N...has done something to correct these bad habits. In Rome, it is the arrested assassin who is pitied and if the pious and retrograde government which has succeeded Cardinal Consalvi's is popular in any way, it is because it rarely employs capital punishment for any other crime than *carbonarismo*...[29]

Energy for Beyle, in general, has an equivocal value – necessarily, in so far as, by his own definition, it is liable to threaten the interests of any living man. It is a law unto itself, and in all its manifestations a terrifying or breathtakingly beautiful reminder that morally there is no other kind of law. This may account for its fascination for Beyle, for in innumerable ways, whatever energy may destroy, it merely confirms the reasonableness of the Beyliste point of view. Though it is worth remembering also that for Beyle who was a pioneer in the form of *Kultur-geschichte* that we find in his travel books and history of painting (Nietzsche's friend, Burckhardt in his *Civilisation of the Renaissance in Italy* was among those who were to pursue it more methodically) the strain of violence running through Italian history had something of the fascination of a new discovery.

To summarise all that Beyle ever wrote about energy is, however, an even more hopeless task than to indicate the broad outlines of his writings on Italy. The loose, deliberately un-schematic and freely digressive form of the latter, which is that of a diary kept by an enthusiastic traveller, overflows with facts, in Beyle's own sense of the word: that is, particular insights and pointed anecdotes, almost any one of which throws light on some different aspect of the Italy as Beyle saw. The fascination with energy was to remain with him till he died. Even his early republicanism and veneration for the heroes of Plutarch, Corneille and Alfieri can easily be seen as a deep interest in one particular kind of energy; though, with the discovery of Shakespeare and of the Italian Renaissance, the growing dissatisfaction with Alfieri and, coinciding with this, the realisation that, with the advent of Napoleon, the early promise of the Revolution had gone, one might say that it was the diversity of forms that energy might assume that absorbed him rather than the single heroic model he had worshipped as a boy.

The true meaning of energy as Beyle uses the term can only be determined by reference to his deepest and most thoughtful writing, and this is to be found in his three major novels rather than in the works with which this chapter is concerned. The *History of Painting in Italy* was undertaken partly to cover the expenses of a further tour of Italy and partly in order to acquire something of the grace of a Correggio, to rid himself of the 'detestable dryness and precision' into which he was afraid of falling as a dramatist,[30] drama being still his chosen vocation, as it was to remain until he decided that the would-be dramatist in the nineteenth century would have to resort to the novel. There is no account in the books on Italy of the nature of energy and of its growth comparable in its logic and inwardness to that which is offered in *Le rouge et le noir*, germane though we may find such thoughts as the following from the *Promenades dans Rome*:

The other assassination took place near St Peter's in the Trastevere district; this is also a bad area, one is told, which makes it sublime for me. One finds *energy* here, that is, the quality most absent in the nineteenth century. Today, we have found the secret of being brave without either energy or character. No one knows how to *will what he desires*[31]; our education simply unteaches this most important subject of all. The English know how to will what they desire; but it is not without difficulty that in doing so they violate the whole spirit of modern civilisation; their life, as a result, is one constant effort... (27.1.1828)

The almost prophetic tentativeness of such remarks, which makes one see why Nietzsche said that it had taken 'two generations to catch up with him', is not that of systematic thought. Which is why Taine's eulogy of Beyle as a historian and chronicler seems always entirely inappropriate. It is Beyle, according to Taine,

...who has explained the most complicated of the internal mechanisms, pointed out to us the principal springs of behaviour and introduced into the study of the human heart the methods of science and the arts of calculation, analysis and deduction. It is he who has shown us the fundamental causes, by which I mean climate, nationality and temperament, and who has approached the study of human feeling as one has to, namely as a natural scientist...[32]

Among those whom Beyle influenced was the Breton aristocrat Gobineau, who, in *Les Pléïades*, his study of the *Renaissance* and his *Essai sur l'inégalité des races humaines*, set out to be systematic in the way Taine describes. The nearest Beyle himself comes to finding reasons in nature for the Italians being as they are is to refer occasionally to their 'beautiful climate'. He differs, in fact, from those who have tried to establish the causes of superior energy and intelligence and then to ensure their survival by maintaining the purity of races and castes, in his readiness to acknowledge energy and intelligence in all their forms and irrespective of their source: in his admiration, for example, both for the 'sublime' assassins of the Trastevere district and the firm measures of Cardinal Consalvi which succeeded in keeping the crime rate down. What makes his writings on Italy so unique, in other words, is the breadth and fearlessness of his sympathies, which presumably owe something to the circumstances of his life. Like Nietzsche, who followed him so eagerly in his study of energy, he was a childless bachelor, and his works on Italy are those of a traveller writing under an assumed name. It is difficult to believe that this has nothing to do with his exceptional ability to appreciate the justice and truth of rival claims.

Saying this leads one to conclude that there may be some justification after all for Professor Cordiè's saying that his love of Italy was 'aesthetic'. The vantage point from which Beyle looks down on society is a privileged one, in that it is so detached and adventurous. But this is not to say that it is one from which no practical lesson can be learned. Beyle's fears for the Europe of his time and our own were that as society became more prosperous and democratic, it would become more American too – more dominated, that is, by the spirit of mutual surveillance and mutual servility that he was to see after 1830 as the price of American popular democracy.[33] (The lawlessness and energy of the American expansion westward were something he did not predict.) And his allegiance to the democratic ideals of his boyhood and to the utilitarian principles of later years was to be qualified only by his fear lest society should lose that energy that he still finds among those who have to 'struggle with real needs'[34] and without which life can no longer be lived as an individual or collective destiny.

The chronicler of contemporary France

Beyle's account of the life of his own contemporaries in France is to be found principally in the articles he contributed to various English periodicals after his return from Milan in 1821 and which were to furnish his main source of income for a number of years, in the *Mémoires d'un touriste* and, most important of all, his own novels. The point of view from which he writes is that of a liberal of the period before 1830, an admirer of the liberal orators Benjamin Constant and General Foy, of the popular Bonapartist and democratic poet Béranger, and the pamphleteer Paul-Louis Courier. The society he describes is one dominated by the Jesuit conspiracy, by the new Puritanism introduced by Napoleon (who had made marriage respectable by insisting that women should never appear at court without their husbands), by the new literary and journalistic industry made possible by the relaxation of censorship under the Restoration, and by the mysticism and religiosity which had invaded philosophy, literature and the fashionable salons. Beyle's diagnosis of the ills of the Restoration is not in itself very unusual. Even Chateaubriand was afraid of the Jesuits,[35] Sainte Beuve and Balzac have left their own accounts of the new commercialism in literature;[36] while the contrast between the melancholy and earnestness of the nineteenth century and the life of pre-Revolutionary France has struck many other contemporary observers of the so-called *mal du siècle*. No other contemporary commentator that I know of, however, seems to have understood the relation between these phenomena so clearly; there is, surely, no better contemporary critic of the literature of the period; none writes with that combination of intellectual excitement, anger and amusement that makes even Beyle's lightest journalism unlike that of anyone else; and few were able to see France, as Beyle was, from the cosmopolitan point of view which enabled him to discuss, for example, the different kinds of freedom enjoyed by the English and French respectively, a subject which continues to baffle both nationalities.[37]

The gossip and the fecundity of ideas that make the articles in the English reviews so readable, even today, may owe something to Beyle's frequenting liberal salons, such as those of Mme d'Aubernon, where he would meet among others Victor Cousin, and on leaving which he had been known to say, 'Now my article's done!'.[38] And their frequent facetiousness may be due both to this and to the fact that they were written to order and with an immediate audience in mind: a foreign audience, in addressing which Beyle seems to have felt even more conscious than usual of the possible absurdity of his claims to be telling the truth. The variety of pseudonyms he chose for his articles and which seems to have enabled him to review at least one of his own books – with reservations, though warmly and with a sense of its true merits[39] – released him from the obligation to be an unfailingly honest reporter; and even when he is carried away by heartfelt enthusiasm or anger, much of his journalism is characterised by an evident reliance on hearsay and a high spirited simplification of the facts.

Beyle seems, moreover, to have flattered his English readers, at least to the extent of concealing from them his dislike of the English character, his disapproval of the Old Corruption of the English governing classes, his anger at the treatment of Napoleon after Waterloo, and his belief that Napoleon should have crossed the Channel and imposed on the country a constitution similar to that of the United States.[40] He was not, on the whole, one of those who utters the truth as they see it fearlessly to anyone who cares to hear. He feared, like Julien Sorel and often with justification, allowing his secret thoughts to be known, a tendency perhaps originating in the days when, as a ten-year-old Jacobin during the Terror and civil war, he lived in a family of political enemies. And this may account partly for the sunnily optimistic view of the future and his seeming faith in the wisdom of the July monarchy expressed in the *Mémoires d'un touriste* of 1837 and which come remarkably near to obsequiousness.

His private views of the new order established in 1830 seem very different, at least during the period before the *Mémoires d'un touriste* appeared. Despite his nomination, through the good offices of the liberal Count Molé as consul in Civita Vecchia, Beyle was one of those who first welcomed the Revolution of 1830 but were speedily disillusioned by its outcome. His novel *Lucien Leuwen* is his most extended and passionate expression of his dislike of the reign of 'this most crooked of kings', and was a book that he knew he could not possibly publish as long as he remained in the service of the crown. His private correspondence of 1831 expresses his indignant sympathy with the unjustly imprisoned Auguste Blanqui and his anger that his former school-friend Félix Faure, in his capacity as President of the Royal Court of Justice in Grenoble should be 'allowed to insult continuously for a whole fortnight all those who think and are twenty-five years old...' (1.2.1831).[41]

The social disturbances that marked the opening years of the July monarchy: the sacking of St Germain l'Auxerrois, the violent repression of popular demonstrations in the Rue Transnonain in Paris and the rising of the *canuts*, the silk workers of Lyon, demanding the right to collective bargaining[42] are often taken as marking the end of the alliance of interests between the liberal bourgeoisie and the urban proletariat, and the beginnings of what was to become in 1848 and 1871 open war between the two classes. M. Jean-Paul Sartre has spoken of 1831 as the year in which the bourgeoisie 'recognised itself for what it was...'[43] and began to live out the contradictions between its avowed beliefs and its actual behaviour as the governing class in society. And in his recent study of Flaubert, *L'idiot de la famille*, Sartre has portrayed Flaubert's father, the distinguished Rouennais surgeon, as one of those who chose to accept such a contradiction and Flaubert himself as one of its spiritual victims.[44]

The terror of the proletariat among the middle classes after the first rising of the *canuts* is expressed in a letter to Beyle by his friend Prosper Mérimée, whose relish of energy however ferocious when it is that of Corsicans and Spaniards, deserts him when it is that of his fellow citizens. After alleging that the rising was the result of the preaching of Saint-Simonian agitators, an allegation that Beyle was later publicly to deny,[45] Mérimée offers his friend the following advice: 'Please note that what happened in Lyon has happened in Bristol and Dresden too. Which proves that those who eat hard tack now want white bread and have just realised that nothing is easier. Believe me, you had better deposit a million or two in Turkey. It's the only country where a man who loves tranquility will be able to live from now on...' (1.12.1831). This note is conspicuously absent from Beyle's own private correspondence; the inhuman callousness of the upper classes after the defeat of the *canuts* is dwelled on at length in *Lucien Leuwen*,[46] and even in the *Mémoires d'un touriste* he will note how, whatever errors they committed in 1831 and again in 1834, the *canuts* of Lyon gave proof of 'super-human courage'.[47]

His admiration for their courage does not prevent him from dwelling in the same work on the mean-spirited enviousness of both the *canuts* and their masters, and that 'unfortunate thirst for enjoyment and rapid fortune which is the folly of all young Frenchmen today', for which the rise of Napoleon created an unforgettable precedent, and to which, more than any actual misery, he attributes the silk workers' revolt:

It is in vain that the voice of philosophy cries out to them: 'But all the odious abuses are now abolished in France; if the Almighty himself put a pen in your hand to correct such abuses, you would be at a loss; you wouldn't know what to write; there are no more radical reforms needed in France, no great upheavals *to hope for or fear*. France has been deceived by the glory of Napoleon and tormented by absurd desires. Instead of *inventing* its destiny, it wishes to *copy* it; it wants to see, starting once again in 1837, the century that began in 1792 with Carnot and Dumouriez...[48]

Like Beyle's new-found admiration when he visits Chambéry, for the Jesuits, whose fanatical devotion to their own order makes them the most exemplary of schoolteachers (as many liberal parents have discovered to their advantage),[49] these thoughts on Napoleon indicate a point of view very different from that of *Le rouge et le noir*, though how literally, or un-ironically, we ought to take such judgments is never clear. The *Mémoires d'un touriste* are ostensibly the work of an iron merchant travelling through the length and breadth of France on business as well as for his own amusement, and the assumed personality of the traveller gives Beyle a freedom to express views he may not actually have held; such as those on the 'wise government of a king who is also a superior man, who refuses to authorise the insolence of the rich towards the poor that one sees in England...'[50] or on the 'growing prosperity of France under the government of Louis Philippe', in expressing which he hopes that no one will think he is in the pay of the crown.[51]

Sincere or not, the *Mémoires d'un touriste* and their unfinished sequel, the *Voyage dans le midi de la France,* leave us with the most attractive impressions he was ever to form of the lives of ordinary Frenchmen and of the diversity and uniqueness of the French provinces; and despite his dislike of the landscape and people of the region of Fontainebleau and his yearning to thrash the wealthy bullying liberals he meets in the coach to Saint Malo, they convey what seems like an unsimulated pleasure after more than two years abroad at the general state of France. Henry James found him still the ideal companion half a century later, and in his *Little Tour of France*, recommended him to every traveller, comparing him in his digressiveness with Sterne;

though a more obvious comparison might have been with Sterne's admirer Diderot, to whom Beyle pays homage during a visit to Langres in the Haute-Marne:

No doubt this writer is guilty of over-statement, but how superior he will seem in 1850 to most of the grandiloquent writers of the present day! His overstatements are not the result of poverty of ideas and the need to hide it! On the contrary, he is weighed down by all he is bursting to say...[52]

Beyle's devouring interest in the human scene and in the organisation of local trade and industry, his delight in painting and architecture (to which James does rather less than justice) and his many digressions on literature remind one of the Diderot of the *Salons* and the *Encyclopédie*, though without the obtrusive excitable self-consciousness which Beyle characterises in a deceptively laconic aside:

Diderot's talent was lacking in one respect only. He never had the good fortune to pay court when he was twenty to a young woman of distinction, and the courage to appear in her salon. His habit of over-statement would have disappeared...

M. Lucien Jansse has paid tribute to Beyle's insight into the economic needs of France at the dawn of her industrial revolution,[53] his understanding of the dangers of inflated credit,[54] of the arguments for and against protectionism[55] and above all, of the real purchasing power of money,[56] of the physical well-being, for example, of the Italian weaver compared with his better-paid and more hard-working French counterpart. M. Rude has drawn attention to Beyle's remarkable receptiveness in the *Mémoires d'un touriste* to the new social ideas; though he perhaps exaggerates Beyle's admiration for Fourier and says nothing of what has come in our own century to seem like the truth of his forecast of the development of the spirit of Fourieresque 'association':[57]

Fourier, living in solitude, or what amounts to the same thing, with disciples who never dared to raise an objection (in any case, he never answered objections) never saw that in each village, an active scoundrel with a glib tongue (a Robert Macaire) will put himself at the head of the association and pervert all its fine consequences. It is, none the less, true that the *competition* which still exists between one individual and another will end up by being exercised only between one big company and another. This characteristic of the industry of the future is already apparent today... [58]

If Beyle is not a distracting or obtrusive presence in his own travelogue, nor is he obviously a neutral one. The clarity and depth of his impressions of France are the effect rather of that lifelong joy in discovering how others find happiness without which no one can be a novelist or even, one is tempted to add, a historian. His willingness to learn about different ways of being happy and of evolving one's way of life accordingly is apparent, for example, in his account of a bird-shooting expedition in the hills above Marseille, where the inhabitants wait for their prey in little cabins made with the branches of thorn trees:

It must be confessed that one derives the most enchanting pleasure from the lovely climate in these cabins of dead wood, that the sea breeze penetrates from every side. There reigns here an enchanting silence, a silence such that one can *hear one's soul*; one can enjoy here a total liberty; no care can penetrate this peaceful retreat. Even if one gave a Marseillais millions to go and live in Paris, I am sure he would miss his little 'post' and I must say I almost agree with him... [59]

By contrast, the wealthy liberals travelling to Saint Malo who 'drag his imagination in the mud', see liberty as 'the power to prevent one's neighbour doing what he likes' and, during the period of their enforced company, 'convert' Beyle himself to their way of thinking. The enjoyment of the diversity of human pleasures is a precarious one, as Beyle is the first to confess, and his own interest in his fellow men never purports to be that of a disembodied mind. Beyle is often intolerant. As in the polemic against Saint-Simon, moreover, he makes his own interests clear before judging society as a whole; and by adopting the rôle of a prosperous iron merchant, he confesses that these are the social and economic interests of a typical member of the middle bourgeoisie.

In the articles in the English reviews, for which a model is the *Correspondance littéraire* of Diderot's friend, the German born Grimm (and in which one of his most frequent pseudonyms is 'Grimm's grandson'), there is no such clearly defined point of view; though this may also be attributed to historical circumstances, to the unsuccessful attempt by powerful factions in the Church and the aristocracy to reverse history, which made a liberalism like Beyle's perhaps inevitably seem like the noble all-too-obvious enlightenment of all parties in opposition. The *Mémoires d'un touriste* and the *Voyage dans le midi de la France* are written from a more unequivocally committed standpoint and with a corresponding sobriety. The image that pervades them is that of a superb mountain torrent, in which the dramatic cascades are compared with the inevitable revolutions of the past and are now seen winding through a prosperous plain.[60] The truth of the comparison may be contested (though the second of the great social revolutions predicted by Marx has still not, at the time of writing, occurred). The value of the *Mémoires* as a document lies in the candour and completeness with which, if nothing else, they express the bourgeois point of view.

M. Sartre has no difficulty in pointing out the contradiction between the interests and commitments of writers like Vigny and Flaubert and their professed contempt for their own way of life and the social order on which it depended.[61] There is no such contradiction in Beyle's writings on France and the aristocratic pseudonym he insisted on retaining, to the amusement of his friends, is no more than a carnival disguise.

History and truth

'Take up history', he wrote to Pauline from his regiment in Italy when he was eighteen years old, 'but only that philosophical history which shows in all events the consequences of men's actions...'.[62] Plutarch was at this time one of the favourite authors of the young republican, and Roman history the reading he most enjoyed. He admired particularly the *Révolutions romaines* of the Abbé Vertot, which had enjoyed considerable currency throughout the eighteenth century, and his continuing interest in the subject and desire to keep up with the latest works on ancient history can be seen in many passages in the *Promenades dans Rome*.

It is perhaps Volney, however, who more than anyone else, helped to 'crystallise', in the sense defined in *De l'amour*, the relation for Beyle between 'history' and 'philosophy' and we should be grateful to Professor del Litto for having dwelled at length on the affinities between their ways of thinking of the past.[63] Beyle read Volney's *Voyage en Syrie et en Egypte* and his *Leçons d'histoire* during his period of service in Brunswick and may have learned in doing so that memory (which Tracy sees as the source of all our errors and the training of which is tantamount to the training of reason itself) is not merely a function of the individual mind. 'The more I have analysed the daily influence exerted on the actions and opinions of men by history', Volney writes, 'the more convinced I have become that it is one of the most fertile sources of men's prejudices and errors....'[64] Volney's plea for critical history, including the critical interrogation, if possible, even of first-hand reporters, may well have impressed Beyle at a time when he was in a position to judge the difference between official bulletins and what was happening in reality. 'Posterity', he writes in *La vie de Henry Brulard*, 'will never know the grossness and stupidity' of Napoleon's immediate underlings 'off the battlefield. And their prudence on it...or how I would laugh when reading in Vienna, Dresden, Berlin and Moscow the *Moniteur*, which no one in the army ever received, in case all the lies were seen and ridiculed...' (chapter 23). In Volney too, he would have found one of the principal models for his own method of writing the history of the present and the past, in the travel books on Italy and France. For Volney – and the view is now well established in France, where history and geography are thought of as the same academic subject – travel is not merely an interesting complement but one of the principal means to our understanding of the past.[65]

Few writers, none the less, have been less suited by nature and the influences of their early years for the career of an exact historian than Beyle, and his writings bear out his confession in *La vie de Henry Brulard* that 'the only memory' he can claim is of his own feelings. 'As for *facts*, I've never had any memory at all, which is, incidentally why the famous Georges Cuvier always beat me in the discussions he sometimes deigned to hold with me in his salon every Saturday from 1822 to 1830...' (chapter 11). The recounting of events in his lives of the composers and of Napoleon, in his travel books and his *History of Painting in Italy* is, sometimes avowedly, unreliable; while in his recollections of his meetings with Byron in Milan, which enjoyed considerable success in his own day and have been regarded as a reliable source by many biographers of Byron even in recent years, it is now clear that he invented almost all he retails.[66] Significantly perhaps, the pseudonym he used as a chronicler was the same that he used as a novelist, and the comic deception involved in its use is a virtual admission that, whether he appears to be writing fact or fiction, the distinction should not be too readily assumed.

Something akin to Volney's concern for truth in history is to be found, nonetheless, in all that Beyle writes of the past, however extravagant his own imagination and however inclined we may be to agree at times with Nietzsche that the Europe he discovered was very much 'his own'.[67] Beyle will sometimes express what seems like almost total scepticism as to the possibility of reaching the truth about the past,[68] and he recommends in his articles in the English reviews the German historian Niebuhr, whose sceptical approach to the best-known sources of Roman history was one of the common topics of conversation in the salons of the day.[69] It is, nonetheless, in the name of truth itself, even if in pursuing it one has to 'know how to be ignorant', that Beyle attacks those historians who are in the pay of a prince or a church or who, like Montesquieu himself, pay more attention to the history of laws than to that of their application.[70] The historians Beyle recommended with enthusiasm were those who, like General Philippe de Ségur, author of the *Histoire de Napoléon et de la Grande Armée en 1812*, were prepared to give the lie to official history; though the enthusiasm here may admittedly derive from the fact that he is writing for an English public:

This young officer has revealed things which, say the partisans of the *national honour*, ought never to have escaped the lips of a Frenchman. As a historian, he has ventured to tell the truth. He says there existed a secret agreement between Napoleon and his army. This army was mowed down by the cannon as rapidly as the English regiments which you send to Ava or the Cape are destroyed by the diseases of India or Africa. The French army submitted to this horrible lottery and in return, Napoleon promised his brave fellows, not only the advantage of pillage (that would have been a peccadillo) but licence to murder the citizens on whom they were billeted (the baker at Cassel in 1809, for instance), to murder the *maires des communes* in France; to pillage their own waggon-train (as in Spain in 1809), which pillage caused the defeat of the French army. M. de Ségur has committed a crime which the French army will never forgive – he has forced the attention of the French people on the military leprosy introduced into France by Napoleon...[71]

He also recommended and was to edit and translate the unknown unofficial sixteenth-century chroniclers, like the author of the story of Vittoria Accoramboni, who prudently 'never judges a fact, never prepares it in any way' and whose 'sole preoccupation is to tell the truth...'.[72] Beyle would probably have agreed with Professor Marrou that good writing is not an incidental quality but indispensable to good history.[73] And it is the good writing which consists in boldness and simplicity of utterance which he valued in the *Life* of Benvenuto Cellini and the tales of the sixteenth century *novelliere* Bandello, both of whom, he believed, give us more of the actual history of the Italy of their day than any historian as such.[74]

How a work of fiction like Bandello's or the testimony of a Cellini, who Beyle admits is sometimes 'un peu Gascon', gives us a true picture of the life of their age, and how we can know this is so are not questions on which Beyle has left any extended thoughts; though in the articles in the English reviews written immediately before his own first novel, *Armance*, he frequently recommended even minor novels as an aid to the study of social history, and in Rome in 1834 in the margin of a book he was carrying, he sketched out the following tentative explanation:

I wrote biographies in my youth, which are a kind of history, lives of Mozart and Michelangelo. I regret it now. With the biggest just as much as with the smallest things, it seems to me impossible to get to what is true, at least to what is true in *some detail* [du moins un vrai *un peu détaillé*]. M. de Tracy once said to me: 'One can no longer reach the truth [atteindre au vrai] except in a novel...'[75]

The novelist's advantage over the historian lies in his freedom to speculate on what might happen and in the reality of the possibilities he imagines; in his devotion to the 'interests of the imagination', as Beyle calls them,[76] without which a historian cannot interpret his evidence and is therefore left with no evidence at all. To say this, however, is to give a very approximate idea of Beyle's meaning; and what is meant by the underlined 'un vrai *un peu détaillé*' is something we can almost certainly best decide by referring specifically to Beyle's own work. The remarks were scribbled in a copy of *Le rouge et le noir* and it is to this work, which Beyle describes as a 'chronicle of 1830' that any discussion of Beyle the historian must lead.

5

Le rouge et le noir

The problem of form

The jotting quoted at the end of the last chapter indicates one of the most important senses in which Beyle discovered he was a novelist. It was as a novelist only that he could be a historian. The claim is by no means inconsistent with the observation developed in his essay of 1835, *La comédie est impossible*, that the would-be dramatist of this phrase of history could only hope to write for individuals not too different from himself and not for the heterogeneous audience of the theatre. Nor obviously is it contradicted by another claim, made on several occasions in the 1820s, that 'all systems of philosophy are addressed to the young' and that many philosophers, such as Plato, Abelard and Victor Cousin, have in fact written *novels* for the young, in the guise of systems of philosophy.[1]

'The novel is a great discovery: far greater than Galileo's telescope or somebody else's wireless. The novel is the highest form of human expression so far attained....'[2] Beyle might have endorsed at least the first of these propositions, though he had no Dickens, Flaubert or Tolstoy to look back to and could not have said it, as Lawrence was able to, with a sense of this being overwhelmingly evident. The great creative work of the past, according to his own account, was that of Shakespeare, Dante, Michelangelo and Mozart. He never spoke in the same terms of Cervantes, Mme de Lafayette or Fielding, thoroughly though he enjoyed and admired the latter. Among his own contemporaries, he welcomed the fact that Mme de Flahaut-Souza showed a delicacy in the portrayal of human feelings lacking in the novels of Sir Walter Scott,[3] that Constant's *Adolphe*, despite its 'affectations', 'does say something, well or badly, which distinguishes it from most other modern books'[4] and that *Le Père Goriot* shows what the government of M. de Villèle is like, much as Scarron's *Roman comique* shows the real France of Colbert.[5] There was no living contemporary, however, on whom he was to model himself. In grasping the possibilities of thought and expression that novels, by their very nature reveal, Beyle was, even more than Lawrence, a discoverer and a pioneer. For the possibilities opened up by the novel as such, on which he seems to have begun to dwell during the 1820s (there is no dateable sudden inspiration) were possibilities that, as we know, he was to develop in practice. Had he not done so, it is perhaps worth adding, it is most likely that *War and Peace* would not have been written in the way that it was. For, though Tolstoy is unfortunately not on record as having said much specifically about the influence of Stendhal, he claimed that it was very considerable indeed.[6]

The relation in which Beyle stands to the great European novelists who succeeded him and of which he was conscious towards those whom he read is not one which encourages us to look in the work of the latter for a significant foreshadowing of the techniques or the sense of life which we find in *Le rouge et le noir*. For this reason a study of the education of the novelist that Beyle became will not be much concerned with novels as such. Beyle wrote little on the technique of the novel, far less than on that of the drama. The most extensive commentary that survives on the former are his notes on the manuscript of *Lucien Leuwen*, the one novel, he tells us, he wrote to a plan – and it is perhaps significant that he was unable to finish it. His most illuminating statement on the history of the novel is the short article which appeared in *Le National* on 19 February 1830, entitled 'Sir Walter Scott et *La Princesse de Clèves*.' (The argument is presented more succinctly than any summary of which I am capable):

Everyone knows the story told by Voltaire. He was instructing a young actress in tragic diction and she was reciting a very moving passage in a cold straightforward way. 'But you ought to act as if you are possessed by the Devil', cried Voltaire. 'Mademoiselle, what would you do if a cruel tyrant had taken away your lover?' 'I would find another one' was the reply.

I don't say that all creators of historical novels think as *reasonably* as this prudent young lady; but the most sensitive among them will not want to accuse me of slander if I say that it is infinitely less difficult to describe in a picturesque fashion the costume of a character than to say what he feels and to make him speak. Don't let's forget another advantage of the school of Sir Walter Scott; the description of a costume and of the posture of a character, however minor he may be, take up at least two pages. The movements of the soul, which first of all are so hard to detect and then so difficult to express, with precision and without exaggeration or timidity, will provide the material for barely a few lines. Open at random one of the volumes of *La Princesse de Clèves*, take any ten pages and then compare them to ten pages of *Ivanhoe* or *Quentin Durward*...

Every work of art is a *beautiful lie*; all those who have written know this well. There is nothing so ridiculous as the counsel given by members of the fashionable public: 'Imitate nature'. Confound it, I know we have to imitate nature; but to what extent? That is the whole question...Art then is only a beautiful lie but Sir Walter Scott has been too much a liar...[7]

The obvious antithesis to Beyle in this respect, as in so many others, is to be found in the theory and practice of his contemporary, Balzac, the Balzac who aspired to be the 'French Walter Scott'[8] and who commended Scott for having 'elevated the novel to the philosophical dignity of history'.[9]

Balzac's attitude to Scott varied more over the years and was less simple than these phrases taken in isolation might suggest, and there are indications that he had read and been impressed, if not moved to any fundamental reappraisal, by *Sir Walter Scott et la Princesse de Clèves*.[10] The novel, as he conceived it, as well as history itself, are, none the less, radically and (for the purposes of definition, conveniently) different from what they were for Beyle. And though both stress the importance of 'detail', it is obvious that for Beyle this was not something whose value lay in a merely external verisimilitude or in the accumulation that might eventually reveal the laws and configurations of society. Beyle never sought, in the way that Balzac did, 'to compete with the Registrar of deaths, marriages and births' (*'faire concurrence à l'état civil'*). There are no social laws that can be easily extrapolated from *Le rouge et le noir* and *La chartreuse de Parme*, certainly none as inclusive and predictable as those invoked in the introduction to *La comédie humaine*. Beyle's own sense of verisimilitude is indicated defiantly (to the point of exaggeration) in the review he wrote of his own novel and which he was hoping would be translated into Italian (it is reprinted conveniently as an appendix to the Garnier edition of *Le rouge et le noir*): 'M. de Stendhal, bored by all the talk of the middle ages, the Gothic arch and the costume of the fourteenth century, has had the audacity to recount an adventure which takes place in 1830 and to leave his readers in total ignorance of the style of costume worn by Mme de Rênal and by Mlle. de la Mole, his two heroines...'

Beyle came to the novel along paths very different from those of his younger contemporary (Balzac indignantly denies in his introduction to *The Human Comedy* that he himself is a 'sensualist', a 'materialist' or, in other words, an 'idéologue') and his early experiments in fiction have very little in common with those of the young Balzac in the best-selling *genres* of the day, the 'Gothic' novel and the historical novel à la *Waverley*. The term 'experiment' misrepresents, in fact, the intention of at least some of the earlier fiction by Beyle. 'I like *examples*, and not, like Montesquieu, Buffon and Rousseau, systems...' he wrote to Pauline (August 1804) and according to Henry James, it was 'this absorbing passion for example, anecdote and illustration that constituted Beyle's distinctive genius...'[11] Narrative, in other words, was for Beyle at first a way of thinking rather than of merely exercising or indulging the imagination, and one of his first completed *nouvelles* was appropriately included by his first posthumous editor as an appendix to *De l'amour. Ernestine* is the story of the only child of a wealthy landowner, brought up in the mountains of Dauphiné and passing through the 'seven stages' of the awakening of love and self-esteem when she is pursued ardently but discreetly by an unknown and at first mysterious neighbour, an eligible bachelor considerably older than herself; '...it is no more than thirty pages long', as George Eliot was to write in a review of *De l'amour*,[12] 'and at the expense of only half an hour's reading, we have the story of a naïve girlish passion, given with far more finish, that is, with more significant detail, than most of our writers can achieve by the elaboration of three volumes'. The significant detail and the fable-like (almost fairy-tale) simplicity of the story spring obviously from the clarity and completeness of Beyle's thoughts on the subject that meant so much to him, and *Ernestine* resembles, in this respect, his best and most mature fiction. Its relative lack of substance and reality is due only, as in a play by Marivaux, to the exclusion of almost any other interest than the dictates of passion and pride. It is easy to imagine that the real Ernestine may have been Mathilde Dembrowski and certainly, if this is true, it would account for the lack of contact or intimacy between herself and her eminently well suited admirer, whose love, though she is too proud to tell him, she returns. It would explain too the one serious weakness in the story: her unaccountably cruel behaviour towards her lover and herself in marrying another man.

Life as it presents itself to the man or woman with exceptional intelligence as well as strength and delicacy of character; that is the focal and developing preoccupation in most of Beyle's stories and novels, and in all those we think of as characteristic. And this perhaps more than anything else is what distinguishes him from Balzac both as a novelist and a historian. It is this too which accounts for the difficulties we see him at times only partially overcoming: technical difficulties in so far as his fiction could only succeed on any level in so far as they were solved, but also difficulties of belief; the difficulty especially of believing in a man or woman whose pursuit of happiness was worthy of interest (and the contemplation of which would afford the 'greatest possible pleasure') and yet whose demands on life were not impossible. Ernestine, in what we can only imagine as a fit of unaccountable perversity, turns down an ideal match; Vanina Vanini, in the story of that name, confesses unnecessarily to her *carbonaristo* lover that she has betrayed his comrades in order to save him for herself and loses him for ever, after he has almost throttled her in rage. The unnecessary confession of a crime inspired by passion leads at the end of *Mina de Wanghel* to a more decorous but no less final estrangement between lovers. Beyle seems incapable in all these stories of imagining either a happy ending or a good reason for the lack of one. All of them clearly are to this extent failures. And in noting this, one suspects that the difficulties he experienced in imagining a life worth living were due to a failure to succeed in what he wanted to achieve rather than to want of trying. A settled pessimism concerning the possibilities of such a life would presumably have led him to show it as being doomed from the very outset rather than thwarted at the end by nothing more than a perverse whim or a mere error of judgment. By contrast, in Balzac, since Charles Grandet and Eugène de Rastignac are already corrupt when we first meet them, or at least patently corruptible, the melancholy and bitter endings of *Eugénie Grandet* and *Le père Goriot* are in perfect harmony with what has gone before.

Armance has the weaknesses and faults of all Beyle's fiction before *Le rouge et le noir*. The crudity of the stratagem by which its hero is deceived into thinking that the bride he loves feels coldly towards him is so obvious as to require no comment. He 'finds' a letter forged by a scheming relative in his bride's handwriting addressed to a friend. His suicide by passion when on his way, ostensibly, to take part in the War of Greek Independence is a piece of conventional romanticism in the tradition of *Werther*, no less romantic or conventional for being at the same time 'ironical'. Yet it is a novel which goes a considerable way towards overcoming the difficulties I have in mind and hence one which anticipates in often impressive ways the achievement represented by *Le rouge et le noir*. For one thing, as in *Le rouge*, exceptional intelligence and unusual delicacy of character are not shown as inexplicable or undefinable virtues. They are, as far as possible, explained by circumstances and shown from the inside in terms of often painful experience rather than as a merely external and enviable impressiveness. Failure, moreover, to find a way of life compatible with the hero's ideal demands does not exclude – on the contrary, it ensues upon – a prolonged examination of what the age has to offer.

The circumstances which make the hero of *Armance*, the young only son of one of the oldest families in France, a man of *strictly* unusual character include the most notorious fact about the novel and the clue, it is often argued, to his enigmatic behaviour: Octave is sexually impotent. The novel appeared shortly after the scandal surrounding Henri de Latouche's *Olivier*, in which the same theme had been discreetly developed, and it is perhaps for this reason that Beyle found it unnecessary to refer to his hero's affliction explicitly. Not that the clue is indispensable or one that cannot be easily guessed at. Octave de Malibert's melancholy and mad impulsiveness, his horror of sexual attraction and his deep love and tenderness for his mother can be taken, in their context, as self-explanatory. Moreover, as a nobleman, he is condemned to impotence of another kind in a constitutional monarchy. He is wealthy and a future peer of the realm, but only on sufferance. The restitution of his future inheritance is due to the vote in the Assembly indemnifying former émigrés, a privilege of which he is reminded by a provincial deputy who congratulates him on the 'two million' he is going to 'vote him' ('these were the very words of this man...'). At the same time his intelligence is that of a well-read and enlightened former pupil of the Ecole Polytechnique, a reader of the Utilitarians and the Idéologues and hence a man fully aware of the absurdity of his position. Octave's physical impotence in this respect is merely one aspect of a general predicament.

It is in the presentation of the latter that Beyle writes as a novelist or rather as the kind of novelist we are to find in *Le rouge et le noir*. 'Detail' here is not an accretion of fictitious accidental facts but the close development of a real possibility. What difference does it make, Octave finds himself asking, after narrowly escaping from being crushed by a passing carriage, whether he goes on living or not? He has no doubt of his mother's love, but his father and his snobbish buffoon of an uncle love only the name he bears:

'I am bound to them by the smallest of obligations...'

The idea of a *duty* to perform, however, is 'like a flash of lightning' to Octave, a sudden illumination:

'Can I really say that it's of little importance if it's the only duty I have left? If I can't overcome the difficulties that chance confronts me with in my present position, what right have I to believe that I am so sure to conquer all the difficulties I may meet in the future? Here am I proud enough to believe that I'm equal to all the dangers and to every kind of harm of which a man can possibly be the victim, and yet when suffering actually presents itself to me, I ask it to go away and come back in some other form that will suit me better, in other words be only half as painful. And I thought I was so firm and resolute! I was merely being presumptuous...

Soon the disgust Octave felt for everything was less violent and he appeared to himself less wretched. His spirits, depressed and disorganised, as it were, by the absence for so long of any happiness, were reanimated and strengthened a little as his self-esteem returned. Thoughts of a different kind began to occur to him. The low oppressive ceiling of his room displeased him beyond endurance; he envied the magnificent drawing room of the Bonnivets' house. 'It's at least twenty feet high', he thought. 'It's a room in which I feel I can breathe...'

He begins to plan a room for himself which only he will ever enter and of which 'the tiny imperceptible key' will be carried always on his watch chain. A servant will dust it once a month but under his own surveillance in case he should guess his thoughts from his books or find what he has written 'in order to guide his soul during his moments of folly'. The room will be decorated with three seven-foot-tall mirrors:

'I have always loved mirrors. They make a sombre and magnificent ornament. How big are the tallest mirrors they make at Saint-Gobain?' And the man who for three quarters of an hour had just been thinking of ending his days climbed up on a chair to find the catalogue of prices. He spent an hour making an estimate of the costs of his own private drawing room. He felt that he was behaving like a child but this made him write with even greater rapidity and seriousness... (ch. 2)

Julien Sorel will, of course, think of 'duty' in terms reminiscent of these, though he will pass beyond the stage at which self-contemplation is not only a necessary precaution in a hostile world but a wholly absorbing pastime. He is far less than Octave a special case and *Le rouge et le noir*, correspondingly, tells us more about the world. For all the beauty and poignancy of the nearly successful love-affair between Octave and his bride, and for all the brilliance of its social comedy, Maurice Bardèche is surely right when he complains that 'those elements within *Armance* which make it resemble a case-history weigh heavily on the novel and reduce its general significance'. Octave's 'condemnation of the world' is, after all, that of 'someone who is ill'.[13] The malevolent trick which wrecks his marriage prevents either the reader or himself from knowing whether he might have been in any way cured through love.

In *Le rouge et le noir*, the difficulties to which the failures of the early fiction bear witness are overcome, most obviously in the last chapters of the novel, and we have the first of his three most complete, that is detailed and self-sufficient, accounts of life as he understood it. The self-sufficiency, even though *Le rouge* is a beautifully finished work of art, is not of the kind that presupposes little or no knowledge of the world. The ideal reader is someone who will be alive to the nuances of its social comedy.[14] Yet at the same time Beyle is at pains to prevent it from being comedy or satire at the expense of a merely *contemporary* world, another version of Lamothe-Langon's *M. le Préfet*. He cannot avoid making oblique references to the politics of the day and this may distract the modern reader. But the social world of *Le rouge et le noir* has its own laws and structure, like those of Manzoni's Lombardy in *I promessi sposi* or Shakespeare's in *Julius Caesar*. How much it corresponds to the actual society of the reign of Charles X is a question that the historian may want to ask. We don't have to answer it, however, or at least not with any professional exactitude, in order to understand and enjoy the novel.

The impression with which the novel leaves us of finish and completeness is also, however, the effect of a kind of romantic rhetoric; not the rhetoric which consists in declamation but the more difficult and less obvious kind which leaves the facts to speak shatteringly for themselves. The guillotine, of which Julien has received a premonition in the church at Verrières in the opening chapters of the novel, falls when his head is at 'its most poetic' and the last two paragraphs of the novel describe the reactions, both violent and very much in character, of the two well-bred ladies who have been his mistresses. The guillotine, which may owe some of its fascination to the fact that it has bathed in royal and noble blood and is the modern version of the sacrificial knife, falls with the same horrifying and yet satisfying thud as at the end of the fourth movement of the *Symphonie fantastique* of Berlioz. There is the same almost ritualistic appropriateness in Julien's shooting of his former mistress during mass as the bell is ringing for the consecration of the Host. *Le rouge et le noir* is a romantic thriller, one that can easily be read as blasphemous and seditious, and the sense of gratifying completeness with which it leaves us is partly that of a point made with an eloquent absence of explanation or apology: 'How could a man as intelligent, sensitive and courageous', the reader may find himself asking, 'a man, moreover, from the working classes, end his life in any other way in such a world?'

When we come to the unfinished *Lucien Leuwen*, which, despite the state of the manuscript, is a finer and deeper novel and in this sense if no other more 'complete', we may be able to look back to the romantic dénouement of *Le rouge* and see it as, potentially at least, a distraction. The public Julien, with his pistols and sensational trial and death, can distract us from the Julien whose inner life is so different from what it seems to others. We can find ourselves forgetting that he has not only committed his crime publicly but left his appeal till too late and gone out of his way to anger the Besançon jury. And we can easily miss the subtlety of the device by which Beyle suggests to us a form of ideal happiness by showing this as a possibility only; as the dream of a man looking back on his life and longing to go on living during his last days in a condemned cell. For in its own way too, like the earlier fiction, *Le rouge et le noir* leaves us in suspense and with many questions unresolved.

'Apprendre à vouloir'

The possibility of ideal happiness is of course that of 'living with Mme de Rênal', a possibility frustrated by the guillotine. Mme de Rênal is shown to us as more than worthy of Julien's yearning for her. The measure of the devotion of which she is capable is given by the fact that she believes quite sincerely that she is damned to eternal torment for loving him. Yet she remains human and not in herself ideal – and conceivably, in so far as a life shared with Julien *can* be imagined, a far too timorous and conscience-ridden companion for her adventurous free-thinking lover. The value of the life that Julien longs for is something quite distinct from what that life itself might have been, however blissful and profitable.

This, however, is different from saying that Mme de Rênal, as a person, is unimportant to Julien or Julien's creator or that she is *unworthy* of the ideal estimate made of her, like Proust's Odette de Crécy, or else conveniently held at a distance and, as a result of this alone, enigmatic and appealing, like Flaubert's Mme Arnoux in *L'Education Sentimentale*. Julien's dreams of happiness are nourished by real and undeluded memories. The ideal value she comes to represent is due to the peculiar circumstances of her life and Julien's and to the perspective in which she is now seen. Thinking of her as he does in prison gives Julien the greatest possible happiness.

In the last two chapters of the novel, the difficulties Beyle had wrestled with in his earlier fiction are overcome. For if Julien is an 'interesting' character it is because he is capable of knowing what he wants and hence what he values more than anything else. The question whether he will be fortunate enough to get what he wants, or would have been had a reprieve come through, could only be answered in a different novel. After Julien's meditations in the penultimate chapter, *Le rouge et le noir* can end with at least one point well made.

What does it mean to be capable of knowing what one wants? *Le rouge et le noir* is concerned with this question, and its usefulness and corresponding beauty are those of the answers it offers. We are told that this is a rare accomplishment, at least in the middle and upper classes, and we are shown many times that it is far from easy. This is the point of much of the comedy of the novel, such as that of Julien's ordeal during the first visit he pays in his life to a café:

But the young lady behind the counter had noticed the charming features of the young farmer or tradesman from the country, as he seemed to be, who, with his package under his arm, was standing three yards from the stove studying the fine white plaster bust of the king. She was tall and had the attractive figure of the young women of Franche-Comté; she was smartly attired and in such a way as to make the café seem all the more elegant; and she had already called out twice in a tiny voice intended to be heard only by Julien: 'Monsieur, Monsieur!'

He walked eagerly towards the counter and the pretty girl standing behind it as if he were marching on the enemy. And in the middle of this sudden manoeuvre he dropped his package on the floor.

What pity the schoolboys of Paris are going to feel for our young man from the provinces, those schoolboys who already at the age of fifteen know how to walk into a café with so distinguished an air. But these children who are so well trained at fifteen, by the time they are eighteen have *turned common*. The passionate timidity one meets in the provinces is sometimes overcome and when this happens it teaches a man to know what he wants and the will to get it ['*elle enseigne à vouloir*']. As he walked up to the beautiful girl who had deigned to address him, Julien thought: 'I must tell her the truth' and as he overcame his shyness, became all the more courageous.

'Madame, this is the first time in my life I've ever been in Besançon and I should like some bread and a cup of coffee, which I'll pay you for.' (book 1, ch. 24)

Julien is comic throughout much of the novel, with his would-be scoundrelly and often touchingly ineffectual show of hypocrisy, his habit of treating everyday life as a hazardous military operation and even during his fateful struggle to work up the courage to hold Mme de Rênal's hand. But he is comic above all in that he seems so unusual. The joke, as so often in Beyle, can become a joke at the expense of the more conventional reader. Not only does Julien go far in society, much further than almost anyone ever goes. He is shown to us as a 'superior being', even when his preoccupation with his own dignity has gone far beyond a joke. We see this during the first night he spends with Mme de Rênal:

But during the best moments [*les moments les plus doux*], the victim of a curious pride, he continued to aspire to the rôle of a man accustomed to conquering women: he took incredible pains to spoil what was most lovable in himself. Instead of noticing attentively the transports he aroused and the remorse which so clearly betrayed their depth and passion, he never once ceased to consider the idea of carrying out his *duty*. He dreaded a fearful remorse and an eternal humiliation if he forgot to follow the ideal model which he had set up for himself. In fact what made Julien a superior being was precisely that which prevented him enjoying the happiness which lay at his feet...

'Is there nothing more to happiness than this? Is this all that it means to be loved?' These were Julien's first thoughts on returning to his room. He felt all the astonishment and misgiving of someone who has just obtained something he has long desired and who still feels the habit of desire, finds that there is nothing left to desire and yet still has no memories. Like a soldier returning from an exercise, he was absorbed in going over every detail of his own behaviour. 'Have I failed in any way towards myself?' he thought, 'Have I played my rôle as I should?'

And what rôle? That of a man who is accustomed to shining in front of women. (book 1, ch. 15)

Beyle's attitude to his hero is far from simple hero-worship[15] and even if it may be true that in some ways Julien is a self-portrait, it is by no means an indulgent one. The novel shows us the cost as well as the immense advantage of learning to know what one wants. And it is not necessarily because they have failed to understand him that some readers have been shocked or horrified by the form that Julien's single-mindedness takes.

Julien is, of course, born into circumstances in which he can survive only by defending himself and if necessary without mercy, circumstances too in which his puny physique forces him to rely on ruse as his principal weapon, though the use of the more ungentlemanly forms of violence is also characteristic of his class. Beyle's interest in the trial of the poor seminarist Antoine Berthet, who was accused of shooting a former mistress, to whose children he had been engaged as a private tutor is well known. And in *Promenade dans Rome*, written only a year before *Le rouge et le noir*, he comments on and reproduces the newspaper account of a similar case judged by a court at Tarbes in the Pyrenees:

> While the upper classes of Parisian society seem to have lost the ability to feel anything with either force or constancy, passion is manifested with a frightening energy in the petty bourgeoisie among the young people who, like M. Laffargue, have received a good education but are obliged to work and struggle for the real necessities of living.
>
> Exempted by the need to work from the thousand tiny obligations imposed by polite society and by its ways of thinking and seeing... they still have the strength to know what they want and get it ['*ils conservent la force de vouloir*'] by the very fact that they feel strongly. All the great men of the future will probably come from the class to which M. de Laffargue belongs. Napoleon himself once combined the same circumstances: a good education, an ardent imagination and extreme poverty.

Only the artist perhaps may benefit from wealthy parentage and hence freedom from charlatanism and the 'fatal temptation of title and crosses'.

> But if one is born rich and noble, how can one be exempt from elegance, delicacy, etc. and maintain that superabundance of energy which makes artists and renders men so ridiculous?
>
> I hope with all my heart that I may be completely wrong.[16]

The description, incidentally, that we are given of Julien in the first chapter of *Le rouge et le noir* reminds one of the portraits of the young Bonaparte, but he has one trait reminiscent of Laffargue himself, whose 'expression and fine-looking eyes, which are normally gentle, become sinister when he stares and his eyebrows meet'.[17]

Le rouge et le noir is a chronicle of 1830, as the title page indicates, a novel about the life of typical social groups in the France of Charles X.[18] Julien is himself typical to a considerable extent of his class and an anomaly only in that he lacks the physique which will enable him to work in his father's sawmill or survive in the brutal world of his brothers and other young men of his class. In the games played on Sundays and feast days, he had always been beaten, we are told in the opening chapters. Critics of the novel have tended very much to underestimate the extent to which Julien's temperament and even his intelligence can be explained by the circumstances in which he has grown. And they have underestimated accordingly the extent to which his career can be seen as *exemplary*: the story of Everyman when Everyman grows up in those circumstances rather than that of the rise and downfall of a romantic freak and an inexplicable genius. Even the extraordinary gifts to which Julien owes his initial rise in society are a reflection of what that particular society expects of the children of his class who seek to improve their lot and win the world's approval. His famous Bible-recitation show, for example, is an exhibition not only of cerebral vigour but of time spent in more worthy occupations than thinking or reading for oneself, and it is for this reason that it impresses not only children and servants but their masters who are men of the world:

Adolphe, the eldest child, had picked up the Bible.

'Open it anywhere', Julien went on. 'Tell me the first word in a verse and I shall recite the Holy Scripture by heart, the rule of conduct for all of us, until you tell me to stop.'

Adolphe opened the Bible, read out a word and Julien recited the entire page as easily as if he had been talking French. M. de Rênal looked at his wife with an air of triumph. The children, seeing their parents' astonishment, stared. Soon Mme de Rênal's chambermaid and the cook were to be seen near the open door. By then, Adolphe had opened the Bible in eight different places and Julien had recited with the same ease.

'Gracious heavens, listen to the pretty little priest!' cried the cook, who was a very devout young woman.

M. de Rênal's self-esteem was becoming perturbed by now and far from thinking about the tutor he had just engaged for his children, he was busy hunting in his memory for one or two Latin phrases to quote. At last, he managed to recite some lines from Horace. Julien, however, who knew no other Latin than the Bible, replied with a frown that the Sacred Ministry which he was destined to enter prohibited him from reading an author so profane.

M. de Rênal quoted quite a fair number of verses that he claimed that Horace had written. He also explained to his children what Horace was. But his children, overcome with admiration, hardly paid any attention to what he said. They were staring at Julien...
(book 1, ch. 6.)

A repeat-performance at the house of M. de Rênal's rival, the governor of the local workhouse, brings him invitations to dinner from the head of the gendarmerie, the tax inspector and a number of 'wealthy liberals' who talk even of voting for a scholarship for Julien to be paid out of communal funds. The dining room echoes with this 'imprudent idea', while Julien, after making his farewells, escapes with 'agile' steps into the night. (Later, with the benign scholarly Bishop of Besançon, he will find that he can unbend and discuss not only Horace but Virgil, Cicero and the subversive Tacitus.)

The pious parrot-learning and the show of saintliness are all part of Julien's strategy to survive. As M. Sartre would put it, it is his way of 'being in the world'. Julien has chosen 'the uniform of his century' and particularly of a period in which the Church was seeking to extend its domination throughout the whole of society. Under Napoleon, he believes that he would have risen from obscurity by being killed in battle or made a general at thirty. Under the Restoration it is necessary to compete with the Jesuits on their own terms. His own studied duplicity has its counterpart in the spying and intrigue of which we hear so much in the novel and which lends it its (characteristically Stendhalian) conspiratorial atmosphere. He is part of this world in so far as he has adapted himself to it, so much so that the local Jesuits think of him as *récupérable* and intrigue to save him from the guillotine. And for all his inner pride, he is able to sympathise readily with the shameless servility of his companions in the Besançon seminary:

Not to smile with respect at the mere mention of the Prefect's name is deemed imprudent by the peasants of Franche-Comté and imprudence is soon punished if you are poor by your having no bread to eat...the fathers of many of his comrades had often known what it is to come back to one's cottage on a winter's evening and find no bread, chestnuts or even potatoes. 'Why should it seem strange then', thought Julien, 'if a happy man, as far as they're concerned, is first and foremost, someone who's eaten a good dinner?' (book 1, ch. 26)

Yet he remains distinct from the other seminarists. He tries diligently to imitate them and finds that there is even a devout-seeming way of eating a boiled egg. But as a hypocrite he is an conspicuous amateur whom they instinctively persecute until his air of superiority, that is his failure to subordinate himself utterly to his rôle, is justified in their eyes by his promotion to the post of *répétiteur* and the gift of a slain boar sent by a friend and proof seemingly of powerful connections in the world.

Julien *is* unusual, unusual in being completely unhypocritical towards himself about the rôle he is playing, though this again is something that his creator explains, or rather enables those readers whose lives are very different to think of not only as a psychological phenomenon but as an experience that could be shared. Deprived in early life of a mother, and brought up brutally in a small provincial town by a man whom we may suspect is not his natural father, one of his few friends as a boy is the old army surgeon who bequeaths him the only books he owns and fills his imagination with stories of the Grande Armée. The surgeon dies and Julien is left alone in a world which his imagination has taught him to see in military terms. And it is impossible for him to believe in his rôle as a future priest as anything but a necessary ruse in a world in which he is despised and oppressed and in which there are only dead heroes to turn to as guides.

He is superstitious though a secret atheist, and, prophetically as it happens, sees portents in the light falling like drops of blood through the red stained glass of the church in Verrières. He owns a miniature portrait of Napoleon which he treats like a secret talisman and he is terrified of allowing his feelings for the Emperor to be known, not only because this would be indeed imprudent but lest it should be seen by others that this is the god he adores. The superstition and the terrible discipline that Julien imposes constantly on himself are those of a lonely man in a dangerous world. They are those of any man who finds that, over long periods of time, he can rely only on his own nerve and presence of mind. The novel is sometimes comic, of course, in that his fears on occasions, like those of Catherine Morland at Northanger Abbey, are groundless.

It is Julien's response even to those challenges he has merely imagined which makes him, however, a 'superior being', this and the discipline he exercises to prove his nerve. It is a truly stupendous feat for the timid suspicious Julien to seize Mme de Rênal's hand, when they are sitting in the garden on a hot summer night, overjoyed though she is as well as dismayed by the liberty. And the record Beyle gives of Julien's thoughts and feelings up to this moment are a sign of the importance he himself attaches to moments of this kind.[19] For it is here that we are shown the reasons for Julien's eventual ability to know what he wants and values in the world. The idea of seizing Mme de Rênal's hand has occurred to Julien the previous evening when it has brushed accidentally against his own:

The hand quickly withdrew; but it occurred to Julien that it was his *duty* to see that it would not be drawn back when he touched it. The idea of a duty to be carried out and a feeling of ridiculousness or rather inferiority to be undergone if he should fail, immediately deprived him of all pleasure.
(book 1, ch. 8.)

He vows the following evening that if he has not taken her hand by the time the strokes of ten have ceased chiming he will walk upstairs and blow out his brains. His voice trembles as he chats to Mme de Rênal and her companion. So does that of Mme de Rênal who wonders what is wrong with him, though he fails to notice this. 'The fearful conflict between duty and timidity was so powerful that he was unable to notice anything outside himself.' At last the hand is grasped on the last stroke of ten, Mme de Rênal tries to pull it away and then surrenders it. Julien's soul is 'inundated with happiness' not because he loves her but because a 'frightful torment' has now ended (book 1, ch. 9). Love for Mme de Rênal is something he will experience later.

Beyle gives us nothing but Julien's thoughts and feelings, 'the movements of his soul', to use a phrase from 'Sir Walter Scott et la Princesse de Clèves'. (As the clock strikes ten, each stroke 'echoes in his heart' and causes 'something like a physical movement'.) He leaves the reader to draw his own conclusions from these essential data, or to use his own word, 'details', and among these conclusions it may occur to us that it is by no means a coincidence that duty should present itself to Julien in this particular form. As Julien's previous and subsequent feelings towards Mme de Rênal reveal, this is more than a Gidean 'acte gratuit'.

'Duty' is none the less the word Julien uses to describe this and his other self-imposed challenges and the irony and, for the reader, humour of the word lies in the fact that this is not duty in any ordinary sense of the word, though the obligation imposed on himself is as strict as if he were carrying out a mission on the battlefield. The idea of a duty to be performed *occurs* to Julien unexpectedly. (We are reminded of the often forgotten truism that all decisions, however long premeditated, are in their origins spontaneous and without conscious motivation. We may decide to do something long before we do it, but we never decide to decide to do it.) It occurs to him as an absolute obligation, an unevadable test of his will. Passing the test gives Julien freedom because of the *sense* of freedom he has now acquired from his previous weaknesses and fears. The next day he oversleeps, is scolded by M. de Rênal and retorts with confident uncontrollable anger that he can easily find another post in Verrières if M. de Rênal is dissatisfied. The confrontation ends with his winning a series of running victories including a rise in his wages and permission to absent himself for the rest of the day, and part of this he spends on a tall rock exulting in the beauty of an immense landscape on a glorious summer afternoon.

Julien, to put with crude explicitness what Beyle conveys by more poetic means, is at one with nature here in the mountains inasmuch as he is at one now with his own nature. Tall beech trees, beneath which there is a 'delicious freshness', reach almost as high as the rock on which he stands and, rooted in the mountains, they prefigure the tree of which Julien speaks during his last days alive when he is recalling what duty has always meant to him:

'I am isolated in this cell; but I have not lived in *isolation* on this earth; the thought of duty has always given me strength. The duty which, rightly or wrongly, I have always forced myself to accept has been like the trunk of a solid tree against which I leaned during the storm; I wavered, I was shaken. After all, I was only a man...but I wasn't swept away.' (book 2, ch. 44)

Significantly, it is near this spot in the mountains that Julien will ask to be buried.

Julien's duty has been of his own choosing but, as the word itself suggests, it has the effect on him of an external obligation. It is something of which he has been acutely conscious and yet it has its origins beyond the conscious self.[20] The life and intelligent purpose to which Julien remains faithful and to which he clings for support are his own and yet, literally, not his alone. Paradoxically, the more utterly dependent he has made himself on his own resources, the more strength he has derived from this other source. A similar paradox occurs in the history of religious experience and it is significant that he is befriended by the two priests in the novel whose Christian faith is most exacting and sincere, even though both of them doubt the sincerity of his own professed vocation. It is significant too that just before these thoughts on duty, Julien should have longed consciously for the consolation of genuine belief:

He was troubled by all his memories of the Bible that he knew by heart...'But how, when as many as *three are gathered together*, can one believe in the great name of GOD, after the fearful way it has been abused by our priests...'

It is significant, finally, that immediately afterwards he should realise what it is that he really wants, what it is of which he is now deprived and what, despite this, gives his life its value:

'So I shall die at the age of twenty-three. Give me five years more to live with Mme. de Rênal...'

Julien, we are told in the scene in the Besançon café, has the 'passionate timidity' of the young provincial which, when it is overcome, '*enseigne à vouloir*'. The phrase cannot be translated directly into English. 'It teaches one to will' is an inadequate rendering, as is also 'It teaches one to desire.' The novel shows us the relation between these two meanings and gives meaning itself to the words 'commonness' and 'vulgarity'; the common-ness and vulgarity that can ensue upon failure to conform to one's own standards and satisfaction if one has conformed to the wishes of the powerful or the numerous or at least what one imagines these wishes to be. The Parisian schoolboys who may laugh at Julien's way of ordering a coffee for the first time 'turn common' by the time they are eighteen. Julien, by contrast, though he dreads doing what he believes he ought to, dreads even more surrendering to his own fear. In this he is the most exacting judge of his own behaviour, and the confidence he acquires in carrying out his self-imposed challenges makes it that much easier for him to do what he thinks right. In Julien, in other words, we are shown a man in whom the common distracting tension between duty and inclination is overcome and who is capable of the single-mindedness which is also whole-hearted desire.

'Scènes probantes' and the historical revelation

We are also shown a man who is capable of learning from experience and his own mistakes. 'Every novel by Stendhal', M. Bardèche has written, 'is the story of an education'[21] and this is certainly true of *Le rouge et le noir*. This is one of the main differences between Stendhal's novel and a novel whose ostensible subject may remind us of it, Flaubert's *Education sentimentale*. One of the most striking impressions of all given by Flaubert's novel and one of its most impressive ironies is that it isn't really the story of an education at all. By the end of the story, as Flaubert himself makes it clear, the hero, Frédéric Moreau has learned nothing. An epigraph to *Le rouge et le noir* might have been: 'Ask and it shall be given you; seek and ye shall find; knock and it shall be opened unto you...' (Matthew VII, 7). For it is because Julien knocks and seeks that he goes into the world and because he goes in that he and hence the reader himself are able to learn from his experience. Throughout his life, by contrast, Frédéric evades confrontation and towards the end of his life can only attribute its uneventfulness to ill-fortune including the fact that he was born at the wrong time. This, as much as anything else, accounts for George Sand's criticism of the lack of *drama* in the novel.[22] Frédéric is in love with the beautiful Mme Arnoux, who is neglected and wronged by her affable brute of a husband; with what is clearly her own grateful assent he spends hours with her alone in her house in Auteuil; yet the dread of intimacy and responsibility (presumably) paralyses his will; his *liaisons* are all with women who mean less to him and the relationship with Mme Arnoux comes to nothing. In the same way, despite his ambition, he fails to take advantage of his many opportunities. He is discouraged by the world of politics as rapidly as by the world of business and he reaches old age as a much travelled but completely undistinguished gentleman of means. The principal result of this infirmity is that we are told remarkably little about the world of politics, the world of business or even Mme Arnoux. We are told a great deal about what they seem like to Frédéric – Flaubert, in contrast to Stendhal, deals painstakingly in external appearances – but the realism of the novel lies in what they seem like to a man who is lacking in curiosity and whose contact with the world is so slight as to seem accidental. Flaubert's intention, in fact, in writing his story of an education was wholly different from Beyle's.[23]

Julien's resolute ambition and his determination not to be sat upon are of the kind that bring out the best and the worst in those he meets and it is in this sense that *Le rouge et le noir* is more 'dramatic' than *L'éducation sentimentale*, not only, that is, more vivid and engaging but psychologically and morally more revealing. It is this too which bears out Beyle's own claim that *Le rouge et le noir* is a 'chronicle of 1830' and, as such, a study of *mœurs*.[24] The good looking, high principled and unsuccessfully domineering mayor of Verrières; his devout, retiring aristocratic wife; his rival, M. Valenod, the affable, mercilessly opportunistic governor of the local workhouse; the Besançon seminarists and their passionately devout director; the clever, powerful Marquis de la Mole and his brilliant, rebellious daughter; all, as a result of their encounter or rather collision with Julien reveal themselves for what they are and leave us to draw our own conclusions about the true nature of their class and background. The revelation of character corresponds to what Beyle in his *Racine et Shakspeare* calls 'des scènes *probantes*', that is 'scenes which *give proof* of the characters or the passions of the personages who take part in them.'[25] The revelation is not only something from which the reader can learn, it is also part of Julien's education. He learns, for example, that Mme de Rênal, the Marquis de la Mole and his daughter Mathilde are not the contemptuous snobs he had thought they were. Nor are the members of their class, at least

146

not always and by no means necessarily. As he loses his dread of being treated 'like a servant' and comes to recognise in Mme de Rênal the deepest devotion of which a woman with her beliefs and in her position is capable and, in the Marquis de la Mole, genuine respect and cordiality, he forgets his former distrust of the world. Interestingly too, he forgets his former cult of Napoleon. He acquires ease and openness of manner and is only at moments of unusual strain – for example, when Mathilde invites him to her room and he suspects that this may be a plot to have him killed on his way through the window – 'an unhappy man at war with the whole of society' (book 2, ch. 13).

This last description of Julien has often, I find, been quoted out of context and taken to refer to something both constant and predictable in his character. Yet there are few novelists who have remained more faithful to the ways in which not only mood but the entire corresponding code of behaviour and philosophy of life can change from one moment to the next. The development of Julien's character is so erratic that many readers will protest that they are unaware that it develops at all. Yet take the account we are given of Julien's *ambition* when we first meet him:

For Julien, to make one's fortune meant first getting out of Verrières; he abhorred his native town. Everything in it he saw chilled his imagination.

Since his early childhood, he had known moments of exaltation when he would dream rapturously of the day when he would be presented to the beautiful ladies of the town of Paris and attract their attention by some daring exploit. Why should he not be loved by one of them, as Bonaparte had been by the brilliant Mme de Beauharnais in the days when he was still poor?

(book 1, ch. 5)

and compare this with what we are told after the attempt on Mme de Rênal's life when this dream has been realised in every particular:

Julien felt unworthy of so much devotion; to tell the truth, he was tired of heroism. He would have responded gladly to an unassuming, naïve and almost timid tenderness, but Mathilde's proud soul needed constantly a public and a sense of what *others* might think.[26]

(book 2, ch. 39)

To take a young man setting out on his career is Beyle's principal method in all his major novels of showing what a society has to offer to those whose courage, capacity for enjoyment and intelligence are unimpaired. The intensity and yet haziness of his dreams of the future are necessary to the process of growth and discovery and, as in the case of Julien, the realisation of a dream can itself be the cause of disenchantment and lead the dreamer to know better what he really wants.

The very form that Julien's ambition takes, moreover, is a sign of his conditioning. He is not born into the conspiratorial world of the Restoration in innocence, innocent or unrepentant though he may feel in the privacy of his own heart. The adoration of Napoleon, whom, unlike Beyle, he fails to distinguish from Bonaparte, is adoration for a ruler who built a new dynasty on the ruins of the old and who chose ostlers' and innkeepers' sons to play the roles of princes and kings. Julien is no Jacobin, despite his tears of sympathy for the inmates of the work-house who are forbidden to sing when their master, M. Valenod, is entertaining guests to dinner and despite his revolutionary fervour in the salons of the Marquis de la Mole when the exiled eccentric Count Altamira is confiding in him as if he were a fellow-radical. Their conversation is overheard, rather too obviously, by Mathilde de la Mole whom he later submits to a deliberately provocative tirade on the virtues of ruthlessness in any reformer of mankind, so that she reverently thinks of him as 'another Danton'. Yet this Danton can act with pride in his efficiency and in the trust placed in him as the secret emissary of the Marquis de la Mode and a group of fellow conspirators who are prepared to seek foreign aid to maintain the power and privileges of the throne, the Church and the ancient nobility of France. Even his speech to the Besançon jury, in which he tells them that they are 'outraged bourgeois' judging him not for his ostensible crime but for having dared to rise in society, is provoked by the triumphant expression in the eyes of its president, M. Valenod. And his speech is directed not against class distinctions as such but against those who would deny a man's right to move into the class he prefers.

Beyle was not himself a socialist by any means, despite some recent attempts to pass him off as one, or at least a *socialiste avant la lettre*.[27] And Julien has certainly nothing in common with the hero of the Communard Jules Vallès's semi-autobiographical trilogy, *L'enfant, Le bachelier* and *L'insurgé*. Julien's political attitudes are more irresponsible and inconsistent than those of Vallès or his hero and in this sense far more commonplace. Yet a Marxist may find interest in the fact that the realisation of Julien's early dreams turns out to be an empty victory. He may also find historical significance in the fact that this is not even really a victory. Julien has striven to overcome his weaknesses and prove equal to any challenge to his self-esteem. But his rise in society has been due entirely to patronage, and to patronage he has not even sought. He has proved to be an excellent choice as personal secretary to the great Marquis de la Mole and once introduced into the noble household, his success in society has been due to his ease and liveliness, which are those of a man with no pretensions to being anything other than he is and with the good sense to behave accordingly.[28] His elevation to the title of Chevalier de la Vernaye is due to the most formidable social asset he will ever possess: the fact that he is a plebeian and that Mathilde de la Mole is prepared to acknowledge him as the father of her child. The normally adroit, imperturbable and courtly Marquis de la Mole goes almost out of his mind with grief and rage. No greater or more final and effective blow to his pride and interests can be conceived. Even Julien is at first mortified by what he has done to his benefactor and offers to lay down his own life if this will be of any assistance. And it is true that fifty years before, he *might* have been disposed of – or at least Julien and Mathilde put away, Julien permanently. But in Restoration France the old nobility, with its mystique of caste, is without defences, history is on the side of the Julien Sorels, and Julien has immense advantages of which he is not even aware. 'My novel is finished', he tells himself in a mood of dazed wonderment when he receives, in addition to his title, a commission in the Hussars, 'and the credit is mine alone' (book 2, ch. 34). Both the events that have led up to this moment and the sequel show that he is deluded, however, on each of these scores.

The mind of the assassin and the language of the author

The by now irresistible-seeming course of Julien's career is checked dramatically by the letter of denunciation which Mme de Rênal sends to the Marquis de la Mole, a letter written, as it turns out later, under the dictation of her confessor and in reply to a request from the Marquis for information concerning the man who is to marry his only daughter:

'Poor and avid for gain, it is with the aid of the most consummate hypocrisy and by the seduction of a weak and wretched woman that this man has sought to make for himself a place and become something in society. It is part of my painful duty to add that I am compelled to believe that M. Julien Sorel has no religious principles. In conscience, I am constrained to think that one of his ways of succeeding in a household is to seek to seduce the woman who enjoys the principal credit in that house...'

(book 2, ch. 35)

The Marquis decides to prohibit the marriage and offers Julien 10,000 francs a year if he will agree to live outside France and preferably in America. The setback to Julien's fortunes is unmistakable though by no means permanent. Many possibilities of action remain open to him. Yet he voluntarily ends his career by travelling to Verrières and shooting Mme de Rênal in a crowded church during Mass. And after this, despite the sympathy with which he is regarded during his imprisonment and trial by the public, by Mathilde and even by Mme de Rênal, he deliberately attacks the integrity of the jury at the moment when they are about to consider their verdict.

Has Beyle spoilt what might otherwise have been a good novel by making his hero forget his former astuteness and ambition and behave like the desperate Antoine Berthet, who, when he shot and killed Mme Michoud de la Tour, his former mistress, also publicly in church, had so much less to lose than Julien? Critics of the novel have disagreed over this for many years, and in so far as they feel that Julien's act is consistent with what we have been shown of him in the novel, they have offered various explanations of his behaviour. The most convincing of these that I have read, convincing in that it is the most scrupulously related to the text itself, is the one given by Mme Henriette Bibas in her article on *Le double dénouement et la morale du 'Rouge'* in *La revue d'histoire littéraire de la France* for January 1949. Mme Bibas points out that the most shocking and wounding phrase in the letter written by Mme de Rênal is the one in which we are told that Julien is 'poor and avid for gain' and has used seduction as a way 'to make for himself a place and become something in society'. It is an accusation all the more intolerable to Julien in that there is so much seemingly to justify it. ('I could have forgiven everything', the Marquis himself writes in a letter to Mathilde 'except the plan to seduce you because you are rich.') We laugh off usually only those accusations which are not only untrue but utterly implausible. Julien may have wanted to 'be presented to the beautiful ladies of Paris and attract their attention by some daring exploit' but he has always despised cupidity. '"I cannot blame M. de la Mole"', he tells Mathilde, '"he is just and prudent. What father would want to give away his beloved daughter to such a man?"' He leaves at once for Verrières and there demonstrates, in the only possible way in the circumstances, that, when weighed against honour, social success and riches mean absolutely nothing to him.

This is how Mathilde de la Mole sees his gesture. At last, here is a man who is going to be condemned to death, 'the one distinction which cannot be bought'. '"What you call your crime"', Mathilde tells him '"...is only noble vengeance which shows me what a proud heart beats in your breast."' The novel, however, as Mme Bibas reminds us, brings out the depth and complexity of Julien's motivation. It also confronts us with an apparent contradiction in the fact that Julien repents bitterly of his crime and only, moreover, when he knows that the person for whose principal benefit it was performed is alive, with nothing worse than a broken shoulder, and fully aware of what he has done.

Mme Bibas very rightly points out how much the Faguets, Blums, Thibaudets and Prévosts, who have argued over the motivation of Julien's crime, have ignored Stendhal's text and spoken of Julien as if he were not a fictitious personage every one of whose characteristics is given us by the author but a real person concerning whose real state of mind no one can make more than reasonable guesses. Yet, when discussing the sequel to the crime, Mme Bibas herself falls into the same error – an error, of course, which it is very difficult to avoid – and in doing so, she reiterates the views of Sainte-Beuve and almost every other critic since him that Beyle was 'naturally deaf and blind to poetry':[29]

If so many readers fail to respond to this great theme of the descent into the self, this can only be blamed on the language. There is no doubt that Stendhal's language remains constantly unequal to the emotion that he wishes to communicate. Nor is there any doubt that this is eminently suited to poetry. He will fall back unhesitatingly on expressions like 'no word can describe...'

How is it, one naturally asks, that if 'the emotion that Stendhal wishes to communicate' is eminently suited to poetry and if this is something we can know, he *fails* to communicate it? Perhaps if Mme Bibas had followed the text of the last chapters of the novel with the same scrupulousness as those concerned with Julien's crime, she would not have wanted to reduce them to the level of significance of Tracy's *Traité de la volonté*, a work which may have helped Beyle to write the novel but which he certainly didn't need in the way that Bunyan needed the New Testament, to quote Mme Bibas's own analogy.

Beyle's debt to Tracy was very real, and especially to the *introspective* Tracy of the *Logique* who had taught himself to distinguish between the real and apparent precision of language and in doing so realise our utter dependence, in all that we think or say, on memory, our 'most deeply rooted habits' and on the language of those among whom we live. And, as I have argued in an earlier chapter, this must have influenced the way in which Beyle simultaneously thought and wrote. By contrast, the *Traité de la volonté* is highly speculative writing, involving much deduction from a few original premisses and very little observation. It is an example of the kind of reasoning which both Beyle and Tracy, at his best, thought that we should try to avoid[30] and it may be for this reason that, unlike *Le rouge et le noir*, it is now read by scholars alone.

The kind of attention we find ourselves paying to the prose of *Le rouge et le noir* is obviously very different from that which is demanded by Tracy's more speculative writing. Consider only the music of the prose and, to take a single instance, the meaning that is conveyed (either unmistakeably or not at all) by the note we hear in Julien's voice and in Beyle's:

Julien entra dans l'église neuve de Verrières. Toutes les fenêtres hautes de l'édifice étaient voilées avec des rideaux cramoisis. Julien se trouva à quelques pas derrière le banc de Mme de Rênal. Il lui sembla qu'elle priait avec ferveur. La vue de cette femme qui l'avait tant aimé fit trembler le bras de Julien d'une telle façon, qu'il ne put d'abord exécuter son dessein. Je ne le puis, se disait-il à lui-même; physiquement, je ne le puis...

    (book 2, ch. 35)

[Julien entered the new church in Verrières. All the tall windows of the edifice were hung with crimson curtains. Julien found himself a few feet behind Mme de Rênal's pew. It seemed to him that she was praying with fervour. The sight of a woman who had loved him so dearly made Julien's arm tremble in such a way that at first he was unable to carry out his plan. 'I can't do it', he said to himself. 'Physically, I can't do it...']

The sense of unbearable strain that is conveyed at this point has no possible substitute in an *idea* of strain. Beyle is not presenting ideas in fictitious form. Nor is he making the book more interesting by refusing to explain what is happening and leaving this as a puzzle for his cleverer readers to work out. One of the necessary clues to Julien's behaviour is given when the news reaches him that Mme de Rênal is alive. The tension gives way to joy, wonder and a sense of overwhelming humility:

Dans ce moment suprême, il était croyant. Qu'importent les hypo-crisies des prêtres? peuvent-elles ôter quelquechose à la vérité et à la sublimité de l'idée de Dieu?

Seulement alors, Julien commença à se repentir du crime commis. Par une coïncidence qui lui évita le désespoir, en cet instant seulement venait de cesser l'état d'irritation physique et de demi-folie où il était plongé depuis son départ de Paris...

    (book 2, ch. 36)

[During that supreme moment, he was a true believer. Why care about the hypocrisies of the priests? Is there anything they can take away from the truth and sublimity of the idea of God?

Only then did Julien begin to repent of the crime he had committed. Through a coincidence which saved him from despair, it was at that moment only that the state of physical irritation and semi-madness ended, in which he had been plunged since his departure from Paris...]

The 'semi-madness', as Mme Bibas points out, is one of the clues to Julien's behaviour that critics tend to overlook. And when it has been noted, it is perfectly easy to say what is happening to him, in that one can readily think of other cases in which men have gone mad from a blow to their pride, 'over-reacted' and then repented with a correspondingly full heart. Yet this is not really an *explanation*: we know that such reactions follow one another commonly but not that they follow inevitably. Moreover, Beyle does not try to explain them. Hence perhaps the difficulties that so many readers have in following the text. The text reminds us of what is unaccountable in such an experience, commonplace though it may be.

We are given no explanation either of why it should be that Julien repents of his crime not as soon as he has committed it (as far as he knows, successfully) but only when he knows that Mme de Rênal is alive and well. M. Georges Blin has described Julien's feelings at this moment in terms of Sartrean psychology and in particular Sartre's study in *L'être et le néant* of those cases in which we know suddenly that someone else knows what we are doing so that its whole significance *for us* is transformed.[31] But this is not an explanation either, and for Sartre himself such experiences are among the given facts of consciousness and not susceptible to further analysis. That such experiences are not only unaccountable but commonplace is something of which Sartre wishes to remind us and he does so with solemn amusement at his readers' possible baser instincts by taking as one of his main examples a peeping Tom aware suddenly that he is himself the object of interested observation. The comic situation, as so often in Sartre, depends for its effect on its sleazy familiarity. By contrast, Beyle reminds us of what is unique in Julien's experience and hence more obviously beyond comprehension. For Julien, learning that Mme de Rênal is alive is literally learning of a miracle.

The prose in which such an experience is conveyed is not the poetic prose or *style noble* that Beyle detested because of its obscurity.[32] But we have to respond to it as we respond to genuine poetry if we are not going to reduce it in our minds to banality or incoherence. We have to read it, that is to say, with the sense of living through a real situation and with the full and undistracted response to detail which for Beyle constituted the poetic experience.[33] It is unfortunate that Mme Bibas should refer only to the *boutade* in his letter to Balzac about reading the *Code Civil* every day as a model of style and not to the passage in the same letter in which he tells him of the one rule he understands: '*to be clear*. If I am not clear, *my whole world is annihilated.*'[34]

The usefulness of prose of this kind is that it can give us, if not explanations of why men behave in certain ways, at least the clearest possible sense of all that their behaviour and experience imply. The undistracted imagination of the author and reader is, of course, an advantage they have over the desperate protagonist and also the economy of the novel which enables author and reader to see crucial moments in the protagonist's experience with the simultaneous wisdom of hindsight and foresight. But these are advantages any novelist enjoys. Beyle's exploitation of the possibilities of the novel can be seen in what he conveys to us of these crucial moments themselves: the dominant physical sensation, for example, the 'physical irritation' which ends suddenly, together with the state of 'semi-madness' and which makes the madness itself an experience that can be understood in the sense at least of being more easily shared in imagination; the sense of how much life itself – one's own life or another person's – matters. Standing behind her in the church, Julien is unable to fire at Mme de Rênal until her head is 'almost hidden in the folds of her shawl'. Afterwards, he is indifferent to what has happened to her and what will happen to himself, as he lies in gaol. It is the knowledge that she is alive that startles him into awareness of who and what she is.

The chapter leading to the final collapse of Julien's morale and, following this, to the self-interrogation which leaves him ready to face both life and death depend in the same way on our ability to conceive a whole outlook, involving far more than the immediate focus of consciousness. *Le rouge et le noir* is a wonderfully constructed novel and to say this is to point not only to the striking dramatic effects which, like superb rhetoric, speak for themselves but to the way in which circumstances combine to produce something analogous to the conditions of a controlled experiment. In the prison cell, Julien is visited continually by those who have known him in the past: Mathilde whose efforts to turn him into a public hero are like those of an actress in a play that bores him, Fouqué, the semi-literate timber merchant who loves money but loves Julien even more, and his father, the justice of whose reproaches he can now no longer deny. 'The trouble with prison is that one cannot close one's door', he jokes unhappily. One of the first visitors is the priest who has taught him Latin and whom we have seen in the third chapter of the novel with 'eyes in which, despite his advanced age, the sacred fire is shining which tells of pleasure at carrying out a fine deed which is also a little dangerous'.

The features which had once been so animated and which had expressed with such energy the most noble feelings were now sunk in apathy. Someone who must have been a peasant soon called to fetch the old man. 'We mustn't tire him', he said to Julien, who realised that he was the nephew. This apparition left Julien in the depths of a misery too cruel for tears. He saw nothing that was not sad and unconsoling; he felt as if his heart were frozen in his breast.

This was the cruellest instant which he had had to endure since his crime. He had just seen death and in all its ugliness. All the illusions he had ever entertained of greatness of soul and of generosity were scattered like a cloud before the tempest.

If life (his own and Mme de Rênal's) had seemed a matter of indifference to him before, so too obviously had death; whereas now:

There was no longer anything rough and grandiose about him, no more Roman virtue; death seemed more formidable than he had ever imagined [*à une plus grande hauteur*] and something far less easy...
(book 2, ch. 37)

Two kinds of heroism

This is not the place in which to argue at any length a claim I should like to throw out in passing, but it is relevant to my general thesis concerning the education of Stendhal the novelist and his immediate relation to his predecessors, a relation which is a matter not of passive inheritance but of the living continuity which T. S. Eliot sought to define in his essay on 'Tradition and the individual talent' and one might say even more, an evolution of awareness. I believe that there is much in Shakespeare that Beyle was unable to surpass and his veneration for Shakespeare is an acknowledgement of the fact. There is nothing, for instance, in Beyle corresponding to what is appealed to in us or rather wrenched out of us by Macduff's cry, 'He has no children.' Yet the comparison with Shakespeare does not always force us to conclude that Beyle's was the inferior intelligence and imagination. The best known speech in *Hamlet*, for instance, though it suffers now from its excessive familiarity, suffers also as a meditation on the actual choice between 'To be and not to be...' when we read it after the last nine chapters of *Le rouge et le noir*. Despite the nightmare focus on 'a bare bodkin' and the swift sequel of events, including the encounter between Ophelia and the distracted prince, we are carried along too thrillingly to register the shock of an actual thought about death of the kind we have after the visit to Julien of the Abbé Chélan. We may be reminded, if we make the comparison, of Beyle's misgivings soon after he first read Shakespeare concerning the facility of Shakespearean rhetoric:

> Shakespeare's characters have perhaps a fault which is very brilliant but none the less a fault: they are too eloquent.
> Eloquent with the poetic eloquence which speaks to the soul while exercising the mind as little as possible, as was necessary with an uncouth people. Eloquence is a falsity of passion. Well no, if you assume that the character has a natural talent for it...[35]

and we may feel that Beyle's prose in passages such as those I have quoted has some of the characteristics not only of genuine but also of great poetry.

Beyle knew *Hamlet* well, both in French and English, and at the age of twenty saw Talma play the rôle in the version by Ducis. But the Shakespearean tragedy to which he alludes directly in the final chapters of *Le rouge et le noir* is the one which seems always to have fascinated him most. In his letter to Mathilde written after his arrest and before he knows Mme de Rênal is alive, he orders her to take a false name for a year and never once to mention his name, far less his crime, even to his child. 'From this time forth I never will speak word', he writes to her in English, remembering Iago. An earlier chapter of this study touched on the question of Beyle's deep lifelong interest in the heroic, and in the violent noble passions of Othello in particular. Julien, like Othello, commits a *crime passionnel* and afterwards bitterly regrets it, though why this should be and what it means is something we are shown in more 'detail' than by Shakespeare. Beyle's sense of the heroic came to be far closer, as he acknowledged, to that of Shakespeare than to Corneille or Alfieri. It was, none the less, very much his own and involved distinctions between different kinds of heroism with which Shakespeare was not apparently concerned.

Julien's self-imposed challenges take a form dictated by his boyhood reading of the *Memorial of St. Helena* and the Bulletins of the *Grande Armée*. The duty he forces himself to perform is always a 'heroic' duty. Like Octave de Malibert, he broods vigilantly on his own resilience and temerity, though, far more than Octave, he is able to enjoy the freedom to know and do what he wants to. Julien's very distinction, in fact, that which saves him from the 'commonness' of the young schoolboys of Paris who merely imitate a distinguished model *lies* in this freedom; a freedom he achieves, of course, with enormous difficulty and, presumably, if he were to live, would have to fight for again. But knowing what he wants and values at the moment when he dies allows him to go to the guillotine 'without affectation'.

After reading *Cinna* in 1811, Beyle and his friend Louis Crozet had noted that 'in what we have seen of the play, we do not acquire an intimate knowledge of the characters. Basing our judgment merely on what they say, we are able to form three or four totally distinct impressions of their character...'.[36] And a few years earlier, he had noted in his diary that 'there is no sensibility *without detail*. Their failure to remember this is one of the principal failings of French dramatists...Shakespeare is much closer to the kind of tragedy I have in mind but shall probably never write' (12.12.1804). (See page 55 above.) Beyle is far closer, obviously, in *Le rouge et le noir* to Shakespeare than to Corneille. And the Shakespearean freedom and precision of his writing would have been impossible were it not for something akin to Shakespeare's freedom of spirit and lack of servility (as expressed by Falstaff and Thersites, it is often a deep cynicism) with regard to any model of behaviour, however sublime. Julien himself grows 'tired of heroism', though it is clear at the point at which this occurs that he is tired specifically of the form of heroism that he is being required to conform to by Mathilde de la Mole:

Mathilde's plans included not merely the sacrifice of her reputation; she cared little if the whole of society learned of the condition she was in. To throw herself on her knees in front of the king's carriage as it galloped past and to draw his attention to beg for mercy for Julien, at the risk of being crushed a thousand times to death, was one of the least of the dreams pursued by her exalted and courageous imagination. Thanks to her friends who were employed at court, she was sure to be admitted to the private enclosures of the park at Saint-Cloud.

Julien found himself on the whole unworthy of so much devotion on her part; to tell the truth, he was tired of heroism. He would have responded gladly to a simple, naïve and almost shy tenderness, whereas the proud soul of Mathilde needed constantly a public and a sense of what *others* might think.

Amidst all her anguish and all her fears for the life of her lover, with whom she wanted to die, she had a secret need to astonish the public by the excess of her love and the sublimity of all that she undertook on his behalf...

(book 2, ch. 39)

The distinction between Mathilde's idea of heroism and Julien's is crucial to our understanding of the novel and, of course, more than the novel alone, and it is a distinction for which I know of no precedent in Shakespeare or elsewhere. Mathilde, by her own standards, is wholly equal to the rôle she imagines for herself as the mistress of a free man. Beyle invites us to share the dreams of her courageous and touchingly schoolgirlish imagination, all the more touching for being more than just dreams. ('Thanks to her friends employed at court, etc.' is both her own and the author's assurance that she is perfectly capable of putting her plans into effect.) Yet there is a profound contradiction in Mathilde which 'the idea of a public and a sense of what *others* might think' and its antithetical juxtaposition with 'the proud soul of Mathilde' makes clear and for which we have been prepared ever since her first appearance in the novel. The italicised 'others' (which clearly mystifies the author of the Penguin translation) refers us back to her thoughts after they first meet:

'Is it my fault if the young men at court are such devoted partisans of all that is *fitting* and go pale at the idea of the least adventure which happens to be a little strange? A little journey to Greece or Africa is for them the height of audacity and even then, they can only march in a troop. As soon as they are alone, they are afraid not of the Bedouin's lance but of ridicule and this fear drives them mad.

My little Julien, on the other hand, likes only to act on his own. Never in this privileged being, is there the least idea of relying on others for support or help. He despises the others and that's why I don't despise *him*...'

(book 2, ch. 12)

It also refers us forward to Julien's exasperated cry to her and to his friend Fouqué who tell him how public opinion is being mobilised on his behalf:

'Leave me my ideal existence. All your fussing, all your details about the real world grate on my nerves and would pull me out of heaven. One dies as best one can; I only want to think about dying in my own way. What do the *others* matter to me? My relations with the *others* are about to be cut short abruptly. For heaven's sake, stop talking to me about all those people; it's quite enough to have to see my judge and my lawyer...'

(book 2, ch. 40)

Mathilde's intelligence and spirit (she is very much her father's daughter) lead her, like the Marquis de la Mole himself, to see the absurd dependence of her class on public tolerance[37] and hence on established form. She wears mourning once a year to honour an ancestor who had been executed for breaking the law and sees in the plebeian Julien the self-reliance which, far more than pedigree, make the true aristocrat. Yet flouting the opinion of others, as she does by her displays of cruel wit at her suitors' expense and by her unabashed acknowledgment that she is to be the mother of Julien's child, she paradoxically depends upon it. The audience, whether it is shocked or admiring, is necessary to her, and this is what Julien cannot stand. The contradiction is symptomatic of a deeper flaw in Mathilde's nature, of a profound inability to know what she wants. Beyle summarises it in his own review of *Le rouge et le noir* and in doing so reminds us of one of the best-known of the categories defined in *De l'amour*. Why, he asks, does the brilliant noble Mathilde fall for her father's secretary?

Because it so happens that, out of sheer pride, Julien has behaved in the way necessary to goad the vanity of Mlle de la Mole. Two or three times, with every intention of doing so and not in the least in order to play with her, he has been on the point of *throwing her over completely*. This is all one need do today in order to win the love of a Parisian lady...This depiction of love in Paris is absolutely new. We have the impression that no other book has touched on it. It makes a fine contrast with the simple, genuine and *unselfregarding* love of Mme de Rênal. It's the *love of the head* [*l'amour de tête*] as opposed to the love of the heart.

However, the intelligence of the novelist, as opposed to the self-advertising reviewer, is seen in his rejection of such facile categories and in his compassionate presentation of the inner life of this (in many ways) unpleasant girl. Mathilde, after she has invited Julien to her room for the first time in the middle of the night, is almost overcome with horror at her own foolishness:

As she listened to him, Mathilde was shocked by his air of triumph. 'So now he's my master', she thought. She was already feeling remorse. Her reason was horrified by the astonishing act of folly she had committed. If she had been able to, she would have annihilated both herself and Julien. During the moments in which, by an effort of will, she succeeded in overcoming her remorse, she suffered agonies of timidity and shame. She had never anticipated for an instant her present horrible state.

'Still, I must say something to him', she thought to herself. 'That is the custom. One is supposed to talk to one's lover...'

In spite of the fearful violence she was doing herself, she was in perfect command of every word she spoke.

No reproach, no regret occurred to spoil a night which seemed to Julien less happy than singular. What a difference between this and his last stay of twenty-four hours in Verrières. 'These fine Parisian manners are capable of spoiling everything, even love', he thought to himself in his extreme injustice...

(book 2, ch. 16)

Mathilde's brave loneliness of spirit is part of her appeal. On another occasion, despite her customary haughtiness, she can be described without incongruity as 'like a poor girl living on the fifth floor of a tenement' (book 2, ch. 42). After their first assignation, however, her overwhelming attractiveness for Julien has a more obvious cause: after the dry tense nightmare horror of her night with Julien, she recoils from him utterly. Julien's pride is, of course, mortified and he becomes obsessed with the desire to reassert his rights, obsessed, that is, with longing for the love and submission of a woman he regards as a 'monster of pride'. He succeeds by simulating an indifference even greater than her own, but meanwhile becomes a 'maniac'. Mathilde 'absorbs every other thought'. He 'sees her everywhere in the future'. 'Everywhere in this future he saw lack of success. This young man whom we first saw so proud and full of presumption in Verrières had fallen into an excess of ridiculous modesty' (book 2, ch. 24). His own vacillations when Mathilde finds she is pregnant, his absurdly considerate offer to the Marquis of his own life as a convenient sacrifice and his state of dazed self-contemplation when a commission is bought for him, he becomes a chevalier and marriage with Mathilde seems imminent, can all be seen as symptomatic of a state of extreme distraction and an (uncharacteristic) inability, akin to Mathilde's, to know what he wants. It is significant, of course, that it should be when he is in this state of mind that he reads Mme de Rênal's letter of denunciation and travels to Verrières to end her life and his own.

Mathilde, with her desire to relive the middle ages, her contempt for the social virtues and her constant need for an audience, has three at least of the characteristics of early nineteenth-century Romanticism. She is formidably intelligent and alive but her feeling for the sublime and the heroic is, in the last analysis, self-frustrating and parasitic on what she scorns. In the salons of the aristocracy 'Mathilde was often bored', we are told. 'It is possible that she would have been bored anywhere' (book 2, ch. 11). Yet there is a great deal more to Mathilde than to her poor Norwegian counterpart Hedda Gabler or to Madame Bovary, whose true capabilities neither she nor the reader has the chance to find out. Her gestures of defiance and her sense of what is wrong with an age in which the young leaders of society are the slaves of the conventions to which they owe their position (this anticipates Beyle's warning after 1830 against the imminent Americanisation of society) cannot be dismissed with contempt, and it is for this reason, presumably, that she is made, for all her faults, to seem so impressive and sympathetic, a suitable partner for Julien in many ways, despite their eventual profound differences. She has the makings of an actress in the grand manner, yet she is portrayed by an author who could be carried away by grand gestures and spectacles.[38] In *Le rouge et le noir*, moreover, ceremonies, and specifically ecclesiastical ceremonies, are described with gusto and appreciation of the fact that they bring life to a dreary age. Julien admires, as Beyle himself seems to, though with a great deal more amusement than Julien, the aristocratic young Bishop of Agde whom Julien catches unawares in front of a mirror practising benedictions and trying to look old; while the celebrations at the shrine of the martyred Saint Clément are described with admiring delight as well as a tingling sense of their sheer absurdity. It is the Marquis de la Mole who has financed the ceremonies, and the enjoyment with which every detail is dwelt on reads like appreciation not only of a wonderful show but of the fact that the Marquis is playing politics with panache and masterful efficiency. Beyle writes as a member of the liberal opposition but with a characteristic *Beyliste* (in English here, sportsmanlike) relish of the cool acumen of the traditional enemy:

There was a *Te Deum*, billowing clouds of incense, an infinite number of discharges of musketry and artillery; the peasants were drunk with happiness and piety. A day like this undoes the work of a hundred issues of the Jacobin press...

Julien himself is so carried away that he would have 'fought for the Inquisition and in perfect good faith' (book 1, ch. 18).

M. H.-F. Imbert has drawn attention to the parallel between the ceremonies at the shrine of Saint Clément and those that accompany Julien's funeral on the last pages of the novel when Mathilde, like her father, distributes largesse to the peasants.[39] What M. Imbert does not bring out is that there is an essential difference, none the less, between the shrine of an improbable Roman saint and the graveside of Julien Sorel. Beyle does not tell us what we ought to think of Mathilde, but the facts speak eloquently for themselves when she stage-manages Julien's funeral and, with a characteristic effort of will, forces herself to imitate Marguerite de Navarre kissing the severed head of her lover before the appalled eyes of the unassuming Fouqué and at the funeral trying to bury the head herself. The word 'vulgarity' is not used to describe either the ceremonies at the graveside or the expensive embellishments she chooses for Julien's tomb on the mountainside where he had asked to be left and forgotten. Yet the associations for Julien of the mountainside and his inability when he dies to take an interest in either Mathilde or her brand of heroism make explicit condemnation unnecessary:

Through Mathilde's cares, this wild grotto was adorned with marble sculptured at great expense in Italy.

The marble monument, like so much of nineteenth-century art, is out of place. The Romanticism which is so powerful an element in the novel's appeal has by now been shown as insensitive to more lasting human needs and desires.

6

Lucien Leuwen and autobiography

Souvenirs d'égotisme

Beyle's dissatisfaction with *Le rouge et le noir* after its publication in 1830 is expressed in numerous jottings in the margin of a copy that was found after his death in his library in the consulate of Civita Vecchia[1] and in the manuscripts of other novels and stories. The style seemed to him too 'abrupt' and 'dry', the 'tone' of the novel insufficiently 'familiar'. 'How familiar ought the tone of a novel to be? Doesn't the extreme familiarity of Scott and Fielding predispose one to follow them in their moments of enthusiasm?' And then, the decisive question indicating how different the next novel was to be: 'Isn't the tone of *Le rouge* too Roman?'

Even more than to *Le rouge*, these objections can be made to the two short stories that appeared in the *Revue de Paris* for May and June 1830, *Le coffre et le revenant* and *Le philtre*, and that may have been inspired by a first brief visit to Spain the previous year. These and *Le juif*, written during hours of boredom after his appointment as consul to Trieste are of minor interest in any case, though they anticipate the narrative manner of much of *La chartreuse de Parme* and *Les chroniques italiennes* and indicate what after *Les promenades dans Rome*, was to become a growing fascination with the psychology of human cruelty. His dislodgement from Trieste at the behest of the Austrian government and his removal to Civita Vecchia coincide with a period when he wrote little, but from the summer of 1832 until four years later, he was to become increasingly absorbed in and was to write prolifically on subjects deriving from his own experience and obviously close to his heart. And he was to leave unfinished the manuscripts of *Lucien Leuwen* and the two volumes of memoirs, *Souvenirs d'égotisme* and *La vie de Henry Brulard*.

One can only guess the reasons that led him to plunge into the record of his own recent past, abandon it, take up what was to become his longest and most penetrating work of fiction and then go back in *La vie de Henry Brulard* to salvage what remained alive in his memory of his childhood and youth. But the same tensions calling for release seem common to all three works and the same preoccupation is made explicit in all three manuscripts concerning the crucial differences between fiction and fact.

I have tried to show already that it would be wrong to conclude from Beyle's thoughts on history that he ever despaired of man's ability to understand the past, clear though he became in his own mind that most historians were really novelists in disguise and that the novel was definitely his own vocation. Presumably he would have agreed that 'where the historian really differs from the poet is in his describing what has happened, while the other describes the kind of thing that might have happened',[2] even if, like Aristotle, he considered the knowledge the poets (and novelists) can give us as potentially more true and important than that of historians. Our sense of what might have happened, however, depends on what *has* happened, at least to us personally. And Beyle was deeply imbued with the beliefs of Locke, Condillac, Helvétius, Tracy and Richard Payne Knight that there is nothing in our experience of the world or in our wildest fancies concerning it that has not come to us originally through our five senses. As a critic, he preferred those poets whose imagination was nourished by their contact with the world:

I am perfectly aware that a poet is permitted to be ignorant of the realities of life. I will go further, it is necessary to his success as a poet that he should be so. If a man of honour and sensibility like M. de Lamartine knew as much about mankind as a Sir Robert Walpole or a Villèle, his imagination, his sensibility, would become arid. This I have always thought the sense of the reply made to Hamlet by the ghost of his father.

If Lord Byron had not enjoyed the advantage of being born an Englishman; if he had not been compelled by his pride, as a peer, to take at least a tinge of the prevailing good sense of his country; if he had not associated with Douglas Kinnaird, the Hobhouses and others,

well versed in the real state of interests and parties; if he had not
seen a little of the world *as it goes*, which he could not avoid doing
in his quality of Member of the Literary Committee of Covent Garden,
never would he have written *Don Juan* – never, in my opinion, would
his genius have risen above the level of that of M. de Lamartine.

(*London Magazine*, July 1825)

As Alain was to point out in 1935, he never 'echoes the commonplace that one now hears everywhere that we can never really
know other people'.[3] And it is unlikely that he would have
endorsed Marcel Proust's belief that for a writer, there is only
one 'true life' and that is 'the life of his novels'[4] or that he
would have relished the quasi-solipsism that is so powerful an
element in *A la recherche du temps perdu* and defended in *Le temps
retrouvé*.

Souvenirs d'égotisme and *La vie de Henry Brulard* are unmistakably
autobiography, and *Lucien Leuwen* a novel. The distinction is
crucial and the fear of turning the one into the other admitted
repeatedly in the margins of the latter and the text of the memoirs
themselves. It seems necessary to insist on the distinction, even
at the risk of doing so pedantically, because scholars and critics
are constantly denying that it exists. We cannot, of course, check
more than a few episodes in the latter for their actual veracity, and
we know that on occasions Beyle suffered from what the French
politely call mythomania.[5] But the difference between illusion
and reality is itself one of Beyle's main preoccupations in the
autobiographies and in *Henry Brulard* in particular. Both are
concerned with the nature of memory and with what makes it
at the same time precarious and indispensable, a way of remaining
alive. In *Henry Brulard* he tells us that in making his inventory
of what remains of his past, he is seeking to know what he is
and has been; and his conception on what, in any other context,
would seem like wholly unimportant details suggests that the
autobiography is serving a need far deeper than what is normally
meant by self-knowledge. In *Souvenirs d'égotisme* he is writing
about a more recent past and the fear that the past may be
irretrievable is less pressing; though the same preoccupation
with the exact truth is expressed and the same fear of the
'egotism' which is, presumably, referred to in the title,[6] the
endless 'I's and me's' to which he sees an antidote only in a
'perfect sincerity'.

As it happens, the fears are much exaggerated – certainly if one compares this one with most other autobiographies; and the title, if it is intended to be apologetic, misleading. *Souvenirs d'égotisme* is a record of the period following his departure from Milan and his life in Paris and London after he had broken finally with Mathilde Dembowski. And it can be enjoyed, if nothing else, for the vivid and economical, since utterly candid portraits of other people: Lafayette, Destutt de Tracy, Mérimée, Charles de Rémusat and other influential figures of the day, as well as the shy lady-like London prostitutes in whose suburban villa off the Westminster Road Beyle and two of his French companions spent much of their time during a visit to England in the autumn following his departure from Milan.

This last, if one likes to think so, reprehensible episode has the virtue at least of bringing to life an often forgotten corner of the London of Blake and Dickens. It is recounted with a simple affectionate appreciativeness and it records Beyle's first awakening from the grief ensuing upon the break with Mathilde Dembowski. It is Mathilde herself who is conspicuously absent from the memoirs and for that matter from Beyle's writings as a whole; absent, that is, as an identifiable voice and personality with recognisable virtues and faults, and it is perhaps significant that in one of the few physical descriptions he has left of her, she is compared with the type of 'Lombardian' (and notoriously enigmatic) beauty to be found in the paintings of Leonardo da Vinci.[7] It is she who inspired, as the marginal notes testify, the portrait in *Lucien Leuwen* of Mme de Chasteller, though even here she is a woman of mainly unrevealed possibilities who enjoys solitude and virtuous seclusion and betrays her fascination with Lucien most freely when she is watching him go by beneath her window.

The real Mathilde may well have resembled what we are allowed to imagine of Mme de Chasteller. She was as whole-heartedly devoted to the seemingly lost cause of Italian freedom after 1815 as Mme de Chasteller to that of the traditional monarchy. She was proudly sensitive and, as Beyle tells us in the *Souvenirs*, easily wounded by the imputation of loose and dishonourable behaviour, and all the more so as she was publicly separated from her husband. Hence probably her shrinking from Beyle's indiscreet and unintentionally comic advances when disguised ineffectually by a pair of green spectacles he pursued her to Volterra, where she was visiting her sons' college. Yet the unguarded affection of which she was capable, as well as the pride and spirit, can be seen if one reads the letters to her 'stimabile amico' Ugo Foscolo, for whom she expresses a devotion almost certainly more warm and intense than anything she felt for the importunate Beyle.[8] 'When will you come back?', Mathilde asks the latter in the first chapter of *Souvenirs d'égotisme*. '"Never, I hope." After which, there was an hour of beating about the bush and useless words of which one alone might have changed my life, though not for long, for this angelic soul hidden in so beautiful a body departed from this life in 1825.'

The memory of Mathilde seems to dominate both *Souvenirs d'égotisme* and the first half of *Lucien Leuwen*. In the second half, attention is turned abruptly to the hero's father and the relations between father and son are explored before the novel is abandoned and Beyle takes up the story of his childhood and family circle in *La vie de Henry Brulard*. The need to write during this period seems to be one that takes him through the memories of his most formative relations with others. A psychoanalyst may find this significant and may note that Beyle had adored his mother with a fierce sensual passion before she died when he was seven years old. And he may wish to account for Beyle's worship of a woman whom he could never love physically by showing this to be a re-enactment of the bitterly thwarted passions of the child. This may be a helpful and revealing exercise but it would be overlooking an essential part of the case if one were to regard the value for Beyle of his experience as merely private and symptomatic.[9] Mathilde's influence in the memoirs can be seen as that of a woman who brought him grief and deprivation – which are at the same time a sense of what might have been supreme happiness and hence, paradoxically, an astounding awareness of being alive.

Landscapes have always been like a *bow* drawn across my soul and especially the aspects of which no one ever speaks (the line of rocks as one approaches Arbois – I think it is – along the main highway coming from Dôle, was for me an evident and sensible image of the soul of Mathilde...)

(*La vie de Henry Brulard*, ch. 2)

As Beyle admits, such an experience is, in one sense, *strictly private*, but there may be many readers who, for this very reason, will be able to understand immediately what he means.

The differences between the memoirs and the novels are crucial, but in both we find the same disconcerting potency of detail, in other words the same confidence in an overwhelming impression which is characteristic of poetry. Prose which is so intensely alive is almost bound to be fragmentary, and in the memoirs it lapses frequently into wandering reminiscence and often mere gossip. The outstanding passages in the *Souvenirs d'égotisme* themselves include the accounts of the journey from Milan in the first chapter, the visit to London in chapter 6 and, perhaps most remarkable of all, in chapter 3, of the sexual fiasco he experienced during a first attempt to console himself for the break with Mathilde. All these episodes are related with a simple wonder at the unexpected things that may happen to anyone, in other words a total lack of egotism. In so far, moreover, as Mathilde played a part in Beyle's life not unlike that of Laura de Noves in Petrarch's, they more than justify comparison with some of the better known expressions in verse of that kind of love and tribute.

The difference between Beyle's autobiography and his novels is not that the former is, in any obvious way, more prosaic. Nor is it, as so often is claimed, that in the latter the imaginary hero succeeds where Beyle himself had hopelessly failed in real life. M. Victor Brombert may be right when he says that the story of Lucien and Mme de Chasteller is the story of Beyle and Mathilde told in a form soothing to the former's vanity.[10] Lucien still, partly through his own foolishness, fails to reassure or conquer Mme de Chasteller, and if day-dreaming vanity had been Beyle's only creative impulse, Lucien would have been happier, more perfect and certainly far less interesting than he is. The most obvious difference between the memoirs and *Lucien Leuwen* is that the latter is sustained by many more interests and takes in a far wider panorama of contemporary life. For all his memories, presumably, of Mme de Chasteller, Beyle is literally, as a novelist, carried out of himself, and though he may be unable to forget his former state of mind, he relives it with an exploratory zest and a concentration of his mental powers which is unequalled in his writing before or afterwards.

Lucien Leuwen, part one

The inspiration for *Lucien Leuwen* and the outline of the story seem to have occurred to Beyle in much the same way as those of his other novels. Like the newspaper account of the trial of Antoine Berthet and the manuscript relating the adventures of Alessandro Farnese, the draft of a novel by a friend seems to have provided the branch, to adopt a metaphor from *De l'amour*, round which a whole novel was to 'crystallise'. Having an idea and developing it straight away on paper seem to have been for Beyle always much the same thing, and having the freedom to do so one of the advantages of the life of a self-professed 'dilettante'. He had been only for a few years – and even then not completely – dependent on writing for a livelihood and he was in the habit of thinking pen in hand. The novel, entitled *Le lieutenant*, is the subject of two letters from Civita Vecchia of May and November 1834, in which Beyle recommends the authoress, Mme Jules Gaulthier, for instance, to

...efface in each chapter at least fifty superlatives. Never write: 'the burning passion of Olivier for Hélène.'

The poor novelist has to try and make the reader believe in the *burning passion* but he must never name it: to do that is slightly immodest and indecent [*cela est contre la pudeur*]...

Don't make your characters too rich and let your hero commit some little blunder at times, because we heroes do make blunders. We run; the dull man hardly ever even walks; and even then it's with a stick; that's why he never falls...

Why not call the novel, Beyle suggested as well, *Leuwen or the student expelled from the Ecole Polytechnique*? How much else he was to add to or borrow from the novel we don't know, since the manuscript has been lost. But realising what could be made of such a story and with many hours of solitude to fill, he began immediately to sketch out and then write the novel that was to occupy him for more than a year.

That it was never finished may be due to his realising, by the time he reached the end of the second part, that it could only be published after his retirement or death. 'As long as I serve the Budget, [i.e. the government] I shan't be able to print it, for what the Budget detests most of all is that one should give oneself the air of having ideas.'[11] The ideas, moreover, and the portrayal of Louis Philippe's ministers (based on a good deal of embarrassing inside information) could easily be thought of as seditious, despite his assurances in the second sketch for a preface that he would rather have to pay court to the Minister of the Interior than to his grocer, that he is by no means a whole-hearted democrat and that he would be in despair if he had to live in New York. By the time he gave up the novel, he had well and truly unburdened himself of his contempt for the government of this 'most crooked of kings', as he called him in private. (The *memoires d'un touriste* written two years later for publication are, of course, far more discreet.) He had also left in the margins of the manuscript the most valuable guide we possess to his method of composition, in the form of notes for his *own* guidance in rewriting the text. Not surprisingly, among these is the admission that he had deliberately made the manuscript of *Lucien Leuwen* too long, unlike that of *Le rouge et le noir*. Hence, 'among other faults' in the latter 'the abrupt phraseology and the absence of those little expressions which help the imagination of the benevolent reader to picture to himself what is happening'.[12] 'I want the style and any indecencies corrected', he wrote in the notes for a will,[13] 'but leave all the extravagances.'

The uninhibited portrayal of the social and political worlds that Beyle knew more intimately than any other, and the general copiousness of detail contribute towards making *Lucien Leuwen* the most profound and penetrating of his novels, despite its unfinished state and a lapse at the end of the first part into absurd contrivance. One can make too much of the fact that the novel would have benefited in parts from revision and lacks the third volume Beyle had originally planned. The manuscripts end with the death of M. Leuwen *père* and the winding up of his affairs by Lucien, who then sets off via Switzerland to take up a post as secretary to a French embassy. Within its context, this is an eloquent dénouement to and comment on what has gone before, and there is no reason why the novel should not have ended there; though Beyle himself seems to have had other ideas, and among them possibly the conventional one that a novel should end in a death or a marriage. Beyle's plans for and comments on the novel, however, for all the acuteness of the latter, are by the nature of things completely different from the intention revealed in his art. (Paul Valéry, in his clever, confusing and much too often quoted preface to the novel refuses to see that they are different.)[14] And I should like to suggest that it is in the very nature of his art that the novel should have been left unfinished. A solution to the issues it raises, and a happy or a tragic ending, would have been almost certainly a falsification both of the issues themselves and the spirit in which they are brought home to the reader.

What that spirit is can be best pointed out by saying what is, in any case, obvious. Much of *Lucien Leuwen* asks to be read as high-spirited social comedy, and this is apparent from the very first page. Lucien has been expelled from the Ecole Polytechnique for taking part in the demonstrations that accompanied the funeral of the republican General Lamarque and which may have seen the first appearance in Paris of the red flag.[15] Before deciding to make the army his career, he lives at home in luxury with his mother and father, the celebrated banker and wit, who pays the debts and pulls the leg of his only child mercilessly:

'A son is a creditor provided by nature...Do you know what we'd put on your marble tomb in the Père Lachaise if ever we had the misfortune to lose you? "*Siste viator*! Here lies Lucien Leuwen, a republican, who for two years waged an incessant war against cigars and his new pairs of boots."'

At the moment when our story begins, this enemy of cigars hardly thought any longer about the republic, which is taking far too long to appear...
     (ch. 1)

The opening chapters of the novel have something of the effect of the overture and first act of a comic opera and this is not merely because of the brilliant dialogue and swift sequence of events but the boisterousness of the comedy, which leaves us wondering from the outset how far Lucien is irredeemably naïf and Quixotic. The principal themes of the novel are briefly stated, as it were, and the wind knocked straight away out of any illusions that the hero or reader may share about easy paths to glory or self-respect. Lucien is ribbed also by his energetic and candidly opportunistic cousin Ernest Dévelroy, a contributor to the leading literary reviews and a candidate for election to the Academy of Moral Sciences (today he would be a candidate

for a university chair) who cheerfully recommends him at least
to appear more grave:

'To look at you, one would say you're a child and, what is worse, a
contented child. You're beginning to be taken at your own valuation,
I warn you, and in spite of your father's millions, you don't count
anywhere; there's nothing solid about you, you're just a nice schoolboy.
At twenty, that's almost ridiculous and worst of all, you spend hours
attending to your appearance and this is known...'
      (ch. 1)

The banker and the man of letters have come to terms with
their age (though Ernest temporarily miscalculates by accompanying an influential academician to the waters at Vichy, where
the old gentleman dies on his hands; having 'lost four months',
Ernest vows that next time he will attach himself to one who
is younger.) Lucien has not. An age in which glory means being
a millionaire or elected to the Academy of Moral Sciences is not
one in which he would have chosen to live; though the comedy
of the first two chapters lies partly in the good humoured,
merciless and very Parisian way in which he is assured that in
being so unworldly, he is merely a fool. What right has he not
to care for worldly success or, after he has obtained his commission in the lancers, to feel disgust on his first meeting with
Colonel Filloteau at the vile and calculating unction of the man
who, to his dismay, is now to be his superior? Doesn't he feel
ashamed, Ernest asks him, that he can't even pay for his own
cigars? '"Vile or not, M. Filloteau is a thousand times your
superior. He has been active and you have not...He's probably
supporting some old peasant who's his father and your father's
supporting you..."' Lucien can only reply in despair:

'I can see you'll be elected to the Institute at the next vacancy and
I'm just a fool, I know it. You're right a hundred times over, I'm
sure, but I really deserve pity as well. I can't stand the thought of the
gate I must go through. There's too much dung lying underneath
it...'
      (ch. 2)

His hopes that he will be able to silence Ernest and his father
and step round or over the dung are to survive many intolerable
humiliations and many hours of boredom and disillusion. And
the fact that they stay alive may explain why the reader is left

in a state of constant suspense throughout the novel and why the comedy of the opening chapters is sustained with such power, variety of mood and inwardness.

The most sympathetic and helpful account of the comedy I know is the one given by Maurice Bardèche in his chapters on the novel and on Beyle's marginal notes to the manuscript in *Stendhal, romancier*. M. Bardèche brings to the novel the eye of a historian who knows the period well and of a committed politician who is able to enjoy many of Beyle's bitterer ironies, and he provides what can be valuable for the reader who is not French: an account of how many of the social types whom Lucien encounters are still alive in France today or at least were alive in 1947, when the book first appeared – a great deal, of course, has changed in France since then. I find, none the less, that M. Bardèche tends to underestimate as literature the comedy he enjoys and admires, for according to his account, this is a matter of wonderful separate portraits *à la Célimène*, a kind of 'magic lantern show' throughout the first half of the novel giving us the identifiable features, and nothing more, of the officers and genteel inhabitants of Nancy, where Lucien spends the whole of his short military career. As M. Bardèche points out, almost none of the characters thus portrayed influence his destiny or are heard of or seen again when he returns to Paris; though M. Bardèche concludes too rapidly, I think, that the inhabitants of Nancy are therefore merely 'amusing', with 'no more life or weight than the comic characters of Walter Scott' and that Lucien remains a mere witness of their absurdities. The admirer of Tolstoy will not, it is true, find anything in Beyle's Nancy comparable to the crowded, varied and yet always individually focused portraits of the society of Moscow and St Petersburg in *Anna Karenina* and *War and Peace* and one of the obvious reasons for the greater range in Tolstoy is that we are not merely being shown, as in *Lucien Leuwen*, the experience of one onlooker and protagonist. Yet Beyle is more like Tolstoy, surely, in the way he brings a whole society to life than he is like his contemporary, Balzac to whom, as a social historian, he is still commonly judged inferior. Compare, for instance, Beyle's Nancy with the world of the *Curé de Tours* or the Angoulême of the first half of *Illusions perdues*. It may occur to the reader that M. Bardèche's description of Beyle's social comedy applies, if anything, more aptly to the last two works and we may be reminded, if we re-read them, that it was Balzac who, of the two, was the greater admirer of Scott. A crucial difference between the minor characters of Beyle and Balzac lies in the point of view from which they are seen, a point of view which, in Beyle, is not merely, or principally, that of the omniscient novelist. Among the 'amusing characters', as M. Bardèche calls them, in *Lucien Leuwen* is Colonel Malher de Saint-Mégrin, who has his officers watched carefully and who forbids Lucien to visit the local reading room, his usually unsmiling brother lieutenants and his protector and 'uncle' the vile Colonel Filloteau. They do not, it is true, decisively affect his destiny. But they serve a dramatic – in the Beyliste sense; that is, a psychologically revealing – function. His determination to go through with a military career having once embarked on it, and despite these vexations, is the first sign we have that his cousin Ernest may have under-rated him. The horrors of a provincial garrison are no less real for being the horrors of seemingly endless hours spent in rented lodgings and darkened streets or, for a change, gambling and drinking in the company of officers who have no objection to seeing him provoked into a duel, wounded and then, fainting from loss of blood, left to make his way back to his rooms alone. The 'life and weight' of the members of the garrison corresponds to the degree to which Lucien himself is unavoidably aware of them. After the duel, he makes a joke 'which must have been a bad one, as it was not understood' (ch. 7) and the narrator's rueful irony reads like that of Lucien; the narrative manner, here as elsewhere, pre-supposes an identity of views between the narrator, the reader and the hero himself. The question touched on but not pursued by M. Bardèche is what makes any depiction of *mores* in a society remote from our own worthy of more than accidental or expert interest, what makes us, the readers, whose imagination alone has the requisite recreative powers, find more 'life and weight' in some characters than others. Novels, particularly very original ones, differ completely in this respect. My suggestion for an answer in the case of *Lucien Leuwen* is that the interest for us of Nancy and its inhabitants is due more than anything else to what Lucien expects of them and to the kind of man that Lucien is: in other words, that it is the very unusual light in which ordinary people are seen and scrutinised that makes their portraits so life-like and memorable. This is perhaps what Beyle had in mind when, after a year's work on the novel, he wrote:

...each sentence tells a story, so to speak, if I compare them with those of M. de Balzac's *Médecin de campagne* or M. Sue's *Koatven*. Now the first thing one asks of a novel is that it should do this, amuse us by what it narrates and, so that it can amuse readers endowed with sense, portray characters who exist in nature.

Like Beyle himself, we may feel like protesting: 'Confound it, I know we have to imitate nature; but to what extent? That is the whole question',[16] but he goes on to suggest an answer in the same note:

In general, *idealise*, as Raphael *idealises* in a portrait in order to make it more life-like. But idealise in order to approach the perfectly beautiful in the figure of the heroine only. Excuse: the reader will have only seen the woman he has loved through idealising eyes...[17]

This note can be interpreted in many different ways, but one of them at least is consistent with the notion that imaginative fellow-feeling with Lucien is necessary to our realising of what he sees; furthermore, this may be a matter of our recalling what is private and incommunicable in our experience, as well as what it has in common with that of other men. In what is both communicated and incommunicable, for example, in the allusion to the idealising eyes of the reader, we may be reminded of those particular aspects of landscape of which 'no one ever speaks'.[18]

Many critics tell us, nonetheless, that *Lucien Leuwen* is an attempt – and some, including M. Bardèche himself, find that it is an unsuccessful one – to write a novel in the manner of Balzac. He had, it is true, thought of dividing it according to the Balzacian categories of *Scènes de la vie de province, Scènes de la vie parisienne*, and so on. But he also left instructions that if any other writer were to correct the style and cut out the repetitions after his death, it should *not* be Balzac.[19] And, as the note I have just quoted suggests, style for Beyle was anything but a separate or secondary consideration. Far from being an imitation of Balzac, as Mr Michael Wood has recently argued,[20] and a departure from the kind of thing he was good at, namely the manner of *Le rouge et le noir*, *Lucien Leuwen* can be seen as a development out of Beyle's earlier work and evidence of what he had learned in writing it. In *Lucien Leuwen*, for example, it seems clear that Beyle needed a hero as *unformed* as Julien Sorel and whose capacity for enjoyment, courage and intelligence were as unimpaired and unfathomable in order to answer the question: what does this particular world and its civilisation have to offer such a man and what potentialities for living, can be realised within them? The most obvious difference between the two novels is that in Lucien Beyle has chosen a hero as privileged as Julien Sorel is deprived, and who lacks the ferocious energy and mental powers that Julien needs to overcome his disadvantages. It is true that Lucien has to brace and assert himself many times, and that he learns the value of self-imposed obligations, including a military punctiliousness in carrying out some very hard work and several missions of which he disapproves. But the obligations are chosen *faute de mieux* – constantly, he will compare his various duties ruefully with those he would have had to carry out on the battlefield – and meeting them does not give him the immense satisfactions which Julien can enjoy and which count for so much in the total effect of *Le rouge et le noir*. In other words, Lucien is less self-preoccupied, less mistrustful of himself and the world and, as a result, Beyle is far more free to present his hero's career as a chronicle of his time.

Why Nancy, however? It would be absurd to attribute the interest of a series of portraits and interiors merely to the intelligence of the eye through which they were seen. There are many possible valid answers to the question and one is that, not only in the garrison but in certain of the homes of local inhabitants he enters, we are shown the common experience of enforced company and the consequent need for sensitiveness and skill on the part of those who are free to escape, without which life for the virtual prisoners can be rendered intolerable. In the household of Mme de Serpierre, for example, with her six plain unmarried daughters, Lucien finds himself in a world which is by no means remote from that of the novels of Jane Austen[21] and his own (and his author's) evident understanding of and respect for it are shown by the fact that though the eldest daughter, Théolinde, is clearly in love with him and she and her sisters enjoy happy excursions in his company, he is able to avoid behaving in a way of which either Colonel Brandon or Mr Knightley would have disapproved. The Serpierres are loyal to the exiled Charles X and live in semi-poverty. Hence the usefulness for the daughters' excursions of Lucien's large private carriage. M. de Serpierre has his old military uniforms turned into coats and trousers he can wear around the house. The town, moreover, serves as a refuge and a capital for others like him. It keeps alive as far as possible the allegiances and the social order of the past and in this sense is provincial in a way that no English town has been since the seventeenth century. (Its way of life is still perpetuated as M. Bardèche points out, in certain quarters of the cathedral towns of Vendée and Anjou.) And it stands in contrast and opposition to the Paris of the July monarchy that has overthrown for the last time the principle of hereditary monarchy and, at least in theory, hereditary privilege and power.

This, in any case, is what it represents in the novel. Beyle himself had never actually visited Nancy, and there is no evidence that he tried to inform himself, while writing it or beforehand, of the actual politics of the town. Nancy offers – and this is perhaps the principal reason for his devoting so much attention to it – an obvious alternative to the democratic ideals and way of life to which Lucien has felt until now half-committed; though characteristic of the way in which the novel works is the fact that Lucien enters the legitimist circles of the town, not on principle or out of a kind of sociological curiosity but from weariness with the company of his fellow-officers and in search of amusing or even ordinarily pleasant company. It is in a mood of high-spirited exasperation, after his duel, that he buys his *carte d'entrée* into the circles he wishes to enter in the form of a sumptuously bound missal, attends benediction in the exclusively aristocratic Chapelle des Pénitents and willingly exposes himself to the series of invitations which follows. He has already, before this, repudiated in the officers' mess the unnecessarily damaging charge that he is a 'republican' and he has been condemned as a 'renegade' in a note from his conspiratorially silent republican fellow-officers. Though what principles is he betraying anyway? It is easier for him to say what he doesn't believe than what he is prepared to die for. He comes to realise this during one of the evenings he spends with his friend, the mathematician Gauthier, the utterly honest and wholly committed editor of the local republican newspaper.[22] In the course of an earnest lecture from

Gauthier on 'America, democracy, prefects chosen by law from among the elected representatives of each department' and other arguments 'that can be found in print anywhere', Lucien finds that despite his 'profound esteem' for his friend, he has difficulty in keeping himself awake.

> 'Can I really call myself a republican after this? This shows me that I'm not made to live in a republic; for me it would be the tyrannical rule of all the mediocrities and I'm incapable of calmly tolerating even the most estimable of mediocrities. I need a prime minister who's an amusing scoundrel, like Walpole or M. de Talleyrand.'
>
> At that moment, Gauthier ended his discourse with the words: 'But we have no Americans in France.'
>
> 'Take any shopkeeper in Rouen or Lyon who's avaricious and without imagination and you'll soon have an American', Lucien replied.
>
> 'Ah! you really grieve me', cried Gauthier rising sadly to his feet and leaving, as the hour after midnight struck.
>
> > 'Grenadier, you grieve me...'
>
> Lucien sang when he was gone [a song from a vaudeville in the Théâtre de Variétés] 'And yet, I esteem you with all my heart.'
> (ch. 8)

Lucien, like Beyle, is no doubt unjust to Americans. But, a century later, his inability to share the Utopian view of America can scarcely seem like incorrigible naïvety.

In the emphatic retort to Gauthier, however, there is a force that comes not from mature reflection on politics and not only from a mounting revulsion against his friend's sincere addiction to numbers and equations, but from an instinct which, without attempting to define or name it, Beyle makes us recognise as profoundly corrective and springing from an undeniable need. The vexations and above all disappointments of his life until now can be easily imagined as contributing to his outburst to Gauthier and to the balefulness with which he tells himself that he'd prefer the rule of an 'amusing scoundrel'. And his instinctive reaction leads him to cultivate the acquaintance of Gauthier's principal political rival in Nancy, Dr Du Poirier, an 'amusing scoundrel' *par excellence* and Lucien's guide into the aristocratic society of the town. Du Poirier is a type of politician and intriguer who is to reappear as Rassi of the *Chartreuse de Parme* and Dr Sansfin of *Lamiel*, and he is 'as crooked as Gauthier is honest'. Lucien's astonished admiration for the histrionic unction, patently false plebeian self-abasement and dialectical brilliance of this self-appointed organiser of the legitimist and aristocratic cause is the uncensurious delight one is able to feel in an exuberantly and perfectly incorrigible rogue. Able to feel, that is, in certain circumstances such as those in which Lucien finds himself at this moment. This is not life to which he might normally have been drawn and the description of Du Poirier's remarkable features, which are compared successively to those of a boar, a hyena and a fox, conveys Lucien's astonished wonder during their first encounter at the sheer and unaccountable otherness of the life in this childless, landless advocate of a return to – of all things – the pre-Revolutionary laws of primogeniture.[23] Lucien suspects immediately, and correctly, that he is a natural traitor – a fox, not a boar – and M. Bardèche argues that after his election to the Chamber of Deputies, he becomes a type of the modern French deputy. Du Poirier is also – a typically Beyliste detail, calling for no further explanation – a man who, despite his tireless scheming, lives in perpetual terror of retaliation.

The usefulness to Lucien of Du Poirier is not merely that he offers much needed entertainment – the need prompting him to cultivate his acquaintance is less desperate, in other words, than that which leads a Prince Hal to consort with a Falstaff; it is above all, and in a way that suits Du Poirier as well, that Lucien can be shown off as a convert to the cause of throne and altar, in front of people whom he is far more happy to know. Both commoners, Lucien and Du Poirier, simulate piety in order to deceive the noble inhabitants of Nancy – they make a good pair to this extent – but in order to gain very different kinds of advantage. Mme de Commercy, for example, noting Lucien's glances at her beautiful English garden, modelled on that of Louis XVIII's house during his exile at Hartwell, begs him to come and walk round it when he wishes and 'without calling to see the old proprietor'.

After this invitation made with cordial simplicity, Lucien was no longer in a mood to mock; he felt as if he were returning to life. It was several months now since he had last seen polite company...
(ch. 10)

This sensation is one that neither Gauthier nor Du Poirier have been able to give him, and that he experiences again when M. de Serpierre, seeing a look of horror on Lucien's face and correctly interpreting it, explains that, though a lieutenant at Colmar in 1822, he had been absent at the time of one of the more shameful crimes of the régime to which he owes his allegiance, the ambush prepared by his fellow-officers for Colonel Caron, and his subsequent execution. The reply 'sanctifies his entire household' in Lucien's eyes and he is unable any longer to mock inwardly at the sour-tempered Mme de Serpierre and her red-headed daughters, tall as grenadiers. The scruples and generosity of Mme de Commercy and M. de Serpierre outweigh for Lucien the injustice and absurdity of the social order they represent.

Yet Lucien does not commit himself to a belief in inherited privilege as a guarantee against barbarism, as his presence in the salons seems to imply, any more than in the past he had seen any positive hope in the prospect of its final elimination. And the novel fails to offer any such final or simple answer to the question: what makes civilisation possible? The local aristocracy is prone, like any other, to the accidents as well as the advantages of birth and includes the vindictive Roller brothers, impoverished ex-officers embittered by their poverty, and the prosperous Marquis de Sanréal, whose yelping voice repeats at full pitch the word *'voleur'* (thief), whenever Louis Philippe is mentioned. 'The noble ladies of Nancy' never tire of the joke, and Lucien is soon 'shocked by the eternal repetition and the eternal gaiety' (ch. 11). Lucien could never, in any case, have hoped to find in the legitimist circles of Nancy company by which he would never have been offended or bored; and if this had been the only point for the novelist of his taking this particular social plunge, his surprise at finding himself in such shallow water would have been merely farcical and surprising to himself alone. The attraction of the world he enters is far deeper: specifically, it is that of Mme de Chasteller, who, as he rides beneath her windows, has twice seen him thrown and on one occasion with unconcealed amusement. Attending benediction at the Chapelle des Pénitents is the first step in a progress that is to lead him to this beautiful retiring young widow who is a willing semi-prisoner in her father's house and the most sought-after match among the noble young bloods of Nancy.

Mme de Chasteller occupies the centre of Nancy, in a manner verging on the symbolic. Her father's Gothic house with the huge white wall, from which her green-shuttered window looks out, is like other buildings in the novels of Beyle in that it is obviously something more than a piece of incidental décor. Newly decorated, it stands in contrast to the lugubrious buildings surrounding it and to the peeling walls of the other houses of Nancy between which flow rivulets of slate-coloured mud, into one of which Lucien falls. Lucien is drawn to the house at first by its appearance, then by pique at having looked foolish to the occupant of the window with the green shutters, and finally by curiosity at the many stories that circulate concerning this wealthy widow of a general, whose father has no wish to see her fortune bestowed on another husband, and this former mistress, according to certain rumours, of the colonel whose lodgings Lucien has inherited.[24] Soon he falls into the habit of spending hours at night strolling beneath Mme de Chasteller's windows, and she, without his knowing, for as long as he is there, watches the glow of his cigar in the darkness below. The setting and Lucien's nocturnal vigils, together with his increasingly deep respect for Mme de Chasteller, suggest a form of courtly romance. And certainly in so far as Mme de Chasteller represents an extreme form of the aristocratic spirit, the hint of mediaeval overtones is not irrelevant. Nor is it more than a hint.[25]

Mme de Chasteller, as we discover, is more truly an aristocrat and more profoundly in revolt against her age – in that she has no desire even to shock those she cannot respect – than Mathilde de la Mole, whose conscious re-enactment of mediaeval dramas is a form of nineteenth-century romanticism. She is unlike Mathilde also in that even her profound indignation at the Jacobins who have sought 'to shake the throne of the Bourbons' never 'troubles her heart for more than an instant'. Before she meets Lucien, her devotion to the cause of the exiled monarchy is the main object of her thoughts, and since other considerations fail to disturb her, she enjoys an 'imperturbable gaiety'. The tears she sheds are tears of pity at the spectacle, for example, of the sun-tanned flesh under the tattered dress of an old pauper in the street. In this respect, one might say that she is more like Mme de Rênal, to whom the language of love, until she meets

Julien, evokes the embraces of her husband and the advances of M. Valenod. Mme de Chasteller too has been profoundly un-affected, both by her marriage and her early bereavement. 'Her most marked characteristic', we are told, 'was a profound non-chalance. Beneath an air of complete seriousness, rendered more imposing by her beauty, her character was happy and even gay. Her greatest pleasure lay in her thoughts and dreams. One would have thought she paid no attention to the little things going on around her: but, on the contrary, not one escaped her; she could see very well what was happening and it was these trivial occurrences which nourished the reverie that others assumed was mere aloofness...' (ch. 15). One might say that she is an aristocrat in the sense that she knowingly does what she wants, like the very different but, in this one respect very similar Mme d'Hocquincourt, her future rival as far as Lucien is concerned, who is good-naturedly promiscuous, indifferent to her reputation and, with her admirably philosophical lover of the moment, very like the courtiers who, presumably, helped to set the tone in pre-Revolutionary Versailles.

The attractions of Mme de Chasteller, as contrasted with Mme d'Hocquincourt, are obvious, if only in so far as they constitute a poignant challenge to Lucien's pride. Pride too is what makes the most profoundly disturbing demands on the normally serene nature of Mme de Chasteller herself. As a model for Mme Jules Gaulthier to follow, Beyle has recommended *La vie de Marianne*. And in the circumstances which bring Mme de Chasteller and Lucien into conscious and compromising intimacy, we can follow, as in a novel or play by Marivaux, the kind of predictable, yet for the lovers themselves wholly un-predictable, chain-reaction of pride, humiliation, reassurance and gratitude that are entertaining only for those who are uninvolved.

If pride counts for a great deal in their relationship, as well as mutual attraction, it would be wrong, nonetheless, to argue as if their relationship could be explained in such conveniently simple terms. If it could, much of the first part of the novel would be merely an all too predictable *marivaudage*, reminiscent, that is, of the worst of Marivaux. Even as it is, the contest of wills between them goes on, I find, just a little too long and can weary those readers who ask in what direction, if any, not only the lovers are moving but also the novelist and the readers themselves. Certainly, anyone looking for an ending along the lines of Musset's *Il faut qu'une porte soit ouverte ou fermée*:

> *Le comte*.... You, my mistress? No, my wife.
> *La marquise*. Ah! Well, if you'd said that when you came in, there'd have been no need to argue...

is bound to feel cheated when he comes to the end of Part one. And it is the absence of any such dénouement that I had in mind when I said that a tragic or happy ending to the novel would have been almost certainly a betrayal of Beyle's inspiration and art. Marriage itself, as it happens, hardly occurs to the two lovers, even during the calm periods of unchaperoned truce they eventually spend together and of which the all too happy Lucien fails to take advantage in order to consolidate or advance his position. And the modern reader will certainly regret that Beyle doesn't tell us what sacrifices and obligations marriage would have entailed between the daughter of a wealthy nobleman and the son of a plebeian millionaire in the 1830s. Yet marriage itself would not have disposed of the problem posed by the story; for this is once again, rethought in an entirely new situation, the problem implicit in the novels and tales: namely, how can any happiness we pursue or simply know that we lack be anything other than a perpetual possibility? And how can even a semblance of satisfaction be achieved without our denying what we genuinely desire? Beyle does not resolve the problem by recommending to mankind in general the divine dissatisfaction which ensures ultimate salvation for Goethe's Faust. Like the greatest of the French Petrarchan poets, he believes that the realisation of desire can take place, miraculously, in the real world:

> Car en *mon corps*: mon Ame, tu revins,
> Sentant ses mains, mains celestement blanches,
> Avec leurs bras mortellement divins
> L'un coronner mon col, l'aultre mes hanches.
> (Maurice Scève, *Délie*, 367)

[For in *my body*, you came back my soul, feeling her hands, hands celestially white, with their arms mortally divine, one crown my neck, the other my hips.]

It is with the man or woman capable of experiencing the miraculous, that is, unable to forget or deny what he genuinely desires, that the novels of Beyle are concerned. And one might say that it is in this sense that Julien Sorel, Mme de Chasteller or Lucien Leuwen are, in their widely differing ways, humanly representative and at the same time exceptional.[26] Lucien and Mme de Chasteller are well matched – during their long conversations, they can agree easily on a *political* truce; they both agree to sacrifice to their friendship their former republican and legitimist sympathies – and because of their obvious suitability and the length at and detail in which the story of their turbulent, idyllic and unrelentingly chaste relationship unfolds, we may find that Beyle comes closer than in any novel to imagining how the ideal possibilities of mutual love might come to be fulfilled in reality.

The failure of the relationship is partly the fault of Lucien, who is alternatively first tactless and importunate in his advances and then unnecessarily submissive and respectful; though the clumsiness and frequent miseries of his courtship and his total lack of worldliness in these matters are, Beyle tells us, commensurate with the genuineness of his feelings:

Given the present state of good sense and somewhat elderly wisdom that characterises our nation in matters of the mind and spirit, I agree that we shall have to make an effort in order to understand the fearful struggles to which Lucien was the prey and not to laugh at them...
    (ch. 29)

His troubles are made worse by memories of the jibes of his cousin Ernest, who has told him that in his dealings with women, as in every other respect, Lucien is incapable of what Ernest calls 'success'. Yet the humiliations alternate with moments when both partners find that they can meet in pride, joy and peace of mind. After an exchange of letters, for example, ending in an imperious note from Mme de Chasteller indicating that the correspondence must promptly cease, they meet accidentally at the Serpierres' before there has been time for the note to be delivered. Mme de Chasteller feels that she has behaved both honourably and decisively in writing as she has and allows herself the pleasure of a last encounter with Lucien. They join Mme de Serpierre's daughters in an excursion to the cabaret in the woods outside Nancy which has already been the scene of some of the happiest and most carefree moments in the novel and afterwards, walking back to their carriages, Mme de Chasteller on Lucien's arm, find themselves more gladly and irrevocably involved than before.

Le chasseur vert, as the cabaret is called, is one of the titles Beyle had thought of giving the novel; and if it is the setting for some of the most idyllic moments in Beyle's fiction as a whole, it is all the more so for being wholly conceivable in reality. It has perhaps a modern equivalent in the *guinguettes* where on a summer afternoon and evening, friends and strangers dine, drink or dance together on the banks of the Garonne, the Loire and the Marne. Compare the beautiful wistful *unreality* of the Arcadian setting of *Le grand Meaulnes* or of Verlaine's evocations of an enchanted world, which were to haunt the end of the nineteenth century and inspire some of its most exquisite music. I described the opening of *Lucien Leuwen* as an 'overture' and the metaphor will perhaps not seem wholly pretentious when one thinks of the function served by music in Beyle's novel as well. There are many occasions when we may be reminded that his sense of comedy had been formed not only by Molière (as in the portrait of the Tartuffe-like Du Poirier) but by Mozart and Cimarosa.[27]

A number of episodes in the second half of the novel take place in M. Leuwen's box at the Opéra, while at the *Chasseur vert*, a German wind band, handsomely tipped by Lucien, plays extracts from *Don Giovanni* and *Figaro*. The plain enthusiastic Serpierre sisters, the troubled Mme de Chasteller and the love-sick Lucien forget themselves in their chaperoned, uncompromising and hence uninhibited freedom as they sit or dance beneath the trees. The music follows them as they walk back to their carriages and the reader may find that every detail of the episode, including whatever he likes to remember of Mozart, adds to his sense of what it is like to be Lucien and of the calm, deep and yet matter-of-fact reality of the scene. Only Tolstoy, among the authors I know, allows us to enter into the spirit of a festivity or a holiday as freely and unwistfully as Beyle in *Lucien Leuwen* – in the excursions and masquerades of the Rostov children in *War and Peace*, for example. And it is strange, while one is on the subject, why Jane Austen should so often associate such occasions with a menacing thundery atmosphere, wounded susceptibilities and the release of deadly instincts, as in the trip to Box Hill in *Emma* or to Sotherton in *Mansfield Park*. *Lucien Leuwen*, however, reminds us not only of the moments when, as in Jane Austen, we are thrown violently back onto ourselves but of those too when we are released from ourselves and leap forward, as it were, into a new and welcome sense of what we are and of our relation to others. Lucien's relationship with Mme de Chasteller 'comes to nothing' in one respect only: the memories of moments such as these give him an awareness, in the second half of the novel, that he would presumably have lacked otherwise, both of what he wants and emphatically doesn't want in any foreseeable future; and this is particularly evident in his dealings with the very different and distinctly *bourgeoise* Mme Grandet. Even the thought of Mme de Chasteller's supposed infidelity cannot alter or spoil the memories. The memories, in other words, are the form through which Mme de Chasteller exerts the purifying and strengthening influence that, in the few expressions that have survived of courtly or Platonic love that are an honest account of experience and not just specious flattery, can be seen as emanating from the object of adoration with a power greater than that of the lover's will.

One answer to the question to which I have claimed that Beyle repeatedly seeks an answer as a novelist (though it is not explicitly stated) seems to be that the realisation of the greatest conceivable happiness is, possibly by its very nature, a matter of astonished wonder at the unforeseen. Which does not mean that such happiness cannot be sought or even that it is possible *not* to seek it, with more or less success and corresponding assurance. Lucien's failure with Mme de Chasteller is a partial failure only, a failure to regain what he loses after their last meeting and to transform their relationship into what would presumably have had to be something else: marriage, for example, whatever that would have entailed. But Beyle also fails himself to see beyond the moment of perfect understanding between the two, and to pursue the story of the relationship to the point at which it would have been crucially affected by and itself affected Lucien's pursuit of a career compatible with his desire for a sense of purpose and the demands of his self-esteem. One can only imagine that if in Mme de Chasteller Beyle was showing us Mathilde Dembowski as he remembered her, and if the novel was a way of trying to satisfy in imagination the irrepressible hopes and curiosity thwarted by the failure of his own love affair, then, as a novelist, Beyle paid the price of owing so much to Mathilde for his sense of the possibilities of life; he could not imagine a life shared with her other than he had known or could at least persuade himself, recalling his happiest moments with her, that he had known in reality. 'You are only a *naturalist*', he told himself in a margin of the manuscript. 'You don't *choose* your models, but you always take as a model for *love* [in English in the manuscript] Métilde and Dominique...' [one of Beyle's own favourite names for himself.] Whatever the explanation, Mme de Chasteller, except when we are introduced directly into the privacy of her thoughts, is too shadowy a figure, her longing for calm and retirement is too much a simple *donnée* to be taken on trust, and the reader may find that she resembles too closely the Princesse de Clèves, another young widow tempted by a very eligible bachelor, in the novel Beyle had recommended four years earlier as a more worthy model for a modern novelist than the fashionable works of Sir Walter Scott. She resembles, that is, the Princess in her shrinking from anything that will disturb her 'repose' after the death of her mother and the Prince. In a way uncharacteristic of his practice as a whole, Beyle fails to give us as many essential details as the authoress of *La Princesse de Clèves* does concerning the childhood, upbringing and marriage of his heroine; to this extent she is less real and more enigmatic than her seventeenth-century predecessor. The first part of *Lucien Leuwen*, furthermore, ends ludicrously as the result of an improbable diabolical plot reminiscent of the one that brings about the dénouement of *Armance*. Beyle is unable to hit on a device as effective as that used in *Le rouge et le noir* for leaving the questions raised by the novel in effective abeyance, and resorts to comic melodrama. The Roller brothers and the Marquis de Sanréal vow that the plebeian outsider who has stolen the heart of the noblest lady in the town will have as many duels to fight as he now has enemies; and they are only dissuaded from executing this plan of semi-legal assassination by Dr Du Poirier, who knows how to outwit both the would-be assassins and their victim. Taking advantage of an attack of nerves, he confines Mme de Chasteller to her bed and then arranges for Lucien to be present when a howling blood-stained babe is brought out of her bedchamber by a servant he has bribed. Lucien asks for no explanations: this is clearly, he tells himself, the child of a rival and Mme de Chasteller is not as 'chaste' as he had foolishly thought. He returns to Paris without even asking for leave of absence and finds himself once again in the genial ironic presence of his father who, as usual, is interested to know what his son intends to do.

Lucien Leuwen, part two

In the first part of *Lucien Leuwen*, we are taken into a world of the past, alive still in the present but in conscious opposition to it and offering those who belong to that world the security of an inherited and an unearned superiority. After Lucien's return to Paris, we come back to what, even to the twentieth-century reader, and to a Frenchman in particular may seem like the modern world. Some of the political intrigues are extraordinarily reminiscent of what went on, notoriously, under the successive governments of the Third and Fourth Republics, though there is a more profound sense – of which I shall say more later – in which *Lucien Leuwen* is a comedy of our times, for it turns on a dilemma peculiar to an age which believes in the necessity of progress. The failure to resolve it can have grimly farcical consequences both in public and private life.

To say that the second part of the novel is a political comedy is to make a fairly obvious remark. It is less easy to find adequate terms to describe the kind of comedy it is and the point of view it presupposes. One difficulty is that almost no one in the novel is ever what he seems. Dissimulation and the playing of assumed rôles are as tireless and time-consuming an activity as in Shakespearean comedy, and for no one more than Lucien's father, who dominates the second part of the novel like an omnipotent, though more human and fallible Prospero.[28] Lucien could, if he chose, work, without any need for dissimulation, in his father's bank, but also with no purpose; he doesn't love money, the 'metal' itself, enough to pursue the career seriously. His father proposes instead that he accept the post of *maître des requêtes* in the Ministry of the Interior and with it responsibility for the correspondence of the minister himself, for whom M. Leuwen acts as a stockbroker using confidential information received on the ministerial telegraph. Only

'Think about this: how much do you feel that you have the strength to be a rogue, that is, to assist in the execution of some minor skulduggery, for there's been no question of shedding blood for the last four years...'

'Merely of stealing money', interrupted Lucien.

'*From the poor unfortunate people*!' M. Leuwen interrupted him in turn and affecting an air of contrition. 'Or rather, using it a little differently from the way the people would have used it otherwise', he added in the same tone of voice. 'But then, the people are really a little stupid and their deputies not quite as intelligent as they should be and more than a little concerned with their own interests...'

'So what do you want me to become?' asked Lucien with an air of ingenuousness.

'A rogue', replied his father. 'I mean a politician, a Martignac, I won't go so far as to say a Talleyrand. At your age and in your newspapers, that is what is known as being a rogue. In ten years time, you will realise that Colbert, Sully, Cardinal Richelieu, in fact anyone who has been a genuine politician, that is someone who has been able to *direct and control other men*, has raised himself at least to the level of roguery that I wish to see in you. Don't go and behave like N..., who was appointed secretary general of police and then, after a fortnight, resigned because he found the job too dirty.'

(ch. 38)

Resigning too is a matter of playing a rôle; a virtuous one, but ineffectual. M. Leuwen approves of those who find that there are limits to the skulduggery to which a man may go and mentions as an example the murder of a political prisoner a few years earlier by the police, on the pretext that he had sought to elude arrest, an incident that had helped to precipitate N...'s resignation and for refusing to condone which a prefect called C... was dismissed. The prefect, M. Leuwen's esteemed friend, had not been enough of a rogue; the secretary general was not ready to be a rogue at all. Does this mean that his decision was any less harmful in its consequences? As in *La chartreuse de Parme*, we discover as soon as we enter the Paris of the second half of *Lucien Leuwen* that appearances in politics are deceptive, whether or not they are deliberately assumed.

Beyle's irony about professions of virtue on the part of politicians has led many commentators to conclude that the novel was written in the mood of disillusionment and exasperation into which Beyle often and easily relapsed, and which he would sometimes express after the age of fifty by the letters S.F.C.D.T., *se foutre complètement de tout*; in other words, not give a damn for anything. This may be partly true, but it fails to take into account how volatile his temperament was and the tonic restorative effect on him of 'blackening a page', as he put it. The conversation from which I have just quoted is pursued with eager seriousness, all the more so in that both Lucien and his father have definite standards of behaviour, standards, moreover, which Beyle presents without any of the amusement or contempt with which Flaubert invites us to contemplate practically all of the political discussions in *L'éducation sentimentale*. M. Leuwen is serious in his preference that cruelty and injustice should be prevented as far as possible, and judges the government of the day accordingly; serious too in his probity about money. His fortune is based on the reputation of his banking house for honest dealing, and the independence, esteem and power he enjoys are a guarantee that his ethic is a practical one. He enjoys an immense advantage over the Minister of the Interior because it is the minister who is acting improperly (and knows it) in using state secrets to his private advantage on the stock exchange; though the King of France, we are told, does the same. M. Leuwen is merely, having received the information, acting as any other stockbroker would. The virtue he practises is its own reward and we may not be surprised to learn from a chance remark of Lucien's that his father is a personal friend of Jeremy Bentham. In politics, we are told, he looks forward to the day when justice, probity and prosperity will prevail in every sector of public life, but knows that it would be foolish to behave or expect his contemporaries to behave as if that day had arrived. This does not make him an enthusiastic partisan of the 'July monarchy'.

He had dined once or twice with the king shortly after the July revolt. It then had another name and Leuwen, whom it was difficult to deceive, had been one of the first to discern the hatred inspired by so pernicious an example. He had then seen clearly written in the august eyes: 'I am going to frighten the property holders and persuade them to believe that there is a war taking place between those who have something and those who have not.'

In order not to seem as stupid as the country deputies invited with him, Leuwen had made a few not too obvious jokes at the expense of this idea that nobody would express directly.

He feared for a short while that the small shopkeepers of Paris would find themselves compromised by being made to shed blood. He found the idea in bad taste, and without hesitation resigned the post of battalion commander in the National Guard to which he had been appointed with the support of the shopkeepers to whom he would lend, with a certain generosity, a few thousand franc notes from time to time and which they would even occasionally pay back later. He had also stopped accepting invitations to dinner from ministers, on the pretext that he found them boring.

The Comte de Beausobre, Minister of Foreign Affairs, would say to him, however, 'A man like you...' and pursue him with invitations. But Leuwen had resisted such adroit eloquence...

(ch. 60)

As a young man, we are told, he had fought in one or two campaigns in the Revolutionary wars and the name of the French Republic is now like that of 'a mistress one has loved and who since then has misbehaved.' 'Meanwhile', he believes, 'her hour has not yet struck.'

By the end of the novel, in fact well before then, Lucien has come to resemble his father in all these respects, and there is no question of his revolting against his father's standards. The standards are impressive, particularly from a hedonistic and utilitarian point of view, M. Leuwen is himself impressive because in observing them he is so exuberantly and with so much vitality to spare his own master, despite his small frame, delicate health and fear of exposure to cold, humidity and boring conversation. It is their inadequacy when observed with no regard to other standards that the novel finally reveals. And that M. Leuwen should have nothing better to which to devote his remarkable mental energies may explain why he seems throughout the novel, as Beyle puts it, 'a little mad'. To say that his standards are shown as inadequate, is not to say that, as far as Beyle is concerned, they are basically misconceived. And I find nothing in the novel or elsewhere to suggest that they are seen from any other standpoint than that of a middle-class liberal, 'a moderate supporter of the constitution of 1830', as Beyle puts it in one of his prefaces, contemptuous certainly of the king and the ministers who had betrayed the hopes of the July Revolution, but seeing no necessity for revolutionary social or economic changes to eliminate mere temporary abuses, and looking forward to eventual fulfilment of the promise of that dawn in which, for Beyle as for Wordsworth, it was 'bliss to be alive'.

The confidence and buoyancy of the comedy are due to the effective presence throughout the novel of these positive implied beliefs. Yet they do not provide a simple code of conduct in the present and they are necessarily (and even hearteningly) imprecise as far as the more distant future is concerned. Even M. Leuwen, for instance, is never deluded by the ardent tragic hopes which Conrad's Gould in *Nostromo* invests in the automatically humanising benefits, as Gould imagines them, of capitalist enterprise; or by the semi-religious Saint-Simonian cult of productivity against which Beyle had protested in his pamphlet of 1825. One of M. Leuwen's fears for his son is that he too might be taken for an ardent Saint-Simonian because of the deep gloom in which he has been plunged since leaving Mme de Chasteller, though it is obvious that this is not all that M. Leuwen fears in the spectacle of his son's real unhappiness; M. Leuwen's own dissembling with Lucien and his insistence that Lucien too should conceal *his* true feelings are evidence of how little mutual confidence there is between them, though they have so much in common and though Lucien has never so far questioned M. Leuwen's authority. M. Leuwen, we realise as the novel unfolds, cannot afford not to dissemble. Even his immense fortune, it turns out after his death, is based to an alarming degree on credit and on the personal confidence that he has been able to inspire. And Lucien, in winding up his father's affairs, has difficulty in saving his name and business from the scandal of bankruptcy.

It is obvious that M. Leuwen carries duplicity to an extreme, but then he is an unusually successful business man who, from any moral viewpoint, has earned the right to be known as the 'Talleyrand of the Stock Exchange'. And his success has not blinded him to the even greater need for duplicity on the part of many ordinary men who have been less successful and on whose confidence in himself his fortune is founded. We are never given to understand that he deludes himself that he has any other than a legal right to his fortune or that the morality he practises is anything other than a conventional one and a matter of personal convenience. Nor, of course, does his creator, who, in this respect, remains faithful to the precepts of Helvétius. In reading the novel we are never, as a consequence, made to feel that a natural order is being violated and, however menacing or despicable the behaviour of a number of the characters, never left with the sense of evil or sacrilege that are evoked in the presentation of the same society in *L'éducation sentimentale* or *Le père Goriot* and *La maison Nucingen*. For the same reason, presumably, Beyle shows no sign in the novel or his other writings of having shared the traumatic horror that Sartre has attributed to the bourgeoisie in general in 1831 (see page 117 above), during 'the moment of truth', as Sartre puts it, 'when the bourgeoisie for the first time knew itself for what it was'[29] – no longer the enlightened and successful representatives of general humanity but a class threatened in its very being by a lower order with an alien culture and morality. M. Sartre quotes as an example of this state of mind the article, which caused a sensation at the time, by Saint-Marc Girardin on 'the new barbarians'.[30] There is no evidence that Beyle shared either the mood or the opinions of the young journalist and he was more probably struck by the author's appeal to Christian charity in urging that the conditions of the alleged barbarians should be raised as soon as possible to those of the civilised middle classes. 'The function of this Saint-Marc Girardin', he wrote in a note to *Lucien Leuwen*, 'is to render somnolent the passions of the young who are alarming the power that subsidises *Le journal des débats*.' And he declares that he is too lazy to imitate his style.[31]

The violent suppression of the 'Republican' demonstrations in the Rue Transnonain in Paris and the second rising of the *canuts* of Lyon, followed by the bombardment of the city by the forces of the crown and the killing, wounding and imprisonment of hundreds of workers, are referred to several times in the novel, and without attributing to Lucien or his father the sense of frightened class-solidarity to which Sartre refers and which Beyle's younger contemporaries, Balzac and Mérimée, had both expressed in their different ways.[32] We are repeatedly shown the reactions of the upholders of the new established order, but it goes without saying that these are not those of the novelist himself. One has only to think of Colonel Filloteau, who disgusts Lucien after their first meeting by trying to impress him with his talk of 'loyalty to the king' and the need 'to repress the seditious'; of Mme Grandet, whom Lucien is unable to forgive for her disapproval of a public subscription for imprisoned *canuts* in transit to Paris in open carriages, many of them sick and wounded and without blankets or coats in the depth of winter; of Colonel Malher de Saint-Mégrin who tells his officers, loudly enough to be heard by his troops, to have no pity for the wretched weavers who have dared to form themselves into a trades union and that there are crosses to be won when they occupy the offending weavers' town; and of the absurd young prefect of Nancy, M. Fléron riding beside the troops with an enormous sabre:

The dull murmur of the lancers' talk turned into shouts of laughter from which the prefect endeavoured to escape by forcing his horse into a gallop. The laughter redoubled, like the cries of 'Look, he's going to fall off. No he's not. Yes he is.'

But the sub-prefect soon was avenged; hardly were the lancers obliged to make their way through the narrow dirty streets of N... when they were jeered at by the wives and children of the workmen stationed in the windows of the poor houses and by the workmen themselves, who from time to time appeared at the corners of the narrowest alleys. The shops could be heard rapidly closing their shutters everywhere.

At last the regiment emerged into the main shopping thoroughfare of the town; all the shops and stores were closed, there was not a head to be seen at any of the windows and a death-like silence reigned. They came to a long irregular square adorned by five or six stunted mulberry trees and divided along its entire length by a filthy gutter bearing all the sewage of the town; the water was blue because the gutter was also used as a drain for a number of dying factories.

The washing hung out to dry at the windows was horrifying in its wretchedness, tattered condition and dirtiness. The windows of the houses were dirty and small and a number of them, instead of glass, were covered with oiled paper on which handwriting could be seen. Everywhere was a vivid image of poverty which gripped one's heart, though not the hearts of those who were hoping to win a cross by distributing sabre blows among the inhabitants of this poor little town.

The colonel lined his regiment along the gutter as if they were on the battlefield. There the unfortunate lancers, overcome by thirst and fatigue, spent seven hours exposed to the burning August sun without food or drink. As we have mentioned, when the regiment arrived all the shops had closed and the estaminets most quickly of all.

'They've got us where they want us', one lancer said loudly.

'We look a right lot of fools', replied another.

'Keep your f...g observations to yourself', yelped some lieutenant or other who was a political moderate.[33]

Lucien noticed that all the officers with self-respect maintained a deep silence and a very serious air. 'So this is the enemy we have to fight', he reflected...

  (ch. 27)

Lucien's own reaction is not one of solidarity with the workers or one that tempts him to go in for zealous intervention on their behalf. It is rather one of compassionate and self-respecting chivalry. It is dishonourable, as he later explains, to 'cut down workers with one's sabre and become 'a hero of the rue Trans-nonain.' 'You can forgive the soldier who sees a Russian defending an enemy battery in the inhabitants of the home he is told to attack; but could you forgive me, an officer, who understands what is happening?' (ch. 49). These bitter reflections occur after he has himself been mobbed by an indignant crowd who have recognised him as an agent of the Ministry of the Interior, pelted him with mud, nearly thrown him into a river and told him that the mud on his face is the image of his character. It is an occasion on which Lucien might have been expected to behave in the way that M. Sartre sees as characteristic of his class during this phase of history. His reaction, however, is that of a proud individual. He is ready to brave the mob in order to find and fight the man who has jeered at the mud on his face, and he is thrown into the deepest humiliation afterwards at the thought that the insult is in many ways deserved and the mission he is engaged on is indeed dirty.

I have so far been speaking of Lucien and his creator as virtually indistinguishable, so far as what they most value is concerned, and the reader may agree that on the many occasions when he is invited by the novelist to feel contempt for Lucien, the invitation is a trap for the literal-minded and the very opposite of what it seems. He may agree too that he never feels that he is being entertained to an irony at Lucien's expense as unsparing and as indicative of incorrigible inadequacies as Balzac's at the expense of Eugène de Rastignac or Flaubert's at the expense of Frédéric Moreau. I would suggest that this is because Beyle neither knows, nor writes as if he knew, what a wisdom superior to Lucien's would entail. The story of Lucien is exploratory, in other words, in a way that those of Rastignac and Frédéric Moreau are not; it lacks the inevitability that in Balzac's novels is repeatedly made explicit and in *L'éducation sentimentale* is the constant point of Flaubert's ironic rhetoric; and it is perhaps for this reason that it takes place in an atmosphere less confined and oppressively picturesque than that in which lovers of Balzac or Flaubert feel at home and others, like myself, find claustrophobic. Beyle, of course, was a liberal with eighteenth-century Jacobin nostalgias, and a self-professed Utilitarian unable to abandon hope of progress towards a better world, whatever this would mean; and in this he differed from his two younger contemporaries. And the hope – certainly not sustained by a belief in the *inevitability* of progress; it is difficult to imagine that he would ever have been able to accept the metaphysical presuppositions of Marxism, as witness his somewhat scornful indifference to German historicism in general,[34] is apparent in the acute seriousness with which he dwells throughout the novel on the problem of what this young representative of the governing class is to make of his life and career. The problem is not only that of doing but of discovering what will be for the best, and Lucien's lack of positive political conviction, his inability to believe in Gauthier's egalitarianism, or in any natural right of his or any other class to privilege and power renders the problem not less but more pressing and acute. Throughout the novel and to a degree which is often maddening and bewildering to Lucien, his pride and honour are constantly at stake.

Lucien's first opportunity to take an active part in affairs of state, and to do so in a way consistent with honour, comes when the Minister of the Interior entrusts him with the task of silencing Kortis, the *agent provocateur* shot by a sentry whom he has tried to disarm in an all too successful attempt to test the sentry's loyalty, and now dying of his wound in a Paris hospital and the object of scandalous disclosures in the press. The episode, based on a number of exact details (including the name of the *agent provocateur*) of an incident that occurred in Lyon while the novel was being written, is a typical drama of the age of uncensored journalism, and Lucien's mission is the thankless one that many idealistic young men have had to shoulder, as the only alternative to resigning their posts: that of saving the reputation of the government he serves, at the risk of sacrificing his own. As at the time of the *affaire des fuites* in the 1950s, when the leaking of state secrets was divulged at such a time as to cause the utmost embarrassment to the allegedly responsible Prime Minister,[35] the scandal in *Lucien Leuwen* is complicated by the existence of more than one police force working independently. The branch of the police responsible directly to the king, and by which Kortis is paid, has tried to suppress the scandal by having Kortis silenced with an overdose of opium, but the outraged surgeon whom they have attempted to bribe has responded by knocking the police emissary down and making a scene throughout the entire hospital. It is this situation that the Ministry of the Interior, in the person of Lucien, has now to prevent from deteriorating further.

Lucien's handling of the ghastly affair turns out to be as successful as it possibly could be, not only as far as he is concerned but from the very different point of view of his anxious minister. Kortis dies in loyal and willing silence, the doctors in the hospital are placated, and no further crimes are broached or committed. The episode includes some of Beyle's most powerful and sustained dramatic writing: the unobtrusively symbolic description, for example, of the dark foul-smelling hospital ward into which affairs of state have led both Lucien and the dying man, who lies awake in the darkness while two male nurses sleep in their chairs with their feet stretched out on a lavatory seat.

Lucien looked at his watch. 'To think that in an hour, I shall be at the Opera', he thought...
    (chapter 45)

It brings home to us, moreover, how much matters of immense moment can turn on the tact, firmness and sense of timing of those whose job it is to persuade other men to follow their lead in dangerous situations. (Unlike the modern conventional liberal, Beyle had the utmost respect for the military virtues.) Lucien wins the confidence of the surgeons by assembling them and entreating them to ensure that the patient receives no treatment other than that which they agree together that he needs. And he reassures the dying man by speaking to him as a fellow-soldier, assuring him of his protection and pressing into his hand an advance on a pension for his wife ('The hand was burning; Lucien felt ill as he touched it'). Though it is a typical stroke on the part of the novelist that the suspicions of the dying man should be allayed finally when he realises that Lucien is the son of 'the rich banker Leuwen who keeps Mlle Des Brins of the Opera' and that if the son of such a man is involved in this affair, it is not because he is in need of money and is ready, as Kortis has been, to do almost anything to earn it. The confidence Lucien has been able to inspire has been due not only to his genuine comradely regard for Kortis and his determination that he should not be murdered in his bed, but to a reasonable calculation by both of the parties to the agreement that Kortis will hold his tongue. Lucien, to his surprise, feels happy as he brings the affair to a conclusion. '"I am sailing close to the public's contempt and to death", he repeated to himself a number of times, "but at least I've known how to steer my boat."'

The assurance Lucien acquires, however, is short-lived and though the episode has shown how it may be possible to make the best of a bad job in the world as it is, the sequel leaves us with no excuse for assuming that he has found a way of guaranteeing for the future a sense of his own usefulness compatible with his self-respect. 'Being a rogue', as his father puts it, and thus keeping out an even greater scoundrel may be more generally useful and personally satisfying than merely wishing that politicians and policemen were better men. But it is a gambler's choice. M. Leuwen has persuaded Lucien to embark on a game which is one both of skill and chance. How much of a rogue can one afford to be by one's own standards, so far as these can be distinguished from those of the public at large? It is by trial and error, and therefore often too late, that one finds out; which is what happens to Lucien on his next important mission: to ensure the election of the government's candidates to the Assembly at Champignier in the Cher and at Caen. Pamphlets written for this purpose fall off his coach as it passes in front of a Republican café, and Lucien and his companion are pelted with mud, some of which finds its way into Lucien's mouth. He escapes with the help of the local gendarmes, whose own amusement is plain, and he is then plunged into the most atrocious mortification he has known in the course of his recorded career.

Any anthology of French prose should include, among other extracts from Beyle's writing, the account in chapter 49 of the sequel, in which Lucien pours out his bitterness to his companion and friend (the impassive former Polytechnician, Coffe, whom he has rescued from a debtor's jail) and in which Lucien is then watched writhing 'like St Lawrence on his grill'. Technically, it is superior to those passages in *Armance* and *Le rouge et le noir* in which we are allowed into the privacy of the hero's thoughts, and it is as if Beyle had found yet another way of improving on what, twenty-five years earlier, he had seen as a weakness of the monologues in Corneille's *Cinna*.[36] The heroine of *Cinna*, he had written then, talks to herself with all the 'clarity and eloquence of a woman addressing a stranger'. Octave de Malibert and Julien Sorel may also strike us as unnaturally eloquent in their moments of solitude[37] and this may be why even the portrayal of Julien has seemed to certain readers like a series of notes for a novel, rather than an evocation of what can be taken without further thought as a living presence. It may also be why Beyle himself found that the tone of *Le rouge et le noir*, when he read it again, was insufficiently 'familiar' and 'too Roman'. The disadvantage of the clarity and eloquence of Corneille's poetry, he had written in 1811, is that they do not allow 'an *intimate knowledge* of the characters'. And intimate knowledge, he could have added, is not always the same as the awareness one has or believes that one has of one's true state and feelings. Hence the importance in this chapter of his friend's unpitying eye as he watches Lucien's silent anguish and reflects on his presumptuousness and endless talk as a student and on the suffering which he has brought on himself since then, when he could be enjoying his health, youth and riches:

'But I have to admit, and it's a *capital point in his favour*, that he said nothing I could possibly object to when he took a fancy to the idea of getting me out of prison...yes, and in order to turn me into an executioner's apprentice...The executioner himself is more worthy of esteem...It's out of sheer childishness and as a result of their usual stupidity that men can't stomach the thought of him. He is fulfilling a duty, a necessary duty...indispensable...Whereas, we! we who are on our way to every honour of which society disposes, we are on our way to commit a turpitude as well, a *harmful* turpitude. The common people, who are so often mistaken, as it happens are completely right this time. In this sumptuous English coach, they have found two scoundrels...and called them by that name. Well spoken', he laughed. 'Notice carefully, the crowd didn't say: "You, Leuwen are a scoundrel," but "You are *both* scoundrels!"'

And Coffe pondered this word for himself. At that instant, Lucien sighed aloud.

'There is he suffering from his own absurdity: he thinks he can enjoy the benefits of his office and the delicate susceptibility of the man of honour as well. How stupid can one be! If you're going to wear an embroidered coat, my friend, you'll need a thick skin, I can tell you...'

(ch. 49)

The contrast between Lucien's view of himself and that of his pitiless friend may leave many readers feeling more free to form their own impressions of his state of mind than if only the hero's own thoughts had been given, as in some of the principal monologues of *Le rouge et le noir*. And Coffe's own thoughts and example oblige us to ask what indeed Lucien thinks he is up to, playing a game he despises and weeping with anger and shame when his own contempt for it is expressed by others? Coffe is a mathematician, but, unlike Gauthier a misanthropic one, and he would gladly retire to a small property in the south of France if he could afford to do so. Why should Lucien then, with all his wealth, pursue success of a kind he despises in a world he so obviously loathes? As a rational man, Coffe fails to see the necessity.

For their different reasons, Lucien and Coffe continue on their mission with what might be described as zeal if it were inspired by devotion to the cause they serve; and their collaboration with the prefects of Champagnier and Caen is an extended study of administrative *moeurs* of a kind which the Consul of Civita Vecchia and former high-ranking member of the Imperial civil service was particularly well qualified to write. According to a note in the margin, Lucien's quarrels with the stubborn, vain and politically inept man of letters who has been appointed prefect of Caen is a reminiscence of the scenes in which Beyle had himself taken part during his mission in 1814 to assist in organising the defences of his native Grenoble. And he is able to show, as very few other novelists have been able or ready to, how every official decision, however impersonal it may seem, is the expression either of an all-too-human childishness or simple adult good sense. If some readers find the scenes in Caen lacking in credibility, it may be because they are unable to credit how often power is wielded by childish men. The mission to Caen fails because of the prefect's refusal to countenance Lucien's scheme to have a legitimist elected rather than the government candidate, who has no chance on his own of defeating the much-feared representative of the republican cause. The republican, a man with a reputation for integrity, sense and an unsparing tongue, wins the election, despite the battle of wits in which Lucien, Coffe and a retired general in government service engage against an adversary whom all three admire. And the strength, confidence and consequent generosity of the republican supporters become apparent when the General registers his own vote.

'Well, the time has come', said the General with evident emotion. He put on his uniform and left the observation room with deep emotion to register his vote. The crowd opened to allow him to walk the hundred yards to the door of the booth. The general went in and just as he approached the electoral officers, he was applauded by all the Republicans who were there.

'He's not a dull rogue, like the prefect', a voice was heard saying. 'He's only got his pension and salary and he's got a family to keep...'
(ch. 54)

Lucien is rewarded on his return to Paris for his part in the riot in which he was pelted with mud. As Mr Michael Wood puts it, 'the only decoration he receives is for a wound to his pride'. But his outrageous acting on his own initiative, together with the speed and efficiency with which he has begun to conduct his official affairs in Paris, have brought him into evident disfavour. An administrator himself, Beyle knows how the notorious inefficiency of bureaucracy can be the result of a constant evasion of responsibility by those who know that their promotion will be jeopardized far more by a single mistake than by the lack over the years of any success. Lucien's father decides to intervene in his career once again; having, on a caprice, had himself elected to the Assembly, he plots how to bring down the government of Lucien's ungrateful minister. He creates a party united merely by the common interests of its members: hungry and simple-minded deputies, new to Paris, whom M. Leuwen invites to dinner and treats as personal friends and who, at his instigation, vote as a single man, even on the most absurd motions. The government is repeatedly within a few votes of defeat, and the instability of successive administrations in the 1830s, as under the Third and Fourth Republics, is simultaneously parodied and explained. M. Leuwen's own speeches, which are his normal caustic conversation pursued from the tribune of the Assembly, become newspaper sensations. The king, unknown to his own ministers, anxiously consults him, and M. Leuwen finds himself close to becoming the most powerful public figure in France.

It is at this point that much which has been until now enigmatic in the novel suddenly becomes clear, as M. Leuwen confesses that, having acquired the power to influence the destiny of others, he is at a loss to find any purpose in his own. The confession is made during a conversation between himself, his wife, whom he adores, and Lucien:

'There is another disadvantage in my becoming a minister: I would be ruined. We are feeling more than ever the loss of my partner, poor Van Peters. We've been *caught out* by two bankruptcies in Amsterdam simply because I haven't been to Holland since we lost him. It's because of this accursed Assembly and this accursed Lucien, who is the principal cause of all our troubles. First of all, because he has robbed me of one half of your heart and secondly, because he ought to know the price of money and take charge of my bank for me. Have you ever heard of a man born rich who had no thought of doubling his fortune? He deserves to be poor. I was amused by his adventures at Caen. And if it hadn't been for the idiotic way his Minister received him when he came back, I would never have thought of making a *position* for myself in the Assembly. Now I've taken a fancy to this fashionable plaything. And I shall have a great deal more to do with the fall of the present government, if ever it does come down, than I ever had with its formation.

But there's one terrible objection to all this: *what can I take for myself?* If I take nothing substantial, the government I shall have helped to form will laugh at me in two months time and I shall be in a *ridiculous position*. Suppose I am appointed to the Treasury, the income will mean nothing to me and it will be too small an advantage, given my present position in the Assembly. If I make Lucien a prefect, whether he likes it or not, I shall provide whichever of my friends becomes Minister of the Interior with the means of throwing me into the mud by dismissing him from his post, which he is bound to after three months...

Mme Leuwen, who has 'the severe morality appropriate to a new despotism' of Napoleon's Empire, makes what, to almost any reader, may seem an obvious suggestion:

'Wouldn't it be nice just to do some good and take nothing?' asked Mme Leuwen.

'Our public would never believe it. M. de Lafayette played that rôle for forty years and was always on the point of being ridiculous. The French are too gangrened to understand such things. For three quarters of the inhabitants of Paris, M. de Lafayette would have been an admirable man if he had stolen four millions. If I refused a ministry and built up my business by spending a hundred thousand a year, at the same time investing in land, in order to show that I'm not ruining myself, people would think I was even more of a genius than they do already and I would maintain my superiority over the semi-crooks who are going to fight for a ministry...'

(M. Leuwen, as a banker and speculator on the stock exchange, understands the value of public confidence and the public mistrust of a man whose motive in seeking power is not obvious. Why is it, after all, that in so many societies the public tolerates not only the wealth but the ostentation of dictators and demagogues? M. Leuwen's answer tells us something about the nature of what we choose to call 'corruption' and the word 'gangrened' slips too easily off his tongue to suggest that he is himself censorious. We may be reminded here of the dying Kortis's calculating trust in Lucien when he hears that he is the 'son of the rich banker Leuwen, who keeps Mlle Des Brins of the Opera' and of the Republican crowd in Caen applauding the old general who has sold himself to the government because he has, after all, 'a family to keep'.) M. Leuwen turns to his son laughing:

'If you don't solve this problem for me: *what can I take for myself?* I shall look on you as a man with no imagination and I shall have nothing else to do but tell people I'm ill and go off to Italy for three months, so that they can form a new government without my help. I shall be forgotten when I return but at least I shan't be ridiculous...'
(ch. 60)

The responsibility then is his. Lucien is being asked to find a justification for his father's wealth and power.

Why, Coffe has wondered, should Lucien go to such immense

pains to put himself in a humiliating position which he could so easily afford to leave to others? The reason has been becoming increasingly obvious as Lucien's Parisian career proceeds and as he has come to realise how much his self-esteem and his desire to prove worthy of his advantages have been partly a desire to pay off a debt of his gratitude to his father, a debt, furthermore, of which his father's good natured jokes and advice have been a constant reminder. The burden of gratitude is so heavy as to outweigh other feelings:

'When I think of how much I owe my father! I am the motive for practically all he does; it's true that he wishes to conduct my life in his own way. But instead of ordering, he persuades me. I shall have to watch myself carefully.'

He had to confess to himself something of which he was profoundly and secretly ashamed. He had no tender feelings for his father at all. The thought of this tormented him and, during his 'black' days, caused him almost more bitterness and pain that having been, as he put it, 'betrayed by Mme de Chasteller'...

    (ch. 60)

M. Victor Brombert alone among critics of the novel I have read, seems to have been struck by the crucial importance of M. Leuwen's subtle domination of his son,[38] though even M. Brombert, I think, underestimates its significance; for his account of the novel tells us nothing of the ways in which the family drama turns on the wider political issues raised in the novel and nothing of the general human relevance of both, which makes *Lucien Leuwen* in its way a moral allegory. M. Leuwen's arranging of his son's affairs, his refusal to allow him a quarter of an hour's solitude between his work at the Ministry and his attendance at the Opera and his insistence that Lucien should go through all the throes, publicly at least, of a grand passion are not only obstacles to Lucien's search for an 'identity'; though they are certainly this and M. Brombert describes the process well. Lucien also has the task of enjoying the benefits of his father's life-long endeavours and skill:

'He is like all fathers, which I hadn't realised till now. With infinitely more wit and sentiment than any other, he none the less wishes to make me happy *according to his own ideas*...'

    (ch. 65)

The reasons for Beyle's choosing to make Lucien an only child
and hence the sole beneficiary of paternal solicitude become
clear when we reflect how common ('like all fathers') and
perhaps inescapable the dilemmas of both M. Leuwen and
Lucien are. As in Racine's *Britannicus*, the fact that there are no
other children brings to a focus the dangerous mutual dependence
of two generations and we are shown how the conduct of life
for both can be determined both by the parent's ambition for
the child and by the forms that gratitude and honour correspondingly assume:

> C'est le sincere aveu que je voulois vous faire.
> Voilà tous mes forfaits. En voicy le salaire.
> Du fruit de tant de soins à peine jouïssant,
> En avez-vous six mois paru reconnaissant,
> Que lassé d'un respect, qui vous gênoit peut-estre,
> Vous avez affecté de ne me plus connoistre...
> (acte IV, scène ii)

[This is the sincere confession I have been meaning to make to you.
These are all my crimes. This is my reward. You have hardly begun
to enjoy the fruit of all my cares on your behalf and you have shown
your gratitude for a mere six months and now you're weary of the
respect you owe me, and which probably embarrassed you anyway,
and you have pretended that you no longer recognise me...]

M. Leuwen's parental solicitude may be less terrifying than that
of Agrippine, but it is scarcely more conducive to complacency.
Few of us become millionaires or Roman empresses and not
all of us have children. But we care for the future and do all we
can to create a world fit for future generations, or at least we
encourage one another to think of this as the justification for
our lives and what is meant by 'responsibility'. How, other than
by not caring at all, as the prematurely aged Coffe seems able
to, or by postponing any concern for the future by acquiring more
wealth and power, as Lucien could if he were to work in his
father's bank (and how even then?) can we avoid that simultaneous
assumption and evasion of responsibility to which M. Leuwen
confesses in the end? Beyle does not tell us, though he makes
it clear that the magnitude of the problem is proportionate to
the power and opportunities that the older generation has made
available to the young. And he leaves us with the reminder that
the child too is responsible for his destiny and not necessarily

incapacitated by his elders – though he may be badly led astray –
from finding the road to happiness. The novel ends with Lucien
acting more responsibly than his father had in his final years,
more responsibly moreover by his father's standards and, by an
ironical reversal of rôles, with a readiness to sacrifice his own
inherited fortune to save his father's posthumous reputation.
The freedom he acquires in paying back what he has always
thought of as a debt of honour is felt in the elation of the journey
through Switzerland on his way to begin his diplomatic career.

Lucien Leuwen and the critic

Anyone who knows the novel at all will realise how little of
what is memorable in it an account as short as my own can
describe and how many different and no doubt better arguments
could be put forward for regarding it as an important novel.
I have said, for instance, nothing of M. Leuwen's fear that his
son should be taken for a Saint-Simonian or of the irony of this
being at a time when, under the editorship of Bazard and
Enfantin, the *Producteur* was taking a more obviously socialist
line than during Saint-Simon's own lifetime and inveighing
particularly against the scandal of inherited wealth. And I have
only referred in passing to the comedy of Lucien's affair with
the ambitious Diana-like Mme Grandet, anxiously stage-managed
by Lucien's father. The revelation that even Mme Grandet's
passion for him has been roused, not as Lucien at first believes,
by his own attractions but by the promise of a ministry for her
husband leads to Lucien's final recognition of how much he has
been 'serving the passions of another' and is a further blow to
his fortunately resilient pride. I have no wish to suggest that
these episodes are inferior to others to which I have referred at
greater length, though they are obviously of minor interest
compared with those which concern Lucien's relationship with
his father or Mme de Chasteller. The same can be said of his
portraits of the would-be overbearing Minister of the Interior,
perpetually obliged to remind himself that France is now a
Parliamentary democracy and of the Minister's beautiful pathetic
wife, Lucien's flirtation with whom is so much better observed
than the very similar relationship in *Une position sociale*. The latter
novel, fortunately left unfinished in 1833, gives us, incidentally,

in the principal character what Beyle himself in a note calls an 'idealised' self-portrait. It takes place in the French Embassy in Rome where the hero tries to seduce the wife of the ambassador, and Beyle thought at one stage of adapting it to form the third part of *Lucien Leuwen*. Having written the first two parts, however, he may probably have realised that it would require a great deal more than adaptation and that even the idealised self-portrait was a poor vehicle for the pursuit of interests such as those he had already brought to life in creating Lucien.

I have said that there are many reasons for regarding *Lucien Leuwen* as an important novel and this is obviously true of any important work of art; the greater the art, the more often and unexpectedly one is likely to find it relevant. It is equally obvious that any account of its importance is, by its nature, restricted and likely to restrict the significance of the work in the minds of those who cling to this one single interpretation, unless they are able at the same time to see its inadequacy as a description or definition of the art. My own argument follows on from and is intended as a qualification of two different interpretations of *Lucien Leuwen* that have been put forward in the past. And one of these is that the novel is interesting (like all Beyle's novels) because it contains a self-portrait and the personal reminiscences, transformed into a fictitious setting, of an uniquely interesting and complex man. The most persuasive version of this argument I know is M. Victor Brombert's in *Stendhal et le voie oblique*. I have no wish to contradict it and no special information that gives me the right to do so, but I have tried to show how much more there is both to Lucien's adventures and to the mind of his creator than is suggested by this view when it is taken on its own, and I have tried to draw attention to what I see as Beyle's concern with the human as well as Lucien's and his own condition.[39] In saying this, I am probably revealing my inability to share the view which tells us that though there is much literature can teach us about the laws of history and men's response to *particular* conditions, there is no human condition as such and it is a sentimental delusion to speak as if there were. One of the most influential advocates of this view had been George Lukács and it is against his interpretation of *Lucien Leuwen* that I have also found myself arguing here. For Lukács, Beyle is a romantic because he is 'unable to accept the fact that the heroic period of

the *bourgeoisie* has ended and that the "antediluvian colossi" –
to use a Marxian phrase, have 'perished for ever'. Beyle's
optimistic forecast of what the bourgeois society of the year
1880 would be like 'was a pure illusion, but because it was an
historically legitimate, basically progressive illusion, it could
become the source of his literary fertility...40 This account of
Beyle's allegiances and nostalgias is obviously apt, though
whether the hopes he placed in the future were an illusion is
more debatable. By 1880, in spite of the atrocities accompanying
the suppression of the Paris Commune, the franchise had been
extended, trades unions were recognised and a repetition of the
suppression of the *canuts* in the 1830s an impossibility. By the
time of the Second World War, partly as a result of the legislation
of the government of Léon Blum (as it happens, one of Beyle's
most enthusiastic commentators), the condition and education
of the poorer peasantry and working classes were almost certainly
superior to what they had been when Beyle wrote *Lucien Leuwen*.
I say this not because I am convinced that Lukács is wrong but
because it is by no means obvious that he is right, or that Beyle's
hopes for the future were misconceived.41 The hopes, moreover,
as expressed by either M. Leuwen or Beyle, are never more
than hopes and, unlike Lukács, Beyle was under no self-imposed
obligation to think of ultimate progress as inevitable. Beyle's
disillusion with his age is accordingly less intolerably at variance
with his ideas of what the world ought to be like than Lukács
claims. What Beyle is showing us, Lukács writes, in the destinies
of Julien, Lucien and Fabrice del Dongo, is 'the vileness, the
squalid loathesomeness of the whole epoch – an epoch in which
there is no longer room for the great, noble-minded descendants
of the heroic phase of *bourgeois* history, the age of the Revolution
and Napoleon. All Stendhal heroes save their mental and moral
integrity from the taint of their time by escaping from life.
Stendhal deliberately represents the death of Julien Sorel on the
scaffold as a form of suicide and Fabrice and Lucien withdraw
from life in a similar way, if less dramatically and with less
pathos...'42 Lucien, of course, doesn't 'withdraw from life...
and though Lukács's saying he does is unimportant in itself, it is
in keeping with a widely held view of Beyle's writings as a
whole and one which, as I have argued in talking of *Le rouge
et le noir*, superficially his art invites. Lukács fails or chooses

not to remember how much Lucien, like Julien, experiences welcome surprises as well as unwelcome ones in his dealings with his contemporaries of every class, and how sensitively Beyle's prose registers not only the immense changes of mood but also of the hero's whole *character* and outlook on life as an immediate result of these surprises. He overlooks, in other words, what other critics, who are either far more settled in their outlook or who have bad memories, refer to as Beyle's hopeless inconsistency. (Take, as an example of this inconsistency, the superb account in chapter 3 of Lucien's arrival in Nancy.) It is unfortunately common for critics to write of Beyle either as if he were inconsistent to the point of buffoonery or as if the freedom with which he can convey disgust at his contemporaries were like a final defiant slamming of the door on them followed by contemptuous contemplation from a superior vantage point of all except those who share the same disgust, suffer intolerably and long to escape as well.[43] This is not the reaction of the sympathetically portrayed General Fari as he makes his way through the crowd to register his vote in the election he has helped unsuccessfully to rig. Nor is it that of the crowd itself, which is able to forgive him for selling himself since it knows that he needs the money. It *is* the attitude of Flaubert, and the point of his irony throughout much of *L'éducation sentimentale*, and it is expressed with painful directness on one of the few occasions when he drops his rhetorical irony and recalls the horrors of 1848:

...and in spite of the victory [of the forces of law and order], equality (as if to chastise its defenders and deride its enemies) was made triumphantly manifest, an equality of stupid brutes, a common level of sanguinary turpitudes; for the fanaticism of self-interest was balanced against the delirium of need, the aristocracy gave vent to all the fury of the lowest scum...Public reason was shaken as after one of the great natural catastrophes. And intelligent men became imbeciles for the rest of their lives...

(part 3, ch. 1)

It is also the attitude of Balzac, as Lukács himself admiringly describes it, in *La maison Nucingen*. (M. Bardèche as well in his chapter on *Lucien Leuwen*. The right-wing M. Bardèche and Lukács make the same comparison and draw the same conclusions.) And because Balzac, as a conservative catholic, was even more contemptuous of his age than Beyle, it makes him for Lukács the greater realist of the two. Lukács praises the portrayal of M. Leuwen père, for example, 'the embodiment of a superior spirit and superior culture...' and a 'very lifelike transposition of the pre-revolutionary traits of the Enlightenment into the world of the July monarchy. But however delicately portrayed and lifelike the figure is, Leuwen is an exception among capitalists and hence greatly inferior to Nucingen as a type...' What Balzac shows in *Le père Goriot* and *La maison Nucingen* 'is how the rise of capitalism to the undisputed domination of society carries the human and moral degradation and debasement of men into the innermost depths of their hearts'.[44]

A comparison of the biographies of the principal Parisian bankers from 1810 to 1835 may well show that Nucingen was in fact the prototype of them all; though among the exceptions in this case would be not only Leuwen but the politician and banker Laffitte, whom commentators have seen as a model in some respects for the portrait of Leuwen himself. Though, even if in our ignorance, we may have to concede that Nucingen may have been the typical capitalist of his time (and we have only Lukács's word for it), M. Leuwen has a representativeness that makes him a more ominous as well as a more sympathetic figure than Balzac's monster, and this whether or not we know anything about the France of the 1830s and whether we think of him as a successful man of the world, as a politician or as being 'like all fathers'.

La vie de Henry Brulard

Well Moore, what are you thinking about now?
I've been thinking about memory, because of what Russell says in the *Outline of Philosophy*.
What is it that you're thinking of particularly?
Well, the whole problem of memory hadn't struck me before. You see, I want to say that you have an immediate knowledge of some things you remember.
Yes, and does Russell deny that?
Yes, he denies that. He says that memory is entirely a matter of inductive consideration from the fact that you remember. He says that it's merely a matter of probability, and he makes what I consider is the fundamental mistake of supposing that when we say that a

person remembers so-and-so, we are talking merely of his present state, do you see, and not also saying that the thing did happen...

> (From a broadcast conversation between G. E. Moore and G. A. Paul, 15 May 1957.)

Beyle's own father is a dominating presence in *La vie de Henry Brulard*, though, like Mathilde Dembowski in *Souvenirs d'égotisme*, largely an invisible one, as far as the reader is concerned. Practically all we are told of the relations between father and son is that they failed to understand one another. Most of Beyle's recollections of his childhood and youth after the death of his mother are consequently a record of years of loneliness in the enforced company of the family circle, which because of his father's royalist and religious allegiances, lived in near isolation in the fortunately peaceful and law-abiding Grenoble of the 1790s, untouched by Civil War or Terror. Beyle left home at the age of sixteen a few days before the 18 Brumaire:

What I am going to say is not very pleasant. When the exact time for my departure arrived, my father received my farewells in the municipal gardens beneath the windows facing the Rue Montorge.

He was crying a little. The only impression his tears made on me was that I found them very ugly to behold. If the reader feels horrified by my reaction, will he deign to remember the hundreds of compulsory walks I was forced to take *for my own pleasure*? It was this hypocrisy that irritated me most and which has led me since to execrate this particular vice...

(ch. 35)

There are few similarities between Chérubin Beyle and the fictitious François Leuwen and the astonishing feat of imagination that went into the creation of the latter shows, among other things, how much Beyle had learned of what fathers are capable of after he had himself left home. Yet neither Lucien nor Beyle are able to feel 'tenderness' for their fathers; both adore their mothers who, none the less, are never shown as seeking to influence their lives; and both have fathers who in their very different ways are far more mercenary than their sons and who seek to make them happy 'according to their own ideas'. The bleak northern valley of the Alps in which Grenoble stands and the even more cheerless Paris that Beyle discovered when he first left home (and in which the absence of mountains made him physically ill) are the background to *La vie de Henry Brulard* and Grenoble is associated with his father who was to become its deputy mayor under the Restoration. His mother's family was originally from Provence and, he liked to think, descended from an Italian who had sought refuge in France after committing a crime of passion. *Henry Brulard* ends with Beyle crossing the St Bernard pass to join his regiment in Italy in the June of 1800 and with the discovery of the southern slopes of the Alps, the Lombard plain and his beloved Milan. The same journey is described briefly in the last chapter of *Lucien Leuwen*; like the young Beyle, Lucien is overjoyed to find himself passing through the country of St Preux and Julie Wolmar in *La nouvelle Héloïse*.

In *Henry Brulard* there is an unmistakeable desire on Beyle's part to pay posthumous justice to the father against whom he had rebelled as a child and railed as a young man in Paris for depriving him for long periods of his personal allowance. And the desire is apparent in the plainness with which the facts of the relationship are stated and in the absence of any self-exoneration on the part of the adult for his hostility as a child. We are given only the reasons he had as a child for this hostility: the fact, for example, that he was never allowed to play with other children of his own age. And the reader is repeatedly told that he may well be shocked to learn of the depth of his animosities. Beyle emulates, in other words, as in all his autobiographical writings, the freedom from either self-exoneration or self-condemnation, or as he puts it himself, the simple 'truthfulness' of the *Life* of Benvenuto Cellini; though without Cellini's very real egotism, the egotism that makes him not only the most but almost the only interesting personality in his book. Chérubin Beyle is described briefly but unforgettably: an 'arch-Dauphinois' constantly preoccupied with the buying and selling of land, 'excessively wrinkled and ugly, awkward and silent in the company of women and yet needing them', a quality which enabled him to 'understand *La nouvelle Héloïse* and Rousseau's other writings of which he would talk with adoration while cursing him for his impiety, for the death of my mother had thrown him into the extremes of the most absurd devoutness...' (ch. 7). The last trait is in revealing contradiction with what we have been told of his acquisitiveness and incapacity for 'noble folly' and we may not be surprised that as deputy mayor of Grenoble, he ruined himself in the legitimist cause.

We are given *only* the salient facts of the relationship between Beyle and his father in *Henry Brulard*. There is no imaginative exploration of the kind we have in *Lucien Leuwen* of all that such a relationship might involve and determine and it is as if the writing of the novel had left Beyle more sure of his own feelings in the matter and with the moral detachment of a man who has done his utmost to know the truth about others as well as himself. But the author's truthfulness in *Henry Brulard* cannot simply be taken on trust. Beyle himself confesses to his poor memory for facts and dates as opposed to feelings, and Stendhalian scholars such as Arbelet, Chuquet and Henri Martineau have devoted much research to checking the most innocent details of Beyle's autobiographical narrative.[45] The first performance that Beyle ever heard of an opera by Cimarosa seems to have taken place, for example, not at Ivrea, as he tells us, but at Novara (though he may well be right in telling us that one of the actresses had a front tooth missing) and it is highly improbable that he read Shakespeare 'continually from 1796 to 1799'.

However, the worst that scholars have discovered of Beyle's inaccuracies suggest that his memory was not so much poor as erratic and, as M. Ernest Abravanel has recently argued, on the evidence that we have, often astonishingly good;[46] particularly Beyle's visual memory. I have therefore followed the usual practice in the preceding chapters of relying on the testimony of the memoirs in my own account of Beyle's childhood and youth; though I would not have done this if I had been concerned with strict chronology, as Beyle's memory for dates was obviously wild. And I find myself agreeing with M. Abravanel that 'Henry Brulard' is a portrait of the child Beyle was, rather than of the ageing author forty years later recreating the child in his own image.[47]

In intention at least, G. E. Moore, in the dialogue I have quoted as an epigraph, sees the 'immediate knowledge' of the past implied by the word 'memory' as a necessary presupposition, Russell's attempted refutation of which is untenable even in its own terms. The desire to achieve and be sure of having achieved such knowledge is something of which Beyle constantly tells his readers and is apparent in the gladness with which he will seize on remembered details with no possible interest for anyone other than himself, unless incidentally, as an example of how memory is bound to operate if it operates at all:

> But the reader, if ever there is some one to read these puerilities, will soon realise that all my attempts to say *why*, all my explanations may be errors. I have only some very clear images, all my explanations are those that occur to me, as I write this, forty-five years later...
> (ch. 5)
> I can still see myself in the Municipal Library listening to my grandfather in the main hall which is full of people and to me seems immense. But why all these people? On what occasion? The image won't tell me. It is only an image...
> (ch. 5)
> I see myself going on an errand for my father to Allier's bookshop in the Place Saint-André with fifty francs to buy Fourcroy's manual of chemistry which gave him his passion for agriculture. I understand very well how this taste developed. He could only walk freely in his property at Claix.
> But then, wasn't all this caused by his love affair with Aunt Séraphie, if ever there was an affair? I can't see the actual shape of events [*la physionomie des choses*]. My only memory is that of the child...
> (ch. 17)

Professor Francesco Orlando has pointed out the contrast between this purported knowledge of the past and that of Rousseau in the *Confessions* and Chateaubriand in *Les mémoires d'outre-tombe*,[48] in both of which the evenly eloquent narration and the omniscient eye of the narrator are made possible by a freedom from any over-riding concern with the *difficulties* of reliving the past. And Professor Orlando compares Rousseau's minor confession, as far as he is himself concerned, that

> ...if I happen to have employed some incidental ornament, I have done so only to fill a void occasioned by some failure of memory on my part...[49]

with Beyle's

> The great difficulty of writing these memoirs is that of having and writing only those recollections that are those of the period I have succeeded in gripping hold of by the hair...
> (ch. 10)

To the names of Chateaubriand and Rousseau, Professor Orlando could, I think, have added that of Marcel Proust, and one of the reasons for recommending *Henry Brulard* to almost any reader and not merely those who wish to know about Beyle's childhood is that it offers an alternative to what many have come to think of as the truth and finality of Proust's thoughts on what a genuine reliving of the past is like, and to the instances of it he offers in his novel. Admirers of Proust tend at times, I think, to forget that *A la recherche du temps perdu* is a novel, not only when we are learning of the adventures of Swann, Charlus and Albertine but in the passages in which the revelation of an unsought memory gives him sudden access to the past. The famous instance of the madeleine dipped in a cup of tea and awakening the sudden poignant realisation that this has happened before, whatever *this* may be, derives no doubt from Proust's experience, but not the beautifully written sequel which plunges us into the world of the novel with something resembling total recall (*Pléïade* edition, vol. 1, p. 47). Proust has described his wrestling with the elusive memory before this revelation[50] and, significantly, in the following terms:

Grave uncertainty whenever the mind feels that it is being overtaken by itself; when it, the seeker, is at the same time the obscure country in which it must search and in which all its baggage and equipment are useless. Seek? Not only seek: create as well. It is confronted by what is not yet what it alone can make real and then bring into its own light...
    (*Pléïade*, vol. 1, p. 45)

Later, when he revisits the little town of his childhood, we learn how different it is from what he had remembered of it earlier (vol. 3, pp. 691–3). And this prepares us for the meditation in which Proust defines that realm which is neither past nor present but 'outside time' and which is that of 'beauty', 'art' and 'reality' itself. 'The true paradises', Proust tells us in a mood of paradoxically exultant reassurance, 'are the paradises that one has lost' (vol. 3, pp. 869–75).[51]

To 'create' in Proust's sense of the word is for Beyle, a distraction, though a tempting one:

No doubt I am enjoying immensely writing as I have been for an hour and seeking to depict *just as they were* my sensations at the time of the arrival of Mlle Kubly, [the actress]. But who the devil will have the time and energy to sink to the bottom of all this, to read this excessive quantity of 'I's and 'me's'? Even I find that it *stinks*. This is the main disadvantage of this kind of book and, moreover, I'm unable to add a little savour by spreading on to it the sauce of charlatanism. And dare I add, as Rousseau does in his *Confessions*...

(ch. 25)

and he does not abandon, as the narrator of Proust's novel seems able to, his 'search' for the past as it was. Hence, presumably, his continual precautions against common tricks of memory such as the following:

I was very adventurous and consequently had two accidents which my grandfather would relate with terror and regret. Near the rock by the Porte de France, I stuck a pointed stick into a mule which had had the impudence to plant its hoofs into my chest and knock me down. 'A little more and he'd have been killed', my grandfather would say.

I have an impression of the event but probably it isn't a direct memory, only a memory of the image I formed of it long ago when I was first told about what had happened...

(ch. 5)

The philosophical work which had influenced Beyle's ideas of the nature of memory more probably than any other is Tracy's *Eléments d'idéologie*, in which the accuracy of memory is seen as the only possible guarantee against errors of judgment, even in logic, as Tracy defines it.[52] And Beyle's journal and letters to his sister Pauline are full of exhortations to remember the past in order to judge correctly in the present. In *Henry Brulard*, memory is referred to, particularly in the opening chapters, as a means to self-knowledge. 'What have I been?' and 'What am I?' are clearly for Beyle two ways of asking the same question. Yet 'what eye can see itself?' (ch. 1). The questions which Beyle feels at a loss to answer are: 'Was my character a melancholy one?' 'Was I a man of wit and intelligence?' 'Did I have a talent for anything?' Self-knowledge as a means to self-perfection is in any case an ambition he had abandoned years before.[53] Hence his inability to reply to Albarthe de Rubempré's accusation, as he saw it, that Julien Sorel was a self-portrait.[54] *La vie de Henry Brulard* is therefore not a moral evaluation nor a psychological analysis of the author; that is an exercise for the reader to perform. The self that Beyle knows or believes he can know is known only in so far as he is able to relive what he has seen, heard and desired in the past. On a number of occasions, he will tell us that he is the same now as when he was a child. And the fact of memory presupposes that identity of awareness, that 'immediate knowledge', as Moore puts it, 'of some things you remember'.

There are no doubt ontological and epistemological implications of these assumptions that it would be fascinating to pursue. Beyle himself does not pursue them, though he takes us some of the way towards their discovery and with a care and intensity of purpose that arise from his characteristic need to be 'clear. If I am not clear, *my whole world* is annihilated.' *Henry Brulard* might have been a longer and more profound work than it is. But on 26 March 1836, he received the news of his leave of absence from Civita Vecchia, which was to last more than two years and enable him to settle in Paris and travel throughout France. His pleasure and excitement were too keen for him to continue. The manuscript of *Henry Brulard* ends in disjointed notes. And having evoked the joys of arriving in Italy, he himself a few weeks later took the boat to Marseille.

7

La chartreuse de Parme

Le rose et le vert and Les chroniques italiennes

Beyle's leave of absence from the early summer of 1836 until the August of 1839 was to be the last period of intense activity before the first of the serious heart attacks and the onset of the crippling gout that were to affect him during the last years of his life. During his absence from Civita Vecchia he travelled through France, Savoy, Switzerland and northern Spain and wrote continuously, in the way he most enjoyed, in the bed-chambers of unfamiliar inns, sometimes after ordering up a bottle of champagne, or in an 'attic' in Paris off the Boulevard des Capucines, where in seven weeks during the winter of 1838, he was to dictate the whole of *La chartreuse de Parme*. The period was also one in which he wrote and published the *Mémoires d'un touriste*, tried again unsuccessfully to complete a life of Napoleon, began to publish his *Chroniques italiennes* in *La revue des deux mondes* and completed nine chapters of one of the best of his unfinished novels, a new version of *Mina de Vanghel*.

Like *Mina de Vanghel*, *Le rose et le vert* is the story of a wealthy heiress from Königsberg who travels to France in search of civilisation, and a lover or husband who will neither bore nor disgust her like her suitors at home. It is Beyle's version of the international theme which Henry James was to explore in *The Portrait of a Lady* and other stories; and Mina has in common with James's American heroines candour and independence as well as a willingness to admire and be carried away by whatever she may find in her promised land which make her the most exacting as well as intrepid of judges. It is not Beyle's first attempt to show his contemporaries how they seem through foreign eyes: there is the American visitor, for instance, in the dialogue on *France in 1821*[1] and the incorrigible German scholar in chapter 48 of *Lucien Leuwen*, holding forth on the origins of the mass in defiance both of French piety and French irony, both of which he counters with well-documented facts. But it is Beyle's most serious and sustained attempt to write in a way which, if it anticipates James, has a distant precedent as well in Montesquieu's *Lettres persanes*. And it was also an opportunity to write about a country in which he had lived as a public administrator for several years, in which he had fallen both happily and unhappily in love and some of whose ways of setting out on 'the hunt for happiness' he had always admired, particularly in so far as the Germans, like the Italians, were free from the French dread of social ridicule.

None the less, the story moves slowly, all the more so in that Mina is almost at once disappointed, after what she has been led to expect from the plays of Marivaux, by what she finds in post-Revolutionary France: the very ungallant talk among business-men and aspiring academicians who are afraid to utter a personal opinion, the amusement, such as it is, afforded by the intrigues of a Jesuit who tries to convert her, and the self-doubts of the decent young aristocrat, who is a less profoundly disturbed (and potentially more interesting) version of the hero of *Armance*. Much of the dialogue too is, for Beyle, uncharacteristically sententious: an opportunity to comment explicitly on *mores* rather than bringing them immediately to life. Yet if the novel moves slowly, it is by comparison chiefly with Beyle's other fiction and its weight is partly that of thought and reflection on two social worlds he had known at first hand. It is this, in fact, which makes it seem like the beginnings of a far more rewarding work than the superficially more gripping *Chroniques italiennes*.

The first of the stories usually collected under this title is *Vanina Vanini* of 1829, a work entirely of Beyle's own invention. *Vittoria Accoramboni, Les Cenci* and *La duchesse de Palliano* are taken directly from his collection of Italian manuscripts, now in the Bibliothèque Nationale, and are remarkable chiefly for their fidelity to the original sixteenth-century texts; to say which is to comment on the sensitiveness of his prose and the unobtrusiveness of his own personality. He lacks, for instance, the cultivated simplicity and terseness of his friend Mérimée, which, for the modern reader, far from putting him *en rapport* with the primitive passions of his Spanish or Corsican heroes, merely gives to his stories their now overwhelmingly obvious nineteenth-century literary flavour. These three more or less direct translations are noteworthy also for the reflections which precede them and in particular those in *Les Cenci* on Don Juan, which form an admirable rider to chapter 59 of *De l'amour*. The character of Don Juan, Beyle argues, is a product of Christian civilisation, as can be seen in the case of the incestuous Francesco Cenci, who sought to assert his individuality by flouting the common Christian morality of his day. Beyle adds almost nothing otherwise to his original sources and it is only in *l'Abbesse de Castro* and the stories he planned for a second series, to be published in *La revue des deux mondes*, that he uses the Italian manuscripts as a point of departure for a story of his own; also, of course, in *La chartreuse de Parme*, though the connection here between the novel and the seventeenth-century text from which it derives is as tenuous as between *Le rouge et le noir* and the story of Antoine Berthet.[2]

L'Abbesse de Castro was Beyle's opportunity to show what he could make, as an imaginative novelist, of the authentic chroniclers of an age he admired; that it is even less superficially gripping than the stories he had merely translated and edited suggests that his understanding of sixteenth-century Italy may have been less real and imaginative than he would have liked to believe. The world of *La chartreuse de Parme*, in which he had taken a chronicle of the sixteenth century and placed it in a nineteenth-century setting, is obviously one in which he was more at home, and *L'Abbesse de Castro* is a failure if one compares it with either *La chartreuse* itself or Manzoni's *I promessi sposi*, which has the same violent lawless setting as the former and similar dramatic contrasts between Christian virtue and ferocious lust and cruelty. It is true, of course, that the innocence of Manzoni's lovers, the saintly heroism of Don Cristoforo and the barbarity of the Innominato are so obvious as to make the book eminently suitable as a school classic. When I told an Italian lady once how much I admired it, she told me that she found its morality 'too tidy'. Yet it is the depth of Manzoni's veneration for a

Don Cristoforo and of his feeling for the moral and civil law – it is not only in his technique as a historical novelist that he resembles Walter Scott – that makes this seventeenth-century 'chronicle' read like a moral allegory and hence an account of Manzoni's own world.[3] In *L'Abbesse de Castro*, the agnostic Beyle has no such deep sympathetic involvement with either the peace-loving Jules Branciforte, forced into the life of a brigand and mercenary, or with the woman he loves, Hélène de Campireali, 'the long degeneration of whose soul' after their enforced separation the novel describes. There are many effectively sinister touches: the glimpses we are given, for instance, of Hélène's clandestine lover, the local bishop, after she has been made Abbess:

Since their first rendez-vous in November, he had continued to visit the convent more or less regularly every week. A slight air of triumph and silliness about him on these occasions was noticed by all who saw him and this gave him the privilege of outraging the proud character of the young Abbess. On Easter Monday, as on a number of other days, she treated him as if he were the most abject of men and addressed him in a way that the poorest labourer employed by the convent would never have borne. In spite of which, a few days later, she conveyed a sign to him that brought him without fail to the chapel door. She had sent for him to tell him she was pregnant. On hearing which, according to the report of their trial, the handsome young bishop became pale with horror and altogether *stupid with fear*...

    (ch. 6)

Effects such as these belie, however, the author's claim in the opening pages to be showing us customs 'marvellously suited to the creation of men worthy of that name' and that 'produced the Raphaels, Giorgiones, Titians, Correggios'. Not surprisingly, Augustin-Thierry, in his book on the Princess Belgiojoso, who kept the embalmed corpse of her lover and secretary in a cupboard in her villa, regrets that Stendhal had not lived to hear the tale and feels sure that in a novel like *L'Abbesse de Castro*, he would have succeeded somehow in fitting it in.[4] The novel seems to fall, in fact, between the heroic drama Beyle seems to have wanted to write and the morbidity that was to be expressed uninhibitedly in the fiction of writers like Gautier and Poe.

La chartreuse de Parme presents us with an Italy very different from that which is exalted at the beginning of *L'Abbesse de Castro*:

During the middle ages, the republican citizens of Lombardy had given proof of a bravery equal to that of the French and had earned the distinction of seeing their city rased to the ground by the Emperors of Germany. Since becoming *faithful subjects*, their principal concern had been the printing of sonnets on little handkerchiefs of rose coloured taffeta whenever the marriage took place of a girl belonging to some rich or noble family. Two or three years after this great event in her life, the same girl would choose a *cavaliere servente* and sometimes the name of the *sigisbeo* chosen by the husband's family occupied an honourable place in the marriage contract. It was a far cry from these effeminate customs to the profound emotions aroused by the unexpected arrival of the French army. Soon there came into being new and passionate ways. An entire people realised, on the 15th of May 1796 that everything it had respected till then was supremely ridiculous and sometimes odious...

The natural voluptuousness of the countries of the south had once reigned in the courts of the Visconti and Sforze, those famous dukes of Milan. But since 1635, when the Spaniards had taken possession of the Milanese and assumed the character of proud, taciturn and suspicious masters living in constant fear of revolt, gaiety had fled. The people had learned to imitate its masters and were far more concerned to avenge the least insult with a dagger than to enjoy the present moment...

(ch. 1)

After the fall of Napoleon, the effeminate ways return, together with the morbid vanity which is the enemy of voluptuous gaiety, and the novel shows us what it is like to live in such a society when one has known and acquired the habits of a different way of life.

Fabrice and Clélia

'...and in this beautiful country, the only thing to do is to make love; the other pleasures of the soul encounter obstacles and constraints; in so far as one feels a citizen of the country, one will die poisoned by melancholy.'

Rome, Naples et Florence en 1817 (17.11.1816)

Beyle's attitude to the way of life which his principal characters are compelled to lead has often, I believe, been misunderstood, and the fault may well lie with his first publisher, Ambroise

Dupont, who miscalculated what would go into two volumes, objected to providing an absurdly short third volume and, as Beyle put it, 'sabred' and 'strangled' the end of his manuscript, making him compress into a few pages what presumably was a far more detailed and circumstantial version of the novel we now possess.[5] We can only guess what the original ending was like, though we know that Beyle thought of expanding it even further. But we can assume from the title of the novel that it included the events leading to Fabrice del Dongo's retirement from the world and that it was at least as obviously a tragic ending as the disconcertingly abrupt ending we know.

It will probably be generally agreed, however, that the overall effect of *La chartreuse* is not tragic; even though its dominating personality, Gina Sanseverina, suffers agonies of yearning for her nephew and both shame and despair at the thought that he can never be hers; even too though she, Fabrice and Clélia Conti die heart-broken at the end. Beyle told Balzac that he was exaggerating the merits of the novel by comparing Gina with Racine's Phèdre and it is true that we never enter into Gina's consciousness with the same horrifying completeness of immersion with which we enter that of Racine's heroine. The novel distracts us constantly with its swiftly unfolding intrigue and its varying degrees of seriousness and high spirited farce. Even the melancholy which underlies so much of the novel has a full-bodied energy of the kind a musician might convey by deep sustained chords on unmuted strings. Critics are fond of describing it as 'operatic'. And if the ending is tragic, it is tragic in the sense in which D. H. Lawrence uses the word in a letter from Lake Garda in October 1912:

I hate England and its hopelessness. I hate Bennett's resignation. Tragedy ought really to be a great kick at misery. But *Anna of the Five Towns* seems like an acceptance – so does all the modern stuff since Flaubert...

Lawrence himself was disappointed by a second reading of *La chartreuse* in 1928, as he mentioned casually years later when writing to his friend Aldous Huxley:

Am reading again *Chartreuse de Parme* – so good historically, socially and all that – but emotionally rather empty and trashy...

We cannot be sure what it was in the novel he disliked so much, though it is more than likely that the grand passion of Fabrice del Dongo for Clélia Conti, which brings the novel to an end was what stayed in his mind when he laid it down and that what Lawrence found 'trashy and empty' is what many readers like the late Henri Martineau have deeply enjoyed and admired:

It is the expression of a dream of tenderness which the author only ever fulfilled in his imagination and of which the most poignant note is heard in the very last pages of the novel in Clélia's appeal to her lover: '*Entre ici ami de mon cœur...*' ['Come to me here, beloved of my heart'].[6]

The idyll of Fabrice and Clélia is certainly presented sympathetically, and as a highly amusing and at the same time almost miraculous-seeming triumph of life over adversity. Fabrice, when he is led into prison in the Citadel of Parma, has every reason to think that he will suffer all the horrors of solitary confinement but as the result of a chance encounter with Clélia at the entrance, knowing that she will be near him, goes to the window of his cell and admires the view of the plain of Lombardy and the distant Alps in the afternoon sun. Seeing Clélia from his cell feeding her caged birds on the terrace of her own lofty apartment, hearing her sing and devising a means of signalling to her, give him happiness and a sense of purpose he has never known until now. The two of them, in spite of the obstacles separating them, live in a world of their own high above the city below; and, after escaping from prison, Fabrice returns voluntarily to his cell, pining away when Clélia marries and finding relief only in the heart-rending eloquence of sermons which draw crowds and which move Clélia herself to become his mistress.

The appeal of the story of Fabrice and Clélia is that of an almost dream-like abandonment to love as the one supreme emotion claiming precedence over every other. Enhanced and deepened by the absence of any obvious designs on the reader's sympathy ('I don't wish by artificial means to fascinate the reader's soul', he told Balzac), it is the appeal of *All for love, or the world well lost* or *If you were the only girl in the world and I were the only boy*. And it is this most obviously that runs counter to the spirit and letter of what Lawrence has written of love: his dislike of the relationship which leaves the man in a state of helpless child-like dependence on the woman, of 'love' in this sense and, for that matter, of any 'supreme emotion'.[7] What Lawrence may have overlooked is that, for all the sympathy and fellow-feeling with which the story of Fabrice is told, it has a catastrophic ending, the ending 'strangled' by Dupont and briefly sketched in the one surviving version of the novel. The 'dream of tenderness' which, Henri Martineau seems to imply, is all the more beautiful for being only a dream, leads to an unpleasant awakening. Clélia bears Fabrice a son and Fabrice wishes him to be brought up as his own. The child's legal father, the Marquis Crescenzi, is kidnapped with the complicity of the police and during his enforced absence, little Sandrino removed to his new secret home. On his return, Crescenzi is told that the child has died, but Sandrino's simulated absence and enforced confinement impair his health in reality. He dies soon afterwards and Clélia, convinced that this is divine retribution, follows him to the grave, while her lover retires from the world. The catastrophe is complete and if its pathos and absurdity are not overwhelmingly manifest, this can only be because it is related so abruptly and with such apparent nonchalance. 'I wrote *La chartreuse* with the death of Sandrino constantly in mind', Beyle wrote afterwards, 'an event I had found acutely touching in real life. M. Dupont has left me no space in which to present it.'[8]

The absurdity and pathos of the ending of *La chartreuse*, even in the version we possess, however, should be apparent if we take the trouble to weigh the full implications of the last few pages. It is foreshadowed, moreover, by what we are told at the very beginning of the novel, of northern Italy before the arrival of the French and of the way of life to which it returns after their final departure. And it is scarcely inconsistent with the kind of comedy for which the novel is justly famed: that of an almost wholly farcical social order in which, even more than in *Lucien Leuwen*, appearances are maintained only to impress and deceive, in which the Prince of Parma can dictate anonymous letters to his own Prime Minister alleging the faithlessness of the latter's mistress, the Prime Minister himself help his rival to escape from prison and the rival, Fabrice, live like an Italian version of Byron's Don Juan, while remaining a high-ranking, highly esteemed and sincerely devout priest of the Church. What tempers the comedy, gives it its weight and edge and prevents it becoming wholly farcical – makes it utterly different, that is, from other comic studies in decadence such as those of a Firbank or a Roger Peyrefitte – is the grim realism on the part of the author and at least one of the actors in the drama itself, which is at the same time a strong antipathy to a great deal of what such a way of life involves and an awareness of its human consequences. Its most obvious victims are the political prisoners in the Citadel of Parma, who subscribe to a *Te Deum* in thanks for the recovery of their principal gaoler who has been seemingly poisoned, and who even compose sonnets in his honour:

> May he who blames them be led by his destiny to spend a single year in a cell three feet tall with eight ounces of bread a day and *fasting* every Friday...
>
> (ch. 21)

Their chief persecutor is the minister Rassi, of whom the Prime Minister Mosca writes, with unindulgent amusement, when the people of Parma rise in revolt:

> They are intent on hanging him; they would be doing him a great wrong; he deserves to be drawn and quartered...
>
> (ch. 23)

Fabrice and Clélia are among the most privileged members of this society – Fabrice can stand and move around in his cell – but their tragedy is yet another consequence of its absurd values and the arrangements it tolerates, in so far as they are its children and have been trained to conform to its ways.

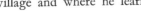

The early education of the aristocratic Fabrice, as of all Beyle's major figures, is of crucial relevance to what he becomes, and despite the rapidity of the narration, the essential features of his upbringing are dwelled on and emphasised at very adequate length. He is brought up, we learn, for a time under the influence of the French court in Milan at which his aunt Gina is one of the most brilliant personalities. And we are shown from the outset that the French rule in Italy, for all the 'enlightenment' it brings or rather seems to promise, does little to discourage the aristocratic spirit or the serene unquestioning acceptance of privilege on which a vigorous aristocracy depends:

> Fabrice spent his earliest years in the family castle at Grianta where he exchanged many blows with his fists among the peasant boys of the village and where he learned nothing, not even how to read.

Later, he was sent to school with the Jesuits in Milan where his father, the Marquis, insisted that he learn Latin not by reading ancient authors, who are always talking of republics, but in a magnificent tome illustrated by more than a hundred engravings, a masterpiece of the artists of the seventeenth century: the Latin genealogy of the Valserras, Marquesses of Dongo, published in 1650 by Fabrice del Dongo, Archbishop of Parma. As the fortunes of the Valserras had been, above all, military, the engravings depicted a great many battles, in all of which could be seen some hero bearing this name and dealing mighty blows with his sword. The book gave Fabrice a great deal of pleasure...

When Fabrice had made his first communion, the Countess, his aunt, obtained permission from his father to fetch him occasionally from college. She found him a singular, intelligent, very serious little boy, but attractive-looking and not altogether out of place in the salon of a fashionable lady; ignorant as one could wish, moreover, and hardly capable of writing a word. The countess, whose enthusiastic nature expressed itself in all that she did, promised her protection to the principal of the college if her nephew Fabrice had made astonishing progress by the end of the year and won lots of prizes to prove it; and to help him earn them, she would send for him every Saturday evening and often return him to his teachers only on the Wednesday or Thursday. The Jesuits, although lovingly cherished by the Prince Viceroy, had been banished from Italy by the laws of the kingdom, and the superior of the college, who was an astute man, was fully alive to the advantages to be gained by his relations with a lady all-powerful at court. He took care not to complain of Fabrice's absence from his lessons and the latter, now more ignorant than ever, at the end of the year obtained five first prizes...

(ch. 1)

His father in alarm has him brought back to Grianta, where he runs wild once again and is sent to school with the village priest, an astrologer who seems more like a venerable Pagan magus than a priest of the Church, and from whom he derives that belief in prophecies and miracles which had been deliberately revived by the Italian church, so Beyle tells us elsewhere,[9] in its reaction against the Enlightenment and the rational spirit of Jansenism. The early influences are decisive and the contradictions of the mature Fabrice dwelled on explicitly on a number of occasions later on in the story: his love, for example, of French newspapers with their advanced ideas, which he will go to pains to obtain, though

The taste for liberty, the fashion and cult of *the happiness of the greatest number* with which the 19th century has become infatuated, seemed to him nothing more than a *heresy* which will disappear like others, but after destroying many souls...
(ch. 7)

and above all, his incapacity, even when he is at his most sincerely penitent, for anything resembling self-criticism:

This is one of the most remarkable features of the religion he owed to the teachings of the Jesuits in Milan. This religion *weakens one's courage and resolve to think of unaccustomed things*, and forbids above all *self-interrogation*, as the most enormous of sins; for it is a step towards Protestantism...
(ch. 12)

Yet Beyle is more than a moralist or social historian. What is bound to disconcert any reader who hopes to find in *La chartreuse* an opportunity to indulge simple feelings of approval or condemnation is the positive attractiveness in so many respects of a boy who has been brought up in such an appalling way and the constant reminder, though it is usually only implied, that this is the only life Fabrice knows and that any beauty or significance in the world as he understands it is due to the beliefs he has been brought up to hold. Do our own beliefs, we may find ourselves asking, give us more satisfaction and joy?

Thus, without lacking intelligence, Fabrice was unable to see that his semi-belief in portents was for him a religion, a profound impression received during his emergence into life. To think of this belief was to feel, was happiness. And yet he persisted in his endeavours to see how it might be shown to be a proven science like geometry, for instance. He sought ardently to recall all those instances in which a portent he had observed had, surely, been followed by the event, either happy or unhappy, the portent had seemed to foretell; and, as he searched in his memory, his soul was overwhelmed with respect and with something like tender awe. He would have experienced an invincible repugnance for anyone who denied the truth of these portents and especially if this person had indulged in irony...
(ch. 8)

Fabrice's superstition, like Julien Sorel's, is presented all the more sympathetically in that, whether through a coincidence or not it is left for us to decide, the premonitions they experience are all fulfilled.

Beyle's own irony at the expense of Fabrice is without malice. It is expressed, moreover, in a way that suggests that it is, in any case, irrelevant to the story of his life, as when he explains to Gina his decision to join Napoleon after seeing an eagle flying northward at the moment that he hears of the return from Elba. The novelist tells us that he is amused by Fabrice's solemn effusions and in doing so, he reminds us, as so often throughout the novel, of the sheer *otherness* of Fabrice, the immeasurable distance separating his life and beliefs from those of his worldly French creator. It is Fabrice's life as he himself lives it on which the focus of our attention constantly falls rather than the novelist's judgment of what is right or wrong with it; which is perhaps why readers have so often failed to notice that Beyle *is* judging this life, explicitly even, and without envy or sentimentality; for however deep and fine, it is a life of aspiration mainly and of promises tragically unfulfilled. This is the essential point, as I see it, of the Waterloo episode, which now has a recognised classical status as an account of the reality as opposed to the official historian's view of war. It is this, no doubt, but it is an indispensable part of the story of Fabrice's life as well and of the kind of man he becomes and is capable of becoming and not, as it may seem at first, a brilliant *tour de force* worked into the novel in the freely romantic way in which Berlioz, for example, worked the Rákóczy March into the *Damnation of Faust*. It has that kind of impact and we may read it also as 'picaresque' comedy, especially at the outset when Fabrice gallops into what he hopes is action, his head filled with scenes from the *Gerusa-lemme Liberata*. Yet 'picaresque' is not really the word. Nor is it comedy at the expense of an incorrigible simpleton. As an aspiring soldier, Fabrice turns out to be the most apt as well as the most willing of pupils. And it is the veterans he encounters who notice this: the motherly camp-follower, whose name we never learn, with her travelling canteen and the resourceful Corporal Aubry: both the most genuine of warriors, as it happens, in so far as they treat a battle as part of a day's work and a defeat as a natural disaster to be coped with accordingly; though Fabrice never realises that these ordinary folk are the true heroes of Waterloo, any more than he is able to tell whether this is a battle or not.

The stark vividness of every detail of the battle, that of the dirty feet and blood-soaked trousers of the first corpse he encounters or of the flying twigs and branches of a line of willow trees scythed by a cannon-ball, is the vividness of all that Fabrice experiences. Nowhere in the novel is the reader's impression of what it is like to be Fabrice more intimate and real; and nowhere are we so aware of what he might have become if Napoleon had won, if the course of history had been different and if he had been able to lead the life of a soldier in the Imperial Army for which his 'fanatical' education at the hands of the Jesuits, his childhood reading of the family genealogy and his Tom Sawyer-like rôle in the escapades of the Grianta peasant boys have prepared him as well as any military academy. To his aunt, he seems suddenly a man after Waterloo, though his baptism of fire and initiation into manhood have been a military débâcle and the downfall of Napoleon's empire and the only wound he has sustained a blow from the sabre of a retreating French hussar. It is true that his devotion to the Emperor has been very much that of a young Italian aristocrat. ('He wanted to give us a country and he loved my uncle', he tells Gina before leaving to join Napoleon.) But it is the only political dispensation in which he will ever be able to believe whole-heartedly. His political mentors when he returns to Italy will be his aunt and her lover Count Mosca, and conformity to the prevailing social order, he will be told, neither more nor less reasonable than to the rules of whist.

The principality of Parma in which Fabrice lives as an adult is a satellite of the Austrian Empire and owes its existence to the Congress of Vienna and the determination of the rulers of Europe, after twenty-five years of living with the sanguinary consequences of French egalitarian and nationalistic ideas, to restore the no doubt absurd institutions of the past. Fabrice is not accustomed, because of his Jesuit education, to criticise the prevailing order or criticise himself and realise to what extent his immense privileges depend upon it; and it is for this reason, presumably, that he becomes so serenely and engagingly indifferent to the world in which he lives. He enjoys, like his creator, digging up Etruscan remains, and his affairs with women, whom he has the courage and refinement never to deceive himself that he loves. But there is a painful void at the centre of his life, a profound aimlessness which leaves him the most amiable and least solemn of men and a man given, more than others, to distraction and dreams (which the people of Parma will later take for saintliness) but not by any means the most contented. Perhaps this is why one is left with the impression that the story of his life takes place in an almost uninhabited Italian landscape on a glorious, though slightly melancholy afternoon. Fabrice does not analyse his predicament in terms of what M. Sartre would call his *situation*, the connections, that is, between his own personal history and that of his fellow men in the Europe of his day. He is aware only, as he tells himself repeatedly, of his inability to love, to love even his aunt Gina in the way he realises, with some alarm, that she loves him. His deep sense of inadequacy and his indifference to the rôle he should be playing in society as a future Archbishop of the Church, are evident in the recklessness of the escapades in which he tries to fall in love and (according to Beyle's letter to Balzac, at the same time make it clear to Gina that he cannot love her), in which he kills a jealous travelling actor who assaults him and is thrown into prison to await trial for murder.

The uncharacteristic care that Beyle takes to describe the citadel of Parma, in which Fabrice becomes the most willing of prisoners, has been often noted and is obviously more than a piece of external verisimilitude in the manner of Scott and Balzac. (M. Robbe-Grillet is able to intrigue us in a superficially similar way when he reminds us that the known significant world may be for certain individuals that which is measured by the dimensions and shape of a single room; though, unlike Beyle, he is usually content with an impression of sinister suggestiveness and leaves us to imagine for ourselves what could have so badly damaged the mind whose experiences we share, that it can live with such unearthly fixity in its immediate surroundings, whatever these may be.) To Fabrice, for reasons which have become eminently clear, the prison is more real than anywhere in the world outside, and he comes to enjoy it as if it were his home, for he finds in Clélia what he had always craved, a woman he can love and who can give his life the purpose and meaning it lacks. His love excludes the world and is all the more compelling for his previous indifference to the world. And it is his absurd scheme years later, after their child is born, to take the child out of the world and bring him up in secrecy that precipitates the catastrophe which brings the novel to its close.

The education of Clélia, who is an accomplice in what she sees as their crime, is as crucial as that of Fabrice to an understanding of the tragedy that overtakes them. And though it is sketched far more briefly, its nature is no less clear. One obvious *donnée* is that her mother is dead and that her most agonising and vital decisions are made in solitude, like those of the unknowingly heroic Princesse de Clèves after the death of Mme de Chartres; and they are made with the same alternating terror and resolution. Clélia is also, despite her father's professed liberalism, the product of an Italian Catholic upbringing; though, thrown on supernatural guidance for lack of any human being to whom she can turn, she practises her religion with an earnestness far greater than her Church usually requires. Hence, presumably, her determined efforts to respect her father, who is so patently unworthy of either respect or trust, and the solemnity of her vows to the Virgin. After betraying her father, as she imagines, in aiding Fabrice to escape from prison, she vows never to see him again. And when she eventually becomes his mistress, their assignations take place in a darkened room,

for we have to confess what will seem strange anywhere north of the Alps, namely, that, despite her faults, she had remained perfectly faithful to her vow...
    (ch. 28)

She is indeed admirably sincere according to her lights, but the lights, unfortunately, are somewhat dim.

Fabrice and Clélia should have married. Their suitability for each other is never in doubt. And there is no other visible road to fulfilment and continuing happiness open to either of them. It should have been possible for Clélia to see the folly of her father's wish that she should marry the opulent foolish Crescenzi, and for herself and Fabrice to take their places in the world as husband and wife and bring up their child accordingly. As it is, they meet furtively, out of the light of day and they are borne along, as they see it, by the supernatural forces to which Clélia attributes little Sandrino's death. And they fail utterly to understand the nature and extent of their own responsibility. A more frivolous couple, a man and woman less capable of whole-hearted commitment and desire and more skilled in the arts of conventional hypocrisy would have been more contentedly irresponsible, would have accepted the need for a *mariage de convenance* and afterwards met in either discreet or open adultery, for they live in a society in which both are tolerated. Before the arrival of the French, the bride's lover, as we have been reminded on the opening page of the novel, had been known to be named in the marriage contract. And it is something like the life of a typical *cavaliere servente* that Gina proposes to Fabrice after his return from Waterloo:

'Can you see yourself on the *Corso* of Florence or Naples,' said the Duchess, 'with your thoroughbred English horses! And in the evening, a carriage and an elegant apartment', etc. She dwelled at length on the delights of this vulgar species of happiness, that she could see Fabrice rejecting with disdain. 'He's a hero', she thought...
    (ch. 6)

The hero-worship is characteristic of Gina, and on this occasion undeserved, for the priesthood, for which he settles, means little more to him than the life of a wealthy man about town.

The marriage code and sexual *mores* of the Italian aristocracy of the 1820s is the subject of an article which appeared in *The London Magazine* for October 1826 and which, for many years, has been attributed to Beyle himself;[10] though it seems far more likely that it was written by another friend and passionate admirer of Mathilde Dembowski in Milan, the poet Foscolo. Whoever the author was, its relevance to the story of Fabrice and Clélia is evident. A young Italian girl of good family, we are told,

...knows full well that the man she loves can never be hers, unless by some extraordinary accident, which she wishes but never dares to hope for. Yet she loves on – and the more noble is her blood, the more ardently does she persist in her attachment. But every passion which is not nourished by some hope either leads to madness or the grave, or yields to time and reason. She resigns herself, at length, to a marriage with a man chosen by her tyrants and revenges herself by refusing him any share in her heart. Marriage, instead of surrounding her, as it does here, with increased *surveillance* and more conventional restraints and decorums, invests her with complete liberty; so that, with greater facility and innocence she can converse with her first love and see him whenever she pleases. Some few, out of a feeling of self-respect or of religion, rather than go to the altar with perjury on their lips, choose the melancholy lot of dying alone...

She may, of course, though Clélia does not, openly choose a *cavaliere servente*:

A true *cavaliere servente* is a constant guest at his mistress's house; he acts as her steward and superintends her household; he always stands behind her while she sits at the pianoforte, and punctually turns over the leaves of her music-book; he sits by her and assists her in her embroidery, or any other work; he never goes out without her; or if ever he does walk out alone, it is to take out her lap-dog for exercise...

The enforced innocence of the unmarried Italian girl and the widespread toleration of her adultery after marriage are, of course, a well-known social phenomenon of the nineteenth century, however much or little the code of behaviour may have corresponded to what happened in reality. Henry James's Duchess in *The Awkward Age* stoutly defends the arrangement in its initial phase and is shown as answerable for its consequences. The author of the article in *The London Magazine* sees its cause in the custom of discouraging all but the eldest son and one daughter of an aristocratic house from marrying (for obvious social and economic reasons) and in the far from disinterested co-operation of the convents and the Church, many of whose leading prelates were recruited, like Fabrice, from among the younger sons of the aristocracy and led the lives of pleasure-seeking men of the world. And he praises Napoleon for having curbed the Church's influence and, through the Code Civil, having ensured the equal distribution among all the children of the parents' property and wealth. He concludes by seeing the political ineptitude of the Italian upper classes and their subjection to those who have divided their country, as a direct consequence of their marriage customs:

Thus, in a country, in which nature has, perhaps, endowed her daughters more liberally than in any other, with the treasures of the mind and heart calculated to render them the mothers of free citizens and the nurses of patriots, bad government and consequent bad usages have rendered them so degenerate, that their domestic life corrupts every germ of virtue in their children. We wish that we may be false prophets; but until such an abominable system of marriage is wholly extirpated, it appears to us that the aristocracy, and the great landowners of the country, will always be contemptible to themselves and others; inert and unfit for any attempt to liberate their country; that their lives will be spent in intriguing, their minds stupefied by idleness and their souls corrupted by sensuality.

The sombre peroration makes it seem more likely that this is a translation from the Italian of the author of *I sepolcri* and *Jacopo Ortis* than from the French of Beyle.[11] But there is nothing in *La chartreuse* to indicate a fundamentally contrasting view. The tragedy of Fabrice and Clélia is that of a man and woman brought up in such a world, who are unable to adapt themselves to its arrangements and who have the misfortune to be neither 'contemptible' nor 'corrupt'.

Mosca and Gina

Lawrence was wrong, surely, to say that '*La chartreuse* is so good historically, socially and all that – but emotionally rather empty and trashy'. Beyle never describes social and historical conditions better than when he is showing their effects on individual lives; for much the same reason, I find that I disagree with those critics who have said that Beyle's concern with the individual is fundamentally anti-social, or, as Mr Irving Howe puts it, that of a 'profoundly unpolitical man'.

Mr Howe's chapter on Beyle in his book on *Politics and the Novel* contains some of the most helpful comments I have read on *La chartreuse* and the point of view it presupposes. Much more can be said than he has space for about the paradoxes of political life in Parma, the ambiguous rôle, for example, of the official opposition ('God alone knows what kind of liberals', as Mosca puts it) who are tolerated and used by the authoritarian prince.[12] But Mr Howe points out 'the seriousness beneath the stillness' of *La chartreuse* and reminds us that even if the point of view of the author cannot be pinned down in conventional terms, it is obvious that Beyle was acutely intelligent about politics. He also provides the best reasons I have come across for thinking of *La chartreuse* as 'Machiavellian' and explains the terms by referring us not only to the Machiavelli of *The Prince* but the more idealistic and 'republican' *Discourses on Livy*.

What Mr Howe means, presumably, when he describes Beyle as a 'profoundly unpolitical man' is a man who was incapable of the servility of mind any political allegiance is likely to require. But this profound indifference is made, as the argument proceeds, to sound like indifference of a more commonplace kind: namely, a belief that politics is one thing; if one succeeds, it is a means to personal survival (Mr Howe's chapter is entitled 'The politics of survival') and the personal life something to be considered apart. Mr Howe is not the only critic of *La chartreuse* to assume that both Beyle and his heroes are 'unpolitical' in this way. 'The Happy Few' to whom the novel is dedicated, according to this view, compromise with society and observe its rules, while leading a life which excludes any other thought or care for the world outside.[13] If this is really true of the novel, Beyle would presumably have sympathised not only with the fierce outburst of Lawrence's Birkin in *Women in Love* against the tyranny of egalitarianism: 'I want every man to have his share in the world's goods, so that I am rid of his importunity', but also with Gerald Crich, on the same occasion (in chapter 5) when he argues that 'society' is a 'mechanism' and that every man is fit for his own little bit of a task – let him do that and then please himself'.

'...Between me and a woman, the social question does not enter. It is my own affair.'

'A ten pound note on it', said Birkin.

'You don't mean that a woman is a social being?' asked Ursula of Gerald.

'She is both', said Gerald. 'She is a social being, as far as society is concerned. But for her own private self, she is a free agent, it is her own affair what she does.'

'But won't it be rather difficult to arrange the two halves?' asked Ursula.

'Oh no', replied Gerald. 'They arrange themselves naturally – we see it now, everywhere.'

'Don't you laugh so pleasantly till you're out of the wood', said Birkin.

Gerald knitted his brows in momentary irritation.

'Was I laughing?' he said.

If *La chartreuse* can be seen to have been written in the belief expressed by Gerald Crich, then this may be yet another explanation of why Lawrence disliked it.

It is true that we are never shown in *La chartreuse* or even, for that matter, in *Women in Love*, how the common human dilemma which Birkin sees might be successfully resolved. But this is not to say that the problem is never posed or the dangers of ignoring it never contemplated. In fact, if there is any profound affinity between Beyle and Lawrence as novelists, it lies, I would suggest, in their refusal to treat the novel as anything other than a provocation to thought, one that however helpful and absorbing the process may be, leaves the responsibility for solving the problems it raises with the reader himself, rather than relieving him of it temporarily by inviting him to dream of enviable and successful lives. In saying this, I seem to disagree with Mr Howe, particularly when he is telling us how Mosca 'triumphs' over circumstances and his own nature:

When Mosca fails, it is precisely because he lives too closely by his own precepts, by his inured political habits. It is he who on behalf of Ernesto IV omits the phrase 'unjust proceedings' from the paper Sanseverina dictates to him, and it is this omission that allows Ernesto IV to throw Fabrizio into jail. Sanseverina rightly describes Mosca's behaviour as that of a 'miserable fawning...courtier'; she jabs him at his weakest point – the weakest point of all professional politicians and parliamentarians – when she says, 'He always imagines that to resign is the greatest sacrifice a Prime Minister can make.' On the other hand, Mosca's triumph, that is, his transcendence of his public self, comes when he breaks from the machiavellian system and allows his passion for Gina to imperil his career and perhaps his life. It is then that he becomes a truly magnificent figure, a man capable of every precaution, yet discarding all, a man for whom love is the means of recovering Fortune. In moving away from the Machiavelli of *The Prince*, Mosca approaches the other Machiavelli, the one who wrote that Fortune favours the young and impetuous: 'like a woman, she is a lover of the young because they are less respectful, more ferocious and with greater audacity command her.'

Mosca, it is true, is 'young' (at heart) and 'impetuous', even when we first meet him and he impresses Gina by his simple humanity and seeming 'shame' at 'the gravity and importance of his position'. Both the human warmth and vulnerability and the over-confident simplicity with which he regards his rôle in the world become apparent during one of their first meetings:

As the only other occupant of the opera box was the lady of strong liberal views to whom it belonged, the conversation continued with the same frankness as before. When questioned, he spoke of his life in Parma. 'In Spain, under General Saint-Cyr, I allowed myself to be shot at in order to win the Legion of Honour and a little glory at the same time. Now I dress like a character in a comedy in order to set up a house and earn a few thousand francs. Once I'd started playing this game of chess and as I was shocked by the insolence of my superiors, I decided I would like one of the leading posts in the state. I succeeded, but my happiest days are still those I spend occasionally in Milan; here, I feel, the heart of your Army of Italy beats on...'

(ch. 6)

His simplicity is studied. The ever wakeful self-observation which makes him a master of ruse and diplomacy – the name Mosca is a hononym for 'a fly' while his illustrious family name means literally 'of the oak tree' – is apparent in the comic yet moving, almost elegiac scene in which we are shown him falling and watching himself fall in love:

Towards six o'clock, he mounted and rode to the *Corso*, where he had some hope that he might find Mme de Piatranera; not seeing her, he remembered that the doors of the Scala opened at eight; he entered and found less than ten people in the immense auditorium. He felt slightly ashamed of being there. 'Can it be', he thought 'that at forty-five, I am committing follies that would make a second lieutenant blush?' He fled and tried to spend the time strolling through the delightful streets around the Opera House occupied by cafés which, at this hour of the day, are bursting to capacity. In front of each of them, inquisitive crowds sit on chairs in the middle of the road eating ices and commenting on the passers-by. The count happened to be an unusual passer-by; so he had the pleasure of being recognised and accosted...He returned to the Opera House and decided that it would be a good idea to hire a box high up in the third tier, from which he could look down, without being observed by anyone, on the second tier boxes in one of which he was hoping that the Countess would eventually appear. Sure of not being seen, he abandoned himself to his folly. 'What is old age, anyway?' he thought. 'Merely not being able to enjoy oneself as I am now, behaving in an absurdly childlike way...'

He rose to go down to the box in which he could see the countess; but suddenly, he felt almost as if he didn't want to call on her, after all. 'But this is wonderful', he exclaimed and paused half way down the staircase. 'I'm feeling shy! I haven't felt shy for twenty-five years.'

He entered the box almost forcing himself to do so; and then, like an intelligent man of the world, took advantage of what had happened to him; he made no attempt to appear at ease or to show off his wit by plunging into some amusing story; he had the courage to be shy, he employed his wits in allowing his shyness to be apparent and yet not ridiculous. 'If she takes it the wrong way, I'm lost for ever', he thought...

(ch. 6)

He is ready to give up his position as minister in order to live with Gina in Naples or Florence:

...this is at least what he succeeded in making the woman he loved believe. In all his letters he beseeched her with ever increasing passion and recklessness to grant him a second meeting in Milan and to this the Countess agreed. 'If I were to swear to you that I am madly in love with you', she said to him one day, 'I would be lying; I would be only too happy to love at more than thirty as I once did at twenty-two! But I have seen too many things fall that I had thought eternal! I feel for you the most tender affection, I place in you an infinite trust and of all men you are the one I prefer.' The Countess believed herself to be perfectly sincere in uttering these words and yet her declaration included a little lie towards the end. Perhaps if Fabrice had wished to, he would have taken precedence over everyone else in her heart...

(ch. 6)

If the love of Fabrice for Clélia excludes any other care in the world, this is never the case with Mosca and Gina. For Mosca, the passion and recklessness are a glorious reprieve from advancing age. He enjoys falling in love as if he were a young lieutenant once more, gives himself excellent reasons for being 'mad' and relives the experience so authentically as to forget that young lieutenants are liable to fall in love with the sheer novelty of their own feelings.

The test of Gina's 'infinite trust' in Mosca and of his actual devotion to her comes unexpectedly – it is the unexpectedness that makes it a test – in the episode in chapter 14 to which Mr Howe refers. It is one of the supreme instances in the whole of Beyle's fiction of 'scènes probantes' of the kind he admired in Molière, that is 'scenes which prove the character or the passions of those who take part in them...'[14] and it testifies to the seriousness of his ambition to be a dramatist, even if it is impossible to imagine it rewritten for the stage. For much of the dramatic effect depends on the actors' unspoken thoughts as they watch one another and on our sense of the virtually uncontrollable situation they create, by which they are borne along as if on a swift current and which makes the timing of every word they utter and expression they assume as decisive and revealing as the words they use. Mr Howe says nothing of the drama and thus overlooks the possibility that the responsibility for the disastrous upshot of their encounter may well be not merely Mosca's alone. Gina does not even consult him before defying protocol, confronting Prince Ernest Ranuce in his palace and delivering her ultimatum that she will leave the city and the court (of which it is well understood that she is the most distinguished ornament) unless an unconditional pardon for her nephew is signed. She is carried away by her furious protective instinct and but for Mosca's attempted diplomacy in drawing up the pardon and omitting the crucial phase on which she had insisted: 'this unjust procedure will have no sequel in the future...', would have triumphed over the easily disconcerted Prince's calculations. He is tired and 'would have signed anything'. Only the fact that she has ignored Mosca – he has to support himself by holding on to the back of a chair when he realises this – is not lost on the Prince:

'What must we do?' said the Prince to Count Mosca, not very sure what he was saying and carried away by his habit of consulting the Count in everything.

'I really haven't the least idea, your most serene Highness', replied the Count with the air of a man heaving his very last sigh. He could hardly pronounce the words and the tone of his voice gave the Prince the first consolation his wounded pride had received in the course of the entire audience; this minor satisfaction inspired him with the thought of a little speech he might make that would soothe his pride even further.

'Well then', he said. 'I appear to be the most reasonable of the three and I am perfectly willing to overlook my position in the world. I am going to talk *as a friend* and', he added with a charming smile of condescension reminiscent of the happy days of Louis XIV, '*like a friend talking to friends*. Mme la Duchesse, what must we do to make you forget a decision which may have been somewhat ill-judged and hasty?'

'I honestly cannot say', replied the Duchess with a heavy sigh. 'I honestly cannot say, I loathe Parma so deeply.' There was no epigramatic intention in these words. It was the voice of sincerity itself that spoke.

The Count turned away with a sudden impulsive movement; his courtier's soul was scandalised; then he turned on the Prince an imploring gaze. With much dignity and calm, the Prince allowed a moment to elapse; then said, addressing the Count, 'I see that your charming friend is no longer herself. The reason is perfectly simple. She *adores* her nephew...'

> (ch. 14)

The Prince, profiting from the temporary advantage he enjoys over his humiliated Prime Minister, outwits them both. The bold unhesitating devotion to Gina's interests which, we are told, would have won the day – he needed merely to write the words that Gina dictated – is something of which he now proves incapable. Yet it is as if no trust had ever existed between them. Gina's face registers the utmost contempt for him, though there is no indication that she either knows or cares what her feelings are or how they will be understood.[15] The unhesitating devotion of which he proves incapable is a devotion for which she does not even ask. Mosca has this justification, though he has courage and intelligence enough to know that there are no excuses for a failure of this kind. When the consequences of his omission are known and Fabrice is arrested, he assumes the full responsibility and Gina does not hesitate either to condemn him for what both agree to describe as his 'courtier's instinct':

I shan't reproach you for having left out the words 'unjust procedure' from the letter you wrote out for him to sign; it was a courtier's instinct that gripped you by the throat; without even realising it you preferred the interests of your master to those of the woman you loved. You have placed your actions at my disposal, my dear Count, and for a long time now, but it is beyond your capacity to change your nature; you have great talents as a minister but you have the instinct of the trade as well [*vous avez aussi l'instinct du métier*]...

> (ch. 16)

Mosca's desperate attempts to redeem himself in her eyes, and thus in his own, first by writing out his resignation and sending it to her to read – she tears it up and sends him back the pieces – and then by leading an armed guard to cover Fabrice's escape from prison are ineffectual. It is as a statesman only that he is able to live down his humiliation and this time, significantly, without needing to profess that utter devotion to her which both of them had thought of as evidence of his freedom of soul.

The revolt of the people of Parma is the occasion to which Mosca rises with the *brio* and decisiveness he has lacked in the conduct of Gina's affairs, as it bursts with a violent and exhilarating release of pent-up energy and feeling over the little Principality. Mosca enjoys himself hugely, relieving the arch-conservative commander of the royal guard of his rank when the latter talks in front of his troops of negotiating with the rebels, leading a battalion to defend the Prince's statue and relating the news in letters to Gina in which, despite 'the most lugubrious terms', the 'liveliest joy' breaks through. Mosca is faithful to the Prince and Princess but servile neither to the old nor the new potential masters of the state; unlike the general of the guard who basely flatters the people as once he flattered the Prince. And it is this that makes Gina decide that 'all things considered', she will 'have to marry him after all' (chapter 23). Yet the reconciliation is based on a more realistic understanding of the extent of their mutual devotion than the liaison to which they had agreed when they first met. There is no question of their going off to Naples or Florence together, and eventually they even live apart, Gina outside the frontiers of the state and Mosca seeing her when he can absent himself from his ministerial responsibilities. Gina, moreover, lives only for a short time after the death of Fabrice, whom she still adores, and Mosca is left alone, according to the last words of the novel, 'immensely rich' in a Parma in which the prisons are empty and the son of Prince Ernest Ranuce IV is adored by his subjects, who compare his rule to that of the Grand Dukes of Tuscany.

The equivocal-seeming conclusion to the novel and the nature of Mosca's rule as Prime Minister have understandably intrigued almost every critic of *La chartreuse*. Mr Martin Turnell, for example, finds the concluding sentence 'characteristically ambiguous':

The prisons are empty either because Ernest V is really a benevolent despot or because all the liberals are dead or in exile or because liberalism itself has died out. The Grand Dukes of Tuscany, to whom the Prince of Parma is compared, were notorious despots. It follows from this that his people worshipped him either because they really like despotism or because they had become so downtrodden that they were not aware of it. The only other alternative is that Stendhal is pulling our leg and that his people secretly detested Ernest V...[16]

I'm not quite sure what Mr Turnell means by 'notorious despots', but there are good reasons for thinking that the public personality of Mosca was based to some extent on that of Vittorio Fossombroni, the mathematician and prime minister of Tuscany, to whom Beyle attributed the relatively enlightened rule of that admittedly despotic state.[17] And I see no reason to think that Beyle regards the emptiness of the prisons of Parma as anything other than evidence of good government; though it is perhaps the most serious weakness of the novel that we have to make so many guesses about the régime which Mosca presumably helps to fashion and in any case agrees to serve, and hence about the kind of man he is in the exercise of what, despite his protestations to the contrary, remains his most absorbing passion; for Mosca forgets when he compares the rules of politics with chess, that both politics and chess can become lifelong addictions.

We are given, it is true, some idea of the kind of politics in which Mosca believes, though very little, apart from what we are told in the final sentence, of their practical and human consequences. One has the impression, for example, that having served in the armies of Napoleon, he wishes to bring about within the state of Parma something resembling the Napoleonic order, with institutions founded on the rule of law and guaranteed liberties allowing for dynastic continuity and the possibility even of peaceful evolution towards more democratic forms of government in years to come. Another precedent for such a régime is to be found in the Austrian states of Lombardy, the 'reasonableness' of whose administration is mentioned more than once in the opening chapters.[18] It is not the Austrians, for example, but their fanatical Milanese supporters who assassinate the Napoleonic minister Prina with their umbrellas and afterwards, in a so-called duel, dispose of Gina's first husband, Count Pietranera; the 'good hearted' Austrian General Bubna, we are told, 'a man of intelligence and feeling seemed altogether ashamed of the assassination of Prina' (chapter 2). It is perhaps for this reason that Balzac thought of Mosca as a fictitious portrait of Metternich (which Beyle denied, adding that he hadn't seen Metternich since 1810, at Saint-Cloud, when he carried a bracelet of the hair of the beautiful Caroline Murat). Mosca rules Parma like an arbitrary tyrant when he first assumes office, and shocks Fabrice by telling him how he has thought of ensuring that the authors of the abominable anonymous letters he has received would be not only tried but sentenced by his 'good judges'; though his retort to Fabrice's protest suggests that in a state like Parma, there is no other way to rule:

'I would rather have seen them condemned by magistrates judging according to their consciences', replied Fabrice, with a naïveté which in a court like Parma seemed comic.

'Since you travel so much for your instruction, perhaps you will give me the names of some of the magistrates you have in mind. I'll write to them before I go to bed...'
(ch. 10)

It is significant that when Fabrice himself has to be tried and found innocent of the murder of the travelling actor, he ensures that judgment will be passed by the twelve judges whose integrity and learning are least in doubt, explaining to Gina that if he is not tried with the 'utmost solemnity', the name of the man he has killed will be an embarrassment to him for the rest of his ecclesiastical career. Characteristically, he is concerned with the practical advantages of proper procedure and his political principles are frankly opportunistic. He is a hedonist rather than a utilitarian:

The Count had no virtue; one may even say that what the liberals call virtue (i.e. seeking the happiness of the greatest number) struck him as fraudulent; he believed that he was under an obligation to seek the happiness of Count Mosca della Rovere...
(ch. 16)

But the pursuit of his own happiness induces him to seek power in a way compatible with his own needs and temperament and hence to avoid, among other things, being responsible in any way for the execution of helpless prisoners. He has had to do this once already, in his career as an officer in Spain, and the memory, he tells Gina, still returns to torment him, 'particularly in the evenings'. And in this he differs from his rival for office, the humble plebeian Rassi, for whom reassurance lies in being insulted and even thrashed by the Prince and who has ensured his royal master's dependence upon him by having two liberals executed in the Prince's name. The vicious circle of official terror, reprisal and the fear of reprisal which Rassi has deliberately set in motion, in order to make himself indispensable, is one that Mosca promptly ends. This does not prevent him ordering the troops to fire on the crowd which tries to overturn the Prince's statue. And on this occasion, Mosca has no remorse. But the statue is worth preserving. Its bullet holes serve as a warning to the Prince's heir that this is what comes of hanging Jacobins. ('And if he says this, I will tell him you must either hang ten thousand or none at all.') While to the people, it is the symbol of triumphant order:

But for me Parma would have been a republic for a month with the poet Ferrante Palla as dictator...
    (ch. 23)

Mosca has no objection on principle to republics, though he believes that it will take 'a hundred years for a republic' in Italy 'not to be an absurdity' and it is obviously preferable for a republic to last longer than 'two months'. He has the utmost admiration also for the revolutionary poet, Ferrante Palla, but cannot think of him as the ideal head of state.

It is Mosca's apparently reasonable as well as energetic behaviour in suppressing the revolt that epitomises more than anything else he does the kind of man he is (and in saying this, I disagree with Mr Howe) as well as the equivocal blessings of his kind of rule. Nothing in the novel suggests that he is wrong in thinking that victory for the insurgents would have been a disaster for Parma and for the insurgents themselves within a very short time:

The troops would have fraternised with the people, there would have been three days of murder and assassination (for it will take a hundred years in this country for a republic not to be an absurdity), then a fortnight of pillage, until two or three regiments provided by some foreign power were sent in to impose order...
    (ch. 23)

Yet the insurrection, however impractical, affects us as a revolt not only against institutions and rules but—what makes it seem so just and natural – against the intolerable boredom and constraint they have imposed. Even the court is normally plunged in boredom; which is why Gina with her grace and vitality has become indispensable to it. And it is significant that it should be her 'gold' that is distributed to the insurgents (even if this was not her intention) and the most devoted of her lovers who in carrying out her orders to assassinate the Prince unleashes the movement to overthrow the state.

The uncalculating devotion to Gina of Ferrante Palla has its counterpart in the untiringly self-watchful astuteness that gives Mosca, as Gina puts it, both the 'talents' of a prime minister and 'the instinct of the trade'; Mosca's candid egoism has its counterpart in Palla's total dedication to the happiness of the greatest number; and Mosca's readiness to make a fortune in the service of an ungrateful Prince its counterpart in Palla's proud integrity with regard to money: as a 'tribune of the people', he keeps a strict account of the riches Gina bestows on him in order to wreak her vengeance on the Prince. The fact that neither Palla nor Palla's ideals can hope to prevail in a state like Parma is one of the most melancholy realities on which the story turns. The valour and energy of the Lombardians of the middle ages, of which we are reminded in the opening pages, has gone *alla macchia* and is now to be found only among the brigands in the woods. It is in the forest surrounding her palace on the River Po in which Gina loves to wander and in which Mosca has told her to beware of brigands that Palla first darts out to confront her, looking like the survivor of some natural disaster or like the disguised Edgar in *King Lear*:

The stranger had the time to approach her and throw himself at her feet. He was young and very handsome but atrociously dressed; his clothes had rents in them a foot long; but his eyes blazed with all the fire of an ardent soul.

'I have been condemned to death. I am the doctor Ferrante Palla. I am dying of hunger and so are my five children...'

(ch. 21)

For Balzac, Palla was the most sublime and beautiful figure in the book, whom he preferred even to his own Michel Chrestien in *Illusions perdues*, and he described him as 'sincere, mistaken, full of talent but unaware of the fatal consequences of his doctrine'.[19] Beyle is far less solemn about him and about the kind of danger he represents – his republic wouldn't last – and shows him as a beautiful but sublimely comic figure, even in the deadly quasi-professional efficiency with which, in the excess of his adoration for Gina, he has the Prince poisoned in the course of a royal bird-shooting expedition on Palla's own ground in the marshes by the Po. If the comedy is not exactly uproarious, it is because Palla is wholly serious, in fact alarmingly so and especially when he is at his most extravagant; and because he is a living reproach in the innocence of his heart and his profound energy to those who regard him as a madman or a 'great poet'. After the abortive revolution, he disappears once more – presumably back into the woods and marshes – and peace and order return to the state. The poignancy of what he represents is not the poignancy of pathos – for he is fierce and proud – but of the life that is banished from Mosca's Parma.

Ferrante Palla's rôle in the novel is clearly symbolic; for example, though he himself is condemned to death, his poems circulate and are universally admired, and it is difficult not to see this as typifying the part played by *romanticismo* in Metternich's Italy. It is, in fact, both a weakness of *La chartreuse* and the source of much of its imaginative appeal that so much of what happens in Parma should be indicated by such indirect means rather than by the detailed evocation of everyday life as in the more Tolstoyan *Lucien Leuwen*. Beyle had, in other words, already written much better 'historically, socially and all that...' Commentators, understandably, dwell on the novel's symbolism;[20] Croce readily forgave Beyle for giving us not the true historical Italy of the 1820s but the 'Italy of his dream';[21] and Professor J. D. Hubert, who draws our attention to the importance of play-acting in the novel – both the dissimulation to which even Clélia resorts and acting in the literal sense: the charades that Gina organises to cheer a dreary court – goes so far as to describe the overall effect of the novel as a 'devaluation of the real'.[22] If it is difficult not to think of Palla as having a significance that transcends his immediate rôle, the same is true of Gina, and increasingly so as the novel proceeds and as we see her not as she appears to herself but as an awe-inspiring and even sinister figure. One thinks of her light step and affected nonchalance as she comes to deliver her ultimatum to the Prince, the look that terrifies her servant as she orders the signal to be given for the Prince's assassination, and her self-possession as she persuades the

Prince's heir to burn the documents that could incriminate her and then flees from his burning palace with the most relevant of the documents wrapped in her shawl.

Gina associates herself with the best and the worst in the Italy of *La chartreuse* and those critics who think of her only at her most admirable, splashing water over the powdered hair of her elder nephew, the solemn Ascagnio, or persuading the Prince that it would be a kindness occasionally to address a few charming words to his wife, speak of her at times as if she were somehow above the intrigues which, together with amateur theatricals, form the main pastime of the court. Yet she is the life and soul of both activities, merciless even to the man she loves more than any other creature in the world:

'Is it in my interest to let Conti be dishonoured? Definitely not. If he is, the wedding of his daughter and that nice dull Marquis Crescenzi will be impossible...' The Duchess believed she no longer loved Fabrice, but still passionately desired that Clélia should marry the Marquis; she had a vague hope that if she did, the preoccupation weighing on Fabrice would disappear...
    (ch. 25)

And nothing makes her more representative of the Italy of her day than the fact that she is worshipped simultaneously – and with an unquestioning adoration that many readers of the novel seem to find it incumbent on themselves to share – by the leader of revolution in Parma and the authoritarian minister who puts the revolution down.

Beyle's apology for his characters in the preface to the novel clearly refers to Gina more than to anyone else:

I confess that I have been bold enough to leave my characters as they were, with all their natural imperfections; but none the less, I declare for all to hear that I condemn many of their actions and in the most moral terms. What use would it be to give them the high moral standards of the French, who love money more than anything else and never commit sins out of hatred or love?...

Gina's blind yearning for Fabrice is what turns her in the end into an accomplished criminal and politician, a figure more reminiscent of Racine's Agrippine in *Britannicus* than of the Phèdre with whom Balzac compared her. It is also the source of her repeated protestations, despite her youthful looks and energy, that she is an ageing woman, unable to love as she once loved at twenty-two, of the smiling resignation with which she grasps what she sees as the few pleasures fate and time have in store for her and of her self-consoling angry pride, after Mosca has unintentionally betrayed them, when she tells herself that she and Fabrice belong to a class of beings apart and that even the soul of Mosca is 'vulgar' compared with theirs, a declaration that the novel almost persuades us as being literally true.

Gina lacks self-knowledge: understandably, in so far as any approach to an admission of the true state of her feelings is an acknowledgment of how little right she has to expect anything from Fabrice in return; though she is predisposed to blindness of this kind as well. The astonishing confidence, impulsiveness and on one occasion at least, overwhelming rightness of her instinct are those of a nature unaccustomed to self-questioning. She is a del Dongo and as such regards it as perfectly right and proper to take little Fabrice away from his lessons and offer her protection to his Jesuit masters on condition that he be given a number of first prizes; while she owes to her serene assurance of the rightness of her instinct and the innocence of her desires the grace and daring by which her many lovers are drawn. It would be a very humourless and dull-spirited reader of the novel who wanted Gina to be fundamentally different, for all her crimes: even though she is one of the most powerful personalities in an oppressive state and even though she has to bear much of the blame for the catastrophe that overtakes Fabrice. And to say this is to touch on the question of that extraordinary moral ambivalence which makes *La chartreuse de Parme* unlike any other novel and which Henry James has described better than any other critic I know:

His notion was that *passion*, the power to surrender oneself sincerely and consistently to the feeling of the hour, was the finest thing in the world, and it seemed to him that he had discovered a mine of it in the old Italian character...It is easy to perceive that this doctrine held itself quite irresponsible to our old moralistic canons, for *naïveté* of sentiment in any direction, combined with great energy, was considered absolutely its own justification. In the *Chartreuse de Parme*, where everyone is grossly immoral, and the heroine is a kind of monster, there is so little attempt to offer any other, that through the magnificently sustained pauses of the narrative we feel at last the influence of the writer's cynicism, regard it as amiable, and enjoy serenely his clear vision of the mechanism of character, unclouded by the mists of prejudice. Among writers called immoral there is no doubt that he best deserves the charge; the others, beside him, are spotlessly innocent.[23]

One of the great merits of James's criticism, though Ezra Pound thought otherwise (when talking of French literature, according to Pound, he tries to 'square all things to the ethical standards of a Salem mid-week Unitarian prayer meeting...') is that he tells us whenever there is a difference between his own notions of decent responsible behaviour and those of an author or his characters. He did not habitually read novels or poems as an escape from reality and would not therefore have been discountenanced if placed in the situation imagined by Yeats in 'The Scholars'. Those twentieth-century critics who talk less severely about Gina, Mosca and Fabrice don't always do so because they would approve of their behaviour in actual life and I am not convinced that it is by being less stern than James that one becomes a better critic of what Beyle had to say. Beyle's own preface and many of his passing comments on the action of the novel are addressed to the consciously moral public of his day; with the most unflattering sarcasm and yet with an acknowledgment – in the preface it is earnest and insistent – that he too judges his characters by standards very different from the characters' own.

The irony and amusement with which the story is told are characteristic of Beyle, but the difficulty of understanding their effect on us is greater than in either *Lucien Leuwen* or *Le rouge et le noir*. For one thing, there is no character in *La chartreuse*, not even Mosca, who appears to be invested by the author with the same hopes as Lucien or Julien Sorel or who is shown as being as capable of assuming the responsibility for his own destiny. M. Bardèche's claim that 'every novel of Stendhal is the story of an education' is far more obviously true of the two earlier novels, for much of the amusement that the principal characters can give, even to readers whose standards are very different from their own, lies in their shameless and perfect incorrigibility.

One of the clues to an understanding of the unsettling effect of opening the novel and being thrown into such a world is to be found, I believe, in the first chapter, where we are told of the arrival of the French in 1796. Bonaparte's army is not an army of moral reformers. (It is the propaganda of the priests in Milan which has portrayed them with a guillotine carried in front of every regiment.) And it is not the laws and institutions of the French but their infectious gaiety and youthfulness on which the story dwells. In the villages, we are told, the soldiers learn the Italian dances, the steps of their own *contredanses* being too difficult for the local inhabitants, and in doing so they encourage the Italians to become themselves again, for gaiety such as this has been long forgotten. The tumultuous joy of the opening pages is inspired by personal memories. 'I felt too keen a pleasure, I admit', Beyle wrote to Balzac, 'in talking of these happy times of my youth...' and some readers may feel that it is all too good to be true and that it is too much an expression of merely personal nostalgia. Yet it is the immense promise of these happy times that the novelist evokes, and the mood of

> Bliss was it in that dawn to be alive,
> But to be young was very heaven...

and if the enlightenment the French bring with them appears so brilliant as to escape all definition ('...the statues of Charles V and Philip II were overturned and the people suddenly found themselves flooded with light...') it is partly because the promise is not kept and because Italy returns to its old institutions and ways. (Palla's revolt will fail to overturn the royal statue and Gina's attempts to flood the streets of Parma will cause merely a few puddles, as if it had rained, while the defiant illumination of her own palace, when Fabrice escapes from prison, is on private property on the frontiers of Parma and Lombardy.) It is in any case in the nature of the French enlightenment as Beyle himself understood and believed in it – and of course not merely Beyle alone; the chapter helps us to understand the appeal to popular and nationalistic instincts of the French example – that it should liberate the oppressed peoples of Europe by helping them to liberate themselves. How they should do that, how, to use one of Beyle's favourite expressions, they should find their own 'path to happiness' is their own affair, and however intolerable the thought of the mistakes they make, their tragedy will lie in their depriving themselves of happiness as they themselves understand it. This is one of the points, as I see it, of

Beyle's many jokes at the expense of his French readers of the 1830s, who are so different from the young Frenchmen of 1796. And it is this 'Beyliste' attitude – in Beyle's own sense of the term – which enables us to contemplate the protracted catastrophes which overtake the main characters without censoriousness or resignation. Beyle's own dissatisfaction with Italy as it is in *La chartreuse* is a tribute to what Italy is capable of becoming again. It is a novel about men and women of wonderful spirit and courage and though so much of it shows us the thwarting of energies, it is not like *L'Abbesse de Castro* a study of 'the long degeneration' of souls.

Lamiel and *Suora Scolastica*

If *La chartreuse de Parme* is concerned with a way of life and an ethical code radically different from those of the public to which it is addressed, the same appears to have been true of *Lamiel*, the novel on which Beyle was working at the time of his death. Lamiel, the heroine, is a foundling brought up by a village beadle, and belongs, like Adrien Laffargue to the class of those who have to 'struggle with real needs'[24] and who alone in France are endowed with 'energy'. Astonished and then bored by the lack of energy and the weakness of character of two aristocratic lovers, she was to have fallen in love with a professional criminal, modelled partly on Lacenaire, whose sinister reputation in his own time has been revived in our own by Marcel Carné's film *Les enfants du paradis*. And according to one plan for the novel, she was to have set fire to the law courts in which he had been condemned to death and to have been found afterwards dead among the ruins.

The sensational ending, however, is only a sketch, and the substance of the novel, which can be read with sustained enjoyment for two or three hours, consists of two versions, which until recently have always been presented as one.[25] The first of these, written out in Civita Vecchia in 1839, includes her adventures with her two disappointing lovers; the second, which was dictated shortly afterwards, gives us only the story of Lamiel's childhood and youth among the leading personalities of her Norman village. And a comparison between the two shows that Beyle was working hard to produce an easy and highly finished narrative: he takes care in the second version, for instance, to make the narrator a character in his own right and a plausible observer of the provincial *mores* he describes; it also suggests that he may have had difficulty in making his Lamiel sufficiently sympathetic and appealing to seem plausible and interesting to himself and his reader. It is the brutal shock to her affectionate nature that we are shown, for instance, in the second version, when her foster parents tell her of her material obligations to them and not merely, as in the first version, her naturally aristocratic aversion to the vulgarity of a reminder of this kind.[26]

'The interest of the novel will become evident when Lamiel experiences actual love', Beyle wrote at the end of the first draft and her criminal lover was to have performed the miracle. Meanwhile, it is because she can feel no love for any man, doesn't know what she wants and is intelligent enough to know she doesn't know, that the novel creates its own suspense and unfolds with the natural precipitate energy of Beyle's comedy at its most outrageous. Lamiel, as Jean Prévost has suggested,[27] is reminiscent of Mathilde de la Mole and of the two Minas of *Mina de Wanghel* and *Le rose et le vert* in her innocence, her intense curiosity and her cruelty towards men who are unwise enough to seek to influence or dominate her in any way; and the most enjoyable scenes in either version are those in which she torments the good-hearted young local priest, who, to his horror, has fallen in love with her and the young Duke whose habitually divided allegiances (he wants to take part in the July Revolution in Paris and his mother insists on his staying at home) and deep self-misgivings make it so easy for Lamiel to throw him off balance; though he has a youthful resilience which Lamiel also enjoys. He is a devoted horseman and when they meet on a rainy day in a half-flooded wood, Lamiel sees that he is thinking more of Greyhound, his drenched thoroughbred than of himself or of her:

'...You've no blanket. He may catch cold. Why don't you take your coat off and put it on his back? Instead of talking to me, you should walk Greyhound round the wood for a while.'

The Duke couldn't reply, he was so worried for his horse and it was so obvious to him that Lamiel was right.

'That isn't all: now something worse is going to happen to you. Happiness is about to fall into your arms.'

'What do you mean?' said the Duke in great alarm.

'I'm going to run away with you and we're going to live together in the same apartment in Rouen,...the same apartment, you understand.'

The Duke stood motionless and frozen with astonishment; Lamiel laughed in his face and then went on:

'As being in love with a peasant girl may dishonour you, I'm seeing if I can kill this so called love of yours with my own hands; or if you'd rather I put it that way, I want to make you agree that your heart isn't strong enough to *feel any love*!'

He looked so funny that Lamiel said to him for the second time since they had first met:

'Now take me in your arms and do it passionately, but don't knock my cotton bonnet off.'

It should be explained perhaps that there is nothing more hideous and absurd than the Phrygian shaped cotton bonnets worn by the young women of Caen and Bayeux.

'You're right', said the Duke laughing.

He took off her bonnet, put his own hunter's cap on her head and embraced her with an impulsive passion which, for Lamiel, had all the charm of the unforeseen. The sarcasm vanished from her lovely eyes...[28]

To say that the comedy here is characteristically Stendhalian is to point to the qualities that make it read like a process of swift developing thought and discovery, to the qualities, in other words, that make it unlike anything by Balzac.[29] The Duc de Myossens, like the hero of *Armance* and the young aristocrat in *Le rose et le vert*, is a student of L'Ecole Polytechnique and a type of young Frenchman whom we always see torn between his natural aristocratic instincts and his sense of the overwhelming reasonableness of the new social enlightenment.[30] But it is Beyle's sympathetic interest in the type that leads him to imagine him responding to the challenge of a Lamiel and revealing new possibilities of character within himself; we last see the Duke after she has run away from him, peering from his saddle into every coach he passes on the road she tricks him into thinking she has taken. Another type by which Beyle was obviously intrigued is that represented by the hunchback Dr Sansfin, a clever physician and an amusing and unprincipled opportunist, like Dr Du Poirier in *Lucien Leuwen*. Sansfin occupies a dominant rôle in Beyle's second version of the novel and various sketches for episodes in which he was to appear (and which read a little like a modern *Roman de Renart*) are to be found among the manuscripts on which Beyle was working during the very last weeks of his life. Sansfin has an alarmingly candid and brutal version of the philosophy of Helvétius to offer, and a reason for his importance may be that he is Lamiel's spiritual mentor during the most impressionable years of her life. Beyle may well have felt that the reasons for her eventual lack of almost any moral scruple and her readiness to become the accomplice of Lacenaire needed the kind of explanation Sansfin's influence provides. His own flamboyant and almost exclusive concern with the interests of his own vanity – he is a marksman and shoots his own dog in the village street when it fails to obey him – has a natural explanation, like Richard III's, in his deformity; though it is the plausibility of his cynicism and what Lamiel sees as the 'granite-like' unshakeable quality of his arguments that Beyle may have wanted to test by imagining them put into practice by an intelligent girl setting out on a journey of discovery in the world.

Nothing in *Lamiel* or in the other story on which he was working at the same time suggests that when he died he was not in full possession of his powers as a novelist, despite the severe illnesses of his last two years. *Suora Scolastica*, though unfinished, is by far the best, or at least the most promising of the *Chroniques italiennes* which are primarily of Beyle's own invention and was begun, if we go by a letter written to the Comtesse de Tascher in March 1839, in an attempt to improve on *L'abbesse de Castro*. Like *L'Abbesse* itself and another of the later chronicles, *Trop de faveur tue*, it is a story of the intrigues of a convent and of the long desperate sieges laid to it by lovers ready to lay down their lives. It is also – in the version on which Beyle was working on the morning of his death – an evocation of the life of an eighteenth-century Neapolitan court, that of the young Don Carlos, son of Philip V of Spain, who, 'though educated by priests and in all the rigours of etiquette, was not, as it happened, an unintelligent man'. The magnificence and geniality of the life over which Don Carlos presides, despite the jealousies by which it is later to be poisoned, contrast with what we are shown of northern Italian society in *La chartreuse de Parme*, while in the preface to the story, we are introduced to an Italy in which politics, though clandestine, are an absorbing universal concern:

In Naples, no one ever talks, even a little clearly, about politics. This is the reason: a Neapolitan family consisting, for example, of three sons, a daughter and the mother and father, will belong to three different parties, which in Naples go by the name of *conspiracies*. The daughter belongs to her lover's party; each of the sons belongs to a different conspiracy; the father and mother sigh for the days of the court which reigned over them when they were twenty years old. As a result of this isolation of each individual, no one ever talks about politics seriously. At the least assertion with an incisive ring and which does not sound commonplace, you will see two or three faces turn pale...

Lamiel and *Suora Scolastica* testify to Beyle's ability to renew radically his sense of human possibilities. It is pointless to speculate on what he would have written had he lived, but it seems unlikely that he would have tried to repeat in any way his previous achievements as a chronicler and novelist. The work which he tried to re-write was work with which he was *dissatisfied*, like *La chartreuse de Parme* itself, for which he planned a new version, encouraged partly by Balzac's enthusiastic review in *La revue Parisienne*. There is nothing to suggest that when he died he had acquired that satisfaction with his achievements that would have led him to merely imitate himself, in other words, no longer to be himself and to become instead what he fortunately never became, a consciously respectable man of letters.

8

Some conclusions

The sense of something uncompleted in Beyle's finest work is conveyed by Tolstoy in a letter to his wife of November 1883:

I read it [*Le rouge et le noir*] some forty years ago, but remembered nothing save my relations to the author: sympathy with his boldness and a feeling of kinship – yet an unsatisfied feeling. And strangely enough I feel the same now, but with a clear consciousness of why and wherefore...[1]

It is significant perhaps that he should have been able to understand his 'unsatisfied feelings' after forty years and after he himself had written *War and Peace* and *Anna Karenina*; it is significant too that he should have continued to regard the influence of Stendhal on his work as greater than that of anyone else.[2]

If Tolstoy's thought and writing is in many ways a development and deepening of what he had found in Beyle, this is not necessarily because he was the more intelligent man – the comparison can easily become impertinent and we are concerned, in any case, if we dwell on these questions at all with something more than individual intelligence; it has something to do as well with the immeasurable advantages he enjoyed, as a sophisticated European, a combatant officer, an aristocrat, a landowner and a husband and father, in having intimate knowledge of so much more of life than Beyle was ever able to experience at first hand. It is not only the experience and growth of the individual consciousness that Tolstoy is able to give us or the moments that test and reveal what we are, but what takes shape in the course of everyday life and in particular the life of a home and family to which all generations can know they belong. This is the most obvious difference between Fabrice del Dongo and Nikolay Rostov in *War and Peace*, who on the field of battle have so much in common. It is because of historical circumstances that Fabrice is unable to follow the destiny for which he is prepared as a child, unable, for example, to live as a dedicated soldier like Nikolay and then as a devoted husband and father enjoying his responsibilities to the full; and it is on the tragic consequences of his fate that Beyle dwells, leaving his potentialities for living pointedly unfulfilled.

It is easy enough, in other words, to say in what ways Tolstoy offers a much wider range of experience than Beyle and why his principal figures are given more opportunities to discover their individual destinies. It is far less easy to account for the greater depth of Tolstoy, the depth that is apparent in the text locally, and, since he never formulates a critique of Beyle, to justify one's belief that he is speaking truthfully of his 'clear consciousness after forty years of the 'why and wherefore' of his dissatisfaction with *Le rouge et le noir*. All I can say is that I know of no one in France who gives the impression of having spoken of Beyle's limitations with Tolstoy's (unassuming) authority. Certainly not Sainte-Beuve. Nor even the André Gide whom Arnold Bennett hailed as 'the Stendhal of our time, but, thank God, better educated and more sensitive...'.[3] Gide is probably the most gifted and entertaining of the many novelists in France who have been influenced by Beyle and the gift can be seen in the reflective wit and the highly personal idiom which never, as in the later novels of Giono, for instance, lapses into virtual pastiche.[4] His Lafcadio in *Les caves du Vatican* cultivates hypocrisy and freedom from his own weaknesses like Julien Sorel, punishes himself for his lapses and in a scene reminiscent of Julien's self-imposed challenges, persuades himself that he has an obligation to push a fellow passenger out of a fast-moving train; while Bernard, in *Les faux monnayeurs*, is shown poignantly at the moment of his entry into the adult world, baffled by what he is to make of his inner freedom, while struggling to maintain it at the same time. Yet neither novel is completely realistic or serious, and Gide's intelligence and artistic gift lie in his not pretending for a moment that they are. The parody of conventional romance in the coincidence by which Lafcadio unknowingly chooses as his victim his own relation by marriage, and the comic ramifications of the crime distract both Lafcadio and the reader from pursuing its moral and psychological implications; while in *Les faux monnayeurs*, Bernard is left by Gide at an early stage in his struggle and the novel becomes increasingly a parody of itself and an eloquent admission, through the characterisation of the novelist within the novel, of his own lack of creative power and inhuman curiosity. It is an inhuman impulse too which dictates the particular form of Lafcadio's self-imposed challenge, when contrasted with Julien's suddenly wanting to hold Mme de Rênal's hand, and it is possibly for this reason that Gide did not attempt to show it as a crucial moment in the development into fuller humanity of a representative fellow-being.

Gide's recorded considerations of Beyle's work are far more copious than Tolstoy's, though his account of Beyle's limitations is not the most convincing evidence that he was 'thank God, better educated and more sensitive'. I mention them because they illustrate the extraordinary range of the appeal of Beyle's writings and also how rare it is to find a man who is more educated in that he is able to recognise and account for Beyle's limitations as a novelist. Beyle was obviously in advance of his time in many ways, but 'catching up with him', as Nietzsche puts it, involves more than the passage of time. Gide's preface to *Armance* of 1925 is a personal tribute of the best possible kind, in that it can remind those readers who are not all that interested in the torments and joys of the hero why these can seem of crucial significance to someone else. The dissociation between love and sexual desire in Octave de Malibert, Gide maintains, brings home to us the easily forgotten likelihood that the sexually impotent may, by the very fact of their impotence, be capable of the 'most fervent and tender love'. It is fairly obvious that Gide had a special interest in the novel, which served to illustrate his defence of homosexual love, in *Corydon* published the year before, as conducive, among other things, to a better understanding between men and women. It is clear too that, though what Gide is saying is in many ways true of *Armance*, it is not the whole truth; for the novel gives us the swift development of Octave's feelings and is virtually unfinished. We never know what Octave might have become.

It is in the preface to *Lamiel* of 1947 that we find Gide's most eloquent account of what he sees as Beyle's limitations, and here he talks of

> ...certain strata of the soul, into which Stendhal doesn't even seek to penetrate because he had no knowledge of them, those profound strata in which the religious feelings have their place that Stendhal dismissed so lightly; where the great Goethean *Schaudern* (for which I find no proper equivalent in our language) hold their sway over and grow in our minds, the region of trances and enchantments. It may be that these mysterious regions exist only in the imagination of men and are only constructions and substructions of the mind; but they matter none the less, and without them, the human being is utterly impoverished...

The preface has the merit of expressing a fundamental misgiving that is shared by many other readers of Beyle, and it is perhaps the judgment least susceptible to confirmation or refutation by reference to any text. I should like, none the less, to invite those readers who share Gide's feelings of dissatisfaction, as he expresses them here, to re-read the chapters in *Le rouge et le noir* giving us Julien's thoughts and experiences in the prison cell[5] and Fabrice's reflections on the beliefs he has derived from the Abbé Blanès in chapter 8 of *La chartreuse de Parme*. Gide, like many of Beyle's most intelligent readers, like Mme Henriette Bibas, for instance,[6] may well have been misled by Beyle's impatience with mere religiosity and his determination, whatever strata of the soul he had in mind, to write with boldness and in an honest language.

The most influential French thinker of our time, M. Jean-Paul Sartre, has made no attempt that I know of to assess Beyle's achievement as a whole or the quality of his intelligence, and though his occasional allusions to him are friendly, has never brought the intense scrutiny to his mind and work that we find in his writings on Baudelaire, Genet and Flaubert. Beyle is, if anything, conspicuous so far by his absence from Sartre's critical writings and in particular from Sartre's massive work on Flaubert, *L'idiot de la famille*, since much of it is devoted to an analysis of the self-delusions of Flaubert's older contemporaries and peers, torn between hatred of the Philistinism of their class and fear of the rising proletariat and seeking a false solution in the cultivation of art as a refuge from the horrors of contemporary society. One may be glad that M. Sartre does not try to pretend that Beyle also fits into the psychological and historical patterns he has traced, though the probability that he does not is one of the principal reasons for doubting whether the patterns correspond to any historical necessity. The incompleteness of M. Sartre's admirably documented picture of the age is apparent particularly when one reads of the influence of Condillac, Helvétius, Tracy and Bentham on men of the generation of Flaubert's own father, which happens to be that of Beyle himself. Sartre gives us only the most repellent and implausible aspects of their combined influence: the mechanistic interpretation of living phenomena and the encouragement they offer to self-love,[7] to which they no doubt lend themselves. But if this were the entire truth, we would have to assume that Beyle, in so far as he was very different from Flaubert's father (whom Sartre portrays as a French Gradgrind) either failed to understand them or, despite his assertions to the contrary, never really underwent their influence at all.

This has often been claimed, or, as an alternative, that it didn't matter with what philosophy Beyle began; what mattered was what he made of it as a creative artist.[8] My purpose in writing this study has been partly to argue against this view and to suggest that the astonishing intelligence of his art was a consequence of many years of self-training in which reflection on the basic tenets of the thinkers whom M. Sartre castigates played a crucial part. Beyle's allusions to Bentham may be sometimes deliberately provocative, an invocation of the name of a *chef de file*, as when he tells us that ' Jeremy Bentham helps us to understand the sense of beauty in antiquity a hundred times better than Plato and all his imitators...',[9] the *boutade* possibly being directed against the author of *Du vrai, du beau et du bien*, the apostle of disinterestedness both in art and in life and possibly the first person to talk of 'art for art's sake', the fashionable young philosopher Victor Cousin. And Beyle's professed Utilitarianism seems to owe more to Helvétius than to Bentham and even then to little of which Helvétius himself was the originator. ('In all ages of philosophy', Mill reminds his readers in his essay on Bentham, 'one of its schools has been Utilitarian – not only from the time of Epicurus but long before...') while Beyle's insistent defence of Helvétius is in part a response to the denigration from which he suffered in France, and not only in France, throughout most of Beyle's lifetime. The whole of the moral philosophy inspired by Kant, according to Nietzsche, was an attack upon Helvétius, 'the most maligned of all good moralists and all good men...'[10] and though Nietzsche himself speaks far less highly of Bentham than Beyle or even Mill, he too acknowledges their common master:

Consider, for instance, those indefatigable, inevitable English utilitarians, so heavy and respectable who tread up and down (a Homeric comparison would express it better) over the footsteps of Bentham, who in turn treads up and down over those of the respectable Helvétius...[11]

Nietzsche too reminds us that Utilitarianism has a longer history than the name of the modern school, he accuses the English Utilitarians of seeking not the happiness of the greatest number but the happiness of England (the organisation of the colonisation of New Zealand by the Utilitarian Edward Gibbon Wakefield might be taken as illustrating the point) and of being, despite the Utilitarian cloak, essentially puritanical, that is the antithesis of '*Ein Moralist*':

For the moralist is a thinker who considers morality as dubious, hypothetical, in other words a problem. And is it not immoral to think of morality as problematic?[12]

The supreme modern example of the questioning moralist for Nietzsche was, of course, Beyle himself.

Beyle's questioning of the economic orthodoxies of his day – Say's theory of markets, for example, and Saint-Simon's cult of productivity (the early versions, that is to say, of the modern subordination of all interests to those of economic growth)[13] is pursued from the point of view of a man who avowedly wishes the happiness of the greatest number, everything, as he makes clear, depending on what we mean by happiness; while in *Lucien Leuwen*, the delusions inherent in the creation of wealth for others to enjoy and in making others happy 'in one's own way' are made to emerge from his presentation of M. Leuwen père, the financial genius and personal friend of Bentham. In Beyle, perhaps more than in any other thinkers of the school with which he identified himself, the pleasure principle and the general theory of utility take a critical and interrogative as well as an affirmative form: what is happiness? what do men really want? being, as he told Balzac, the questions he habitually asks. In Paris, as a young man, he studied, he tells us,[14] together with Adam Smith, Say and Shakespeare, Montaigne. And as in Montaigne, the interrogative cast of mind proves to be incompatible with systematic thought – that is, thought which seeks to demonstrate its consistency by defending itself against all possible objections – and to demand, far more than in most other men, enlightenment from particular instances. It is the scepticism which is dissatisfied with vague generalities or general propositions that ask to be taken on trust that led Beyle to evolve his own highly idiosyncratic idiom and to become a novelist; and in doing so he showed that readiness to rely on what is felt and perceived which is fundamental to the utilitarian method. 'It is the introduction into the philosophy of human conduct, of this method of detail', Mill tells us in his essay on Bentham, 'of this practice of never reasoning about wholes till they have been resolved into parts, nor about abstractions till they have been translated into realities – that constitutes the originality of Bentham in philosophy, and makes him the great reformer of the moral and political branch of it.' The inhuman abstractness, none the less, of Bentham's systematisation of the pleasure principle (which Mill goes on to demonstrate) may remind us that Bentham's ostensible concern with 'realities' by no means corresponded always with his actual 'practice'. I have suggested earlier that a similar contrast between practice and avowed method can be found in Tracy's *Traité de la volonté*, especially when contrasted with *Le rouge et le noir*.[15] Beyle learned certainly from Tracy, as he learned from Helvétius and to a lesser extent Bentham. But in learning, I should like to conclude by suggesting, he expressed the beliefs he shared with them more consistently than they had themselves, at the cost of neglect throughout his lifetime and by becoming the first of the great modern novelists. We see this whether we consider the form that the basic principles of utilitarianism take in his writings or his simultaneous reliance on and questioning of experience. It is for this reason, presumably that he should today prove so much more readable, on any level of seriousness, than the thinkers whose influence he underwent. And it may be for this reason too that he counts for so much in the formation of Nietzsche and Tolstoy, who belong to the age succeeding that of Beyle and have had a by no means negligible influence on our own.

Notes

NOTES TO CHAPTER ONE

1 F. Nietzsche, *Untimely Considerations*, book 1, ch. 2.
2 *La vie de Henry Brulard*, ch. 1 in *Oeuvres intimes* (Paris, Gallimard, 1955), p. 41.
3 *Correspondance*, 16.10.1840.
4 F. Nietzsche, *Beyond Good and Evil*, VIII, p. 254.
5 A. Lamartine, *Cours familier de littérature* (Paris, 1864), vol. 17, entretien 102.
6 J. Prévost, *La création chez Stendhal* (Paris, 1951), p. 29.
7 *Pensées* (Paris, 1931), vol. 1, p. 123.
8 See Picavet, *Les idéologues* (Paris, 1891), p. 585.
9 *Henri Brulard*, ch. 2, p. 53.
10 *Ibid.*, ch. 40, p. 375.
11 J. Prévost, *La création chez Stendhal*, p. 23.
12 H. James, *Literary Reviews and Essays*, ed. Mordell (New York, 1957), p. 157.
13 T. S. Eliot, 'Tradition and the Individual Talent' in *Selected Essays* (London, 1932), p. 14.
14 See A. Latreille, 'Le catéchisme impérial de 1806', *Annales de l'Université de Lyon*, 3e série, 1935. Dr A. P. Kerr has drawn my attention to this paper.
15 Chateaubriand, *Le génie du christianisme*, part 1, book 1, ch. 1.
16 C. Morazé, *La France bourgeoise* (Paris, 1947), ch. 3, p. 82.
17 *Ibid.*, p. 85.
18 Gérard de Nerval, *Quintus Aucler*, ch. 1, in *Les Illuminés*.
19 A thorough examination of Vigny's lifelong concern for public order and the maintenance of the established creed, despite his own religious scepticism, is to be found in M. Henri Guillemin's excellent *M. de Vigny, homme d'ordre et poète* (Paris, 1955).
20 Preface to *Mémoires sur Napoléon*.
21 *Courrier Anglais* (Paris, Le Divan, 1935), vol. 1, p. 330. *Paris Monthly Review*, June 1822.
22 F. Nietzsche, *Ecce homo*, II, 3.
23 In the essay on Balzac in *Portraits contemporains*.
24 C. A. Sainte-Beuve, *Causeries du lundi*, vol. 9 (Paris, 1856), pp. 264–5.
25 A. de Tocqueville, *L'ancien régime* (Paris, 1952), vol. 1, pp. 175–6.
26 *Ibid.*, vol. 1, pp. 207–8.

27 Reprinted in Charles de Rémusat, *Passé et présent* (Paris, 1859).

28 *Oeuvres intimes*, ch. 9, p. 119.

29 *Ibid.*, ch. 10, p. 127.

30 *Ibid.*, ch. 15, p. 172.

31 See the essay on Milton in *Etudes critiques sur la littérature contemporaine*.

32 See Emile Durkheim, *L'évolution pédagogique en France* (Paris, 1969), ch. 10.

33 See V. del Litto, *La vie intellectuelle de Stendhal* (Paris, 1959), pp. 12–15.

34 Beyle is alluding, presumably, to his *Vie de Mozart* (1815) and the chapter on Michelangelo in his *Histoire de la peinture en Italie* (1817).

35 *Mélanges de littérature* (Paris, 1933), vol. 3, p. 417.

36 L. Blum, *Stendhal et le Beylisme* (Paris, 1947), p. 7.

37 *Ibid.*, p. 9.

38 *Correspondance*, 19.2.1831.

39 *Ibid.*, 8.8.1804.

40 *Ibid.*, 29.8.1804.

41 Beyle's conduct towards his sister is one of the least attractive episodes in his life. For many years after leaving Grenoble he wrote to her the long persistent letters in which he tried to form her mind and character and transform her into another Mme Roland, the ideal embodiment, for Beyle, of enlightened femininity. Her marriage with François Périer-Lagrange was, as Beyle had advised, a marriage of reason rather than love and not, as it turned out, a happy one. (See 'Sur Pauline Beyle. Documents inédits présentés par V. del Litto' in *Stendhal Club*, no. 24, 15 July 1964.) After her husband's death, childless and in reduced circumstances, she joined her brother in Milan. He had many times in the past suggested that they might one day live together with a few friends and form an ideal community. (See, for instance, *Correspondance*, 22.8.1805.) Beyle describes in *Souvenirs d'égotisme* the outcome of her journey to Milan: 'I was severely punished for having advised a sister of mine to come to Milan, in 1816 I think it was. Mme. Périer attached herself to me like a barnacle, making me responsible for her destiny, virtually for the rest of her life. Mme Périer possessed all the virtues and considerable sense and amiability. I was obliged to quarrel with her in order to rid myself of a barnacle tediously clinging to my keel and who, for good or ill, placed on me the future responsibility for her happiness. It was a horrible business.' (*Oeuvres intimes*, p. 1,483.)

42 C. A. Sainte-Beuve, *Causeries du lundi*, vol. 9, p. 254.

43 *Oeuvres intimes*, pp. 38–9.

NOTES TO CHAPTER TWO

1 *La vie de Henry Brulard*, chapter 3 in *Oeuvres intimes* (Paris, Gallimand, 1955), p. 57.

2 *Racine et Shakspeare* (Paris, Le Divan, 1928), p. 35.

3 *Pensées* (Paris, Le Divan, 1931), vol. 2, p. 60.

4 *Mélanges de littérature* (Paris, Le Divan, 1933), vol. 3, p. 105.

5 See the article by Lucien Jansse in *Stendhal Club*, 36, 15 July 1967, 'Stendhal et la constitution anglaise.'

6 In this respect, his criticisms are similar to those made by Helvétius to Montesquieu himself. See *Oeuvres complètes d'Helvétius* (éd.) Didot, vol. 14, p. 61.

7 See V. del Litto, *La vie intellectuelle de Stendhal* (Paris, 1959), pp. 67–70.

8 'If Mme de Staël hadn't wished to be more passionate than nature and her early education have made her, she would have written masterpieces. She has tried to adopt something other than her natural style, she has written works full of excellent thoughts which are the fruit of a *reflective character* and which show nothing of a *tender* character. And as she has tried to display tenderness, she has fallen into mere gibberish.' Letter to Pauline Beyle, 20.8.1805.

9 Montesquieu, *L'esprit des lois*, part 3, book 14, ch. 2.

10 Stendhal, *De l'amour*, ch. 2.

11 Rousseau, book 5 (p. 448 in the Garnier edition, Paris, 1957).

12 *La vie de Henry Brulard*, ch. 44, p. 407.

13 *Ibid.*, ch. 46, p. 421.

14 See, for example, the letter to Pauline of 29 October 1804.

15 *Mélanges de littérature* (Paris, Le Divan, 1933), pp. 95–6.

16 See *Emile*, the seventh paragraph of *La profession de foi du Vicaire Savoyand*.

17 *Ibid.*, pp. 114–15.

18 *Correspondance*, 2.10.1812.

19 See, for example, Chateaubriand, *Le génie du christianisme*, part 3, ch. 2 and Mme de Staël, *De la littérature*, part 1, ch. 6.

20 *Pensées*, vol. 1, p. 119.

21 *Mémoires d'un touriste* (Paris, le Divan, 1837), vol. 3, p. 38.

22 In a note to *Lettres de la Montagne* quoted by Guy Besse in his very useful preface to Helvétius's *De l'esprit* (Paris, Editions sociales, 1959).

23 *Courrier anglais* (Paris, 1935), vol. 2, p. 166.

24 *Mélanges intimes* (Paris, Le Divan, 1936), vol. 2, pp. 166–7.

25 Cf. the epilogue to *L'histoire de la peinture en Italie*: 'A great genius mistrusts his discoveries...In a matter in which his happiness is so much at stake, he thinks of all the objections to them he can. Thus a man of genius can only make a certain number of discoveries. It is rare for him to have the courage to take his discoveries as an unassailable point of departure. Consider Descartes, who abandoned a sublime method and, after the second step only, began to reason like a monk...'

26 See the article on Kant in *Courrier anglais*, vol. 1, pp. 327–31.

27 *Correspondance*, 24.1.1806.

28 See Otto Gierke, *Natural Law and the Theory of Society*, translated by Ernest Barker (Boston, 1957), p. 97. The whole of this, I am told, still classical study – extracted from *Das deutsche Genossenschaftsrecht* – is relevant to the crucial issue of natural law and its social and metaphysical implications. See particularly ch. 2 for its bearing on the Enlightenment.

29 *Correspondance*, 8.2.1803.

30 *Courrier anglais*, vol. 1, pp. 301–4.

31 *Loc. cit.*

32 Helvétius, *De l'esprit*, discourse 2, ch. 5.

33 *La vie de Henry Brulard*, ch. 37, pp. 353–4.

34 Robert M. Adams: *Stendhal, notes on a novelist* (London, 1959), p. 184.

35 In Book I, part 4, section 6.

36 *Courrier Anglais*, vol. 3, p. 412 (*New Monthly Magazine*, September 1828).
37 See p. 16 above.
38 G. Cabanis, *Oeuvres complètes* (Paris, 1956), vol. 2, p. 348.
39 See A. Girard, *Le journal intime* (Paris, 1963). M. Girard's thesis is that the intimate journals of Benjamin Constant, Maine de Biran, Stendhal and other contemporaries mark a totally new departure in the recording of personal experience.
40 *Oeuvres intimes*, p. 962.
41 Stendhal's ideas of human perfectibility and of the nature of the known and knowable self came increasingly in fact to resemble those of D. H. Lawrence in the two versions of his essay on Benjamin Franklin in the *Spirit of Place* and *Studies in Classic American Literature*. Both these versions, together with the sketch for an essay on the influence of Rousseau, 'The Good Man' published in the first volume of *Phoenix*, provide an excellent foil against which Stendhal's own writings on the same themes stand out in peculiarly clear relief. The contrast, of course, between Lawrence and Stendhal is as illuminating as the resemblances.
42 See the letter to Alberthe de Rubempré quoted on p. 23, above.
43 In K. Marx, *The German Ideology*, vol. 1, 3 (pp. 447–54 in the Lawrence and Wishart edition, London, 1965).
44 In K. Marx, *The Holy Family* (Moscow, 1956), pp. 168–77.
45 Mme de Staël, *De la littérature*, part 1, ch. 6.
46 Preface to *De la religion* quoted by Beyle in the *Courrier Anglais*, vol. 4, p. 29. Beyle describes this passage as worthy of any commonplace fanatical preacher.
47 Victor Cousin, *Cours d'histoire de la philosophie morale au dix-huitième siècle* (Paris, 1839), lesson 4, p. 166.
48 *Correspondance*, 16.10.1840.
49 F. R. Leavis, *The Great Tradition* (London, 1948), p. 191.
50 *Pensées*, vol. 2, p. 294.
51 Utilitarianism, it is true, is often presented ironically in the novels themselves. Count Mosca in *La chartreuse* regards 'the greatest happiness of the greatest number' theory as a naïve absurdity, while the solemn Utilitarianism of the conspiratorial Liberal, Count Altamira in *Le rouge et le noir*, makes him something of a Pangloss or a Don Quixote. Beyle's own readiness to quote and stand by Utilitarian and specifically Benthamite principles seems on the whole, none the less, to characterise his writings from 1810 onwards after his discovery of the *Treatise of Civil and Penal Legislation*. In a letter to Mareste (24.10.1818) he describes Bentham as 'Montesquieu perfected' comparing Bentham again with Montesquieu to the former's advantage in *Mémoires d'un Touriste* (vol. III, p. 318 of the 1929 edition), in *De l'amour* he quotes Bentham several times on the nature of asceticism and in an essay of 1829, *Philosophie transcendentale* (see *Mélanges de littérature*, vol. II) he makes what is virtually a Utilitarian and Benthamite profession of faith.
52 George Santayana, *Five Essays* (Cambridge, 1934), p. 21.
53 In a letter to Stendhal of 22 December 1825 their mutual friend Victor Jacquemont told Stendhal that although Tracy had admired *Rome, Naples et Florence*, he had never believed 'and still doesn't believe that you've written this book *seriously*'. Henri Martineau points out in his preface to his 1957

edition of *De l'amour* that Tracy was personally, for one thing, unable to believe in any form of what is usually called Platonic love.

54 *De l'amour*, ch. 24.

55 Most obviously at the beginning of ch. 3.

56 Adams, *Stendhal, notes on a novelist*, p. 55.

57 See the unsigned article by George Eliot on *De l'amour* and other recently published or republished works in *The Westminster Review*, 65 (April 1856) included in volume 7 of George Eliot's letters (London, 1955).

58 See *The Second Sex* (London, 1953), pp. 247 and 652.

59 *De l'amour*, ch. 55.

60 L. Jansse, 'Stendhal et l'économie politique' in *Stendhal Club*, 28, 15 juillet 1965.

61 In an article in *The New Monthly Magazine* for February 1827 (see *Courrier Anglais*, vol. 3, pp. 287–98), Beyle resumes for his English readers Dupin's statistical survey for the whole of France showing the relative numbers of those in various regions attending schools and institutes of learning.

62 In his essays on *Saint-Simonian economic doctrine* to be found in *The Era of Tyrannies* (London, 1967).

63 How it is that Beyle did not apparently read Sismondi's *Nouveaux principes d'économie politique* of 1819 is by no means clear. He knew Sismondi's work, on the whole, very well and particularly his *Littérature du midi de l'Europe* and *Histoire des républiques italiennes*. As an economist, Sismondi, like Beyle, foresaw the saturation of markets and his critique of the theory of markets strongly influenced Robert Owen, whom he met in 1818, Proudhon and the early Marx. See the essay on Halévy's *Era of Tyrannies*. For Beyle's views on Fourier see *Mémoires d'un touriste* (1929), vol. II, p. 22 and vol. 3, p. 279. Also *Stendhal et la pensée sociale de son temps* (Paris, 1967), pp. 238–42.

64 Notice that Beyle says 'a sacrifice of interest to some noble end' ('*sacrifice* de l'intérêt à quelque noble but') and not 'sacrifice of *all* personal interest'. I mention this because one recent critic, Miss Margaret Tillett in *Stendhal, the Background to his Novels* (London, 1971) sees in this phrase a contradiction of 'his Helvetian principle' that 'self-sacrifice is simply a form of self-interest' (p. 96). The confusion and self-contradiction of which Miss Tillett complains stem perhaps from her use of the English phrase 'self-interest' of which there is no equivalent in Beyle's own French.

65 Beyle claims in *La vie de Henry Brulard* (*Oeuvres intimes*, p. 177) that, as a lieutenant of dragoons, at the Battle of Castel-Franco in January 1801 he took part in a head-on charge against the Austrian artillery. He also mentions an attestation written to confirm this by General Michaud to whom he served as aide-de-camp. Paul Arbelet in *La jeunesse de Stendhal* (Paris, 1914, 2 vols.) and Henri Martineau in *Le calendrier de Stendhal* (Paris, 1950) both give interesting arguments for believing that Beyle was lying ill at the time in Milan and that Michaud's certificate was one in which he perjured himself as a favour to Beyle.

NOTES TO CHAPTER THREE

1 See Martin Turnell's reviews of my edition of Stendhal's *Selected Journalism* in *The Spectator* for 26 July 1959 and in *The Twentieth Century* for October 1959.

2 Mme de Chasteller finds Lucien Leuwen, when they first meet and he is tongue-tied, a mere 'hero out of Ariosto'. *Lucien Leuwen*, ch. 17.

3 *Pensées*, vol. 1, p. 30.

4 *Pensées*, vol. 1, p. 95.

5 See Helvétius, *De l'esprit*, discourse 2, ch. 16 and discourse 4, ch. 2.

6 *Oeuvres intimes*, ch. 7, p. 94.

7 *Correspondance*, 8.8.1804.

8 *Oeuvres intimes*, p. 1,174 (27.9.1811).

9 *Ibid.*, p. 563.

10 See V. del Litto, *La vie intellectuelle de Stendhal*, pp. 503–63 for a detailed account of Beyle's comments on and borrowings from *The Edinburgh Review*.

11 *Rome, Naples et Florence en 1817*, entry for 11 May 1817.

12 *Pensées*, vol. 1, p. 158.

13 *Mélanges de littérature*, vol. 3, pp. 81–3.

14 *Ibid.*, p. 86.

15 *Ibid.*, p. 87.

16 *Rome, Naples et Florence, en 1817*, entry for 11 May 1817.

17 *Oeuvres intimes*, pp. 620–1.

18 *Ibid.*, p. 614.

19 See *D'un nouveau complot contre les industriels* quoted on page 51.

20 *Molière, Shakespeare, la comédie et le rire* (Paris, 1930), p. 208. This is in Crozet's handwriting.

21 *Ibid.*, pp. 208–9 (in Beyle's handwriting).

22 *La vie de Rossini*, ch. 18.

23 C. A. Sainte-Beuve, *Causeries du lundi*, vol. 9, p. 254.

24 Georges Blin, *Stendhal et les problèmes du roman* (Paris, 1954), p. 19.

25 *Rome, Naples et Florence en 1817*, entry for 11 May 1817.

26 Alfieri, *Vita*, epoca quarta, ch. 1.

27 *Mélanges de littérature*, vol. 3, p. 98.

28 *Ibid.* p. 110.

29 Cf. D. H. Lawrence's introduction to his volume of poems entitled *Pansies*: 'Each little piece is a thought; not a bare idea or an opinion or a didactic statement, but a true thought which comes as much from the heart and genitals as the head.' More relevant in this connection, however, is the claim by Lawrence's one-time friend, John Middleton Murry that this definition of style is the best that has ever been formulated. See Murry's Oxford lectures of 1921 on *The Problem of Style*. Murry's own translation of the definition reads as follows: 'Style is this: to add to a given thought all the circumstances fitted to produce the whole effect that the thought ought to produce.' He adds, however: 'A more truly accurate translation, I think, would be: "the whole effect which the thought is intended to produce." At any rate the French hovers between the two meanings.' The reader will obviously choose as he prefers between Murry's translation and my own, but I believe that if Beyle had wished to convey the two meanings which Murry finds in the single word '*doit*' he would have done so more clearly. A very free translation of the whole phrase might be: 'the total effect which this thought must produce if it is to be adequately conveyed'. The last seven words would contribute, however, only to making misunderstanding impossible and I hope that my translation is clear enough as it stands.

30 In, for example, an article on Italian poetry in *The London Magazine* for January 1826. See *Le Courrier Anglais*, vol. 4, p. 280.

31 In *The New Monthly Magazine* for September 1826 (*Courrier Anglais*, vol. 3, p. 154).

32 *Oeuvres intimes*, p. 568.

33 *Pensées*, vol. 1, ch. 23.

34 See *Eléments d'idéologie*, part 3, *Discours préliminaire*.

35 *Oeuvres intimes*, p. 621 (11.2.1805).

36 See *Horace*, act 3, scene 6.

37 See *Andromaque*, act 5, scene 3.

38 For Beyle's debt to Reynolds see V. del Litto's *Vie intellectuelle de Stendhal*. The 'moment of repose' in *Macbeth* marked by the 'temple haunting martlet' speech is one to which Reynolds draws attention in his eighth Discourse. Beyle uses the example again in book 2, ch. 34 of *The History of Painting in Italy*.

39 See again del Litto, *Vie intellectuelle de Stendhal*. Beyle's allegation that Reynolds exaggerated his admiration for Michelangelo and that he was far more influenced in his depiction of the human form by Rembrandt, whom he feigned to disparage, is almost certainly one of his many borrowings from Knight (cf. del Litto, p. 499). William Blake makes a similar point in his annotations to Reynolds' *Discourses*: 'If Reynolds had really admired Mich. Angelo, he never would have followed Rubens.'

40 See Mill's *Autobiography*, ch. 5.

41 Beyle appears particularly as he grew older, to have had a limited confidence in the usefulness of reasoning in any discussion of music or poetry. In a dialogue, for instance, in *Racine et Shakspeare* between the Romantic and the Academician, the former talks of the moments of 'perfect illusion' which he claims are more frequent in Shakespeare than Racine. He adds, however: 'If you are dishonest or insensitive or petrified by Laharpe, [the most influential academic critic of the pre-Romantic period; he lived from 1739 to 1803] you will deny my little moments of perfect illusion. And I admit there is nothing I can say in reply. Your feelings are not something material I can extract from your heart and place under your nose to prove you are wrong . . . I have reached the limits of what logic is able to grasp in poetry.'

42 *De l'homme*, section 8, ch. 17.

43 Helvetius, *De l'esprit*, discourse 2.

44 There is no need to insist on the parallel with Augustan criticism in England.

45 *Lettres philosophiques*, 21. It is true that Voltaire, like Johnson, is sensitive to the kind of poetic effect of which he disapproves and, in the *Lettres philosophiques*, when writing of English poetry, he transcends his own prejudices.

46 In the *Commentaires*, in a note on Corneille's *Le Cid*, act 1, scene 6. Cf., from ch. 22 of *Le siècle de Louis XIV*, 'It must not be thought that the great tragic passions and sentiments can be varied indefinitely in a new and striking way. There are limits to everything.'

47 *Eléments d'idéologie*, *La grammaire*, ch. 6.

48 *Loc. cit.*

49 *Seconde lettre à M. de Voltaire*.

50 *Loc. cit.* cf. Voltaire in his *Discours à l'Académie.* 'The style of Montaigne is neither pure, correct, precise or noble...'

51 Cf. the remarks attributed to Goethe by Beyle on the 'purging' of the French language in *Racine et Shakspeare*, pp. 369–70 in the Divan edition.

52 Clément, *Seconde lettre à M. de Voltaire.*

53 Hobbes on *Human Nature*, ch. 10.

54 *Quatrième lettre à M. de Voltaire.*

55 *Stendhal et le Beylisme* (Paris, 1947), p. 7.

56 *Eléments d'idéologie, La grammaire*, ch. 6.

57 *Loc. cit.*

58 *La vie de Henry Brulard*, ch. 1.

59 *Correspondance*, 4.5.1834. Cf. the opening pages of *La vie de Marianne*, where Marivaux's heroine and narrator confesses that she has no idea what 'style' means. 'Is good style the kind of style I see in books? Why then do I dislike it so often? What do you think of the style of my letters? Will it do? In any case, this is the one I intend to use.'

60 *Racine et Shakspeare*, ch. 3.

61 *Loc. cit.*

62 *Mélanges de littérature*, vol. 3, p. 430.

63 *Ibid.*, p. 431.

64 See R. G. Collingwood, *The Principles of Art*, ch. 14, section 9. The whole of this chapter corroborates Beyle's general attitude to the question of the artist and his audience.

65 See Pierre Mélèse, *Le théâtre et le public à Paris sous Louis XIV* (Paris, 1934).

66 Cf. *Rome, Naples et Florence* (the entry for 27 February 1817): 'Alfieri lacked a public. Just as generals need soldiers, so are the common people necessary to great men.'

67 Eugène Scribe, *La camaraderie*, a thinly disguised satire of Chateaubriand and his literary circle.

68 *Racine et Shakspeare*, part 1, ch. 2.

69 *La comédie est impossible* in *Mélanges de littérature*, vol. 3, p. 431.

70 *Ibid.*, pp. 432–3.

71 In a note written in a copy of *Le rouge et le noir* two years before the essay appeared, Beyle remarked that the 'society of Mme de Sévigné approved of the nonsense that La Bruyère utters on religion and government, but what an admirable judge it would have been of a scene as that between Mme de Rênal and her husband.' (See *Mélanges de Littérature*, vol. 3, p. 418.)

72 In Remy de Gourmont, *Promenades littéraires*, 2nd series, pp. 97–8.

73 *Mélanges de littérature*, vol. 3, p. 263.

74 *La vie de Henry Brulard*, ch. 9.

75 *Correspondance* (letters to Stendhal), 28.12.1805.

76 *Journal* (13.7.1810).

77 Gourmont, *Promenades littéraires*, 4th series, p. 178.

78 *Ibid.*, p. 206.

79 *Bouvard et Pécuchet* anticipates, as Mr Hugh Kenner has recently argued in his study of *The Stoic Comedians*, the novels of Samuel Beckett.

80 F. Nietzsche, *The Birth of Tragedy*, section 1 of the 1886 preface.

81 Paul Bourget, *Essais de psychologie contemporaine* (Paris, 1885), p. 325.

82 *Mélanges de littérature*, vol. 2, pp. 165–8.

83 *Molière, Shakspeare, la comédie et le rire*, p. 76.

84 See G. E. Moore, *Principia Ethica*, ch. 3, section A.

85 Similar arguments are adduced and given substantiation from a psychological point of view by I. A. Richards in the chapter on 'Pleasure' in his *Principles of Literary Criticism*.

86 In his memoir, *H.B.* (Paris, 1850), p. 12.

87 In *La Revue des deux-mondes*, 1837. Quoted by J. Starzynski in the preface to his useful selection from Beyle's writings on art, *Du romantisme dans les arts* (Paris, 1966).

88 An extraordinary claim by Lionello Venturi in his *History of Art Criticism* (New York, 1964), p. 35 is that before Stendhal 'nobody was aware that Leonardo expressed a melancholy mind in his painting'.

89 *Histoire de la peinture en Italie* (Paris, 1929 Divan edition), vol. 2, p. 361.

90 *La chartreuse de Parme*, ch. 5.

91 *Ibid.*, vol. 1, pp. 158–60.

92 *Mélanges d'art* (Paris, 1932), p. 175. See too *Promenades dans Rome* (17.3.1828): 'Jeremy Bentham helps us to understand the sense of beauty in antiquity a hundred times better than Plato and all his imitators.'

93 M. Bardeche, *Stendhal romancier* (Paris, 1947), p. 64.

94 In the *Mémoires d'un touriste* (15.6.1837), Beyle claims that Giotto would have admired Delacroix's battle scenes, but his judgment of the latter's *Massacre of Chios* in his *Salon* of 1824 is far more severe. See *Mélanges d'art*, pp. 67–71 and 168–9 in the Divan edition, for his judgments of Delacroix and David. One should mention also among contemporary artists whom Beyle admired the Neapolitan choreographer Salvatore Vigano who had 'advanced expression in every genre' and whom Beyle compares to Shakespeare. See *Rome, Naples et Florence en 1817* (10.2.1817).

95 See p. 20.

96 *Histoire de la peinture en Italie*, vol. 2, p. 111.

97 In the concluding chapter of *L'histoire de la peinture en Italie*, moreover, Beyle argues that the true 'beau idéal moderne' has still to be found.

98 *Histoire de la peinture en Italie*, vol. 2, p. 183.

99 For the method by which the *Histoire de la peinture* was composed, see Jean Prévost, *La création chez Stendhal* (Paris, 1951), pp. 120–41.

100 *Histoire de la peinture*, vol. 2, pp. 362–3.

101 *Ibid.*, p. 334.

102 In his article on Rossini in the *Paris Monthly Review* for January 1822 (*Courrier Anglais*, vol. 1), Beyle makes the point he repeats in different forms in *La vie de Rossini* and his reviews of productions of his works: '...the first composer who has the courage *not* to copy him and who abandons the various forms of *allegro* and rapid *crescendo*, to return to a slower measure and to the authentic, natural expression of the words of the libretto, will certainly see Rossini's glory fade to his own advantage...it is perhaps because of its general dash and its continual and disconcerting variations that Rossini's music never leaves any profound impression. One might say with Shakespeare that

It is too rash, too unadvised, too sudden;

Too like the lightning which doth cease to be
Ere one can say it lightens...
Romeo and Juliet.'

In ch. 14 of his *Memoirs*, Berlioz makes a similar though far more strongly worded protest against Rossini's musical vices. He too, however, notably in the articles collected in *Les soirées de l'orchestre*, speaks with amusement, sympathy and admiration of Rossini.

103 See ch. 14 of the *Memoirs*.

104 The recommendation, like a great deal in the *Life of Mozart*, seems to have been lifted from C. Winckler's *Notice biographique sur Mozart*. See Professor Coe's excellently documented account of Beyle's musical experiences in Vienna and elsewhere in *Stendhal Club*, nos. 39 and 40, 1968. Professor Coe, incidentally, questions whether Beyle's discovery of Cimarosa was quite as sudden and early as he claims in *La vie de Henry Brulard*. See pp. 31 and 215, below.

105 See the *Lettre sur Mozart* which concludes the *Vie de Mozart*.

106 *Histoire de la peinture en Italie*, vol. 2, p. 172.

107 See del Litto, *La vie intellectuelle de Stendhal*, p. 496.

108 *La vie de Rossini*, introduction.

109 *L'histoire de la peinture en Italie*, vol. 2, p. 171.

110 *La vie de Rossini*, introduction.

NOTES TO CHAPTER FOUR

1 See p. 7, above.

2 It is commonly assumed by both historians and critics that it was Balzac who was the better historian of his time. See pp. 211–12 below.

3 See *Stendhal Club*, nos. 28, 36 and 56 (1965–72).

4 H. Marrou, *Connaissance de l'histoire* (Paris, 1954), p. 47.

5 See T. S. Lindstrom, *Tolstoï en France* (Paris, 1952), pp. 107–10.

6 *Mémoires sur Napoléon*, ch. 1.

7 Tolstoy, *War and Peace*, epilogue, ii, ch. 6.

8 *Mémoires sur Napoléon*, ch. 10.

9 Tolstoy, *War and Peace*, epilogue, i, ch. 3.

10 Peter Geyl, in *Napoleon: for and against* (London, 1964), pp. 32–3, bases his severe account of the book partly on the assumption that Beyle himself published it in 1837.

11 See the autobiographical sketch of 1837, *Oeuvres intimes*, p. 1,531.

12 *Journal*, 9.2.1804.

13 See the *Lettres écrites de Méry-sur-Seine* in *Mélanges II, Journalisme* (Geneva, 1972), pp. 1–10.

14 See the final letter in the *Vie de Metastasio*.

15 *Journal*, 25.7.1815.

16 See Lord Broughton (John Cam Hobhouse), *Recollections of a long life* (London, 1909), vol. 2, pp. 45–57. Hobhouse comments: 'I have every reason to think that Beyle is a trustworthy person – he is so reported by Brême. However, he has a cruel way of talking and looks and is a sensualist...'

17 Chateaubriand, *Mémoires d'outre tombe*, 4, ch. 60 (quoted by Peter Geyl).

18 *Mémoires sur Napoléon*, ch. 1. As a corollary of this distinctly 'Roman' point of view, Beyle expressed the private conviction, just after abandoning the *Mémoires* (See *Mélanges intimes*, 2, p. 338) that it would have been better 'for the happiness of the greatest number' if Napoleon had been killed after Austerlitz, a view he admits would shock his young friend, Mlle de Montijo, the future Empress Eugénie.

19 See the essay on *Aristocracy* in *Reflections on the Death of a Porcupine*.

20 See particularly the *Vie de Napoléon*, chs. 19 to 23.

21 K. Popper, *The Poverty of Historicism* (London, 1961), p. 148.

22 *Del principe e delle lettere*, 3, ch. 9 (quoted by del Litto, *La vie intellectuelle de Stendhal*).

23 Sismondi, *Histoire des républiques italiennes*, vol. 4, ch. 25 (Zurich, 1808), quoted by del Litto.

24 C. Cordiè, *Ricerche stendhaliane* (Naples, 1967), p. 522.

25 For an extended discussion of this idea, see the fragments appended to *Rome, Naples et Florence en 1817* in Henri Martineau's edition (Paris, Le Divan, 1956, pp. 263–6) in which Beyle is paraphrasing Sismondi.

26 *Ibid.*, p. 265.

27 See especially *Rome, Naples et Florence en 1817*, pp. 279–86 and *Promenades dans Rome* (4.12.1828).

28 For the difficulties of translating *vouloir* into English, see pp. 144–5 below.

29 *Promenades dans Rome* (27.1.1828). The *carbonari* were members of a secret society dedicated to Liberalism and the unification of Italy.

30 *Journal*, 5.3.1812.

31 This is an inadequate translation of 'Personne ne *sait vouloir*...' See pp. 144–5.

32 See the introduction to Taine, *L'histoire de la littérature anglaise*.

33 Beyle's ideas of America derived to a great extent from Frances Trollope's *Domestic Manners of the Americans*, which he read soon after its publication in 1832. He also mentions Tocqueville with respect in the *Mémoires d'un touriste* (29.4.1837). Beyle's dislike of American-style democracy seems to have been strengthened partly by his misgivings concerning the pro-American faction among the French republicans of the 1830s and especially Armand Carrel, editor of *Le National*. Lucien Leuwen expresses what is probably Beyle's own view of the Utopian pro-Americanism of the period (comparable with the idealisation until recently of Soviet Russia) in his discussion with the decent idealistic republican Gauthier in *Lucien Leuwen*. See pp. 179–80 below.

34 See the portrait of Adrien Laffargue in *Promenades dans Rome* (23.11.1828).

35 See the extract from *Mémoires d'outre-tombe* quoted by H. Martineau in the Garnier edition of *Le rouge et le noir* (1960), p. 550.

36 See part 2 of *Illusions perdues* and Sainte-Beuve's essay on *La littérature industrielle* in *Portraits contemporains*, vol. 2 (Paris, 1876).

37 See the letter from Paris in the *New Monthly Magazine* for October 1826, the main argument of which is taken up in the discussion on the stage coach in ch. 1, part 2 of *Le rouge et le noir*.

38 See the *Souvenirs de soixante années* by E. Delécluze (Paris, 1862), p. 245.

39 For an extended discussion of the possible authenticity of these articles, see

Dr K. G. McWatter's article, 'Du faux Stendhal?' in *Stendhal Club*, no. 44, 1969.

40 *Vie de Napoléon*, ch. 32.

41 An interesting defence of Félix Faure, and an attack on what he sees as Beyle's undiscriminating radical sympathies, is made by M. Jacques Félix-Faure in *Stendhal Club*, no. 13, 1961.

42 It is not always realised in Britain that the history of the right to collective bargaining is closely parallel on both sides of the Channel. The English Combination Act of 1799 has its counterpart in the legislation of all successive governments from 1789, in France, until the advent of the Third Republic. There is, of course, an excellent precedent for this prohibition of autonomous institutions within the state in Rousseau's *Social Contract*.

43 J.-P. Sartre, 'La conscience de classe chez Flaubert' in *Les temps modernes*, May 1966.

44 J.-P. Sartre, *L'idiot de la famille* (Paris, 1971).

45 *Mémoires d'un touriste*, 21.4.1837.

46 See p. 196, below.

47 *Mémoires d'un touriste*, 4.6.1837.

48 *Ibid.*, 12.9.1837.

49 *Ibid.*, Chambéry...1837.

50 *Ibid.*, 10.4.1837.

51 *Ibid.*, 12.6.1837.

52 *Ibid.*, 9.5.1837.

53 In T. Jansse, 'Stendhal et l'économie politique' in *Stendhal Club*, no. 28, 1965.

54 *Mémoires d'un touriste*, 21.4.1837.

55 *Ibid.*, especially 17.4.1837.

56 *Ibid.*, 18.5.1837 and 12.9.1837.

57 G. Rude, *Stendhal et la pensée sociale de son temps*, pp. 238–42.

58 *Mémoires d'un touriste*, 12.9.1837.

59 *Ibid.*, Marseille...1837.

60 *Ibid.*, 12.9.1837 and 12.6.1837.

61 In 'La conscience de classe chez Flaubert' in *Les Temps Modernes*, May 1966.

62 18.11.1801.

63 del Litto, *La vie intellectuelle le de Stendhal*, pp. 348–60.

64 *Leçons d'histoire*, avertissement de l'auteur (quoted by del Litto).

65 Volney, *Voyage en Syrie et en Egypte* (Paris, 1787), vol. 1, p. vi and vol. 2, p. 457 (quoted by del Litto).

66 See Doris Langley Moore, *The late Lord Byron* (London, 1961), pp. 372–95.

67 See p. 3, above.

68 E.g. 'Except for events which are very close to us, such as the conversion of the Protestants by Louis XIV's dragoons or insignificant facts like Constantine's victory over Maxentius, history is only, as they say, a fable on which men agree...', *Promenades dans Rome*, 26.10.1827.

69 In the *New Monthly Magazine*, January 1826. (*Courrier anglais*, vol. 2, pp. 413–14). See too the unfinished novel, *Une position sociale*, ch. 3.

70 *Mélanges intimes* (Paris, Le Divan, 1936), vol. 2, p. 337. Beyle here refutes Montesquieu with arguments taken from Niebuhr.

71 *London Magazine* (*Courrier anglais*, vol. 5, pp. 128–33), August 1825. This judgment is completely reversed in chapter 4 of *Souvenirs d'egotisme*, written seven years later.

72 See the introduction to *Vittoria Accoramboni* in *Les chroniques italiennes.*

73 *Connaissance de l'histoire*, pp. 284–6.

74 *Promenades dans Rome*, 5.4.1828 and *Mélanges intimes*, vol. 2, pp. 174–5.

75 *Mélanges de littérature*, vol. 3, p. 417.

76 *Le rouge et le noir*, ch. 22, part 2: the passage beginning 'Politics is a stone round the neck of literature. . .'

NOTES TO CHAPTER FIVE

1 *Paris Monthly Review*, June 1822 (*Courrier anglais*, vol. 1, p. 329).

2 From the essay on 'The Novel' in *Reflections on the Death of a Porcupine.*

3 *New Monthly Magazine*, December 1822 (*Courrier anglais*, vol. 1, p. 47).

4 *London Magazine*, October 1825 (*Courrier anglais*, vol. 5, p. 206).

5 *Correspondance*, 30.10.1840. In *Mémoires d'un touriste*, 27.4.1837 and 15.7.1837, Beyle mentions enthusiastically *Le curé de Tours* and *Le lys dans la vallée*, though he deplores the 'pretty neological style' in which he imagines that Balzac *rewrites* his novels.

6 See T. S. Lindstrom, *Tolstoï en France* (Paris, 1952), pp. 107–10.

7 In *Mélanges de littérature*, vol. 3, pp. 305–11 in the Divan edition.

8 See Maurice Bardèche, *Stendhal romancier* (Paris, 1947), ch. 1.

9 In the 'Avant-propos' of the *Comédie humaine.*

10 In the 'Avant-propos' itself, for instance, he suggests that Scott is poor at depicting women and love, a point made by Beyle, though Balzac adds that this was probably because Scott was at a disadvantage in being brought up in a Protestant country. In *Illusions perdues*, the dedicated D'Arthez tells the young Lucien Chardon what is wrong with his own Scott-like historical novel in terms strongly reminiscent of Beyle's (See book 2, *Un premier ami*).

11 H. James, *Literary essays and reviews* (New York, 1957), p. 152. My quotation and the slightly paraphrased translation of the letter of August 1804 are taken from James's review.

12 In an unsigned article in *The Westminster Review*, 65 (April 1856) attributed to George Eliot by G. S. Haight. See *The Letters of George Eliot* (London, 1955), vol. 7 (appendix).

13 M. Bardèche, See *Stendhal romancier* (Paris, 1947), p. 138.

14 Cf. Beyle's comment in the margin of his copy of *Le rouge et le noir* that 'the society of Mme de Sévigné approved the absurdities uttered by La Bruyère on religion and government but what an admirable judge of a scene like that between Mme de Rênal and her husband'. (*Mélanges de littérature*, vol. 3, p. 418.)

15 I disagree with Middleton Murry that 'Stendhal was even less a creator of heroes than a hero worshipper.' (See the essay on Stendhal in *Countries of the Mind*) but the argument which leads him to this conclusion is one of the most intelligent I know about his writings as a whole, for all its brevity.

16 *Promenades dans Rome* (23.11.1828), vol. 3, pp. 200–2 in the Divan edition.

17 'Dark brown hair brushed low left only a tiny brow visible and in moments of anger, an air of vindictiveness. . .' (book 1, ch. 4).

18 The chronology of events takes no account, of course, of the Revolution of July 1830. The novel was almost entirely completed when Charles X was forced into exile. Henri Martineau in the Garnier edition of the novel provides a chronology of events according to which the action of the novel, going by Beyle's few precise indications of time, can be seen as covering a period from September 1826 to July 1831.

19 Julien is in many ways reliving Beyle's own torments with the wife of his cousin, Count Pierre Daru. See his diary for 31 May and 3 June 1811.

20 Beyle disapproved of the 'mystical' Cartesian system of the contemporary philosopher Victor Cousin but respected the man. It is possible that his thoughts on obligation which transcend the conscious self owe something to the following idea enunciated in Cousin's *Cours d'histoire de la philosophie au 18e siècle*. See, for instance, this account of the authority of Reason: 'Since Reason commands and governs me, it is superior to me and if it is superior to me, it is not me...Perhaps I shall never succeed in penetrating its essence but what I feel very well is that whenever it appears to me, I have an intuition of the immutable, the necessary and the absolute...' (pp. 30–1). A very interesting account of the philosophical significance of Julien's sense of 'duty' is offered by Colin Smith, 'Aspects of Destutt de Tracy's Linguistic Analysis as Adapted by Stendhal' in *The Modern Language Review*, vol. li, no. 4, 1956. Professor Smith points out how Beyle, in the penultimate chapter of the novel 'moves away from the position of his idealogical mentors'.

21 Bardèche, *Stendhal romancier*, p. 264.

22 See George Sand's letter to Flaubert of 19 December 1875: 'One is a man before anything else. One wishes to find the man behind every story and every deed. That's what's wrong with *L'éducation sentimentale*, which I've spent so long thinking about...wondering why a work so solid and so well constructed should have given rise to so much bad feeling. What's wrong is the absence of *action* on the part of the characters directed towards each other or themselves. They undergo various acts and never make them their own...'

23 In his 1902 essay on Flaubert in *Notes on Novelists*, Henry James calls Frédéric 'too poor for his part, too scant for his charge...' Flaubert 'apparently never suspects either our wonder or our protest – "Why, why *him*?"' I cannot myself believe that Flaubert had not foreseen these objections. I have indicated the way in which I think they might be answered in my essay on 'Flaubert. T. S. Eliot and Ezra Pound' in *The Cambridge Quarterly*, vol. 2, no. 3, 1966.

24 In the article on *Le rouge et le noir* reprinted as an appendix to the Garnier edition.

25 *Racine et Shakspeare*, p. 308. The term is also used a great deal in Beyle's marginal notes to *Lucien Leuwen*.

26 The Penguin translator's 'people of the other sort' is a surely inaccurate guess at what Beyle means here by 'l'idée d'un public et *des autres*'. On page 159, I offer a suggestion as to how one should understand the italicised words.

27 Notably by Louis Aragon in *La lumière de Stendhal* (Paris, 1954) and Fernand Rude in *Stendhal et la pensée sociale de son temps* (Paris, 1966). Rude, it should be said in fairness, quotes several passages from *Mémoires d'un touriste* which go against his argument that ideologically Beyle was somewhere 'between liberalism and socialism'. Aragon is less scrupulous.

28 In an article in *The New Monthly Magazine* for May 1826 (*Courrier anglais*, vol. 3, p. 57), Beyle compares the young aristocrats of the 1820s who cannot openly subscribe to the liberal and Utilitarian views which their fellow-students profess as a matter of course without seeming in absurd position. Here and in *Armance*, he points out the positive disadvantages, from the point of view of social ease, of belonging to the *noblesse d'épée*.

29 Cf. pp. 63–6 above.

30 See particularly the *Discours préliminaire* and ch. 8 of *La Logique* (*Eléments d'idéologie*) in which Tracy argues against particular perceptions (or 'ideas') being replaced in discourse by conventional signs, insists that general ideas depend upon and are incorporated in particular perceptions and rejects Aristotelian logic, reducing all syllogisms to sorites. Quoting Maine de Biran, he insists that in all our thinking and speech, we should '*bear perpetually the double burden of the sign and the idea*'.

31 See G. Blin, *Stendhal et les problèmes de la personalité* (Paris, 1858), vol. 1, pp. 191–205. See also J.-P. Sartre, *L'être et le néant* (Paris, 1943), part 3, ch. 1, iv.

32 See the remarks on the style of Chateaubriand in the letter to Balzac of 16.10.1840 and *The New Monthly Magazine* for September 1826 quoted on p. 65–6, above.

33 See the remarks quoted on pp. 66–7, above.

34 In the letter to Balzac referred to on p. 2.

35 In *Molière, Shakspeare, la comédie et le rire*, pp. 197–8.

36 *Mélanges de littérature*, vol. 3, p. 87.

37 The Marquis de la Mole is the only one of the assembled noblemen plotting counter-revolution in the episode of 'The secret note' (book 2, ch. 22) to argue in favour of firmness and independence with regard to possible allies abroad. This gives the episode a relevance which it otherwise seems to lack to the rest of *Le rouge et le noir*.

38 See, for instance, the accounts of the ceremonies at the Vatican in *Promenades dans Rome* (23.4.1829).

39 In M. Imbert, *Les métamorphoses de la liberté* (Paris, 1967), pp. 580–2.

NOTES TO CHAPTER SIX

1 See *Marginalia*, vol. 2, pp. 137–45 and *Mélanges de littérature*, vol. 1, p. 143, both in the Divan edition.

2 Aristotle, *Poetics*, Everyman's Library edition, p. 17.

3 In Alain, *Stendhal* (Paris, 1935), ch. 2.

4 M. Proust, *Contre Sainte-Beuve* (Paris, 1954), p. 198.

5 Cf. pp. 122–3 above.

6 A useful history of the term and interpretation of it is given by del Litto in his introduction to the Cercle du bibliophile edition of *Souvenirs d'égotisme* (Geneva, 1970).

7 Quoted by del Litto in *La vie de Stendhal* (Paris, 1965), p. 196.

8 Foscolo, *Edizione nazionale delle opere di Ugo Foscolo*, vol. 19 (Florence, 1966). See particularly Mathilde's letters to Foscolo of 10.9.1815, 15.3.1816, 10.6.1816, 26.6.1816 and 10.8.1816.

9 A more extreme instance of the kind of intensely painful but, in its way,

privileged insight I have in mind is the motherless Gérard de Nerval's idealisation of the woman who is identified in his novels with Sylvie and Aurélia.

10 See V. Brombert, *Stendhal et la voie oblique*, pp. 118–25.

11 All my page references are to the Pléiade edition, volume 1, 1952 of the *Romans et nouvelles*; p. 1,398.

12 *Ibid.*, p. 1,401.

13 *Ibid.*, p. 1,397.

14 See Brombert's excellent comments on this in *Fiction and the Themes of Freedom* (New York, 1969), p. 184.

15 See Lavisse, *Histoire de la France contemporaine*, vol. 5, pp. 77–8.

16 In 'Sir Walter Scott et *La Princesse de Clèves*' quoted on p. 128.

17 *Romans et nouvelles*, p. 1,400.

18 Cf. pp. 169–70, above.

19 *Romans et nouvelles*, p. 1,397.

20 In M. Wood, *Stendhal* (London, 1971), pp. 115 *et seq.*

21 There is no evidence that Beyle ever read Jane Austen. A minor French novelist whom he admired is Mme de Flahaut-Souza, author of *La comtesse de Fargy*. Another is Mme de Cubière, author of *Marguerite Aymon*. (See *The New Monthly Magazine*, December 1822 and *Courrier anglais*, vol. 1, pp. 44–8.) The realistic social comedy he admired in these two authors suggests that he might have found Jane Austen even more congenial than her French contemporaries.

22 Gauthier is partly a portrait of Louis-Gabriel Gros, who taught Beyle mathematics as a boy and refused to receive payment for his lessons on the days when he would comment on the latest news and preach his Jacobin principles. Gauthier has also something of Armand Carrel, editor of *Le National*, a republican in the tradition of La Fayette rather than a follower of Blanqui, the 'Amis du peuple' and the advocates of proletarian solidarity. This, at least, can be inferred from his idealisation of the United States and from his embarrassment at the activities of the weavers whom Lucien's regiment is sent to put down.

23 Du Poirier has probably a number of traits borrowed from Beyle's friend Maurice Rubichon, who visited Civita Vecchia while the novel was being written. Du Poirier's views on the harmful consequences of abolishing the laws of primogeniture are the same as Rubichon's in his *Du mécanisme de la société*, which Beyle admired and compared with the works of Tracy and Helvétius himself. See F. Rude, *Stendhal et la pensée sociale de son temps*, pp. 209–23.

24 Margaret Tillett has suggested in *Stendhal, the background to the novels* (Oxford, 1971, p. 63) that the colonel is a rueful self-portrait and a confession of how he must have truly seemed to Mathilde Dembowski with his 'failure to understand the welcome accorded him and oblivious of his bulky girth, his common expression and his forty years...' (*Lucien Leuwen*, ch. 14).

25 Beyle had studied Raynouard's history and anthology of the troubadours and in chapter 52 of *De l'amour*, quotes several examples of courtly love. See too the appendix in which he quotes several of the judgments of the twelfth-century 'Courts of love' and finds particular interest in the question, highly relevant to *Lucien Leuwen*, 'Can true love exist between husband and wife?'

26 My own use of the term 'representative' owes a great deal to F. R. Leavis's essay on Conrad's *The Shadow Line* in *Anna Karenina and other Essays* (London, 1967), see particularly pp. 102–3.

27 Cf. pp. 96–8, above.

28 Beyle read, enjoyed and quoted *The Tempest* as an epigraph to ch. 20, book 1 of *Le rouge et le noir*; though he seems always to have preferred *Cymbeline*. Miss Tillett discusses very interestingly the influence of the latter in *Stendhal, The Background to the Novels*, pp. 84–91. Disguise and assumed rôles are, of course, very much part of the comedy here as well.

29 See J.-P. Sartre, *Les temps modernes*, May 1966, p. 1.924.

30 In the *Journal des débats*, December 1831. It is to this article that Sartre is specifically referring.

31 *Romans et nouvelles*, p. 1,389.

32 For Mérimée's reaction, see the letter to Beyle of 1 December 1831 on the atrocities allegedly committed by the silk-workers in Lyon.

33 Beyle calls him 'juste-milieu', which is virtually untranslatable, i.e. an upholder of the new régime, which is neither conservative and legitimist nor revolutionary and republican. It is an illusion, a Greek communist has told me, to believe that the 'centre' parties are *ipso facto* the most 'moderate', in the sense of being the least sanguinary, and one can easily agree that, indeed, this does not follow inevitably.

34 There is no evidence that Beyle ever read Hegel and even Niebuhr, whom he admired, 'gets lost', he claims, 'among the Platonic reveries of Kant'. See *New Monthly Magazine*, February 1827.

35 See Jacques Fauvet, *La Quatrième République* (Paris, 1959), pp. 280–2, on 'l'affaire des fuites' which took place under the premiership of M. Pierre Mendès-France.

36 'Notes sur Corneille' quoted on pp. 57–60, above.

37 Cf. pp. 84, 85 and 132 above.

38 V. Brombert, *Fiction and the themes of freedom*, pp. 123–7.

39 Since the term 'human condition' originates in Montaigne, it is worth mentioning in passing that Beyle professed his admiration for Montaigne on a number of occasions and obviously preferred him to Descartes. In *Henry Brulard*, he claims that it was Montaigne, Tracy, Shakespeare and Cabanis whom he principally studied during the important period from 1800 to 1805. Lucien, after his return from Nancy (ch. 39) quotes Montaigne on the need to '*se colleter avec la nécessité*' ('come to grips with necessity'). Montaigne's concern with 'the human condition' was certainly neither foreign nor antipathetic to Beyle.

40 In G. Lukács, *Studies in European Realism* (New York, 1964), pp. 81 and 83.

41 Lukács, for example, believes that Beyle underestimates the 'revolutionary' potentialities of the proletariat and 'did not and could not see the part the proletariat was to play in the creation of a new society, nor the perspectives opened up by socialism and by a new type of democracy...' (*Studies in European Realism*, p. 83). I don't myself get this impression from the account of the attempted suppression of the weavers in ch. 27, where, as one of the lancers points out, they have 'the troops where they want them'. In failing to predict a proletarian *revolution*, furthermore, he was merely failing to predict what has so far never happened.

42 Lukács, *Studies in European realism*, pp. 72–3.

43 Bardèche, for instance, sees *Lucien Leuwen* as the novel of 'contempt' *par excellence* and Martin Turnell in *The Novel in France* puts it in the following terms: 'He [the nineteenth-century artist] was socially and intellectually out of place. The only course was for him to found a new intellectual aristocracy, a minority which lived inside society but which was at odds with every section of it. This explains Stendhal's interest in the "happy few" and Baudelaire's "dandyism". Stendhal's attitude bears a certain resemblance to Baudelaire's but in reality it was much more extreme...' (Peregrine Books, p. 141).

44 Lukács, *Studies in European realism*, pp. 78 and 80.

45 See Paul Arbelet, *La jeunesse de Stendhal*, 2 vols (1909), Arthur Chuquet, *Stendhal-Beyle* (1902) and Henri Martineau, *Le coeur de Stendhal* (1953).

46 See 'Stendhal à la recherche du temps perdu' in *Stendhal Club*, 20, July 1963.

47 Cf. George Blin, *Stendhal et les problèmes de la personnalité*, p. 570. 'One only writes one's confessions by making a confession in the present and hence a confession about the present [sic]. Thus Stendhal, who, while striving to go over once again the legacy of his former impressions, develops willy-nilly the self-portrait of the ageing consul...' Michael Wood says something similar in *Stendhal*, p. 143: 'The force of an autobiography lies not in its subjective rendering of objective occasions but in its capacity to erase just that distinction to make us attend to it as history, although we know much of it may be invented...' Both M. Blin and Mr Wood generalise about our ability to tell the truth about the past and I am personally relieved that I am unlikely ever to find myself being tried by a jury of which they are members for a crime of which I happen to remember I am innocent.

48 'Su Chateaubriand e Stendhal memorialisti' in *Annali della Scuola Normale Superiore di Pisa*, 1965.

49 Rousseau, *Oeuvres complètes* (Bibliothèque de la Pléiade, 1959), vol. 1, p. 5.

50 Compare with Proust's account of his struggle and his vision, when he has succeeded in locating the source of his memory, of 'all the flowers in our garden and in the park of M. Swann...all Combray and its surroundings', etc. with Edward Thomas's evocation of a very similar experience in his poem *Old Man*. By contrast with Proust's more famous reliving of the past, Thomas's poem has the kind of authenticity I find in *La vie de Henry Brulard*.

51 I think Etiemble is right to point out that these are not, and probably could not be, thoughts consistent with Proust's keen interest, as shown elsewhere, in the kind of 'realism' he condemns in these pages. 'Imbued, as he is, with Ruskin, seeped in the fashionable confusions of his time (encouraged by Bergsonism) between the beautiful and the sacred, the artist and the priest, between inspiration and the "moments" prized by the current mystique, between the eternity of the Platonic idea and the perenniality attributed to the work of art, it is true that Proust, appalled by the flow of time and change, will attempt to build up in his last volume the puerile hypothesis – the hypothesis, anyway – of *time* allegedly *found once more*...' (*Hygiène des lettres*, vol. 5, p. 144). One shouldn't, as Etiemble goes on to say, take any of these thoughts too literally.

52 *Eléments d'idéologie. La logique*, ch. 4.

53 Cf. p. 42, above.

54 Cf. p. 23, above.

NOTES TO CHAPTER SEVEN

1 In *Mélanges de politique et d'histoire*, vol. 1 (Paris, Le Divan, 1933).

2 For an exact account of Beyle's use of his original sources in *La chartreuse* and *Les chroniques italiennes*, see Charles Dédéyan, *Stendhal et les chroniques italiennes* (Paris, 1956).

3 Beyle seems to have been more interested in Manzoni as a poet than as a novelist and speaks on one occasion of *I promessi sposi* being over-praised, though it 'depicts extremely well the existence of the *bravi* under the Spanish government...' (*Mélanges de littérature*, vol. 3, p. 391.)

4 Quoted by Mario Praz in *The Romantic Agony* (London, 1960), p. 140.

5 See Beyle's marginal notes quoted by Henri Martineau in his edition of *La chartreuse* (Paris, Garnier, 1961), p. 528.

6 See Martineau's introduction to the Garnier edition of *La chartreuse*, p. xiii.

7 See *Morality and the Novel* in *Phoenix*.

8 See the first draft of Beyle's letter to Balzac of 16.10.1840 and the note in the manuscripts of *Lamiel* dated 25.5.1840: 'I was thinking of the death of Sandrino: that alone made me undertake the novel...'

9 For a detailed account of the religious background to *La chartreuse de Parme*, see H.-F. Imbert's *Stendhal et la tentation janséniste* (Geneva, 1970), book 3, ch. 2 and book 4 and the same author's *Les metamorphoses de la liberté* (Paris, 1967).

10 Henri Martineau includes the article in his collection of Beyle's writings in the English reviews, *Le Courrier Anglais*, 5 volumes (Paris, Le Divan, 1935). I also plead guilty to the charge of attributing it without question to Beyle in my edition of the *Selected Journalism* of Stendhal (London, 1959).

11 See too Foscolo's own letter to Fortunato Prandi of 7 May 1826.

12 L. F. Benedetto (in *La Parma di Stendhal* (Florence, 1950), part 2, ch. 3) sees the principal model for Ernest Ranuce in Francesco IV of Modena. (There was, of course, no autonomous principality of Parma in the nineteenth century.) Francesco IV saw himself as a possible ruler of an united Italy and for this reason encouraged liberalism of the nationalistic kind. In *La chartreuse de Parme*, Ernest Ranuce and his son play off the 'liberals' of Parma against the ostensibly more conservative Mosca.

13 Maurice Bardèche is the most persuasive of those who have presented this view. He describes Parma as Lilliput and Gina, Mosca and Fabrice as giants. See chs. 10 and 11 of his *Stendhal romancier*.

14 See *Racine et Shakespeare* (Paris, Editions du Divan 1928), p. 308.

15 This is not the only occasion which Beyle leaves the reader himself in sudden ignorance as to what is happening, though he will subsequently enlighten him at times, as in the course of the joke at the expense both of Mosca and the French reader in ch. 6: '...what will seem utterly improbable on this side of the Alps is that the Count would have given his resignation happily; *this is at least what he succeeded in making the woman he loved believe*...' (my italics). Dr Giulio Lepschy has an interesting note on the 'illiterate' scribe to whom

the Prince dictates his anonymous letters (ch. 7) in *Strumenti Critici*, 12, 1970, which analyses a similar probably deliberate effect.

16 M. Turnell, *The Novel in France* (London, 1962), p. 216.

17 See one of the footnotes in *Promenades dans Rome* (1.6.1828) in which he talks of the unlikelihood of revolt in Florence: 'They still enjoy in 1829 the wise just government of the minister Fossombroni. What a difference it would make to Italy if this great man were only forty years old.' See too the detailed account of his administration in the letter to the Minister of Foreign Affairs in Paris (6.1.1834) and the letter to Count Salviati of 28.4.1831. We may be reminded of Mosca's objection to liberals like Ferrante Palla – 'They prevent us from enjoying the best of monarchies...' in Beyle's telling Salviati that Fossombroni is one of the 'gentlemen' who 'are profoundly irritated with France, whose *bad example* has disturbed the tranquility in which their old age might have otherwise followed its peaceful course...'

18 Cf. p. 110, above.

19 See Balzac's article on *La chartreuse* in *La revue Parisienne*, September 1840.

20 Notably Gilbert Durand in *Le décor mythique de la Chartreuse de Parme* (Paris, 1961).

21 See B. Croce, *Philosophy, poetry, history* (Oxford, 1966), p. 935.

22 See *Stendhal Club*, no. 5, 1959.

23 *Literary reviews and essays* (ed. Mordell) (New York, 1957), p. 156.

24 *Promenades dans Rome*, 23.11.1828.

25 Until the appearance of Professor del Litto's edition of *Lamiel* (Geneva, 1971), all editions of the novel were based on those of Casimir Stryienski (Paris, 1889) and Henri Martineau (Paris, 1928). Both Stryienski and Martineau took Beyle's first version of the novel written between October and December 1839 and, keeping only the story of Lamiel's adventures with the Duc de Myossens and the Comte d'Aubigné, inserted Beyle's second draft of the novel at the beginning. Neither offers any indication or explanation of this surgical operation.

26 Compare in the Cercle du Bibliophile edition, pp. 61–3 and pp. 305–8.

27 In his *Essai sur les sources de Lamiel* (Lyon, 1942).

28 Pp. 79–80 in the Cercle du Bibliophile edition.

29 When Josépha, one of the courtesans in *La cousine Bette*, addresses the Baron Hulot as 'mon bonhomme', Balzac tells us that this word 'addressed to a man placed so high in the administration of the state, admirably typifies the audacity with which these creatures bring down to their own level the most illustrious existences...' (ch. 19). This too, of course, can be read as a process of thought and discovery, though scarcely 'swift' and Balzac's capacity for wonder, whether real or simulated, is clearly very different from Beyle's.

30 See the account of the plight of young noblemen who feel the victims of this kind of contradiction in *The New Monthly Magazine* for May 1826 (*Courrier anglais*, vol. 3, p. 57).

NOTES TO CHAPTER EIGHT

1 Quoted by E. J. Simmons in *Leo Tolstoy* (London, 1949), p. 417, and by F. A. Ivanova *et al.* in *L. N. Tolstoy on Literature* (Moscow, 1955), p. 172.

2 See T. S. Lindstrom, *Tolstoï en France* (Paris, 1952), pp. 107–10.

3 See the *Correspondance* of Gide and Bennett, edited by L. F. Brugmans (Geneva, 1964), 28.5.1922.

4 In *Le hussard sur le toit*, the hero, Angélo asks himself at one point (ch. 2): 'What kind of figure will I cut on the battlefield? I will have the courage to charge, but would I have the courage of the gravedigger? I'll have not only to kill but know how to look at the corpses without getting upset. If one can't do that, one is ridiculous. And if one's ridiculous when doing one's job, in what else can one hope to be elegant?' This sounds like one of Julien's, Fabrice's or Lucien's inner monologues, but the word 'elegant' is betraying. Angélo's behaviour during a cholera epidemic is shown as unquestionably commendable but in their moments of serious self-interrogation, Beyle's heroes are usually less fatuous.

5 In his *Journal* (11.12.1942), Gide notes with surprise that the last chapters of *Le rouge et le noir* have a haunting quality and a depth he had failed to notice in previous readings.

6 See pp. 150–3, above.

7 See J.-P. Sartre, *L'idiot de la famille* (Paris, 1971), vol. 1, pp. 37–8 and 471–512.

8 Valéry, for instance, in a letter to Gide (5.7.1897) argues that Beyle's 'psychological theory', though poor from the point of view of 'analysis', 'gave a clear view of things and was therefore good for literary expression'. The correspondence of Gide and Valéry of this period when both were in their twenties and discovering Beyle has a freshness and pointedness lacking in their later published deliberations on his work. See, for instance, the memorable letter by Valéry to Gide of 19.4.1897, in which he claims that Beyle is the only writer he can bear to read on the subject of love.

9 *Promenades dans Rome* (17.3.1828).

10 Quoted by W. D. Williams in *Nietzsche and the French* (Oxford, 1952), p. 65. Dr Williams' book is by far the most useful guide I know to Nietzsche's reading both of Helvétius and Beyle.

11 Nietzsche, *Beyond Good and Evil*, IV, 228.

12 *Loc. cit.*

13 See pp. 48–51, above.

14 *La vie de Henry Brulard*, ch. 30.

15 See p. 152, above.

Chronological Table

Life	Work	Date of first publication of Beyle's principal writings

1783
Henri Beyle born in
Grenoble, 23 January.

1786
Birth of Pauline Beyle.

1790
Death of Beyle's mother,
23 November.

1796
The Ecole Centrale opens
in Grenoble on 21 No-
vember. Beyle becomes a
pupil on the first day.

1799
Receives first prize in
mathematics and leaves
for Paris on 30 October
to take the entrance
examination for the Ecole
Polytechnique.

1800–2
Works in the offices of
the Ministry of War be-
fore being commissioned
as a second-lieutenant of
dragoons. Joins his
regiment and sees active
service in Italy.

1802–6
Lives on an allowance
from his father, chiefly in
Paris. Studies philosophy,

Begins his two comedies,
Les deux hommes and
Lettellier and writes his

Life	Work	Date of first publication of Beyle's principal writings
literature, acting and English. The actress Mélanie Guilbert becomes his mistress.	*Penseés* and *Filosofia Nuova.*	
1806 After an unsuccessful business venture in Marseilles, enters the Ministry of War and leaves for service in Germany.		
1806–14 Receives rapid promotion in the Imperial service, appointed administrator of the Imperial domains in the region of Brunswick, then Inspector of the property and buildings of the Crown. Attached to the Commissariat during the Moscow campaign. Takes part in the retreat from Moscow and the organisation of the defences of Grenoble. Unsuccessfully seeks employment after the abdication of Napoleon under the new régime.	Begins the *Histoire de la peinture en Italie*, plans a treatise on 'Population, wealth and happiness' and, together with Louis Crozet, writes the notes 'On style' and the commentaries on Corneille and Shakespeare referred to in ch. 3.	*Lettres écrites de Méry-sur-Seine sur la Constitution* in the *Journal de l'imprimerie et de la librairie,* May 1814.
1814–21 Lives unemployed on his pension in Milan. Love affairs with Angela Pietragura, whom he had first met fourteen years before and with Mathilde Dembowski. Meets regularly Monti, Pellico and the contributors to *Il conciliatore*; also Byron during the latter's visit to Milan in 1816. His father dies, financially ruined, in 1819.	Begins a life of Napoleon, writes the first of his travel books and finishes *L'histoire de la peinture en Italie*. Becomes an enthusiastic reader of *The Edinburgh Review,* of Byron and contemporary Italian poetry. Takes sides in the issue of whether the language of literature in Italy should continue to be the Italian of Florence.	*Lettres écrites de Vienne en Autriche, sur le célèbre compositeur, Jh. Haydn, suivies d'une vie de Mozart, et de Considérations sur Metastasio...*Par Louis-Alexandre-César Bombet (1814). *Histoire de la peinture en Italie.* Par M.B.A.A. (1817). *Rome, Naples et Florence en 1817.* Par M. de Stendhal, officier de cavalerie (1817).
1821–30 Obliged to leave Milan, Beyle settles in Paris, travelling twice to Italy and twice to England. On the second of these trips,	Financial difficulties, after his pension is reduced, compel Beyle to live by his pen. He becomes a regular contributor to the	*De l'amour,* par l'auteur de l'*Histoire de la peinture en Italie...*(1822).

Life	Work	Date of first publication of Beyle's principal writings
he accompanies his friend, the barrister Sutton Sharpe on the northern circuit and sees Birmingham, Manchester and the Lake District. Love affairs with La comtesse Curial and Mme Alberthe de Rubempré. Friendship with Prosper Mérimée and meetings with Destutt de Tracy, Delacroix, Lamartine and Cuvier.	*Paris Monthly Review, The London Magazine* and the *New Monthly Review* and publishes most of what he writes. He becomes an art and music critic for the *Journal de Paris*.	*Racine et Shakspeare*. Par M. de Stendhal (1823). *La vie de Rossini*. Par M. de Stendhal (1823). *Racine et Shakspeare*, no. II. Par M. de Stendhal (1825). *D'un nouveau complot contre les industriels*. Par M. de Stendhal (1825). *Armance, ou quelques scénes d'un salon de Paris en 1827* (1827). *Promenades dans Rome*. Par M. de Stendhal (1829). *Vanina Vanini* published in *La Revue de Paris*, December 1829.
1830–6 Appointed consul in Trieste and then, having been declared *persona non grata* by the Austrian government, consul in Civita Vecchia. In 1830 seeks the hand of Giulia Rinieri in marriage, who in 1833 marries a cousin. In 1835 receives the cross of the Legion of Honour for his services to literature.	During this period, Beyle, isolated for long periods in Civita Vecchia, wrote and left unfinished *Souvenirs d'égotisme, Lucien Leuwen* and *La vie de Henry Brulard*.	*Le coffre et le revenant* and *Le philtre* published in *La Revue de Paris*, May and June 1830 and 'Sir Walter Scott et *La Princesse de Clèves*' in *Le National*, February 1830. *Le rouge et le noir, chronique du XIXe siècle*. Par M. de Stendhal (1831).
1836–9 Leave of absence from Civita Vecchia during which he travels through France, northern Spain and Switzerland and settles in Paris. In 1838, he is reunited with Giulia Rinieri.	A period of intense activity. Much of what he wrote during his leave of absence he published immediately. He also, however, began and left unfinished the *Mémoires sur Napoléon* and *Le rose et le vert*.	*Vittoria Accoramboni* and *Les Cenci* published in *La Revue des Deux-Mondes*, March and July, 1837. *Mémoires d'un touriste*. Par l'auteur de *Rouge et Noir* (1838). *La Duchesse de Palliano* published in *La Revue des Deux-Mondes*, August 1838 under the pseudonym F. de Lagevenais.

Life	Work	Date of first publication of Beyle's principal writings

1839–42
Returns to Civita Vecchia in August 1839. Struck down by a fit of apoplexy in March 1841. Returns to Paris, November 1841. Dies after a second stroke on 23 March 1842.

Works on *Lamiel, Suora Scolastica, Trop de faveur tue* and a revised version of *La chartreuse de Parme.*

L'Abbesse de Castro published in *La Revue des Deux-Mondes,* February and March, 1839.

La chartreuse de Parme. Par l'auteur de *Rouge et Noir* 1839).

*Romans et nouvelles par de Stendhal (Henry Beyle) précédés d'une Notice sur de Stendhal par M. R. Colomb (1854). (This includes *Mina de Vanghel* and *Armance*.)

De Stendhal (Henry Beyle) Nouvelles inédites (1855). (This includes the first published version of *Lucien Leuwen*).

De Stendhal (Henry Beyle) – Correspondance inédite précédée d'une introduction par Prosper Mérimée de l'Académie Française (1855).

Vie de Napoléon – Fragments – De Stendhal (Henry Beyle) (1876).

Oeuvre posthume. – Journal de Stendhal (Henri Beyle) 1801–14 publié par Casimir Stryienski et François de Nion (1888).

Stendhal (Henri Beyle) – *Lamiel.* Roman inédit publié par Casimir Stryienski (1889).

Stendhal (Henri Beyle) – *Vie de Henry Brulard.* Autobiographie publiée par Casimir Stryienski (1890).

Stendhal (Henri Beyle) – *Souvenirs d'égotisme.* Autobiographie et lettres inédites publiés par Casimir Stryienski (1892).

Index

Abelard, P., 126
Abravanel, E., xi, 215
Adams, R.
  Stendhal, notes on a novelist, 40–1, 47
Alain (Emile Chartier)
  Stendhal, 167
Alfieri, V., 20, 34, **54–61**, 63, **64**, 65, 66, 72, 104, 110, 112, 157, 274n.
  Cleopatra, 64
  Del Principe e delle lettere, 108
  Oreste, 55, 56, 66
  Vita, La, **54–5**, **64**, 65, 66
Amyot, J., 20
Antony, Mark, 40
Aragon, L.
  La lumière de Stendhal, 280n.
Arbelet, P.
  La jeunesse de Stendhal, 215, 271n.
Ariosto, L.
  L'Orlando furioso, 53, 66, 272n.
Aristophanes, 77
Aristotle, 36, 166, 281n.
  The Poetics, 166
d'Aubernon, Mme, 115
Austen, Jane, 142, 178, 187–8, 282n.
  Emma, 178, 187–8
  Mansfield Park, 187–8
  Northanger Abbey, 142
  Sense and Sensibility, 178

Balzac, H. de, 2, 14, 16, 43, 76, 115, **127–8**, 129, 130, 131, 154, 175–6, 177, 195, **197–8**, **211–12**, 225, 226, 233, 245, 248, 250, 253, 256, 258, 265, 276n., 277n., 279n., 286n.
  Avant-propos à la Comédie Humaine, **128**, 129

La cousine Bette, 286n.
Le curé de Tours, 175, 279n.
Eugénie Grandet, 131
Les illusions perdues, 175, 248, 277n.
Le lys dans la vallée, 279n.
La maison Nucingen, 195, 197–8, 211–12
Le médecin de campagne, 177
Le père Goriot, 131, 195, 197–8, 212
Bandello, M., 124
Bardèche, M.
  Stendhal romancier, **92–4**, 133, 145, **175–9**, 181, 211, 252, 283n., 284n., 285n.
Bassano, Il (Jacopo da Ponte), 91
Baudelaire, C., 262, 284n.
Bazard, A., 208
Beaumarchais (P. A. Caron de)
  Le mariage de Figaro, 96–7
Beauvoir, S. de
  Le deuxième sexe, 47
Beccaria, C., 110
Beckett, S., 274
Beethoven, L. van, 95
Belgiojoso, Princess, 223
Benedetto, L. F.
  La Parma di Stendhal, 285
Bennett, A., 225, 260
  Anna of the Five Towns, 225
Bentham, J., 35, 88, 89, 192, 263–5, 270n., 275n.
  A treatise of civil and penal legislation, 270n.
Bentivoglio, family of, 109
Béranger, P., 115
Bergson, H., 87, 284n.
  Le rire, 87
Berlioz, H., 95, 134, 231, 276
  La damnation de Faust, 231

Berlioz, H. (*cont.*)
  Mémoires, 95, 276n.
  Soirées de l'orchestre, 276n.
  Symphonie fantastique, 134
Bernard, Samuel, 51
Berthet, A., 62, 138, 150, 171, 222
Besse, G., 269n.
Beyle, Chérubin, 7, 9, **18–19**, 33, 39, 169, **213–15**, 289
Beyle, Henri, *passim*
  L'Abbesse de Castro, 109–10, **222–4**, 254, 257, 291
  Armance, 4, 124, **131–3**, 158, 189, 201, 221, 256, 261–2, 281n., 290, 291
  articles in the English reviews, 13, 38–9, 41, 65–6, 79, **115–16**, 121, 123–4, 269n., 281n., 282n., 283n., 285n., 286n., 289
  Les Cenci, 221, 290
  La chartreuse de Parme, 2, 3, 43, 44, 91, 110, 111, 128, 165, 180, 191, 222, **223–54**, 257, 258, **260**, 262, 270n., 285n., 291
  Chroniques italiennes, 130, 165, **220–4**, 251, 257–8, 283n., 290, 291
  Le coffre et le revenant, 165, 290
  'La comédie est impossible', **74–9**, 98, 126
  correspondence, 2, **23–5**, 33, 42, 43, 44, 55, 73, 129, 154, 218, 226, 233, 257, 269n., 291
  De l'amour, 28–30, **44–8**, 121, 129, 171, 221, 282n., 289
  Les deux hommes, 54, 288
  La duchesse de Palliano, 221, 290
  'D'un nouveau complot contre les industriels', xi, 44, **48–51**, 61, 290
  'Du style', 28, 32, **64–5**, 289
  Ernestine, **129–30**
  'La France en 1821', 221
  Histoire de la peinture en Italie, 33, **89–94**, 95, 108–9, 112, 122, 269n., 289
  Journal, **42**, 55, 56, 60–1, 66–7, 102, 103, 158, 218n., 291
  Le juif, 165
  Lamiel, 180, **254–8**, 262, 286n., 291
  Letellier, 4, 288
  Lettres écrites de Méry-sur-Seine, 102, 289
  Lucien Leuwen, 3, 117, 127, 134, 167, 168, **170–212**, 213, 221, 252, 256, 264, 277n., 290, 291

Mémoires d'un touriste, 107, 114, **116–21**, 172, 220, 290
Mémoires sur Napoléon, 13, **101**, **106**, **107**, 220, 290
Mina de Wanghel, 130, **220**, 255, 291
'Notes sur Corneille', **57–61**, 158, 201, 289
Pensées, 28, 54, 289
Le philtre, 165, 290
Promenades dans Rome, **111–14**, 121, **138–9**, 286n., 290
Racine et Shakespeare, xi, 27, 52, **73–4**, **76–7**, 79, 87, 92, 96, 146, 241, 290
Rome, Naples et Florence en 1817, **56–7**, **59–60**, 75, **110**, 224, 270n., 275n., 277n., 289
Le rose et le vert, **220–1**, 255, 256, 290
Le rouge et le noir, 3, 22, 23, 24, 37, **62–3**, **82–6**, **93–4**, 112, 116, 118, 125, **126–64**, 165, 172, **177–8**, **183–4**, 186, 189, 201, 218, 230, 252, 255, 259, 262, 290
Salon de 1827, 92
'Si la comédie est utile', 44, **86–7**
'Sir Walter Scott et la Princesse de Clèves', **127–8**, 142, 290
Souvenirs d'égotisme, 80, **166–70**, 279n., 290, 291
Suora Scolastica, **257–8**, 291
Trop de faveur tue, 257, 291
Une position sociale, **208–9**, 278n.
Vanina Vanini, 130, 221, 290
La vie de Henry Brulard, 2, 5, 7, **18–19**, 26, **31**, 40, 55, 73, **80**, 122, 166, **169**, **213–19**, 283n., 290, 291
Vies de Haydn, Mozart et Metastasio, 22, **94–8**, 102, 124, 289
La vie de Napoléon, **104**, **105–6**, 289, 291
La vie de Rossini, 62, 95, 97–8, 110
Vittoria Accoramboni, 124, 221, 290
Voyage dans le midi de la France, 118, 121
Beyle, Henriette (mother of Henri Beyle), 18, 169, 213, 288
Beyle, Pauline, 20, **23–4**, 38, 39, 55, 121, 129, 218, **268n.**, 269n., 288
Beylisme, **26–51**, 88, 112, 163, 254
Bezenval, P. S., 92
Bibas, H., **150–4**, 262
Blake, W., 37–8, 66, 168, 273n.
Blanqui, A., 116, 282n.

Blin, G., **63–6**, **154**, 284n.
  *Stendhal et les problèmes de la
    personnalité*, **154**, 284n.
  Stendhal et les problèmes du roman,
    63–6
Blum, L., **22–3**, 25, 77, 151, 210
  Stendhal et le Beylisme, **22–3**, 25, 77,
    151
Boileau (Nicolas Despréaux), 3
Bologna, 56, 109
Bonaparte, N., *see* 'Napoleon'
Boswell, J., 3
Boucher, F., 92
Bouhours, Le père, 64
Bourget, P. 23, **83–4**
  Essais de psychologie contemporaine, **83–4**
Brême, L. de, 103, 277n.
Brombert, V., 170, **206**, 209, 282
  Fiction and the themes of freedom, **206**,
    282n.
  Stendhal et la voie oblique, 170, 209
Brosses, Président de
  Lettres sur l'Italie, 74
Brunswick, Duke of, 9, 105
Brutus, Marcus Junius, 55, 61, 62
Buchman, Frank, 13
Bunyan, J., 152
Burckhardt, J.
  Civilisation of the Renaissance in Italy,
    112
Bussière, A., **14**
Byron, Lord, 8, 12, 15, 80, 103, **122–3**,
    166–7, 227, 289
  Beppo, **80**
  Childe Harold, 15, **80**
  Don Juan, 15, **80**, **167**, 227

Cabanis, G., 42, 283
Camillus (second founder of Rome),
    19
Canova, A., 110
Canuts, Les (silk workers of Lyon),
    117–18, **195–6**, 210
Carbonarismo, 45, 111, 130, 277n.
Carlyle, T., 49
Carné, M.
  Les enfants du paradis, 254
Carnot, L., 118
Carpani, G., 94
Carrel, A., 277n., 282n.
Cassius Longinus, Caius, 62
Catéchisme impérial, Le, 10, 267n.

Catholic Church, **8–12**, 74, 110, 121,
    140, 234, 236
Cellini, B.
  La vita, 124, 214
Cenci, F., 222
Cervantes, M.
  Don Quixote, 53, 81, 126, 270n.
Charles X, 10, 134, 139, 179, 280
Chartier, P., xi
Chateaubriand, F. R., **10–11**, 24, 33,
    65–6, **103–4**, 105, 106, 115, 216,
    269n., 274n.
  Le dernier des Abencérages, 65–6
  Le génie du christianisme, **10–11**, 33,
    269n.
  Mémoires d'outre-tombe, **103–4**, 105,
    216
Chuquet, A.
  Stendhal-Beyle, 215
Ciachi, Mgr, 111
Cicero, 140
Cimarosa, D., 26, 31, 95, 96–8, 187,
    215, 276n.
  I nemici generosi, 97
Cincinnatus, 19
Civil constitution of the Clergy, 8
Clément, J.-M.
  Lettres à M. de Voltaire, **70–1**
Code Civil, Le, 106, 154, 236
Codrus (last king of Athens), 51
Coe, R. N., 95, 276n.
Collingwood, R. G.
  The Principles of Art, 75, 274n.
Colomb, R., 291
Comte, A., 49
Il conciliatore, 289
Concordat, 11, 21, 105
Condillac, E., 21, 34, 69, 166, 263
Condorcet, A., 20
Congress of Vienna, 232
Conrad, J., 44, 194, 283n.
  Nostromo, 44, 194
Consalvi, E., 111, 114
Constant, B., 43, 115, 127, 270n.
  Adolphe, 127
  De la religion, 43
  Journal, 270n.
Cordiè, C.
  Ricerche stendhaliane, 108, 114
Corneille, P., 20, 27, **54–61**, 63, 64, 67,
    69, 112, 157, 158, 201, 289
  Cinna, **57–62**, 158, 201
  Horace, 67

Correggio, A., 33, 91, 94, 96, 110, 112, 223
Courier, P.-L., 78, 115
Cousin, V., 43, 115, 126, 263, 280n.
  Cours d'histoire de la philosophie au XVIIIe siècle, 43, 280n.
  Du vrai, du beau et du bien, 263
Croce, B., 249
Crozet, L., 32, **57–62**, 65, 158, 289
Cubière, Marie de
  Marguerite Aymon, 282
Curial, Clémentine, 4, 290
Cuvier, G., 122, 290

Daily Worker, 13
Dante
  Divine Comedy, 55, 64, 90, 94, 107, 126
Danton, G., 148
Daru, P., 280n.
Daru, Comtesse P., 280n.
David, L., 20, 92, 275n.
Dédéyan, C.
  Stendhal et les chroniques italiennes, 285n.
Delacroix, E., 90, 92, 275n., 290
  Massacre of Chios, 275n.
Delécluze, E., 277n.
del Litto, V., xi, 1, **122**, 268n., 269n., 272n., 273n., 276n., 281n., **286**n.
  La vie de Stendhal, 281n.
  La vie intellectuelle de Stendhal, **121–2**, 268n., 269n., 272n., 273n., 276n.
Dembowski, Matilde, 45, 80, 130, **168–70**, **188–9**, 213, 235, 281n., 282n., 289
Desaix, General L., 9
Descartes, R., 32, 36, 269n., 280n., 283n.
  Discours de la méthode, 32, 269n.
Destutt de Tracy, A., **20–1**, 28, 40, 42, 46, 66, **69–70**, 71, **72**, 89, 122, 124, **152**, 166, 168, 218, 263, 265–6, 270–1n., 280n., 281n., 282n., 283n., 290
  Commentaire de L'Esprit des lois, 28
  Eléments d'idéologie, **20–1**, 66, **69–70**, 72
  La grammaire, **69–70**, 72
  La logique, **152**, 281
  Traité de la volonté, **152**, 265–6
Dickens, C., 126, 168

Diderot, D., 10, **119**, 120
  Encyclopédie, 119
  Salons, 119
Don Carlos of Naples (son of Philip V of Spain), 257
Dryden, J.
  All for love or the world well lost, 226
Dubois-Fontenelle, J., 21
Ducis, J. F., 55, 157
Dumouriez, C.-F., 118
Dupin, C., 48, 271n.
Dupont, A., 224–5, 227
Durand, G.
  Le décor mythique de la Chartreuse de Parme, 286
Durkheim, E.
  L'évolution pédagogique en France, 268n.

Eckermann, J. P.
  Conversations with Goethe, 3
Ecoles centrales, 5, **20–1**, 288
Edinburgh Review, 56, 272n., 289
Eliot, George, 47, 129
Eliot, T. S.
  'Tradition and the individual talent', **6–7**, 52, 156
Encyclopédie, 11, 119
Enfantin, P., 208
Epictetus, 93
Epicurus, 264
Etiemble, R.
  Hygiène des lettres, 284n.
Eugène de Savoie, Prince, 39
Eugénie de Montijo (Empress Eugénie), 277n.

Faenza, 109
Faguet, E., 151
Farnese, A., 171
Faubourg Saint-Germain, 13, 74
Faure, F., 33, 40, 116, 278n.
Faure, J.-F., 278n.
Fauvet, J.
  La Quatrième République, 283n.
Fénelon, F., 32
Fielding, H., 15, 126, 165
  Tom Jones, 15
Firbank, R., 228
Flahaut-Souza, Mme de, 126–7, 282n.
  La comtesse de Fargy, 282n.
Flaubert, A.-C., 117, 263

Flaubert, G., 5, 17, **81-2**, 117, 121,
    126, 135, **145-6**, 162, 192, 195,
    197-8, **211**, 225, 262, 263, 280n.
  Bouvard et Pécuchet, **81-2**
  L'éducation sentimentale, 135, **145**-6,
    192, 195, 197-8, **211**, 280n.
  Madame Bovary, 17, 162
Florence, 55, 56, 64, 65, 109, 286
Florian, J.-P., 4
Foscolo, U., 45, 169, **235-7**, 281, 285n.
  I sepolcri, 237
Fossombroni, V., 245, 286n.
Fourier, C., 50, 119-20
Fournier, A.
  Le grand Meaulnes, 187
Foy, M.-S., 115
Fragonard, J.-H., 92
Francesco IV of Modena, 285n.
Franklin, B., 42, 270n.
Frederick the Great, 106
French Revolution, **8-9**, 17, 40, 43,
    49, 74, 105, 112, 116, 153, 193,
    210, 253-4

Gagnon, Elizabeth, 19, 54
Gagnon, H., 81
Gagnon, Séraphie, 18, 19, 39, 216
Gaulthier, Mme J., 73, 171, 184
Gautier, T., 14, 223
Genet, J., 262
Geyl, P.
  Napoleon: for and against, 276n.
Gide, A., 143, **260-2**, 287n.
  Les caves du Vatican, 143, **260-1**
  Corydon, 261
  Les faux monnayeurs, **260-1**
  Journal, 287n.
Gierke, O.
  Natural law and the theory of society,
    269n.
Giono, J., 260, 287n.
  Le hussard sur le toit, 287n.
Giorgione (Giorgio da Castelfranco),
    110, 223
Giotto, 275n.
Girard, A.
  Le journal intime, 270n.
Gobineau, J.-A. de
  Essai sur l'inégalité des races humaines,
    113
Goethe, W., 3, 62, 131, 185, 262,
    274n.

Faust, 185
  Werther, 62, 131
Gourmont, R. de, 79-86
Grenoble, 1, 6, 9, 18-21, 53, 80, 116,
    202, 213-14, 289
Grimm, F.-M.
  Correspondance littéraire, 120
Gros, J.-L., 282n.
Guilbert, Mélanie, 289
Guillemin, H.
  M. de Vigny, homme d'ordre et poète,
    267n.

Halévy, E., 35, **49**
  The era of tyrannies, **49**
  The growth of philosophic radicalism, 35
Hartley, D., 67
Haydn, J., 94
Hegel, F., 111, 283
Helvétius, C.-A., 10, **33-44**, 48, 52,
    54, **68-9**, 71, 89, 166, 195, 257,
    263, 264, 265, 269n., 271n. 282n.
  De l'esprit, **33-44**, 54, **69**
  De l'homme, **33-5**, 68
Henri IV, 38, 157, 181
Hobbes, T., 37, 71, 83
  On Human Nature, 37, 71
  The Leviathan, 37
Hobhouse, J. C., 103, 166, 276-7n.
  Recollections of a long life, 276-7n.
Hohenlinden, Battle of, 9
Homer, 54
Horace, 140
Howe, I.
  Politics and the novel, 237-42, 247
Hubert, J. D., 249
Hugo, V., 11, 13
Hume, D.
  A treatise of human nature, 41
  History of England, 41
Huxley, A., 225

Idéologues, les, 33, 35, 45, 46, 65, 129,
    132
Imbert, H.-I.
  Les métamorphoses de la liberteé, 99,
    163, 285n.
  Stendhal et la tentation janséniste, 285n.
Imola, 109
Ingres, D., 92
Ivanova, F. A., 286n.

Jacquemont, V., 270n.
James, H., **6**, 118, 119, 129, 220, 236, **251–2**, 280n.
    The awkward age, 236
    A little tour in France, 118, 119
    The portrait of a lady, 220
Jansenism, 229
Jansse, L., **48**, 99, 119, 268n.
Jeffrey, F., **56–7**, 59
Jesus, Society of, 20, 115, 118, 140, 221, 229, 230, 232, 251
Journal de Paris, 96, 290
Journal des débats, 195, 283n.
Johnson, S., 3, 273n.
Julius Caesar, 100
Julius II, Pope, 111

Kant, I., 36, 88, **89–90**, 264, 269n., 283n.
Kenner, H.
    The Stoic Comedians, 274n.
Kerr, A. P., 267n.
Keynes, J. M., 48
Knight, R. Payne
    An analytical enquiry into the principles of taste, **67–8**, 98, 166, 273n.
Kutuzow, General M., 100

La Bruyère, J. de, 274, 279
Lacenaire, P., 254, 257
La Fayette, M.-J., Duc de, 168, 205, 282
La Fayette, Mme M. de
    La Princesse de Clèves, **126–8, 189, 234**
Laffargue, A., 138–9, 254, 277
Laffitte, J., 212
La Fontaine, J., 24, **66, 67**, 70, 71
La Harpe, J. F. de, 273n.
Lamarque, General M., 173
Lamartine, A. de, 4, 11, 24, **166–7**, 290
Lamothe-Langon, Baron de
    M. le Préfet, 79, 134
Lanzi, L.
    Storia pittoresca dell'Italia, 94
Latouche, H. de
    Olivier, 131
Latreille, A., 267n.
Laura de Noves, 45, 170

Lauzun, Duc A. de, 77
Lavisse, E.
    Histoire de la France contemporaine, 282n.
Lawrence, D. H., 106, 126, 127, **225, 226–7, 237, 238–9**, 270n., 272n.
    Studies in classic American literature, 270n.
    Women in Love, **238–9**
Leavis, F. R., 44, 283n.
    Anna Karenina and other essays, 44
    The Great Tradition, **283** n.
Le Brun, Mme P., 5
Leibnitz, G. W., 36
Leonidas, 93
Lepschy, G. 285–6n.
Le Tourneur, P., 60
Ligne, Prince de, 92
Lindstrom, T. S.
    Tolstoï en France, 276n., 279n., 287n.
Livy, 40, 107
Locke, J., 21, 34, 35, 38, 46, 166
London, H., 118, 168, 170
London Magazine, 8, 79, 235, 290
Louis-Philippe, King, 7, 16, 118, 172, 182, 192, 199, 204
Louis XIV, 37, 73, 74, 76–7, 242
Louis XVI, 18–19
Louis XVIII, 181
Lukács, G.
    Studies in European realism, **209–12**, 283n.
Luther, M., 27
Lyon, 117–18, 195–6, 198, 210

Macaire, R., 119
Machiavelli, N., 237, 239
Maine de Biran, F., 270n., 281n.
Maistre, J. de, 49
Malthus, T.
    Essay on population, 48
Manfredi, family of, 109
Manzoni, A.
    I promessi sposi, 134, **222–3**, 285n.
Mareste, A. de, 42, 270n.
Marivaux, Pierre de Chamblain de, 73, 75, 130, 184, 221, 274n.
    Le jeu de l'amour et du hasard, 75
    La seconde surprise de l'amour, 75
    La vie de Marianne, 73, 184, 274n.
Marrou, H.
    Connaissance de l'histoire, **99–100**, 124

Marseille, 81, 120, 289
Martineau, H., xi, 1, 215, 226, 227, 270n, 271n., 277n., 280n., 285n., 286n.
Marx, K., 43, 121, 149, 198, 210, 270n., 271n.
  The German Ideology, 43
  The Holy Family, 43
Marxism, 149, 198, 210, 270n., 271n.
Masséna, General A., 101
McWatters, K. G., 278n.
Medici, family of, 109
Mélèse, P.
  Le théâtre et le public à Paris sous Louis XIV, 274n.
Mendès-France, P., 199, 283n.
Mérimée, P., **3–4**, 42–3, **90**, 109, 117, 168, 195, 222, 283n., 290, 291
  H.B., **3–4**, 42–3, **90**
Metastasio, P., 94
Metternich, Prince K., 245–6, 249
Michaud, General C., 271n.
Michelangelo, 10, 22, 90, 92, **93–4**, 96, 111, 124, 126, 273n.
Michoud de la Tour, Mme, 62, 150
Milan, 26, 45, 80, 103, 108, 109, 122, 168–9, 170, 214, 224, 228–9, 230, 240, 245, 253, 289
Mill, J., 48
Mill, J. S., **68**, 88, **263–5**
  Autobiography, **68**
  Essay on Bentham, **263–5**
Milton, J., 56
Modena, 285n.
Molé, L.-M., 116
Molière (J. B. Poquelin), 17, 41, 54, 73, 74, 75, 77, **86–8**, 98, 241
  Le bourgeois gentilhomme, 77
  L'école des femmes, **86–7**
  Georges Dandin, **87–8**
  Le misanthrope, 17, 76
  Tartuffe, 187
Le moniteur, 122
Montaigne, M. de, 70, 265, 274n., 283n.
Montesquieu, C. de Secondat, Baron de, 2, 28, **28–9**, 37, 81, 106, 123, 129, 221, 269n., 270n., 278n.
  L'esprit des lois, **28–9**, 123
  Les lettres persanes, 221
Monti, V., 103, 289
Moore, D. L.
  The late Lord Byron, 278n.

Moore, G. E., **88–9**, **212–13**, **215**, 219
  Principia Ethica, **88–9**
Morazé, C.
  La France bourgeoise, 11
Moreau, General J.-V., 9, 102
Moscow, 4, 32, 40, 103, 175, 289
Mozart, W. A., 22, 26, 42, **94–8**, 124, 126, 187
  Così fan tutte, 98
  Don Giovanni, 98, 187
  Magic Flute, 95
  Marriage of Figaro, **95–7**, 187
Murat, Caroline, 246
Murat, J., King of Naples, 103
Murry, J. M., 272n., 279n.
  The Problem of Style, 272n.
La muse française, 13
Musset, A. de, **14–15**, 75, **185**
  Confessions d'un enfant du siècle **15**
  Fantasio, 75
  Il faut qu'une porte soit ouverte ou fermée **14–15**, 75, **185**

Nancy, 175, 178–83
Naples, 257–8
Napoleon, 3, 4, 7, 9, 10, 11, 13, 21, 28, 33, 56, **100–7**, 110, 111, 112, 115, 116, 117–18, 122, **123–4**, 138, 140, 141, 147, 148, 158, 205, 210, 224, 231, 232, 236, 245, 253, 277n., 289
  Mémorial de Ste Hélène, 158
Napoleon III, 49
  Idées napoléoniennes, 49
National, Le, 127, 277n., 282n.
Nero, Emperor, 56
Nerval, G. de (Gérard Labrunie), **11–12**, 43, 281–2n.
  Les illuminés, **11–12**
New Monthly Magazine, 13, 41, 65, 271n., 277n., 281n., 282n., 286n., 290
Ney, Marshal, 102
Niebuhr, B. G., 123, 278n., 283n.
Nietzsche, F., **2**, **3**, 7, 13, **82**, **85**, 86, **89–90**, 102, 112, 113, 114, 123, 261, **264**, **266**
  Beyond good and evil, **3**, **264**, **266**
  Birth of tragedy, **82**, **85**, **86**
  Ecce homo, 13
  Genealogy of Morals, **89–90**
  Untimely considerations, **2**, 102

Orlando, F., 216–17
Owen, R., 271n.

Paris, 33, 95, 111, 136, 145, 173, 174,
    190, 213–14, 220
Paris Monthly Review, 38, 42, 275,
    290
Pascal, B., 36
Paton, A. A., 6
Pellico, S., 103, 289
Périer-Lagrange, F., 268n.
Peter the Great, 106
Petrarca, F., 45–6, 109, 170
Peyrefitte, R., 228
Philip V of Spain, 257
Picavet, F.
    Les idéologues, 35, 267n.
Pietragura, A., 289
Plato, 36, 126, 283n.
Plutarch,
    Lives of illustrious men, 20, 55, 62,
        107, 112, 121
Poe, E. A., 223
Polentini, family of, 109
Pope, A., 93
Popper, K.
    The poverty of historicism, 106
Pound, E., 252
Praz, M.
    The romantic agony, 285n.
Prévost, J., 4, **5–6**, 53, 151, 255, 275n.
    La création chez Stendhal, 4, **5–6**, 53,
        151
Producteur, Le, 208
Proudhon, P., 271n.
Proust, M., 22, 135, 167, **217–18**,
    284n.
    A la recherche du temps perdu, 22,
        135, 167, **217–18**, **284**n.
    Contre Sainte-Beuve, 167

Racine, J., 27, 54, 57, 67, 70, 73–4, 75,
    207–8, 225, 250, 273n.
    Andromaque, 67, 73–4
    Britannicus, **207–8**, 250
    Phèdre, 225, 250
Raphael, 10, 110, 177, 223
Raynouard, J.-F.-M.
    Les Troubadours, 282n.
Regulus, 39, 43
Rémusat, C. de, 16, 17, 168

Revue de Paris, La, 165, 258, 290
Revue des deux mondes, La, 14, 220,
    222, 290, 291
Rey, Abbé G., 18
Reynolds, J.
    Discourses, 67, 273n.
Ricardo, D., 48
Richards, I. A.
    Principles of literary criticism,
        275n.
Riego y Nunez, R. del, 51
Rinieri, Giulia, 290
Robbe-Grillet, A., 233
Robespierre, M., 30, 37, 40
Roebuck, J. A., 68
Roland, Mme M., 268n.
Roman de Renart, Le, 257
Romanticism, **10–16**, 30, 52, **73–4**, 76,
    92, 162, 164, 183, **209–10**, 249,
    273n.
Rome, 16, **110–14**, 121, 123
Rossini, G., 62, 95, 96, 97, 275
Rousseau, J. J., **30–3**, **34–7**, 54, 63, 65,
    73, 129, 214, **216–18**, 269n.,
    270n., 278n.
    Les confessions, **31**, **32**, **33**, 34, **216–
        18**
    Du contrat social, **34**, **36**, **37**, 278n.
    Emile, **30**, **32**, **34**, **35–6**
    Lettres de la montagne, 35, 269n.
    La nouvelle Héloïse, **31**, 73, 214
Rubempré, Mme. A. de, 23, 218, 290
Rubichon, M.
    Du mécanisme de la société, 282
Rude, F.
    *Stendhal et la pensée sociale de son
        temps*, 48, **99**, 119, 271n., 280n.,
        282n.
Rue Transnonain, massacre of, 117,
    195, 197
Ruskin, J., 284n.
Russell, B., 212–13, 215

Saint-Cyr, General Gouvion, 240
Sainte-Beuve, C. A., 11, **15–16**, **24–5**,
    63–6, 71, 115, 151, 260, 277n.
    Causeries du lundi, **15–16**
    Les consolations, 16, **24–5**
    Portraits contemporains, **63–6**, 71, 115,
        151, 277n.
Saint-Just, L., 37
Saint-Marc Girardin, 195

Saint-Simon, C. H. de, 44, **48–51**, 107, 117, 120, 194, 208, 264n.
  Catéchisme des industriels, **49–51**
  Le nouveau christianisme, 49
  Le système industriel, 49
Salviati, Count, 286
Sand, George (Aurore Dupin), 145, 280n.
Santayana, G., 46
Sartre, J.-P., 117, 121, 140, **154**, 195, 197, 233, **262–3**, 281n.
  L'être et le néant, **154**
  L'idiot de la famille, 117, **262–3**
Say, J.-B., 48, 50, 264, 265
Scarron, P., 127
Scève, M., 185
Schérer, E., 20
Scott, W., **127–8**, 129, 165, 175, 176, 189, 223, 227, 233, 279n.
  Ivanhoe, 128
  Quentin Durward, 128
  Waverley, 129
Scribe, E.
  La camaraderie, 76
Ségur, P. de, 123, 279n.
  Histoire de Napoléon et de la Grande Armée en 1812, 123
Sévigné, Mme de, 76–7, 109, 274, 279
Sforze, family of, 224
Shakespeare, W., 40, **54–62**, 63, 64, 65, 66, 67, 71, 93, 95, 96, 112, 126, 134, **156–7**, 158, 159, 166, 181, 190, 215, 248, 265, 273n., 275n., 276n., 283n., 289
  Cymbeline, 283n.
  Hamlet, **156–7**, 166
  Henry IV, part one, 61, 158, 181
  Julius Caesar, **61–2**, 134
  King Lear, 248
  Macbeth, 55, 59, 67, 156, 273n.
  Othello, 59, 60, **62**, 157
  Romeo and Juliet, 276n.
  The Tempest, 190, 283n.
  Troilus and Cressida, 61, 158
Shapira, M., 61–2
Sharpe, Sutton, 290
Shelley, P. B., 12
Siéyès, E.-J., 20
Simmons, E. J.
  Leo Tolstoy, 286n.
Sismondi (L. Simonde de), 50, **108**, 271n., 277n.
  Histoire de la littérature du midi de l'Europe, 271n.
  Histoire des républiques italiennes, **108**, 271n., 277n.
  Nouveaux principes d'économie politique, 271n.
Smith, A.
  The wealth of nations, 48, 265
Smith, C., 280n.
Socrates, 93
Spinoza, B., 36
Staël, Mme de, 28, 33, 43, 67, **102**, 106, 269n.
  Considérations sur la Révolution Française, **102**
  De la littérature, 33, 43, 269n.
  Delphine, 67
Starzynski, J., 275n.
Stendhal, *see* 'Beyle, Henri'
Stendhal Club, 1 and *passim*
Strickland, G., 271n., 280n., 285n.
  Selected journalism of Stendhal (editor), 271n., 285n.
Stryenski, C., 286n., 291
Sue, E.
  Koatven, 177

Tacitus, 140
Taine, H., 2, 109, **113**
Talleyrand, Prince C.-M. de, 20, 180, 191
Talma, F.-J., 55, 157
Tascher, comtesse C. de, 257
Tasso, T.
  La Gerusalemme liberata, 42, 53, 231
Tell, William, 51
Thibaudet, A., 151
Thierry, A., 223
Thomas, E., 284n
Tillett, M.
  Stendhal, the background to his novels, 271n., 282n., 283n.
Timoleon, 55
Titian (Tiziano Vecellio), 110, 223
Tocqueville, A. de, **16–17**, 42, 277n.
  L'ancien régime, **16–17**
  De la démocratie en Amérique, 42, 277n.
Tolstoy, L., **99–102**, **106**, 126, 127, 175, 187, 249, 259, **259–60**, 261, 266
  Anna Karenina, 175, 259

Tolstoy, L. (*cont.*)
    War and Peace, **99–102**, **106**, 127,
      175, 187, **259–60**
Tracy, *see* 'Destutt de Tracy'
Trollope, F.
    Domestic manners of the Americans,
      277n.
Turnell, M., 52, 244–5, 271n., 284n.
    The Novel in France, 244–5, 284n.
Tuscany, Grand Dukes of, 244–5
Twain, Mark
    Tom Sawyer, 232

United States of America, 50, **114**,
    116, 162, 172, **180**, 221, 277n.,
    282n.
Utilitarianism, **33–44**, 48, 106, 107,
    110, 132, 193, 198, 246, **263–6**,
    270n., 281n.

Valéry, P., 173, 287n.
Vallès, J.
    Jacques Vingtras trilogy, 149
Vasari, P.
    Lives of the painters, 94
Vatican, 9, 11, 110–11, 281n.
Venice, Republic of, 110
Venturi, L.
    History of Art Criticism, 275n.
Verlaine, P., 187
Veronese, P., 94
Vertot, R. A. de
    Les révolutions romaines, 121
Vigano, S., 275n.
Vigny, A. de, 11, **12–13**, 14, 121,
    269n.
    Eloa, **12–13**, 14
Villèle, J. de, 127, 166
Villeroy, N. de, 77
Vinci, Leonardo da, 90, 92, 168,
    275n.

Virgil, **38**, 44, 54, 90, 140
    Aeneid, 90
    Eclogues, **38**, 44
Visconti, family of, 109, 224
Viscontini, Matilde, *see* 'Dembowski,
    Mathilde'
Volney, C. de, 12, **121–3**
    Leçons d'histoire, **122**
    Voyages en Syrie et en Egypte, **122**
Voltaire, 10, 11, **27–8**, 58, 67, **69**,
    70–1, 78, 93, 127, 273n., 274n.
    Candide, 27
    Commentaire sur Corneille, **69**
    Discours à l'Académie Française,
      274n.
    Lettres philosophiques, **69**, 273n.
    Mérope, 67
    Le siècle de Louis XIV, 273n.
    Tancrède, 58
    Zadig, 27

Wakefield, E. G., 264
Walpole, Sir R., 166, 180
Waterloo, Battle of, 100, 103, 231–2
Wellington, Duke of, 100, 102
Williams, W. D.
    Nietzsche and the French, 287
Winckler, C.
    Notice biographique sur Mozart, 276n.
Wood, M.
    Stendhal, 177, 203, 284n.
Wordsworth, W., 68, 194, 253
Wurmser, General D., 101

Yeats, W. B.
    'The scholars', 252

Zamet, S., 51
Zola, E.
    La curée, 91

The International Business Environment

The International Business Environment

Second Edition

Leslie Hamilton and

Philip Webster

OXFORD
UNIVERSITY PRESS

Great Clarendon Street, Oxford OX2 6DP

Oxford University Press is a department of the University of Oxford.
It furthers the University's objective of excellence in research, scholarship,
and education by publishing worldwide in

Oxford New York

Auckland Cape Town Dar es Salaam Hong Kong Karachi
Kuala Lumpur Madrid Melbourne Mexico City Nairobi
New Delhi Shanghai Taipei Toronto

With offices in

Argentina Austria Brazil Chile Czech Republic France Greece
Guatemala Hungary Italy Japan Poland Portugal Singapore
South Korea Switzerland Thailand Turkey Ukraine Vietnam

Oxford is a registered trade mark of Oxford University Press
in the UK and in certain other countries

Published in the United States
by Oxford University Press Inc., New York

British Library Cataloguing in Publication Data
Data available

Library of Congress Cataloging in Publication Data
Data available

Typeset by Graphicraft Limited, Hong Kong
Printed in Italy on acid-free paper by L.E.G.O. S.p.A. — Lavis TN

ISBN 978–0–19–959682–9

3 5 7 9 10 8 6 4

New to this edition

This second edition has been completely updated throughout. The changes include a more in-depth treatment of the global financial crisis, new cases both at the start and end of chapters, new mini cases, and new learning tasks. The cases are drawn from a wide range of geographical areas including emerging markets. A chapter on assessing country attractiveness has also been introduced.

A brand new pedagogical feature has been incorporated for this edition: 'counterpoint' boxes, which give an alternative critical viewpoint on the issue under discussion.

Author acknowledgements

We are indebted to all of the Oxford editorial team for their terrific support throughout, especially Angela Adams (Commissioning Editor) for encouraging us to develop the idea for the book, and Helen Adams and Gina Policelli (Development Editors) for their constant support and guidance.

Over the years spent teaching at Leeds Met we have been grateful for the comments and reflections of our domestic and foreign students who have taken the International Business Environment module and we hope that we have learned from these to produce a book which meets the needs of the intended wider audience of future students.

Oxford University Press acknowledgements

In listing those whom OUP would like to thank, we include the many reviewers who made a direct contribution to the way this book was put together. We express our gratitude to all who helped us, but especially:

Steve Rodgers, University of Gloucestershire
Fragkiskos Filippaios, Kent Business School
Rob Haywood, University of Brighton Business School

Colin Turner, Heriot-Watt University
Nuran Fraser, Manchester Metropolitan University
Sharon Loane, University of Ulster
Ron Thomas, Portsmouth Business School
John Hart, London Metropolitan University
Chengang Wang, University of Bradford
David Edelshain, City University London
Eleanor Davies, University of Huddersfield
Deli Yang, Bradford University School of Management
Kurt Pedersen, Aarhus University
Jends Graff, Umeå University
Mo Yamin, University of Manchester
Bill McCormick, University of Sunderland
Peter Chadwick, University of Gloucestershire
Steve Millard, Bucks New University
Kirsten Foss, Copenhagen Business School
Sonny Nwankwo, University of East London
Caroline Burr, Bournemouth University
Sangeeta Khorana, Aberystwyth University
Jonathan Murphy, Cardiff Business School
Mike Smith, Leeds Metropolitan University
Jakob Lauring, Aarhus School of Business
Markus Kittler, University of Stirling
Maria Benson, Manchester Metropolitan University
Catherine Welch, University of Sydney Business School

The authors and publisher are grateful to those who granted permission to reproduce copyright material.

Every effort has been made to trace and contact copyright holders but this has not been possible in every case. If notified, the publisher will undertake to rectify any errors or omissions at the earliest opportunity.

Brief contents

List of figures   xii
List of tables   xiv
List of counterpoint boxes   xvi
Guide to the book   xvii
How to use this book   xx
How to use the Online Resource Centre   xxii
About the authors   xxv
Map of the world   xxvi

PART ONE Global Context   1

1 Globalization   3

2 The Global Economy   35

3 Analysing Global Industries   66

4 The Global Business Environment   92

5 Assessing Country Attractiveness   120

PART TWO Global Issues   155

6 The Socio-cultural Framework   157

7 The Technological Framework   191

8 The Political Environment   221

9 The Legal Environment   252

10 The Financial Framework   280

11 Corporate Social Responsibility   310

12 The Ecological Environment (Dorron Otter)   339

Glossary   366
Index   376

Detailed contents

List of figures   xii
List of tables   xiv
List of counterpoint boxes   xvi
Guide to the book   xvii
How to use this book   xx
How to use the Online Resource Centre   xxii
About the authors   xxv
Map of the world   xxvi

PART ONE Global Context   1

1 Globalization   3
   Introduction   5
   The Process of Globalization   5
   The Indicators of Globalization   7
   Globalization is All-Pervasive   17
   The Drivers of Globalization   20
   Barriers to Globalization   24
   The Benefits and Costs of Globalization for Business   28
   Chapter Summary   30

2 The Global Economy   35
   Introduction   37
   Measuring the Size of the Global Economy   37
   The BRIC Economies   43
   International Trade   48
   Chapter Summary   62

3 Analysing Global Industries   66
   Introduction   68
   The Market and the Industry   68
   Market Structures   70
   Market Power   72
   Analysing Industries—A Framework   75
   Chapter Summary   87

4 The Global Business Environment   92
   Introduction   93
   The External Environment   94
   The Macroenvironment   104
   Chapter Summary   116

5 Assessing Country Attractiveness   120

The Internationalization Process   122

Screening and Evaluating Foreign Markets   128

Chapter Summary   150

PART TWO **Global Issues**   155

6 The Socio-cultural Framework   157

Introduction   158

Culture   159

The Social Environment   172

Chapter Summary   183

7 The Technological Framework   191

Introduction   192

What is Technology?   193

Waves of Innovation   195

Who Innovates?   200

Why Technology is Important for Business   206

Protecting Technology   214

Chapter Summary   216

8 The Political Environment   221

Introduction   222

What is the Political Environment?   223

The Size of the State   231

The Demise of the Nation State?   234

Functions of the State and their Importance for Business   235

How Organizations Influence the State   241

Chapter Summary   248

9 The Legal Environment   252

Introduction   253

The Importance of Law for Business   254

Systems and Sources of Law   257

Important Aspects of the Law for Business   264

International Law and IPRs   269

European Union   270

The Internet   274

Chapter Summary   275

10 The Financial Framework   280

Introduction   282

Money   282

Financial Institutions—Who Are They and What Do They Do?   284

Financial Markets   296

Financial Crises 297

Financial Regulation 301

Chapter Summary 305

11 Corporate Social Responsibility 310

Introduction 311

Debates about CSR 312

Global CSR 321

Chapter Summary 335

12 The Ecological Environment 339

Introduction 341

The Ecological Problem 341

Perspectives on the Role of Business 343

Environmental Regulation 346

Global Cooperation—Establishing Effective Environmental Regimes 349

Global Climate Change 352

The Effects of Climate Change 357

The Progress on Climate Change Action 360

Chapter Summary 361

Glossary 366

Index 376

List of figures

Figure 1.1	World export of goods and services as % of global GDP	8
Figure 1.2	Exports of goods (volume)—annual change %	8
Figure 1.3	Exports (FOB) value and numbers	10
Figure 1.4	Profits	10
Figure 1.5	Inflows FDI (US$ billions)	12
Figure 1.6	FDI inflows 2008–09 (US$ billions)	13
Figure 1.7	FDI outflows 2008–09 (US$ billions)	13
Figure 2.1	Real GDP growth 2006–08	41
Figure 2.2	Relative size of the G7 and E7 economies US$ billions (real value)	45
Figure 2.3	Determinants of national competitive advantage	54
Figure 2.4	How many Chinese Renminbi for US$1	61
Figure 3.1	Global beer % market share by volume 2009	73
Figure 3.2	Porter's 'Five Forces' model	75
Figure 4.1	Strategy	99
Figure 4.2	The stakeholder view of the corporation	101
Figure 4.3	Stakeholder mapping	102
Figure 4.4	The external environment	105
Figure 4.5	Estimated annual growth rate	109
Figure 4.6	Old age dependency ratios	112
Figure 5.1	World urban and rural population	127
Figure 5.2	The twelve pillars of competitiveness	132
Figure 5.3	The process of assessing country attractiveness	136
Figure 6.1	Major religions of the world	167
Figure 6.2	Language skills of Europeans	170
Figure 6.3	Language and trade	171
Figure 6.4	Social expenditure % of GDP	174
Figure 6.5	Asia social expenditure as % of GDP	176
Figure 6.6	Fertility rate 2010	180
Figure 6.7	Percentage of population in urban areas	181
Figure 6.8	Africa's biggest cities (population millions)	182
Figure 7.1	R&D performed by US affiliates of foreign companies in United States, by host region 2006 (billions US$)	195
Figure 7.2	Location of estimated worldwide R&D expenditures: 1996 and 2007 (%)	203
Figure 8.1	General government expenditures as % of GDP	232
Figure 8.2	General government revenues as % of GDP	233
Figure 8.3	Profit tax rates %	233
Figure 8.4	State aid to industry EU 2009 (US$ billions)	241
Figure 9.1	Legal systems across the world	259
Figure 9.2	Legal systems across Europe	261
Figure 10.1	Inflation rates %	284

Figure 10.2 Global concentration—banks and hedge funds 291
Figure 10.3 Global daily foreign exchange turnover 296
Figure 10.4 Sub-Saharan Africa: real GDP growth % 303
Figure 11.1 Corruption Perceptions Index 2010 326
Figure 12.1 Rising CO_2 levels 354
Figure 12.2 Global air temperature 354

List of tables

Table 1.1   The world's top 25 non-financial TNCs, ranked by foreign assets, 2008   14
Table 1.2   Country of origin of films on show in Catalonia   18
Table 2.1   Gross Domestic Product 2009   39
Table 2.2   Economic growth (annual % change in GDP)   42
Table 2.3   BRIC economies 2005 and 2050   46
Table 2.4   Projected relative size of economies and relative per capita income levels   46
Table 2.5   World exports of merchandise and commercial services 2005 (billion dollars and percentage)   48
Table 2.6   Leading exporters and importers in world merchandise trade 2009 (billion dollars and percentage)   49
Table 2.7   Leading exporters and importers in world service trade 2009 (billion dollars and percentage)   49
Table 2.8   Intra- and inter-regional merchandise trade 2009 (billion dollars)   49
Table 2.9   GATT/WTO rounds   57
Table 3.1   Types of market structure   70
Table 3.2   Market share by volume—Europe 2009   74
Table 3.3   Market concentration natural gas 2008   76
Table 3.4   Russian market—cars, % share by volume 2009   79
Table 3.5   Rank and value of international brands 2010   81
Table 4.1   Average tariffs on imports 2009   107
Table 4.2   Total Gross Domestic Product 2009   110
Table 4.3   Japan's declining and ageing population   112
Table 5.1   The traditional model of internationalization   123
Table 5.2   Income thresholds for establishing stages of development   132
Table 5.3   Global Competitiveness Index rankings 2010   133
Table 5.4   Economic Freedom Index 2008 (%)   140
Table 5.5   Country attractiveness grid   149
Table 6.1   Women and the workplace   165
Table 6.2   Health indicators for the USA, Sweden, China, India, and Mexico 2008   175
Table 6.3   World population 1950, 1975, 2009   177
Table 6.4   The ten most populous countries 2010 (millions)   178
Table 6.5   Public social expenditure (as a percentage of GDP)   184
Table 7.1   Innovation activity   200
Table 7.2   Top ten innovators by patent applications (PCT) 2008   201
Table 7.3   Top 25 global companies by R&D expenditure   202
Table 8.1   Public investment by government level as % of GDP   231
Table 9.1   Protection of IPRs   270
Table 9.2   Ten highest cartel fines by company   273
Table 10.1 Growth in output %   281

Table 10.2 Payment method 289
Table 10.3 Global daily foreign exchange turnover 292
Table 10.4 World's top ten banks by assets (US$ billion) 295
Table 11.1 UN Global Compact Principles 323
Table 11.2 Millennium Development Goals 331
Table 12.1 Total emissions by sector (*excluding LULUCF) 355
Table 12.2 Total emissions by gas (*excluding LULUCF) 355

List of counterpoint boxes

Counterpoint Box 1.1	Cross-border mergers & acquisitions	15
Counterpoint Box 1.2	Globalization: the free market	24
Counterpoint Box 2.1	GDP and the quality of life	41
Counterpoint Box 2.2	Is economic growth a good thing?	43
Counterpoint Box 3.1	Market power—good or bad?	74
Counterpoint Box 3.2	International joint ventures—cooperation not competition	80
Counterpoint Box 3.3	Porter's 'Five Forces' model and its critics	86
Counterpoint Box 4.1	What's wrong with PESTLE?	106
Counterpoint Box 4.2	Is China's growth sustainable?	110
Counterpoint Box 5.1	How useful are competitiveness indices?	133
Counterpoint Box 5.2	Investing in Africa	144
Counterpoint Box 6.1	Homogenization of management?	160
Counterpoint Box 6.2	Hofstede and his critics	163
Counterpoint Box 6.3	The clash of social models	175
Counterpoint Box 7.1	The internet—how revolutionary?	199
Counterpoint Box 7.2	Patents—a help or hindrance to innovation?	215
Counterpoint Box 8.1	The nation state—dead or alive?	235
Counterpoint Box 8.2	Tax avoidance	237
Counterpoint Box 9.1	How big a role for law?	257
Counterpoint Box 9.2	Regulating the internet	275
Counterpoint Box 10.1	The IMF and World Bank	286
Counterpoint Box 10.2	The financial meltdown and the free market	300
Counterpoint Box 11.1	Executive responsibility—to whom?	313
Counterpoint Box 11.2	Corruption—is it always a bad thing?	328
Counterpoint Box 12.1	Tragedy of the Commons	345
Counterpoint Box 12.2	European emissions trading system	356

Guide to the book

This book is aimed at undergraduate students and Masters level students taking an introductory module on either the Business Environment or International Business Environment on business or related courses. It will provide a thorough underpinning for those modules which deal with International Business Management or Strategy.

The International Business Environment takes, as its starting point, a global perspective with a focus on understanding the global economy, the globalization process, and its impact on international business organizations. It examines the institutions and processes of the global economy and the economic, political, technological, and socio-cultural environment within which business organizations operate.

The International Business Environment is based on a module which the authors have successfully taught for a number of years. The authors have combined experience in academia of module development, and delivery at undergraduate and postgraduate level and this has provided the foundation for this text. Les and Phil have vast experience of teaching International Business Environment and Business Strategy and the text benefits from this experience and the feedback from students, including many international students, on these modules.

Why use this book?

This book is aimed at undergraduate students studying the International Business Environment as part of a Business or International Business degree. It also offers an essential knowledge base for postgraduate students in Business, especially those specializing in the International Business Environment.

The text provides comprehensive coverage of the core topics that are central to the International Business Environment. Each topic is presented with a balance of theory, case studies, and exercises aimed to develop the reader's ability to understand and analyse the internal and external environmental factors affecting the business environment.

The case studies and examples used throughout the text identify the opportunities and threats to business organizations arising from changes in the global business environment. Detailed case studies, highlighting key concepts and issues from the chapter, are provided at the start and the end of each chapter.

Structure of the book

The book is divided into two parts. The first section, The Global Context, includes Chapters One to Five and sets the context for the international business environment, while in the second section, Global Issues, Chapters Six to Twelve deal with a range of global issues.

The first chapter of the book describes the process of the globalization of markets and production, and examines the key drivers and barriers to that process. It emphasizes the increasing complexity and interdependence of the world economy, concluding that the opportunities and threats arising from the global business environment can have consequences for all business organizations. Chapter Two examines in more detail some of the more important features of the world economy. It identifies the pattern of global wealth and poverty and the pattern of inter-national trade. Chapters Three, Four, and Five include detailed analytical frameworks which pro-vide the tools to enable students to undertake an analysis of external environmental issues and how these impact on business organizations. Chapter Three looks at the analysis of industries while Chapter Four places this analysis within an examination of the global macroenvironment using the familiar PESTLE framework. These frameworks are then used in Chapter Five to assess country attractiveness as markets or locations for production. Chapters Six to Twelve analyse in detail the issues in the socio-cultural, technological, political, legal, financial, and ecological environments with Chapter Eleven providing an analysis of corporate social responsibility.

How to use this book

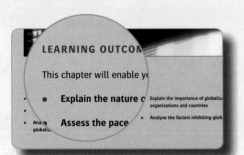

Learning outcomes

A bulleted outline of the main concepts and ideas starts every chapter. These serve as helpful signposts to what you can expect to learn from each chapter.

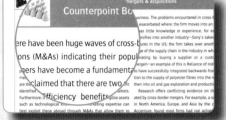

Counterpoint boxes

Counterpoint boxes have been introduced throughout all chapters and serve as a useful pedagogical feature to provide an alternative critical viewpoint.

Case study

Each chapter begins with a case study that provides you with an introduction to the topic area and helps to set the scene.

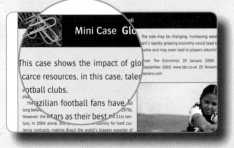

Mini case

The book is packed with examples that link the topics to real-life organizations and help you gain an understanding of the international business environment.

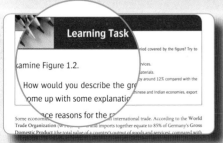

Learning tasks

Short questions and examples put the topic into context and give you the opportunity for discussion.

End-of-chapter case study

A longer case study with questions at the end of each chapter provides an opportunity to apply what you have learnt and analyse a real-life example.

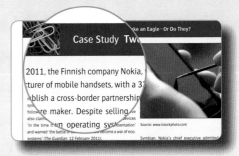

Chapter summary

Each chapter ends with a brief summary of the most important arguments developed within that chapter to help you recap on what has been covered.

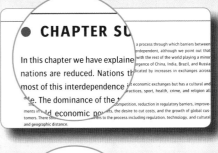

Review questions

These are designed to test what you have learnt in the chapter and extend your understanding. These questions may also be used as the basis for seminar discussion and coursework.

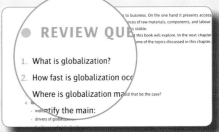

Further reading

An annotated list of recommended reading will help guide you through the literature in each subject area.

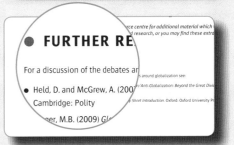

Glossary

Key terms are highlighted in blue where they first appear. They are also defined in the glossary at the end of the book.

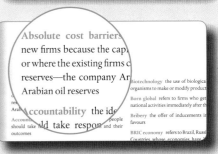

How to use the Online Resource Centre

www.oxfordtextbooks.co.uk/orc/hamilton_webster2e/

For students

Multiple choice questions

Ten multiple choice questions for each chapter provide a quick and easy way to test your understanding during revision. These self-marking questions give you instant feedback, and provide page references to the textbook to help you strengthen your knowledge and focus on areas which may need further study.

Web exercises

A set of exercises to help further your knowledge of the international business environment. You will be asked to find out information and answer questions based on web links to relevant articles and websites.

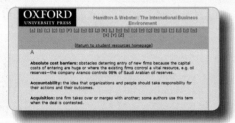

Glossary

A list of all key terms from the text.

Web links

A set of links to organizations which feature in the text is listed to help you with research.

Interactive world map

Bringing together up-to-date information from a variety of sources, this interactive world map contains statistical country data, including imports and exports expenditure, population growth rate, CO_2 emissions, and inflation rates.

Library of video links

Throughout the book reference is made to videos which will enhance your understanding of the international business environment. Go online to click straight through to these videos.

For lecturers

PowerPoint lecture slides

A suite of PowerPoint slides has been designed by the authors for use in your lecture presentations which highlight the main points from each chapter. These can easily be customized to match your own lecture style.

Answers to review questions

Suggested answers to the end-of-chapter review questions in the book succinctly highlight the main points students should be covering in their answers.

Answers to case study questions

Guidance on answering the questions in the end-of-chapter case studies is provided to emphasize the key points students should be including in their responses.

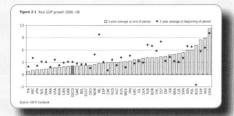

Figures and tables

All figures, tables and photographs from the text are provided for downloading into presentation software or for use in assignments and exam material.

Exam and assignment questions

Additional questions are provided for use in your group tutorial work, exams, and assignments.

About the authors

Leslie Hamilton is currently an associate member of staff at Leeds Metropolitan University and holds an MSc in Economics from the University of Hull. He has more than 30 years' experience of teaching at both undergraduate and postgraduate levels, mostly in the areas of the International Business Environment, and the European Union. In the Business School at Leeds Metropolitan Les was responsible for developing and leading a large module on the Global Business Context. He has taught in France, Germany, Hong Kong, Russia, and Spain. Les worked for two years in the Netherlands researching the economic and social implications of EU policies towards the regions, and examining issues around migration. His other publications cover a variety of topics including the EU, international business, and the business environment.

Philip Webster is an associate member of staff at Leeds Metropolitan University. He was formerly Director for Undergraduate Studies at Leeds Business School and Principal Lecturer in Business Strategy and International Business. He graduated from the University of Leeds with an MA in Economic Development and worked in financial services and the computing industry before moving into education. Phil has over 30 years' experience of teaching International Business Environment, Business Strategy and Business Ethics, and Corporate Social Responsibility. He has taught mainly in the UK but also in India, Sabah, and Hong Kong. Phil has also worked and lived in Malaysia.

Contributor

Dorron Otter is Head of Economics and International Business at Leeds Metropolitan University. Dorron has extensive experience of developing new approaches to learning and teaching in introductory economics and business modules, and has led wider curriculum developments in these and other areas. While he has wider research interests, in the political economy of global development and responsibilities as an academic manager, Dorron retains his passion and commitment to teaching issues relating to the business environment.

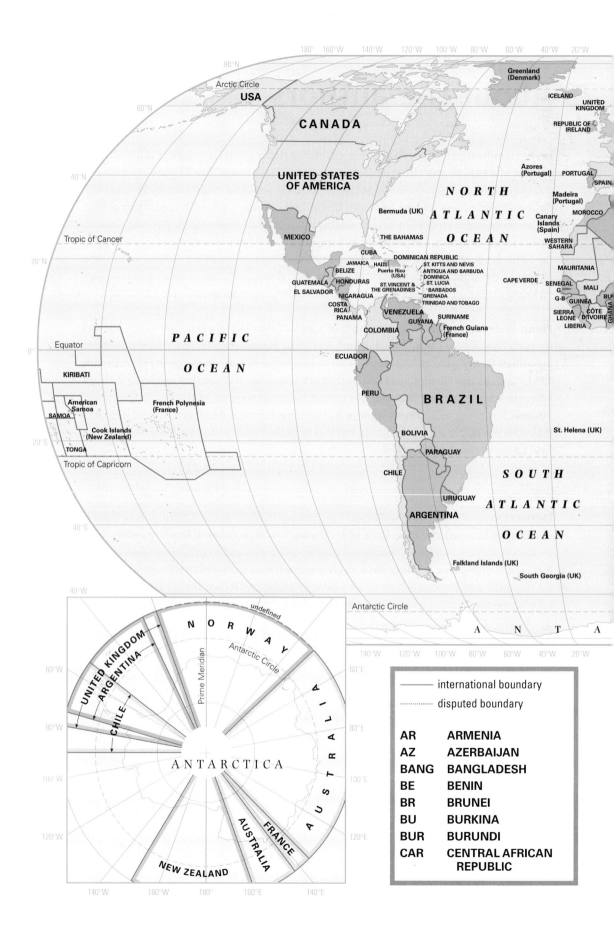

180° 160°W 140°W 120°W 100°W 80°W 60°W 40°W 20°W

80°N

Arctic Circle
USA

Greenland
(Denmark)

ICELAND

UNITED
KINGDOM

60°N

CANADA

REPUBLIC OF
IRELAND

40°N

UNITED STATES
OF AMERICA

NORTH

Azores
(Portugal)

PORTUGAL

SPAIN

Madeira
(Portugal)

ATLANTIC

Bermuda (UK)

Canary
Islands
(Spain)

MOROCCO

Tropic of Cancer

OCEAN

MEXICO

THE BAHAMAS

WESTERN
SAHARA

20°N

CUBA

DOMINICAN REPUBLIC

MAURITANIA

JAMAICA HAITI ST. KITTS AND NEVIS
BELIZE Puerto Rico ANTIGUA AND BARBUDA
(USA) DOMINICA

CAPE VERDE SENEGAL

GUATEMALA HONDURAS ST. LUCIA
EL SALVADOR ST. VINCENT & BARBADOS
THE GRENADINES GRENADA

G

MALI

BU

G-B GUINEA

COSTA
RICA NICARAGUA TRINIDAD AND TOBAGO

SIERRA CÔTE
LEONE D'IVOIRE

GHANA

PANAMA VENEZUELA SURINAME

LIBERIA

COLOMBIA GUYANA French Guiana
(France)

ECUADOR

0° Equator

PACIFIC

KIRIBATI

PERU

OCEAN

BRAZIL

American
Samoa

French Polynesia
(France)

SAMOA

BOLIVIA

St. Helena (UK)

Cook Islands
(New Zealand)

20°S

TONGA

PARAGUAY

Tropic of Capricorn

CHILE

SOUTH

URUGUAY

ATLANTIC

ARGENTINA

OCEAN

40°S

Falkland Islands (UK)

South Georgia (UK)

Antarctic Circle

A N T A

40°W

140°W 120°W 100°W 80°W 60°W 40°W 20°W

undefined

NORWAY

Antarctic Circle

60°W

60°E

UNITED KINGDOM

ARGENTINA

Prime Meridian

A
U
S
T
R
A
L
I
A

80°W

CHILE

80°E

ANTARCTICA

100°W

100°E

FRANCE

AUSTRALIA

120°W

120°E

AUSTRALIA

NEW ZEALAND

140°W 160°W 180° 160°E 140°E

—————— international boundary

·············· disputed boundary

AR   ARMENIA
AZ   AZERBAIJAN
BANG BANGLADESH
BE   BENIN
BR   BRUNEI
BU   BURKINA
BUR   BURUNDI
CAR   CENTRAL AFRICAN
      REPUBLIC

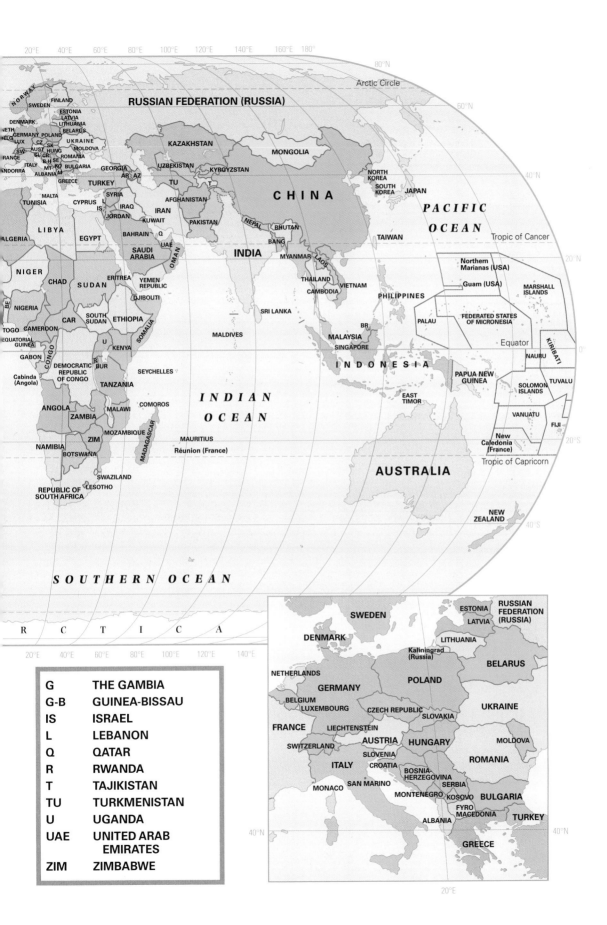

20°E 40°E 60°E 80°E 100°E 120°E 140°E 160°E 180°

80°N

Arctic Circle

60°N

RUSSIAN FEDERATION (RUSSIA)

NORWAY
SWEDEN
FINLAND
ESTONIA
LATVIA
DENMARK
LITHUANIA
NETH
GERMANY POLAND
BELARUS
BELG
LUX
CZ
SK
UKRAINE
KAZAKHSTAN
MONGOLIA
FRANCE
AUST HUNG
MOLDOVA
SW
SE
ROMANIA
ITALY
MT
KO
BULGARIA
GEORGIA
UZBEKISTAN
KYRGYZSTAN
ANDORRA
B-H
GR
ALBANIA
M
AR
AZ
TU
ALBANIA
GREECE
TURKEY
T
CHINA
NORTH
KOREA
SOUTH
KOREA
JAPAN

40°N

MALTA
TUNISIA
CYPRUS
SYRIA
IS
IRAQ
IRAN
AFGHANISTAN
PACIFIC
JORDAN
KUWAIT
LIBYA
EGYPT
BAHRAIN
Q
PAKISTAN
NEPAL
BHUTAN
TAIWAN
OCEAN
Tropic of Cancer
ALGERIA
SAUDI
ARABIA
UAE
OMAN
INDIA
BANG
MYANMAR
LAOS

20°N

NIGER
CHAD
SUDAN
ERITREA
YEMEN
REPUBLIC
THAILAND
VIETNAM
Northern
Marianas (USA)
BE
DJIBOUTI
CAMBODIA
PHILIPPINES
Guam (USA)
MARSHALL
ISLANDS
NIGERIA
SOUTH
SUDAN
ETHIOPIA
SRI LANKA
FEDERATED STATES
OF MICRONESIA
TOGO CAMEROON
CAR
PALAU
EQUATORIAL
GUINEA
U
KENYA
MALDIVES
BR
Equator
GABON
SOMALIA
MALAYSIA
NAURU
KIRIBATI
Cabinda
(Angola)
DEMOCRATIC
REPUBLIC
OF CONGO
R
BUR
SINGAPORE

0°

CONGO
SEYCHELLES
INDONESIA
TANZANIA
PAPUA NEW
GUINEA
ANGOLA
MALAWI
COMOROS
INDIAN
EAST
TIMOR
SOLOMON
ISLANDS
TUVALU
ZAMBIA
MOZAMBIQUE
OCEAN
VANUATU
ZIM
MADAGASCAR
MAURITIUS
FIJI

20°S

NAMIBIA
BOTSWANA
Réunion (France)
New
Caledonia
(France)
Tropic of Capricorn
SWAZILAND
REPUBLIC OF
SOUTH AFRICA
LESOTHO
AUSTRALIA

NEW
ZEALAND

40°S

SOUTHERN OCEAN

R C T I C A

20°E 40°E 60°E 80°E 100°E 120°E 140°E

G	THE GAMBIA
G-B	GUINEA-BISSAU
IS	ISRAEL
L	LEBANON
Q	QATAR
R	RWANDA
T	TAJIKISTAN
TU	TURKMENISTAN
U	UGANDA
UAE	UNITED ARAB EMIRATES
ZIM	ZIMBABWE

SWEDEN
ESTONIA
RUSSIAN
FEDERATION
(RUSSIA)
LATVIA
DENMARK
LITHUANIA
Kaliningrad
(Russia)
BELARUS
NETHERLANDS
POLAND
GERMANY
BELGIUM
UKRAINE
LUXEMBOURG
CZECH REPUBLIC
SLOVAKIA
FRANCE
LIECHTENSTEIN
MOLDOVA
SWITZERLAND
AUSTRIA
HUNGARY
SLOVENIA
ROMANIA
ITALY
CROATIA
MONACO
BOSNIA-
HERZEGOVINA
SAN MARINO
SERBIA
MONTENEGRO
KOSOVO
BULGARIA
FYRO
MACEDONIA
ALBANIA
TURKEY
GREECE

40°N   40°N

20°E

PART ONE

Global Context

Chapter 1   **Globalization**

Chapter 2   **The Global Economy**

Chapter 3   **Analysing Global Industries**

Chapter 4   **The Global Business Environment**

Chapter 5   **Assessing Country Attractiveness**

CHAPTER ONE

Globalization

LEARNING OUTCOMES

This chapter will enable you to:

- Explain the nature of globalization

- Assess the pace and extent of globalization

- Analyse the factors driving and facilitating globalization

- Explain the importance of globalization for organizations and countries

- Analyse the factors inhibiting globalization

Case Study Globalization and Dell

The globalization process involves the establishment of economic, political, social, and technological links among countries. This case illustrates how one company, Dell, got involved in, and profited from, the process of globalization. It shows: how Dell took advantage of the freeing up of cross-border trade and investment to set up a global supply chain across four continents and to penetrate foreign markets; how it had to adjust its products to different country contexts; and how its production methods have been influenced by foreign firms.

The Company

Dell, based in Texas, is the world's third largest manufacturer of personal computers and has grown very fast. In the ten years up to 2007, sales increased from US$5 billion to US$57 billion but then, with the global recession and fierce competition from HP and low-cost competitors such as Lenovo and Acer, they fell to US$53 billion in 2009. Profits were around the £1.4 billion mark. The company sells more than 110,000 computers every day, most of them direct to the final customer via the internet.

The Global Supply Chain

To manufacture its products, Dell coordinates a global production network that spans four continents, North and South

Source: www.dell.com

America, Europe, and Asia. Dell assembles most of its machines in its own plants but outsources the supply of many components such as motherboards and DVD drives to other companies and, as a result, is heavily reliant on foreign suppliers like Samsung and LG Display of South Korea, Infineon of Germany, Foxconn in China, and Toshiba of Japan. The whole production operation from the design to assembly stage can involve a dozen countries. The Dell Notebook illustrates the complex global nature of Dell's supply chain. The machine was designed by Dell engineers in Texas and Taiwan and assembled in Malaysia from parts made in China, the Philippines, Germany, Singapore, Costa Rica, Israel, India, Thailand, and Mexico.

Dell's production system aims to minimize the number of components held in stock. It does this by applying principles of lean manufacturing and just-in-time production first employed by Japanese manufacturers such as Toyota.

Selecting Locations

Dell's decisions about where to locate are driven by the desire to minimize costs and to extend the build-to-order, direct sales model around the world. Dell has taken advantage of the reduction and removal of barriers to trade and investment to locate in regions and sites that best meet its needs. Given the necessity to have production and support capabilities in the major markets, the company selects specific locations based on a combination of factors including the quality of labour and its cost. To keep costs low, the company relocated manufacturing units from the USA to lower cost locations and from Ireland to Poland where labour costs are lower and where workers are well-educated but much cheaper and less strongly unionized than in other EU countries. Also important in location decisions are: the quality of transport and telecommunications infrastructure; the availability, quality, and cost of telecommunications bandwidth especially for call centres and data centres; access and proximity to markets—Malaysia is centrally located for emerging markets in the Asia-Pacific region; government incentives such as low corporate tax rates; avoiding barriers like tariffs that would make Dell's products uncompetitive—locating in Brazil and China not only gave good access to the South American and Chinese markets but also got around tariffs that would make Dell imported products too expensive.   →

→ As the US market matured, Dell expanded into 180 countries across the world searching for higher revenues. Company
sales in the emerging and fast-expanding markets of Brazil,
Russia, India, and China have grown rapidly. It has had to adapt
its business activities and organizational structure to the different markets in which it operates. While product development is
largely centralized in the USA and the same base products are
sold worldwide, Dell has to customize its products for different

regional and country markets with appropriate power supplies,
keyboards, software, and documentation.

Sources: Thomas Friedman (2005); Datamonitor, The Top 10 Consumer
Electronics Manufacturers, September 2010; www.dell.com; http://
content.dell.com/uk/en/corp/d/corp-comm/cr-ca-list-suppliers.
aspx; see video: www.youtube.com/watch?v=oB3qRAr-up8

Introduction

How is it that a teenager in the UK can press a key on his computer and immediately bring chaos
to Houston, the biggest US seaport? Why is it that a collapse in the US housing market causes
banks to be nationalized in the UK? Why should a demand for democracy in the Middle East be
good news for BP and Shell shareholders? Why should an earthquake in Japan cause an increase
in the price of computer chips and a fall in stock markets worldwide, or the expansion of the
Chinese economy cause unemployment among Dell employees in the USA? How is it that a
decision by an obscure bureaucrat in Brussels causes the giant US multinational, Microsoft to
change its product policy?

These are all examples of globalization—a major theme of the book. They show that events in
one corner of the globe can have a major impact on others, sometimes good, sometimes bad.
Business operates in a world where globalization is going on at an accelerating rate. As globalization progresses, it confronts business with significant new **threats** and **opportunities** in the
external environment to which it has to respond. So globalization is important for business, but
what is it and why is it so important?

The Process of Globalization

Globalization involves the creation of linkages or interconnections between nations. It is usually understood as a process in which barriers (physical, political, economic, cultural) separating
different regions of the world are reduced or removed, thereby stimulating exchanges in goods,
services, money, and people. Removal of these barriers is called liberalization.

As these exchanges grow, nations, and the businesses involved, become increasingly
integrated and interdependent. Globalization promotes mutual reliance between countries.
Globalization can have many advantages for business such as new markets, a wider choice of
suppliers for goods and services, lower prices, cheaper locations for investment, and less costly
labour. It can also carry dangers because dependence on foreign suppliers and markets leaves
businesses vulnerable to events in foreign economies and markets outside their control.

The example of the EU and its dependence on foreign countries like Russia for energy illustrates how important the interlinkages brought about by globalization can be, and what can
happen when things go wrong. The EU depends on Russia for 40% of its natural gas needs, much

Mini Case Globalization and a Natural Disaster

In 2011, Japan experienced its biggest earthquake in 140 years followed by a tsunami causing a humanitarian disaster, major economic disruption, and a meltdown in a nuclear energy plant. Shock waves went through financial markets in North America, Europe, and Asia leading to a drop of around 4% in world share prices. The natural disaster also led to volatility in the foreign exchange markets. The yen rose significantly in value against other currencies as speculators bought in anticipation of Japanese insurance companies and other large firms needing to repatriate funds held abroad to meet multibillion dollar claims and to pay for reconstruction. This caused central banks in the USA, the Eurozone, the UK, and Japan to sell billions of yen to lower its value. The World Bank reported that around 25% of East Asia's long-term debt was denominated in yen and that a 1% appreciation in the Japanese yen would translate into about a US$250 million annual increase in debt payments for East Asia's developing nations.

The disaster also led to disruptions in supply from Japan particularly of electronic components. General Motors was forced to halt production in plants in Louisiana in the USA and Zaragoza in Spain while Renault cut production in South Korea. The quake also adversely affected output at Volkswagen and Sony/Ericsson. Prices of memory chips and display panels for computers and game consoles increased due to problems at Japanese factories. The disaster was bad news for the nuclear industry. Safety concerns were raised in China and in Europe, where

Germany closed two nuclear plants and reviewed plans to extend the life of others.

Renewable energy and construction companies foresaw an increase in business as a consequence of the earthquake. US car buyers flocked to Toyota dealers to buy the hybrid battery/petrol-driven Prius on fears of disruptions in supplies from Japan.

Sources: *Financial Times*, 18 and 19 March 2011; *The Guardian*, 18 March 2011; www.guardian.co.uk 14 and 16 March 2011; www.ecb.int; http://siteresources.worldbank.org/INTEAPHALFYEARLYUPDATE/ Resources/550192-1300567391916/EAP_Update_March2011_ japan.pdf

Source: www.istockphoto.com

of which is transported through the Ukraine. Squabbling between Russia and the Ukraine led to repeated cuts in supply with the result that Bulgarians and Slovaks ended up shivering while Russia was in dispute with the Ukraine over its gas bill. As a result, the EU started to diversify its sources of supply to Central Asia, the Middle East, and Norway (EU Commission 2011; *The Economist*, 16 July 2009).

Globalization also poses a threat insofar as it removes protection from domestic producers by opening up their markets to foreign competitors. Manufacturing in footwear, textile and clothing, and toys in the USA and EU has shrunk as a result of competition from low cost countries such as China, Vietnam, Pakistan, and Bangladesh.

Nations may also find that globalization causes them to specialize in producing those goods and services in which they are relatively more efficient. While this could generate benefits from economies of scale in production, it could also create dependence on a smaller range of products, and leave their economies more vulnerable to external events.

Globalization is not Global (yet)

Globalization is something of a misnomer because most foreign trade and investment takes place within and between the three great economic blocs:

- Western Europe dominated by EU member states;
- NAFTA comprising the USA, Canada, and Mexico; and
- Japan.

They are called the triad. A significant proportion of world trade takes place either within each triad member or between the blocs. However, most of this trade is internal: NAFTA is not heavily dependent on trade with either the EU or with Japan and over 60% of EU trade takes place between the member states (Eurostat 2010).

This situation is reflected in the strategies pursued by big multinational companies. These organizations focus their strategies on the bloc where they produce. This concentration of trade in their own bloc is largely due to the size of their markets. Globally, rich countries make up less than a fifth of the world population but consume more than four fifths of the goods produced (www.globalissues.org).

The countries making up the triad have changed over time. For example, membership of the EU increased to 27 in 2007 with the entry of ten Eastern European countries, Cyprus, and Malta. Although the triad still accounts for nearly 40% of world exports and imports, its predominance is under threat from China whose share of world trade in manufacturing has grown very rapidly. China has become the largest trader ahead of both Germany and the USA. In 2009 it accounted for almost 10% of world merchandise exports (WTO, World Trade Report 2010).

The triad is dominant in foreign investment, but even here emerging countries such as China and India are making their presence felt. This aspect is dealt with in the next section.

The Indicators of Globalization

There are three main economic and financial indicators of globalization, these are:

- international trade in goods and services
- the transfer of money capital from one country to another
- the movement of people across national borders.

Of the three, international trade and foreign investment are the most important. Each of the three indicators will be examined in turn.

International Trade

International trade means that countries become more interconnected through the exchange of goods and services, that is, through imports and exports. Between 1950 and 2006, world trade grew 27-fold in volume terms, three times faster than world output growth (WTO 2007). We can conclude from this that importing and exporting were becoming an ever more crucial component of global and national economic activity, at least up until 2009 (Figure 1.1). Merchandise

Figure 1.1 World export of goods and services as % of global GDP

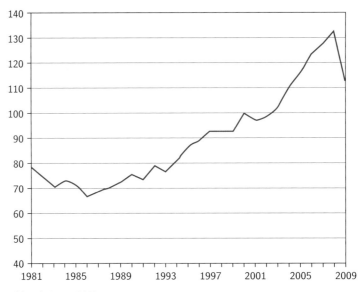

Source: WTO, World Trade Report 2010

Figure 1.2 Exports of goods (volume)—annual change %

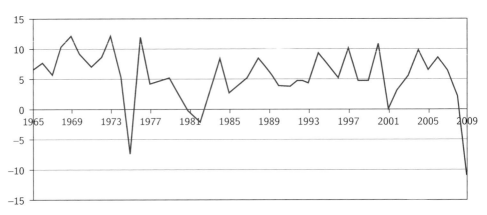

Source: WTO, World Trade Report 2010

trade grew very quickly particularly in manufactures which increased tenfold between 1950 and 1975. While the rate of growth subsequently fell, it was still very rapid.

Trade, particularly trade in services, grew exceptionally fast in the period between 2000 and 2008, at an average rate of 14% per annum. But the financial crisis in 2007/08 and the subsequent global economic downturn turned the growth in world trade negative (Figure 1.2). In 2009, the global recession caused the sharpest decline in world trade in 70 years but it recovered strongly in 2010 (UNCTAD 2010).

In 2009, ten countries accounted for more than half of merchandise exports. China with almost 10% was the largest exporter of goods followed by Germany, the USA, and Japan, Similarly, the ten leading countries supplied around half of service exports. China with around a 4% share in exports of services trailed behind the USA, the UK, Germany, and France (www.wto.org).

Learning Task

Examine Figure 1.2.

1. How would you describe the growth path of exports over the period covered by the figure? Try to come up with some explanations for your findings.

2. Advance reasons for the rapid growth in exports of commercial services.

3. The WTO (2010) showed increasing exports of fuels and mining materials.
   In 2010, the price of metals rose by more than 30% and energy by around 12% compared with the previous year.
   What links could there be between the rapidly expanding Chinese and Indian economies, export growth, and price rises in metals?

Some economies are particularly dependent on international trade. According to the World Trade Organization (WTO), exports and imports together equate to 85% of Germany's Gross Domestic Product (the total value of a country's output of goods and services), compared with around 60% for China and the UK, but only a little more than one quarter for the USA (http://stat.wto.org). Furthermore, the UK depends on customers in only two countries, the USA and Germany, for a quarter of its exports of goods (Office for National Statistics 2010). Events in those economies are outside the control of UK business but could have a major impact on it. For example, a rapid and simultaneous expansion of both economies would be very good news for sales of British manufactures but a recession, as occurred in 2008/09, could mean a significant fall in turnover and profits. Dependence is also reflected in particular industries. For example, the ratio of UK imports of chemicals to domestic demand is 97%. At the same time, the UK chemical industry is very dependent on foreign demand because it is equivalent to 97% of total sales (Annual Abstract of Statistics 2010).

Multinational companies (MNCs) are major traders and account for a large proportion of international trade, with significant proportions accounted for by trade between subsidiaries within the same company—this is called intra-firm trade. So for example, Ford makes gearboxes in its factory in Bordeaux and exports them to its assembly plants in other European countries. For the US, intra-firm trade flows are estimated at around one half of imports, and one third of exports. Intra-firm trade takes place in both goods and services like bank and IT call centres which have been moved offshore (Maurer and Degain 2010; Lanz and Miroudot 2010).

Financial Flows

Foreign Indirect Investment

The second main driver is the transfer of money capital across borders.

This can take two forms. The first, Foreign Indirect Investment (FII, or Portfolio Investment), occurs where money is used to purchase financial assets in another country. These assets can

Mini Case The Global Environment and Tata Motors

Tata Motors, a division of the Tata Group, the giant Indian multinational conglomerate, employs some 50,000 people and produces around 700,000 vehicles per year in countries as far afield as India, South Korea, South Africa, Thailand, Bangladesh, Singapore, UK, Spain, Morocco, and Brazil. Its products include heavy trucks, vans and passenger cars such as Jaguar, Land Rover, and the ultra cheap Nano.

In 2010, Tata Motors reported that the world economy was recovering from the devastating 2007–09 global financial crisis which had hit car makers very hard particularly in North America, Continental Europe, and the United Kingdom. Sales of cars in the United States declined by more than one fifth in 2009 and in Continental Europe and the United Kingdom by 11.9% and 6.4% respectively. This depressed Tata's exports and profits (see Figures 1.3 and 1.4).

By contrast, the automotive sector in Asia experienced growth, with China and India the main drivers. China, now the world's largest car producer, saw its passenger car sales increase by almost one half from 5.7 million units in 2008 to 8.4 million units in 2009. India too witnessed growth in passenger vehicle

Figure 1.3 Exports (FOB) value and numbers

Figure 1.4 Profits

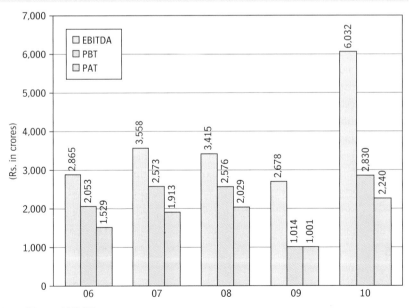

Source: Company Annual Report 2009/10
EBITDA: earnings before the deduction of interest, tax, depreciation, and amortization   PBT: Profit before tax   PAT: Profit after tax   ➜

➜ sales of 25% from 1.5 million units to about 1.9 million units in 2009–10.

Regarding market prospects, the company noted signs of recovery in the world economy which augured well for car sales. In particular, it saw growth in China, Russia, and the Middle East, key markets for products such as Jaguar and Land Rover but only moderate growth in the USA and UK. Tata also foresaw the global recovery leading to a rise in commodity prices that would increase its input costs. It also anticipated an intensification of competition in the vehicle sector and inflationary pressures resulting in increases in interest rates.

Finally, climate change was forcing car manufacturers globally to concentrate on new technologies to meet the stringent forthcoming emission goals being set by governments. Hybrids and plug-in electric cars were being introduced in the market in increasing numbers.

Source: Tata Motors Annual Report 2009/10; Datamonitor, MarketWatch: Tata Motors, October 2010; *New York Times*, 9 December 2010

comprise foreign stocks, bonds issued by governments or companies, or even currency. Thus, UK financial institutions such as HSBC and Barclays often purchase bonds or company shares quoted on foreign stock exchanges such as New York or Tokyo. Purchasers buy them for the financial return they generate. This activity has been increasing very rapidly—in the 1990s such trading was expanding at more than 20% per annum, helping to bring about an increased integration of **financial markets**. Growth faltered after the East Asian financial crisis of the late 1990s but picked up again in the new century. The interlinkages created by FII were demonstrated in 2006 when it was estimated that foreign financial institutions held more than 10% of the US$8 **trillion** in outstanding US residential mortgages in the form of mortgage-related securities. This left them vulnerable to the downturn in the US housing market which started in 2007 and led to a worldwide credit crunch (International Monetary Fund 2006) (see the section on financial crises in Chapter Ten). In 2009, total portfolio investment reached around US$1 trillion. The biggest receivers were the Eurozone, the USA, and UK with the latter two being the largest sources (International Monetary Fund 2010).

Activity on the foreign exchange market is enormous. The average daily turnover worldwide in 2001 was US$1.4 trillion with most business taking place in the main financial centres of the triad: New York, London, and Tokyo. By 2010, turnover had almost trebled to US$4 trillion. Only a very small proportion of currency trading is associated with the financing of trade in goods and services—most goes on the buying and selling of financial assets (Bank for International Settlements 2010).

Another example of cross-border flows of money is **migrant** remittances. Migrants often send money to their home countries and the total amount has grown over time. They exceeded US$400 billion in 2010 with India, China, and Mexico as the three largest recipients, each receiving more than US$20 billion. The USA was the biggest source, sending some US$48 billion in 2009 (www.worldbank.org). Remittances are a vital source of foreign currency for some poor countries—Tajikistan, Moldova, Lesotho, and Lebanon are countries whose remittances from abroad equate to 25% or more of their GDP (World Bank 2010).

Foreign Direct Investment

The second form of capital movement is **Foreign Direct Investment** (FDI). FDI occurs when a firm establishes, acquires, or increases production facilities in a foreign country. MNCs are

Figure 1.5 Inflows FDI (US$ billions)

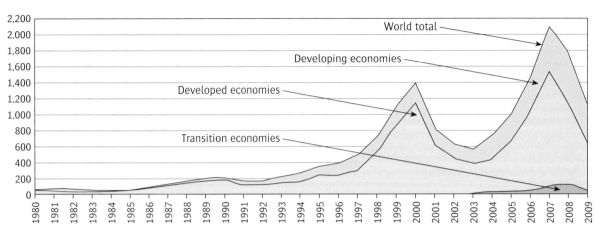

Source: UNCTAD, World Investment Report 2010

responsible for foreign direct investment and the massive increase that has occurred in FDI in the last 50 years.

The distinguishing feature between FII and FDI is that MNCs not only own the assets but also wish to exercise managerial control over them.

FDI grew spectacularly in the 1990s but declined steeply after 2000 due to weak growth of the world economy. Following a five-year upward trend from 2003, FDI inflows declined by 16% in 2008. This was followed by a further decline of 37% in 2009 to US$1,114 billion, while outflows fell some 43% to US$1,101 billion. Outflows from rich countries fell much more than those from developing economies (Figure 1.5; UNCTAD 2010).

Countries can receive inflows of investment but they can also be sources of investment. Up to recently, the major recipients of FDI were the **developed countries**, mainly because of their large and affluent markets. In 2006, they received around 60% of FDI inflows whilst accounting for the vast majority—between 80 and 90%—of the outflows (UNCTAD 2007; World Bank 2008; Figure 1.5). By 2010, rich countries were receiving just under one half of inflows but, remained predominant in outflows (WIR 2010). Poorer countries, for the first time ever, received more than half of FDI inflows with much of the investment going to Asia and Latin America. (UNCTAD 2011; Figure 1.5).

The USA heads the league of FDI recipients, followed a long way behind by China (even after adding the figures for Hong Kong to those of China) and France. Russia was sixth in the rankings; India, ninth; and Brazil, fourteenth. The USA is also, by far, the biggest source of FDI followed by France, Japan, and Germany. Hong Kong, China, and Russia ranked fifth, sixth, and seventh respectively (see Figures 1.6 and 1.7).

Up to 2010, FDI largely involved MNCs in rich countries investing in production facilities in other rich countries, the **developing countries** and Eastern Europe, having smaller and less lucrative markets, playing only a minor part. Where FDI did take place in poor countries it was often to exploit natural resources such as oil or other minerals, to take advantage of cheap labour or, sometimes, to penetrate a market. China was favoured by foreign multinationals because labour was cheap and there was great market potential. Firms like Volkswagen, Toyota, Caterpillar,

Figure 1.6 FDI inflows 2008–09 (US$ billions)

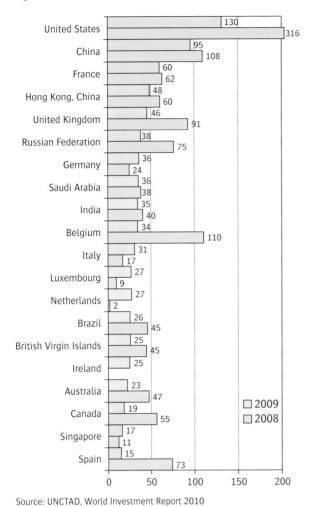

Source: UNCTAD, World Investment Report 2010

Figure 1.7 FDI outflows 2008–09 (US$ billions)

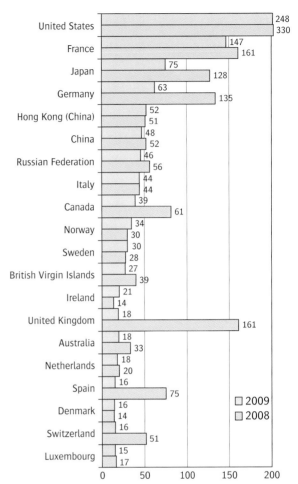

Source: UNCTAD, World Investment Report 2010

and Tesco invested there to take advantage of cheap resources or to exploit the market. Now markets in countries like India, China, and Brazil are large and fast-growing and a major attraction for MNCs.

According to UNCTAD (2010) there are some 82,000 multinational companies employing 80 million workers. While the vast majority are based in rich countries, there are an increasing number of MNCs to be found in developing economies such as Tata of India, China's Lenovo, Vale of Brazil, and Russia's Gazprom.

Big MNCs are the most important foreign direct investors. Table 1.1 shows the 25 biggest global companies ranked by the value of their foreign assets. The list is dominated by companies based in the **advanced economies**. Five are US companies, 17 are Western European (5 German, 3 French, 3 British and 1 in Luxembourg), and two are based in Japan. Many of the largest companies are extremely international in their operations. Oil companies like ExxonMobil, BP, Shell, and Total, and others such as Siemens and Vodafone, all generate more than 50% of

Table 1.1 The world's top 25 non-financial TNCs, ranked by foreign assets, 2008

Rank	MNC	Home economy	Industry	Assets US$m	
				Foreign	Total
1	General Electric	United States	Electrical & electronic equipment	401,290	797,769
2	Shell Group	United Kingdom	Petroleum	222,324	282,401
3	Vodafone Group	United Kingdom	Telecommunications	201,570	218,955
4	BP	United Kingdom	Petroleum	188,969	228,238
5	Toyota Motor Corporation	Japan	Motor vehicles	169,569	296,249
6	ExxonMobil	United States	Petroleum	161,245	228,052
7	Total	France	Petroleum	141,442	164,662
8	E.On	Germany	Utilities (Electricity, gas, and water)	141,168	218,573
9	Electricité De France	France	Utilities (Electricity, gas, and water)	133,698	278,759
10	ArcelorMittal	Luxembourg	Metal and metal products	127,127	133,088
11	Volkswagen Group	Germany	Motor vehicles	123,677	233,708
12	GDF Suez	France	Utilities (Electricity, gas, and water)	119,374	232,718
13	Anheuser-Busch InBev	Netherlands	Food, beverages, and tobacco	106,247	113,170
14	Chevron Corporation	United States	Petroleum	106,129	161,165
15	Siemens	Germany	Electrical & electronic equipment	104,488	135,102
16	Ford Motor Company	United States	Motor vehicles	102,588	222,977
17	Eni Group	Italy	Petroleum	95,818	162,269
18	Telefonica	Spain	Telecommunications	95,446	139,034
19	Deutsche Telekom	Germany	Telecommunications	95,019	171,385
20	Honda	Japan	Motor vehicles	89,204	120,478
21	Daimler	Germany	Motor vehicles	87,927	184,021
22	France Telecom	France	Telecommunications	81,378	132,630
23	Conocophillips	United States	Petroleum	77,864	142,865
24	Iberdrola	Spain	Utilities (Electricity, gas, and water)	73,576	119,467
25	Hutchison Whampoa	Hong Kong, China	Diversified	70,762	87,745

Source: UNCTAD, World Investment Report 2010

turnover from foreign sales. Wal-Mart, the world's biggest retailer has expanded its foreign activities very rapidly. By 2010, it was employing more than 2 million workers in around 9,000 stores in 15 countries, and across four continents (www.walmartstores.com).

However, the reality is that only a few of the 500 MNCs that dominate international business have a genuinely global presence. Most have focused primarily on sales within their part of the triad. So American MNCs concentrate strategy on North America, European companies on Western Europe, and Japanese MNCs on Asia. However, FDI statistics show that the growth of developing economies such as China, India, and Brazil has caused many MNCs to invest there.

Greenfield and Brownfield Investment

MNC investment overseas can be broken down into **greenfield** and **brownfield investment**. Greenfield investment involves the establishment of completely new production facilities, such as Ford setting up its new car factory near St Petersburg in Russia. Brownfield investment entails the purchase of already existing production facilities—the **acquisition** of Asda, the British supermarket chain, by Wal-Mart, is an example of brownfield investment. MNCs have undertaken massive brownfield investment. In 2000 they were involved in around 11,000 cross-border mergers and **acquisitions** (M&As) to a value of more than US$1.1 trillion, two to three times greater than the figures for 1995. However, after 2000 there was a significant drop in **merger** activity to around US$380 billion by 2004. Merger activity then started to pick up so that by 2007 the total had again reached US$1 trillion. The main purchasers were rich country MNCs, but companies from China, India, and Russia also played a prominent role. The global crisis caused a significant decrease in 2009 in the number (4,239) and value (US$250 billion) of cross-border M&As. Over two thirds of cross-border M&A transactions still take place in rich countries, but the share of developing economies is on the increase reaching almost one third in 2009. The service sector is the dominant player in cross-border mergers with finance firms like banks, **hedge funds**, and commodity firms playing a significant role. The oil and gas and telecoms sectors are also important (UNCTAD 2007 and 2010).

 Counterpoint Box 1.1 Cross-border mergers & acquisitions

There have been huge waves of cross-border mergers and acquisitions (M&As) indicating their popularity with business. Such mergers have become a fundamental tool of business strategy.

It is claimed that there are two major benefits of cross-border mergers. Efficiency benefits arise when takeovers increase economies of scale in production, finance, and marketing or economies of scope leading to a reduction in unit costs. Strategic gains are generated if M&As, by reducing the number of competitors, permit the company to raise prices and profits. Horizontal mergers (i.e. between firms producing the same good or service) are the most likely type to yield these benefits. Another benefit identified includes the spreading of risk over several markets. Furthermore, it is argued that firms with lots of intangible assets such as technological know-how or marketing expertise can best exploit these abroad through M&As that allow them to control the use of these assets rather than ceding, and perhaps losing control, to foreign firms through licensing or franchising.

However, cross-border mergers also pose significant challenges that threaten the ability to realize these gains. For example, the acquirer may face difficulties and extra costs in dealing with language barriers and cultural differences, customer preferences, business practices, and in the political and legal environment which could act as major impediments to integrating the new business. The problems encountered in cross-border M&As can be exacerbated where: the firm moves into an activity of which it has little knowledge or experience, for example where it diversifies into another industry—Sony's takeover of Columbia Pictures in the US; the firm takes over another at a different stage of the supply chain in the industry in which it is currently operating by buying a supplier or a customer (a vertical merger)—an example of this is Reliance of India which appears to have successfully integrated backwards from textile production to the supply of polyester fibres into the refining of oil and then into oil and gas exploration and production.

Research offers conflicting evidence on the results generated by cross-border mergers. For example, a survey of business in North America, Europe, and Asia by the consultancy firm, Accenture, found most firms had not achieved the expected cost and revenue gains from cross-border M&As. However, this has apparently not deterred business which still sees cross-border M&As as an essential part of their competitive strategy.

Sources: Accenture, *Globalization and the Rise of Cross-Border Mergers and Acquisitions*; Finkelstein 2009; European Central Bank 2009; www.ril.com; Aybar and Ficici 2009; Conn *et al.* 2005; Chakrabarti *et al.* 2009; Steigner and Sutton 2011.

Migration

The globalization of markets has not been paralleled by the liberalization of labour flows. While globalization has led to the dismantling of barriers to trade in goods, services, and capital, barriers to cross-border labour movements are not falling as fast. Nevertheless, **migration** between developing and developed countries has risen. Flows of migrants are greatest to two triad members, North America and Europe—while Asia, Latin America, and Africa are major sources. The immigrant population in the USA numbers 43 million (World Bank 2011). That is the official figure, however Camarota and Jensenius (2009) estimate that a further 11 million people are living in the USA without permission.

According to the International Organisation for Migration, the number of migrants (people currently residing for more than a year in a country other than where they were born) is 214 million—which is around 3% of the world's population. This means that the migrant population more than doubled in 25 years. Europe has most migrants with 70 million (9.5% of the population), Asia has 61 million (1.5%), and North America 50 million (14%) (http://esa.un.org/migration). This increase in numbers has occurred despite the fact that during the last 30 years of the 20th century migration had become steadily more difficult—particularly for people in developing countries wanting to enter Europe. Migrants constitute a significant proportion of the population in some countries. In Australia, Canada, New Zealand, Luxembourg, and Switzerland the percentage exceeds 20%. The USA, along with certain European countries such as the UK, France, Germany, the Netherlands, and Sweden, has a percentage, between 10 and 15%, of immigrants. None of these compares with the Middle Eastern state of Qatar where more than four fifths of the population are migrants. Care needs to be taken regarding the accuracy of migration statistics because countries differ in their definition of 'migrant' and clandestine migrants are unlikely to be picked up by official statistics (http://esa.un.org/migration; http://iom.int).

People move for a variety of economic, social, and political reasons. They may move voluntarily to find work, to earn higher wages, to study, or to reunite with their families. Widening inequalities in income and job opportunities increase the pressures to move. Movement may also be stimulated by employers in developed countries actively recruiting labour from abroad. At the start of the new century, the attitudes of certain governments towards migration changed, as shortages of skilled workers emerged. For example, the USA, UK, and Germany started to look much more favourably on the entry of workers with high levels of education and skills in areas such as IT. The 2007 global crisis caused a hardening of attitudes to migration in rich countries.

Migration may also be involuntary where people, often in large numbers, are forced to migrate by political instability and violations of human rights—as we have seen for example in Zimbabwe, the Balkans and the civil unrest in 2010/11 in North Africa. Natural disasters, such as hurricanes, earthquakes, and floods can also force people to move. Global warming is expected to cause extensive flooding in coastal areas of South East Asia which will cause large waves of migration.

Large short-term movements of people also occur as a result of executives going on foreign business trips, students involved in study abroad, and tourism. France, the most popular tourist destination, receives 79 million tourists annually the USA around 55 million, and China 50 million (http://data.un.org). Some small countries are heavily dependent on tourism for their income. In the Caribbean countries of St Lucia, Antigua and Barbuda, and the Bahamas, tourism contributes more than 45% to their GDP (http://wttc.org/eng).

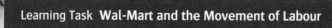

Learning Task Wal-Mart and the Movement of Labour

It was reported that more than 300 illegal workers had been arrested at 61 Wal-Mart stores in the USA as part of an investigation into contract cleaning crews at the world's largest retailer. The investigation involved allegations that a contractor had recruited illegal immigrants, mainly from Eastern Europe. The company ended up paying millions of dollars in fines in 2005. But the story did not end there. In 2010, a group of migrant workers took Wal-Mart to court for, amongst other things, failing to give them over-time pay, and coercing them into forced labour. They claimed that Wal-Mart employed undocumented workers to evade taxes and government regulations and to avoid having to pay for health benefits.

1. What are the advantages to Wal-Mart of employing illegal migrants to clean its stores?

2. What risks might Wal-Mart face by taking on such workers?

3. Google the class action taken by the migrant workers to find the outcome of the 2010 case.

Source: *The Observer,* 26 October 2003; *Financial Times,* 24 October 2003; www.courthousenews.com

Globalization is All-Pervasive

Although globalization is often seen as an economic phenomenon involving trade and invest-ment, it also has many other cultural and social dimensions. Held (1999) argues that globaliza-tion is all-pervasive. He defines globalization as:

> the widening, deepening and speeding up of worldwide interconnectedness in all aspects of contemporary social life, from the cultural to the criminal, the financial to the spiritual (p 2).

As Held observes, globalization is not confined to economic life but also influences many other areas of society. And he contends that each of these areas is becoming more deeply affected by the phenomenon. Cultural life involving the attitudes, behaviour, and values that are charac-teristic of a society, can be influenced by the process. Globalization can influence culture through the transfer of knowledge, ideas, and beliefs across national borders.

Mass media, such as television and film, illustrate how culture has been influenced by global-ization. American programmes such as *The Simpsons, Twilight,* and *House* are watched worldwide. While the USA is the by far major exporter of TV programmes, countries with large internal markets such as Brazil, Japan, and the UK are also active exporters (Bielby and Harrington 2008). Similarly, US films like *Inception* and *Avatar* are widely shown around the world. The collapse of communism in Eastern Europe and the arrival of cable and satellite system opened up more markets to US media companies. However, commentators such as Tunstall (2008) see a chal-lenge to the American TV and film industry from the growing capacity of China and India to become global media players, and the increasing competition from Latin America.

Diet is another area influenced by globalization. In France, the consumption of fast food such as hamburgers, and soft drinks like Coca Cola has increased and this is attributed by some com-mentators to the globalization of fast food chains like McDonald's, Subway, and Burger King. The movement of people can also have an impact on diet. In the second half of the 20th century, many migrants came to the UK from India and Pakistan. With around 9,000 Indian restaurants

Learning Task

One of the authors, while holidaying in Spain, looked at the films showing in cinemas in Catalonia. This is what he found:

Table 1.2 Country of origin of films on show in Catalonia

	2003	2010
Total on show:	59	57
Number made in:		
USA	28	27
Spain	10	9
Other countries	21	21

Source: *La Vanguardia*, 4 August 2003; El País 26 August 2010

Examine Table 1.2 and answer the following questions:

1. What conclusions can be drawn regarding the cultural interconnectedness of Spain with other countries? Does there appear to have been much change between 2003 and 2010?

2. How do you explain the position of the USA?

Now look at the film listings for your town or local area and work out to what extent it is connected with foreign countries. You could, if you wish, carry out a similar exercise on television programmes to see how many are of foreign origin.

in the UK, now almost all British towns and cities have an 'Indian' and it is claimed that the favourite meal, when eating out, is curry.

Another obvious route for transfer of culture across borders is through education. Universities in the USA, Western Europe, and Australia have enthusiastically embarked on campaigns to recruit students from abroad. Some have also gone in for FDI by setting up education facilities in other countries or have established partnerships with foreign colleges. The EU, through its Erasmus and Socrates programmes, has led to large numbers of students studying in other member states. In a further move to facilitate the movement of students and workers across borders, more than 40 European countries have initiated a programme of reform of their university systems. The idea is to standardize the structure of university studies with degrees taking from three to four years and the introduction of a common system of assessment, the European Credit and Transfer System.

Another conduit for such transfers is through the world of work. For example, the UK and the USA have been favoured locations for Japanese car companies, in other words, capital has been moved to these countries from Japan. The movement of capital across national borders brings with it different ways of working such as Just-in-Time where suppliers deliver raw materials and components immediately before they are needed in the manufacturing process, or quality circles where small groups of employees meet together to identify how production could be improved. Domestic firms have, in turn, been influenced by this, e.g. Nissan has persuaded suppliers to alter their production methods. And Nissan's rivals such as General Motors and Ford finding their market shares slipping because of their inability to compete with the Japanese, have responded to the threat by introducing some of their working methods. As a result, in the UK and USA, car industry working methods have become similar to those in Japan. Another example concerns McDonald's setting up in Moscow in partnership with the City Council. It had to devise a strategy for dealing with a Russian workforce that had a reputation for being surly and slovenly. McDonald's introduced expatriate managers and training pro-grammes to show the Russian staff how things should be done. Moscow City Council officials could not believe that the employees in the fast food outlet were Russian because they were so friendly.

The globalization process can also be seen in sport, where football players like Lionel Messi and Cristiano Ronaldo cross borders to play abroad. In a 2011 European Championship match between Chelsea and Copenhagen no fewer than 14 nations were represented on the field. There has also been a rush of foreign direct investment into the English premier football league. Chelsea is owned by a Russian businessman, while Liverpool and Manchester United were acquired by US tycoons. Manchester United is promoted and known worldwide—it is marketed as an international brand and there is a lucrative trade in Manchester United team kits and other products outside the UK. Furthermore, many of the top teams in England are now managed by foreigners.

A further impact of globalization is on health. A new treatment for disease, discovered in one country, can be quickly transferred to others, helping to limit the spread of disease and improve the quality of health care. On the other hand, diseases may also spread more quickly as people move across borders, for example the outbreak and spread of swine flu in 2009/10.

The swine flu pandemic originated in Mexico, a popular tourist destination for the USA, Canada, and the UK. So it was these countries that were most quickly affected. It then spread to other European countries, and, with the onset of winter, to countries in the southern hemisphere. In all, 171 countries were affected (go to the map at news.bbc.co.uk/1/hi/uk/8083179.stm to see the worldwide spread of the virus). Illness can also be spread through trade. In 2004 it was found that poultry farmers in Vietnam and Thailand had contracted the virus associated with avian flu. The infection spread to other countries through cross-border trade in poultry and the movement of migratory birds.

With regard to crime: globalization, by removing barriers to movement, can make it easier for criminals to operate in other countries. Criminals can move more easily across borders, as can pornography, prostitution, and illegal substances such as drugs. Large amounts of cocaine are produced in Colombia and gangs there ensure that the drug finds its way to users in the USA. The Russian mafia is involved in trafficking women for the vice trade in Amsterdam. Communications technology facilitates the electronic movement across borders of money generated by these ille-gal activities into countries where the criminals can portray it as being derived from a legitimate source. Or they may move the money to countries where the laws regulating such **money laun-dering** activities are deficient.

Religion, or the spiritual dimension as Held calls it, is another area that is globalized. Major churches, for example the Catholic, Anglican, Muslim, and Jewish churches all operate multinationally and have been spreading their values over large parts of the world for the last 2,000 years. In the UK the established churches, such as the Church of England, are in decline in contrast to evangelical churches which have their roots in the USA and, ironically, have their origin in English Puritanism.

The Drivers of Globalization

In 1983 Theodore Levitt claimed:

> Gone are accustomed differences in national or regional preferences. Gone are the days when a company could sell last year's model—or lesser versions of advanced products—in the less developed world. Gone are the days when prices, margins and profits were generally higher than at home.

Although he was overstating the case, he was making the point that **technology**, through communication, transport, and travel was driving the world towards convergence. In the business world the process of competition would drive firms to seek out these markets and force down prices by standardizing what was sold and how it was made in an effort to cut costs and to maintain profit. International competition is not a new business phenomenon, nor is FDI or international trade but, as we have seen in the first section, the process of globalization appears to be accelerating. The organization of trade is also different, with much of it taking place between and within large multinational organizations across borders which are increasingly irrelevant. It is supported by international organizations like the WTO and agreements which did not exist a century ago.

The process also embraced an increasing number of countries, as free **market ideology** was accepted as the dominant economic philosophy. The countries of South East Asia, Latin America, India, Central and Eastern Europe, and even China have one by one bowed to the power of market forces. However, the global financial crisis of 2007 did raise questions about giving markets free rein and led to calls for more government intervention (see Chapter Ten on The Financial Framework for discussion of this).

The big MNCs have not been passive participants in the liberalization process. They are usually to be found at the forefront, pushing governments to open up their economies by removing barriers to trade and investment. Indeed, Rugman (2002) argues that their managers are the real drivers of globalization. MNCs encourage governments through pressure groups such as The European Round Table (ERT) which was set up by MNCs from 17 countries. It brings together leaders of around 45 of the biggest MNCs with a combined turnover exceeding around US$1,400 billion, supporting nearly 7 million jobs in Europe. It was instrumental in promoting the idea of a single market for the EU and is very keen to integrate the former **communist** countries and the developing nations into a globalized system (see the ERT website at www.ert.be). Similarly, the National Association of Manufacturers in the USA has pressed for markets to be opened up from Cape Horn, the southernmost tip in South America, to Alaska.

Competition is one of the dominant drivers in the process of globalization of the world economy. If your competitors are globalizing and capturing new growth opportunities, scale efficiencies, and gaining invaluable knowledge of global operations then you are likely to cease to exist or be forced into small domestic market niches unless you follow suit.

There are other drivers, although some might be more correctly labelled as 'facilitators'. In the next sections we look at the forces driving the globalization of business, the facilitating factors, and those forces which act as barriers, helping to keep business 'local'.

Political/Regulatory

Governments have taken steps to remove barriers to trade and the movement of finance through international organizations such as the General Agreement on Tariffs and Trade (GATT) and its successor organization the World Trade Organization and they have also set up **free trade** areas, customs unions, or common markets.

- **Free trade area**—member states agree to remove tariffs and **quotas** on goods from other members of the area. Members have the freedom to set the level of tariff imposed on imports of goods from non-members of the area.

- **Customs union**—this is a free trade area but with the addition that members agree to levy a common tariff on imports of goods from non-members.

- **Common market**—this is a customs union but with the addition that member states agree to allow free movement of goods, services, capital, and labour.

There have been major reductions in the barriers to movement, particularly for goods and capital brought about by liberalization. These have been brought about multilaterally through negotiations in international institutions such as GATT and its successor organization, the WTO, or bilaterally between individual governments. Governments help bring about increased economic and political interlinkage by signing treaties setting up **regional trade areas** (RTAs) such as the North Atlantic Free Trade Area (NAFTA) with the involvement of the USA, Canada, and Mexico where barriers to movement such as tariffs and quotas are abolished among the members. Other examples are, The Association of Southeast Asian Nations (ASEAN) incorporating ten countries in South East Asia, and Mercosur comprising four countries in South America. The number of RTAs rose dramatically from about 30 in 1990 to 474 in 2010 (www.wto.org), 90% of which are free trade areas and 10% customs unions. While such bodies do promote integration among the members they often limit integration with non-members by maintaining barriers against imports from them.

Sometimes governments push integration further by agreeing to the establishment of customs unions which comprise a free trade area plus a common import tariff against non-members. Or they may set up a common market where there is complete freedom of movement for goods, services, capital, and people. One result of this removal of barriers to the movement of people in the EU is that someone in Southern Spain could drive to Lapland without necessarily having to stop at a single border. Some members of the EU have taken the integration process even further by removing currency as a barrier by agreeing on the introduction of a common currency, the euro. Economic integration often then leads on to political integration. So EU member states are subject not only to EU laws but also to common policies in areas such as agriculture, the regions, and social policy.

Changes in political regimes have also helped reduce barriers, e.g. the collapse of communism in the late 1980s and early 1990s led to Eastern European countries becoming more interconnected economically, politically, and militarily particularly with Western Europe and the

USA. Many of the former communist countries joined NATO and the EU. China opened up its economy to foreign investors and joined the WTO.

Governments, particularly in poorer countries in Asia, Africa, and Latin America, anxious to promote economic development, facilitate the movement of capital into their countries by setting up export processing zones (epz) where MNCs can invest, produce, and trade under favourable conditions. China has 15 zones employing 40 million people. Kenya has 45 zones, while Honduras has 24. MNCs are usually given financial incentives to invest and often they are allowed to import goods and produce output free of tax. Boyenge (2007) estimated that there were 3,500 epz in 130 countries employing around 66 million people. There are also many free trade zones or freeports which are supposed to act as entrepots and be used for storage purposes.

Technological

Improvements in communications and reductions in transport costs have facilitated the movement of goods, services, capital, and people. Modern communications technology makes it easier for businesses to control far-flung empires. It further allows people to connect and interact over long distances, and with transport becoming easier and cheaper, goods and people are able to travel long distances quickly and at a relatively low cost (see Golub and Tomasik 2008 for changes in the cost of transporting goods).

The internet and cheaper telephony not only make it easier for MNCs to control their foreign operations but also for migrants to maintain links with their countries of origin. Furthermore, it has been a major force in integrating the world's financial markets. A trader in a bank in New York can use the computer to monitor movements in share prices, interest rates, and currency rates in all the major financial markets and can respond by buying and selling almost simultaneously. Vast amounts of money can be transferred across borders at the press of a button.

In 1930, it cost more than a week's average wage in the UK for a three minute telephone call from London to New York. Now it costs a fraction of the average hourly wage. Demand for telecommunications has increased very rapidly. The number of mobile phone subscribers worldwide more than doubled between 2005 and 2010. Access to a mobile network is available to 90% of the world population (International Telecommunications Union 2010).

The growth in demand for telecommunications services has been driven by the development of the cellular technology associated with mobile phones. Another factor, the internet, has revolutionized telecommunications. It has become a very cheap and reliable method of communicating text, data, and images and it is also being increasingly used for voice communication. The number of people in the world with internet access grew more than tenfold from less than 100 million in the mid 1990s to 2 billion in 2010 with China having around 420 million users and India 81 million. However, although their numbers are huge, the proportion of people with internet access is lower in these countries compared with the rich countries of North America and North Western Europe (www.internetworldstats.com).

India is a good example of a country that has benefited from the impact of advances in communications technology. It has a ready supply of relatively cheap educated labour and has become an increasingly popular location for call centre jobs. This has come about as a result of the advances in communication technology which have significantly reduced the costs and improved the quality and reliability of telephony. Consequently, there has been a movement of jobs from the UK and the USA to South East Asia. More than half of the world's top 500 companies outsource either IT or other business processes to India.

Technology can also have the effect of reducing movements of people. Improvements in the costs and quality of video links may mean that business executives do not need to attend meetings abroad. They can be virtual travellers interacting electronically through teleconferencing with fellow managers in other countries.

Economic

In many modern industries the scale of investment needed for research and development (R&D) and production facilities can mean that the size of a single domestic market is insufficient to support that industry. The production of electronic components requires high levels of investment in both R&D and the manufacturing process, and this drives firms to go global. This is especially so when **product life cycles** are shortening, increasing the pressure to recover investment quickly. Competitive pressures on costs also push firms to reduce product lines and to expand globally to seek every possible saving from economies of scale in R&D, manufacturing, and marketing.

The desire to cut costs can be seen in the aluminium industry. Aluminium is a relatively expensive metal to produce as it takes a lot of electricity to turn ore into metal. This is why aluminium firms locate their smelters in locations with access to cheap energy. Other industries will seek out cheap sources of labour. In the footwear industry, which uses relatively simple technology and is therefore **labour intensive**, labour costs represent about 40% of total costs. Hourly wages in some countries are very low. For example, in manufacturing, those in Mexico are just one sixth and Brazil a quarter of those in the USA. As a result manufacturing has been relocating to countries with low labour costs. (Bureau of Labour Statistics at www.bls.gov).

Firms may globalize because they have outgrown their domestic market. Furthermore, the pace of growth in mature, developed economies for many industries is relatively modest. To maintain a rate of growth required by **capital markets** will mean for most of the world's leading companies that they must seek opportunities beyond their domestic borders.

Ikea, based in Sweden and the world's largest furniture retailer, is an example of this. The Swedish market is relatively small so, in order to grow, Ikea had to go abroad. In the decade up to 2010, it trebled global sales operating through 280 stores in 26 countries in North America, Europe, Asia, and Australasia (*Financial Times*, 14 January 2011).

The rapid improvements in technology and the consequent reduction in communication and transport costs have enabled people to experience other societies' lifestyles first hand or through the medium of TV and film or the internet. This has led to a convergence in tastes which MNCs have been quick to exploit by creating global brands such as Coca Cola, Levi, Sony, Nike, and McDonald's. This has been called the 'Californiazation' or 'McDonaldization' of society (Ohmae 1985; Ritzer 2004, respectively).

Global companies mean global customers. Global customers require basic supplies of input materials, global financial and accounting services, and global hotel chains to house travelling executives. Dealing with one supplier of a standard product or service has many advantages for the global buyer; lower purchase costs, a standard product of consistent quality, lower administration costs, and more opportunities for cooperation with suppliers. For example, Japanese banks became more global following the globalization of Japanese car manufacturers (an important customer).

Counterpoint Box 1.2 Globalization: the free market

Supporters of globalization claim that free movement of goods, services, and capital increases economic growth and prosperity and leads to a more efficient allocation of resources with benefits to all countries involved. It results in more competition, lower prices, more employment, higher output and standards of living. Countries, therefore should open up their economies to free movement by removing barriers such as tariffs, quotas, laws and regulations, subsidies, and the purchase by public bodies of goods and services on nationalist grounds. It is also argued that a liberalized world economy would eradicate global poverty.

Critics see an element of hypocrisy when rich countries use the arguments above to persuade poor countries to open up their economies to imports and inward investment. Historically, almost all rich countries, including the USA and UK, protected domestic industries from foreign competition with subsidies,

tariffs, quotas, regulation and through state-owned enterprises. Many such as Japan, Finland, and South Korea tightly controlled foreign investment whilst France, Austria, Finland, Singapore, and Taiwan developed key industries through state-owned enterprises. But despite this, they grew rich. Critics also point to the period after 1980 when developing countries liberalized their economies and their economic growth rates fell compared with the 1960s and 70s when they protected their domestic industries from foreign competition. Opponents claim that globalization increases inequality between countries, and also results in economic instability citing the 2007–09 financial crisis which spread rapidly from the USA around the world.

Sources: Sachs 2005; Bhagwati 2004; Wolf 2005 and 2010; Stiglitz 2002; Chang 2008 and 2010; Chua 2003

Barriers to Globalization

Despite the fast pace of globalization, it remains the case that goods, services, capital, and people move more easily within nations than across borders. Trade between regions within nations is generally much higher than trade across borders even when adjusted for income and distance levels. This occurs even when trading restrictions appear to be low, for example, between Canada and the USA.

Government Regulation

Governments pursue policies that can hinder the flow of goods and services and the movement of capital and people across borders. Surprisingly, the global economic crisis did not lead governments to resort to protectionism, the head of the WTO describing it as 'the dog that hasn't barked' (*The Guardian*, 27 January 2011). However, there are still a number of barriers to globalization.

Tariffs and Subsidies

There remain numerous tariffs on imports of goods. Rich countries impose particularly high tariffs on goods coming from poor countries. The EU, Japan, and Norway levy high tariffs on imports of agricultural products that are important to developing economies while tariffs imposed on manufactured goods from other rich countries are lower. Such differences in tariffs help to explain why trade tends to take place within and between the rich countries of the triad. Poor countries also impose tariffs. India and Brazil apply maximum average tariffs of over 30% on imports of non-agricultural products (WTO 2010).

Rich countries also subsidize their farmers. In 2009, OECD countries subsidized agriculture to the tune of US$253 billion. The EU, Japan, Norway, and Switzerland are amongst the biggest subsidizers (OECD 2010).

Subsidies can also be used to promote globalization. In export processing zones they are often used to attract foreign investors.

Foreign Aid

Rich countries usually give financial assistance to poor countries. Frequently, such aid, for example from the USA and Japan, is used to promote the interests of domestic firms by requiring the recipients to buy goods and services produced by firms in the donor country irrespective of whether they give best value for money.

Controls on Capital

Controls on capital can take the form of either controls on inflows or outflows of foreign direct and indirect investment.

Big steps have been made in liberalizing the movements of capital. However, some countries have been more amenable to this than others. Thus India and South Korea have been reluctant to remove restrictions on capital inflows, and Japan has one of the most closed financial systems of all the advanced countries. In 2009, Brazil introduced controls on inflows of portfolio investment because they were driving up the value of the currency and affecting the country's international competitiveness. Countries are often reluctant to accept inflows of foreign direct investment where it involves sectors they regard as strategically important such as the basic utilities of gas, electricity, and water. The USA and the EU are not prepared to cede control of their airline companies to foreign organizations. US law prevents foreign firms from buying more than 24.9% of an American airline (the corresponding figure for the EU is 49%).

Public Procurement

Government departments, nationalized industries, public utilities in telecommunications, gas, and water often spend large amounts of public money purchasing goods and services. **Public procurement in the EU equates to 16% of GDP or €2,600 billion.** Governments are very important customers for firms, particularly those producing goods and services for the defence, health, and education sectors. When issuing **contracts**, governments will often favour domestic producers over their foreign rivals even when domestic firms are more expensive.

Border and Immigration Controls

Border controls affect trade in goods. They can require the filling in of export/import forms and also customs officers stopping vehicles and checking goods at the frontier. This can take time, add to traders' transport costs and make goods less competitive in the foreign market.

Many barriers remain to the movement of people. These include stringent visa requirements, quotas, requiring employers to search for a national employee before employing a foreign one, and refusal by the authorities to accredit foreign educational and vocational qualifications.

Technical Standards

Technical standards and regulations can be formidable barriers. There are thousands upon thousands of different technical specifications relating to goods and services which can effectively protect domestic markets from foreign competition and consequently restrict trade. The EU has tried to deal with this through its Single Market Programme. It uses the principle of mutual recognition whereby countries accept products from other member states so long as they do not constitute a danger to the consumer. Companies in the service sector can be hampered by the myriad of technical standards and requirements. Financial institutions such as banks may find it difficult to use the internet to sell their services in foreign markets because countries may lay down different solvency requirements, or different levels of liquidity for financial institutions operating in their territory.

In addition, new barriers can appear: where several companies are competing to develop a new product, the first to do so may establish its technical specifications as a standard for the new product which then acts as a barrier to trade for competitors.

Protection of Intellectual Property Rights

Different national policies towards what are called intellectual property rights (IPRs) could constitute barriers as well. IPRs relate to new products and production processes, brand names, logos as well as books and films. Their owners argue that they should have the legal right to prevent others from commercially exploiting them. However, the extent of protection and enforcement of these rights varies widely around the world. Some countries such as China and Malaysia do not offer the firms creating the ideas and knowledge much protection against counterfeiting. Firms contend that the lack of protection of IPRs stunts their trade and FDI in those countries.

Cultural and Geographical Distance

Culture

Cultural distance can constitute an important barrier. Differences in language, religious beliefs, race, national and regional tastes, social norms and values, and business practices which regulate what is regarded as acceptable behaviour and attitudes can constitute major impediments to globalization. Culture can be an important influence on consumer behaviour, work culture, and business practices. Thus, McDonald's cannot sell Big Macs in India because to Hindus the cow is sacred, nor can it assume that staff in Eastern Europe will have the same attitudes to work as its workers in the USA. Another example concerned Tyrrells, the UK crisp company; the founder described how it encountered difficulties when trying to sell parsnip crisps in France not realizing that the French saw parsnips as pig feed (*Financial Times*, 21 March 2011).

Some goods and services are more sensitive than others to cultural differences. Ghemawat (2001) researched the impact of culture and found that products such as meat, cereals, tobacco, and office machines had to be adapted to local cultures, whereas firms producing cameras, road vehicles, cork and wood, and electricity did not need to adapt their products—or were under less compulsion to do so.

Corruption

Another area where cultural distance can cause problems for firms, is corruption. In some countries, in Africa and the Middle East for example, it is the norm for firms to reward individuals who help it to get business. However, in other countries such behaviour would be seen as corrupt and would be deemed illegal. The prospect of prosecution in their home countries

Mini Case Cultural Distance—Domino's Pizza

This case illustrates how companies wishing to profit from globalization have to take into account cultural differences in taste and eating habits.

The US firm Domino's Pizza is the world's second largest pizza chain with sales of US$6.2 billion of which US$2.9 billion was made outside the USA. It has over 9,000 outlets in 69 markets across five continents. As it expanded around the world, the company found that it had to adapt both the product and the service to appeal to local consumers.

Icelanders prefer their pizza topped with fish while the French go for goat's cheese and lardons. In Taiwan, the favourite toppings are squid, crab, shrimp, and pineapple, whereas in Brazil pizza lovers go for mashed bananas and cinnamon. In Japan, mayonnaise, potato, maize, and bacon are the preferred options. Mexicans favour chorizo sausage and jalapeno peppers.

Domino's has found simply by changing the toppings that pizza is acceptable to consumers all round the world. But there can still be cultural complications. In India, the fact that Hindus cannot eat meat from cows meant Domino's had to replace pepperoni with a spicy chicken sausage. Most pizzas sold there are vegetarian. In Japan, where no word for pepperoni existed, they introduced it.

Domino's was able to export the idea of home delivery almost everywhere but not to China. In the capital, Beijing, Domino's had to fit tables in its restaurants. People in China, paying for a prepared meal, want to have somewhere to sit and eat it. Delivery can also be challenging in some markets. In Tokyo, where buildings are numbered not in sequence along streets but according to the date they were constructed, Domino's outlets each have a full-time employee whose job is to find locations on the map and tell drivers where to go.

Source: www.dominosbiz.com; www.release-news.com; *Financial Times*, 26 November 2003; www.franchise-international.net

Learning Task

Some goods and services are more sensitive than others to cultural differences. Ghemawat did some research on the impact of culture and found the following:

More Sensitive Products	Less Sensitive Products
Meat	Cameras
Cereals	Road vehicles
Tobacco	Cork and wood
Office machines	Electricity

Discuss and advance explanations for Ghemawat's findings.

might deter firms from trading with, and investing in, countries where such behaviour is the norm.

Cultural differences can be a significant barrier to globalization and ignoring them can be very costly (see Ghemawat 2001).

Geography

Geographical distance can also be a barrier. It has been shown that the more distance there is between countries, the less will be the trade between them (Ghemawat 2001). Geographical distance can make trade difficult, particularly for firms producing goods that are low in value but high in bulk, such as cement or beer. The cost of transporting cement or beer over long distances would be prohibitive. Fragile or highly perishable products like glass and fruit may suffer similar problems. Firms respond to the barrier posed by geographical distance in various ways. Brewers have responded either by taking over a foreign brewer or by granting a licence to firms in foreign markets to brew their beer. Thus barriers to one aspect of globalization, trade, result in globalization in another form, investment or **licensing**. Historically, geographical distance is likely to have declined in importance as transport has become cheaper and techniques for carrying fragile or perishable products more effective.

The Benefits and Costs of Globalization for Business

Globalization can comprise major changes in the external environment of business. On the one hand, it creates opportunities for business, particularly for the big MNCs who are in the best position to take advantage. On the other hand, it can pose threats for business as well. We examine the benefits and costs in turn.

The Benefits for Business

Removal of barriers to trade or investment can:

* open up markets to businesses that were previously excluded giving them the possibility of higher revenues and growth. The activities of car producers and tobacco firms in South East Asia illustrate this. As their traditional markets in North America and Western Europe have matured, General Motors, Ford, Volkswagen, Toyota, and others have all looked to the fast-expanding markets of South East Asia as a source of growth. China, with its rapidly growing car market, has been a particularly favoured location for car industry investment. Similarly, the fall of communism gave banks from the USA and Western Europe the opportunity to move into the former Communist bloc countries and, in many countries such as the Czech Republic, Bulgaria, and Croatia, have ended up controlling a majority of banking assets;

* give business access to cheaper supplies of final products, components, raw materials, or to other **factors of production** such as labour which lowers their costs and makes them more competitive. It is hardly surprising that firms such as HSBC, Tesco, ebookers, and BT have been relocating activities to India where graduates can be employed for a fraction of the corresponding salaries in the USA or the UK. The relatively low cost of IT professionals has also resulted in the biggest computer firms establishing operations in India. Similarly, China is not seen by Western MNCs simply in terms of its market potential but also as a very cheap source of supply. And many MNCs relocated manufacturing production to China where there was an abundant supply of cheap labour;

- allow firms to obtain previously denied natural resources. For many years Saudi Arabia was unwilling to give foreign firms access to its energy deposits. The Saudi authorities had a change of heart allowing Shell to explore for gas.

The Costs for Business

Globalization can also have costs for business:

- the environment is likely to become more complex and risky. Business is confronted by new sets of factors in the form of different political regimes, laws and regulations, tax systems, competition policies, and cultures. In extreme cases, they may find that the host government seizes their investment or takes discriminatory action against them. For example, Bolivia nationalized natural gas production and took four electricity generating companies, including power stations owned by France's GDF Suez and UK's Rurelec, into public ownership (PRS Group 2010);

- inefficient firms may find that it removes the barriers protecting them from foreign competitors. National airlines such as Lufthansa, or telecommunications companies like France Telecom found it difficult to face up to the more intense competition engendered by the liberalization of civil aviation and telecommunications in the EU. Often the endangered businesses will pressurize governments to leave the protective barriers in place or to reintroduce the barriers previously removed. Removal of the barriers may allow the entry of new competitors from abroad or it may permit existing customers to switch their custom to foreign suppliers who are cheaper or who can offer better product quality. Weaker domestic firms may find that their access to **factors of production** is threatened (see Mini Case on Brazilian Football for an example of this);

- globalization can raise the dependence of plants and firms on foreign markets and suppliers. As a result of NAFTA, more than 3,000 plants (called **maquiladoras**) were set up along the Mexico/USA border employing some 1,300,000 workers, producing goods for the North American market. They accounted for half of Mexico's exports. When the US economy went into recession in 2008, the maquiladoras began shedding workers. By 2009, nearly 30% of jobs had disappeared and exports had fallen by more than one third (Muñoz and Martinez 2010). In the Mexican border towns they say that when the US economy catches cold, Mexico gets pneumonia (Rosen 2003);

- globalization can cause the environment to become more volatile. Firms generally prefer to operate in an environment where the financial and macroeconomic systems are stable and predictable. However, there is evidence from global financial crises, for example in the late 1990s and in 2007/08 that the economies of developing economies, whose financial systems have integrated most with the rest of the world, are more subject to greater instability than other developing countries (Prasad *et al.* 2003; Green *et al.* 2010). Increasing integration of financial markets allows enormous sums of money to be moved effortlessly across borders leaving financial markets more vulnerable to instability, and the world financial system more prone to violent fluctuations in **exchange rates** and interest rates. Such fluctuations can pose a major risk to business costs, revenues, and profits.

Mini Case Globalization and Football

This case shows the impact of globalization on the supply of scarce resources, in this case, talented footballers, to Brazilian football clubs.

Brazilian football fans have long lamented the loss of their football stars as their best players leave for big contracts abroad.

Arguably one of the largest sources of football talent in the world, Brazil itself has hardly any stars left. Fans and officials blame global capitalism. Brazil is a developing economy and is poor relative to its European counterparts. So the best Brazilian players seek greener grass in Europe.

The process is not new. Brazilian football icons went abroad long before Pele was lured to the New York Cosmos in the 1970s. However, the exodus reached new proportions in the 21st century. In 2004 alone, 850 players left the country for hard currency contracts making Brazil the world's biggest exporter of footballers. There are almost 600 Brazilian footballers playing in major European leagues. It is hardly surprising that the national team comprises many foreign-based players. Kaka plays for Real Madrid, Ramirez for Chelsea, and Robinho for AC Milan. The attraction for foreign clubs is that buying players from Brazil costs less than local footballers of equivalent talent.

As the head of a Brazilian fan club put it, 'Brazil has the best football in the world but we are losing all our top players, we feel betrayed.'

The tide may be changing. Increasing wealth generated by Brazil's rapidly growing economy could lead to players staying at home and may even lead to players returning from abroad.

Sources: *The Economist*, 20 January 2005; *Financial Times*, 15 September 2003; www.bbc.co.uk 25 November 2010; http://soccerlens.com

Source: Brand X Pictures

● CHAPTER SUMMARY

In this chapter we have explained the nature of globalization as a process through which barriers between nations are reduced. Nations thereby become increasingly interdependent, although we point out that most of this interdependence is between members of the triad, with the rest of the world playing a minor role. The dominance of the triad is being challenged by the emergence of China, India, Brazil, and Russia as world economic powers. Increased interdependence is indicated by increases in exchanges across borders of goods and services, financial capital, and people.

We also make the point that globalization is not just about economic exchanges but has a cultural and social dimension. The media, our diet, education, work practices, sport, health, crime, and religion all demonstrate the impact of globalization.

The main drivers of globalization are identified as competition, reduction in regulatory barriers, improvements in technology, saturated domestic markets, the desire to cut costs, and the growth of global customers. There still remain important barriers to the process including regulation, technology, and cultural and geographic distance.

Globalization presents both opportunities and threats to business. On the one hand it presents access to new and bigger markets and to different and cheaper sources of raw materials, components, and labour. On the other hand, the environment is more complex and less stable.

It is this environment and the implications for business that this book will explore. In the next chapter we will look at the global economy and explain in more depth some of the topics discussed in this chapter.

● REVIEW QUESTIONS

1. What is globalization?

2. How fast is globalization occurring?

3. Where is globalization mainly taking place? Why should that be the case?

4. Identify the main:

    - indicators of globalization

    - drivers of globalization

    - facilitators of globalization

5. What are the important barriers to globalization?

Case Study Two Turkeys Do Not Make an Eagle—Or Do They?

In 2011, the Finnish company Nokia, the world's biggest manufacturer of mobile handsets, with a 33% market share agreed to establish a cross-border partnership with Microsoft the biggest software maker. Despite selling millions of phones each year with its own operating system, Symbian, Nokia found itself operating at the low margin end of the market. Furthermore, profits were in decline and Symbian's market share had fallen from 36% in 2009 to 29% the following year and it was being outsold by Apple's iPhone and devices using Google's Android system. Apple was the most profitable company in the sector, followed by RIM with its BlackBerry. The Nokia chief executive also claimed that Chinese rivals were turning out new devices 'in the time it takes us to polish a PowerPoint presentation' and warned 'the battle of devices has now become a war of ecosystems' (*The Guardian*, 12 February 2011).

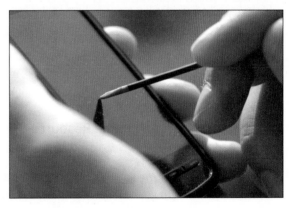

Source: www.istockphoto.com

The smartphone market is seen as a key battleground because it is expected to become the dominant means by which people use the internet in the near future. At the end of 2010, smartphones were outselling PCs worldwide.

Nokia's adoption of Windows Phone was seen by some analysts as a final admission of defeat in its efforts to promote Symbian. Nokia's chief executive admitted that he had privately compared the group's predicament to a man standing on a burning North Sea oil platform, torn between being burnt alive and jumping into icy waters.

The agreement allowed Nokia to use the US company's smartphone operating system, Windows Phone. Nokia hoped that Microsoft's operating system would enable it to fight ➜

➜ back against Apple and Google. Nokia also planned to combine its app store, which had more than 30,000 apps, with Microsoft's Marketplace, which had 8,000. But that was still just a fraction of the 350,000 apps in Apple's store and the 200,000 in Google's Android. Nokia claimed that big mobile phone operators like Vodafone, Telefónica, and Everything Everywhere supported the partnership fearing that a Nokia tie-up with Google to use its Android system would create a duopoly thus reducing the operators' bargaining power. The partnership with Microsoft left three rivals competing for their business.

Microsoft went into the partnership hoping to secure a bigger global foothold in mobile software. Microsoft was a leader in smartphone software before the iPhone's launch in 2007, but Windows Phone's market share had slipped to around 4% in 2010. With Nokia, the largest mobile maker, using Windows Phone, Microsoft hoped to see its operating system prosper. Microsoft also saw Nokia's use of Windows Phone boosting search advertising business on Bing, its internet search engine, which would be used on the Finnish company's smartphones. Under the agreement, Microsoft would carry out R&D on the Windows Phone system which would lead to a reduction in Nokia's research spending. Nokia agreed to pay its partner royalty fees of between US$10 and US$20 per smartphone for use of the Windows software. Microsoft announced that it would continue to sell its software to other mobile producers like Samsung.

The Google vice president of engineering described the tie-up thus, 'Two turkeys do not make an eagle' (*The Guardian*, 12 February 2011).

Sources: *The Guardian, Financial Times, The Independent*, 12 February 2011; http://press.nokia.com 11 February 2011; www.microsoft.com 11 February 2011; http://mobithinking.com/mobile-marketing-tools/latest-mobile-stats

Questions

1. Given that the alliance between Microsoft and Nokia is cross-border, what potential problems might be encountered?

2. Why is the smartphone important for:

- mobile handset producers
- software producers
- PC manufacturers

3. Analyse the role played by competition in the tie-up of Nokia and Microsoft.

4. Outline the benefits and disadvantages of the tie-up between Nokia and Microsoft to each company.

5. Discuss the implications of the partnership for rivals such as Apple and Google.

 Online Resource Centre

www.oxfordtextbooks.co.uk/orc/hamilton_webster2e/

Visit the supporting online resource centre for additional material which will help you with your assignments, essays, and research, or you may find these extra resources helpful when revising for exams.

● FURTHER READING

For a discussion of the debates and controversies around globalization see:

● Held, D. and McGrew, A. (2007) *Globalization/Anti-Globalization: Beyond the Great Divide*, 2nd edn. Cambridge: Polity

● Steger, M.B. (2009) *Globalization: A Very Short Introduction*. Oxford: Oxford University Press

For an examination of the various theories around globalization and how the world economy has been transformed by MNCs, states, and interest groups see:

● Dicken, P. (2009) *Mapping the Changing Contours of the World Economy*, 5th edn. London: Sage

The next book discusses the relationship between globalization and climate change, terrorism, energy supply, population, and business:

● Moynagh, M. and Worsley, R. (2008) *Going Global: Key Questions for the 21st Century*. London: A&C Black

● REFERENCES

Aybar, B. and Ficici, A. 'Cross-border Acquisitions and Firm Value: An Analysis of Emerging-market Multinationals'. *Journal of International Business Studies*, Oct/Nov 2009, Vol 40, Issue 8

Bank for International Settlements (2010) Triennial Central Bank Survey of Foreign Exchange and Derivatives Market Activity, September

Bhagwati, J. N. (2004) *In Defense of Globalization*. Oxford: Oxford University Press

Bielby, D. and Harrington, C. L. (2008) *Global TV: Exporting Television and Culture in the World Market*. New York: New York University Press

Boyenge, J.-P. S. (2007) ILO database on export processing zones, International Labour Office, April

Camarota, S. A. and Jensenius, K. (2009) A Shifting Tide: Recent Trends in the Illegal Immigrant Population, July, Center for Immigration Studies, July

Chakrabarti, R., Gupta-Mukherjee, S., and Jayaraman, N. (2009) 'Mars–Venus Marriages: Culture and Crossborder M&A'. *Journal of International Business Studies* 40

Chang, H.-J. (2010) *23 Things They Don't Tell You About Capitalism*. London: Allen Lane

Chang, H.-J. (2008) *The Myth of Free Trade and the Secret History of Capitalism*. New York: Bloomsbury Press

Chua, A. (2003) *World on Fire: How Exporting Free Market Democracy Breeds Ethnic Hatred and Global Instability*. New York: Doubleday

Conn, R., Cosh, A., Guest, A., and Hughes, A. (2005) 'The Impact on U.K. Acquirers of Domestic, Cross-border, Public and Private Acquisitions'. *Journal of Business Finance & Accounting* 32

EU Commission (2010) State Aid Scoreboard, Autumn

EU Commission (2011) Background on Energy in Europe, 4 February

Eurostat (2010) External and intra-European Union trade, Data 2004–2009

Finkelstein, S. (2009) *Cross Border Mergers and Acquisitions* available at www.tuck.dartmouth.edu

Friedman, T. (2005), *The World is Flat: Brief History of the Globalized World in the 21st Century*. London: Allen Lane

Ghemawat, P. (2001) 'Distance Still Matters: The Hard Reality of Global Expansion'. *Harvard Business Review*, September, 137–47

Golub, S. S. and Tomasik, B. (2008) Measures of International Transport Cost for OECD Countries, OECD Economics Department Working Papers, No 609

Green, D., King, R., and Miller-Dawkins, M. (2010) The Global Economic Crisis and Developing Countries: Impact and Response, Oxfam Research Report, January 2010

Held, D., *et al.* (1999) *Global Transformations*. Stanford: Stanford University Press

International Monetary Fund (2006) World Economic Outlook, September

International Monetary Fund (2010) Global Financial Stability report, October

International Telecommunications Union (2010) The World in 2010: ICT Facts and Figures

Lanz, R. and Miroudot, S. (2010) Issues and Challenges for Measuring Intra-firm Trade, OECD, 6 October

Levitt, T. (1983) 'The Globalization of Markets'. *Harvard Business Review*, May–June, 91–102

Maurer, A. and Degain, C. (2010) Globalization and trade flows: what you see is not what you get!, WTO 22 June

Muñoz Martinez, H. (2010) The Double Burden on Maquila Workers: Violence and Crisis in Northern Mexico, available at www.global-labour-university.org

OECD (2010), Agricultural Policies in OECD Countries: At a Glance

Office of National Statistics (2010) Monthly Review of External Trade Statistics, December 2010 Edition

Ohmae, K. (1985) *Triad Power: The Coming Shape of Global Competition*. New York: Free Press

PRS Group (2010), Bolivia: Country Report, 1 May

Prasad, E., Rogoff, K., Wei, S.-J., and Kose, M. A. (2003) 'Effects on Financial Globalization on Developing Countries: Some Empirical Evidence'. IMF Occasional paper No 220, September 3

Ritzer, G. (2004) *The McDonaldization of Society*. London: Pine Forge Press

Rosen, D. H. (2003) 'How China Is Eating Mexico's Lunch'. *The International Economy*, Spring, 78

Rugman, A. and Hodgetts, R. M. (2002) *International Business*. London: Prentice Hall

Sachs, J. (2005) *The End of Poverty*. New York: Penguin Press

Steigner, T. and Sutton, N. K. (2011) 'How Does National Culture Impact Internalization Benefits in Cross-Border Mergers and Acquisitions?'. *The Financial Review* 46

Stiglitz, J. (2002) *Globalization and its Discontents*. London: Penguin

Tunstall, J. (2008) *The Media were American: US Media in Decline*. Oxford: Oxford University Press

UNCTAD (2007) World Investment Report

UNCTAD (2010) International Trade After the Economic Crisis: Challenges and New Opportunities

UNCTAD (2011) Global Investment Trends Monitor 17 January

Wolf, M. (2005) *Why Globalization Works*. Yale: Yale University Press

Wolf, M. (2010) *Fixing Global Finance*. Baltimore: Johns Hopkins University Press

World Bank (2008) MIGA Perspectives, January

World Bank (2008b) The Migration and Remittances Factbook

World Bank (2010) 2010 World Development Indicators

WTO (2010) World Tariff Profiles 2010

WTO (2010) World Trade Report

CHAPTER TWO

The Global Economy

LEARNING OUTCOMES

This chapter will enable you to:

- **Identify the global pattern of wealth**

- **Analyse the pattern of international trade**

- **Explain why countries trade with each other**

- **Identify the controls on trade**

- **Assess the significance of exchange rates for the business environment**

Case Study China and the World Economy

Globalization is a process whereby nations become increasingly interdependent largely through the exchange of goods and services, financial capital, and people. This case illustrates China's entry into the world economy. It shows how China transformed itself from a centralized, closed economy into a very open one and in the process became a leading world player: how growth has raised the living standards of some sectors of the economy but not all, and that rapid growth can also have its costs.

China joined the World Trade Organization (WTO) on 11 December 2001 submitting itself to a universal set of rules giving up some of the independence it had for so long defended. The process of moving the centrally **planned economy** of China to a more market oriented economy actually started in 1978 with the phasing out of **collectivized** agriculture. Other liberalization measures in relation to state-owned enterprises, prices, domestic labour mobility, external trade, and foreign direct investment (FDI) followed and by 2009 it had become the world's second largest economy with an estimated Gross Domestic Product (GDP) of over US$9 trillion (PPP) (**Purchasing Power Parity**—a measure which takes into account the relative cost of living). The USA was the biggest at over US$14 trillion.

The Chinese economy grew rapidly after 1978 averaging around 10% per year although with some wide fluctuations with growth as low as 4% and as high as 14% per annum. This resulted in a sixfold increase in GDP from 1984 to 2004. Growth has been much more stable since 2000 with 2007 being the fifth year in a row with growth above 10% per annum. Growth was 9.6% in 2008 and an estimated 8.7% (IMF World Economic Database) in 2009 when the world was in recession. This has been very much an export led growth with exports growing at over 30% per year for five years up to 2007. In 2009 China had the largest **trade surplus** in the world. It is also a very **open economy** with trade (imports plus exports) as a percentage of GDP measuring 58.7% between 2007 and 2009 (WTO) up from 44% in 2001. Visit the supporting **Online Resource Centre** for a link to these statistics.

China is now a major world player and changes in that market have a significant knock-on effect on the rest of the world economy. In 2004 China accounted for a third of the growth in world demand for oil and was a major reason for the dramatic rise in oil prices in that year. 'China is the world's second largest

Source: photodisc

oil consumer, using one in every 10 barrels produced. China is also the top consumer of iron ore, copper and aluminium and the world's largest buyer of soybeans.' (*International Business Times*, 16 December 2010).

The sectors of the economy to benefit have been industry and services with agriculture now in decline. The main cities to benefit alongside Beijing have been those along the coastal region, and the well-to-do residents of those cities can now afford to buy imported luxury goods, such as the Mercedes, and can choose from a greater variety of goods available in the retail stores.

But it is not good news for all. The reduced tariffs on agricultural products have threatened the livelihoods of hundreds of millions of farmers. More than 100,000 people have lost jobs in state-owned banks as they adjust to a more competitive →

→ climate. While the economy may be the fastest growing, according to the **World Bank**, the poorest 10% of the population have seen their incomes fall in absolute terms. In 1998 the share of wages and household income was over 53% but by 2005 this had fallen to 41.4%.

China may well be the world's second largest economy but with a population of 1.3 billion the average income is still only US$3,735 (2009) although this has risen significantly from US$285 in 1985 and US$1,290 in 2005. 150 million Chinese people still live on less than US$1 per day and income inequality has risen.

Twenty of the world's 30 most polluted cities are in China. Coal is the major energy source and there are plans to build more than 500 coal fired power stations to add to the 2,000 that already exist. Most of these are unmodernized and spew out clouds of carbon dioxide and sulphur dioxide. China's mines have the world's worst casualty rate. According to the Chinese media there were 2,456 accidents underground in 2005 leading to 3,818 deaths.

Sources: IMF; World Bank; WTO; *International Business Times*, 16 December 2010.

Introduction

What is going to happen to the world economy next year? Which economies will grow the fastest? Which are the richest? Which are the poorest? Where are the new markets of the world? What sort of goods and services do they require? Who trades with whom? What trade restrictions are there in place? What's happening to exchange rates?

These are just a few of the many questions international businesses will be asking as globalization spurs their search for new markets and new locations to site their increasingly global activities. This chapter seeks to answer some of these questions. It looks at the incidence of global wealth and **poverty** and how this is likely to change in the future. It examines the pattern of international trade, why countries trade, regulation of trade, and exchange rates.

Measuring the Size of the Global Economy

The most common method of measuring the size of an economy is by calculating Gross Domestic Product. This is the market value of total output of goods and services produced within a nation, by both residents and non-residents, over a period of time, usually a year.

In comparing the relative size of different economies one obvious problem is that the calculation of GDP is in a country's national currency. A common currency is required and this is normally the US$ using foreign exchange rates. This is not without its problems as foreign exchange rates reflect only internationally traded goods and services and are subject to short-term speculation and government intervention. For example, in the 1940s £1 sterling bought US$4. This rate was fixed as part of an international regime which considered that it was best for business if there was certainty about future exchange rates. In 1949 the UK government, for domestic reasons, decided to devalue the £ to be worth only US$2.80. It remained at this rate until 1967 when it was further devalued to US$2.41. In 1971 the USA moved to a **floating exchange rate** and other currencies followed suit. In the 1970s the £ floated and has varied from US$2.5 in the early 1970s to almost parity (US$1=£1) in 1984, back to about US$2 in 2007 and around US$1.5 in

2010. So measuring and comparing the wealth of the UK with the USA using foreign exchange rates would have indicated sudden changes in wealth which is clearly not the case, as the wealth of a mature economy such as the UK tends to change slowly, and fairly smoothly, over time.

This way of measuring GDP may indicate a country's international purchasing power but doesn't adequately reflect living standards. Most things, especially the basics of food, transport, and housing tend to be much cheaper in low income countries than in high income countries. A Western European travelling in much of Asia or Africa will find hotels, food, and drinks on average a lot cheaper than at home. The opposite of course is also true that people from those countries will find that their money does not go very far in Western Europe. A better indicator of living standards can be achieved by calculating GDP by what is known as the purchasing power parity (PPP) method. This calculates GDP on the basis of purchasing power within the respective domestic market, i.e. what you can buy with a unit of a country's currency. The International Comparison Program, housed in the World Bank, collects information from 170 countries to establish PPP estimates. When these rates are used the relative size of developed economies is very much reduced and that of lower income countries much increased as indicated in Table 2.1. This table compares GDP and GDP per capita, both at current prices and PPP, of some of the richest and the poorest countries of the world. The data is derived from the International Monetary Fund's World Economic Outlook database.

Learning Task

The World Bank, using a slightly different measure (Gross National Income which is GDP plus net income flows from abroad), classifies 209 countries into four different per capita income groups: low income, US$995 or less; lower middle income, US$996–US$3,945; upper middle income, US$3,946–US$12,195; and high income, US$12,196 or more. (http://data.worldbank.org/about/country-classifications)

From the information in Table 2.1 complete the following tasks:

1. Explain why, if the countries were ranked according to their nominal GDP or their PPP GDP, the rankings vary depending on which measure of income is used.

2. Use your answer to Q1 to explain why the USA is more than 20 times richer than China according to GDP per capita but less than ten times richer using the PPP figures.

3. Group the countries according to the World Bank classification of different income groups. Comment on their regional spread.

GDP as an Indicator of the Standard of Living

GDP tells us the absolute size of an economy and will indicate that in nominal terms, according to the table overleaf, India is slightly larger than Australia, and China and Japan are roughly the same size. However if we look at their respective GDPs using PPP we can see that India's GDP is more than four times that of Australia and China's is more than twice that of Japan. What does this tell us? Not a lot really because both India and China have big populations. When we take this into account to calculate on average how much of that GDP accrues to each person then,

Table 2.1 Gross Domestic Product 2009

	GDP current prices US$ mills	GDP PPP US$ mills	population (,000)	GDP per capita current prices US$	GDP per capita US$ (PPP)
Angola	74,474	107,011	17,312	4,302	6,181
Argentina	310,057	582,953	40,134	7,725	14,525
Australia	994,246	848,862	21,955	45,285	38,663
Benin	6,650	13,507	9,381	709	1,440
Bolivia	17,464	45,523	10,227	1,707	4,451
Botswana	11,6384	25,955	1,815	6,437	14,321
Brazil	1,574,039	2,010,332	191,481	8,220	10,499
Bulgaria	47,101	89,940	7,569	6,223	11,883
China	4,984,731	9,046,990	1,334,740	3,735	6,778
Egypt	187,954	468,997	76,704	2,450	6,114
France	2,656,378	2,094,048	62,632	42,413	33,434
Germany	3,338,675	2,811,771	81,767	40,832	34,388
Ghana	15,330	35,997	23,108	663	1,558
Haiti	6,560	11,973	9,923	661	1,207
India	1,236,943	3,615,326	1,199,062	1,032	3,015
Indonesia	539,377	961,106	231,547	2,329	4,151
Italy	2,118,264	1,737,657	59,779	35,435	29,068
Japan	5,068,894	4,152,301	127,551	39,740	32,554
Malaysia	192,955	383,095	27,761	6,950	13,800
Oman	46,115	73,902	2,883	15,996	25,635
Pakistan	174,792	439,439	163,774	989	2,683
Poland	438,884	687,916	38,111	11,302	18,050
Russia	1,476,912	2,116,119	141,900	8,681	14,913
South Africa	354,414	504,497	49,320	5,824	10,229
Sweden	444,585	334,306	9,299	43,668	35,951
Turkey	729,051	879,319	70,538	8,711	12,466
UK	2,258,565	2,125,128	61,798	35,257	34,388
USA	14,624,184	14,119,050	307,374	45,934	45,934
Venezuela	285,214	348,587	28,611	11,383	12,184
Vietnam	101,987	256,546	87,211	1,068	2,942

Source: International Monetary Fund, World Economic Outlook Database, October 2010

using PPP, we can see that Australia has a per capita income of US$38,910, over 13 times that of India's US$2,940 and Japan has a per capita income of US$32,607 compared with China's US$6,567.

Does this mean that Japanese citizens are five times as well off as Chinese citizens? It might but GDP only measures activity that takes place in the formal, officially recorded, economy. If an electrician does jobs for cash and doesn't declare the income to the tax authorities then there is additional output in the economy but it is not recorded. This is an example of activity in the so-called 'shadow economy'. This would include all activities (legal and illegal) which produce an output but do not get recorded in official statistics. Schneider, Buehn, and Montenegro (2010) used a narrower definition than this to include 'all market-based legal production of goods and services that are deliberately concealed from public authorities . . .' in a survey of the shadow economies of 162 countries from 1999 to 2007. They found that the unweighted average size of the shadow economy was 31% in 2007 (down from 34% in 1999).

The countries with the largest average size of shadow economy over the period were Zimbabwe (61.8%), Georgia (65.8%), and Bolivia (66.1%). The lowest were Switzerland (8.5%), USA (8.6%), and Luxembourg (9.7%). By region Sub-Saharan Africa has the highest estimate with a mean of 40.8%, followed by Latin America and Caribbean (38.7%). The lowest is the OECD (Organization for Economic Co-operation and Development—33 of the most developed economies) at 16.8%. Within the last group Greece had an average of 27.5% and Italy, 27.0%.

Learning Task

How would the shadow economies change the picture, were they to be included in official GDP figures?

Another problem with these measures is that they do not take into account environmental degradation and the depletion of natural resources. When oil is taken from the ground it is irreplaceable. The value of that oil is added to GDP but the depletion of reserves is not accounted for, even though it will affect the welfare of future generations. When the oil is turned into petrol that again adds to GDP but the damage done to the atmosphere when we use it in our cars is not deducted. GDP simply measures the additions to output without taking into account the negative effects of pollution, congestion, and resource depletion.

Economic Growth

Regardless of the comments in the counterpoint boxes growth in national output (**economic growth**) is a key objective for all national governments as they believe it is fundamental to raising standards of living. It is measured by the annual percentage change in a nation's gross domestic product at constant prices as GDP can grow through the effects of inflation. Quite modest rates of growth can have a significant effect on living standards if they are maintained. A growth rate of 2% would double real incomes every 36 years. We saw in the opening case study that China's GDP had increased sixfold in just 20 years from 1984.

According to the **International Monetary Fund** (IMF), world GDP between 2006 and 2008 grew on average by 4.7% per year but in Figure 2.1 which shows average growth rates for the

Counterpoint Box 2.1 GDP and the quality of life

GDP per person is often used as an indicator of human progress, welfare, and happiness but GDP tells us only about income. It doesn't tell us if GDP is spent on health and education projects or on armaments or space projects. To emphasize that development is about people The United Nations Development Programme (UNDP) has developed a set of measures which capture some other elements of development, the Human Development Index (HDI). This is an aggregate measure of three features of development, life expectancy, education, and standard of living (PPP per capita income). Its purpose is to emphasize those other elements of development not captured by GDP. The top countries in the 2010 HDI rankings are Norway, Australia, and New Zealand. The latter two would rank only 13th and 33rd respectively in a table ranked in order of GDP but do very well on the other measures of welfare. On the other hand Qatar ranked 2nd in GDP terms slumps to 38th in HDI terms and Kuwait from 5th to 47th. (See http://hdr.undp.

org/en/ for more information and the full tables or visit the **Online Resource Centre** for a video of an interview with Amartya Sen.)

Does more money make people happier? In the 1970s Richard Easterlin drew attention to the fact that within a society rich people seemed to be happier than poor people but that rich societies seemed no happier than poor societies and getting richer didn't necessarily make people happier. It became known as the Easterlin paradox. Others have claimed the evidence is not so clear. Visit the **Online Resource Centre** for a video link on this topic.

Nicholas Sarkozy unhappy with current measures of economic performance (i.e. GDP) set up a commission in 2008, chaired by Joseph Stiglitz, to see if the present measures properly reflect societal well being as well as economic, environmental, and social sustainability. A link to this report can be found on the supporting **Online Resource Centre**.

Figure 2.1 Real GDP growth 2006–08

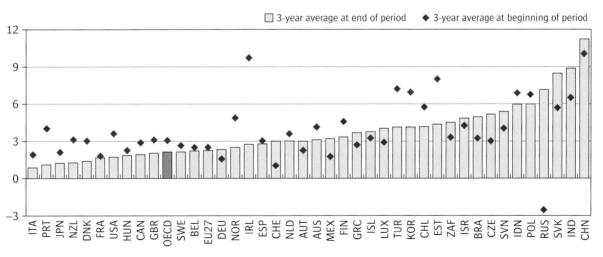

Source: OECD Factbook

period 2006–2008 we can see that average growth rates for individual countries can vary quite markedly, from less than 1% in Italy to more than 11% in China. Growth in the most advanced and mature economies of the developed world, which account for 77% of world GDP, tends to be much lower than in the developing economies of the world. Table 2.2 shows world growth rates since 2002 have varied from −0.6% to 5.3% but for the G7 (the most advanced economies of the world) the corresponding figures are −3.5% and 2.9% and for developing economies 2.5% and 8.7%. This is especially so in latter years, as some of the developing economies, especially China and India, have grown more quickly and taken a slightly larger share of world GDP. In late 2008 and 2009 after the financial crisis (see Chapter Ten) the world economy went into recession. World output shrank in a recession which lasted longer and was deeper (the fall in output from its peak to its trough was about 4%) than any other post-war recession.

This affected some economies more than others. The developed economies suffered worst with Japan's economy shrinking by 5.2%, Germany by 4.7%, and the USA and the UK by 2.6% and 4.9% respectively. At the same time China continued to grow at a slightly slower rate than hitherto, 9.1% and India by 5.7%. In 2010 the world economy began to recover although the European debt crisis still threatened that recovery. The World Bank expected global GDP to expand by 3.3% in 2010 and 2011 and by 3.5% in 2012. Again developing countries were expected to grow faster (on average over 6%) than high income countries (2.3% to 2.7%). Visit the **Online Resource Centre** for a link to the Global Economic Prospects Report on the World Bank's website.

Table 2.2 Economic growth (annual % change in GDP)

	2002	2003	2004	2005	2006	2007	2008	2009	2010(e)
World	2.9	3.6	4.9	4.5	5.2	5.3	2.8	−0.6	3.7
G7	1.3	1.8	2.9	2.4	2.6	2.1	0.1	−3.5	2.5
EU	1.4	1.6	2.7	2.2	3.5	3.2	0.8	−4.1	1.7
Developing Economies	4.8	6.2	7.5	7.3	8.2	8.7	6.0	2.5	7.1
Sub-Saharan Africa	6.8	5.0	7.2	6.3	6.4	7.0	5.5	2.6	5.0
Australia	3.9	3.2	3.6	3.2	2.6	4.8	2.2	1.2	3.0
Brazil	2.7	1.1	5.7	3.2	4.0	6.1	5.1	−0.2	7.5
China	9.1	10.1	10.1	11.3	12.7	14.2	9.6	9.1	10.4
Germany	0.0	−0.2	1.2	0.7	3.4	2.7	1.0	−4.7	3.3
India	4.6	6.9	8.1	9.2	9.9	9.4	6.4	5.7	9.7
Indonesia	4.5	4.8	5.0	5.7	5.5	6.3	6.0	4.5	6.0
Japan	0.3	1.4	2.7	1.9	2.0	2.4	−1.2	−5.2	2.8
Kenya	0.3	2.8	4.6	6.0	6.3	6.9	1.3	2.4	4.1
Nigeria	21.2	10.3	10.6	5.4	6.2	7.0	6.0	7.0	7.4
Russia	4.7	7.3	7.2	6.4	8.2	8.5	5.2	−7.9	4.0
Tanzania	7.2	6.9	7.8	7.4	6.7	7.1	7.4	6.0	6.5
United Kingdom	2.1	2.8	3.0	2.2	2.8	2.7	−0.7	−4.9	1.7
United States of America	1.8	2.5	3.6	3.1	2.7	1.9	0.0	−2.6	2.6
Vietnam	7.1	7.3	7.8	8.4	8.2	8.5	6.3	5.3	6.5

(e) estimate
Source: International Monetary Fund, World Economic Outlook Database, October 2010

Counterpoint Box 2.2 Is economic growth a good thing?

Not everybody agrees that the pursuit of economic growth is necessarily a good thing. Edward Mishan in his book, *The Costs of Economic Growth* (1967), pointed out that economic growth brought with it social costs such as pollution, traffic congestion and 'the frantic pace of life'. In a later book (1972), *The Limits to Growth*, the authors explored the relationship between growth and resources and concluded that if growth continued at its present pace then the limits to growth would be reached some time in the 21st century.

Visit the link on our **Online Resource Centre** for an interview in January 2010 with Dennis Meadows, one of the authors. (See Chapter Twelve for a fuller discussion of these issues.)

Nor is everybody agreed that growth is necessarily the solution for poverty as the benefits of growth can be highly unbalanced. For a recent discussion of this and the problems of climate change and resource depletion see *Growth Isn't Possible*, a New Economics Foundation publication by Andrew Simms, Dr Victoria Johnson, and Pert Chowla. You can find the link on the supporting **Online Resource Centre**.

The BRIC Economies

Looking further ahead the World Bank (2007) estimates that the world economy will grow at an annual rate of 3% up to 2030 which will result in a more than doubling of world output (at constant market exchange rates and prices) from US$35 trillion to US$72 trillion. Growth will be higher in developing countries (4.2%) than high income countries (2.5%) with developing countries' share of total output increasing from one fifth to a third and their share of global purchasing power increasing to more than one half. There will be a modest convergence of per capita incomes but developing country incomes will still be only one-quarter of those of rich countries at US$11,000 in 2030. The number living below the poverty line of US$1 per day will halve to 550 million people despite there being an additional 1.5 billion people.

Goldman Sachs (2003) looked further ahead to 2050 and others such as Pricewaterhouse-Coopers (2006) have followed suit. In their report Goldman Sachs paint a picture of a very different world economy by 2050 with growth in the developing economies and especially Brazil, China, India, and Russia making them a much greater force. In 2050, China and India are predicted to be the world's biggest and third biggest economies sandwiching the USA in second place.

For China and India this would be more like their positions in the 19th century when they were the world's two biggest economies. In the 19th century together they accounted for around 30% of world GDP (Maddison 2003). Their populations were large then, as now, so per capita incomes were lower than Western Europe. In fact China remained the largest economy until 1890 when the lead was lost to Western Europe and the USA following the **industrial revolution** that originated in the mid-18th century in Britain. This transformed Western society from an agricultural economy with small-scale cottage industries to an industrialized economy with mass production carried out in factories in towns. There was mass migration from the countryside to the cities as a result of this.

The driver for all of this was the application of steam power not just in factories but also transport allowing the movement of relatively low value goods across large distances over both land and water. The benefits of this transformation were confined to the industrialized nations of the time largely because they held the advantage in technological progress but also because many of the countries of Africa, Asia, and Latin America were the colonies of the Western powers supplying primary products to the industrialized nations. In the case of Africa they also supplied young men and women as unpaid, slave labour.

In the 19th century the UK was the dominant power producing 30% of total world industrial output but this position was changing as the USA and other Western European powers developed. By 1913, the USA was producing 36% of world industrial output and the UK only 14% (Dicken 2004). This pattern continued until World War II when the world divided into three different spheres.

The first sphere was the Western world led by the USA and organized along capitalist lines. It set up world institutions such as the World Bank, the IMF, and the GATT in order to aid recovery of the war torn Western European economies and to establish a 'world system' to combat the power of the Soviet bloc. The 1950s also saw the emergence of Japan as a new competitor for the developed western world so that the bi-polar world of trade in manufactures became a tri-polar world dominated by the triad discussed in Chapter One.

The second sphere to emerge after World War II was the Eastern communist bloc led by Russia. Russia had become a communist state after the 1917 revolution, but it was after World War II that communism took hold in other countries. Some Eastern and Central European coun- tries were invaded by Russia and others, Cuba and China, experienced revolutions. The Soviet Union was a centrally planned economy and this system was imposed on the satellite states of Eastern and Central Europe so that trade and investment between the two spheres was minimal. China became the People's Republic of China in 1949 and for the next 30 years had little to do with the world economy following a policy of self reliance. The Soviet bloc ushered in some political and economic reforms in the 1980s in a move towards becoming a democratic market economy and this was a prelude to popular revolutions which swept across Eastern Europe following the withdrawal of Soviet Union support for the communist regimes. In 1991, the Baltic states declared themselves independent and by the end of that year the whole Soviet sphere unravelled with the Soviet Union itself ceasing to exist. China had started its move towards becoming a market economy in 1979, but unlike the Soviet bloc, communism still prevails there.

The world is now less divided along political lines but there is still an enormous gap between those who have and those who have not. In East Asia a number of newly industrialized econom- ies have emerged (initially South Korea, Taiwan, Singapore, and Hong Kong and later, Malaysia, Thailand, and Indonesia) to become global players, but for much of the rest of the world poverty remains a major problem and narrowing this gap will be a major challenge. We have already noted the growth prospects for the BRIC economies and to these PricewaterhouseCoopers (2006) added Mexico, Indonesia, and Turkey to form what they called the E7. They also identified 13 other emerging economies including Vietnam, Nigeria, Philippines, Egypt, and Bangladesh with strong growth prospects (above 7% per annum) to 2050 and therefore of major interest to business as markets and investment opportunities. They estimate that by 2050 the E7 emerging economies will be 50% bigger than the current G7 economies of USA, Japan, Germany, UK, France, Italy, and Canada (see Figure 2.2 and Table 2.3).

It is estimated that by 2050 China's economy will be some 30% bigger than the US economy and India's about 12% smaller. Brazil, Russia, Indonesia, and Mexico will all be bigger than any of the European economies, with Turkey not far behind. These economies will provide oppor- tunities for outsourcing manufacturing activities, opening new offices, mergers, acquisitions, and alliances but of major significance will be the emergence of a global middle class. In 2050 Russia, Mexico, Brazil, Turkey, China, Indonesia, and India will still have per capita incomes less than the USA, Japan, and Western Europe but they will be very much greater than today (see Table 2.4). The World Bank foresees an extra 800 million people in developing countries

Figure 2.2 Relative size of the G7 and E7 economies US$ billions (real value)

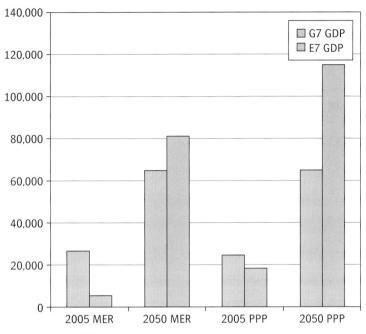

MER – market exchange rate   PPP – purchasing power parity
Source: PricewaterhouseCoopers 2006

Mini Case Tesco in Asia

Tesco, the world's third biggest supermarket chain, is planning further expansion in Asia to take advantage of rapid economic growth in the region. Tesco's first foray into Asia was in Thailand in 1998 through a joint venture (Tesco Lotus) with a Thai company, Charoen Pokphand. They now have 663 stores (and are planning more) making it Thailand's leading grocery retailer controlling 12.7% of the grocery market and 40.4% of the supermarket trade. According to the IMF, Thai GDP per capita has grown from less than US$2,000 in 2002 to an estimated US$4,402 in 2010 (US$8,470 in PPP terms) and the economy is expected to continue growing to 2015 by over 5% per annum. After success in Thailand, Tesco has ventured further into Asia by entering South Korea in 1999, Malaysia in 2002, Japan in 2003, and China in 2004. According to Tesco, China has now been identified as one of its most important markets for growth. It is planning to quadruple sales in China to US$6.36 billion within five years. At present it has 88 stores in China, a mixture of hypermarkets and 'lifespace' shopping malls (a mix of shops, leisure outlets, eating places, and a Tesco hypermarket). They want to more than double the number of stores to over 200 hypermarkets and over 50 shopping malls by 2015, such is the size and pace of growth in China, a country which is forecast to have 221 cities of over 1 million people by 2025, compared with 35 in Europe now.

Sources: *Financial Times*, 23 October 2010; IMF World Economic Outlook database, 2010; www.TecsoPLC.com

Source: photodisc

Table 2.3 BRIC economies 2005 and 2050

| Country | 2005 | | | | | 2050 | | |
	Pop (m)	GDP (US$bn)	GDP per head (US$)	Growth to 2050 (% per annum)		Pop (m)	GDP (US$bn)	GDP per head (US$)
				Pop	GDP			
Brazil	186	1,536	8,258	0.8	3.5	266	7,223	27,131
Russia	142	1,584	11,155	0.2	3.4	155	7,131	45,903
India	1,103	3,666	3,324	0.9	6.4	1,651	59,781	36,215
China	1,313	8,883	6,765	0.5	6.0	1,643	122,271	74,402
USA	298	12,310	41,309	0.7	2.7	408	40,825	100,089

Source: International Business Report 2007, Emerging Markets, Grant Thornton

Table 2.4 Projected relative size of economies and relative per capita income levels

Country (indices with US = 100)	GDP at market exchange rates in US$ terms		GDP in PPP terms		GDP per capita in PPP terms (000s of constant 2006 US$)	
	2007	2050	2007	2050	2007	2050
US	100	100	100	100	44.4	93.3
Japan	32	19	28	19	29.3	70.5
China	23	129	51	129	5.2	34.5
Germany	22	14	20	14	32.4	72.1
UK	18	14	15	14	33.6	77.5
France	17	14	15	14	37.0	78.3
Italy	14	10	13	10	32.1	70.0
Canada	10	9	10	9	39.2	83.3
Spain	9	9	10	9	30.1	72.4
Brazil	8	26	15	26	10.4	39.0
Russia	8	17	17	17	16.2	60.5
India	7	88	22	88	2.5	19.9
Korea	7	8	9	8	25.0	72.3
Mexico	7	17	10	17	12.6	48.0
Australia	6	6	5	6	35.9	79.2
Turkey	3	10	5	10	8.7	36.3
Indonesia	3	17	7	17	4.1	20.9

Source: PricewaterhouseCoopers 2008

joining the middle classes by 2030, bringing the total to 1.2 billion, 15% of the world population; 361 million of these people will be in China. This will mean hundreds of millions of new consumers in developing countries with spending patterns similar to current residents of high-income countries, providing enormous opportunities to international business in the form of new markets. The Bank includes in its definition of the middle class all those with incomes of US$4,000 or more at 2006 prices.

In the next section we go on to look at two other aspects of international business: trade flows and exchange rates.

Learning Task

Given the above scenario:

1. What are the implications for international business and its markets?
2. Explore the impact on the demand for, and the prices of, natural resources.
3. In light of your answer to question 2, analyse the effects on natural resource companies in Brazil and Russia.

Mini Case Africa to join the BRICS?

The World Bank uses as its extreme poverty line an income of about US$1.25 (at 2005 prices) per person per day. Using this measure poverty has fallen in all regions since 1990 except in Sub-Saharan Africa where in 2005 nearly 300 million people still lived on less the US$1 per day, up from 240 million in 1990. Sub-Saharan Africa stands out as the poorest area. The situation didn't change much in the nineties largely because of low and sometimes negative rates of economic growth but since 2000 growth has been around 6% (see Table 2.2). Some, such as Nigeria and Tanzania with growth rates of 10% and 7%, respectively, have done much better. This has lead Jim O'Neill of Goldman Sachs to speculate that Africa, thought of as a whole, could have the same bright future as the BRIC countries. He picks out South Africa, Nigeria, and Egypt as critical to this success. Michael Keating (Executive Director of the Africa Progress Panel) writing in the *Financial Times* points out 'The continent's advantages include abundant natural resources, whether commodities, land or energy, whose strategic and financial value is generally increasing. It also has a vast, inexpensive pool of labour; a growing middle class that brings growing demand for consumer goods (and better governance); and an increasing recognition that business can play a much greater role in reducing the costs

of goods and services to all of Africa's billion people, including the hundreds of millions living on or below the poverty line.' But as McKinsey points out in a survey of African economies, Africa has over 50 individual economies which are extremely diverse. It identifies four different development paths. The diversified economies are the most advanced and have large (as a % of GDP) manufacturing and services sectors. The four largest are Egypt, Morocco, South Africa, and Tunisia of which only South Africa is in Sub-Saharan Africa. The oil exporters such as Angola, Chad, Libya, and Nigeria are the richest but least diversified and need to invest in infrastructure and education. The transition economies, e.g. Ghana, Kenya, and Tanzania have begun the process of diversifying but their income per head remains below the first two groups. The poorest countries such as the Democratic Republic of the Congo, Ethiopia, Mali, and Sierra Leone remain in the pretransition stage.

Sources: *Financial Times International Business Insight*, Part Three: Middle East and Africa, 22 October 2010; www.FT.com 'How Africa can Become the Next BRIC', Jim O'Neill, 26 August 2010; IMF World Economic Outlook Database, 2010; *McKinsey Quarterly*, 'What's Driving Africa's Growth', June 2010

International Trade

One of the key drivers of globalization is international trade, the exchange of goods and services between nations. In this section we will look in more detail at the pattern of global trade and put forward several theories to answer the question 'why do countries trade'? We will also look at the regulation of trade through the WTO.

The Pattern of Trade

International trade grew very quickly in the second half of the 20th century and more quickly than global output which had been rising at 3% per annum. In 1950 world exports were approximately US$0.5 trillion rising to US$12.5 trillion dollars in 2005. Of this US$12.5 trillion, most (US$10.1 trillion) was in merchandise trade, and the rest—US$2.4 trillion—was in services. Apart from a three-year period from 2003–05 service trade has grown more quickly than merchandise trade (see Table 2.5). Exports as a percentage of world output were about 13% in 1970, 25% in 2005, and are predicted to be 34% in 2030 (World Bank 2007).

Merchandise trade comprises three categories, manufactured goods, mining, and agricultural products. The share of primary commodities in total world exports of merchandise trade has fallen dramatically. In 1960 primary commodities (excluding fuels) accounted for 38% of world exports, but by 2001 had fallen to only 12%. Over the same period the share of manufactured goods has increased from 51.3% to 74.1%. Developing countries have increased their share of world trade in manufactured goods from less than 25% in 1960 to less than 33% in 2002 with South East Asian countries being the main contributors to this growth. Other developing regions' exports did not see the same growth. African states' exports have averaged only 2% growth since 1980, while world exports have grown at 6% per annum. Developed economies still account for the majority of traffic—see Tables 2.6, 2.7, and 2.8.

Table 2.5 World exports of merchandise and commercial services 2005 (billion dollars and percentage)

	Value 2009	Annual percentage change			
		2000–09	2007	2008	2009
Merchandise	12,178	3	6.5	2.0	−12
Commercial Services	3,350	9	20	13	−12

Source: WTO

Table 2.6 Leading exporters and importers in world merchandise trade 2009 (billion dollars and percentage)

Exports				Imports			
Rank		Value	Share	Rank		Value	Share
1	China	1,201	9.6	1	USA	1,605	12.7
2	Germany	1,126	9.0	2	China	1,006	7.9
3	USA	1,056	8.5	3	Germany	938	7.4
4	Japan	581	4.6	4	France	560	4.4
5	Netherlands	498	4.9	5	Japan	552	4.4
6	France	485	3.9	6	UK	482	3.8
7	Italy	406	3.2	7	Netherlands	445	3.5
8	Belgium	370	3.0	8	Italy	413	3.3
9	Korea, Republic of	364	2.9	9	Hong Kong, China	352	2.8
10	UK	352	2.8	10	Belgium	252	2.8

Hong Kong imports includes re-exports   Source: WTO

Table 2.7 Leading exporters and importers in world service trade 2009 (billion dollars and percentage)

Exports				Imports			
Rank		Value	Share	Rank		Value	Share
1	USA	474	14.1	1	USA	331	10.5
2	UK	233	7.0	2	Germany	253	8.1
3	Germany	227	6.8	3	UK	161	5.1
4	France	143	4.3	4	China	158	5.0
5	China	129	3.8	5	Japan	147	4.7
6	Japan	126	3.8	6	France	126	4.0
7	Spain	122	3.6	7	Italy	115	3.6
8	Italy	101	3.0	8	Ireland	103	3.3
9	Ireland	97	2.9	9	Spain	87	2.8
10	Netherlands	91	2.7	10	Netherlands	85	2.7

Source: WTO

Table 2.8 Intra- and inter-regional merchandise trade 2009 (billion dollars)

Origin	Destination							
	North America	S & C America	Europe	CIS	Africa	Middle East	Asia	World
North America	769	128	291	9	28	49	324	1,602
S and Central America	115	120	90	6	13	11	96	459
Europe	366	75	3,620	147	162	154	426	5,016
CIS	23	5	239	87	7	14	63	452
Africa	66	9	149	1	45	12	85	384
Middle east	60	5	76	4	34	107	357	690
Asia	627	95	640	57	102	163	1,846	3,575
World	2,026	437	5,105	311	390	510	3,197	12,178

(Asia includes Japan, Australia, New Zealand, China, and other Asia)   Source: WTO

Learning Task

Using the information in Table 2.8

1. For each region calculate its share of world merchandise trade.

2. What proportion of world trade is accounted for by North America and Europe?

3. For each region calculate the share of intra-regional trade, e.g. what proportion of Europe's trade is within Europe?

4. What conclusions can you draw from these and any other calculations in terms of the economic self-reliance of different regions?

Why do Countries Trade?

The earliest theory (17th and 18th century) in relation to international trade was that of **mercantilism**, which held that countries should maximize exports and try to limit imports as much as possible. Mercantilists viewed the accumulation of precious metals (gold and silver being the medium for settling international debts) as the only way to increase the wealth of the nation. Generating a trade surplus (when the value of exports exceeds the value of imports) was the aim of governments as this would result in an inflow of gold and silver. The governments of mercantilist nations such as Britain, The Netherlands, France, Spain, and Portugal restricted or banned imports with tariffs and quotas and subsidized domestic industries to encourage exports. At the same time they developed large colonies which provided cheap raw materials to a growing manufacturing base. They in turn exported finished goods to the colonies at much higher prices.

Mercantilists viewed exports as a good thing, as they stimulated industry and increased the number of jobs at home, and imports as bad, as this was a loss of demand and jobs. Although the mercantilist era ended in the 18th century, **neo-mercantilism** or, as it is also known, **economic nationalism** continues. The USA and Germany in the late 19th century were able to erode Britain's dominance through protectionist policies. More recently post-war Japan has subsidized its domestic industries and protected them from foreign imports. It also had very tight controls on foreign exchange and foreign investment within Japan. These policies resulted in large trade surpluses. The current problems besetting the world economy are threatening a new waive of mercantilist policies as countries look to exports of goods to deliver economic growth. Whereas mercantilists viewed trade as a zero sum game (i.e. one country could only gain if another lost), Adam Smith (1776) set out to prove that all could gain by engaging in free trade. Smith demonstrated that if countries specialized in producing the goods in which they were most efficient (i.e. in which they had an absolute advantage), then world output would be increased and the surpluses could be exchanged.

David Ricardo (1817) extended this theory to show that even when a country had an absolute advantage in the production of all goods, total output could still be increased if countries specialized in the production of a good in which they had a **comparative advantage**. A country has a comparative advantage over another country if it can produce at a lower **opportunity cost**. In other words it has to forgo fewer resources than the other in order to produce it.

These theories help to explain the pattern of trade but don't tell us why one country should be more efficient than another and therefore what that country should specialize in. The factor proportions theory (or factor endowment theory), developed by Eli Heckser and Bertil Ohlin, explains that countries will produce and export products that utilize resources which they have in abundance, and import products which utilize resources that are relatively scarce. So Australia, with lots of land and a small population, exports mainly minerals (about 40% of total exports), beef, cereals, and dairy products. Its main imports are petrol, road vehicles, telecoms equipment, and industrial machinery (in total about 35% of total imports). China and India export goods and services which take advantage of cheap labour, whereas in Western Europe (where labour is expensive) there tends to be a concentration on relatively high value **capital intensive** industries such as the chemical industry.

Trade patterns seem to correspond quite well with this theory but there are weaknesses which Wassily Leontieff (1953) discovered in a study of US exports—some of which he found to be highly labour intensive and imports which were capital intensive. This became known as the Leontieff paradox. A weakness of the Heckser–Ohlin theory is that it treats all factors as homogeneous, when in fact they are not. Labour, for example, varies enormously in skill levels depending on the training and development undertaken. When this was taken into account and skill intensity was measured then the results were more as predicted. The theory is further complicated when technology is considered. It had been assumed that technology is universally available, but there are in fact major lags in the diffusion of technology. However, one of the features of globalization is that this diffusion is becoming more rapid, especially the reduction in cost of collecting, analysing, and communicating information.

For much of the less developed world the pattern of trade predicted by these theories holds true, but this pattern has tended to favour the richer nations at the expense of the poor. This is especially the case for Sub-Saharan Africa. These countries produce and export primary products (other than oil) for which they have a comparative advantage and import manufactured goods for which they are at a comparative disadvantage. The problem is that the theories predict that total output is increased but say nothing about how that increase will be shared between countries. History shows that the demand for primary produce does not rise as quickly as the total rise in demand for all goods and services so there tends to be long run deterioration in the terms at which primary produce exchanges for manufactured goods. In other words the price of manufactured goods tends to rise more quickly than the price of primary products. This, together with a very narrow range of products, probably goes a long way to explaining the low levels of income in those countries. Uganda, for example, relies heavily on agriculture which forms 30% of GDP but 80% of the population rely on it for their livelihood. It also forms 90% of export earnings, with coffee being the major export crop (20% of earnings in 2005)—consequently the economy is very susceptible to variations in the price of coffee. The main imports are oil and manufactured goods.

Another model to explain the pattern of trade in manufactured goods was developed in 1966 by Raymond Vernon (the International Product Life Cycle model). The different locations for production, and subsequent exports and imports were explained according to stages in the International Product Life Cycle. According to this theory products move through three phases: new product growth, maturing product, and standardized product.

The new product stage requires high levels of investment in research and design and a market with high purchasing power. Initial production volumes tend to be low with consumers paying a premium price for the new product. The market conditions for this scenario are found in the developed economies and this is where production is first located. During this stage firms monitor demand and make modifications to the product. Towards the end of this stage production increases and some exporting begins.

In the maturing product stage overseas markets become more aware of the product and exports increase. As they begin to account for an increasing proportion of sales then production facilities are set up in major markets either in subsidiaries or through licensing local manufacturers.

In the standardized stage new competitors selling similar products appear, the technology is widely available, and in order to maintain sales prices are reduced. Companies seek low cost production centres, often in developing economies. Products which were once exports now become imports.

Vernon was using this theory to explain the evolution of US firms and the associated pattern of US exports and imports, and at the time it fitted quite well. Since then the pattern of international investment has become much more complex as we saw with the case of Dell (Chapter One). Competition is much more international, product life cycles much shorter, and **innovation** may come from anywhere in the company's global production and marketing network. In an electronic age some firms are said to be 'born global', in that they start international activities right from the outset and move into distant, and sometimes multiple, markets right away.

What none of this explained was, as noted earlier, that most trade takes place, not between nations which are very different but, between similar, developed nations and that it is trade in similar goods—so called intra-industry trade. **New trade theory** in the 1980s explained that there were gains to be made from **specialization** and economies of scale and that those who were first to enter the market could erect entry barriers to other firms. As output increases the unit costs of production fall and new entrants are forced to produce at similar levels. Without a large domestic market to justify producing on that scale constitutes a major barrier to entry. (See Chapter Three for a discussion of entry barriers.) The end result can be a global market supporting very few competitors.

A feature of intra-industry trade is **product differentiation**. Much international trade theory regards products as homogeneous but modern manufacturing firms produce a range of similar products appealing to different consumer preferences. For example a few car producers based in a few developed economies each manufacture a range of models and most of the trade in those products takes place between those countries.

According to the country similarity theory (Linder 1961) this trade is determined not so much by cost difference but by similarity in the markets. As identified in Chapter One there are many barriers to globalization: such as geography, cultural difference, and corruption. It follows that firms will tend to do business with countries which are geographically close, culturally similar, have similar economic and political interests, have similar demand patterns, and are at similar levels of development.

The Competitive Advantage of Nations

In the 1980s Michael Porter undertook a study to find what made the major advanced nations competitive. He studied ten of the most successful exporting nations and found that constant innovation and upgrading, in their broadest sense, were the key to **competitive advantage**. Constant, and often incremental, improvement is the key as almost any advantage could be replicated by others. According to Porter this advantage comes from four related attributes which he called 'the diamond of national advantage'. They were factor conditions, demand conditions, related and supporting industries, and firm strategy, structure, and rivalry.

Factor conditions: traditional theory said that nations would export those goods which made most use of the factors in which they were relatively well endowed. Porter distinguished between basic and inherited factors (such as raw materials and a pool of labour) and the created factors (a skilled workforce and scientific base) essential in modern, knowledge based industries. Where countries can create these advantages then they will be successful. He gave Denmark, a world leader in the export of insulin, as an example where two specialist hospitals existed for the study and treatment of diabetes.

Demand conditions: what is important is the nature of demand rather than the size of the market. Sophisticated and demanding buyers keep sellers informed of buyers' wants and give them early warning signs of shifts in market demand. It helps companies also if consumer tastes and national values are being exported to other countries, as the USA has done so successfully.

Related and supporting industries: the third determinant is the existence of internationally competitive firms within the local supply chain. They provide cost effective inputs and information on what is happening in the industry. Clusters of mutually reinforcing organizations tend to grow within the same geographical area. Porter used the example of the Italian shoe industry which benefits from the close proximity of world class leather-tanning and fashion-design industries.

Firm strategy, structure, and rivalry: the final determinant of national competitiveness refers to the ways in which companies are created, organized, and managed as well as the nature of domestic rivalry. Intense local competition leads firms to be innovative in seeking ways to outdo their domestic competitors. This in turn makes them more internationally competitive. The way in which firms are organized, managed, and the goals they set themselves as well as the structure of capital markets are all key to this rivalry.

Porter emphasizes the systemic nature of this diamond in that the points are dependent on each other. A nation may have sophisticated buyers but if the other conditions are not present then this is likely to lead to imports rather than domestic production. Low cost supplies may be available but if a firm easily dominates the market then this is not likely to lead to greater competitiveness. Domestic rivalry is probably the most important point of the diamond because of the improvement effect it has on all the others but clustering is also important because it magnifies the effect of the other elements (Porter 1990).

Porter also included two other variables as being important for the success of a nation, chance and government. Chance events are those outside the control of firms and even governments which can change very quickly the conditions in the 'diamond'. They include such things as wars, inventions, political decisions by foreign governments, shifts in the world financial markets or exchange rates, discontinuities in input costs such as oil price shocks, major technological breakthroughs, and surges in world or regional demand.

Figure 2.3 Determinants of national competitive advantage

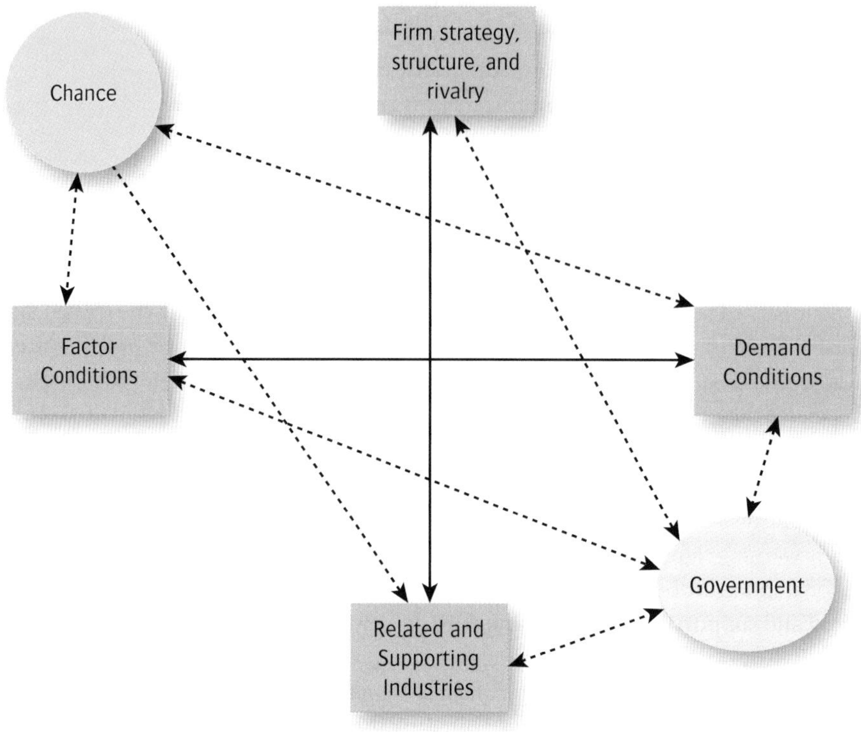

Source: Porter 1990

Governments can influence the four broad attributes either positively or negatively through various policies such as subsidies, incentives, capital market controls, education policy, environmental controls, tax laws, and competition laws.

The complete model is shown in Figure 2.3.

Trade Intervention

All of the theories and models make the assumption that trade takes place freely between nations but, as noted in Chapter One, this is far from the case. Every nation imposes trade restrictions of some description. Generally their purpose is to limit imports by imposing tariff or non-tariff barriers, or to encourage exports by subsidizing exporting firms.

A tariff is a tax or duty placed on an imported good by a domestic government. Tariffs are usually levied as a percentage of the declared value of the good, similar to a sales tax. Unlike a sales tax, tariff rates are often different for every good and tariffs do not apply to domestically produced goods.

Non-tariff barriers can take a number of forms; quotas, licences, **rules of origin**, product requirements (standards, packaging, labelling and markings, product specifications), customs procedures and documentation requirements, local content rules, and exchange rate manipulation.

Subsidies can take many forms and can be difficult to identify and calculate. Financial assistance of any sort including cash payments, low interest loans, tax breaks, **export credits** and guarantees, export promotion agencies, free trade and export processing zones all distort trade in favour of domestic producers. According to the OECD (2010) support to agricultural producers amounted to US$253 billion or €183 billion in 2009.

Yet another way of affecting both imports and exports is by exchange rate manipulation. When two firms in different countries do business the prices they quote will be determined by a combination of their domestic price converted to the other's currency using foreign exchange rates. If £1 exchanges for US$2 then a UK exporter with a domestic price of £100 will quote US$200 to an American buyer. Any change in the exchange rate will affect the foreign exchange price. If the £ strengthens to £1 = US$2.5 then the US price will be US$250. In a competitive market a price rise might not be possible which would then mean that if the UK firm could only charge US$200 then it would only receive £80 of revenue. One way of maintaining the competitiveness of a country's exports would be to keep the value of its currency low in relation to others.

Why Intervene?

National defence—it is argued that certain industries need defending from imports because they are vital in times of war. Weapons, transport, utilities, and food would probably fall into this category but where would the line be drawn? Similar arguments have been put forward to ban exports of technically advanced, especially military, products. The USA banned exports of satellites to China because this would have given the Chinese access to US military technology. It resulted in a fall in the American share of world satellite sales.

When US firms sell high-tech products and military equipment to allies the US government tries to prevent the selling-on of such technology to countries such as China and Venezuela. In July 2007, Saab withdrew from an international trade deal with Venezuela because of an arms ban imposed by the US on Venezuela. Bofors, a subsidiary of Saab, had for 20 years supplied Venezuela with weapons but the ban meant they could not sell any weapons with US-made parts.

To protect fledgling domestic industries from foreign competition—it is argued that industries in their infancy may need protection until they can compete internationally. This gives them time to grow to a size where they can gain economies of scale, learn from doing business, and develop the supporting infrastructure discussed above. Some of the Asian economies, Japan, South Korea, and Taiwan have successfully protected infant industries until they have grown to compete internationally and the barriers have been removed. On the other hand some Japanese industries such as banking, construction, and retailing have remained protected and inefficient.

To protect domestic industries from foreign competition and thereby save jobs—governments often come under pressure to support industries in decline because the human cost involved in the event of sudden closure can be very high. Protection may be justified to delay the closure and allow time for adjustment.

To protect against over dependence on a narrow base of products—the law of comparative advantage tells us that countries should specialize in the production of goods in which they have a comparative advantage. For some countries this will result in a range of primary products for which demand is income inelastic. This could condemn these countries to persistent poverty so protection to expand the industrial base may be the only way to escape from poverty.

Political motives—the USA, for example has an embargo on trade with Cuba because it disagrees with Cuba's politics.

To protect domestic producers from dumping by foreign companies or governments—dumping occurs when a foreign company charges a price in the domestic market which is 'too low'. In most instances 'too low' is generally understood to be a price which is lower in a foreign market than the price in the domestic market. In other instances 'too low' means a price which is below cost, so the producer is losing money. Vietnam took its first case to the WTO (having joined the WTO in 2006—see Mini Case on p 59) accusing the USA of unfair duties on frozen shrimp imported from Vietnam. The USA has charged duties ranging from 2.5% to 25.76% because it fears dumping by the Vietnamese. The case is due to be completed in April 2011. Firms in the USA have accused China of dumping by keeping the value of the Renminbi low (see section below on exchange rates).

Retaliation—to respond to another country's imposition of tariffs or some other restriction or against 'dumping'.

To prevent the import of undesirable products—drugs, live or endangered animals, and certain foodstuffs may be deemed undesirable.

To resist cultural imperialism and/or maintain a particular lifestyle—that is the imposition of one country's culture, politics, systems of governance and/or language on another. Quite often the West and in particular the USA is accused of cultural imperialism. As we noted in Chapter One American movies and television programmes are watched worldwide and most of these promote American values and beliefs.

Learning Task

1. Which of the above reasons for trade intervention do you think is justified and which is not?

2. For each identify the costs and the benefits of the policy for domestic consumers and producers and foreign producers and workers.

Control of Trade

On 7 November 2006 the General Council of the World Trade Organization (WTO) approved Vietnam's accession to membership making it the 150th member. The WTO was the successor organization to the General Agreement on Tariffs and Trade established in 1947 with just 23 members. In the depression of the 1930s many countries had suffered from falling exports and had tried to solve their problems by restricting imports. Of course others retaliated and the net effect was a reduction, by a third, of world trade in manufactured goods. These beggar-my-neighbour trade policies were in part responsible for WWII so there was a determination to devise a system in which there was much more economic cooperation. A much more ambitious scheme, the International Trade Organization, was proposed—covering not only trading relations but also financial arrangements, but this was blocked by the USA. This left the GATT as the only mechanism for regulating trade until the establishment of the WTO. The aim of the GATT was the reduction of tariffs and liberalizing trade giving countries access to each other's markets.

GATT's, and now the WTO's, principles are:

- **Non-discrimination:** a country should not discriminate between trading parties. Under the 'most favoured nation' rule a member has to grant to all members the most favourable conditions it allows trade in a particular product. Once goods have entered a country then the 'national treatment rule applies' in that they should be treated exactly the same as domestic goods.

- **Reciprocity:** if a member benefits from access and tariff reductions made by another member then it must reciprocate by making similar access and tariff reductions to that member.
- **Transparency:** member's trade regulations have to be published so all restrictions can be identified.
- **Predictability and stability:** members cannot raise existing tariffs without negotiation so everyone can be confident there will be no sudden changes.
- **Freeing of trade:** general reduction of all barriers.
- **Special assistance and trade concessions for developing countries.**

Under the GATT these principles were applied only to merchandise trade and then some sectors such as agriculture and textiles were ignored. These have now begun to be addressed under the WTO. Another weakness with the GATT was the lack of any effective process for settling disagreements and a deterrent against offenders. The WTO now has a dispute resolution process and is able to take sanctions against offenders as it did against the USA in 2002. Under pressure from domestic steel producers the American administration imposed tariffs on steel imports. WTO members reported this and the WTO allowed other members to impose retaliatory tariffs. The US tariffs were removed. See also the Mini Case on p 268 concerning online gambling.

Trade negotiations have taken place in a series of 'rounds'. There have been nine of these rounds if we include the current and incomplete Doha round. These are summarized in Table 2.9.

Table 2.9 GATT/WTO rounds

Period	Round	Countries	Subjects
1947	Geneva	23	Tariffs
1949	Annecy	13	Tariffs
1950–51	Torquay	38	Tariffs
1955–56	Geneva	26	Tariffs
1960–61	Dillon	26	Tariffs
1964–67	Kennedy	62	Tariffs, anti-dumping measures
1973–79	Tokyo	102	Tariffs, non-tariff measures and framework agreements
1986–94	Uruguay	123	Tariffs, agriculture, textiles and clothing brought into GATT Agreement on services (GATS) Intellectual property (TRIPS) Trade related Investment (TRIMS) Creation of WTO and dispute settlement
2001–	Doha	141	Not yet resolved

Source: WTO

The GATT was a fairly loose arrangement, but the WTO is a permanent organization dealing with a much wider range of issues. About three quarters of its members are less developed countries. Its top level decision-making body is the Ministerial Conference which meets at least every two years, but below this are other committees which meet on a regular basis. It has permanent offices in Geneva.

The GATT/WTO has been successful in reducing tariffs on industrial products from an average of about 40% in 1947 to something like 4% today, but whether it increases trade is the subject of debate. Trade has increased and, as we have seen, faster than world GDP—but is this because of the measures taken by the GATT/WTO? Not according to Andrew Rose (2004) who found that trade had increased, but for members and non-members alike. On the other hand Subramanian and Wei (2005) found that GATT/WTO had served to increase trade substantially (possibly by US$8 trillion in 2000 alone), but that the increase had been uneven. Industrial countries witnessed a larger increase in trade than did developing countries, bilateral trade was greater when both partners undertook liberalization, and those sectors that did not liberalize did not see an increase in trade.

The WTO is not without its critics, as we have witnessed with the demonstrations by anti-globalization protestors at the Ministerial Council meetings from Seattle in 1999 to Hong Kong in 2005. The major criticism is that it is a club which favours the developed countries, at the expense of the less developed countries. Decision-making is by consensus, often following many rounds of meetings which favour those countries with the resources to have representatives present at these meetings. Many of the less developed countries are excluded from this process. Other arguments against are that market access in industry is still a problem for less developed countries; anti-dumping measures have increased; there are still enormous agricultural subsidies in the developed world; labour standards and the environment are ignored.

Some of these problems have led to the suspension of the latest round of talks which began in Doha, Qatar, in 2001. The previous round of talks in Seattle had ended in failure, and a major disagreement between developed and developing countries—the latter accused the WTO of being for free trade whatever the cost, a charge which the WTO contests (see ten common misunderstandings about the WTO at www.wto.org). Whatever their protestations, the package for discussion at the Doha round has been called the Doha Development Agenda. The concern is to ensure that developing economies benefit from the growth of trade by improving market access to developed economies for developing countries. The most significant differences are between developed countries led by the European Union (EU), the United States (USA), and Japan and the major developing countries led and represented mainly by China, Brazil, India, South Korea, and South Africa. There is also considerable contention against and between the EU and the USA over their maintenance of agricultural subsidies. Nine years after the talks started agreement has still not been reached.

Exchange Rates

An exchange rate is the price of one currency as expressed in another or, to put it another way, the rate at which one currency is exchanged for another. Movements in exchange rates can be an important influence on the business environment—good news for some, bad for others. A rise in the exchange rate can make imports cheaper which is good news for those firms buying a lot of goods and services from abroad. On the other hand it is likely to be bad news for exporters as

Mini Case Vietnam's Entry to the WTO

On 7 November 2006, after 12 years of talks, WTO members voted for Vietnam to become a member. What does it mean for Vietnam? On the positive side it will mean that Vietnam's exports will face fewer restrictions in the form of quotas and tariffs. In particular, US and EU quotas on textile and garment exports will end, and Vietnam will compete on a level playing field with other exporters who, since the beginning of 2005, have enjoyed quota free trade. It will mean more investment from developed economies, keen to take advantage of Vietnam's abundance of young, highly motivated, low waged workers.

WTO accession means that Vietnam has had to open its markets and implement a lot of regulatory reform, thereby making it safer and more attractive to overseas investment.

On the negative side it has had to remove agricultural export subsidies, reduce substantially or eliminate some industrial subsidies, and reduce import tariffs. All of this will make it much more difficult for domestic industry to compete. Foreign ownership ceilings in the services sector have also been raised. It will retain protection in some sectors while the economy adjusts to the new situation.

Source: photodisc

it could make them less competitive in foreign markets. Requena-Silvente and Walker (2007) found that car exporters to the UK reduced their mark up to keep prices stable and maintain market share when their currencies rose against sterling.

Similarly, for businesses producing abroad a rise in the exchange rate could reduce the value of their foreign sales and assets when translated back into their domestic currency.

Mini Case The US Dollar Exchange Rate

The US dollar exchange rate has important implications for non-US firms buying goods and services, like oil, shipping, and aircraft whose prices are expressed in dollars. A rise in the dollar means an increase in the price of oil, the cost of shipping goods and the price of aircraft from companies like Boeing and Airbus.

Falls in the rate have the opposite effect as can be seen in Volkswagen's 2010 results. In the first half of that year the euro declined by around 17% against the US dollar and the Chinese renminbi. This helped VW increase the sale of Audis by more than 20% in the US and Audi exports to China by almost a fifth. Sterling also fell against the dollar making the USA a more expensive tourist destination. The number of UK visitors fell affecting tourism-related businesses such as hotels and car hire firms.

Sources: Bank of England; ITA Office of Travel and Tourism; www.volkswagenag.com; European Central Bank

Source: Photodisc

Adverse long-lasting realignments of exchange rates can have a major impact on business strategy. They may cause firms to: relocate production; change the source of supply; look for new product markets or strong currency markets; make products having a more global appeal to facilitate the switch from weak to strong currency markets; look for ways of increasing productivity.

Learning Task

In 2009, EADS, a Eurozone aerospace company and the parent of Airbus, reported ongoing concerns about the weakness of the US dollar against the euro. Aircraft, internationally, are priced in dollars so Airbus was finding it increasingly difficult to compete with its major rival, the US firm, Boeing. The problem had been a long-standing one because the dollar had fallen by 30% in value against the euro between 2000 and 2009. In 2006, the company estimated that it needed to cut costs by $3 billion annually to offset the losses caused by the decline in the dollar. By the following year, the euro had risen another 20 cents which meant that Airbus had to find a further $3 billion of savings. The company, fearful of being driven out of business, responded by cutting costs, increasing the quantity of supplies bought in the USA, looking to expand in the United States, and trying to sell off European factories. It had also taken out insurance policies, the technical name for this being hedging, to protect itself ➜

➜ against unfavourable movements in the dollar. The costs of the policies had been rising and the company expected an adverse effect of these on its 2010 results to the tune of €1 billion.

1. Explain how the weakness of the dollar makes it more difficult for Airbus to compete with Boeing.

2. Analyse how the responses by Airbus would help it compete more effectively with Boeing.

3. Go to the exchange rate section of the Federal Reserve website to find out how the value of the dollar has changed against the euro since 2009. Do the changes make life easier or harder for Airbus?

Sources: www.BusinessWeek.com, 17 January, 16 November and 20 December 2007; EADS Annual review 2009

Countries may adopt a fixed **exchange rate** policy where they peg the value of their currency against another. Fixed rates give a degree of stability to business whether it be importers, exporters, or investors wishing to move capital in or out of the country. According to the IMF (2009), 10 countries, including El Salvador and Panama, use the US dollar as their domestic currency and 42 others peg their currency against it, while 26 countries peg theirs against the euro. China pegs the renminbi against the US dollar. It came under pressure to revalue the rate from the US authorities who were worried about the burgeoning trade deficit with China. As can be seen in Figure 2.4, China allowed the spot rate—the current exchange rate that the renminbi could be bought at 'now'—to rise against the dollar. In June 2005 US$1 bought about 8.29 renminbi. Four years later, one US dollar only bought around 7 renminbi (see Figure 2.4).

Learning Task

The US authorities put pressure on a reluctant Chinese government to allow its currency to appreciate against the dollar.

1. Explain why the USA would wish to see a rise in the value of the renminbi against the dollar.

2. Explain the Chinese reluctance to let the renminbi appreciate in value.

3. Use the data in Figure 2.4 to calculate:

   • how much the renminbi went up against the dollar between 2005 and 2010

   • how much the dollar depreciated against the renminbi.

Figure 2.4 How many Chinese Renminbi for US$1

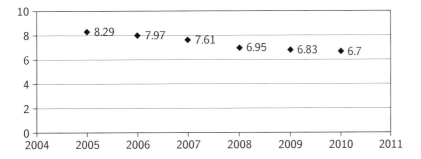

Countries may also choose to have floating exchange rates where the rate is determined solely by the supply and demand for the currency on the foreign exchange markets. There are 40 such countries including those in the Eurozone (IMF 2009). Here the currency value would be determined by the requirement to finance imports and exports, the movement of capital across borders, the country's interest rates relative to others, and the demands of speculators. In this situation the rate could be very volatile and this could create problems for firms that are heavily involved in international trade and investment. They could face wild fluctuations in import prices and in the value of export earnings and foreign assets.

Or it may be that the authorities decide that they are prepared to see the value of the currency fluctuate within prescribed bands against another currency. When the currency looks as if it is going to break through the bands, the authorities intervene to buy the domestic currency when it is sinking too low or to sell it when it is threatening to rise too high in value. This gives business less certainty than the fixed rate regime but more certainty than a floating regime.

● CHAPTER SUMMARY

In this chapter we have looked at the global pattern of wealth, international trade, and exchange rates. One way of comparing countries is to compare their respective GDP. This can be adjusted for purchasing power parity, which has the effect of narrowing the gap between rich and poor. The richest economy is still the USA, but China, in terms of PPP, is catching up quickly.

GDP indicates the different sizes of economies but doesn't say much about the standard of living—population has to be taken into account to give income per capita. In determining the degree of development the UNDP also looks at other indicators such as income inequality, life expectancy, literacy rates, and school enrolments. On any of these measures the world is still a very divided place when comparing the rich with the poor. Economic growth is seen as the key to raising standards of living.

International trade has increased, with exports in 1970 just 13% of world output whereas they are predicted to be 34% by 2030. Developing countries are increasing their share of trade in manufactures but this is still dominated by the triad nations. Countries trade with each other and world output increases, but history shows that the rich nations tend to benefit at the expense of the poor. There have been a number of theories put forward to explain the pattern of trade. Many countries impose restrictions, but the WTO works to liberalize trade. It has faced criticism because it is seen as a club which helps to maintain the established patterns of trade which favour the rich.

An exchange rate is the price of one currency expressed in another. Fluctuations in exchange rates can have a major impact on business. Some countries have been accused of manipulating the exchange of their currencies in order to make their goods more competitive in overseas markets.

● REVIEW QUESTIONS

1. Why would it be useful for business to build up knowledge of the global distribution of income and wealth and how it is changing over time?

2. Discuss the proposition that happiness does not necessarily increase with increased wealth.

3. Analyse and explain the major trends in international trade. Discuss links between these trends and the changing distribution of world income.

4. What are the advantages to countries of foreign trade? In the light of these advantages, explain why, in 2006, the EU accused China and Vietnam of dumping footwear and imposed import duties. In 2010 it decided to continue with the tariffs for a further 15 months.

   To help you answer this see the articles in *The Guardian* by Ross Davidson, 7 April 2006 and David Gow, 20 February 2006 and articles at http://ictsd.org/i/news/bridgesweekly/70138/ and www.wfsgi.org/articles/411 (the latter is by the World Federation of Sporting Goods Industry).

5. Discuss why the level of exchange rates is important for international business.

Case Study Brazil

Brazil is the largest of the South American economies and second only to the USA in the whole of the Americas. It has a population of 191 million people and a per capita income of US$8,220 (2009) more than double that of 1990 with the result that more than 50% of Brazil's population is now middle class. Brazil has a very young population and the growing workforce is likely to make a major contribution to future growth. Brazil's economy is based largely on primary products, especially raw materials. It has large agricultural, mining, manufacturing, and service sectors. Its main exports are transport equipment, iron ore, soybeans, footwear, coffee, and cars to the EU27 (22.3%), China (13.2%), USA (10.3%), and Argentina (8.4%). Its main imports are machinery, electrical and transport equipment, chemical products, oil, and automotive parts to the EU27 (22.9%), USA (15.8%), China (12.5%), and Argentina (8.8%). Brazil is regarded by many as the one BRIC likely to be most challenged by the predictions for growth into the 21st century. Its growth record in the past has averaged around 2% and has been erratic, swinging between −4% and 5.8% between 1990 and 2003. However, since 2004 its performance has been much improved save for 2009, the year of global recession. For these years it has averaged nearer 5% and is expected to grow at 7.5% in 2010 and about 4% per annum up to 2015.

One problem hindering the economy in 2010 and beyond is the struggle to maintain a competitive exchange rate. Since the end of 2008 the Real (Brazil's currency) has appreciated against the dollar by about 35%. Brazil's economy has grown strongly in 2010 but much of the growth in income has been spent on imports and overseas travel as the Real has risen. Other countries, Brazil has complained, have intervened in the foreign exchange markets in what Brazil has called 'a global currency war' in order to prevent their currencies from rising and so aid their economic recovery. They have accused the USA, Europe, and Japan of seeking to devalue their currencies. The USA for

example pumped $600 billion into the US economy. This increase in dollars finds itself spent in countries which have strong growth prospects and high returns, such as Brazil.

As domestic demand in Brazil outstrips supply inflation has also become a worry as the rate has risen above 5% (the ➡

Source: www.istockphoto.com

→ target is to keep the rate below 4.5%). To combat this interest rates are very high. The central bank has a rate of 10.75%, higher than any other major economy. The effect of this is to attract capital inflows and so exacerbate the problem of the exchange rate. In response the Brazilian authorities have recently introduced some new measures to restrict lending.

Sources: CIA Factbook; Grant Thornton International Business Report 2007, Emerging Markets; IMF Economic Outlook Database, 2010; www.xe.com/news/2010-09-21%2014:56:00.0/1409613.htm

Questions

1. What factors might account for the rise of the Brazilian economy?

2. Explain how the growth of the middle class can help and hinder the Brazilian economy.

3. Explain what is meant by a currency war and why it is in nobody's interest.

4. How does the appreciation of the Real threaten the growth prospects of the Brazilian economy?

Online Resource Centre
www.oxfordtextbooks.co.uk/orc/hamilton_webster2e/

Visit the supporting online resource centre for additional material which will help you with your assignments, essays, and research, or you may find these extra resources helpful when revising for exams.

● FURTHER READING

For a book which challenges the idea that the best way of improving the quality of human lives is to raise material living standards see:

● Wilkinson, R. and Pickett, K. (2009) *The Spirit Level, Why Equality is Better for Everyone*. London: Penguin Books

For a historical account of the evolution of world trade up to the 21st century see:

● Findlay, R. and O'Rourke, K. H. (2007) *Power and Plenty: Trade, War, and the World Economy*. Princeton, New Jersey: Princeton University Press

For an in-depth analysis of the Chinese economy and its relationship with global trade see:

● Eichengreen, B., Chui, Y., and Wyplosz, C. (eds) (2008) *China, Asia, and the New World Economy*. Oxford: Oxford University Press

For an application and extension of the Porter diamond to national competitiveness see:

● Stone, H. B. and Ranchhod, A. (2006) 'Competitive Advantage of a Nation in the Global Arena: A Quantitative Advancement to Porter's Diamond Applied to the UK, USA and BRIC Nations'. *Strategic Change*, Vol 5, Issue 6

● Özlem, Ö. (2002) 'Assessing Porter's Framework for National Advantage: The Case of Turkey'. *Journal of Business Research*, Vol 55, Issue 6, June

Rugman has been one of the main critics of the Porter diamond. See:

● Rugman, A., Verbeke, A., and Van Den Broeck, J. (eds) (1995) *Research in Global Strategic Management: Volume V Beyond the Diamond*. Greenwich, Conn.: JAI Press

REFERENCES

Dicken, P. (2004) *Global Shift, Reshaping the Global Economic Map in the 21st Century*. London: Sage

Goldman Sachs (2003) Global Economic Paper No 99. Dreaming with Brics: The Path to 2050

Grant Thornton (2007) International Business Report, Emerging Markets

International Monetary Fund (2009) De Facto Classification of Exchange Rate Regimes and Monetary Policy Frameworks

International Monetary Fund (2010) World Economic Outlook Database, April 2010

Leontieff, W. (1953) 'Domestic Production and Foreign Trade: The American Capital Position Reexamined'. *Proceedings of the American Philosophical Society*, Vol 97 November

Linder, S. B. (1961) *An Essay on Trade and Transformation*. New York: Wiley

Maddison, A. (2003) The World Economy: Historical Statistics. Development Centre Studies OECD

Meadows, D. H. *et al*. (1972) *The Limits to Growth*. New York: Universe Books

Mishan, E. (1967) *The Costs of Economic Growth*. London: Staples Press

OECD (2010) Factbook

OECD (2010) Agricultural Policies in OECD Countries at a Glance

Porter, M. (1990) *The Competitive Advantage of Nations*. London: Macmillan Press

PricewaterhouseCoopers (2006) The World in 2050: How big will the major emerging market economies get and how can the OECD compete

PricewaterhouseCoopers: Updated projections (2008)

Ricardo, D. (1817) *On the Principles of Political Economy and Taxation*. London: John Murray

Requena-Silvente, F. and Walker, J. (2007) 'The Impact of Exchange Rate Fluctuations on Profit Margins: The UK Car Market, 1971–2002'. *Journal of Applied Economics*, Vol X, No 1, May 2007

Rose, A. (2004) 'Do WTO Members have More Liberal Trade Policy?'. *Journal of International Economics*, Vol 63, No 2

Schneider, F., Buehn, A., and Montenegro, C. E. (2010) Shadow Economies All Over the World, New Estimates for 162 Countries from 1999 to 2007, World Bank working paper WPS5356

Simms, A., Johnson, V., Chowla, K. (2010) *Growth Isn't Possible*. London: New Economics Foundation

Smith, A. (1776) *An Inquiry into the Nature and Causes of the Wealth of Nations*. Oxford: Clarendon Press

Subramanian, A. and Wei, S.-J. (2005) The WTO Promotes Trade, Strongly But Unevenly, CEPR Discussion Papers 5122

Vernon, R. (1966) 'International Investments and International Trade in the Product Life Cycle'. *Quarterly Journal of Economics*, Vol 80

World Bank (2007) Global Economic Prospects: Managing the Next Wave of Globalisation

CHAPTER THREE

Analysing Global Industries

LEARNING OUTCOMES

This chapter will enable you to:

- **Distinguish between the concept of market and industry**

- **Identify various market structures and their implications for competition and performance**

- **Measure market concentration, analyse it, and explain the link with market power**

- **Explain and use the Porter Five Forces model for industry analysis**

Case Study Apple

Apple designs, manufactures, and markets personal computers, mobile communication devices, and portable digital music and video players. The company also offers a variety of related software, services, peripherals, and networking products. Its products include the iPod, iPhone, iPad, iPlayer, and iMac, software such as Mac OS, iLife, and iWork and internet applications like Safari and QuickTime. The company provides online distribution of third-party music, audio books, music videos, short films, and television shows. The company sells its products worldwide through online stores, retail stores, its direct sales force, and wholesalers.

In 2009 it recorded sales of nearly US$43 billion, an increase of more than 14% over the previous year and its profits rose by more than a third to more than US$8 billion. It has around 34,000 employees. In 2010, its value on the stockmarket at US$222 billion overtook that of the software giant, Microsoft.

Apple's competitive strategy is based on creating a strong brand name through product design, innovation, and improvement and effective promotion. For example, in the first decade of the new century Apple introduced iTunes, the App store, upgrades to iPhoto, iMovie and GarageBand, and included iDVD, and an updated version of iWeb. In 2009, the company launched the iPhone 3GS, its third generation of smartphone with new features such as speed up to twice as fast as iPhone 3G. In 2010, version 4 of the iPhone and the iPad were launched with the latter selling 300,000 on day one and 3 million in the first 80 days. However, Apple's image was somewhat dented by customer problems with the poor call and data signal strength of the new iPhone. The company has been very successful in differentiating the brand. Martin Lindstrom, a brand consultant, claims, 'Apple's brand is so powerful that for some people it's just like a true religion' (Manjoo 2010). The company is also highly protective of its technology.

The company's main rivals include Dell, HP, IBM, Samsung, Sony and Sony Ericsson, Nokia, Microsoft, Toshiba, and Sun Microsystems. While the company, with 25% of the market, is the largest retailer of music in the USA and has great bargaining power with music companies, it faces competition from digital music providers like Spotify and we7. Apple has gone in for takeovers of companies like Sismo Graphics, Silicon Grail, and Emagic to gain access to their technology. It has also cooperated with rivals such as Ericsson and Sun Microsystems to develop a standard format for delivering multimedia content and with customers like Ford, GM and airlines such as Air France,

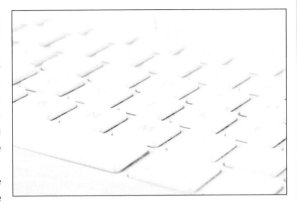

Source: www.istockphoto.com

Emirates, and Delta to incorporate the iPod technology into their entertainment systems.

Apple outsources much of the manufacture of its products and components to Japanese companies like Toshiba, Toshiba-Matsushita, and Elpida, the Korean firm Samsung, and Foxconn and Inventec from Taiwan. Linden (2009) calculated that the cost of supplies and assembly for the 30GB fifth generation iPod were just over US$144 compared with a wholesale price of US$224 and a final selling price in the USA of US$299. More than half of the input cost was accounted for by the hard drive supplied by Toshiba.

Apple has a social responsibility code for suppliers aiming to ensure that working conditions are healthy and safe, workers are treated with respect, and production processes are environmentally responsible. Unfortunately for Apple, problems arose just before the launch of the iPad when a number of employees at a Foxconn plant in China committed suicide due, according to some commentators, to the tough managerial style. (Visit the accompanying **Online Resource Centre** to watch a news report of the issue, and see Steve Jobs, the head of Apple, defend Foxconn.) Foxconn, which also supplies firms like HP and Samsung, is a subsidiary of Ton Hai Precision Industry, the world's largest contract manufacturer for electronic components. Apple is Foxconn's biggest customer.

Sources: Datamonitor, Apple Inc., 21 May 2010; Linden 2009; www.apple.com; Manjoo 2010; *Bloomberg Business Week*, 7 June 2010; *The Guardian*, 26 May 2010 and 30 August 2010; *The Economist*, 27 May 2010; USA Today, 27 July 2010.

Introduction

In this chapter we develop the knowledge and skills necessary to carry out analyses of industries. We start off by examining the concepts of the market and the industry. In line with other authors we see the terms 'market' and 'industry' as being interchangeable. Various market structures are then explored along with their implications for the nature and intensity of competition and company performance. We go on to look at **market concentration**, how it is measured, and the implications of different levels of concentration for the distribution of market power among firms in the industry. The Five Forces of Porter's model provide a set of tools that allow a systematic and comprehensive analysis of industries. Each force is explained and applied to various industries along with a sixth force, **complementary products**.

The term 'global' is used liberally in this chapter. We use it on occasions where multiple countries are involved. This usage varies from other authors who interpret the word as meaning worldwide, that is covering most countries in the world.

The Market and the Industry

Analysing markets and industries involves building up a detailed knowledge of the competing firms in the industry, the goods and services they are selling, and the geographical markets where they compete.

Defining the market involves several steps:

- deciding which goods or services to include;
- identifying the firms competing in the market;
- indicating the geographical area where those firms are competing.

First, it is important to identify products or services that customers see as very similar. Economists use a concept called the **cross elasticity of demand** which measures the response of customers when one firm changes its price. If the price of a product increases and customers switch in large numbers to other cheaper products, then economists conclude that the products can be classified to the same market. In other words, there is a high cross elasticity of demand because customers see the products as being very good alternatives. One would expect to see this effect were an oil company like BP to raise the price of petrol on the forecourt to a level higher than competitors, Esso and Shell. This allows us to identify competitors because the firms making products with a high cross elasticity of demand are then defined as being part of the same industry. However, if very few customers transfer their business to the cheaper goods then the products are not seen by consumers as good alternatives and the firms cannot be classified to the same industry. The concept of cross elasticity, while neat in a theoretical sense, can be difficult to use in practice. Usually, the information required to calculate cross elasticity is not available. In the absence of data on cross elasticity, some observers look for evidence showing businesses reacting regularly to decisions made by other firms. Signs of such interdependence among firms indicate that they see themselves as competitors. For example, if one firm lowers price or increases spending on advertising and others regularly follow suit, then those firms who end up pursuing similar policies could be seen as members of the same industry. Another approach is to identify firms whose actions as regards, for example, pricing, advertising, and sales promotion are constrained by others. To take the example of low cost airlines, it would be understandable were firms such as Ryanair and easyJet constrained in their pricing policies by the possible reaction of the other.

Classifying firms to a particular industry may not be as straightforward as it first appears. Car firms are often seen as operating in the same industry, but it would hardly be sensible to view the Rolls Royce as a direct competitor to a Mini or a Fiat Punto. It would make more sense, for our purposes, to consider car manufacturers as producing for a series of markets, from the most basic models to the luxury end of the market. **Diversified firms** also complicate the picture. Companies, selling a range of goods, may end up being classified to several industries. Take domestic appliance manufacturers such as Whirlpool, Electrolux, or LG, the South Korean multinational. They make various appliances including washing machines, dishwashers, and electric cookers—these products can hardly be seen as close substitutes, so the companies could be seen as competing in various markets, for washing machines, dishwashers, and electric cookers. Of course, the fact that diversified firms such as these can offer customers like retailers the ability to source a range of products from a single company may put such firms at a competitive advantage against rivals offering a more limited range. Companies operating at several stages of production of a product can also complicate the issue of how to classify them. Examples of **vertically integrated firms** can be found in the oil industry where companies like Shell, Exxon, and BP drill for oil, refine it, and sell it on the forecourt. They could be classified to three industries: drilling, refining, and retailing. The media sector also provides an illustration with groups like News International producing films and distributing them through their television and satellite broadcasting companies.

Another aspect of the market that needs to be clarified is its geographical boundaries. Firms located in different places could be producing similar products, but not actually competing against each other in the same geographical market place. Geographical distance may mean that the cost of transporting goods from one area to the other is not economical so, in reality, the firms in one area are not competing with firms in the other. There are a variety of factors which keep markets separate, such as geographical distance, or poor transport infrastructure. For example, in poor countries in Africa and South East Asia the lack of road and rail networks may keep markets fragmented, whereas in the developed economies of Northern Europe improving transport links have integrated previously distinct markets. Firms may also set out deliberately to keep markets separate. Car producers do this in Western Europe. Traditionally, they have charged significantly higher prices in the UK than in countries like Belgium and the Netherlands. They hope that British customers will not realize that prices are cheaper across the Channel and therefore will not hop across to get their cars from Belgian or Dutch dealers. UK customers who recognize that they can get a lower price on the Continent, and try to buy there, have found that distributors may claim that they are out of supplies or that they do not have access to right-hand drive cars. The EU Commission found Volkswagen guilty of discriminating in price between customers in Southern Germany and those in Northern Italy. German consumers were richer than the Northern Italians so they could afford to pay more. VW, so long as it could keep the two markets separate, increased profits by charging more in Germany than in Italy. Economists identify the geographical boundaries of the market by assessing the extent to which a price increase in one area:

- attracts competition from firms elsewhere. For example, had the high prices charged by VW in Southern Germany attracted many car dealers from Northern Italy lured by the prospect of higher profits, then the two regions could be classified as one market;

- drives customers away to cheaper areas. VW's high prices in Germany could have led many German car buyers to go to Italy to get a better deal. The two areas could be seen as part of the same geographical market had many German consumers taken that route. Such behaviour can be seen in Southern England where consumers get the ferry across to France to buy cheaper alcohol and tobacco. Similarly, French buyers of alcohol and tobacco products flock to the small Spanish towns on the border where the prices of these products are much lower than in France.

Market Structures

There is a variety of market structures ranging from pure **monopoly** to the perfectly competitive (see Table 3.1). In a pure monopoly, one firm dominates the market usually protected from competition by high **barriers to entry** (barriers to entry are explained in more detail in the discussion of Force 2 in Porter's model, Competition from new entrants). Such firms control the market and can set prices to extract maximum profit from their customers. Consumers have to pay the price because they have no alternative suppliers to turn to. In a globalizing world economy, one rarely encounters pure monopoly outside the pages of basic economics textbooks although some markets, at times, may come close. For example, Wrigley accounts for more than 80% of the UK chewing gum market, while Microsoft accounts for around 92% of the world market for desktop operating software (Mintel, Gum Confectionery (Snapshots), July 2008; netmarketshare.com).

Market structure can be influenced by the costs incurred by business. Very high **fixed costs** can result in the creation of what is termed a **natural monopoly**. To survive, firms need to produce on a very large scale relative to the size of the market to generate sufficient revenues to cover their fixed costs. Examples of natural monopolies include gas, water, electricity, and telephone networks. It is very expensive to build transmission networks of pipelines for water and gas and electricity and telephone lines. The result is a single producer having an overwhelming cost advantage over potential competitors. Such rivals are deterred from entering the market by the high capital investment involved and the dominant market position of the monopolist.

In perfectly competitive markets, large numbers of firms are completely free to enter and to leave the market, no individual firm can control the market, price is set by the forces of supply

Table 3.1 Types of market structure

Type of market structure	Number of firms	Barriers to entry	Nature of product
Perfect competition	Very many	None	Homogeneous
Monopoly	One	High	Unique
Monopolistic competition	Many	None	Heterogeneous
Oligopoly	Few	Often high	Homogeneous/Differentiated

and demand, and buyers and sellers have complete knowledge of market conditions. Profit levels are just enough to keep firms in business. Any profits above that level are quickly eroded away by competition from entrants attracted to the market by the prospect of high profits. **Perfect competition**, where there are many firms supplying identical products with no entry barriers, is difficult to find in the real world. In reality, markets are usually imperfect—they can be costly to enter and dominated by a small number of firms who set prices, differentiate their products, earn abnormally high profits, and comprise buyers and sellers who have gaps in their knowledge of market conditions.

Another market structure is **monopolistic competition** with large numbers of firms, no barriers to entry, and only a small degree of product differentiation. The corner shop or convenience store segment of the retail market could be seen as monopolistically competitive with a large number of outlets, ease of entry, and each differentiated by their location.

In reality, most manufacturing and many service sector industries operate in oligopolistic markets where there are few firms, often protected by high entry barriers and able to exercise some control over the market. In oligopolistic markets, firms often try to differentiate their products from those of their competitors in the branding, advertising, packaging, and design of their goods and services. Firms that are successful in convincing consumers that their products are different, such as Apple with its Mac computer, the iPod and the iPad, can charge higher prices and not lose custom. Oligopolists, when formulating their policies, have to take into account that their actions could affect their rivals' sales, market share, and profits and are therefore likely to provoke a reaction. For example, a price reduction by one of the players might spark off a price war where competitors try to undercut each other. The end-result could be cut-throat competition with some firms going out of business.

In order to avoid such competition, oligopolists sometimes set up **cartels**. These, usually operating in secret, aim to control competition through the firms in the market agreeing to set common prices or to divide the market geographically amongst cartel members. In the EU 17 steel producers were found guilty of running a cartel for 18 years in which they fixed prices and shared markets (EU Commission press release IP/10/863). Work by Connor (2002) suggests that global cartels are widespread. He talks of 'a global pandemic' of international cartels and a 'resurgence of global price fixing' (p 1).

Market structure can influence the behaviour of firms in the industry and the nature and intensity of competition. In perfect competition, firms cannot set their own pricing policy because price is determined by the market and there would be no point in trying to differentiate one's goods or services in a perfectly competitive market because consumers see the products as identical.

By contrast, a monopolist is free to pursue an independent pricing policy. In addition, monopolists, facing no competition, do not need to try to differentiate their products. On price, oligopolists can usually exercise some influence although they must take into account the possible reactions of their competitors. Furthermore, in **oligopoly**, especially when selling to the final consumer, firms make strenuous efforts to differentiate the product through, for example, their marketing and sales promotion activities. For instance, Procter and Gamble, a leading producer of toiletries and other personal care products, was the leading global advertiser in 2009 with an annual spend of nearly US$10 billion equal to 12% of sales. This was around four times greater than its rival Reckitt Benckiser and nearly double the amount spent by Unilever (www.pg.com; Advertising Age at http://adage.com/datacenter).

Market structure can also influence company performance. The intensity of competition can affect profitability. In very competitive markets, profits are likely to be lower than they would be were those markets to turn into an oligopoly or a monopoly.

Learning Task

The European Commission was asked to decide whether a proposed merger between a firm producing instant coffee and one making ground coffee had any implications for competition. To come to a decision, the Commission had to determine whether the firms were competing in the same market. There was no statistical information available to estimate the cross elasticity of demand between instant and ground coffee.

Do you think consumers see these products as good alternatives?

One way to determine this is to compare the prices for both products. A major price difference could indicate that they are not good alternatives. Check prices at your local supermarket. You could also survey your fellow students to find out whether they see the two products as significantly different. An important indication that they are in different markets would be the willingness of the students to pay more for one than the other.

Market Power

The distribution of power amongst firms in an industry is assessed by the level of market concentration which can be measured by looking at the market share of firms in the industry. Market concentration gives an indication of the competitive pressures in a market. High concentration levels usually indicate that competition will be of low intensity. Big firms in highly concentrated markets will be able to determine prices, the quantity and quality of output they are prepared to supply, and to force policies on reluctant customers. Thus, Coca Cola dominates the EU's carbonated soft drinks market. In France, Coke has more than half the market whilst in Belgium it is nearer 70%. An EU investigation found that the company had stifled competition by obliging customers to stock only Coke drinks and forcing them to take less popular brands such as Sprite and Vanilla Coke (Mintel, Carbonated Soft Drinks (Snapshots) France 2009, and Belgium 2009; Hamouda; EU Commission, IP/04/1247).

In search engines high levels of concentration indicate low intensity competition. Google dwarfs its rivals, holding around 70% of the US search market while in Western Europe its share exceeds 90% (*Financial Times*, 12 July 2010). More than three quarters of all web searchers click on the first three links in Google and only a small minority look past the first page of results. Consequently, Google has the power to make or break firms promoting their products on the web. Online travel firms like Expedia claim that Google ensures that its own travel services appear above Expedia in the rankings. Firms, generally having little bargaining power over Google, sometimes complain to the regulatory authorities—in France Google was ordered to reinstate an advertiser it had excluded from the system.

The European Commission found that Microsoft used its market power to shut out competitors by bundling software programs together in its Windows package and refusing to supply rivals with technical information allowing them to make their products compatible with Windows (see EU Commission, IP/04/382 and *The Economist*, 20 September 2007).

Figure 3.1 Global beer % market share by volume 2009

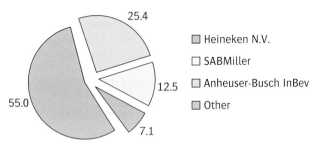

Source: Datamonitor, Global Beer, September 2010

Pure monopoly demonstrates the highest level of concentration with one firm holding 100% of the market. At the other extreme, in perfect competition, power is distributed equally amongst firms and as a result the level of market concentration is low. In oligopoly, a few firms dominate the market and the level of market concentration is usually high. The world beer market is a good illustration of this. As can be seen in Figure 3.1, the three largest firms, Anheuser-Busch InBev, SABMiller, and Heineken account for almost half of global beer sales.

Measuring Market Concentration

There are various ways of measuring market concentration. The most straightforward method is the **concentration ratio** (CR). This is usually calculated by taking the share of the largest firms in industry sales or output by value or by volume. CR2, CR3, CR10, and so on indicate the concentration ratio for the two, three, and ten largest firms in the industry. In 2009, the CR3 for the global brewing industry was 45%. This had changed dramatically compared with 2007 when the CR3 was 33.9%. The increase in concentration was mainly due to the acquisition of Scottish & Newcastle jointly by Heineken and Carlsberg and the takeover of Anheuser-Busch by InBev (Datamonitor, Global Beer, September 2009, September 2010).

A second method of calculating market concentration is provided by the **Herfindahl-Hirschmann Index** (HHI). The HHI is calculated by summing the squares of the individual market shares of all the firms in the market. The HHI gives proportionately greater weight to the market shares of the larger firms. It gives a more accurate picture than the concentration ratio because it includes all firms in the calculation. Sometimes, there is a lack of information about the market shares of very small firms but this may not be important because such firms do not affect the HHI significantly. For example, a market containing five firms with market shares of 40%, 20%, 15%, 15%, and 10%, respectively, has an HHI of 2,550 ($40^2 + 20^2 + 15^2 + 15^2 + 10^2 =$ 2,550). The HHI ranges from close to zero in a perfectly competitive market to 10,000 in the case of a pure monopoly. The EU Commission sees an HHI of more than 1,000 in a market as indicating a level of concentration that could have adverse effects on competition. The Commission is especially concerned where firms are also protected by high entry barriers and where their market position faces little threat from innovation. It feels the same way when the share of the largest firm in the market, that is the CR1, exceeds 40%. Consequently, in these markets, the Commission looks for evidence of firms abusing their market power and examines closely proposed mergers between firms in these markets that would raise concentration to an even higher level (see Verouden 2004; Pleatsikas and Teece 2001).

Concentration figures can also be affected by the geographical focus of the information. In 2009, Lenovo the Chinese multinational held 9% of the world market for personal computers, far behind that of the market leaders HP, Acer, and Dell. However, switching the focus to China changes the picture dramatically where it holds one third of the market (*Bloomberg Business Week*, 4 February 2010).

Learning Task

1. Use the information on market shares in Table 3.2 to work out an HHI for the European beer market. Assume that the remaining firms in the beer market only hold tiny shares and that their inclusion would not significantly distort the result.

2. On the basis of your answer, discuss whether the EU Commission would be concerned, on competition grounds, were Heineken to propose a takeover of Carlsberg.

3. How does changing the geographical focus from the world to Europe affect the picture you get of market concentration? For example, are the same companies the market leaders in both Europe and the world? How does the CR1, 2, 3 in Europe compare with the world concentration ratios?

Table 3.2 Market share by volume—Europe 2009

Company	% share
Heineken	20.4
Carlsberg	17
Anheuser-Busch InBev	15.6
Others	47
Total	100

Source: Datamonitor, Beer in Europe, September 2010

What this shows is that a market can appear to be quite highly concentrated at one geographical level but fragmented at another. While Anheuser-Busch InBev holds around a quarter of the world market for beer, the figure is nearer 70% in Brazil (Datamonitor, Beer Brazil, September 2009).

Counterpoint Box 3.1 Market power—good or bad?

Firms like to have market power because it reduces competitive risk and gives them more control over price and output decisions.

The traditional case against market power is that it concentrates control in the hands of one, or a few firms. Low levels of competition and high barriers to entry allow firms to raise prices above the competitive level in order to reap abnormally high profits. High prices cause customers to buy less of the product, less is produced, and society as a whole is worse off. Furthermore, facing light competitive pressures, monopolists may not press down on costs of production resulting in resources not being used to maximum efficiency. In short, prices are higher, output less, and average cost of production greater under monopoly.

On the other hand, the Austrian School argue that dominant firms gain their position through competing better in the market place whether that be through price, new or better products, more effective advertising or distribution channels, or lower costs due to economies of scale. And higher prices, rather than indicating abuse of market power, simply reflect the value that consumers place on the goods and services provided.

Schumpeter and Galbraith assert that firms need to be large, have a significant market share, and be protected by barriers to entry to induce them to invest in the risky R&D that society needs to advance technologically (also see Threats and Challenges in Chapter Seven, The Technological Framework).

Sources: George J. Stigler, Monopoly, The Concise Encyclopedia of Economics, available at www.econlib.org; Leibenstein (1978); D. T. Armentano, A Critique of Neoclassical and Austrian Monopoly Theory, available at http://mises.org; Schumpeter (1976); Galbraith (1967).

Analysing Industries—A Framework

Porter provides a useful framework for analysing the competitive environment of an industry (Porter 1979; 2008). His Five Forces model can be used to identify and evaluate the main threats to the firms in an industry (Figure 3.2).

The Porter model is often used in combination with other complementary tools such as the PESTLE model (Chapter Four) that focuses on the wider environment or the resource-based view (RBV). While Porter focuses on the firm's external environment, the RBV tool concentrates on evaluating how the firm's internal resources and capabilities such as patents and trade marks or the success of the company in establishing a successful reputation for itself and its brands can be used to achieve and sustain competitive advantage (see Fahy 2007).

Three of the forces are concerned with competition. The first, and most important, is industry rivalry which involves competition from rivals already established in the industry. Next, there is competition from new entrants to the industry. Third, the industry may have to confront competition from products which carry out the same function for customers but provide the service in a radically different way. For example, trains and planes both transport customers from points A to B but in a different way and consumers can get access to music by buying CDs or downloading it from the internet—it is a substitution in use. Porter calls these products, substitutes. The inclusion of this particular force helps get around problems of a precise identification of the industry. For example, in the market for luxury cars we might include firms producing Rolls Royces, Bentleys, and Mercedes because we see them as having a high cross elasticity of demand. Such a definition would exclude competition from sailing yachts or motorized vessels but these could be analysed using the substitution force in the Porter model.

The other forces are concerned with the industry customers and suppliers. We go through each of the forces in turn.

Figure 3.2 Porter's 'Five Forces' model

Source: Porter 2008

Mini Case Market Concentration in the Energy Market

This case concerns the high levels of market concentration in the energy markets of member states of the EU and the attempts by the Union to create a single electricity and gas market out of 27 separate national markets.

In the EU there are very high levels of market concentration in national gas and electricity markets. In 2008, the largest firm held more than 90% of the market for natural gas in six member states indicating low levels of competition in these markets. Germany was an exception with a CR2 of only 17.5%. (see Table 3.3).

Table 3.3 Market concentration natural gas 2008

	No. of main suppliers	%Market Share
Latvia	1	100
Lithuania	1	97.5
Slovakia	1	95
Finland	1	95
Poland	1	93.8
Estonia	1	91
Italy	3	83.2
France	3	83
Spain	8	80.4
UK	7	78.3
Germany	2	17.5

Source: Eurostat 2010

The sector had seen attempts at mergers by the already powerful national producers and also an increasing number of cross-border acquisitions such as the takeover of Scottish Power by Iberdrola, the Spanish energy company and that of Innogy, the UK's largest electricity supplier, by RWE of Germany. In certain electricity markets, there also appeared to be a tendency towards growing vertical integration between generators and distributors which would increase the power of the market leaders.

The EU as part of the Single Market programme set out to increase cross-border competition by removing barriers that were holding back the integration of separate national markets. That the markets were indeed separate was indicated by the significant price differences between the member states and the low level of cross-border trade. The Commission found that price differences for electricity for industrial customers in the EU were more than 100% in some cases.

Establishment of a single market would increase trade and competition and lead to a narrowing of the price differentials across the EU, or at least between adjacent member states or regions. The main barrier to market integration in electricity was identified as a lack of interconnection capacity which made it difficult to produce electricity in one country and sell it in another. Another important obstacle was the tendency by suppliers to tie in their customers through long-term contracts. The Commission found that there had been very few new entrants to the market, hardly surprisingly, given the market power of the established suppliers and the high barriers to entry.

Source: EU Commission 2005 and 2006; *Financial Times*, 7 March 2002; Reuters UK, 23 April 2007

Force 1 Industry Rivalry

Industry rivalry can vary in form and intensity from one industry to the other and in particular industries over time. At one point in the 1980s, telecommunications companies like BT, France Telecom, and Deutsche Telecom in Germany were seen as national flagship companies, with very powerful market positions, and protected by the law preventing other firms entering the industry. There was little competition to speak of. This changed in the subsequent 20 years as barriers to entry fell and they faced up to fiercer competition generated by new entrants, like Vodafone, to the industry.

Competition usually occurs in one or more of the following areas: price, advertising and sales promotion, distribution, and improvements in existing goods and services, or the introduction of completely new products. New and improved products are particularly important in industries such as electronics—as illustrated in the oligopolistic battle between Sony with its PlayStation, Nintendo's Wii, and Microsoft's Xbox in the console market. In the autumn of 2007, Sony managed to quadruple its sales and steal market share in the USA from its rivals after launching a new 40-gigabyte PlayStation 3 model and reducing the price on its old models (www.FT.com, 14 December 2007). Rivalry can also take the form of a struggle for resources. In 2007, with buoyant demand from India and China, mining companies found that capacity at existing mines was stretched. Billiton, the giant Australian mining group, in an attempt to increase its capacity to supply, tried to steal a march on rivals by making a bid for a major competitor, Rio Tinto while in 2009 Xstrata bid for Anglo American (*Guardian*, 9 November 2007; Mining Journal, 23 June 2009). Firms in the oil industry also have to compete for reserves. In 1970 international oil companies controlled 85% of the world's oil reserves whereas, nowadays, state-owned oil companies control 80% of reserves (*Financial Times Magazine*, 15 December 2007; see also the *Wall Street Journal*, 22 May 2010). The difficulties that big oil firms confront in their relationships with oil-rich countries like Russia and Venezuela force them to seek out reserves elsewhere.

Firms, especially international firms, increasingly strive for competitive advantage through mergers and alliances. The value of cross-border M&As reached around US$1 trillion in 2007. While the global recession blunted the business appetite for acquisitions cross-border merger activity started to recover very rapidly in 2010. (UNCTAD 2010) **Horizontal mergers**, that is between firms at the same stage of production of a product, boost market share and reduce competition. An example of this was the Air France merger with the Dutch carrier KLM which made it, in revenue terms, the largest airline in the world. Subsequently it set up an alliance with Delta Air Lines of the USA to make it one of the most powerful forces in North Atlantic aviation and posing a tough competitive challenge for other transatlantic carriers such as BA. BA, in turn, responded by setting up a joint venture with American Airlines and merging with Iberia (www. bbc.co.uk; *Financial Times*, 18 October 2007; www.britishairways.com). Horizontal mergers facilitate the movement into new geographical markets (see Mini Case below). **Vertical mergers**, where companies move closer to their supplies of raw materials or to their final customers, guarantee supplies of materials or distribution. In the late 1990s, with the internet offering new methods of distributing news, music, and film, media companies in newspaper publishing, TV, radio, and film moved to integrate different levels of production and distribution in order to place their products in the largest possible number of different platforms. The motto appeared to be 'Create Once, Place Everywhere!' This enabled companies to produce films or music, register them in DVDs or CDs and distribute them not only through retail outlets but also through the cable, satellite, or mobile telephony networks they owned. Such vertically integrated companies were in a position to exploit their products at every single level of the value chain. Thus, Time Warner, the US media giant, merged with internet service provider AOL, and Vivendi got together with Universal. Vertical integration may also allow firms to squeeze rivals where those rivals have to come to them for supplies or for distribution (see Pleatsikas and Teece 2000).

Competition intensity can range from being cut-throat to weak and depends on the following:

- The number of competing firms—the larger the number of competitors, the more likely is rivalry to be fierce. Conversely, the lower the number of rivals, the weaker the competition is likely to be.

- The relative size of firms—where rivals are of similar size or have equal market shares, then competition can be expected to be strong. This situation can be found in oligopolies such as cars where a small number of leading firms including General Motors, Ford, Volkswagen, and Toyota compete hard for sales. By contrast, in markets where one dominant firm competes with a number of smaller rivals, competition is likely to be less intense.

- Market growth rate—when the market is growing slowly, firms, wishing to grow faster than the market, will try to take market share away from their rivals by competing more fiercely. This is the case in the traditional markets of North America and Western Europe for the beer and car industries. If a beer firm wants to grow in those markets it has to up its competitive performance or take over a rival.

- The extent of product differentiation—when firms have been successful in persuading customers that their products are different from those of their rival's then competition is likely to be less intense. In the beer market, Anheuser-Busch inBev has five well-established international brands, Budweiser, Stella Artois, Beck's, Skol, and Leffe and more than 200 local brands while Heineken manages a large portfolio of beer brands, such as Heineken, Amstel, Cruzcampo, and Tiger. Some firms like Hoover, Sellotape, and Google are so successful that their brand becomes the generic name for the product.

- The importance of fixed costs—fixed costs are those which do not change with output and include, for example, depreciation, rent, and interest payments. Industries operating with large, expensive pieces of capital equipment often have high fixed costs and relatively low running, or variable, costs. Examples include oil refining, nuclear power generation, and mass car production. In such industries, firms will be under pressure to sell their output in order to generate some contribution to their fixed costs. This pressure will be particularly intense when there is spare capacity in the industry, in other words where firms are not using the resources to produce to their full potential, a situation faced by the big car producers in the traditional markets of North America and Western Europe.

- Where production capacity needs to be added in large chunks then expansion by firms can add significantly to the industry's ability to supply and could result in supply outstripping demand, leading to more competition. This is a particular problem for the car industry given that new factories could add significantly to supply in an industry suffering from over-capacity. To be competitive, new factories have to be able to produce several hundred thousand units a year in order to take advantage of economies of scale.

If most or all of the above conditions are met then competition in an industry will be fierce. Conversely, if none of these conditions prevail then firms in the industry are unlikely to be competing fiercely against each other.

Often oligopolists faced with the unpalatable prospect of competition will make efforts to avoid it. There are various devices they can use to achieve this such as forming a cartel which, in many countries, is illegal. The members of the cartel agree to follow certain competition-avoiding policies. This was seen when several large multinational producers of vitamins including Roche of Switzerland, BASF of Germany, and Daiichi of Japan agreed to charge common prices, and when Dutch brewers, Heineken, Grolsch, and Bavaria along with InBev agreed to coordinate beer prices (EU Commission IP/07/509). The USA and the EU found that major airlines including British Airways, Air France, Lufthansa, and Japan Airlines were operating a cartel to fix the prices for carrying cargo (*Financial Times*, 22 December 2007). Often cartels are

Mini Case The Car Industry—The Struggle for New Geographical Markets

This case shows one aspect of Industry Rivalry (Force 1) among car firms, the struggle to tap into new geographical markets, in this case the booming Russian market. In 2005, the car market in Russia generated sales of US$12 billion. In the three years to 2008 the number of cars sold almost doubled to 2.7m units. Although sales slumped in 2009 as a result of the global economic crisis, the market was forecast to grow at a compound annual rate of more than 25% up to 2014. In the middle of the decade, car ownership in Russia was only 160 cars per 1,000 people compared with 508 in Western Europe.

The search for new markets by big car makers was spurred by the slow growth of car sales and the level of spare capacity in the traditional markets of North America, Western Europe, and Japan. Russia, along with other Eastern European countries, was also attractive to car firms because of its cheap labour.

Renault, which also controls Nissan, set out to dominate the Russian car market by agreeing, in 2007, to buy a quarter of Avtovaz, the maker of the Lada, which used to be regarded as one of the world's worst brands. Renault intended to boost output to 1.5m cars a year and to improve the Lada by, for example, incorporating Renault engines and gear-boxes. The French company had to fight off competition from General Motors, Fiat, and Volkswagen to acquire its 25% stake in Avtovaz. The deal gave Renault and Nissan greater access to the fast-growing Russian market that had already attracted GM, Ford, Toyota, and VW.

The Russian car market was highly concentrated. In 2005, Avtovaz with its Lada model held more than half of the Russian market for cars but its share fell to around one quarter due to competition from foreign rivals. It employed 105,000 workers and had a joint venture with GM producing two models. Before the deal with Avtovaz, Renault had built up a presence in Russia with a new plant in Moscow and Nissan was in the process of building a production facility in St Petersburg as was General Motors. Peugeot and Mitsubishi followed Renault by setting up a joint production unit in 2010.

Source: Datamonitor, Russia—New Cars, October 2006 and December 2009; *Financial Times*, 5 December 2007; *The Guardian*, 10 December 2007; Russia Beyond the Headlines, 5 June 2010

Table 3.4 Russian market—cars, % share by volume 2009

Company	% Share
Lada	24.4%
General Motors	7.3%
Volkswagen	6.6%
Ford	5.7%
Other	55.9%
Total	100%

Source: Datamonitor, New Cars in Russia, October 2010

Source: www.istockphoto.com

established by firms producing undifferentiated products where buyers will take their custom to the cheapest supplier. When supply threatens to outstrip demand in such industries firms fear the outbreak of fierce competition and sometimes set up a cartel to prevent this happening. Alternatively, competitors can avoid competition by resorting to price leadership. While cartels bring firms together in an explicit agreement, price leadership can result from implicit understandings within the industry. Under price leadership one firm raises prices and the others

Counterpoint Box 3.2 International joint ventures—cooperation not competition

During the past decade, international joint ventures (IJV) have become increasingly popular, particularly for MNCs trying to enter emerging economies, driven as these MNCs are by sluggish growth in developed economies, increased market competition, and rapid technological change. IJVs involve firms agreeing to combine resources in R&D, or production, or marketing, or distribution. In some emerging economies, foreign firms may be obliged to take on a local partner as a condition of entry. Studies on the performance of individual IJVs have shown mixed results.

The plus points of IJVs for business include: by reducing political and business risks IJVs facilitate faster, cheaper, and more reliable entry into new geographical or product markets and access to technology; greater ability to obtain economies of scale and/or scope in areas like R&D, production, marketing and distribution; more rapid development of new products; mitigation of competition; faster growth. Gaining partners who have knowledge of local markets, can help foreign firms navigate unfamiliar business practices and policies, increase a firm's credibility in the eyes of local consumers, and make connections with government.

The minuses include: difficulties of managing due to the IJV being owned by parent companies that could have very different cultures, managerial styles or conflicting goals, with the added complexities associated with a different political and legal environment; loss of control over strategic and operational decisions; difficulties in monitoring, maintaining, and enforcing intellectual property rights particularly in emerging economies where little protection may be given to them. (see the sections, Protecting Technology in Chapter Seven, The Technological Framework, and, International Law and IPRs, in Chapter Nine, The Legal Environment)

Sources: Teece (1986); Beamish and Lupton (2009); Zhang, Li, Hitt, and Cui (2007); Burgers and Padgett (2009)

follow suit. Price leadership takes two forms. The first is dominant price leadership where the biggest firm in the industry changes price and others, either willingly or through fear of the consequences, follow suit. Barometric is the second type of price leadership. This occurs when firms in the industry are of similar size and the identity of the price leader changes from one period to another.

Force 2 Competition from New Entrants

The entry of new firms is another threat to established firms in the industry. New entrants will be attracted into industries by the prospects of high profits and growth. It may be that established firms are not making high profits but that the entrants can see the potential for profit—this was the case with low-cost entry to the airline industry. Entry increases the number of firms and, if it takes the form of greenfield investment, adds to industry capacity. As a result competition could become more intense. On the other hand, low growth industries with poor profits are unlikely to be threatened by a rush of new firms. Established firms are likely to leave such industries looking for more profitable pastures elsewhere.

The probability of new entrants to the industry is dependent on the height of barriers to entry. Industries protected by very high barriers face little threat of new entry. The following are examples of barriers to entry.

- **Absolute cost barriers**—these are advantages which established firms have over newcomers. In the world of five star hotels where location is of utmost importance, it would be difficult for a new entrant to find a sufficient number of prime sites to set up an extensive chain of hotels because many of these sites would be already occupied by established hotel chains. Similarly firms trying to enter the telecommunications, electricity generation, or rail industries could have problems because existing operators control the physical networks.

- Legal barriers—laws and regulations can constitute insurmountable barriers. Before the telecommunications and airline industries were liberalized, the legal and regulatory framework protected existing firms from new entry. In many countries, firms wishing to enter banking usually have to pass a series of legal tests to get permission to set up in business.

- Product differentiation—this can be a major barrier when firms manage to convince customers that their products are significantly different from those of their competitors. Some firms, especially in consumer goods industries like cars, food, soft drinks, and computer software, spend large amounts of money on advertising, sales promotion, and packaging to differentiate their products. IBM spent nearly US$500 million on advertising in the USA in 2009 but still ranked only 74 in the top 100 advertisers (http://adage.com). Spending on advertising is increasing very fast in countries like China. In 2009, it reached US$74 billion with firms in cosmetics, food and beverages, and pharmaceuticals being particularly active advertisers (*China Daily*, 30 January 2010). Promotional expenditure in the pharmaceutical industry is one of its main areas of cost—GlaxoSmithKline spends nearly US$2 billion alone a year on advertising (http://adage.com). Some pharma companies spend more on promotion than they do on R&D. Massive promotional expenditures can build up brand loyalty and recognition to such an extent that the brands become very valuable. As can be seen in Table 3.5, it is estimated that the Coca Cola, IBM, and Microsoft brands are each worth more than US$50 billion. Product differentiation can therefore be a significant deterrent to new firms entering an industry.

- Economies of scale—these occur when an increase in the scale of organization say from a small factory to a large factory leads to a fall in unit costs. In some industries, such as cars, firms need to operate on a large scale in order to compete with their rivals. If not, then they

Table 3.5 Rank and value of international brands 2010

1	Coca-Cola (US)	70,452 (US$m)
2	IBM (US)	64,727 (US$m)
3	Microsoft (US)	60,895 (US$m)
4	Google (US)	43,557 (US$m)
5	GE (US)	42,808 (US$m)
6	McDonald's (US)	33,578 (US$m)
7	Intel (US)	32,015 (US$m)
8	Nokia (Finland)	29,495 (US$m)
9	Disney (US)	28,731 (US$m)
10	Hewlett-Packard (US)	26,867 (US$m)

Source: Interbrand

will suffer a major competitive disadvantage and some may find it hard to survive. This appears to be happening in China. A local industry has emerged selling about 1.5 million cars a year. However, sales are divided up between some 130 companies, few of whom are anywhere near achieving the economies of scale needed to guarantee long-term survival (*Financial Times*, 9 October 2007; *Autocar*, 13 May 2010).

Other factors deterring entry to an industry are **excess capacity**, declining demand, the ability of established firms to freeze out new entrants by controlling supply of materials, and distribution through vertical integration or long-term contracts with suppliers and customers. The actual or anticipated reaction of established firms can also be an obstacle to entry especially where those companies are large and powerful. The EU found that French banks used discriminatory prices to block the entry of internet banks and supermarket chains who wished to issue credit cards (*Financial Times*, 18 October 2007).

Firms need to be ready to respond to new entrants. In the first decade of the new century, domestic banks in Singapore embarked on a frenzy of mergers when the authorities carried out further liberalization which was expected to lead to the entry of foreign competitors (*Asia Pacific Bulletin*, 17 August 2001). The Chinese car industry cut prices when China's membership of the WTO meant that the measures previously protecting them from foreign competition would have to be removed (*Asia Pacific Bulletin*, 25 January 2002). India's big retailers, like Reliance Industries, fearful that the Indian government would open up the market completely to foreign firms, expanded very rapidly in order to steal a march on rivals such as Wal-Mart and Tesco (*Time*, 15 May 2009).

Force 3 Substitutes

An industry may face competition from substitutes. In the Porter model, substitutes are goods or services produced by firms in an apparently different industry and delivering a similar service to the consumer but in a different way. In the airline industry, firms sell flights to transport customers from point A to B, say London to Paris. All firms selling flights, such as BA, Air France, Lufthansa, and easyJet would be seen as part of the same industry competing in the same market. But trains, ferries, coaches, and private cars could also be used by travellers to get to Paris. If the consumer sees the trains run by Eurostar as being an acceptable alternative to the services provided by airlines then it would seem sensible to include them in any analysis of an industry's competitive environment. The threat from substitutes will be influenced by the cost and ease with which customers can switch to the substitute product. For example, as oil prices rise, customers with central heating might consider switching to a cheaper form of energy. However, the costs, time, and inconvenience of changing the equipment could deter switching. In addition, switching may be deterred by firms using what is called confusion pricing. This occurs where the deals offered to customers are so complicated that it is virtually impossible to compare the value of one firm's offer against another. Examples can be seen in the competitive struggle in the telecommunications sector between mobile and fixed-line telephones. Customers are offered a bewildering variety of tariffs, services, and handsets with different technical capabilities making it difficult to judge which is the best deal for them (see Leek and Chansawatkit 2006).

One problem faced by the industry analyst is that often the information is not available to assess whether customers do see different goods or services as being good substitutes, in other words, whether there is a high cross elasticity of demand.

Mini Case **Pharmaceuticals and the Threat from Substitutes**

Substitutes (Force 3) can constitute a significant competitive threat. Big firms in the traditional pharmaceutical industry face

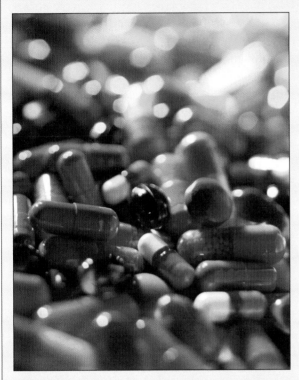

Source: Photodisc

an increasing challenge from fast-growing biopharmaceutical companies that are coming up with new treatments for diseases based on genetic science. Biotech firms use living cells to develop biotech drugs, a very different technology to that used by the traditional pharmaceutical industry. The biotech industry, while still relatively small, has become an increasingly important threat to the traditional pharmaceutical industry. Globally, sales of biotech health products reached US$133 billion in 2009 compared to a total pharmaceutical market turnover of US$837 billion. The pharmaceutical industry has recognized and responded to the growing threat. Roche, the Swiss pharmaceutical firm took over 454 Life Sciences, which makes gene-sequencing technology and NimbleGen, which makes technologies used in identifying the genetic causes of disease. Pfizer, the industry leader, bought up Wyeth which had set up what is claimed to be the biggest biotech plant in the world in Ireland. Merck acquired Schering Plough while AstraZeneca acquired the Cambridge Antibody Technology Group and Medimmune. Top pharmaceutical firms like Pfizer, GlaxoSmithKline, and Merck have also gone in for large numbers of alliances with biotech companies.

Source: *The Economist*, 28 June 2007; *Financial Times*, 12 January 2006; AstraZeneca, *Annual Report* 2006; www.pfizer.com; www.merck.com; Datamonitor, Global Biotechnology, May 2010; www.imshealth.com

Force 4 Customers

Firms sell their output to customers who could be other businesses or the final consumer. For companies like Intel, business customers will be the main purchasers of its computer chips. On the other hand, supermarkets sell to the final consumer. Some firms such as Microsoft sell both to other businesses and to the final consumer. The power relationships that firms have with their customers depend on a combination of factors:

- The number and size of firms: when an industry comprises a small number of large firms facing a large number of small customers then the industry will be in a powerful position. Losing a customer, in this situation, would not be very costly in terms of sales. This is the position of supermarket chains in Western Europe. They are large, few in number but have millions of customers. It is also the case for accountancy services in the Asia-Pacific region which includes Australia, China, Japan, India, Singapore, South Korea, and Taiwan. Four major players dominate the market: PricewaterhouseCoopers, KPMG,

Deloitte Touche Tohmatsu, and Ernst & Young (Datamonitor, Asia-Pacific—Accountancy, June 2010).

On the other hand, where many firms in an industry have a small number of large customers then the power switches to the buyer because loss of a single client could cause much damage to revenues and profits. Firms producing defence equipment, such as BAE in the UK or Mitsubishi and Kawasaki in Japan, are in this position. Usually their domestic governments are, by far, the biggest purchasers of arms and other defence equipment such as tanks, submarines, and aircraft carriers.

- The proportion of customer costs constituted by the product: when a product constitutes a large proportion of a business customers' total costs the more sensitive they will be to price because price increases will have a big impact on their costs and, if they are unable to pass this on, their profits. These buyers, when faced by a variety of sellers, can shop around and play suppliers off against each other in order to get the most favourable prices.

  Where customers are dealing with only a few suppliers then their bargaining power is reduced. This is the case in Europe for intensive energy users like steel makers whose energy bills are a large proportion of their total costs. As we have seen in the Mini Case above, the EU energy sector is highly concentrated indicating low bargaining power for buyers such as those in the steel industry.

- The extent of product differentiation: the less differentiated the product the easier it is for customers to switch to a cheaper supplier. Farmers supplying supermarket chains with meat, fruit, and vegetables will be in a much less powerful bargaining position than firms selling branded washing powders.

- The ability of customers to integrate vertically: sellers will be at a disadvantage where customers are big enough to produce their own supplies either by taking over their suppliers or by setting up new production facilities. Wal-Mart and other supermarket chains built giant warehouses to take over the distribution of supplies direct from the manufacturer thereby cutting out the wholesalers that previously carried out this task. Apple is also vertically integrated because it not only designs and markets Macs, iPhones, and iPads but also distributes them through its retail outlets. In contrast, buyers will have less power when they are unable to integrate vertically.

Force 5 Suppliers

Suppliers refer to businesses selling inputs such as fuel, raw materials, and components to the firms in the industry. The position of suppliers can be analysed in a similar way to those of buyers but in reverse. The only difference, as Grant (2005a) points out, is that it is now the firms in the industry that are the customers and the sellers of inputs that are the suppliers. To illustrate, if the supplier industry is dominated by a few large firms, compared to the buying industry, then the ability of suppliers to get away with price increases, reductions in quality, and a worsening of the terms and conditions of sale will be high. Firms producing computers have little bargaining power faced as they are by the world's dominant producer of microprocessors, Intel. Conversely, where the supply side is more fragmented than the buying side, then the advantage will lie in the hands of the customer. This was the case in the European dairy industry where suppliers of milk, cheese, and yoghurt were faced by a smaller number of big, powerful customers like Tesco, Aldi, and Leclerc. The dairy industry responded to this inequality by consolidating. For example, in the UK, Arla took over Express Dairies while Campina, the Dutch firm took over Germany's Sator (see www.FoodandDrinkEurope.com; www.FoodNavigator.com). (To see Porter discussing his Five Forces model and its application to the airline industry, visit the link on our **Online** @ **Resource Centre**.)

A Sixth Force: Complementary Products

The Porter model pays particular attention to the relationships between competitors' products and also the threat from substitute products. It does not deal with the complementary relationship that can exist between products. Complementary products are those that are used together by customers, in other words they do not compete with each other but operate in tandem. There are numerous examples of complementary products: mobile phones need service providers; DVDs need equipment to play them; computers need software; cars need petrol; and printers require ink cartridges. The suppliers of complementary products can play an important role in the competitive environment for firms in an industry, first because the firms making the products depend on the efforts of the other, for example, in relation to product development. Second, there can be conflict over who gets most of the spoils. Such a relationship is illustrated in the case of software vendors and the producers of PCs and PC components. Most PC manufacturers want new exciting software to be developed that requires customers to upgrade to new PCs, but software providers generally prefer to target the larger market of customers with their existing computers. The schizophrenic nature of complementarity can be seen in the case of Intel, the maker of computer chips, and Microsoft. According to Casadeus-Masanell *et al.* they are 'joined at the hip' (2007, p 584) because more than four fifths of the personal computers sold worldwide contain an Intel microprocessor running Microsoft's Windows operating system. The companies are dependent on each other because consumer demand and revenues depend on how well the different software and hardware components work together. This means that the R&D programmes for both players have got to complement each other. Casadeus-Masanell reports that the two companies have been in conflict over pricing, the timing of investments, and who captures the greatest share of the value of the product. An Intel manager puts it thus:

> Intel is always trying to innovate on hardware platform and thus, always needs software. When software lags, it creates a bottleneck for Intel. Microsoft, on the other hand, wants to serve the installed base of computers in addition to demand for new computers. Therefore, a natural conflict exists between both companies. In addition, the question always remains— Who will get the bigger piece of the pie? The success of one is seen as ultimately taking money away from the other (Casadeus-Masanell *et al.* p 584).

Grant (2005b) shows how Nintendo managed to keep the upper hand in its relationships with the suppliers of games software for its video games console. Nintendo used various methods of establishing a dominant position over developers of games. It maintained control of its operating system, avoided becoming over-dependent on any single supplier by issuing licences to many developers and established a firm hold over the manufacture and distribution of games cartridges.

Analysing an Industry using the Six Forces: A Checklist

- Are there many firms or only a few?
- Are firms a similar size?
- Is the market growing or declining?
- Is product differentiation important?
- How high are fixed costs as a % of total costs?
- Do additions to production capacity increase total industry capacity significantly?
- Are there any significant barriers to entry?
- Is there significant excess capacity in the industry?
- Do existing firms have the power to prevent entry?
- Is there any significant competition from substitutes?
- Is there a large number of small buyers/suppliers or a few large buyers/suppliers?
- Does the product constitute a large proportion of customer costs?
- Do input purchases constitute a large proportion of supplier revenues?
- Do customers/suppliers have the ability to take over firms in the industry?
- Are firms in the industry dependent on complementary products?

Counterpoint Box 3.3 Porter's 'Five Forces' model and its critics

Porter's Five Forces model has become part of the standard tool-kit for managers and industrial analysts. However, it has been criticized on several grounds. Firstly, some of its underlying assumptions have been questioned, for example, the idea that firms develop competitive advantage by strengthening their position vis-à-vis the five forces of rivalry, customers, suppliers, substitutes, and entry barriers.

Critics claim that economic conditions have changed dramatically since the appearance of the model in the 1980s when the business environment was much more certain, making it easier for firms to plan ahead. They cite three developments that have made the environment much more dynamic and uncertain for business: digitalization and, in particular, the development of the internet and e-business; globalization resulting in firms finding themselves increasingly in a global market where customers can shop around and compare prices and where rivals, buyers and suppliers may decide to move production to cheaper locations; and extensive deregulation which led to a reduction in government influence over industries such as airlines, utilities in the energy, telecoms, and finance sectors, and helped lead to major restructuring in these sectors. A further line of criticism holds that a firm can not be evaluated simply by reference to five forces in its external environment. These critics, supporting a Resource-Based View, argue that internal strengths and weaknesses of the firm also need to be taken into account.

Porter's supporters, while accepting the validity of some criticisms, argue that the idea that all firms operate in an environment characterized by rivals, buyers, suppliers, entry barriers, and substitutes remain valid. Some attempts have been made to extend the model. The inclusion of a sixth force, complementary products, has been proposed whilst others have suggested adding government (national and regional) and pressure groups as another force.

The message for managers is that, while the model remains a useful tool, enabling them to think about the current situation of their industry in a structured, easy-to-understand way, they need to be aware of its limitations when applying it.

Sources: Coyne and Sujit Balakrishnan (1996); Downes (1997); Brandenburger and Nalebuff (1996); Porter (2008)

● CHAPTER SUMMARY

In this chapter we set out to explain the concepts and tools that are indispensable to the industry analyst and to show how they can be used to analyse industries. We started off with the concepts of the industry and the market. It was shown that any satisfactory definition of the market needs to specify a set of products and its geographical boundaries. The next issue to be addressed was the various market structures and their implications for business behaviour and industry performance. It was shown that the more highly concentrated is the market, the more power is concentrated in the hands of a few firms able to manipulate prices, the quantity and quality of the good or service, and the terms and conditions of sale. This was followed by an explanation of the Porter Five Forces model and how this could be used to analyse industries. As part of the analysis of Porter's force of rivalry, it was demonstrated how firms sometimes make strenuous efforts to avoid price competition through the establishment of cartels and systems of price leadership. We also revealed the importance of product differentiation as a major element of competitive strategy and as a barrier to entry in certain industries. A sixth force, complementary products was added to the Porter model to make it an even more effective analytical tool.

● REVIEW QUESTIONS

1. A report on the global energy market grouping together oil, gas and coal shows that the vertically integrated MNCs, Shell, Exxon, and BP all had a similar market share of 4%–5%. However, a different report, looking at oil and gas refining and marketing gives Exxon around 10% of the market with the two others trailing. (Datamonitor, Global Energy, April 2010; Global Oil and Gas Refining, March 2010).

   Discuss which of these market definitions would be most useful to oil firms trying to analyse their competitive environment.

2. Geological maps of the world show that:

   - the greatest concentrations of metals and minerals reserves are not located in the same places as population;

   - most metal and mineral deposits are in countries with relatively low populations like Australia, Canada, South America, and Russia;

   - the most populous parts of the world, Asia, the Middle East, and Europe, have a relative deficit of resources. The USA, with its enormous market is deficient in metals, as is the fast-growing Chinese economy;

   - the rate of discovery of major reserves of minerals is in decline.

   What are the implications of this information for the competitive strategy of leading international mining groups such as Rio Tinto, Vale, the Brazilian miner, and Billiton?

3. The Datamonitor Report (June 2010) on Accountancy Services in the Asia-Pacific region showed that the market was dominated by four firms, PricewaterhouseCoopers, KPMG, Deloitte Touche Tohmatsu, and Ernst & Young. The report says that although these firms all provide similar services they have managed to differentiate themselves effectively. They serve thousands of business customers that are required by law to have their accounts externally audited.

   Explain Porter's forces of industry rivalry, competition from new entrants, and the power of buyers. Use these forces to help you analyse the accountancy services market.

4. Rexam, holds around one quarter of the global market for beverage cans. Its top ten customers, including Coca-Cola, Anheuser-Busch InBev, and Procter and Gamble account for 62% of Rexam sales (*The Times*, 29 July 2010). However, at just less than 3%, it has a tiny share of the total metal, glass and plastic packaging market (Datamonitor, Global Metal, Glass & Plastic Packaging, March 2010).

   Given the above information, analyse Rexam's position re buyer power and the threat from substitutes.

5. Online companies offering travel services, maps, weather forecasts, price comparison sites, and news complain that Google gives pride of place in its search results to its own services in these areas. With reference to the structure of the online search market, explain why companies such as Expedia and Mapquest are so incensed by this.

Case Study Global Advertising

This case study looks at the global advertising industry. It requires you to apply concepts, for example from the Porter Five Forces model, to the global advertising sector.

The advertising industry consists of agencies providing advertising, marketing, and corporate communications services. They advise clients on advertising and sales promotion strategies, create and produce advertising campaigns, and negotiate prices with the various media on behalf of their customers. Up to 2008 the market had been growing at about 5% per year. However, the global recession provoked a 10% downturn in the market. Zenithoptimedia expected world advertising expenditure to be around $444 billion in 2009. North America and Western Europe were the biggest markets with the fast growing Asia Pacific region third in the rankings.

The major customers for the agencies are the food, beverage, and personal/health care sectors followed by retailers. Car manufacturers, media and telecommunications firms are also important sources of advertising revenues. Advertising Age reported that, globally in 2008, Proctor and Gamble spent nearly €10 billion on advertising, GM around $4 billion while Disney spent almost $2 billion.

The global market is fragmented with the leading multinational firms together accounting for a small share of market value, just over 8%. The leading company, with a 2009 turnover of about US$14 billion, is the Dublin based WPP Group closely followed by the Omnicom Group Inc. with headquarters in the USA. The French and US firms, Publicis and Interpublic with turnover of about £6 billion lag far behind their two bigger rivals. The picture of fragmentation at global level does not reflect the situation nationally. The advertising market in most developed countries is concentrated, following years of consolidation through mergers and acquisitions, leaving the big four agencies with substantial aggregate market share. In the USA for example, the big four, WPP, Omnicom, Publicis and Interpublic, together hold nearly 60% of the market.

The Asia Pacific market is forecast to grow by 12% between 2010 and 2012. The big players in the industry all recognize the great potential of India and China. Omnicom sees those countries as the markets of the 21st century and, as a result, took over two marketing firms there while WPP sees India as the jewel in its crown.

Competition can be intense because the leading players offer similar services to their clients. However, they try to differentiate themselves by publicizing their prestigious client list, campaign records, and also by the range of services offered. Where successful, such attempts at differentiation discourage customers from switching agencies. However, historically strong growth in the global market takes the edge off competitive rivalry, and along with low barriers to entry, attracts new competitors.

According to Zenithoptimedia, newspapers, magazines, TV, and the internet are the major distribution channels in the global advertising market accounting for almost 75% of the market's value. Radio and cinema also play an important part. However, the dramatic growth in the number of media channels, for example television channels, and the increasing popularity of the internet, has worked to the benefit of advertising agencies. The result has been a fragmentation of audiences, making it more difficult to target the final consumer in a cost effective way. These trends reduce buyer power because they make clients increasingly dependent on advertising agencies to come up with innovative strategies for efficient ways of communicating with target markets. Fragmenting markets and the cost of ➡

➜ developing in-house advertising expertise, make it less likely that customers will integrate backwards, for example, by setting up their own advertising units. The capital costs of entering this market are low. However, potential new entrants could be deterred by the difficulty of recruiting the creative personnel on which agencies depend for their success. Furthermore, building up knowledge of client needs, expertise on the various media channels, and the variations in national regulations limiting advertising content and methods, costs time and money and could also constitute major barriers. Furthermore, the big agencies offer customers a comprehensive range of advertising and marketing services which newcomers might find difficult to match. Finally, leading agencies have got well-established brands and track records which clients might be reluctant to forgo in favour of untried newcomers to the market.

Sources: www.zenithopitmedia.com; Datamonitor, Global Advertising, October 2007, November 2009; *Adweek*, 19 June 2006, 22 Oct 2007; *Campaign*, 28 July 2006; www.omnicomgroup; www.wpp.com; www.interpublic.com

Questions

1. How concentrated is the global advertising industry? Does the global level of market concentration reflect the situation in national markets?

2. Industry rivalry can take various forms. Explain what these different forms are and indicate which you would you expect to be important in this industry.

3. Assess the bargaining power of buyers in the industry. How has this changed with the development of new communications technology?

4. With reference to the barriers to entry to this market, discuss the likelihood of new entry.

5. Why are India and China so attractive to the big advertising agencies? Why might merger and acquisition be an attractive way for big firms like Omnicom and Publicis to enter the Indian and Chinese markets?

For discussion of online advertising see the You Tube clip via our **Online Resource Centre**.

Source: www.istockphoto.com

Online Resource Centre
www.oxfordtextbooks.co.uk/orc/hamilton_webster2e/

Visit the supporting online resource centre for additional material which will help you with your assignments, essays, and research, or you may find these extra resources helpful when revising for exams.

● FURTHER READING

For further discussion of market definition and market power see:

● Weinstein, A. (2006) 'A Strategic Framework for Defining and Segmenting Markets'. *Journal of Strategic Marketing*, 14, June

● Fennell, G. and Allenby, G. M. (2004) 'An Integrated Approach'. *Marketing Research*, Winter 2004, Vol 16, Issue 4

● Pleatsikas, C. and Teece, D. (2001) 'The Analysis of Market Definition and Market Power in the Context of Rapid Innovation'. *International Journal of Industrial Organization*, Vol 19, Issue 5, April and Verouden, V. (2004) 'The Role of Market Shares and Market Concentration Indices in the European Commission's Guidelines on the Assessment of Horizontal Mergers under the EC Merger Regulation'. FTC and US DOJ Merger Enforcement Workshop, Washington, DC, 17–19 February

For discussion and application of Porter's Five Forces Model see:

● Miller, A. and Dess, G. G. (1993) 'Assessing Porter's (1980) Model in Terms of Generalizability, Accuracy, and Simplicity'. *Journal of Management Studies*, Vol 30, Issue 4, July

● Siaw, I. (2004) 'An Analysis of the Impact of the Internet on Competition in the Banking Industry, using Porter's Five Forces Model'. *International Journal of Management*, Vol 21, No 4, December

● Carle, G., Axhausen, K. W., Wokaun, A., and Keller, P. (2005) 'Opportunities and Risks during the Introduction of Fuel Cell Cars'. *Transport Reviews*, Vol 25, No 6, November

● REFERENCES

Beamish, P. W. and Lupton, N. C., Managing Joint Ventures, Academy of Management Perspectives, May 2009.

Brandenburger, A. M. and Nalebuff, B. J. (1996) *Co-Opetition*. London: Profile Books

Burgers, W. and Padgett, D. (2009) 'Understanding Environmental Risk for IJVs in China'. *Management International Review*, May 2009

Casadeus-Masanell, R. and Yoffie, D. B. (2007) 'Wintel: Cooperation and Conflict'. *Added Management Science*, Vol 53, Issue 4, April

Connor, J. M. (2002) *The Food and Agricultural Global Cartels of the 1990s: Overview and Update*. Purdue University Staff Paper #02-4, August

Coyne, K. P. and Sujit Balakrishnan (1996) 'Bringing Discipline to Strategy'. *The McKinsey Quarterly*, No 4

Downes, L., 'Beyond Porter', *Context Magazine*, Fall 1997

EU Commission (2005) Report on progress in creating the internal gas and electricity market. Communication from the Commission to the Council and the European Parliament, COM (2005) 568

EU Commission (2006) Corrigendum, Commission Communication on Progress in Creating the Internal Gas and Electricity Market, COM (2005) 568 and Technical Annex, SEC (2005) 1445, 12 January

EU Commission, Enterprise and Industry: Healthcare industries, 16 June 2010

Eurostat: Data in Focus, Environment and energy 12/2010

Fahy, J. (2007) *The Role of Resources in Global Competition*. London: Taylor and Francis

Galbraith, J. K. (1967) *The New Industrial State*, Woodstock: Princeton University Press.

Grant, R. (2005a) *Contemporary Strategy Analysis*, 5th edn. Oxford: Blackwell

Grant, R. (2005b) *Cases in Contemporary Strategy Analysis*. Oxford: Blackwell

Hamouda, H. M. (Undated) Agreement with Coca-Cola Ends the European Union's Five Year Inquiry into a Potential Abuse of a Dominant Position. Available at www.luc.edu

Leek, S. and Chansawatkit, S. (2006) 'Consumer Confusion: The Mobile Phone Market in Thailand'. *Journal of Consumer Behaviour*, Vol 5

Leibenstein, H. (1978) *General X-Efficiency Theory & Economic Development*. Oxford: Oxford University Press

Linden G., Kraemer K. L., and Dedrick, J. (2009) Who Captures Value in a Global Innovation Network? The Case of Apple's iPod, Communications of the ACM, March 2009, Vol 52, No 3

Manjoo F., 'Apple Nation'. *Fast Company*, Jul/Aug 2010, Issue 147

Pleatsikas, C. and Teece, D. (2000) 'The Competitive Assessment of Vertical Long-Term Contracts' presented at the Trade Practices Workshop, Business Law Section, Law Council of Australia, Queensland, 12 August

Pleatsikas, C. and Teece, D. (2001) 'The Analysis of Market Definition and Market Power in the Context of Rapid Innovation'. *International Journal of Industrial Organization*, Vol 19, Issue 5, April

Porter, M. E. (1979) 'How Competitive Forces Shape Strategy'. *Harvard Business Review*, March–April

Porter, M. E. (2008) 'The Five Competitive Forces that Shape Strategy'. *Harvard Business Review*, Vol 86, Issue 1, January

Schumpeter, J. (1976) *Capitalism, Socialism and Democracy*. London: Routledge

Teece, D. J. (1986) 'Profiting from Technological Innovation: Implications for Integration, Collaboration, Licensing, and Public Policy' *Research Policy*, Vol 15(6)

UNCTAD (2007 and 2010) World Investment Report

Verouden, V. (2004) 'The Role of Market Shares and Market Concentration Indices in the European Commission's Guidelines on the Assessment of Horizontal Mergers under the EC Merger Regulation'. FTC and US DOJ Merger Enforcement Workshop, Washington, DC, 17–19 February

Zhang, Y., Li, H., Hitt, M. A., and Cui, G. (2007) 'R&D Intensity and International Joint Venture Performance in an Emerging Market: Moderating Effects of Market Focus and Ownership Structure'. *Journal of International Business Studies*, 38

CHAPTER FOUR

The Global Business Environment

LEARNING OUTCOMES

This chapter will enable you to:

- **Explain the nature of the global business environment**

- **Understand and apply the PESTLE analytical framework**

- **Identify organizational stakeholders and construct a stakeholder map**

- **Analyse the impact on business of changes in the external environment**

Case Study **Telecommunications and India**

This case demonstrates the difficulties multinational companies face in dealing with the diverse political, legal, and regulatory environments.

In 2007, Vodafone, the UK based MNC, paid nearly US$11 billion for a 67% stake in Hutchison Essar, India's third largest mobile operator. Vodafone was delighted to get such a powerful foothold in the world's second largest and fastest growing telecoms market where prices, and profit margins of 35%, were high. However, within three years prices had fallen by more than 50% and revenues had collapsed. Vodafone was forced to write down the value of its investment in India by US$3.3 billion or more than one quarter. The company found itself in this position due to the intensity of competition in India. Vodafone was not alone in its suffering. All 15 telecoms operators in India, including the market leader, Bharti Airtel, were feeling the pain.

Government regulation was also an issue for telecoms operators. The Indian authorities were accused of implementing a series of policy switches that led to an influx of new entrants and a scarcity of spectrum—the precious airwaves on which mobile calls are transmitted. Bernstein Research, a US investment research company, commented that India was not a good choice for telecoms firms looking to exploit emerging markets: 'The country . . . is a competitive mess, and its regulation grows more capricious and nonsensical by the day' (*Financial Times*, 25 May 2010).

Inhospitable market conditions made foreign investors wary of pumping money into Indian telecoms. This wariness was compounded after the eruption of a major corruption scandal in 2010. In 2011, the telecommunications minister was arrested on allegations that he had been bribed to allocate 122 mobile phone frequency licences at discount rates to a select group of firms. Several of these firms had no experience in the telecoms sector. India ranks 87 out of 178 countries in the Transparency International Corruption Perceptions Index. Auditors estimated that the alleged mis-selling of the licences cost the Indian government nearly US$40bn in lost revenue. As a result of the scandal, foreign multinationals started to distance themselves from their local partners whose licences might get cancelled by the Indian Supreme Court. However, justice might take a long time for Datamonitor (2010) reports that the legal system is plagued by backlogs.

It was not meant to be this way. In 2011 there were almost 800m mobile subscribers and the market was adding 20m customers a month. Unlike China, India welcomes foreign ownership of mobile companies. The Indian authorities see telecoms as one of the country's primary drivers of development. Millions of urban poor and farmers, from Calcutta rickshaw pullers to Himalayan yak herders, now carry mobile phones. Mobiles enable them to do more business and gives them better access to services, such as health care. Every 10 percentage points increase in mobile penetration produces 0.81% economic growth, according to a 2009 World Bank study.

Sources: India Telecom News, 13 April 2011; *Financial Times*, 25 May 2010; bbc.co.uk, 15 November 2010 and 4 April 2011; Transparency International Corruption Perceptions Index 2010 Results; Datamonitor 2010, India: In-depth PESTLE Insights, December

Introduction

In this chapter we are going to examine the global **macroenvironment** and the tools which firms use to analyse it. By macroenvironment we mean the wider external (or general) environment rather than the microenvironment (sometimes referred to as the task environment) which was the subject of Chapter Three. In this chapter we will refer to the macroenvironment as the 'external environment'. The external environment is changing radically and becoming much less predictable due to:

- the accelerating rate of globalization;
- the information technology revolution;
- the increasing economic and political weight of countries such as China, India, and Russia;

- international institutions like the WTO and the EU becoming increasingly important influences on the global environment, as have **NGOs** with their vocal opposition to free trade and investment, and their success in getting environmental issues, such as climate change onto the political agenda of national governments and international agencies.

Firms face great difficulty in monitoring, analysing, and responding to an external environment subject to literally thousands of different forces, both domestic and international. The increasing pace of globalization in recent decades has made the task of monitoring the external environment much more complex and turbulent. Firms can find themselves operating in countries with very disparate histories, political and legal institutions and processes, economic, financial, socio-cultural environments, and physical and technological infrastructures. Firms have to be prepared to cope with various languages, different trading rules and currencies and volatile exchange rates. Given this complexity, organizations may find it difficult to identify forces that could have a critical impact as opposed to those that can be safely ignored. This ability to evaluate the external forces is vital because the environment creates opportunities for firms to achieve crucial objectives, such as profits and growth. However it can also pose dangers to firms that could result, ultimately, in their failing. At the global level the external environment can force organizations to alter policies on prices, modify products and adapt promotional policies. It may oblige them to restructure the organization, to change strategies regarding moves into new product or geographical markets and it can make them vulnerable to takeover. These can be seen as indirect costs for business when operating abroad.

The External Environment

The external environment of the firm comprises all the external influences that affect its decisions and performance. Such influences can vary from firm to firm and industry to industry and can change, sometimes very rapidly, over time. According to many observers, the environment for international business is changing faster than ever in two particular aspects, complexity and turbulence. Complexity relates to the increasing diversity of customers, rivals, suppliers, and of socio-cultural, political, legal, and technological elements confronting international business. Complexity is increased by the forces in the external environment continuously interacting with, and impacting on, each other. An increasingly complex external environment makes it more difficult for firms to make sense of, and to evaluate, information on changes in the environment and to anticipate their impact on the business. This, in turn, makes it more of a problem to formulate an appropriate response. The problems created by complexity are aggravated by the growing turbulence of the environment. A turbulent environment is one where there is rapid, unexpected change, in contrast to a stable environment where change is slow and predictable. Turbulence has increased with the rapid widening and deepening of the political, economic, socio-cultural, and technological interconnections brought about by globalization and facilitated by advances in telecommunications.

What was a fairly static environment may become turbulent and subject to violent change. In the 1990s, the relatively tranquil environment faced by EU airlines like BA, Air France, and Lufthansa was disturbed by the decision made by the EU to liberalize entry into the industry. New aggressive rivals in the form of the low cost airlines like Ryanair, easyJet and Air Berlin entered the industry competing away the established firms' market shares on short- and medium-haul flights. Business operating on a purely domestic basis is likely to confront a safer environment than its international counterparts. Some firms, like corner shops, face a relatively simple and certain environment whereas multinationals, like Nestlé, operating in almost 100 countries have to deal with one that is much more dynamic, complex and in some cases, dangerous and uncertain.

Growing complexity and turbulence in the environment makes it more difficult for firms to predict demand. It leads to competition becoming more disorderly, shortens the time available to make decisions, increases the risk of product obsolescence, and forces business to speed up the innovation process. Mason (2007) suggests that most managers have not been trained to cope with an environment of complexity, uncertainty, and turbulence and goes on to claim that such an environment is not conducive to traditional authoritarian, top-down, command and control styles of management.

Mini Case Complexity and Turbulence—China is Changing the World

This case shows how political and economic developments in China have affected, in expected and unexpected ways, the international business environment. After the decision by the Chinese Communist Party to move towards a more open economy, it has become the fastest growing economy, the world's second largest exporter of goods after Germany, the biggest exporter of capital, and the largest emitter of greenhouse gases.

China's entry into the world economy had a big impact on global prices. With its low unit costs of production feeding into low export prices, it helped to lower world prices of exports, putting manufacturers, particularly in the developed economies under great competitive pressure. On the other hand, its booming demand for commodities such as steel, copper, and oil has caused their prices to rise. Between 2003 and 2008 the world price of metals rose by 180% and energy by 170%—good news for mining companies, such as Billiton and Rio Tinto, but bad news for car manufacturers and transport companies who are big consumers of these commodities. It is forecast that, were Chinese oil consumption to continue to grow at the same rate, deposits of oil and natural gas would be rapidly exhausted and the implications for climate change would be catastrophic. Commodity prices eased somewhat during the recession of 2008–09 but The Economist's commodities index notched up an all-time high in early 2011 largely due to the strength of demand, especially from Asia. Demand for certain foods has also risen. Japan used to be the largest soya bean importer but its imports (3.6 million tonnes) are now dwarfed by China's (50 million tonnes). China's bargaining power puts Japan at a serious competitive disadvantage in the search for soya beans.

There are fears that China's development will provoke a political backlash from other countries. Continued growth in China's trade surplus could trigger protectionism by governments in North America and Europe which could have a serious impact on importers and retailers of Chinese goods. Western economies and the USA in particular are not happy at the huge trade surpluses of China and what they see as currency manipulation by the Chinese. In 2010 they have been trying to bring pressure on China to allow the renminbi to rise which would increase the price of Chinese exports. This may be eased by Chinese ambitions to make the renminbi a global reserve currency as in order for this to happen the renminbi must be allowed greater freedom to be traded internationally. Already some countries, for example Malaysia, are buying renminbi denominated bonds for their reserves. This would put pressure on the renminbi to rise against other currencies.

Political tensions are also rising with Chinese efforts to secure supplies of raw materials in Africa and South America. Chinese oil companies spent US$15 billion in deals in Argentina in 2010. They have also invested heavily in infrastructure projects such as the railways and in minerals and agricultural commodities such as soya beans.

Sources: Financial Times, 3 January, 23 January, and the supplement on Africa–China Trade on 24 January 2008, 5 November 2010, 13 December 2010; The Economist, 26 July 2007, 13 January 2011. The Financial Times published a series of articles in January 2011 entitled 'China Shapes the World'. There are also discussions on video available via the Online Resource Centre.

However, it would be unwise to see firms as simply being the subject of the macroenvironment. Business, especially big businesses like Microsoft, General Electric, ExxonMobil, and Deutsche Bank, can exercise influence over their macroenvironment. The US presidential election in 2000 shows how firms attempt to do this. Large oil companies in the USA, along with other energy interests, gave around US$50 million to the Republican Party in the run up to the presidential election. George W. Bush was elected with Dick Cheney as Vice President. Both Bush and Cheney had previously been involved in the oil industry. Cheney had been the CEO of Halliburton, the world's largest oil field services company (www.bbc.co.uk, 1 May 2001). On his election, the President abandoned the Kyoto Protocol on global warming and moved to allow oil drilling in the Arctic National Wildlife Refuge in Alaska. Just before the EU was about to slap a €300 million fine on Microsoft for abusing its dominant position in computer operating systems, US diplomats lobbied the EU to take a softer line (*EU Observer*, 27 September 2006).

Opportunities and Threats

Globalization, associated with the increased cross-border movement of goods, services, capital, and people, is creating a more closely interdependent world characterized by growing networks and has been a major influence in shaping the external environment of business. The widening and deepening of globalization means that local environments are not solely shaped by domestic events. Equally, increased interdependence causes local, regional, or national events, such as the 2007 credit crunch which originated in the USA, swine flu with its origins in Latin America, and bird flu with its origins in South East Asia to become global problems. Increasing interconnectedness means that threats and opportunities are magnified, especially for organizations operating internationally.

Opportunities

Globalization generates opportunities for business to enter new markets, take advantage of differences in the costs and quality of labour and other resources, gain economies of scale, and get access to raw materials. Over the last decade China and India have opened up their economies to foreign trade and investment. Foreign companies including Tesco, Heineken, Disney, General Motors, and Toyota have taken advantage of the opportunity to invest in China and India.

Many firms have responded to the new environment by globalizing production and reorganizing their supply chains to take advantage of low cost labour, cheap international transport, and less regulated operating environments. Wal-Mart, the largest retailer in the world has located its global procurement headquarters in China and purchases many of its supplies of toys, clothes, and electronic goods there. In 2006, Wal-Mart purchased US$18 billion worth of commodities from China (www.chinatoday.com). Other large retail multinationals like Carrefour and Auchan of France, Metro in Germany, Makro of the Netherlands, UK-based B&Q, IKEA of Sweden, and the US firm Home Depot also source extensively from China (Coe *et al.* 2007). Boeing is another example, with the three million parts in a 777 being provided by more than 900 suppliers from 17 countries around the world (*Guardian*, 18 January 2008). An implication of this trend is that the fates of these companies, and their customers, become intertwined with their foreign suppliers and subject to the external environments in which they operate.

Threats

Globalization is also accompanied by threats which can have devastating effects on business, causing long-term damage or even leading to the collapse of the business. In the past, threats for international firms tended to be seen as country-specific, arising from:

- financial risks, for example, currency crises, **inflation**;

- political risks associated with events such as expropriation of assets by foreign governments or unwelcome regulations; and

- natural disasters such as earthquakes and tsunamis.

For example, the 1999 earthquake in Taiwan cut the supply of computer chips to HP, Dell, and Compaq, and the Chinese earthquake in 2008 forced Toyota to halt production there. In 2011 the Japanese earthquake restricted the flow of many components to industry around the world. But now there is an additional set of threats—these include terrorism, hacker attacks on computer networks, and global diseases such as Aids and bird flu.

Terrorists are more likely to attack business than other targets, particularly US business. Two-thirds of terrorist attacks are against US businesses in the Middle East, South America, and Asia (*Financial Times*, 25 April 2006; Enderwick 2006). Czinkota *et al.* (2010) identifies the main threats to business from terrorism as; interruptions in international supply chains resulting in shortages or delays in critical inputs; government policies to deal with terrorism that alter the business environment and the ease with which global commerce takes place, for example at ports and airports; and declines in inflows of FDI caused by high rates of global terrorism as observed in Greece, Spain, Israel, and Latin America.

As firms become more international they become more vulnerable to threats. For example, with the move towards global sourcing, supply chains can become stretched as they straddle multiple borders and involve more parties (see Braithwaite 2003, for a discussion of global sourcing and its risks). This leaves the supply chain more liable to disruption.

The growth in world trade in goods has resulted, according to the World Bank (www.data.worldbank.org) in around 474 million container trips each year. The 9/11 terrorist attacks led the USA, along with other governments, to tighten up on security at ports. This resulted in a more rigorous inspection of cargoes, which led to increased delivery times. As a result, costs rose for firms who, often facing fiercer competition as a result of globalization, were trying to reduce delivery times and minimize stockholding through the introduction of just-in-time. It also raised costs for shipping firms as it increased the time taken to turn round their vessels.

Another effect of 9/11 was to make it more difficult, and sometimes even impossible, to get insurance cover. Enderwick (2006) reports that Delta Airlines' insurance premium against terrorism in 2002 rose from US$2 million to US$152 million after the attack. In a survey it was found that more than 60% of businesses bought insurance cover against terrorism. (You can view The Marsh Report, Terrorism Risk Insurance 2010 through the link on our **Online Resource Centre**.) Increased international sourcing of supplies means that firms need to pay particular attention to the maintenance of quality standards. In 2007, the giant US toy firms Mattell and Hasbro had to recall millions of toys made for them in China because of hazards, such as the use of lead and small magnets that could be swallowed by children (*Financial Times*, 30 August, 10 September 2007).

Threats for some firms and industries can be opportunities for others. In 2005, the US states of Florida and Louisiana, along with the Gulf of Mexico were devastated by several hurricanes—the city of New Orleans had to be evacuated. Oil firms, operating in the Gulf, suffered extreme losses as a result of extensive damage to oil rigs and onshore pipelines and refineries. The supply of oil was adversely affected, and prices rose hitting big consumers of oil such as shipping and airline companies. On the other hand, some firms benefited. With power lines down, and many houses destroyed, producers of portable power generators experienced a surge in demand, as did producers of mobile homes. And in 2006, Shell, which had only suffered limited hurricane damage, announced its largest profits ever.

Financial risks have become increasingly important because, over the last 40 years, there have been increasing levels of volatility in financial markets. Unexpected movements in exchange rates, interest rates, and commodity and equity prices are major sources of risk for most MNCs. Surveys show that many large MNCs see the management of foreign exchange risks to be as important as the management of other risks.

Mini Case Global Threats—Cybercrime

Increasing global interconnectedness has been accompanied by the development of new threats which can have a devastating impact on business. Advances in communications technology have made it easier to commit crimes using computers and the internet. This fast-growing threat is called cybercrime. It is attractive because it can be done at a distance and with anonymity. It includes identity theft where personal information, for example, from customers is stolen. Users are lured to fake websites where they are asked to enter personal information such as usernames and passwords, phone numbers, addresses, credit card numbers, and bank account numbers. The information can be used to drain bank accounts or to buy goods and services using fraudulently obtained credit card details. It also includes hacking into computers to get access to confidential business information, and the creation and distribution of viruses and worms on business computers. Companies may find themselves being blackmailed by cybercriminals threatening to use the information they have stolen to attack their systems. An example of this was seen when Russian gangsters tried to blackmail gaming companies with threats to attack their online operations.

It is estimated that, in Britain alone, six million people illegally download films and music every year costing film and music companies billions of pounds in lost revenues.

Although cybercrime tends to be under-reported the Association of Chief Police Officers in the UK claim that online fraud generated US$52 billion worldwide in 2007.

As Web technology develops and companies increasingly open their networks to involve communities of customers and suppliers as well as employees so the opportunity for abuse of the systems increases.

Pandalabs (security specialists) issued their annual report in January 2011 labelling 2010 as the year of cybercrime, cyber war and cyber activism. They reported that in that one year cybercriminals created 34% of all the malware that ever existed. Trojans dominated (56%) followed by viruses and worms. One of those worms was the Stuxnet worm. This worm targeted industrial systems such as power stations, water plants, and industrial units. It seems to have been aimed at disrupting Iran's nuclear programme although it wasn't the only country attacked. Experts seem to be agreed that only a state could have engineered something as complex as this worm.

The other new phenomenon was cyber protests or 'hacktivism' most famous of which was the attack by 'anonymous' in defence of wikileaks. (see Counterpoint Box 9.2 in Chapter Nine)

Sources: *Financial Times*, 9 November 2005; *The Independent*, 17 September 2007; *The Timesonline*, 18 March 2005 and 12 February 2008; www.techterms.com. For an update on the incidence of cybercrime go to Symantec's Risk Management report at www. symantec.com and to Pandalabs annual report at http://press. pandasecurity.com/press-room/reports/; ACPO (2008) *National Strategic Assessment*

There are various overlapping risks associated with exchange rate movements that need to be managed. Contractual risk occurs when firms enter into contracts where the revenues or outgoings take place in a foreign currency. A Eurozone firm may agree to buy a good from a US supplier and pay in dollars, or may accept dollars in payment from US customers. If the dollar falls against the euro then purchasers in the Eurozone benefit because they need to exchange fewer euros to buy the goods. On the other hand, French champagne producers, selling to the USA, will lose out because the dollars they receive will buy fewer euros.

The next risk arises when firms earn money abroad and have to translate that into their domestic currency for the purposes of the reports and accounts. Movements in the exchange rate could have a major impact on the profit and loss account and on the balance sheet value of assets held abroad. Acer, the large Taiwanese IT firm, reported a loss of US$45 million on foreign currency exchange and other financial instruments in the first nine months of 2010. An article on this topic can be located on the supporting **Online Resource Centre.**

Fluctuations in exchange rates make it difficult to evaluate company performance. Some companies get round this by stripping out the effects of movements in rates by translating the current year's turnover and operating profit using the previous year's exchange rate, or stating the sales and profits in the appropriate foreign currencies or, like Unilever, stating how much sales or profits were reduced or increased as a result of exchange rate changes.

Scanning the Environment

Big international firms spend time and resources regularly **scanning** their environment in order to identify forces that will have a major influence on them. In particular, they will be looking out for changes in the environment that could have an impact on their operations in terms of helping or hindering them achieving their objectives. These objectives for industrial and commercial firms usually include profits and growth, and they may also set themselves targets with regard to market share or becoming the leading brand. Thus, firms will be particularly sensitive to aspects of the external environment that will affect their ability to achieve their objectives.

This scanning of the external environment is part of what is known as '**strategy**', that is the process by which firms arrive at decisions about the direction the firm should take. Essential parts of that process are understanding the goals of the organization and analysing the resources and capabilities of the firm and the external environment. Indeed strategy is the link between these elements.

Figure 4.1 Strategy

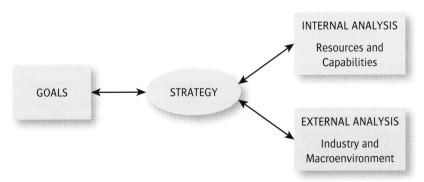

Thinking about strategic management has gone through several phases. In the fifties and sixties when the external environment was much more stable the emphasis was on planning with detailed operational plans being set typically for five years ahead. Instability in the macro-environment in the seventies made forecasting difficult and so the emphasis changed from planning to positioning the firm in the market to maximize the potential for profit using techniques such as Porter's Five Forces (see Chapter Three). This became known as the **industry based view** (IBV) emphasizing that a firm's performance was determined by the macro- and microenvironment. In the nineties the emphasis shifted again from external analysis to internal analysis of resources and capabilities in order to identify what was different about the firm and to look at ways of exploiting those differences—the **resource based view** (RBV). In the first decade of this century change, as noted in the opening section to this chapter, is much less predictable and so there is now increasing emphasis on flexibility and creating short term rather than sustained competitive advantage often in alliances with other organizations. (see Grant, R. (2010) *Contemporary Strategy Analysis*, 7th edn. Chapter 1). It could be argued then that knowledge of the external environment and identification of the main drivers of change for the organization is more important than ever. Indeed strategy must start from an understanding of the major trends in society, where your markets are going to be, who your suppliers will be and where, what new technology is on the horizon and how it will affect products and processes and the way you organize your business.

There has also been a questioning of the role of business in society in the wake of corporate scandals such as Enron and the impact of business on the natural environment which strategists must consider. This questions whether business exists simply to make profits for owners (or increased shareholder value) or if there should be some wider purpose in serving society. At the heart of this debate is the notion of **stakeholders**. According to Freeman (1984) a stakeholder is any individual, group, or organization that is affected by or can affect the activities of a business. They therefore have an interest in the decisions of the business and equally, it is argued, the determination of strategy should take into account the actions and wishes of stakeholders. This would be true whatever the motivations of the firm but for those who argue that firms should have an obligation to society other than their economic role in maximizing shareholder value then the recognition of who and what is affected is fundamental to the realization of that obligation (see Chapter Eleven for a much fuller discussion of the debates around corporate social responsibility and Chapter Twelve for an analysis of the relationship between business and ecology). Stakeholder analysis, or mapping, aims to identify a firm's stakeholders likely to be affected by the activities and outcomes of a firm's decisions and to assess how those stakeholders are likely to be affected.

Post, Preston and Sachs (2002) embracing the concept of the stakeholder put forward a new strategic approach to managing what they called the 'Extended Enterprise' (Figure 4.2). They stressed the role of recognizing stakeholder relationships in managing wealth creation in today's complex 'extended enterprise'. This approach recognized the futility of the controversy between those who preached the RBV rather than the IBV approach to strategy and that both of those approaches ignored the social-political environment. This approach, it is claimed, integrates all three aspects. It recognizes that a network of relationships exists that is not just a matter of contracts but which also needs to be managed through building relationships and that these relationships exist not just between the organization and its stakeholders but also between stakeholders. For this they put forward a new definition of stakeholders as:

Figure 4.2 The stakeholder view of the corporation

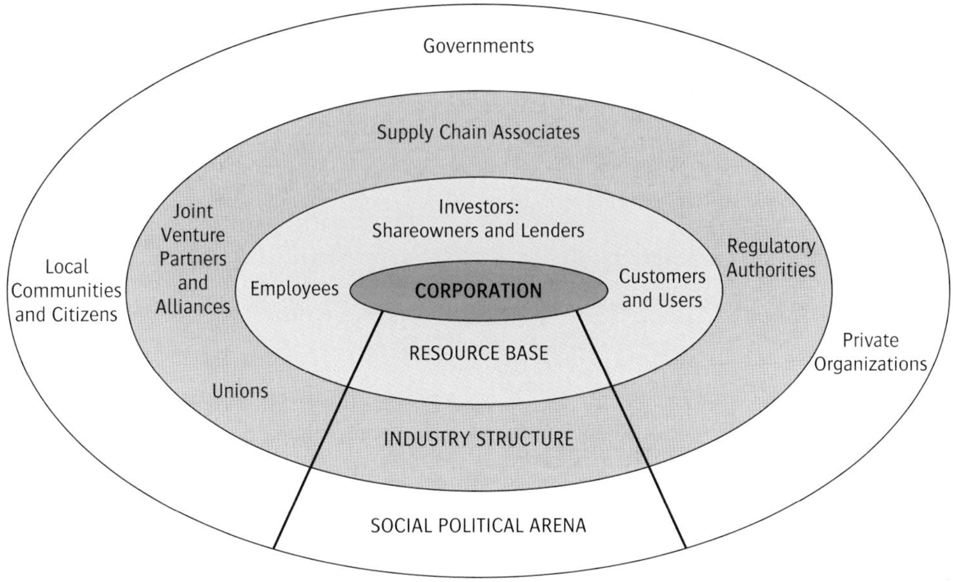

Source: James E Post, Lee E Preston, Sybille Sachs (2002)

individuals and constituencies that contribute, either voluntarily or involuntarily, to its wealth-creating capacity and activities, and who are therefore its potential beneficiaries and/or risk bearers.

Stakeholders for each firm will differ but Post *et al.* put forward typical groups within each of the three dimensions as demonstrated in Figure 4.2.

This idea of the extended enterprise along with the industry structure (see Chapter Three) provides a useful framework for assessing the impact of changes in the external macroenvironment on the structure of the industry and ultimately on the stakeholders of the organization. This approach could also be used for assessing the impact of particular courses of action or future scenarios (see below).

1. Identify the macroenvironmental issues.

2. Assess the urgency and likely occurrence of the issues.

3. Analyse the impact on the structure of the industry.

4. Identify the relevant stakeholders.

5. Assess which are the most important by assessing their impact on the organization.

6. Assess the impact of the issue on each of the stakeholders.

One method of classifying the importance of stakeholders is to map them on to a 2 × 2 matrix according to their power and their interest. Those with the highest level of power and interest are the key stakeholders and need most attention. Others will need to be kept satisfied or informed.

Figure 4.3 Stakeholder mapping

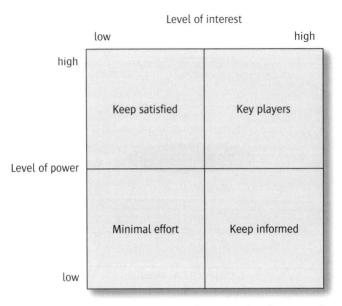

Source: Adapted from A. Mendelow, proceedings of the Second International Conference on Information Systems, Cambridge, MA, 1991 cited in Johnson, G., Scholes, K., and Whittington, R. (2009) *Fundamentals of Strategy*, Pearson Education Ltd

Learning Task

Access the BBC News site at www.bbc.co.uk/news/special_reports/oil_disaster and any other sources available including the opening case to undertake the following:

1. Identify the stakeholders of BP's operations in the Gulf, classifying them into the various categories of the extended enterprise.

2. Construct a stakeholder map such as that above.

3. Assess the impact of the disaster on each of these stakeholders.

Of course the situation regarding stakeholders is not a static one and stakeholder positions change according to the situation. Firms involved in stakeholder engagement keep up a constant dialogue with their stakeholders. Royal Dutch Shell, for example, has incorporated responsibil-ities to its stakeholders into its Business Principles. Visit the **Online Resource Centre** for a link to Principle 7 Communication and Engagement on this topic.

Following embarrassing experiences in the 1990s over the proposed disposal of the Brent Spar Oil storage terminal by sinking it in the sea and its relationships with the Nigerian gov-ernment and local communities in Nigeria Shell now make it a requirement that any new project has a stakeholder engagement plan. Since 2007 Shell has been discussing the decom-missioning of the Brent Oil and Gas Field and has held a series of meetings with over 140 invited

stakeholders and also published a series of e-newsletters (see www.shell.co.uk/home/content/
gbr/aboutshell/shell_businesses/e_and_p/decommissioning/brent_field_decomm_studies/
stakeholder_dialogue).

Shell and other organizations make full use of the social media in keeping in touch with their
stakeholders by developing surveys, websites, chat rooms, emails, e-newsletters, bulletin boards,
blogs, and podcasts.

This **impact analysis**, when done early enough, allows firms the time to consider a range of
responses to exploit the opportunities and defuse the threats. This helps organizations recognize and adapt policies and strategies to their changing regional, national, and global environments. Because of increasing volatility and turbulence in the external environment, firms have
got to expect/prepare for the unexpected. Kotler and Caslione (2009) claim that turbulence, with
its consequent chaos, risk, and uncertainty, is now the 'new normality' for industries, markets,
and companies. Globalization together with communications technology mean the world is
now, as we noted in Chapter One, more interdependent than ever so that change in one country
can soon lead to change in many others. According to Kotler and Caslione (2009, ch 1), the factors
that can cause chaos are:

- The **information revolution** and especially cloud technology which allows instant and
  flexible access to sophisticated software and data storage. Specially useful for new firms.

- Disruptive technologies and innovations which quickly render 'old' technologies/
  products redundant.

- The 'rise of the rest'—a rebalancing of economic power around the world, for example
  China and India.

- Hyper-competition—a situation in which competitive advantage is short lived.

- Sovereign wealth funds—trillions of US$ owned by states such as China, Singapore, Adu
  Dhabi and Kuwait and available for overseas investment purposes, increasing the role
  of some states in other economies.

- The environment—and especially the need to preserve scarce resources and deal with the
  effects of climate change.

- Consumer and stakeholder empowerment gained through the information revolution.

They state that 'even more unsettling is the harsh recognition that whenever chaos arrives, you'll
have little more than a fig leaf to hide behind—unless you can anticipate it and react fast enough
to lead your company, your business unit, your region, or your department through it safely'
(p 11).

Much of the above accords with McKinsey's assessment of the key trends in global forces.
They identify five forces which they label as follows:

- The 'great rebalancing' which, as we have noted above, refers to the likelihood that most
  growth will come from emerging markets which they say will create a wave of new middle
  class consumers and new innovations in product design, market infrastructure, and value
  chains.

- The productivity imperative—to continue to grow developed economies will need to
  generate pronounced gains in productivity.

- The global grid in which the global economy is ever more connected through vast complex networks. Information barriers break down as the walls between private and public information become blurred and economic volatility becomes more likely. The world more than ever before is becoming a single market place.
- Pricing the planet, rising from the tension between increasing demand for resources and sustainability. This will put pressure on using resources more efficiently, cleanly, and in dealing with new regulations.
- The market state in which the role of the state increases rather than withers in protecting individuals from the effect of globalization, intervening to stabilize economies (as in the recent financial crisis) and in bilateral agreements as multilateral agreements become more difficult as more economies demand their say at places such as the WTO and IMF. (Visit the **Online Resource Centre** for a useful link related to this topic.)

Given that forecasting and prediction become ever more unreliable in turbulent and chaotic times one way of anticipating or being prepared for change is through what is known as scenario planning. Scenario planning is an approach to thinking about the future which looks at stories which relate different possible futures so that strategic responses can be considered and managers be better prepared to deal with the issues. Shell has been developing scenarios since the 1970s initially on a three-year cycle but now, indicative of the pace of change, annually. They have developed a tool called Global Scenario which is used to explore various scenarios relating to the legal environment, the role and importance of the market and the state, non-governmental organizations in society, forces bringing about global integration, and the factors leading to fragmentation and economic growth. It is also interested in the impact of the growing concerns about environmental issues, such as global warming, on the demand for fossil fuels such as coal, oil, and gas and consequently produces separate energy scenarios.

For more information on these scenarios and how Shell approaches scenario building see the link on our **Online Resource Centre**.

Another organization busy developing scenarios is the National Intelligence Council of the USA which issued a report in 2008 looking at global trends to 2025. A link to this report can be found on the **Online Resource Centre**.

The Macroenvironment

Macroenvironmental forces comprise the wider influences on the business environment and together with the microenvironment complete the external environment (see Figure 4.4). For the purpose of analysis the macroenvironment can be classified under the headings of political and legal, economic and financial, socio-cultural, technological, and ecological. Each of these can be examined as independent elements but often changes in one area of the external environment can have an impact on others. For example, a government may take a policy decision to carry out a big expansion of public spending on infrastructure. This could influence the economic environment by increasing the total demand for goods and services in the economy and boost the rate of economic growth. If the economy is close to operating at full capacity then it could also lead to an increase in inflation and/or suck in more imports or divert exports to the domestic

Figure 4.4 The external environment

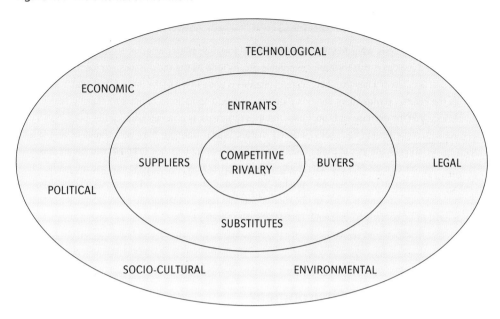

market. The balance of payments could suffer, which could result in a fall in the exchange rate. Another instance of the interconnection between the various elements in the external environment occurred when the Chinese and Indian authorities made a decision to open up their economies to foreign trade and investment. These decisions changed the political environment and helped transform the economic environment as their rates of economic growth soared. This, in turn, had an impact on the microenvironment of business because rapid growth of income and demand for goods and services in China and India made them very attractive markets for foreign firms. On the other hand, the microenvironment can lead to changes in the macroenvironment—the credit crunch of 2007/08 is likely to lead to tighter government regulation of financial services. What is important for the individual firm of course is not just to identify the relevant external factors but to analyse what the implications are of any change for their industry environment and their stakeholders.

Constant monitoring of all external issues might seem desirable but it would not only be very time consuming but also very expensive. It would probably also result in a mass of information much of which might not be very useful. It is usually sufficient to identify the key drivers of change for an organization and monitor those. We are going to examine each element of the macroenvironment in turn, looking in particular at their potential impacts on business. For this we use PESTLE as an analytical framework. PESTLE is an acronym for the Political, Economic/financial, Social, Technological, Legal, and Ecological factors which fashion the environment within which business operates. It is often used to identify opportunities (O) and threats (T) which can be combined with an analysis of a firm's strengths (S) and weaknesses (W), to produce a SWOT analysis. The second part of this book deals with each section of the PESTLE in much more detail.

Counterpoint Box 4.1 What's wrong with PESTLE?

It is common to refer to this kind of analysis as a PESTLE analysis but the great danger of this terminology is that the purpose of the analysis is forgotten, that is to identify key external drivers and their implications for the industry environment and the organization's stakeholders. Too often the exercise ends up with a long list of external issues with something in each section of the PESTLE but with no appreciation or analysis of their implications. Moreover it is often difficult to classify some as say, political, social, legal, or economic. A rise in taxes could be classified in any one of those four categories. The truth is that it doesn't matter. There does not need to be something in each section and it does not matter whether issues are political or economic etc. as long as the main issues are identified and a careful analysis is undertaken of the impact then that is all that is required. It is also sometimes difficult to classify issues as opportunities or threats as often an issue can be both. Again it doesn't matter. Global warming may be a threat in that it is likely to increase energy bills but it could also be an opportunity in the search for new products and new and more efficient production methods. The same could be said about the classification of internal issues as strengths or weaknesses but that is not the subject of this book.

Political and Legal Environment

The political and legal environment is made up of the various political and legal systems under which business operates. We treat these together here because political institutions, such as governments and parliaments, pass laws and establish regulations which shape the legal environment within which business operates. The courts, the police, and prisons ensure that the laws are enforced and lawbreakers are punished. Political regimes range from the liberal democratic systems of North America and Europe, to the Communist regimes of China and Vietnam, to military dictatorship in Burma (Chapter Eight deals with this in more depth).

Some industries, like oil, need to pay particular attention to their political environment because they operate in a very politically sensitive sector, energy. Politicians and civil servants need to be kept on-side because they are the people who decide whether oil companies are given the opportunity to search for, and exploit, oil reserves. Like other areas of the external environment, the political environment can turn nasty. Countries such as Russia, Venezuela, and Bolivia have been taking back control of their energy reserves from the oil majors. BP is a company with many reasons to nurture relationships with political institutions, and the people within them—it was nationalized in Iran, Iraq, and Nigeria, fined millions of dollars for illegally fixing propane prices in the USA, and for oil spills in Alaska and is once again facing heavy fines and possibly criminal charges in the USA.

Business also often looks to its domestic government to protect it from threats abroad (see next Learning Task). Governments in powerful countries such as the USA can exercise their influence over other countries to provide protection for home-based firms. This is particularly reassuring for MNCs given that the majority of the largest multinationals are based in the USA. However, commentators such as Haass (2008) see the USA losing position as the dominant world power. After the collapse of the Soviet Union, the USA was the dominant economic, political, and military power in the world. But in the 21st century, US dominance is being challenged economically and politically by countries such as China whose share of the world economy is growing rapidly (for conflicting views of change in the global balance of power see

Learning Task

Examine the table below which shows the average level of tariff protection afforded by the authorities in Lesser Developed Countries (LDCs) and Developed Economies.

1. Compare and contrast the level of protection given by governments to their domestic producers in developing/emerging economies and developed/rich economies.

2. Discuss the protection given to farmers by:

   a) Developing countries. Advance reasons for this.

   b) Japan heavily protects its rice farmers. Why should that be the case?

3. A more detailed breakdown of tariff protection shows that Vietnam provides a very high level of protection to its processed food sector. What are the implications of that level of protection for domestic producers of processed food products in Vietnam and for foreign food processors wishing to enter the Vietnamese market?

Table 4.1 Average tariffs on imports 2009

	Average Tariffs on Imports 2009		
	Total	Agriculture	Non-Agriculture
China	9.6	15.6	8.7
Colombia	12.5	16.8	11.8
Japan	4.9	21	2.5
Nigeria	11.2	15.5	10.5
USA	3.5	4.7	3.3
Vietnam	10.9	18.9	9.7

Source: WTO
http://stat.wto.org/TariffProfile/WSDBTariffPFHome.aspx?Language=E

Wallerstein (2007) and Wohlforth (2007)). Going along with this line of reasoning would suggest that the USA will not be able to offer the same degree of protection to its international companies.

Firms also have to take account of the increasing importance in the political and legal environment of international institutions like the World Trade Organization (WTO), the EU, and the substantial number of regional trading blocs that have been established, and bodies such as the International Accounting Standards Board that has the task of setting international accounting standards. Countries get together in the WTO to agree the rules and regulations around international trade and investment. The WTO then acts to ensure respect for the rules. In 2008, a WTO panel ruled, in a case brought by the USA, the EU, and Canada, that China had broken the rules by using tax policy to restrict imports of car parts. Saner and Guilherme (2007) point out that the common approach used by the International Monetary Fund and the World Bank towards developing countries included:

- reducing budget deficits by raising taxes and cutting public expenditure;
- giving up control of interest rates;
- reducing barriers to trade and foreign direct investment;
- setting a stable and competitive exchange rate; and
- privatizing public enterprise.

All of these could have significant effects for domestic and foreign firms on the intensity of competition, market shares, prices, costs, and profits.

Mini case Political Turbulence and the Cocoa Industry

According to *The Independent* (8 November 2010) chocolate is heading for £7 per bar. As farmers who produce the raw cocoa beans destined for the multinational chocolate companies see only 2p for each £1 of retail sales they are turning to other crops such as rubber or palm oil, which is used for biofuels, or heading for the cities where they can make more money. Crop disease and soil exhaustion are other problems besetting the industry. The world's third largest producer is Indonesia where changed weather systems have also had an effect. So production is falling at the same time as demand is rising to new highs as millions of new consumers in emerging economies get the taste for chocolate.

The world's largest producer is the Ivory Coast which has seen a decade of political turmoil. An election was held in October 2000 in which Laurent Gbagbo was elected President but a civil war followed in 2002/03. In January 2003 Gbagbo and rebel leaders signed an accord creating a 'government of national unity' but effectively the country was split into two with the rebels running the North and Gbagbo the South. The UN has since had a peacekeeping force in the country but there has been continuing violence. Elections supposed to be held in 2005 were eventually held in November 2010 with Alasanne Outtara (who draws most of his support from the North) announced victor but Gbagbo refused to accept this claiming

widespread vote rigging in the North. Gbagbo controls the army and the constitutional court which swore him back into power. As a result traders fearing further violence and disruption to supplies pushed cocoa prices on the New York and London exchanges up by 10% despite forecasts of a huge crop. (For more on the Ivory Coast see the Trafigura case at the end of Chapter Nine.)

Sources: *Independent*, 8 November 2010; *Financial Times*, 1, November 2010, 3 /10 December 2010

Source: www.istockphoto.com

Economic and Financial Environment

The economic and financial environment comprises forces that affect large areas of the economy like the rate of economic growth, interest rates, exchange rates, and inflation and the policies of domestic and international institutions that influence these economic variables. The rate of economic growth is important for business because it indicates the speed at which the total level of demand for goods and services is changing. In fast-growing economies income and purchasing power is increasing rapidly, leading to an expansion in demand. By contrast, slow growth means that markets are not expanding so quickly and are therefore not so attractive for business. Institutions like the IMF produce information on the world economy and its component parts. Its figures show that advanced economies have been growing relatively slowly whilst developing countries are expanding at a more rapid rate—Chinese growth, for example, topped 14% in 2007, 9.6% in 2008, and in 2009, when most developed economies GDP's were shrinking, China's growth was over 9% (IMF 2010). The IMF also makes predictions of growth rates which could be of use for business trying to identify which markets will be fastest growing. They estimate that the world economy will grow at an average of about 4.5%

Figure 4.5 Estimated annual growth rate

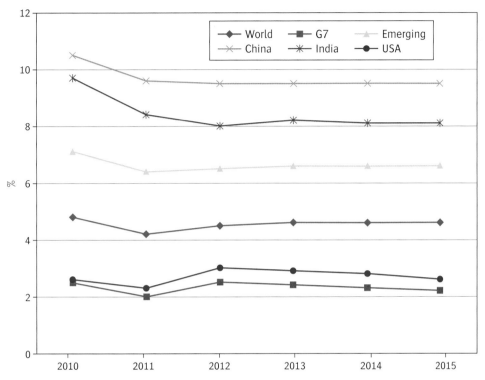

Source: IMF World Economic Outlook Database, October 2010

Learning Task

Using the IMF World Economic Outlook Database look up the estimated future growth rates for the following countries; Colombia, Indonesia, Vietnam, Egypt, Turkey, and South Africa (the so-called CIVETS countries).

Analyse the market implications for foreign producers of telecoms, processed foods, roads, ports, and airports.

per annum to 2015 but that most of this growth will come from emerging economies. China is expected to grow at around 10% per annum and India at 8% compared to the USA's 2.3% (see Figure 4.5).

Despite the higher rates of economic growth in poorer countries they still account for a relatively small proportion of world income and purchasing power, indicating that the biggest markets continue to be located in richer regions. IMF data (2009) show that the advanced economies generate 69% of global income, the USA alone leading the way with around 25% of world GDP. Japan, Germany, the UK, and France together make up a further 23% of income (Table 4.2). China accounts for 8% of the total but Sub-Saharan Africa as a whole only 1.5%.

Table 4.2 Total Gross Domestic Product 2009

Ranking	Economy	US$ millions
1	USA	14,256,280
2	Japan	5,068,060
3	China	4,908,980
4	Germany	3,352,740
5	France	2,675,920
6	UK	2,183,610
7	Italy	2,118,260
8	Spain	1,404,040
9	Canada	1,336,427
10	Brazil	1,574,040
	World	57,937,460

Source: International Monetary Fund, World Economic Outlook Database, April 2010

Counterpoint Box 4.2 Is China's growth sustainable?

Not everybody believes that China's growth will continue at the rate estimated by the IMF. There are those who think the rate could be halved to a very modest, at least by Chinese standards, 5%. Some of the problems very familiar to Western economies are beginning to appear in the Chinese economy, especially inflation, which in November 2010 reached 5.1%. Chinese growth has been export and investment led and it is argued that this is no longer sustainable. Global demand is slowing and internal policies aimed at promoting growth may well lead to further inflationary pressures with easier money going into speculative rather than productive investment. Indeed much of the investment has been in property which has led to another feature familiar to westerners, a property boom. An average size apartment in Beijing can cost US$450,000, way out of the reach of the average Chinese worker. Many of the benefits of Chinese growth have accrued to a small minority with the result that income inequality has risen and with it increased social tensions.

So some argue it is now time to slow growth and restructure the economy by boosting domestic consumption and productive investment and address some of the problems of income inequality, a lack of public services, and pollution.

Sources: *Financial Times*, 17 November 2010, 23 December 2010

Business can also be affected by volatility in the economic and financial environment. In the 20 years after the late 1980s, there were seven periods of turmoil in financial markets:

- the US stock market crash of 1987;
- the crisis in the European Monetary System in 1992 when sterling and the Italian lira were removed and several other currencies had to be devalued;
- Russia defaulting on debt repayments and the collapse of Long Term Capital Management in 1998;

- the financial crisis in East Asia of the late 1990s;
- the dotcom crash of 2000;
- the impact of the attacks on the Twin Towers in 2001;
- the 2007/08 credit crunch.

Such events cause a sudden and, because of globalization, geographically widespread increase in uncertainty in business and finance. Markets become volatile and make the assessment of risk more difficult. As a result, there is a flight from, what are deemed to be, risky to safer assets. Lenders steer away from providing credit to the private sector into lending to governments. It can become more difficult and costly for business and financial institutions to borrow money. Confidence takes a hit, which has a knock-on effect on economic growth because business and consumers become less willing to invest or buy goods and services. The inability to borrow, combined with contracting markets, could result in companies going out of business. These effects can be alleviated, to an extent, when institutions such as central banks, take action to boost confidence by, for instance, reducing interest rates and providing credit to banks, as happened in the USA and the UK during the 2007/08 credit crunch (see Chapter Ten for a more detailed analysis of these events).

Socio-cultural Environment

The socio-cultural environment is concerned with the social organization and structure of society. This includes many social and cultural characteristics which can vary significantly from one society to another. Social aspects include the **distribution of income** and wealth, the structures of employment and unemployment, living and working conditions, health, education, population characteristics including size and breakdown by age, gender and ethnic group, social class, the degree of **urbanization**, and the provision of welfare for the population in the form of education, health care, unemployment benefits, pensions, and so on. The cultural components cover areas like language, religion, diet, values and norms, attitudes, beliefs and practices, social relationships, how people interact, and lifestyles (for more discussion of the socio-cultural framework see Chapter Six). Responding to cultural differences, whether that is producing packaging in various languages or changing ingredients in food products due to different diets, can incur costs for firms.

Learning Task

1. Explain what is meant by an ageing population.
2. What are the implications for Japanese policy makers?
3. What are the implications for Japanese businesses?

(For more on population trends see Chapter Six.)

Mini Case Japan's Demographic Time Bomb

Japan's population in 2009 was 127.5 million but this was 277,000 fewer than in 2004 when Japan's population peaked. It is now in decline with, since 2005, deaths exceeding births and by 2050 it is estimated that it will be just 95,152,000, over 32 million fewer people than in 2004. The birth rate measured as live births per 1,000 of the population was 28.1 in 1950 but has more or less declined continuously since then and in 2009 was only 8.5. The population is also ageing as the Japanese are famous for their longevity. In 2009 the life expectancy for a female was 86.4 years and for a male 79.6 compared to 80.4 and 75.4 for the USA. It means that there are many more elderly households (households with all occupants over 65). In 1975, 3.3% of households were elderly but by 2009 that figure had reached 20%.

So with a declining birth rate the proportion of the younger age population (0–14) is shrinking as is that of working age (15–64) and the only age group which is growing is the over 65s. Consequently the total dependency ratio, measured as the sum of the young and the elderly divided by those of working age, will increase from 56% in 2010 to an estimated 93% in 2050. The old age dependency ratio will increase from 36% in 2010 to 76% in 2050, far higher than other developed economies (see Figure 4.6).

Table 4.3 Japan's declining and ageing population

Year	Population ('000)	Age composition (%)			average annual rate of increase
		0–14	15–64	65+	
2010	127,176	13.0	63.9	23.1	−0.26
2020	122,735	10.8	60.0	29.2	−0.35
2030	115,224	9.7	58.5	31.8	−0.63
2040	105,695	9.3	54.2	36.5	−0.86
2050	95,152	8.6	51.8	39.6	−1.05

Source: Statistical Yearbook of Japan (2010)

Figure 4.6 Old age dependency ratios

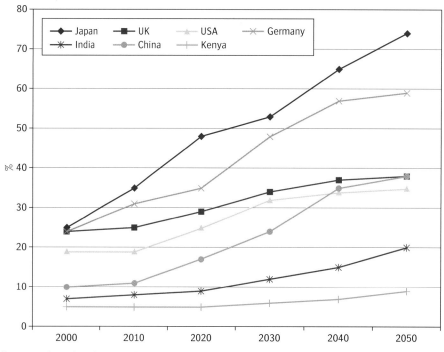

Source: http://esa.un.org/unpd/wpp/JS-Charts/aging-old-dep-ratio_0.htm   →

➔ Japan is not the only country facing this demographic problem. As the graph shows Germany has a similar profile and Italy, Greece, and Spain will all have dependency ratios of around 60% by 2050 so they will be looking to Japan to see how they deal with the problem.

Sources: Statistical Handbook of Japan available at www.stat.go.jp/english/data/handbook/index.htm; United Nations, World Populations Prospects: The 2008 Revision Population database available at http://esa.un.org/UNPP/index.asp?panel=2

Source: Deco

Technological Environment

In simple terms, technology refers to the know-how or the pool of ideas or knowledge available to society. Business is particularly interested in advances in knowledge that it can exploit commercially. Technology offers business the prospect of:

- turning new ideas into new or improved products or production techniques;
- entering new markets;
- boosting revenues;
- cutting costs;
- increasing profits.

However, **technological advance** has been a fundamental force in changing and shaping the patterns of business as regards what it does and how it does it. The advent of microelectronics is a good illustration. In the production process it has cut down the amount of labour and capital required to produce a certain level of output, allowed firms to hold fewer components in stock, improved product quality by increasing the accuracy of production processes and facilitating quality testing, and reduced energy use by replacing machinery with moving parts with microchips (see Chapter Seven for more detailed discussion of the technological framework).

However, technology involves much uncertainty. Firms can pump lots of resources into research and development, be at the cutting edge of technology with new products that technically excel those of their competitors, but that does not guarantee success. Big pharmaceutical companies have increased their spending on research and development significantly but have found that the number of new drugs being generated has fallen. As a result, they have had to rely on old drugs for their revenues, look for ways of cutting costs, and going for mergers (PricewaterhouseCoopers 2007). These technology uncertainties make it more difficult for business to carry out long-range planning.

Mini Case New Technology

Skype is typical of a new technology company developing cheap global communications as part of what McKinsey refers to as the global grid. It was one of the pioneers of voice communication over the internet and provides a service that allows consumers to make free voice calls between computers. It also allows voice and video calling, video conferencing, instant messaging, and SMS. It has also recently (December 2010) launched a video calling app for the iPhone, iPad, and iPod Touch so their owners can make free Skype-to-Skype video calls wherever they are. Low-cost calls can also be made to landlines using a prepaid account or annual subscription.

Skype was founded in 2003 by Niklas Zennström and Janus Friis, Swedish and Danish entrepreneurs respectively. The software was developed in Estonia and most of its engineers are still based in Estonia. Its headquarters are in Luxembourg but it also has offices in Stockholm and London. In 2005 Skype was sold to eBay for US$2.6 billion but in 2009, 70% was sold to a consortium of Silver Lake Partners, Canada Pension Plan Investment Board, Andreessen Horowitz, and Joltid (owned by the original Skype founders). In 2010 Skype filed for an initial public offering in the United States of America to raise up to US$100 million.

Skype is now the world's largest carrier of transnational phone calls with over 500 million registered users worldwide and over 25 million people at peak times. According to TeleGeography (www.telegeography.com) while growth in international call traffic has slumped in 2010, traffic routed through Skype continued to accelerate. It was estimated to grow by 45 billion minutes which was more than twice the volume added by all of the world's phone companies combined. It is not the only VOIP (voice over internet protocol) system but it is the most popular. In the first half of 2010, 88.4 billion minutes of calls were made and something like 40% of these were video calls.

It is mostly used by home consumers and small businesses. For both home consumers and businesses the cost of calling can be much cheaper but there are also other benefits for business. Video and teleconferencing can reduce the requirement for meetings and travel and further reduce costs. Skype can also keep employees in touch with remote workers, home workers, partners, suppliers, and customers and this can be across the world.

There can be problems. Voice quality will depend on a host of factors such as hardware and bandwidth, at both ends of the conversation. It also depends on being connected so if your connection fails so does your Skype ability. Security is also a concern. This is an internet technology so it is subject to viruses and malware, identity and service theft, and other common problems. It is also subject to outages as happened in December 2010 when software problems caused a two-day outage for many of its users. If you are a business then this can be catastrophic.

McKinsey calls Skype 'a disruptive newcomer' but it also makes clear to businesses that 'even if they eschew such radical business models, they need to think strategically about how to use these new networks to advance their existing business models'.

Sources: http://about.skype.com/; www.guardian.co.uk/technology/blog/2010/dec/29/skype-launches-video-calling-iphone-app/; *McKinsey Quarterly*: The Global Grid available at www.mckinsey-quarterly.com/The_global_grid_2626

The Ecological Environment

In recent decades there has been increasing concern, both nationally and globally, about the interaction between human beings, the economic systems they establish, and the earth's natural environment. Business forms a major part of economic systems that impact on the environment by using up resources and altering the ecological systems on which the world depends. The damage to the ozone layer, the impact of global warming, and the rise in sea levels due to greenhouse gases emitted by power generation, industrial, transport and agricultural sectors, have been of growing concern (for more discussion on the ecological environment see Chapter Twelve).

Environmental challenges are a global phenomenon. Global warming is not confined within national borders but affects the whole world. There is widespread recognition that economic growth is harming the environment irrevocably, and that we need to move towards a system that values the natural environment and protects it for future generations.

There is growing pressure on the political authorities to respond to these ecological threats. There are a number of possible policy responses, all of which have implications for business:

- tax the polluter;
- subsidize firms who manage to reduce activities that harm the environment, for example by switching to non-polluting sources of energy;
- use regulations to control the amount of pollution generated by business;
- promote the creation of environmentally friendly technologies.

Mini Case ExxonMobil versus the Environmentalists

This case illustrates attempts by a giant oil major to defuse threats to its business by influencing the debate around global warming.

In 1997, the US President, the Democrat Bill Clinton, agreed to the Kyoto Treaty that would reduce greenhouse gas emissions and prevent climate change. ExxonMobil, the giant US oil company, feared that the treaty would be approved by the US Senate and the result would be greater controls on emissions from fossil fuels, oil, coal, and natural gas. It came up with a plan to stall action on global warming. It set out to raise doubts among the public, and in the media, about the uncertainties in the scientific evidence for global warming. Exxon argued that the theory behind climate change was based on forecasting models with a very high degree of uncertainty. It claimed that there was no convincing evidence that climate change was occurring and that, if it was, there was no convincing evidence that humans had any influence on it.

Its plan was to recruit and train a number of independent scientists who had not been publicly involved in the debate on climate change and to depict supporters of action on global warming as out of touch with reality. A proposal was made to set up a Global Climate Science Data Centre which would undermine the evidence of scientists arguing for measures to be taken against global warming. The Centre would inform and educate members of Congress, the media, business, and educational institutions about climate change. The company spent millions of dollars spreading its message worldwide. It pumped hundreds of thousands of dollars into organizations that also questioned global warming like the American Enterprise Institute and the American Council for Capital Formation. In the event, and much to the joy of Exxon, the US Senate which had fallen under the control of the Republican Party, failed to ratify the Kyoto Treaty.

However, by 2007, with the Democratic Party in control of Congress, the company had changed its position. It had withdrawn funding from bodies sceptical of climate change and claimed that its position on climate had been widely misunderstood.

Sources: Environmental Defense at: www.edf.org; Exxon internal memo available at www.edf.org; *Guardian*, 20 March 2002 and 12 January 2007; *The Independent*, 8 December 2005

● CHAPTER SUMMARY

In this chapter we examined the global external business environment. The factors in this environment are highly interdependent but can usefully be analysed in the following categories: political and legal, economic and financial, socio-cultural, technological, and ecological, the various elements that make up the PESTLE model. This environment is increasingly complex, dynamic, uncertain, and can be hostile. Firms need to scan the environment in order to identify opportunities for new markets, for cost reductions, and for new sources of supply. They also need to look out for the many threats, not just from competitors but from economic and financial volatility, political instability, new technology, and natural disasters. Organizations can assess the impact of external issues by analysing the effect of these issues on the structure of the industry and on the stakeholders of the organization.

● REVIEW QUESTIONS

1. Explain why operating in the international business environment is much more complex than in the firm's domestic business environment.

2. What implications does your answer to question 1 have for planning a firm's strategy?

3. Select an organization of your choice operating internationally. Select one issue from each of the PESTLE sectors and analyse the impact on the organization (consider the industry environment and stakeholders).

4. Look up the National Intelligence Council report mentioned in the text. One of their scenarios is what they call the 'globalizing economy'. Identify the opportunities and threats that might result from this scenario.

5. In 2008, The European Candle Institute, representing four EU candle makers, complained of unfair competition from China. The EU agreed to investigate (see *Guardian*, 19 February 2008). In May 2009 the Council of Europe imposed anti-dumping measures on imports of certain candles originating in China.

   Explain why the Institute wanted measures implementing and why the British Retail Consortium was so opposed.

Case Study   AXA and the Global Business Environment

AXA is a leading insurance group based in France. The company can trace its origins in France to the beginning of the 19th century but the AXA name did not come into existence until 1985 after a number of acquisitions and mergers of French mutual insurance companies. Like many companies it gained strength in its domestic market before taking the riskier step of competing abroad. It now operates in 57 countries, has 216,000 employees and an annual turnover, in 2009, of 90.1 billion euros making it the world's 9th largest company ranked by sales turnover (according to the Global Fortune 500, see:

http://money.cnn.com/magazines/fortune/global500/2010/full_list/).

AXA operates primarily in Europe, North America, Asia Pacific but also in the Middle east, Africa, and Latin America. It has grown organically and through merger and acquisition. For example, in 2006 AXA acquired the Winterthur Group (a Swiss based Insurer) with activities in 17 countries. This increased its presence in a number of high growth markets in Central and Eastern Europe and Asia. Since then AXA has made further acquisitions in South Korea, Ukraine, Russia, and Mexico. ➜

Source: www.istockphoto.com

Its strategy to 2015 is to build a greater presence in Asia to take advantage of higher growth in emerging markets such as Thailand, Indonesia, and Malaysia.

As an insurance company AXA operates in three broad areas, Life and Savings, Property and Casualty Insurance, and Asset Management. It provides services to both personal and commercial customers including large multinational companies covering their risks in operations across the world. In some countries it also offers retail banking services.

An insurance company operates in a highly regulated and supervised environment in terms of who can do business and how it does business. For example, the regulator will define a minimum amount of capital that it must maintain to ensure that the insurer is able to meet any claims made against it. The ratio of the insurer's resources and this regulatory minimum is called the solvency ratio or margin.

At the heart of the insurance business is risk and assessing risk. Insurers provide protection to their clients by assuming the risk of their client. A premium is charged in proportion to the degree of risk and monetary value of the potential loss. The insurer spreads the risk by putting all the premiums into a pool safe in the knowledge that only so many of the insured will make claims in any one year and draw money from the pool. The premiums collected are then invested against the time frame of the commitments made, i.e. some are short term such as car and property insurance while others are much longer term such as retirement savings.

AXA, as an insurance company, is doubly exposed to the unpredictability of the global business environment. On the one hand it must assess the risk of covering its clients from the everyday misfortunes but also from new risks such as climate change and the increased incidence of natural disasters, terrorism, and cybercrime. It must also manage the risk associated with over 1,000 billion euros of assets it manages on behalf of its clients and shareholders. Events such as the 2008 financial crisis could be catastrophic. As a global player exchange rates are also important. It reports its results in euros but an increasing amount of revenue is raised in other currencies before being converted into euros.

A brief survey of some of the major events of the first decade of the 21st century will demonstrate the nature and importance of the global business environment to a company such as AXA. The decade started with a first for the insurance industry, a global economic recession, financial market depreciation after the bursting of the dotcom bubble and a series of severe losses, the worst by far being the terrorist attack on the USA. There was also a series of corporate bankruptcy scandals the worst of which was Enron but this led to a crisis of trust in the corporate world and this affected corporate earnings. 2000 to 2003 saw three years of falling equity markets. All of these events were outside the control of AXA. The slight upside to these losses was the realization by many of the need to insure risks and the importance of risk prevention programmes.

Other major events in the decade have been the Iraq war in 2003 and the war in Afghanistan. There have also been a series of terrorist incidents after 9/11, in Bali, Istanbul, Madrid, London, and Mumbai. There have been a series of natural disasters: the Indian Ocean Tsunami in 2004; hurricanes in the Caribbean such as Katrina; earthquakes in India and Iran; a heat wave in Europe (2003) which killed thousands; bushfires in Australia; floods in Australia, Brazil and Sri Lanka; and SARS and flu pandemics.

As noted above the world economy started the decade in recession but recovered from 2003 until the financial crisis of 2008 when the world once again went into recession. The developed economies' stock markets have followed this pattern with stocks falling from 2000 to 2002, recovering from 2003 to 2007, and then once again falling in 2008 but recovering again in 2009. Interest rates in developed economies started the decade at around 6%, fell to around 1% in 2004, recovered to 2007 but fell again to less than 1% at the end of the decade. ➔

→ One bright note for an insurance company such as AXA is that the populations of their major markets are ageing. The post-war baby boomer generations are now 'grandboomers'. They generally have lots of money and want to spend it on motorbikes, holidays, and the like. As Henri de Castries (Chairman of AXA's Management Board) says 'I think that the outlook for insurance and asset management is very attractive: there really is no alternative to the services that we offer; we have natural growth pipelines in our "old" countries such as demographic ageing, limits to the welfare state and new needs in the quality of life; and emerging markets are sources of both present and future growth.'

Sources: Among many others, AXA Annual Reports 2001 to 2009 available at www.axa.com/en/publications/annualreports/archives

Questions

Using the case and the annual reports and in particular the interviews with Henri de Castries answer the following:

1. In April 2010 AXA moved from a dual board structure of governance (with a Management Board and Supervisory Board) to a single board structure with a Board of Directors. Explain what this means, why they have decided to change, and how it will help AXA to deal with the external environment.

2. The following is taken from the annual reports:

US$/euro exchange rate:

2005	1.2400
2006	1.2661
2007	1.3797
2008	1.4695
2009	1.3955
2010	1.3765

Explain how this and other currency variations with the euro will affect AXA's business.

3. How would the sub-prime crisis of 2008 affect AXA?

4. Explain how an ageing population, such as that of Japan and several European countries, would be beneficial to AXA.

5. Identify and prioritize AXA's stakeholders as at 2010. Justify your decisions.

Online Resource Centre
www.oxfordtextbooks.co.uk/orc/hamilton_webster2e/

Visit the supporting online resource centre for additional material which will help you with your assignments, essays, and research, or you may find these extra resources helpful when revising for exams.

● FURTHER READING

For a very readable view of possible political, social, economic, and technological developments in the global economy see:

● Moynagh, M. and Worsley, R. (2008) *Going Global: Key Questions for the 21st Century*. London: A&C Black Publishers

The next two articles give alternative views on the changing world power of the USA:

● Wallerstein, I. (2007) 'Precipitate Decline'. *Harvard International Review*, Spring, Vol 29, Issue 1

● Wohlforth, W. (2007) 'Unipolar Stability'. *Harvard International Review*, Spring, Vol 29, Issue 1

For an introductory text to strategy see:

● Johnson, G., Scholes, K., and Whittington, R. (2009) *Fundamentals of Strategy*. Harlow: Pearson Education Ltd

● REFERENCES

Braithwaite, A. (2003) 'The Supply Chain Risks of Global Sourcing'. *Stanford Global Supply Chain*, October

Coe, N. M., Kelly, P. F., and Yeung, H. W. C. (2007) *Economic Geography*. Malden: Blackwell

Czinkota, M. R., Knight, G., Liesch, P. W., and Steen, J. (2010) 'Terrorism and International Business: A Research Agenda'. *Journal of International Business Studies*, Vol 14, Issue 5, June/July

Enderwick, P. (2006) 'Managing the Global Threats'. *University of Auckland Business Review*, Vol 8, Issue 2, Spring

Freeman, E. (1984) *Strategic Management: A Stakeholder Approach*. Boston: Pitman

Grant, R. (2010) *Contemporary Strategy Analysis*. Oxford: Blackwell

Haass, R. (2008) 'A Political Education for Business: An Interview with the Head of the Council on Foreign Relations'. *McKinsey Quarterly*, February

Kotler, P. and Caslione, J. (2009) *Chaotics: The Business of Managing and Marketing in the Age of Turbulence*. New York: American Management Association

Mason, R. B. (2007) 'The External Environment's Effects on Management and Strategy: A Complexity Theory Approach'. *Management Decision*, Vol 45, Issue 1

Porter, M. (1990) *The Competitive Advantage of Nations*. London: Macmillan Business

Post, J. E., Preston, L. E., and Sachs, S. (2002) 'Managing the Extended Enterprise: The New Stakeholder View'. *California Management Review*

PWC (2007) *Pharma 2020: The Vision: Which Path Will You Take?*, www.pwc.com

Saner, R. and Guilherme, R. (2007) 'The International Monetary Fund's Influence on Trade Policies of Low-Income Countries: A Valid Undertaking?'. *Journal of World Trade*, Vol 41, Issue 5, October

CHAPTER FIVE

Assessing Country Attractiveness

LEARNING OUTCOMES

This chapter will enable you to:

- Explain the process of internationalization

- Identify reasons for FDI

- Select target markets and sites for exporting and FDI

- Assess global risks

Case Study Tesco in the USA

This case demonstrates the difficulties even mature multi-national companies can face when entering overseas markets.

After transforming itself into the UK's leading supermarket Tesco embarked on an international expansion programme in 1994. Its first foray into overseas markets was into Eastern Europe after the end of Soviet control. It opened in Hungary in 1994, then Poland in 1995 and the Czech Republic and Slovakia in 1996. It first ventured into the Far East in 1998 in Thailand followed by South Korea, Taiwan, Malaysia, Japan, and China. In all these markets, except Taiwan, Tesco has had tremendous success and become, with Carrefour and Wal-Mart one of the world's largest international supermarket chains. Tesco entered the Taiwanese market some ten years after Carrefour, couldn't find a suitable partner and found that Carrefour had built an impregnable position, and so decided to exit.

The USA has been somewhat of a graveyard for British retailers with both Sainsbury and Marks and Spencer trying but failing to establish themselves but nevertheless Tesco decided it would enter that market in 2007. The USA is the biggest retail market in the world and Sir Terry Leahy's (then Tesco CEO) vision was to grow as big a business in the USA as in the UK. He aimed to fill a gap he saw in the market by opening a chain of relatively small local supermarkets selling fresh food under the name 'Fresh and Easy'.

In other markets Tesco had usually sought a domestic part-ner but in the USA they decided to go it alone. Before entering the market Tesco sent a team to undertake extensive research on American shopping habits. They interviewed hundreds of US shoppers, undertook focus group interviews, lived with American families, and even built a shop in a derelict ware-house to see make sure they were getting it right.

They opened the first store in Los Angeles in November 2007 with plans for 200 by the end of 2009 and eventually 1,000 stores across America. But things have not gone to plan. By 2009 only 178 stores had been opened and 13 of those have been mothballed leaving 165 operating stores. Losses in the first half of 2010 were £95 million.

Tesco is blaming the recession, which was particularly severe in the West, but others are not so sure and think that Tesco's market research may have been flawed. The offering is aimed at the 'middle market' between Wal-Mart and the more expensive stores but already Fresh & Easy has had to offer discounts to entice people into its stores. There have been problems with pack sizes and portions too small for Americans. US consumers also prefer to select their fresh produce rather than being pre-packed and prefer branded goods rather than own label. There have also been complaints about self-serve checkouts as US customers like to see a full service checkout.

Unlike some of its predecessors Tesco has not yet turned its back on the USA. It plans to break even by 2012–13 and to have opened nearly 400 stores.

Sources: *Financial Times*, 21 September 2010; *The Economist*, 21 June 2007; *The First Post*, 27 April 2009

Source: Corel

In the last chapter we looked at tools that could be used for making sense of the international business environment. In this chapter we are going explain the internationalization process and why companies would want to invest overseas (FDI). We then go on to show how organizations can assess the attractiveness of countries as markets or production locations.

The Internationalization Process

International business includes firms undertaking imports and exports, producing abroad or being involved in joint ventures, licensing or franchising arrangements with a foreign partner. It ranges from firms producing goods and services in a single country and exporting them to another, to firms like Dell (see Case Study in Chapter One) with complex global production and distribution networks across dozens of countries.

The traditional view of international business is that firms initially establish a stable domestic base before venturing overseas. Pia Arenius quoting a Finnish company executive, provides a reason for this:

> 'it seems easier for a fellow countryman to sell to a fellow countryman.' 'It's easier for a Swedish company to do business with a Swedish person, who is located in the nice city of Stockholm and speaks their native language.' 'There are cultural differences. You need to have an American to sell to an American company.' Pia Arenius (2005)

Carrefour, a French company, is the world's second largest retailer with 12,500 stores in 30 countries. The Carrefour name came into being in 1959 but it wasn't until 1969 that it took its first venture outside France, and that was in Belgium—a country, in terms of its business environment, very similar to France. Its next venture was to Spain and then in 1975 to South America. It wasn't until 1989, when it entered the Taiwanese market, that it ventured into a very different business environment. However, by 2009, nearly 80% of turnover was still being made in France and other European countries (www.carrefour.com).

Traditionally, companies are seen as internationalizing incrementally in three stages, the Uppsala model (see Johanson and Vahlne, 1977). From their domestic base firms develop gradually by exporting to another country which is geographically and culturally similar. Initially, exporting takes place either directly through the company's own export department or, indirectly, via an external export agency. Then as overseas business expands, and with it the experience and confidence of operating in overseas markets, the firm becomes more committed to foreign activities. This can take the form of exporting to more distant and less culturally similar countries and perhaps setting up an overseas sales company. Success, combined with the greater knowledge of foreign markets, according to the traditional model, leads ultimately to the setting up of production facilities across the world which can be done with partner firms through joint ventures or totally owned foreign subsidiaries. Whichever the mode of operations, expanding overseas is always challenging.

This traditional model of slow and incremental development of international business has been challenged in a number of ways. Benito, Petersen, and Welch (2009) argue that the reality is much 'messier' and that rather than a simple sequential process firms may often operate different modes at the same time. Malhotra and Hinings (2010) argue that different types of organization follow different processes of internationalization. The Uppsala model was based on the

Table 5.1 The traditional model of internationalization

Entry mode	
Export from domestic base	Directly through export department or via overseas agent
Licensing/Franchising	An agreement to allow a partner to manufacture or sell abroad
Joint Venture	An alliance in which an equity investment is made with a partner
Wholly owned subsidiary	Either acquisition of existing firms (brownfield investment) or entirely new facilities (greenfield investment)

study of Swedish manufacturing firms but now many different organizations are internationalizing their operations. Many are consumer and professional service organizations such as hotels, restaurants, accountants, solicitors, retailers, and management consultants for whom the process is likely to be quite different. Professional service firms often follow clients into new markets and for consumer services such as retailing and hotels the nature of the service demands a physical presence in the host market.

Many empirical studies of the internationalization process, especially in technology-based, knowledge-intensive sectors, contradict the predictions of the three stage model and it is now claimed that many firms are 'born-global'. A born-global company is one in which foreign sales account for at least 25% of the total within three years of its inception and looks to derive significant competitive advantage from operating multinationally (Andersson and Evangelista, 2006). Such firms take an international perspective from the outset with the intention of trading internationally immediately or within a short period of time. 'These firms view the world as their marketplace from the outset and see the domestic market as a support for their international business' (Rennie 1993). They globalize their business rapidly, entering physically distant markets from an early stage in their life cycle (Shameen Rashantham, 2005). Such companies are usually small, with limited resources but with a global vision (Gabrielson, 2005). They tend to be high technology companies, focused on market niches. Companies in small open economies, like Denmark, Sweden, and Switzerland, because of the limited size of their domestic market and the pressure of competition, are likely to come under more pressure to enter global markets than firms based in bigger markets. Andersson and Evangelista cite the example of Rubber, a Swedish company producing advanced cable entries and seals. From the start-up in 1990, the company saw the whole world as its market. It entered around ten new markets each year, and by 2001 it was present in 80 nations.

The most important macro-trends encouraging the widespread emergence of born-globals, are globalization and advanced information and communications technologies. Globalization provides market opportunities and along with the widespread diffusion of new communications technology and falling transport costs lowers the costs of entering foreign markets. Born-global firms use technology to achieve competitive advantage and develop a range of alliances and collaborative partnerships with suppliers, distributors, and customers. This helps them overcome the traditional constraints to internationalization: being too small to gain economies of scale; lack of resources both financial and knowledge; and an aversion to risk-taking. The financial burden and risk is shared with alliance partners and the partners provide knowledge about foreign markets (Freeman *et al.*, 2006). Although still small in relation to the total, such firms are taking up an increasing share of world trade (Knight, Madsen, and Servais, 2004). Fan and Phan (2007) argue that they are not such a distinct breed and that these firms are subject to many of the same influences as in the traditional pattern of internationalization.

Learning Task

Research the history of an international business organization of your choice. Trace the steps in its growth and see if it fits the traditional path suggested above.

The Reasons for FDI

Businesses invest abroad for various reasons. The main motives can be summarized as:

- the need to get market access;
- the search for lower production costs; and
- a quest for natural resources and other assets.

Market Access

Business is interested in gaining entry to big markets or markets with the potential for growth and profit. Thus Ernst and Young found that France dominated UK outward investment activity because of the size of its consumer market and its proximity (*Financial Times*, 28 May 2007). Europe is the UK's biggest market for outward investment followed by the Americas although in 2009 this fell whereas investment in Asia and Africa increased by £8.3 billion and £7.4 billion respectively (Office for National Statistics, www.statistics.gov.uk/pdfdir/fdi1210.pdf). Emerging markets are particularly attractive markets because of their relatively high rates of economic growth and purchasing power at a time when developed country markets are growing only slowly. According to the IMF (World Economic Outlook Database) emerging markets are estimated to grow at over 6% per annum for the next four years whereas the estimate for developed economies is only just above 2%. China is estimated to increase by almost 10% and India around 8%.

A problem confronted by business is that attractive markets are sometimes protected from imports by barriers, such as tariffs the USA levies on imports of steel, quotas such as those imposed by the EU on Chinese clothing and footwear, and countries such as China and Indonesia trying to ensure that a certain proportion of the cars sold there is manufactured locally. According to the OECD, there is a growing move towards protectionism in its member countries (OECD, 2007). In order to circumvent these barriers, firms set up production facilities in the market. Another reason for locating near the market is that, for bulky, low value goods, transport costs can be prohibitive and it becomes imperative that firms produce close to their customers. Or it may be that retail firms like Tesco and Wal-Mart, construction companies, or providers of medical or education services have to be in face-to-face contact with their customers. It may also be that important customers can precipitate a decision to invest abroad. When big car firms like Volkswagen and Fiat moved into Eastern Europe following the collapse of Communism, a large number of car component suppliers felt obliged to follow, given their customers' requirements for just-in-time deliveries (van Tulder and Ruigrok, undated).

Other firms may feel the need to be close enough to respond quickly to alterations in market conditions, such as changes in taste or to provide speedy after-sales service.

Lower Production Costs

Firms are often driven abroad by the need to find cheaper factors of production so as to cut costs. When jobs are transferred abroad, it is referred to as **offshoring**. This has gone on to such an extent that it is estimated that around 40% of US imports are produced by US companies, many of them in China (*Financial Times*, 10 July 2007).

With the increasing cost of labour in rich countries, industries, particularly labour intensive industries including textiles, clothing, and footwear, and firms assembling electronic components have looked abroad for cheaper locations. Financial institutions have also relocated data processing and call centre activities to countries such as India, as have computer manufacturers and internet service providers. Initially, firms transferred low level, unskilled or semi-skilled work to countries where labour was cheap, labour market regulation loose, and there was a low level of unionization of the work force. However, with the passage of time, firms have started to transfer higher level activities such as product design and development, as they discovered that developing countries also had pools of highly educated, technically qualified, and relatively cheap labour. In India there is an abundance of well-trained programming, software-developer, and systems-engineering talent while China and Taiwan are developing world-class design expertise in specific technologies. Design is one of the most popular subjects at Chinese universities, and hundreds of design consulting firms have sprung up in cities such as Shanghai and Beijing (*CFO Magazine*, 17 March 2003; *CFO Magazine*, 29 June 2004; *Business Week*, 21 November 2005).

The savings in labour costs from offshoring can be substantial. A manufacturing worker in 2009 costs, per hour: in the UK US$30.78, in the USA US$33.53. A comparable worker in Mexico costs US$5.38 per hour, in Taiwan US$7.76 per hour, and in Portugal US$11.95 (www.bls.gov/news.release/pdf/ichcc.pdf). In the computer and car industries, the Mexican production worker comes in at around a tenth of the cost of workers in the UK and the USA. Labour savings also apply to white collar work. Project managers, software engineers, and accountants can all be much cheaper in developing countries.

The advantages of cheap labour in developing countries are likely to be offset to an extent by lower levels of **productivity**. Productivity measured in terms of output (GDP) per head is much lower in Mexico and Portugal than in the USA or UK. In 2010 in Mexico it is US$14,266 per head, in Portugal US$23,114, in the UK US$35,053, and in the USA US$47,132 (www.imf.org).

One effect of these fast expanding economies is that wages and salaries have been increasing in countries like China and India, as demand for educated and technically skilled workers starts to outstrip the supply of suitable candidates. Although the productivity of Chinese workers is rising, in many industries it is not keeping pace with wages. Consequently, some MNCs may look elsewhere, like the Philippines, Thailand, and Indonesia where wages are much lower than in China or India (*The Economist*, 13 January 2007). South Korea is no longer as competitive, as far as blue-collar workers are concerned, but its engineers continue to be of high quality and will work up to 12 hours per day (*Financial Times*, 17 July 2007).

It has also been argued that MNCs, to avoid environmental regulations at home, have intentionally relocated polluting activities to developing countries, including China, where the authorities turn a blind eye to environmental damage (Zheng and Chen, 2006). Christmann and Taylor (2001) contend that pollution-intensive MNCs have not taken advantage of lax environmental regulation in China. They found that MNCs were more likely than local firms to comply with local regulations and to adopt internationally recognized environmental standards.

Learning Task

Find an organization that has offshored some of its activities. Explain the reason for the offshoring activity.

Natural Resources

Businesses in the primary sector are the principal seekers of deposits of natural resources such as oil, gas, and other minerals. But deposits of natural resources are not spread evenly across the globe so resource-seeking firms such as mining groups like Rio Tinto and BHP Billiton and oil companies like Shell and Exxon must locate near deposits of natural resources.

With increasing demand for raw materials from the fast growing economies of China and India pulling up prices, combined with a lack of new deposits, mining companies are also looking to expand their deposits of mineral ores and their capacity to refine them. Rio Tinto expects world demand for iron ore, copper, and aluminium to more or less double between 2007 and 2022. According to Rio Tinto the main driver of the demand for metals is the growth of urbanization as this creates a demand for infrastructure projects and increased wealth also increases demand for consumer durables such as fridges and cars. They estimate that the urban dweller uses five times as much steel as the rural dweller (www.riotinto.com/documents/ReportsPublications/Review_86_-Value_and_Growth.pdf).

The UN (2007c) predicts that, by 2050, urban dwellers will likely account for more than four fifths of the population in the more developed regions and for two thirds in the less developed regions. Overall, the world urban population is expected to almost double from 3.3 billion in 2007 to 6.4 billion in 2050 which would mean that seventy out of every hundred people in the world would be living in towns and cities (see Figure 5.1).

To increase production capacity, Rio Tinto (one of the world's largest mining companies; mines for coal, copper, iron, bauxite, gold, titanium, lead, zinc, cobalt, nickel, and uranium) in 2007 put in a successful bid for the Canadian aluminium company Alcan. In 2010 it also bid for an Australian coal mining company, Riverside (www.riotinto.com). Rio Tinto in turn was the subject of an unsuccessful bid by BHP Billiton in 2010.

Competition from Developing Country MNCs

Western and Japanese MNCs not only compete with each other for access to natural resources, but also face increasing competition from companies based in poorer countries. In 2005, the Brazilian company CVRD bought Inco of Canada to become the second biggest mining group in the world. The following year, Mittal Steel, whose founder Lakshmi Mittal is of Indian origin, bought Luxembourg rival Arcelor for US$34 billion—thereby creating the world's biggest steel maker. Rusal, the Russian minerals company, became the largest aluminium company in the world

Figure 5.1 World urban and rural population

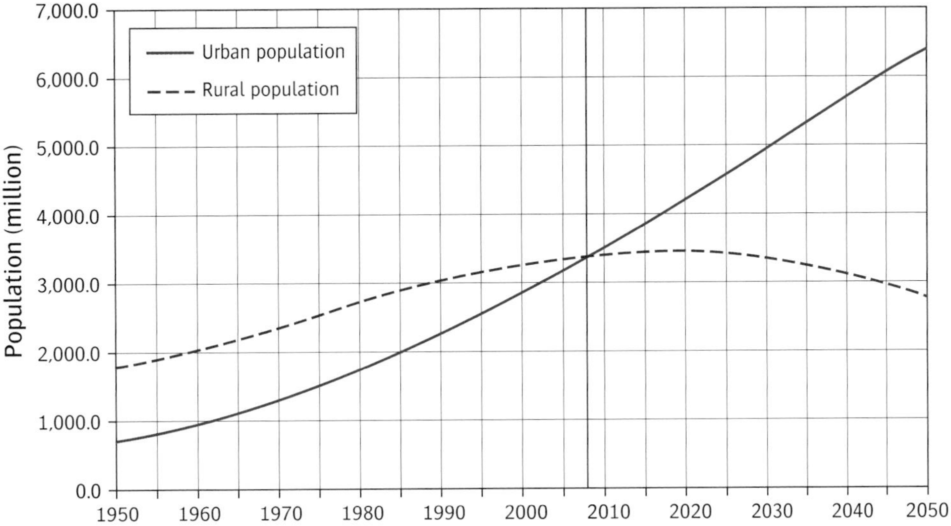

Source: UN (2007c), The World Urbanization Prospects: The 2007 revision

when it took over another Russian company, SUAL, and the aluminium assets of the Swiss firm, Glencore. In the same year, Tata, one of India's biggest conglomerate firms, took over Corus, the European steel firm (Yahoo Finance; *Financial Times*, 22 November 2006 and 6 July 2007).

There is also fierce competition from China for resources. With just over 1.3 billion people, China is the world's most populous country and the second largest consumer of global oil supplies after the USA.

China's oil reserves are limited and its oil consumption, growing at 7% per annum, is almost double that of its output. By 2020, it is forecast that China will need to import 60% of its energy requirements. Ten years later, it is expected to have more cars than the USA, and to be one of the world's largest importers of oil. The Chinese authorities, well aware of their increasing dependence on imported oil, especially from the Middle East, have made aggressive efforts to secure oil and gas supplies all over the globe, in Africa, Latin America, and Central Asia. In 2010 it had spent over £15.2 billion by the end of October on overseas oil and gas acquisitions. This accounted for one fifth of all deal activity in that sector (*Financial Times*, 8 October 2010).

Other assets

Another reason for FDI is to gain other assets such as technological and managerial knowhow. Firms can set up in other countries to more closely monitor competitor activities as Kodak did in Japan to learn from their Japanese competitors. They can also enter into joint ventures to learn from others or acquire the assets of another firm and in so doing acquire access to technology, brand names, local distribution systems, and expertise. A good example of this kind of FDI activity was the acquisition of IBM's personal computer business by Lenovo of China in 2004. Lenovo was able to acquire a foothold in the American market and easier access to Europe (market seeking activities) but also acquired a famous brand (the 'Think' brand), technological and management expertise, and a distribution network.

Mini Case China and Brazil—FDI and Trade

China has become a major force in foreign direct investment. In 2009, with outflows of US$48 billion, it was the sixth largest foreign direct investor. This has been driven by a search for natural resources and by the opportunities to acquire foreign companies created by global restructuring (WIR, 2010).

Brazil, with vast mineral resources and a well-developed agricultural sector has been a major recipient of Chinese FDI. In 2010, China became the biggest foreign direct investor in Brazil accounting for about US$17 billion of Brazil's total FDI inflows in 2010 of US$49 billion, up from less than US$300 million in 2009. The biggest transaction was Chinese oil major Sinopec's US$7.1 billion purchase of a 40% stake in Repsol Brazil.

The Chinese have also invested in infrastructural projects such as the building of an enormous port complex in the state of Rio de Janeiro. This will allow China to transport iron ore for its fast expanding steel industry. The complex will include a steel mill, shipyards, an automobile plant, and factories manufacturing oil and gas equipment. Chinese companies have also invested heavily in Brazil's electric power supply business with the purchase of stakes in the country's power grid. Others are looking to buy land in Brazil for the production of soya beans.

Brazil as the largest and most populous country in South America and with its fast growing economy and appreciating exchange rate, has also become a major attraction for Chinese exports. In 2010, imports of manufactured goods from China rose by 60% compared with 2009. The deficit in manufactured goods was a record US$23.5 billion, up from only US$600 million, seven years previously. The Brazilian finance minister responded to this by calling for a revaluation of the renminbi, the Chinese currency.

However, Brazilian exporters have also benefited from trade with China. Between 2000 and 2009, exports to China rose 18-fold. In 2010, Brazil ran an overall trade surplus with China of US$5.2 billion due to exports of commodities such as iron ore and soya beans. China has overtaken the USA to become Brazil's biggest trading partner.

Sources: UNCTAD, World Investment Report 2010; CIA Factbook 2011; www.investinbrazil.biz, 29 July 2010; *Financial Times*, 31 January 2011; see video, Enter the Dragon? China's Presence in Latin America at www.wilsoncenter.org/ondemand/index. cfm?fuseaction=Regions.play&mediaid=37FD6DB5-AFC3-376F-1CECBB53A20278D5&categoryid=17; Roett, R. (2010) *The New Brazil*, Washington, Brookings Institution

Screening and Evaluating Foreign Markets

In Chapter Four we talked about environmental analysis being part of the strategic process. The decision to 'go abroad' is another aspect of strategy which involves a matching of internal resources with external opportunities aimed at achieving the organization's goals. Although the basic principles of strategy apply, the decision-making in international strategy is much more complex because of the 'barriers created by distance' (Ghemawat, 2001). Ghemawat identified four dimensions of distance; geographic, cultural, administrative, and economic all of which, in different ways, add complexity to decision-making. Managers have to decide not just which countries to target but how they are going to target those countries and they need some idea of the global systems and structures appropriate for their organization. How companies organize will depend very much on the type of product/service they produce. For products, such as commercial aircraft, which are transportable, subject to substantial economies of scale and do not have to accommodate local tastes then production is likely to take place in a small number of sites and output is exported. Boeing Commercial Airlines, for example, has just two main assembly sites in Renton and Everett in Washington. A third is under construction in North Carolina although for its latest development the 'Dreamliner' many of its components come from manufacturers across the world. For service industries where production and consumption are inseparable then direct investment has to take place in the host economy. This will also be the case where products need to be adapted to local tastes and where there are few economies of scale such as in packaged foods. Products such as telecommunications equipment, cars, computers, mobile phones, and pharmaceuticals where some local adaptation is probably necessary and for which there will be some economies of scale (but which can be produced anywhere and shipped around the world) then both direct investment and trade are important. Increasingly firms try to locate each part of the production chain where resource availability and cost is the lowest and this global mode of operations is becoming dominant. It is the most complex form of organization requiring decisions on the most appropriate locations for all aspects of the organization's operations. Whatever method they choose they are faced with the complex task of screening and evaluating foreign markets/countries and this is the subject of this section.

What makes an attractive market or production location? To begin with there has to be an expectation of profit but this must be weighed against the risk of operating in the country. However there is usually a trade-off to be made between risk and return. High attractiveness and high returns are usually associated with high risk and low attractiveness and low returns with low risk. Countries differ in terms of their attractiveness as a result of variations in the economic environment, growth rates, political stability, disposable income levels, available resources, government incentives, level of competition, and they also differ in the associated risk according to economic and political stability.

In this section we are going to build on the general macroenvironmental analysis already established in Chapter Four together with the industry analysis of Chapter Three, to provide a framework to assess 'attractiveness'. We concentrate here on attractiveness as a market or a production site (or for many managers in an increasingly globalized world, both) rather than for sourcing or partners. Much of the literature about evaluating countries is from the marketing world and focuses on international market selection (e.g. Cavusgil 1985) rather than production location but many direct investment decisions are heavily influenced by target market potential (Papadopoulos and Martin, 2011) and the sequential process they advocate can also be applied to decisions to locate albeit with some different considerations. Target market selection will, inter alia, be primarily concerned with indicators such as the size and growth of the market whereas location decisions will be more concerned with the ease of competition. Deciding between over 200 possible country locations is a daunting task and so the process which is usually recommended is that a general screening is undertaken which narrows down the choice to a group or cluster of countries, possibly a region, against some given criteria for which the data is readily available from public sources (Cavusgil et al. 2004). These selected countries may well be ranked before a more detailed analysis takes place in which those countries are compared with each other. For market selection, information on a range of variables which indicate market size and potential growth will be needed as well as information about potential competition and the general macroenvironment and how that might affect demand. For site location, information about the competition, resources, infrastructure, and any government incentives will need to be collected. Some information collected will be relevant to both decisions, for example the ease of doing business and the general attitude of government to business. Infrastructure will also be a common concern as both will require transport, communications, and power to operate. Once the field has been narrowed down to one or two possibilities then the final stage is to select the market or site and at this stage site visits and field research will probably be needed to collect more detailed and specific information and to talk to possible partners and/or suppliers and distributors. This can be an expensive process so thorough initial screening is important. Alongside all of this managers will also need to undertake a **risk analysis** to weigh against the possible returns before a decision can be made.

Collecting Data

In order to undertake an assessment of country attractiveness for markets and production sites companies have to undertake research and analysis which can be both time consuming and expensive. Like all research there has to be a balance between the cost of research and the benefits from the research as it is impossible to gather all the information and this may anyway result in information overload. There is a lot of information which can be obtained from the internet and for companies there are many private sector organizations providing country and industry reports at a price.

IMD World Competitiveness Yearbook

The IMD ranks 58 of the most competitive countries according to economic performance, government efficiency, business efficiency, and infrastructure. (A link to the IMD World Competitiveness Yearbook can be located on the accompanying website for this book.) Each of these four factors is then broken down into a number of sub-factors (327 in all) and scores given to each of these sub-factors. From this an overall total is calculated. These totals are then formed into indices with the most competitive given a score of 100 and the rest ranked below this with their relative score. Of course that is only 58 out of over 200 countries although these countries do account for the bulk of investment and trade. In 2010 Singapore topped their list with Hong Kong second and the USA third although all their scores were above 99 so there was little to choose between the top three. Switzerland was next at 96.126 and bottom of their 58 countries was Venezuela with a score of 27.970 (www.imd.org/research/publications/wcy/upload/scoreboard.pdf).

The Economist Intelligence Unit (EIU)

The EIU ranks 82 countries according to the attractiveness of their business environment (www.eiu.com/public). Their model covers ten different factors, political environment, the macro-economic environment, market opportunities, policy towards free enterprise and competition, policy towards foreign investment, foreign trade and exchange controls, taxes, financing, the labour market, and infrastructure. These categories are then broken down into between five and ten indicators and assessed for the last five years and the next five years. As with the IMD index overall scores are calculated and then countries ranked. (http://graphics.eiu.com/files/ad_pdfs/CF_PDF.pdf). They also produce country reports from over 200 countries.

For students trying to collect information these costly sources are not an option but fortunately there are now many sources of information available free of charge over the internet. The first to mention is the interactive map which is part of the **Online Resource Centre** attached to this textbook. Here you will readily find information on the economy, people, geography, and government of over 50 countries across all the continents of the world.

GlobalEDGE

GlobalEDGE is created and maintained by the International Business Centre Michigan State University. (See the **Online Resource Centre** for a link to this resource.) This is a very extensive resource bank and links to many other sites of interest. In its Country Insights database (http://globaledge.msu.edu/countries/) there are entries for 201 countries with information on the history, government, and culture of each country as well as a range of statistics on the economy. You can find, for example, that Nigeria has a population of 149 million people with a GDP (PPP) per capita of US$2,099 (2008 estimate). It mainly exports to the USA, India, and Brazil and imports from China, Netherlands, and the USA. It is ranked 134 out of 178 countries in Transparency International's Corruptions Perceptions Index (see Chapter Eleven) and 137 out of 183 in the World Bank's Ease of Doing Business Index. (http://globaledge.msu.edu/countries/nigeria/memo/). GlobalEDGE also ranks the market potential of 26 emerging markets. It uses eight factors in its assessment, market size, market growth rate, market intensity, market consumption capacity, commercial infrastructure, economic freedom, market receptivity, and country risk. In 2010 Hong Kong was ranked first followed by China and Singapore with, as for the IMD rankings, Venezuela in bottom spot. (http://globaledge.msu.edu/resourcedesk/mpi/). There is also an industry database with an overview of each industry, trade statistics, main corporations, and links to other resources (http://globaledge.msu.edu/industries/).

The World Economic Forum

The WEF Global Competitiveness Report ranks 139 countries based on publicly available information and its own survey according to national competitiveness. (See the accompanying **Online Resource Centre** for a link to this report.) It takes into account the microeconomic and macroeconomic foundations of national competitiveness based on the ideas outlined in Porter's diamond and the stages of development (see the section on The Competitive Advantage of Nations in Chapter Two). The WEF identifies '12 pillars of competitiveness' as:

- Institutions—the legal framework, government attitudes to markets and freedom, excessive bureaucracy, overregulation, and corruption.
- Infrastructure—quality roads, railroads, ports, airports, electricity supply, and telecommunications.
- Macroeconomy—economic stability.
- Health and Primary Education—a healthy workforce with a basic education.
- Higher education and training—higher grade skills necessary for the economy to move up the value chain.
- Goods market efficiency—sophisticated customers and competitive domestic and foreign markets.
- Labour market efficiency—flexible labour markets with appropriate reward systems.
- Financial market sophistication—with savings channelled to productive investment.
- Technological readiness—access to **information and communications technology**.
- Market size—domestic and foreign markets allow economies of scale.
- Business sophistication—quality of business networks and individual firms' operations and strategy.
- Innovation—high levels of R&D expenditure, collaboration between universities and industry, protection of intellectual property.

Figure 5.2 The twelve pillars of competitiveness

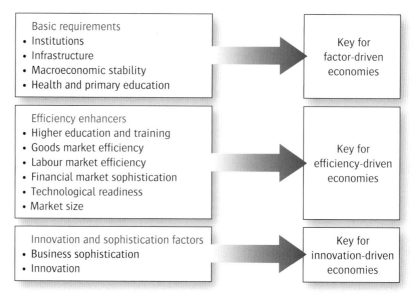

Source: The Global Competitiveness Report 2010–11, World Economic Forum

According to the WEF these 12 pillars are the key to national competitiveness but they are only separated in order to be measured (Figure 5.2). They are interdependent and reinforce each other. For example the 12th pillar of innovation is impossible without an advanced higher education system, or without the protection of intellectual property rights.

The WEF identifies three stages of development linked to the pillars and include the factor-driven stage, efficiency-driven stage, and the innovation-driven stage. The WEF allocates countries to each stage according to two criteria. The first is the level of GDP per capita (see Table 5.2) and the second is the share of exports of primary goods in total exports with the assumption that countries with a ratio of 70% or more are factor driven. Those falling in between are said to be 'in transition'. The full list of countries and which stage they are in can be found in the report.

In 2007/08 the USA topped the overall ranking of the 131 countries included at that time but this spot was taken by Switzerland in 2009 and 2010 with the USA relegated to fourth spot behind Sweden and Singapore (see Table 5.3).

Table 5.2 Income thresholds for establishing stages of development

Stage of Development	GDP per capita (in US$)
Stage 1: Factor driven	<2,000
Transition from stage 1 to stage 2	*2,000–3,000*
Stage 2: Efficiency driven	3,000–9,000
Transition from stage 2 to stage 3	*9,000–17,000*
Stage 3: Innovation driven	>17,000

Source: The Global Competitiveness Report 2007–08, World Economic Forum

Table 5.3 Global Competitiveness Index rankings 2010

Country	Rank	Score/7	Country	Rank	Score/7
Switzerland	1	5.63	Italy	48	4.37
Sweden	2	5.56	Malta	50	4.34
Singapore	3	5.48	Slovak Republic	60	4.25
United States	4	5.53	Latvia	70	4.14
Germany	5	5.39	Rwanda	80	4.00
Canada	10	5.30	Gambia, The	90	3.90
Luxembourg	20	5.05	Libya	100	3.74
Chile	30	4.69	Guyana	110	3.62
Kuwait	35	4.59	Paraguay	120	3.49
Cyprus	40	4.50	Nepal	130	3.34
Slovenia	45	4.42	Chad	139	2.73

Source: The Global Competitiveness Report 2010, World Economic Forum

Counterpoint Box 5.1 How useful are competitiveness indices?

Competitiveness is at the top of business and political agendas all over the world. On the basis of the indices, several countries and regions have established policies and institutions devoted to improving competitiveness. Despite its popularity in business and management literature and public policy, the concept of national economic competitiveness remains unclear and the object of criticism (Johansen, 1977).

Critics of the field of competitiveness research argue that there are limitations to the indices. They often fail to include a national economy's unique characteristics such as geography, culture, and demographics. In addition, the choice of variables and their weight is based on a particular concept of competitiveness and, therefore, a country's competitive rank will be different depending on which index is used. Johansen specifically contends that indices like that of the WEF pay too little attention to the importance of human capital in national competitiveness indices. These critics contend that indices risk diverting country attention towards areas with a lesser potential impact on competitiveness, with critical consequences particularly in developing and transition countries because the indexes can have a major impact on policy-making in these countries. This could lead to an inappropriate allocation of resources, an even less competitive economy, and possibly to protectionism.

Krugman (1994) questions the very concept of competitiveness rankings, challenging the basic assumption that countries compete with each other like companies and that a country's prosperity is based on its success in international markets. A firm can go out of business if it is uncompetitive but an economy does not. This is because all economies produce the bulk of their goods and services for domestic consumption and however uncompetitive an economy may be, most of its business continues regardless. Furthermore, when two firms compete, one wins and the other loses but when two economies compete, through trade, both can gain thanks to the law of comparative advantage. Finally, while an uncompetitive firm may be unable to lower its costs, an uncompetitive economy will do so through a deflation of the economy or a depreciation of the exchange rate or a combination of both.

Sources: Sabadie, J. A. and Johansen, J. (2010) 'How Do National Economic Competitiveness Indices View Human Capital?' *European Journal of Education*, Vol 45, Issue 2, p 236, June; Aridas, T., Global Finance Magazine at www.gfmag.com/tools/global-database/economic-data/10620-global-competitiveness.html#axzz1RbGcyBeJ; Krugman, P. (1994) 'Competitiveness: A Dangerous Obsession', *Foreign Affairs*, March/April

Mini Case Investing in Italy

Italy is the world's seventh largest economy with a GDP of US$1,858 billion (see Table 2.1) and a per capita income of US$35,435. It has a history of weak political structures and, recently, a declining economic base. In 2007 inward investment into the EU grew by 15% to US$610 billion, but in Italy inward investment fell 28% to a very low US$28 billion. In contrast, inward investment into France grew by more than 50% to US$123 billion.

Why? The World Economic Forum lists inefficient government bureaucracy and inadequate supply of infrastructure as the most problematic obstacles to doing business in Italy. In the WEF rankings Italy comes 48th and scores poorly in institutions, macroeconomic stability, labour market efficiency, and financial market sophistication. The most problematic factors for doing business are inefficient government bureaucracy, access to financing, tax rates and regulations, and inadequate supply of infrastructure.

Many tourists will see the Italian towns which retain their traditional shops as quaint, unlike many other European towns and cities which look very much alike with global retail chains and their familiar facades. But the reason for the absence of these chains is not that they don't want to be there, it is because it is made so difficult to invest there. Italy is ranked 87th in the Heritage Foundation's Index of economic freedom.

According to the *Financial Times* (22 January 2008) there are no KFC outlets in Italy and only 37 Burger Kings. McDonald's have managed to open 360 outlets but have battled bureaucracy, nationalism, and corruption to even get that far. The article goes on to say that AT&T pulled out of an investment, in 2007, in Telecom Italia because of political interference from the government. There is a mass of regulations, selective application, and long drawn-out processes for settling disputes.

All this means that many organizations feel Italy is not an attractive country in which to invest, with the consequence being economic growth below the European average, and estimated by the International Monetary Fund to be 1% for 2010 rising to only 1.3% by 2015.

Sources: Global Economic Forum; *Financial Times*; Economist Intelligence Unit, Heritage Foundation

Doing Business

The World Bank also has a very useful website called 'doing business' (www.doingbusiness.org). Again this gives basic information for 183 economies but its major focus is about starting a business in a particular economy and provides answers to such questions as dealing with construction permits, registering property, getting credit, paying taxes, enforcing contracts, and closing a business—as they apply to domestic small and medium-size enterprises. More detailed information about national and international statistics and trends in the world economy can be found at another World Bank site www.worldbank.org with information on over 200 countries. The World Bank is particularly interested in the development of countries and so it provides a lot of indicators of development such as figures on health, education, literacy, the environment, and infrastructure many of which can be good indicators of market potential. For example the number of internet users per 100 people in 2008 was 28.1 for Argentina but 70.8 for Australia (http://data.worldbank.org/indicator/IT.NET.USER.P2).

Other useful sources

The International Monetary Fund has a freely accessible database (www.imf.org/external/data.htm) providing data on economic and financial indicators such as GDP, GDP per capita, economic growth, inflation, government finance, balance of payments, and population.

Other useful sources of data from world organizations:

OECD (www.oecd.org/home/0,2987,en_2649_201185_1_1_1_1_1,00.html),

UNCTAD (www.unctad.org/Templates/StartPage.asp?intItemID=2068)

World Trade Organization (www.wto.org/)

The Economic and Social Data Service (ESDS) International is hosted by Manchester and Essex Universities and provides a useful link to many international datasets (www.esds.ac.uk/international).

UK Trade and Investment also has a useful website (www.ukti.gov.uk/export.html) aimed at supporting UK business to expand internationally through exporting. It offers detailed guides on how to do business in many countries across the world. The USA has a similar site at www.export.gov/index.asp.

The Central Intelligence Agency's World Factbook has information on every country recognized by the USA (https://www.cia.gov/library/publications/the-world-factbook/index.html). It covers each country's geography, people, system of government, climate, natural resources, infrastructure and economic conditions and is a most useful source of information to extract data for country screening. Moreover it is regularly updated.

International data problems

When collecting international data it is important to consider some of the problems associated with the data. Using the IMF World Economic Outlook database as an example most of the information comes from national datasets although the IMF advises countries on the compilation of the statistics in such areas as analytical frameworks, concepts, definitions, classifications, and valuations. Nevertheless compilation of national statistics is highly complex and not all governments have the same resources to allocate to the process so governments with limited funds and/or skills at their disposal may not place too high a priority on collecting information. Often information is not available or is out of date and sometimes it can be 'managed' for political purposes.

There are also definitional problems. Poverty, literacy, and unemployment, for example, can have very different meanings depending on the context or country. Unemployment in Sub-Saharan Africa is not reported in 36 out of 44 countries included in the IMF database. In any case many 'unemployed' workers may not be captured by the official employment statistics as they form part of the informal economy or even if captured there tends to be considerable underemployment in low productivity jobs more concerned with survival.

Even where there is common understanding of the terms capturing the data only takes place in the official recorded economy. Some economies have large informal economies and some have shadow economies where the production of goods and services is deliberately concealed from the authorities. As we saw in Chapter Two this can amount to over 60% for some economies.

Difficulties also arise in comparison when converting to a common currency, usually the dollar. Again as we saw in Chapter Two variations in exchange rates can lead to changes in GDP reported in US dollars when no change has actually taken place. Even when GDPs are converted to PPP terms comparison is difficult to make and care needs to be taken especially when trying to estimate market size.

The Process of Assessing Country Attractiveness

Figure 5.3 Country Assessment

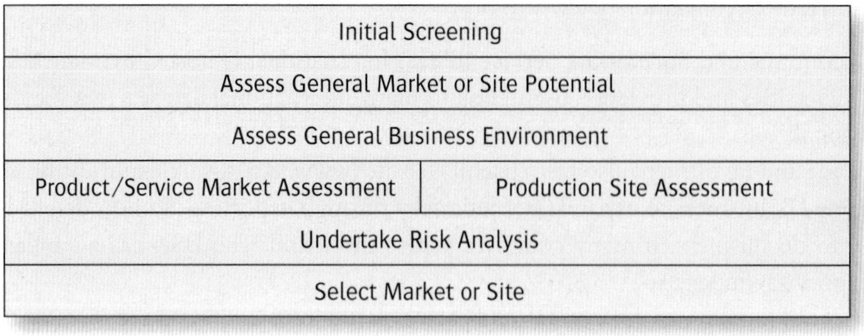

Initial Screening
Assess General Market or Site Potential
Assess General Business Environment
Product/Service Market Assessment   Production Site Assessment
Undertake Risk Analysis
Select Market or Site

Initial Screening

The first stage in any screening process is to eliminate those countries which have little chance of being markets or production sites by assessing if there is a basic demand for the company's products or if the basic resources required are present and that the business environment is acceptable. This is a fairly obvious first step which can eliminate many countries from the search. For example a country's climate can be a significant influence on the pattern of demand. There is no demand for heating in Malaysia, a tropical country with an average year round temperature above 30 degrees Celsius, but a substantial demand for air conditioning. This makes screening fairly straightforward for specialized goods of this nature but less so for other more widely consumed products such as confectionery, computers, and games.

Many businesses, as noted above, target countries which are close not only geographically but also in language, culture, and business environment and this can be a simple way of arriving at a handful of countries on which to do more detailed analysis. This could of course ignore many potentially good targets and is no guarantee of success. The USA would be considered to have more in common with the UK than does Thailand but as we noted in the opening case study Tesco entered Thailand with far fewer problems than it did the USA.

Assessing general market or site potential

Market potential

At this stage the objective is to develop a number of indicators which help firms assess the general potential of a market so that further countries can be eliminated. This assessment often uses broad economic, social, or infrastructural indicators as proxy measures. This is not intended to assess the size of markets for particular products but to be an overall assessment of the market potential of a country. In particular companies will want an indication of:

- Market size—the relative size of the overall economy. Population size can be a useful indicator of the number of potential customers while GDP per head and disposable income per head indicates whether there is a sufficient level of purchasing power—the overall buying power of those within the economy is referred to as market intensity. The distribution of income tells us about whether purchasing power is evenly spread.

- Market growth—size is important but the rate at which the market is growing is also important so that markets which are large but shrinking or growing very slowly can be avoided and those which are small but growing rapidly can be targeted. Growth in population and GDP are often used to assess market growth.

- Quality of demand—refers to the socio-economic profile of the customers within a market.

Learning Task

Using Table 2.1 in Chapter Two, select a high income, a middle income, and a low income country. Using the statistics in that table, and any other secondary data you can obtain, compare the potential markets of the three countries.

A common method of assessing basic potential is to look at macroeconomic indicators such as GDP, GDP growth, and GDP per capita. If you are selling digital cameras, flat screen televisions, and DVD recorders then Japan, with a per capita income in 2009 of US$39,740 is a better starting point than Haiti with a per capita income of only US$661 (IMF World Economic Outlook Database 2010). Other proxy indicators of wealth may also be used to assess market potential such as the ownership of cars, energy usage, televisions, computers, telephones, and internet usage, usually measured per head of population. These indicators are often associated with an expanding middle class and this is often a good indicator of market potential (see Mini Case). These types of figures are often used in combination with other indicators such as demographic changes (population size, growth, and age structure), degree of urbanization, and income distribution. The type of indicator used will depend on the industry. Financial service firms require countries where the population has considerable disposable income.

Another way of targeting countries is to use trade statistics, such as the United Nations' International Trade Statistics Yearbook, to look at the goods and services a country is importing from abroad, or to identify to which countries your domestic competitors are exporting. Looking at the domestic output of an economy to see what local producers are selling is another indicator. Many businesses will also follow their customers into new markets.

Site potential

Similarly, companies intending to produce abroad can do a quick scan of what they consider are essential resources to undertake production. Availability of raw materials is one such consideration, but access to labour and finance are other important considerations. As the reduction in costs is often a major reason for going abroad then the cost of doing business is also an important factor. This refers not just to labour but also the cost of finance, the price of energy, communications, transport, and tax rates. Against the low cost of labour the availability, skill level, and productivity must also be considered. A quick consideration of country risk can also eliminate many countries from the equation.

Mini Case The Expanding Global Middle Class

A recent OECD working paper defined the middle class as 'all those living in households with daily per capita income of between US$10 and US$100 in PPP terms'. On this basis about 28% of the global middle class is in the Asia Pacific region but this could rise to 54% by 2020 and 66% by 2030. China already has a middle class of 157 million people second only to the USA and is now the largest car and cell phone market. India's middle class is not yet so big but in 30 years time 90% of its 1.6 billion population could be middle class.

This has lots of implication for business but the dominant one is the rise of millions of consumers able to pay the bills for basics and have spare disposable income to spend on consumer durables. According to the Asian Development Bank 'Asia's emerging consumers are likely to assume the traditional role of the US and European middle classes as global consumers, and to play a key role in rebalancing the economy.' The demand for refrigerators, washing machines, televisions, computers, mobile phones, cars, and other consumer durables is increasing rapidly in these economies. The *Financial Times* reports that China has taken over from the UK and Germany as the largest export destination (in value) for Bordeaux wines. Burberry, the UK luxury fashion house, has opened 53 stores in China and has plans to extend this to 100 within five years. Vietnam's growth

has averaged 7% per annum for the past decade so HSBC and Standard Chartered banks have entered the market to target the growing Vietnamese middle class who are looking to the banks to manage their savings and investments.

Sources: Asian Development Bank; Key Indicators for Asia and the Pacific 2010; OECD Development Centre, Homi Karas, Working Paper No. 285, The Emerging Middle Class in Developing Countries; *Financial Times*, 17 September 2010, 3 October 2010, 19 November 2010

Source: www.istockphoto.com

Assess the general business environment

Assessing the general business environment can further eliminate some countries and provide useful information to be incorporated into the next steps in the process. In this section the PESTLE framework from Chapter Four is a useful framework to use.

Political and Legal Environment

The main factors in any assessment of the political and legal forces are government regulation, government bureaucracy and law and order.

Most governments impose ownership restrictions which hinder FDI according to the World Bank (World Bank 2010). In their report, Investing Across Borders, the World Bank claim that of the 87 countries surveyed 'almost 90% of countries limit foreign companies' ability to partici-pate in some sectors of their economies'. It was the removal of such restrictions in the retailing sector by the Thai government in the late 1990s that allowed Tesco to enter the country through a joint venture. Governments may also impose trade barriers so a scan for any barriers can soon eliminate a country. In a globalizing world with countries eager for FDI a ban is much less likely than a range of incentives trying to attract FDI.

Typical of the type of incentives are:

- financial incentives—investment grants or credit guarantees;
- fiscal incentives—reduced corporation tax;
- regulatory incentives—easing of health and safety or environmental regulations;
- subsidized services—water, electricity, communications;
- market privileges—preferential government contracts; and
- foreign exchange privileges—special exchange rates.

Other features of the regulatory and legal regime to consider are the tax regime, employment laws, health and safety laws, environmental policy, and competition policy.

Government bureaucracy, in relation to business, refers to the difficulties faced by business in day-to-day operations because of the number of regulations that they have to comply with, and the rigidity with which they are enforced, commonly referred to as 'red tape'. For example, how long does it take to obtain licences to operate and how many forms have to be completed and submitted to government, how often, and in how much detail?

The Heritage Foundation in the USA, a libertarian think-tank, assesses countries according to various measures of freedom—business freedom, freedom to trade, freedom from tax, regulation and corruption, the strength of property rights, and labour, financial, and investment freedom. It then ranks countries according to their scores out of 100. Those scoring between 80 and 100 are classified as free, from 70–79.9 mostly free, 60–69.9 moderately free, 50–59.9 mostly unfree, and less than 50 repressed. Hong Kong with a score of 89.7 was ranked 1st in 2011. The USA with a score almost 12% below Hong Kong was ranked 9th, and North Korea with a score of 1 was ranked 179th (see Table 5.4 below for the scores of a selection of countries). This is used in several of the country rankings including the globalEDGE rankings.

Learning Task

From Table 5.4, select one country in the top ten and one ranked above 100. Using any secondary data you can obtain, explain the differences in the rankings.

Secondary data is available in World Development Indicators on the World Bank website. The IMF produces country reports and the OECD carries out country surveys, reviews, and guides which are available on their websites. More information is also on the Heritage site under each of the country profiles.

Economic and Financial Environment

The major financial considerations will be rates of inflation, interest rates, exchange rates, credit availability, financial stability, and returns on investment. High and variable rates of inflation reduce the value of earnings and make forecasting and planning difficult, adding to the risk of operations. Similarly, exchange rate volatility adds to the uncertainty surrounding the value of any repatriated earnings, and how much capital is needed for investment. On the other hand some firms in the financial sector depend on volatility to make a living. Large industrial and commercial firms quite often have Treasury departments not only trying to protect earnings, but also trying to make money out of movements in exchange and interest rates. Equally

Table 5.4 Economic Freedom Index 2011 (%)

Country	Rank	Score	Country	Rank	Score
Hong Kong	1	89.7	Italy	87	60.3
Singapore	2	87.2	Zambia	91	59.7
Australia	3	82.5	Kenya	106	57.4
New Zealand	4	82.3	Tanzania	108	57.0
Switzerland	5	81.9	Nigeria	111	56.7
Canada	6	80.8	Brazil	113	56.3
Ireland	7	78.7	Indonesia	116	56.0
Denmark	8	78.6	India	124	54.6
United States	9	77.8	China	135	52.0
Bahrain	10	77.7	Argentina	138	51.7
United Kingdom	16	74.5	Vietnam	139	51.6
Germany	23	71.8	Russia	143	50.5
Taiwan	25	70.8	Angola	143	46.2
Norway	30	70.3	Venezuela	161	37.6
Malaysia	53	66.3	Korea, North	179	1.0

Source: www.heritage.org

important are the policies that governments use to try and control their economies and how successful they are as poor economic management can lead to volatility in the above.

Socio-cultural Environment

In assessing countries for markets and industrial locations socio-cultural factors also have to be taken into account. The cultural elements of language, religion, diet, values and norms, attitudes, beliefs, customs, and social relationships can all be important in terms of employment and in the acceptability of the product and any adaptations which need to be considered including labelling and instructions on use of the product. Social factors such as the distribution of income, modes of employment, living and working conditions, population characteristics such as ethnicity, the degree of urbanization, the availability and skill level of labour, the motivational basis of work, levels of pay, working hours, and the level of trade unionization are all important.

The growth of a 'middle class' in many emerging markets is boosting world demand for mass consumer goods and is making these countries the target for global multinational companies. China is at the forefront of this, although estimates of the growth of its middle class vary. What all seem to agree is that during the next 20 years a huge middle class with enormous spending power will emerge. Wal-Mart, Carrefour, Tesco, IKEA, and Kingfisher's B&Q are already well established in China.

Technological Environment

Another key feature of country attractiveness is how well developed the infrastructure is. An efficient transport and communications network is necessary for markets to function properly, and if the intention is to export a well-developed port infrastructure is also necessary. Key elements to assess in the infrastructure are:

- Science and technology infrastructure.
- Extent and quality of road network.
- Extent and quality of public transport network.
- Telephony network.
- Internet capacity.
- Water supply.
- Air transport.
- Quality of ports.
- Electricity production and certainty of supply.

Countries with well-developed infrastructures are attractive to business because they facilitate market growth and offer cheaper and better transport and communication networks. Developing countries with poorer infrastructures in Africa, Asia, or Latin America are less appealing.

Ecological Environment

The natural environment is the source of essential raw materials which are part of any basic screening but the natural environment is also the source of major but difficult-to-predict risks. Natural catastrophes such as earthquakes, flooding, and hurricanes are all unpredictable, although certain areas are more prone to these occurrences than others.

Mini Case Doing Business in Indonesia

Indonesia is an ex Dutch colony situated in South East Asia between the Indian Ocean and the South Pacific. It has a population of 237 million people and the world's largest Muslim population. Its capital is Jakarta, its currency is the Indonesian Rupiah, and the dominant language is Indonesian Bahasa.

The World Economic Forum describes it as a transition economy (see table 5.2) although most of its indicators, e.g. business sophistication, innovation, and especially market size are higher than the average transition scores. It has a per capita GDP US$2,963 (US$4,380 in ppp terms) with a growth rate of 6% in 2010 rising to 7% in 2015. (IMF estimates). Inflation and unemployment are both relatively high.

Its major industries are petroleum and natural gas, textiles, apparel, footwear, mining, cement, chemical fertilizers, plywood, rubber, food, and tourism. Its main export partners are Japan, USA, Singapore, China, South Korea, India, and Malaysia and main import partners are Singapore, China, Japan, Malaysia, USA, South Korea, and Thailand.

It fell six places in the World Bank's ease of doing business rankings from 115 to 121 in 2010. At 155 out of 183 it scores particularly poorly in the ease of starting a business. It fell 7 places to 116 in the ease of getting credit and 5 places to 130 in paying taxes. It also scores poorly in enforcing contracts, closing a business and registering property but does pretty well in trading across borders and protecting investors.

Its political risk rating has been improving moving up the rankings from 112 out of 140 in 2006 to 89 in 2010 and its score from 49.0 to 61.0. It is ranked 110 out of 178 in Transparency International's Corruption Perceptions Index.

Sources: World economic Forum Global Competitiveness Reports; IMF World Economic Outlook Database, 2010; globalEDGE Country reports; World Bank Doing Business reports ➔

Source: www.fotolia.com

Product/Service Market Assessment

Having reduced the number of countries for consideration in the first stage the next stage is to undertake a more detailed assessment of the potential within each of the selected markets. Initial screening is undertaken using broad indicators but at this stage much more specific industry indicators are called for in attempting to measure the total market demand in a particular industry and gaining as much information as possible about the market in each of the countries selected after stage 1. Data is more likely to be available for developed economies than for emerging economies but again this information is likely to cost. A Euromonitor report on alcoholic drinks in Brazil for example would cost in January 2011, US$1,900 (www.euromonitor. com/alcoholic-drinks). It is worth searching your library to see if it has subscriptions to such organizations as Mintel, Datamonitor, and Key Note.

The information that will be needed includes:

- size and growth rate of the market;
- major competitors, products, and market shares;

- prices, marketing, and promotions of competitors;
- distribution networks;
- local standards and regulations including trade mark rules and product liability;
- value of imports and exports of the product;
- tariffs and other trade regulations; and
- local cultural factors that may require product adaptation.

Information on the size of the market may not be readily available and often it is necessary to look at other indicators. For example, a UK company producing protective covering for transporting high value but bulky audio equipment wanted to investigate export markets in Europe. There was no information available on the products they produced but a lot on the music industry they supplied and so comparing this market with the UK market gave them an indication of the potential demand in Europe.

Competitive forces

As well as information on the size of the market an analysis of the competitive environment will be required using a model such as Porter's Five (Six) Forces. This was explained in Chapter Three and a checklist was provided to help in the process (see page 86).

Production site assessment

If FDI is taking place then a more detailed analysis of doing business in each market is required. This will include information on setting up the business, the quality and cost of the resources available, the infrastructure, regulations, taxation, financial reporting, and legal system. In addition it is important to find information on a whole host of practical issues as detailed in the following checklist:

- Foreign ownership of enterprises. What are the regulations restricting the ownership of enterprises and what type of businesses are permitted? What regulations exist concerning governance, procedures, and liability?
- Financial system—how developed is the banking system? What currency is used? Are there any foreign exchange controls? Is there a stock exchange?
- Investment—are there any investment guarantees? Are there any incentives? What business registration procedures exist?
- Labour regulations—what regulations are there covering expatriate employees? Are there social, health, and unemployment insurance payments to be made for local and expatriate employees? Is there a minimum wage?
- Disputes—how are disputes settled? Are there any regulations protecting intellectual property rights? Is there any competition law?
- Taxation—what taxes exist and what are the rates?
- Reporting—what are the statutory requirements for financial reporting?
- Expatriate employees—are entry visas and work permits required? What housing, education, and medical facilities are there for expatriate employees?

Counterpoint Box 5.2 Investing in Africa

According to Ha-Joon Chang (*23 Things They don't Tell You about Capitalism*), the perceived image of Africa is that it is, 'destined for underdevelopment'. It has a poor climate, lousy geography, small markets, violent conflicts, corruption, poor-quality institutions. It is ethnically divided making them difficult to manage and has a bad culture in which people do not work hard, do not save, and they cannot cooperate with each other.

These are sweeping generalizations for a group of over 50 countries but nevertheless probably most people's image of the prospects for Africa. However real GDP growth in Africa averaged 4.9% per annum from 2000 to 2008, dipped in 2008 along with the rest of the world but, according to UNCTAD, has rebounded faster and stronger than from previous global downturns accelerating to 4.7% on average in 2010. The growth was driven by exports, rising public expenditure on infrastructure, increasing FDI, good harvests, and increasing agricultural productivity. Average GDP growth is expected to be 5.0% for 2011 and 5.1% for 2012. For some countries such as Botswana, Angola,

Ethiopia, Ghana, Liberia, Malawi, Mozambique, Nigeria, Rwanda, Tanzania, Uganda, and Zambia growth will be significantly higher than this.

McKinsey is also optimistic about prospects for Africa. They highlighted 'government action to end armed conflicts, improved macroeconomic conditions, and microeconomic reforms' ('What's Driving Africa's Growth?', June 2010) as key reasons behind the growth. Although recognizing individual economies may struggle their analysis suggested that:

> Africa has strong long-term growth prospects, propelled both by external trends in the global economy and internal changes in the continent's societies and economies.

Sources: Chang, Ha-Joon, (2010) *23 Things They Don't Tell You About Capitalism*, Allen Lane; IMF World Economic Outlook Database, October 2010; *McKinsey Quarterly*, June 2010, 'What's Driving Africa's Growth'; UNCTAD, World Economic Situation and Prospects 2011

Risk

All of the above must be weighed against the risks of doing business.

Wars, hurricanes, terror attacks, uprisings, crime, earthquakes, and stock market crashes can bring companies to the brink, and sometimes tip them over the edge. The Gulf oil spill in 2010 cost BP upwards of US$20 billion and severely damaged its future operations in the USA. Earlier Hurricanes Katrina and Rita left the global insurance industry with a bill for US$80 billion. The price of insurance and re-insurance cover for areas of the world exposed to US hurricanes has also rocketed. A construction company agreed a contract in Nepal without seriously considering the implications of the uprising by Maoist rebels. Within weeks, a couple of its workers had died at the hands of rebels, and the roads on which the project relied had been blown up. The company was forced to pull out. More recently uprisings across North Africa and the Middle East have pushed up further the price of oil and following the earthquake in Japan stock markets suffered their biggest two-day fall for 40 years.

In today's more interconnected world, uncertainties can emerge almost anywhere as a result of product innovation, political change, changes in the law, or **market deregulation**. As business becomes more globalized—moving into new markets and transferring production to lower cost locations, it opens itself up to more risks, especially in countries with political instability and more vulnerability to natural catastrophes. International business needs to weigh up the risk factors when making strategic decisions on foreign direct investment.

Country risk

Country risk refers to the possibility of the business climate changing in such a way as to negatively affect the way in which business operates. Sources of risk include:

- change in political leadership;
- radical change in philosophy of political leadership;
- civil unrest between ethnic groups, races, and religions;
- corrupt political leadership;
- weak political leadership;
- reliability of the infrastructure;
- supply chain disruption;
- economic risks such as the volatility of the economy and foreign exchange problems;
- organized crime;
- poor relationships with other countries;
- wars;
- terrorism; and
- piracy.

One source of risk is a change in political leadership. Elections take place every four or five years in all of the advanced industrialized economies of the world, and with this can come relatively minor changes in attitude to business. This might result in changes in trade agreements or general changes in policies and regulations towards business. This is risk which is fairly predictable and shouldn't therefore be a problem. It is risk which is unpredictable that is the bigger problem. Although past patterns can be analysed to assess the risk, this also has its dangers. Kenya was generally considered as one of Africa's more politically stable countries with a thriving tourist industry bringing in about US$1 billion per year. Controversial elections in December 2007 triggered a wave of violent unrest resulting in more than 1,000 deaths and 250,000 forced from their homes. The World Bank was predicting growth in real GDP of 6.5% for Kenya in 2008 (Global Economic Outlook—October 2007), but the violence hit the economy by reducing the number of tourists to a trickle. Horticulture was Kenya's other big earner but this also depended on the tourist industry as did the many local handicraft sellers. According to the IMF estimated growth in 2008 was just 1.5% increasing to 2.4% in 2009.

It is the other sources of political instability that form the biggest risk. The possible consequences are:

- property seizure by:
  - confiscation—assets seized by government without compensation;
  - expropriation—assets seized with compensation;
- nationalization—takeover by government of an entire industry;
- property destruction;
- freezing of funds;
- kidnapping of employees;

Mini Case Piracy

This case illustrates the increased risks of global business operating in unfamiliar territory with lengthening supply chains.

21.03.2011: 0846 UTC: Posn: 03:47N–053:33E, around 495nm NE of Mogadishu, Somalia.

A tanker underway was chased by one mother vessel and two skiffs with four pirates in one skiff and ten pirates in the other skiff. The pirates fired upon the tanker with RPG and guns and attempted to board. The tanker increased speed, took evasive manoeuvres, and activated SSAS. Master, two crew and the unarmed security team remained on the bridge while all the other crew members retreated into the citadel. The vessel managed to evade the boarding. Due to the continuous firing two crew sustained injuries of which one was very serious. The vessel sustained damage as well.

Source: www.icc-ccs.org—weekly piracy report

This was one of three reported incidents that day and ten in the week. Piracy is defined by the International Maritime Bureau as:

An act of boarding or attempting to board any ship with the apparent intent to commit theft or any other crime and with the apparent intent or capability to use force in the furtherance of that act.

In 2011, by the 16 March there had been 119 reported attacks worldwide with 15 hijackings. 83 of the attacks and 14 of the hijackings had taken place in the waters off Somalia. On this date 28 vessels and 587 hostages were being held by Somali pirates.

The number of attacks has been rising. In 2006 there were 239 reported acts of piracy with 188 crew members taken hostage but this had risen to 445 attacks in 2010 and 1,181 hostages. Somali waters remain the riskiest and the attacks are spreading further into the Indian Ocean and Arabian Sea. Other hotspots are Bangladesh, off the coast of Nigeria, Indonesia, and around the South China Sea. There have also been attacks around South America and the Caribbean.

All figures and information have been taken from the ICC IMB Piracy reporting Centre available at www.icc-ccs.org/piracy-reporting-centre/piracynewsafigures.

- market disruption;
- labour unrest;
- supply shortages; and
- racketeering.

Risk assessments

Again many commercial organizations provide assessment of risk but at a price.

The EIU assesses countries for a variety of risks and sells the results to business. Country ratings are based on ten categories of risk:

- security;
- political stability;
- government effectiveness;
- legal and regulatory;
- macroeconomic;
- foreign trade and payments;

- financial;

- tax policy;

- labour market; and

- infrastructure.

They produce several rankings, political instability, operational risk, and overall country risk. The political stability index ranks shows 165 countries according to the level of threat posed to governments by social protest. Zimbabwe headed the list as the most likely to suffer with Norway the least likely. But to show how difficult it is to predict in 2009–10 Egypt was ranked as the 106th government least likely to be threatened by protests. Tunisia was ranked 134 with the USA at 110, and the UK at 132. This report and other related articles on the Economist Intelligence website can be found via the link on the supporting **Online Resource Centre** for this @ book. The least risky countries tend to be the most advanced economies, whilst poorer countries dominate the ranks of the most risky. Countries with good records on economic policy-making such as Singapore, Hong Kong, and Chile tend to do well. Those with poor payment records, institutional failings, and civil violence are the worst rated.

The World Bank has a worldwide governance indicator project which reports governance indicators between 1996 and 2009 for the following:

- voice and accountability;

- political stability and absence of violence;

- government effectiveness;

- regulatory quality;

- the rule of law; and

- control of corruption.

See http://info.worldbank.org/governance/wgi/pdf_country.asp.

Euromoney also produce country risk ratings for 100 countries aimed primarily at financial investors. It ranks countries according to political risk, economic performance/projections, structural assessment, debt indicators, credit ratings, access to bank finance, and access to capital markets. More on their methodology and rankings can be found via the link on the supporting **Online Resource Centre**. Their March 2011 rankings had Norway, Luxembourg, @ and Switzerland in the first three places with Mozambique at the bottom. The protests in the Middle East were reflected in their rankings with Egypt falling 23 places.

The World Economic Forum also produces a global risks report which is available at (http://riskreport.weforum.org/#). It identifies 37 major risks for 2011. Among these it highlights growing economic disparity and global governance failures. It also looks for growing signs of resurgent nationalism and social fragmentation as a result of economic disparity at both national and international levels. Other risks are:

- the global macroeconomic imbalances, currency volatility, fiscal crises, and asset price collapse;

- the illegal economy: state fragility, illicit trade, organized crime, and corruption; and

- the 'water-food-energy' nexus: shortages could lead to political instability.

It identifies five other risks to watch:

- cyber security;
- demographic challenges;
- resource security;
- retrenchment from globalization; and
- weapons of mass destruction.

Learning Task

Using the sources mentioned above compare the risk of doing business in China and Australia.

Select market and/or site

Having reduced the number of countries to a few and undertaken detailed analysis of the market and business environment in those few countries a decision has to be made about which country or countries to enter. This decision will require an estimate to be made of the market share the company is likely to gain.

One useful mechanism for comparing countries is to compile a grid using factors judged important to the decision, giving each of them a weight, according to the importance to the company, and then scoring each country. The factors will be different for a company just considering exporting from one considering FDI and will be different for each company. This idea can be used at any stage of the process with earlier grids using fewer and broader measures of potential. The grid at this stage is likely to be in at least two sections and probably three. One would be for market potential, one for the ease of doing business, and one for potential risk. At its simplest the grid could be just three rows with a score taken from published ranking tables for each of the above three categories but this is unlikely to capture all the factors a company might want to take into account. A grid might look like the following scoring each factor out of five and taking into account the weighting. In the first two categories higher numbers are preferable, indicating higher potential and greater ease of doing business. In the third category a low score is preferred.

From this grid country B and country D would seem to be ruled out given that their total score for the first two sections is 19 and 20 respectively with a risk score of 8 and therefore a net score 11 and 12. Country A has a net score of 21 (14 + 12 − 5) and country C scores 24 (16 + 14 − 6) and would seem to be the preferred choice although the risk is slightly higher. At this stage it is likely that managers would want to undertake field trips to each of the countries in order get a 'feel' for those countries, check the assessments and meet potential customers, suppliers and potential workforce. Only then will the final decision be made and contracts negotiated.

Table 5.5 Country attractiveness grid

Factor	Weight	Country A	Country B	Country C	Country D
Market potential					
Size of market	0.3	4	3	3	2
Growth rate	0.2	2	3	4	2
Market share	0.3	3	1	3	2
Investment required	0.4	3	1	4	2
Tax rates	0.1	2	2	2	2
TOTAL		14	10	16	10
Ease of doing business					
Starting a business	0.3	3	3	4	3
Getting credit	0.1	3	2	3	3
Paying taxes	0.1	3	2	3	2
Employing labour	0.3	3	2	4	2
TOTAL		12	9	14	10
Risk					
Political risk	0.4	1	3	2	3
Supply chain disruption	0.2	2	3	2	3
Foreign exchange risks	0.2	2	2	2	2
TOTAL		5	8	6	8

Learning Task

Carry out a screening of Venezuela for firms involved in:

- the production of newspapers and magazines

or

- oil production.

Comment on the conditions to be faced by US businesses considering setting up operations in Venezuela.

● CHAPTER SUMMARY

In this chapter we examined a process for assessing the attractiveness of countries. We saw that firms tend to follow a gradual process of internationalization, starting by exporting and gradually progressing to the establishment of overseas subsidiaries, although we noted that some firms appear to be 'born global'. Reasons for FDI include market access, lower production costs, and access to resources. China is leading the way in scouring the world for raw materials.

Firms intending to export or invest abroad can systematically screen countries to assess their attractiveness as new markets and/or production locations. This should include an initial assessment of the need for exports or investment before an analysis of the general business environment and the ease of doing business. Many commercial organizations specialize in country and market analysis but at a price. Once the initial need is established then a more detailed analysis of industry potential and operations is required before a final decision can be made.

● REVIEW QUESTIONS

1. The internationalization process is normally a gradual transition from exporting to FDI but some firms may be 'born global'. Explain what this means and why firms should want or need to be 'born global'.

2. Why is it that some firms locate their investments close to their markets whilst others appear to have the luxury of a much greater choice of location? Illustrate your answer with examples.

3. Investigate the factors that attracted Tesco to invest in the USA. Is it just the recession that has caused a problem and will they eventually succeed? Explain your answer.

4. Explain what is meant by political risk. Use examples to illustrate your answer.

5. Your company is looking for investment opportunities abroad and wishes to evaluate various country locations. Select three countries, one from South America (not Venezuela), and one from Africa, and one from Asia: compare the attractiveness of these countries for foreign direct investment.

6. The WEF produces a rank and scores for the 12 pillars for each country it assesses. Access the WEF website and look up the rank and scores for the USA, Italy, and Nigeria. Construct a table to show these and explain how the three countries differ in their attractiveness to foreign investment.

Case Study Starbucks in India

The Indian economy has been growing at record rates and despite the dip in 2008–09 growth in GDP is estimated by the IMF to continue at around 8% per annum to 2015. This growth has meant that India's population of 1.1 billion is becoming substantially richer with a large and growing middle class of more than 50 million consumers with disposable incomes ranging from US\$4,166 to US\$20,833. Its urban population is growing rapidly and it is estimated that it will grow by 230 million in the next 20 years.

It is ranked 134 (out 183) in the World Bank's ease of doing business rankings largely because it is ranked 32 in getting credit and 44 in protecting investors. It does very poorly in enforcing contracts (182), dealing with construction permits (177), and starting a business (165). It is held back by a slow moving bureaucracy, corruption, infrastructure failings, and regulatory and foreign investment controls.

Most people associate tea with India rather than coffee but there is in fact a growing coffee culture, especially among the ➔

Source: www.istockphoto.com

young. *The Independent* reported in 2007 that 'Café culture has taken a firm grip on India's cities' and that 40% per annum growth could be a conservative estimate. The Coffee Board of India estimate that domestic consumption of coffee has risen from 60,000 tonnes in 2000 to 94,400 in 2008 (www.indiacoffee.org/indiacoffee.php?page=CoffeeData). They also report that over 1,200 cafes have sprung up across India in the last decade and they say there is space for another 5,000 or so outlets. India's largest coffee chain is Café Coffee Day followed by Barista Coffee and then Costa Coffee who entered the Indian market in 2005 through a franchise tie-up with Devyani International Ltd.

The UK's Coffee Republic, Malta's Café Jubilee, and Australia's Coffee Club group are all allegedly looking for franchise partners. Meanwhile Starbucks has announced a deal with Tata Coffee. The deal will mean that Tata Coffee supplies Starbucks with the beans and together they will explore sites for establishing retail outlets. Starbucks reportedly attempted to enter the Indian coffee market in 2007 but had difficulty in getting approval from the Indian authorities.

Sources: *The Independent*, 2 December 2007; globalEDGE India country profile; Coffee Board of India (www.indiacoffee.org/default.php)

Questions

Using the above case and any other resources mentioned in the chapter answer the following:

1. India's urban population is estimated to grow by 230 million in the next 20 years. Analyse the consequences of this growth for the Indian economy.

2. Explain the attraction of the Indian economy as an investment location.

3. Investigate how easy it would be for a Western company to establish a new business in India.

4. Starbucks has chosen to enter the Indian economy with a domestic partner. Explain why this might be a more attractive proposition than direct investment.

5. What risks will Starbucks face in entering the Indian economy?

Online Resource Centre
www.oxfordtextbooks.co.uk/orc/hamilton_webster2e/

Visit the supporting online resource centre for additional material which will help you with your assignments, essays, and research, or you may find these extra resources helpful when revising for exams.

● FURTHER READING

For further discussion and ideas about assessing country and market attractiveness see:

● Cavusgil, S., Tamer, Knight, G., and Reisenberger, J. R. (2010) *International Business The New Realities*, 2nd edn. Harlow: Pearson

● Daniels, J. D., Radebaugh, L. H., and Sullivan, D. P. (2010) *International Business*, 13th edn. Harlow: Pearson

For the issues around doing business in China:

● Xiaowen Tian (2007) *Managing International Business in China*. Cambridge: Cambridge University Press

● Buckley, P. J., Clegg, L. J., Cross, A. R., Liu, X., Voss, H., and Zheng, P. (2007) 'The Determinants of Chinese Outward Foreign Direct Investment'. *Journal of International Business Studies*, Vol 38, Issue 4, p 499

● Morck, R., Yeung, B., and Zhao, M. (2008) 'Perspectives on China's Outward Foreign Direct Investment'. *Journal of International Business Studies*, Vol 39, Issue 3, p 337

● REFERENCES

Andersson, S. and Evangelista, F. (2006) 'The Entrepreneur in the Born Global Firm in Australia and Sweden'. *Journal of Small Business and Enterprise Development*, Vol 13, Issue 4, p 642

Arenius, P. (2005) 'The Psychic Distance Postulate Revised: from Market Selection to Speed of Market Penetration'. *Journal of International Entrepreneurship*, June 2005, Vol 3, No 2

Benito, G. R. G., Peterson, B., and Welch, L. S. (2009) 'Towards More Realistic Conceptualisations of Foreign Operation Modes'. *Journal of International Business Studies*, Vol 40, p 1455

Cavusgil, S. T. (1985) 'Guidelines for Export Market Research'. *Business Horizons*, Vol. 28, No 6, p 27

Cavusgil, S.T., Kiyak, T., and Yeniyurt, S. (2004) 'Complementary Approaches to Preliminary Foreign Market Opportunity Assessment: Country Clustering and Country Ranking'. *Industrial Marketing Management*, Vol 33, p 607

Christmann, P. and Taylor, G. (2001) 'Globalization and the Environment: Determinants of Firm Self-Regulation in China'. *Journal of International Business Studies*, Vol 32, No 3, Third Quarter

Fan, T. and Phan, P. (2007) 'International New Ventures: Revisiting the Influences behind the "Born-Global" Firm'. *Journal of International Business Studies*, Vol 38, p 1113

Freeman, S., Edwards, R., and Schroder, B. (2006) 'How Smaller Born-Global Firms Use Networks and Alliances to Overcome Constraints to Rapid Internationalization'. *Journal of International Marketing*, Vol 14, No 3, p 33

Gabrielson, G. (2005) 'Branding Strategies of Born Globals'. *Journal of International Entrepreneurship*, Vol 3, No 3, p 199

Ghemawat, P. (2001) 'Distance Still Matters: The Hard Reality of Global Expansion'. *Harvard Business Review*, September, p 137

Johanson, J. and Vahlne, J. E. (1977) 'The Internationalization Process of the Firm—A Model of Knowledge Development and Increasing Foreign Commitments'. *Journal of International Business Studies*, Vol 8, Spring/Summer, p 23

Knight, G., Madsen, T. K., and Servais, P. (2004) 'An Inquiry into Born-Global Firms in Europe and the USA'. *International Marketing Review*, Vol 21, No 6, p 645

Malhotra, N. and Hinings, C. R. (2010) 'An Organizational Model for Understanding Internalization Processes'. *Journal of International Business Studies*, Vol 41, p 330

OECD (2007) *Factbook*

Papadopoulos, N. and Martin, O. M. (2011) 'International Market Selection and Segmentation: Perspectives and Challenges'. *International Marketing Review*, Special Issue, Vol 28, Issue 2

Prashantham, S. (2005) 'Toward a Knowledge-Based Conceptualization of Internationalization'. *Journal of International Entrepreneurship*, Vol 3, No 1, Issue 5

Rennie, M. W. (1993) 'Born Global'. *McKinsey Quarterly*, No 4

Roett, R. (2010) *The New Brazil*. Washington: Brookings Institution

UN (2007c) *The World Urbanization Prospects: The 2007 Revision*

van Tulder, R. and Ruigrok, W. (undated) *International Production Networks in the Auto Industry: Central and Eastern Europe as the Low End of the West European Car Complexes*. Available at http://repositories.cdlib.org

World Bank (2010) *Investing Across Borders, Indicators of Foreign Direct Investment Regulation in 87 Economies*

Zheng, Y. and Chen, M. (2006) *China Moves to Enhance Corporate Social Responsibility in Multinational Companies*. Briefing Series, Issue 11, August, University of Nottingham: China Policy Institute

PART TWO

Global Issues

Chapter 6   The Socio-cultural Framework

Chapter 7   The Technological Framework

Chapter 8   The Political Environment

Chapter 9   The Legal Environment

Chapter 10   The Financial Framework

Chapter 11   Corporate Social Responsibility

Chapter 12   The Ecological Environment

CHAPTER SIX

The Socio-cultural Framework

LEARNING OUTCOMES

This chapter will enable you to:

- Explain the importance of the social and cultural environment for business

- Apply concepts of cultural theory to international business

- Explain and analyse major social and cultural elements such as demography, urbanization, religion, and language and their implications for business

- Compare and contrast the liberal, conservative, and social democratic social models

Case Study China The Importance of Guanxi

Firms from the West and Japan, attracted by fast growing markets and low production costs, have been rushing to do business in China. To be effective, it is important for business to have a knowledge and understanding of Chinese culture. In this case study we look at guanxi, an aspect of Chinese culture that is particularly important for firms wishing to be successful in China.

Guanxi refers to the networks of social connections based on trust and the reciprocal exchange of favours and mutual obligations. The exchanges taking place amongst members of the guanxi network are not solely commercial, but can involve gifts and banquets and can extend into other areas of social life such as helping a member of the network avoid loss of face or social status which is very important in Chinese society. The network members have an obligation to return favours and if this does not occur then the culprit loses face and incurs damage to their reputation. The degree of obligation is determined by one's ability to help—the weaker party expects to receive more, in exchange for less. Guanxi creates mutual dependence and indebtedness amongst the network members. In the business world, networks can involve customers, suppliers, competitors, partners in joint ventures, research institutes, politicians, and civil servants. Western firms wishing to do business in China need to create effective social networks. McDonalds came to grief in a site in Beijing because of inadequate guanxi. Despite holding a lease on the site, it was evicted in favour of a new-comer with stronger guanxi.

Guanxi has been embedded in Chinese society for thousands of years and is also an important feature of business life in Chinese communities overseas, Taiwan, Korea, and Japan. It is used by business to overcome competitive and resource disadvantages and the problems arising from an underdeveloped legal framework, for example contract law.

There is some debate amongst commentators as to whether guanxi is becoming more or less entrenched. While Guthrie argues that it is on the wane, Park contends that it has become more deeply rooted and that firms, particularly foreign firms, need to understand and use guanxi. He argues that effective use of guanxi is critical to business performance because it can give firms a competitive advantage, facilitate flows of resources, and generally make it easier to deal with the external environment. Li gives some support to this as he found a positive link between the performance of high technology new business ventures in China and political networking by their managers. Research by Gu found guanxi also had a positive effect on sales, growth, and market share of branded consumer products.

Sources: Guthrie 1998; Li and Zhang 2007; Ordóñez de Pablos undated; Park and Luo 2001; Xin and Pearce 1996; Gu, Hung and Tse 2008

Introduction

Why did the merger between two big pharmaceutical companies run into trouble? Why did McDonald's have to employ a queue monitor to control customers in Hong Kong? In a nutshell it comes down to culture. Following the merger between American pharmaceutical company Upjohn and the Swedish firm Pharmacia, it became clear that the cultures of the two parties were incompatible. Upjohn executives did not like the gradualist style of management practised by the Swedes which favoured consensus. The Americans were harder driven, preferred taking the decisions themselves and their main focus was on results. There were also smaller irritations. The Americans found it difficult to understand why the Swedes went on holiday for the entire month of August. On the other hand, the Swedes could not see why the Americans banned alcohol at lunch (*Financial Times*, 10 November 2006). McDonald's want customers to carry their own tray, queue up in an orderly fashion, pay, seat themselves, eat quickly, help clean up afterward, and depart. In Hong Kong, customers, following local custom, crowded round the tills and pushed their money over the heads of the people ahead of them. McDonald's appointed an employee to act as a queue monitor, and within a few months, regular consumers began to enforce the system themselves. But McDonald's also had to accept that customers, rather than paying a brief visit, used the outlets as leisure centres (Watson 2000).

Business operating at the international level has to face a variety of social and cultural environments where social characteristics, structures, and institutions may differ significantly. Societies across the world can differ enormously in terms of **demography**, health, class structures, composition by ethnic group, incidence of corruption, the importance of pressure groups, and in norms and values. To be successful, business has to be aware of the differences that could be important to it regarding levels and patterns of demand, the quality and quantity of labour, and the policies and strategies to be adopted.

This chapter examines the social and cultural environment. This encompasses a vast range of social and cultural characteristics which can vary significantly both within societies and between one society and another. Social aspects include the distribution of income and wealth, the structures of employment and unemployment, living and working conditions, health, education, population characteristics including size and breakdown by age, gender, and ethnic group, the degree of urbanization, and the provision of welfare for the population in the form of education, health care, unemployment benefits, pensions, and so on. The cultural components cover areas like language, religion, diet, values and norms, attitudes, beliefs and practices, social relationships, and how people interact. There are links between certain aspects of culture and social conditions, for example between diet and certain types of disease, values and norms and the role of women in society, religious beliefs and attitudes to contraception and their effect on birth rates.

There are far too many elements to be addressed comprehensively in a single chapter. Therefore, the chapter focuses on a limited number of social and cultural aspects. We start off by considering culture and then go on to consider some important elements in the social environment.

Culture

Culture can be seen as a system of shared beliefs, values, customs, and behaviours prevalent in a society and that are transmitted from generation to generation (Bates and Plog 1990). Hofstede (1994), the management scientist, described these elements of culture as the software of the mind, 'the collective programming of the mind which distinguishes the members of one category of people from another'. The values in the culture are enforced by a set of norms which lay down rules of behaviour. These rules are usually supplemented by a set of sanctions to ensure that the norms are respected. Culture comprises a whole variety of different aspects, including religion, language, non-verbal communication, diet, dress, and institutions to ensure that the values and beliefs are transmitted from one generation to another. Culture is dynamic, in other words, it changes over time not least due to the process of globalization with the increasing cross-border movement of goods, services, capital, and the migration of people.

Different cultures can have significantly different attitudes and beliefs on a whole range of issues. As we will see later, when discussing the various social models, there is a significant divide between the USA and Continental Europe on attitudes to social issues such as poverty. In the USA poverty tends to be seen as the fault of the poor whereas in Europe the poor tend more to be seen as victims of the system. Cultural attitudes can also vary towards issues such as, corruption, women at work, sexuality, violence, suicide, and time.

Cultural attitudes can have important implications for business. Some of the most influential research on culture and the workplace was carried out by Hofstede (1991; 2001). His study, the largest that had then been conducted, surveyed over 100,000 workers in IBM subsidiaries in 40 countries looking for cultural explanations of differences in employee attitudes and behaviour. He concluded that the norms and values embedded in national culture were a very powerful influence on the workplace, and that different approaches would be necessary when managing people from different cultural backgrounds. Hofstede (1994) concludes that the workplace can only change people's values to a limited extent (see Mini Case). The message for multinational companies was that they would be unwise to assume that an **organizational culture** that was successful in the cultural context, for example of the USA, would be equally successful in a completely different cultural context in, say, China (see Counterpoint Box 6.1 for a different view).

Hofstede's work (2007) also contains another message for multinationals. He contends that countries, especially big countries like China, India, Indonesia, and Brazil do not have a single national culture but a variety of cultures that can vary significantly from region to region. A similar point could be made for smaller countries, in Western Europe for instance, where different cultures may be based on ethnic group rather than region.

Counterpoint Box 6.1   Homogenization of management?

Multinationals face a dilemma when they operate abroad whether to standardize their managerial style or adopt local practices.

Work by academics such as Kerr (1960) suggest that this issue should become less important for MNCs as best managerial theory and practice are universally valid and applicable irrespective of the cultural, political, or legal context. According to this school of thought, best practice inevitably spreads across borders leading to a convergence of managerial approach. The idea that shareholder value should be maximized, resources should be allocated rationally, human resources should be systematically selected and developed, and their performance objectively appraised and rewarded are seen as universally acceptable managerial concepts. They see managerial convergence being driven by the forces of globalization and the international diffusion of technology. And because all humans share common needs so motivation theories also have universal validity, independent of any cultural context, examples being Maslow's hierarchy of needs model, Herzberg's two-factor theory, McClelland's achievement motivation theory, and Porter and Lawler's expectancy theory.

An alternative body of thought propounded by Hofstede (2003) and many others holds that managerial practices are heavily influenced by their particular cultural and institutional contexts and can not simply be transferred willy nilly from one culture to another. They cite significant differences in managerial style between rich and poor countries but also between nations such as Japan and the USA which they attribute to important cultural, political, and legal factors. Such authors also point to fundamental differences within the West particularly between the managerial model operational in the US and that in Europe. Work by Maurice indicates major disparities in approach even between European countries. This school emphasizes the continuing national differences in management practices and is sceptical about the possibility of international transfer of best practice. Their message to MNCs is that there is little room for the international convergence of management processes.

Researchers like Shimoni (2006) steer a middle course arguing that a hybrid form of management is developing across borders.

Sources: Hickson 2001; Hofstede 1980 and 2003; Kerr 1960; Child 2002; Shimoni 2006

Research has revealed fundamental cultural differences between East and West that have important implications for Western executives trying to do business in the East. Psychologists have shown that Eastern and Western cultures can vary significantly in terms of perception, logic, and how they see the world around them. Apparently, Westerners focus more on detail while Easterners tend to look at things in the round. For example, when American students were asked to look at a picture of a tiger in a forest, they focused on the tiger while Chinese students concentrated more on the background, that is, the context within which the tiger was located.

Researchers attribute this to different social environments. In East Asia, social environments are more complex, collective, and constrained. As a result, Easterners need to pay attention to the social context if they are to operate effectively. On the other hand, Western societies prize individual freedom and there is not the same need to pay heed to the social environment. With their focus on the individual, Westerners tend to view events as the result of specific agents, while those raised in the East set the events in a broader context.

Cultural differences influence the way firms in the East and West do business. For example, when an applicant for a job appears uneasy, Westerners are likely to see that as an undesirable characteristic of the interviewee which makes them unsuitable for stressful jobs. In the East, they will tend to view the uneasiness in the context of a stressful situation, the interview, and thus be less likely to attribute it to the character of the applicant. Similarly, North Americans, when posing a question, expect a trustworthy person to respond immediately, with any delay inspiring mistrust. In contrast, the Japanese view more favourably individuals who take time to ponder before giving a reply. Attitudes towards contracts also vary. Once a contract is signed, Westerners regard them as agreements set in stone while Easterners, such as the Japanese, take a more flexible view. They are quite happy to renegotiate if circumstances change. They look at the situation of their customers or suppliers in the round and may renegotiate in order to maintain a long-term relationship. In the East there is a desire for consensus and harmony. Westerners sometimes perceive Japanese managers as incompetent or indecisive because, in pursuit of consensus, they continually consult their team and are usually reluctant to challenge the decisions made by others (Nisbett 2005). One of the authors came across an example of this in an interview with the Scottish executive put in charge of Mazda, the Japanese car company, by the parent company, Ford. Coming from a Western culture, he was used to debate, discussion, and disagreement when arriving at decisions. In Mazda he found the reluctance to disagree among his senior managers extremely frustrating.

Hofstede and National Cultures

National cultures can vary significantly from one country to another and the differences can be reflected by employees in the workplace and by consumers in the market. Such variations in the psychology of work and organizations and in the marketplace have major implications for management. Managerial systems and approaches that work well in one country may be inappropriate for another.

Geert Hofstede, when working with IBM, noted that, while the company promoted an organizational culture in the form of common values, assumptions, and beliefs, there remained differences in attitudes and behaviour among IBM's international subsidiaries. He concluded that organizational culture is less influential than the attitudes and values prevalent in the national culture.

In his research, he identified five dimensions of culture:

- Individualism: reflects the degree to which people in a country act as individuals rather than as members of a group. Individualistic cultures value the rights of the individual over those of the group. By contrast, cultures low in individualism and high in collectivism emphasize the interests of the group rather than the individual. The USA, The Netherlands, France, and Germany are highly individualistic while countries in Asia, Africa, and Latin America score low on this dimension.

- Uncertainty avoidance: refers to the extent to which people prefer structured to unstructured situations. Societies tolerant of ambiguity, the unknown, and the unfamiliar score highly on this dimension. They operate with fewer rules and do not attempt to control all events or outcomes. Cultures with an aversion to uncertainty try to cling to rules and seek ways to control their environment. Latin America, Africa, France, Germany, and Japan have low tolerance levels of uncertainty in contrast to China and the UK. The USA lies somewhere in the middle.

- Masculinity: reflects the degree to which masculine values such as competition, assertiveness, a clear role distinction between men and women, money, income, job promotions, and status over feminine values like cooperation, quality of life and human relationships. The USA, Japan and certain South American countries, like Venezuela score highly on masculinity while Nordic countries and Africa score low.

- Power distance: shows the degree of inequality accepted as normal in a society. High power distance cultures accept, and are marked by significant levels of inequality, and hierarchy such as the differences in social class. Low power distance societies value equality and egalitarianism. In Latin America, Africa, Thailand, and Arab countries hierarchies are very important and power is distributed very unequally. Less powerful members of organizations, those on the lower rungs of the hierarchy, expect and accept the unequal distribution of power. In the USA and Nordic countries there is low acceptance of differences in power and a greater desire for equality.

- Long term/short term: long-term cultures make decisions based on long-term thinking and value perseverance and thrifty behaviour such as saving for the future. Brazil, India, and China have a long-term orientation. At the other extreme, the USA, Britain, Spain, Nigeria, and Pakistan focus on the short term while most European countries lie somewhere in the middle.

Counterpoint Box 6.2 Hofstede and his critics

Hofstede's work is widely recognized as a major contribution to the understanding of cross-cultural relationships. He has described his work as paradigm shifting. However, his work has also been criticized on five major grounds: 1) surveys are not a suitable way to measure cultural differences. It is not a good way of measuring phenomena that are subjective and culturally sensitive. Hofstede's response is that methods additional to surveys were also used; 2) nations are not the best units for studying culture. Hofstede retorts that national identities are the only way of identifying and measuring cultural disparities; 3) studying the subsidiaries of a single multinational, IBM, is not a valid method of uncovering the secrets of entire national cultures; 4) the data are old and obsolete; 5) five dimensions are not enough to represent the complexity of culture.

Critics point out that cultures are not limited to the confines of national frontiers but can straddle national boundaries.

Hofstede's assumption that the population of a country is culturally homogeneous has also drawn criticism on the basis that most countries comprise a variety of different ethnic groups. In his 2007 article Hofstede goes along with this argument. Some researchers claim that the study data are too old to be of relevance to modern times, particularly given the subsequent changes brought about by the impact of rapid globalization and the collapse of communism. Hofstede refuted this by claiming that cultural change occurs only very slowly and that cross-cultural differences are inherently stable and based on the evolution of societies over centuries. Hofstede accepts the criticism that five dimensions are too few and that more should be added.

Sources: Bond 2002; Hofstede and Bond 1998; Hofstede 2001 and 2007; McSweeney 2002 and 2002a; Redpath 1997

Implications for Business

Cultural characteristics have important implications for international business. According to Hofstede, centralized corporate control is more feasible in societies with large power distances while decentralization fits better in small power distance cultures. Collectivism is more likely to favour group rewards and family enterprises while job-hopping and individual remuneration systems are more acceptable in individualistic cultures. Masculine cultures prize competition and survival of the fittest while feminine cultures favour solidarity and sympathy for the weak. Uncertainty avoiding cultures are comfortable with strict adherence to rules and principles, while their counterparts are happy to shape policies according to particular circumstances and are more tolerant of deviant behaviour (Hofstede 1994). Studies in many countries show that culture has implications for human resource management, the management of change, entry strategies into foreign markets, the targeting of consumers, and selling to industrial customers (see An and Kim 2007; Eby 2000; Ramamoorthy 1998; Fisher 2001; and Mini Case below).

Business meetings in North America or Europe have formal agendas setting the order in which items are discussed, and each item is resolved prior to proceeding to the next. The Japanese, rather than deal with agenda items in a rigid sequence, may prefer a more flexible approach which enables them to get a better overview. To Westerners, meetings in Japan may appear unstructured, chaotic, and even threatening. However, Japanese managers are well used to such ambiguity.

Mini Case Culture and Purchasing

Hewett (2006) used Hofstede's model to investigate the impact of culture on the behaviour of industrial purchasing managers in Latin America and in the USA. The research results were similar to those found by Hofstede in his research.

Hewett found that the uncertainty avoidance dimension was a major influence on buyer behaviour. Her research showed that Latin American buyers tended to be loyal to suppliers even when there had been problems with the supplier's performance. US buyers were more likely to switch to get a better price or quality or as a result of supply problems. She concludes that, in cultures with low uncertainty avoidance such as the USA, sellers may have to work harder to ensure repeat business because buyers in such cultures will see a decision to switch suppliers as low risk. On the other hand, in cultures with an aversion to uncertainty like Latin America, where customers are loyal to existing suppliers, sellers would be well advised to focus on retaining customers rather than trying to win new customers.

Source: www.istockphoto.com

Source: Hewett 2006

Differences in approach can also be seen in negotiations. Westerners expect to focus on contentious issues and try to achieve the most beneficial outcomes for themselves. In contrast, the Japanese prefer to discuss areas of agreement, with the expectation that harmony will lead to the resolution of details. Such differences can lead to bad feeling in negotiations. Lee (2004) quotes a senior South Korean official involved in trade negotiations with Australia. Even though Australia was running a large trade surplus in agricultural products with South Korea, which was of serious concern to the Koreans, 'Australia, nevertheless, continuously puts pressure on Korea to buy more off them . . . they are self-centred, one-sided, only concerned with self-interest, not in considering another's situation or position' (p 76).

The upshot is that business has to take cultural differences into account when considering entry to foreign markets through exports, joint ventures, or through takeover or greenfield investment. Similarities between the domestic and foreign cultural norms and values may make entry for a firm easier whereas large differences may cause major difficulties due to misunderstandings and conflict where social groups do not want to give up valued elements of their culture (Oudenhoven and van der See 2002).

Learning Task

A survey was carried out in 14 countries where Muslims are either the overwhelming majority or a prominent minority. Questions were asked about attitudes to women and work. The responses are shown in Table 6.1 below. Examine the tables and answer the questions.

1. Which countries are most/least favourably disposed towards women working outside the home? Can a link be drawn with Hofstede's concept of masculinity?

2. In which countries do the majority/minority of respondents think that men should have more right to a job when jobs are scarce?

3. In the light of your answers, which countries would be a suitable location for a call centre employing both men and women?

4. A firm would like to give one of its female managers experience of working abroad. Which countries would appear to be most/least accepting of this?

Table 6.1 Women and the workplace

% Agree	Women should be able to work outside home %	When jobs are scarce, men should have more right to a job %
U.S.	97	14
Britain	97	12
France	97	20
Germany	97	19
Spain	97	12
Poland	92	44
Russia	95	47
Turkey	95	67
Egypt	61	75
Jordan	58	68
Lebanon	96	51
China	97	73
India	95	84
Indonesia	88	74
Japan	94	41
Pakistan	69	82
S. Korea	96	60
Argentina	87	43
Brazil	96	37
Mexico	90	28
Kenya	87	46
Nigeria	84	77

Source: 'Global Gender Gaps', 13 May 2004, Pew 2010

Religion

A core element of the culture in many societies is religion. In such societies religion is a major influence on the attitudes and beliefs that regulate behaviour. Christianity has the ten commandments, Islam has five pillars, and Buddhism has eight precepts. Each religion has a system of rewards for those who are good and punishment for those who are evil. Although there are hundreds of religions in the world, five of them, accounting for around 75% of the world population, predominate. Christianity with 2.1 billion followers has the greatest number of adherents, followed by Islam with 1.5 billion, Hinduism at 900 million, Buddhism with 376 million, followed a long way behind by Judaism with 14 million. Christianity and Islam together account for more than half of the world's population and operate in more regions of the world than all the other religions (Adherents; McFaul 2006). Even in China, where religion declined after the Communist revolution, it is estimated that around 400 million Chinese practise some religion, with 100 million of them Buddhists, 20 million Muslims, and up to 90 million Christians (www.adherents.com; www.bbc.co.uk).

Some religions lay down rules about which foods can and cannot be eaten, and how they should be prepared. For instance, Muslims are not supposed to consume pork, alcohol, foods that contain animal fats, tinned vegetables that include animal fat, frozen vegetables with sauce, particular margarines, and bread or bread products containing dried yeast. Animals have to be slaughtered in a particular way. In Judaism, meat from cattle, sheep, goats, and deer can be eaten but not from pigs and there are rules forbidding the mixing and consumption of dairy products with meats. As in Islam, animals must be slaughtered in a certain way. Only fish with scales and fins can be eaten. Hindus do not eat meat, but dairy products including milk, butter, and yoghurt are considered to enhance spiritual purity, and most Buddhists are vegetarian. There can be differences in dietary rules among faiths of the same religion. Some Christian faiths, such as Protestantism, do not have dietary rules while others, such as the Mormons, avoid alcohol and caffeinated drinks like coffee, and most Seventh Day Adventists do not eat meat or dairy products. The various rules and rituals around eating help religions reinforce their identity and distinguish them from other religions. These rules have implications for food manufacturers and retailers wishing to operate in countries with large numbers of practising Muslims, Jews, Hindus, and Buddhists (Better Health Channel).

Learning Task

The map below (Figure 6.1) shows the geographical location of major world religions (note that space limitations make it impossible for the map to represent the large number of Muslims in areas like Western Europe and North America).

1. Comment on the geographical spread of Christianity, Islam, and Judaism.

2. Discuss the implications for fast food retailers such as McDonald's or Burger King of expanding in the Middle East.

3. Where are the major markets for firms producing goods specifically aimed at Jewish consumers?

→

➜

Figure 6.1 Major religions of the world

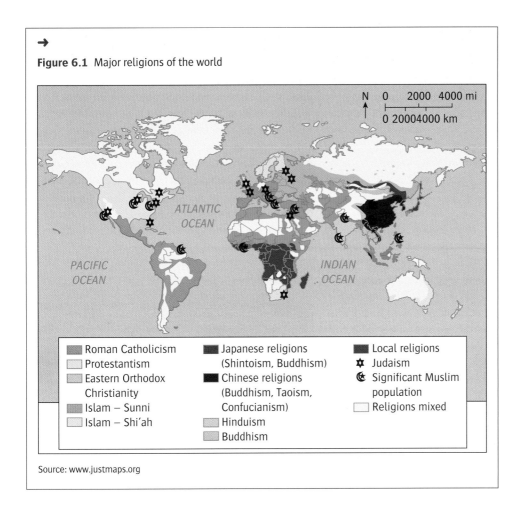

Source: www.justmaps.org

Language

Another important distinguishing feature for many cultures is language.

There is no agreed total on the number of languages spoken in the world today. Estimates vary from between 3,000 and 10,000 with Ethnologue suggesting a figure of about 7,000 (Gordon 2005; www.ethnologue.org). Estimating the number of speakers is complicated because it can vary widely from one decade to another, due to factors such as population growth and armed conflicts. The Asian population is forecast to grow by 25% to over 6 billion in the half century up to 2050, while the number of European inhabitants is expected to fall by some 75 million (UN 2008). As a result the number of speakers of Asian languages like Chinese, Hindi, and Bengali will increase dramatically while those speaking German, French, and Italian will fall. War, civil unrest, abuses of human rights, political instability, and people moving across borders to find work can also cause the figures to change significantly. Climate change could also play an increasing part in causing people to move across borders. The UN estimated the number of refugees at more than 10 million people in 2009 with the vast majority coming from Asia and Africa.

Mini Case Secularism Versus the Church

In many developed countries, and particularly in Western Europe, there has been a trend towards secularism shown by people moving away from religious beliefs and practices. Secularism is seen as a threat to the influence of the church because it rejects religiously prescribed rules, advocates the separation of the church and the state, the freeing of education from church authority, the rejection of church prescriptions about divorce, birth control, abortion, and sex before marriage. Decisions according to the secularists should be made on scientific and rational grounds. Moves towards secularism indicate a decline in the power of religion and religious institutions.

Italy, the home of the Vatican, is a good example for it has one of the world's lowest birth rates despite the opposition of the Catholic Church to contraception, and the incidence of abortion is similar to that of countries in North West Europe. A quarter of young cohabiting couples are unmarried and the share of Italians attending mass at least once a month has been in long-term decline.

But even in Western Europe, religion can still play an important role in politics. In Italy it managed to stop the government extending legal rights to unmarried couples including gays and restricted the scope of a law on the treatment of infertile women.

While secularization spread all over Europe in the post-war decades and grew in pace after the 1960s, in other areas of the world, such as the USA and Latin and Arab countries, there has been a resurgence in the power of religion and religious institutions. In the 21st century, religion appears to be gaining force in society, whether that be reflected in the growth of radical Islam or the spread of evangelical Christianity. Gallup polled 143 countries regarding the importance of religion. In most of Western and Eastern Europe, Australasia and countries such as China, Japan, and South Korea a majority of the population saw religion as unimportant. In contrast, religion was important for more than 75% of the population in many African countries, in Latin American countries like Brazil and Bolivia, and in India.

Source: *The Economist*, 31 May 2007; Swatos 1998; Falk 2006; https://worldview.gallup.com

Source: www.istockphoto.com

Pakistan, Iran, and Syria, with almost 4 million refugees were the largest hosts (UNHCR 2010). It is obvious from the figures given that major changes are occurring in the number and location of speakers of particular languages.

While estimates vary of the most commonly spoken languages, most research identifies Mandarin/Chinese, with over 1 billion speakers, as first in the rankings. Other languages in the top five are Arabic, Hindi, English, and Spanish. The top languages are spoken across many countries. Chinese is spoken in 31 countries, English in 112, and Spanish in 44 mainly Latin American, countries (www.ethnologue.com).

Business will be interested in the speakers of a particular language especially when they congregate together in large enough numbers to constitute a market worth exploiting or present an attractive pool of labour. In the past, language speakers, even where there were lots of them, were not attractive to firms when they were widely dispersed geographically because of high marketing and distribution costs.

Learning Task The Indian Diaspora

It has been estimated that there are some 25 million people of Indian origin settled in 70 countries around the world. In Fiji, Mauritius, Trinidad, Guyana, and Surinam they constitute around 40% of the population and form significant minorities in Malaysia, South Africa, Sri Lanka, the Middle East, Uganda, UK, USA, and Canada. They maintain their cultural identity through Indian films, newspapers, books, stage plays, traditional dances, style of clothing and food (Sahoo 2006; www.henryjacksonsociety.org).

What opportunities does the presence of 25 million people of Indian origin abroad offer to Indian business? Hint: do not simply concentrate on market and investment issues.

Visit the supporting **Online Resource Centre** for a video related to this learning task.

Countries Speaking the Same Language

Even where a single language is the mother tongue in several countries, business may still encounter certain difficulties. English is the mother tongue in the UK, the USA, Australia, and the major part of Canada but that does not mean that communication is always straightforward. Words used in one country may not be understood in another. The British talk about multi-storey car parks while the Americans refer to a parking garage and the Canadians to a parkade. Similarly, Americans go to a convenience store, the British to a corner shop, and the Canadians go to a depanneur. Australians, like Americans, drive on freeways while the British drive on motorways. And some words have completely different meanings. American cars run on gas but British vehicles run on petrol. In the UK mufflers are scarves that are put round the neck for warmth but in the USA it is part of the car exhaust system that deadens noise. Similar concerns are likely to arise with Spanish which is also spoken in many Latin American countries.

Issues also arise in countries where English is an official language, for example in India, Pakistan, and South Africa or where it is widely spoken as a second language. Firms would be foolish to assume that they can conduct business effectively in English because levels of proficiency in the language can vary dramatically. Some may have the ability to read the language but have difficulties speaking or listening to it. Even where people have a good level of proficiency, it does not figure that they can understand it to the required level, especially where the topic of discussion is technical or legal, for instance around product specifications or patents and copyright.

Facing such difficulties, business will often turn to translators and interpreters. However, according to Crystal (2003), translation always involves some loss of information because it is impossible to get an exact equivalence. The slogan 'Come alive with Pepsi' appeared in a Chinese newspaper as 'Pepsi brings your ancestors back from the grave' (2003, p 347).

Even big multinational companies can slip up with language. One of the most well-known gaffes was when General Motors sold the Nova model in Spain. Nova, in Spanish means, it does not go. Toyota offered the MR2 in France which, when pronounced, means excrement. Estée Lauder produced a hair spray for its German customers called Country Mist. Unfortunately, mist in German means manure (*The Times*, 9 November 2002).

For a long time, British and American firms have come in for much criticism for their linguistic insularity, their assumption that English is the global language of business, and that

Figure 6.2 Language skills of Europeans

Aggregate percentage of those with non-mother tongue skills*

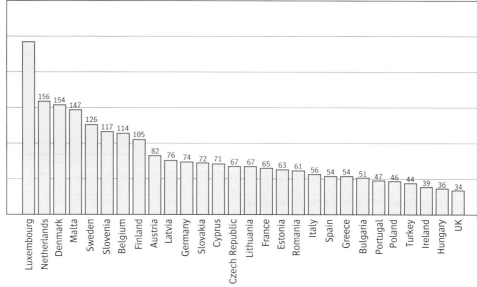

* the percentage saying they speak French plus the percentage speaking German etc.

Source: CILT

foreigners will be happy and able to communicate in English. Therefore, for them building up competence in foreign languages is not a priority. The situation may have improved to a degree, but one US senator said that his country was 'linguistically malnourished' (www.eric.digests.org). International surveys of language skills across Europe tell a consistent tale: the UK is bottom of the league in terms of competence in other languages. A survey of 28 European countries aggregated all non-mother tongue languages spoken and produced the results given in Figure 6.2.

While English is the most widely spoken foreign language throughout Europe and can be seen as the global language of business, it does seem as if competence in foreign languages is essential for international commerce. The evidence in Figure 6.3 suggests that if companies want to buy anything from anywhere in the world, they can manage with only English; if they want to sell something abroad, they need to learn the language of their customers.

Time

Different cultures vary in their attitudes to time. In some cultures the clock directs behaviour, in others behaviour is determined by the natural course of events in which people find themselves. In cultures where people follow the clock, they are careful to turn up on time for meetings and are likely to be irritated and frustrated if others do not. In other cultures, people behave according to event time which means that they organize their time around various events and participate in one event until it reaches its natural end, and then begin the next event. It has been found that the clock directs behaviour in North America, Western Europe, East Asia, Australia, and New Zealand. Event time is often found in South America, South Asia, Mediterranean countries,

Figure 6.3 Language and trade

Where English is the language of our customers, we sell more than we buy:

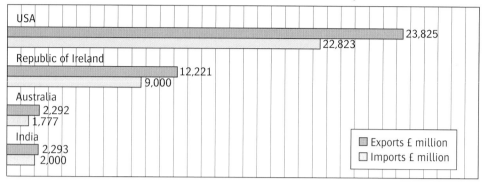

However, where the language of our customers is not English, we buy more than we are able to sell:

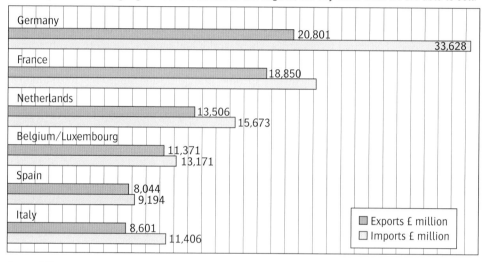

Source: CILT

and in developing economies with big agricultural sectors—in which people operate according to the seasons rather than the clock, and clock time is not yet fully part of people's work habits. North Americans will schedule a meeting for 9am, turn up on time and apologize if they are a few minutes late. In countries like Saudi Arabia, people may turn up 20 minutes late and feel no need to apologize. It may be that in cultures where status is important, this is demonstrated by the high status participants turning up late. In event time countries, a higher proportion of time at work is likely to be devoted to social activities such as chatting, having cups of tea or coffee. People from clock time cultures will often get frustrated by this behaviour, seeing it as time-wasting or an inefficient use of resources. However, these activities could be useful for a business because they may help to build up supportive groups so that when someone comes under pressure, colleagues will be happy to help out on a voluntary basis. Also it may be that important business relationships are made during what appears to be aimless social activity (Brislin and Eugene 2003).

The Social Environment

In this section we move on to examine various elements of the social environment. We start off by examining social divisions and then go on to compare three social models which show how the state looks after the welfare of its citizens. Subsequently we consider demography, the process of urbanization, and then health and education.

Divisions within Societies

All countries are characterized by social divisions. In some societies the major dividing lines are based on social class whilst in others it might be caste, ethnic group, age, or gender. Such divisions are often associated with inequalities between the various social groups in income, wealth such as land, property, shares, levels of health and education, and lifestyles. Such social inequalities are important to business insofar as they can affect levels and patterns of demand for goods and services. For example, countries where a relatively small social group control most of the income and wealth and the rest are relatively poor will have very different levels of demand for luxury goods compared to countries where wealth and income are more evenly spread. Similarly, great inequalities in health and education could affect the quality of the labour force.

Examining one of the areas of inequality, income, Brandolini and Smeeding (2007) found in their study of industrialized nations that, in terms of disposable income (income after deduction of income taxes and social security contributions) the US, among rich countries, had the highest level of inequality with the highest earners earning around six times more than the lowest. Only Russia and Mexico had higher levels of inequality. Most European countries have lower levels of inequality than the USA. The most equal societies were the Scandinavian countries, along with Finland and Holland. Japan and Taiwan lay somewhere in the middle of the rankings.

Social Models

In different countries, the state takes on varying degrees of responsibility for the welfare of its citizens. Today in most developed economies the state spends more on welfare than all other programmes. This spending takes the forms of benefits to the elderly, the disabled, the sick, the unemployed, and the young. It also usually involves spending on health care and education. Welfare policies may vary from country to country in terms of their aims, the amount of money spent on them, the priority given to different programmes, and the identity of the beneficiaries. In some countries the state intervenes only to provide a limited level of support to those who are regarded as deserving of help. This tends to be the dominant system in Anglo-Saxon countries. In others, such as in Scandinavia, benefits are universal, relatively generous, and open to the entire population. In poor countries the provision of welfare is often left to the family. Influences on the various approaches are the levels of economic wealth, different attitudes towards poverty, and towards the proper role of the state.

In the West, there are three social models in operation, the liberal, the corporatist, and the social democratic. Trying to classify different welfare states neatly into separate pigeon-holes is not straightforward, because they are continually adjusting to factors like globalization and to demographic change such as the **ageing population**, or to the feminization of the labour force. And sometimes a country will contain elements of several models. For example, the UK has aspects of both the liberal and the social democratic models. On one hand, as in the USA, unemployment benefits are not tied to incomes and require those out of work actively to seek employment or training or perform community service. On the other hand, the provision of universally provided social services in the UK such as the National Health Service and more generous in-work benefits for those who take low-paid jobs, a policy underpinned by a minimum wage, are more akin to the social democratic model prevalent in countries such as Denmark and the Netherlands.

The Liberal Social Model

The **liberal social model** found in the USA, Canada, and Australia and also, to an extent, the UK, is based on a clear distinction between the deserving and undeserving poor, with limits on the level of benefit payments. In liberal welfare states like the USA and the UK there is a sharp cut-off in unemployment benefits to discourage dependency and to force people back to work.

There is a commitment to keep taxes low and to encourage people to stay in work. While everyone is treated equally, there is a low level of welfare provision as expressed in the level of social expenditure (see Figure 6.4). There is a belief that people can better themselves through their own efforts, and that they may be poor because they do not try hard enough. In the USA, and to a lesser extent in the UK, there is scepticism about the state's effectiveness in tackling poverty. The welfare system, by giving benefits to single parents, is also believed to discourage marriage and to encourage single motherhood (see Lang 2007 on the US system).

Even in countries operating the liberal model, there can be major differences in the level and nature of welfare provision. For example, in the UK and Canada publicly funded health care is provided free to all at the point of delivery. All citizens qualify for health coverage, regardless of medical history, personal income, or standard of living. By contrast, the US system is a combination of private insurance paid for by workers through their employer, publicly provided insurance for the elderly (Medicare), the military, veterans, the poor, and disabled (Medicaid). The implementation of Medicaid varies greatly state by state. In the run up to the 2010 health care reforms around 43 million people in the USA did not have private health insurance, which made it the only developed country not providing health care for all of its citizens (University of Maine 2001). The 2010 reforms to the US system extended health care insurance to a further 32 million Americans but still left 23 million uncovered. (Visit the supporting **Online Resource Centre** for a video on this topic.) Large government budget deficits, brought about by the global financial crisis, have led to countries such as the UK to cut back on welfare benefits.

Now we look at the corporatist and social democratic models operating in many European countries. They share certain distinctive characteristics. There is a commitment to social justice. Neither system abandons those who fail. They aspire to high levels of employment, universal access to health care and education, adequate social insurance for sickness, disability, unemployment, and old age and have a well-developed system of workers' rights. These systems seem better at tackling poverty than the liberal model operating in the UK and the USA (Hemerijck 2002).

The Corporatist Model

The corporatist model is typical of continental European countries such as Germany, France, Austria, and Italy. Japan and Southern Europe also display elements of the corporatist model but spending is not as generous as in France or Germany (see Figure 6.4). In the past, the Church played an influential role on the model with its commitment to the preservation of the

Figure 6.4 Social expenditure % of GDP

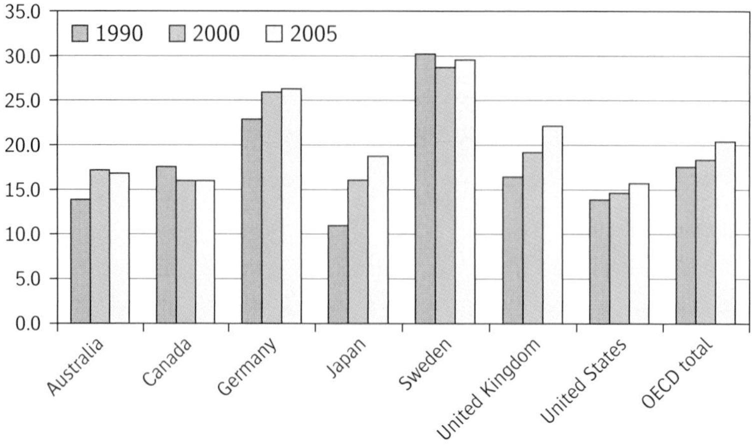

Source: OECD

traditional family. Thus, wives who were not working were excluded while family benefits were paid to those having children. The model emphasizes the importance of work and benefits are based on individual contributions. Benefits are generous relative to those provided in countries operating under the liberal model. In contrast to the liberal model, poverty is viewed as either inevitable or as a result of social injustice. This is why in Germany and the Netherlands, political parties of both the right and the left support an extensive welfare state. While around one in five households in Britain are poor the rate for Germany is one in eight.

In corporatist systems, there is a belief in the value of partnership and dialogue between the government and the various interest groups in society (sometimes called the social partners) such as trade unions and employers' associations. This is seen as a way of avoiding and reconciling conflicts over economic and social policy. It emphasizes solidarity between the various social groups and gives an important role to voluntary organizations such as churches and charities. In Germany, for example, church bodies are important providers of welfare services to groups such as migrants and young people.

The Social Democratic Model

The social democratic model, found in Scandinavian countries, has several defining characteristics. Sweden, where total state spending makes up 60% of the economy, spends almost twice as much on social welfare as the USA (see Figure 6.4). Britain falls between the low-spending USA and the high-spending continental European countries.

There are much lower levels of poverty in Sweden compared to the UK and the USA. According to UNICEF, less than 5% of Swedish children live in poverty while more than one in five are in that position in the USA.

Support is provided through generous welfare benefits for all those who are poor, old, young, disabled, and unemployed, and there is universal access to education and health care. There is a heavy commitment to helping families and to mothers wishing to work. This is financed by high levels of taxation. Secondly, unlike the liberal model, governments usually commit themselves to generating and maintaining high levels of employment and low levels of unemployment. There is an emphasis on taxation and spending policies that redistribute income from the rich to the poor and an active approach is taken to finding jobs for the citizens. As in the corporatist model, dialogue between the social partners is valued (UNICEF 2005).

Learning Task

Examine Table 6.2 which shows some health indicators in the USA, Sweden, China, India, and Mexico.

1. How does the health of the USA population compare with that in Sweden and India?

2. Use your knowledge of the different social models to come up with explanations for your findings.

3. What other explanations might be advanced?

Table 6.2 Health indicators for the USA, Sweden, China, India, and Mexico 2008

	Life expectancy (years)[1]	Adult mortality rate[2]	Infant mortality rate[3]
USA	78	107	7
Sweden	81	62	2
China	74	113	18
India	64	213	52
Mexico	76	121	15

[1] Life expectancy influenced by both positive and negative biological and social factors. Negative biological factors tend to show up quite early after birth so that death rates tend to be higher during the first year of life. Social factors are the main determinants of life expectancy. Positive elements include shelter, health care, educational provision, working conditions. Malnutrition, poverty, armed conflict, stress, and depression are examples of negative social aspects (Chattopadhyay 2010)

[2] probability of dying aged 15–60 years per 1,000 of population

[3] per 1,000 live births

Source: WHO, Global Health Observatory

Counterpoint Box 6.3 The clash of social models

Critics have launched bitter attacks on the social democratic and corporatist social models of Western Europe and blame them for the inferior economic performance of Europe compared with the USA, for example as regards economic growth.

They attribute high and persistent unemployment in France and Germany, declining productivity growth, growing fiscal strains, and the mediocre and inflexible services provided by the state, to high tax and spend policies and over-zealous interference with market forces, for example, the setting of a minimum wage. The essence of the argument is that high taxes and benefits discourage people from seeking employment and working hard and businesses from taking risks. The result is mediocrity—people who do well are penalized by high taxes while nobody is allowed to fail. The answer is to move towards a liberal regime where market forces are allowed much freer rein. Critics accept that the free market can result in undesirable outcomes but argue that it leads to a more creative, flexible, and productive economy. In their view people should take responsibility for their lives and not be protected by the state from the consequences of their own decisions. Thus, if individuals decide ➡

➡ not to buy health insurance then they, not the state, must bear the consequences when they become ill.

Defenders of the social democratic model challenge claims of superior US performance. They argue that growth of GPD per head has grown at roughly the same rate in the USA and the majority of European countries, and that European countries such as Sweden are richer than the USA as measured by per capita income, even though its economy is more highly regulated and has a larger welfare state. They also claim that French and German productivity levels are higher than in the USA. In addition, they say that inequality, poverty, and crime rates are much higher in the USA, and point to the large proportion of the US population not covered by private health insurance.

Sources: Green 1999; Navarro and Schmitt 2005; Pierson and Castles 2006

Asia

Asian countries spend much less as a proportion of their **national income** on social programmes (see Figure 6.5).

Some authors have noted that several East Asian societies do not fit in with any of the models outlined above. In Japan and the four 'tiger' economies of Hong Kong, Singapore, South Korea, and Taiwan, priority has been given to economic growth and welfare policies have been subordinated to that. They do engage in social policy but only after attending to their main objective of growth, and social policies are often geared to the achievement of economic objectives. While welfare arrangements do vary in each of these countries, there are some common elements. In these societies, there is hostility towards the concept of the welfare state, public expenditure on social welfare is low, social rights and benefits tend to be limited, and the family is expected to play a central role in social support.

The Japanese Constitution accords its citizens a minimum standard of healthy civilized life. They have a right to basic health care, and pensions are almost universal. However, benefits are limited and the family is expected to play a role (Holliday 2000). Compared with other OECD members, Japan ranks very low in the level of social assistance it provides (see Figure 6.4). The level of income inequality and relative poverty among the working-age population in Japan has been rising and is higher than the OECD average (Jones 2007). In Hong Kong, around half the population live in rented housing provided by the authorities, and rights to health care and education are universal but limited. The state does not provide pensions, unemployment benefit, or child benefit. In Taiwan, the bulk of welfare spending predominantly goes to groups in the armed

Figure 6.5 Asia social expenditure as % of GDP

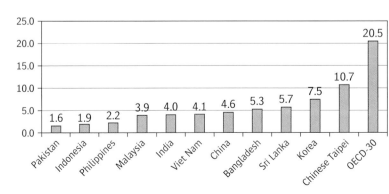

Source: Asian Development Bank 2008

forces, state bureaucrats, and teachers while the less fortunate, the poor, the handicapped, the old, and the young receive almost nothing (Holliday 2000). A lot of resources have been put into the education system in pursuit of the country's economic objectives (Chow 2001).

Welfare policy in China prioritizes three aspects: high growth at the expense of other public goods such as health care, education, and environmental protection; the favouring of those in occupations and sectors that are better off than average, for example, civil servants and high ranking military veterans; a large proportion of expenditures on pensions compared to health care and unemployment (Frazier 2006).

In India social programmes include the provision of education, housing schemes, income and employment-oriented programmes, schemes for providing jobs in government and places in higher educational institutions for lower castes. Social security takes the form of primary health care through government health care centres, nutrition schemes, and old age pensions for the destitute, widows, physically disabled, and informal sector workers. In India, more than four fifths of health care is privately financed putting it out of reach of the poor (Ma 2008; OECD 2009). According to Jayal (1999) the Indian state adheres, philosophically, to welfare based on need. In practice, the basis is one of charity, benevolence, and paternalism.

Demography

Demography is the study of population. It looks, amongst other things, at the size of the population, its rate of growth, the breakdown by age, gender, ethnic group, and the geographical distribution of the population.

World population was 6.8 billion in 2009, 750m more than in 2000. More than 80% of the world's population live in poorer regions, and just less than one fifth in the more developed regions—by contrast, in 1950 almost one third of the world population lived in rich countries (Table 6.3). Poorer countries have increased their share of world population because they have

Table 6.3 World population 1950, 1975, 2009

Area	Population (million)		
	1950	1975	2009
World	2,535	4,076	6,829
More developed regions	814	1,048	1,233
Less developed regions	1,722	3,028	5,596
Least developed countries	200	358	835
Other less developed countries	1,521	2,670	4,761
Africa	224	416	1,010
Asia	1,411	2,394	4,121
Europe	548	676	732
Latin America and the Caribbean	168	325	582
Northern America	172	243	348
Oceania	13	21	35

Source: UN (2009), World Population Prospects: The 2008 Revision

Table 6.4 The ten most populous countries 2010 (millions)

1. China	1.330
2. India	1.173
3. US	310
4. Indonesia	243
5. Brazil	201
6. Pakistan	177
7. Bangladesh	158
8. Nigeria	152
9. Russia	139
10. Japan	127

Source: US Census Bureau

been growing almost three times as fast as the more developed regions (UN, World Population Prospects: The 2006 Revision).

The number of people and their geographical location are of interest to business. Large populations may indicate that markets are there to be exploited. However, to be attractive to business, incomes in such populous areas need to be high enough for consumers to be able to afford to buy goods and services.

The most highly populated countries tend to be found in the less developed regions of the world. China and India are the most populous, each with over 1 billion people. Together they account for more than one fifth of the world population. The USA and Japan are the only rich countries to make the top ten in terms of population (Table 6.4).

Changes in Population Size

Population size is affected by the death rate, the birth rate, and net migration.

With increasing prosperity, advances in sanitation, diet, and medical knowledge, death rates have been declining, not only in the richer countries of the developed world but also in Asia, Latin America, and the Caribbean. However, in some former communist countries, like Russia and the Ukraine, rates have been increasing—largely as a result of deteriorating social and economic conditions, and in some African countries due to the spread of HIV/AIDS.

Birth rates at a world level have been falling. By 2010 they were expected to be at 2.56 children per woman—half the level they were in the 1950s. Women in the least developed countries have more than twice the number of children as their counterparts in the rich world (UN Population Prospects: The 2008 Revision). Birth rates tend to fall as countries become richer. In poor countries, where incomes are low and there is minimal or no welfare provision, people have large families to support them in their old age. Increasing incomes in these countries reduces the need for large families. The OECD suggests that the changing role of women also has a big influence on the number of children they have. As the level of education of women increases, along with their greater participation in the workforce, so the birth rate declines. The attitudes of women, especially in the developed world, are changing away from their traditional role as bearers and nurturers of children. Even in supposedly Catholic countries such as Poland, Italy, and Spain, where the Church condemns contraception, there have been significant declines in the birth rate (d'Addio 2005).

As regards international migration, it has been increasing since the 1970s. Estimates put the number of people living outside their country of origin at about 214 million, or 3% of the global population. At first sight, this seems fairly insignificant. However, as Martin (2008) points out, the picture changes if the inflow of migrants is measured as a proportion of the increase in the labour force. On that calculation, migration accounts for 30–40% of the growth of the labour force in the developed economies. In 2008, foreign-born workers accounted for 10% or more of the labour force in the USA, Australia, France, UK, Italy, Ireland, and in the Benelux countries (www.oecd.org). The global financial crisis and the accompanying recession will cause some of these workers to go home.

Migrants have moved in their greatest numbers to the more developed countries. By 2005, migrants accounted for more than 8% of the population in those countries. In 2005, about 60% of the world's stock of migrants lived in Europe and North America, followed by 26% in Asia, leaving only 15% in the other major regions of Africa, Oceania, and Latin America (Martin 2008). Between 2010 and 2015, the UN (2009) expects net migration into rich countries to be running at more than 2 million per year.

The Ageing Population

Increased life expectancy and falling birth rates mean that the average age of the population in many countries will rise, and this has become a major demographic concern. This will lead in some countries to stagnation and even decline in the population. Europe is the first region in the world to experience demographic ageing. By 2050 it is expected that the population in the EU will fall by nearly 10 million people, while the number of those over 80 years of age will increase by some 34 million (EU Commission 2005). The populations of other regions in Europe, Africa, the Middle East, and Asia will start to age later because their populations are much younger.

Mini Case Hispanic spending power in the USA

One of the major demographic changes in the USA has been the increase in the Hispanic* population. In 2009 there were nearly 50 million Hispanics in the USA, some 16% of the total population. According to the US Census Bureau, the number of Hispanics is projected to rise to 133 million which will double their proportion of the population to 30% by 2050. 35 million US residents speak Spanish at home and in four states, New Mexico, California, Texas, and Arizona, Spanish is spoken by more than a fifth of the population at home.

For business this means that the Hispanic market is one of the fastest growing in the USA. The spending power of these consumers, which was more than US$980 billion in 2008, is estimated to reach US$1.3 trillion in 2013, a much faster rate than that of non-Hispanic groups. Business, particularly in the car, food and drink, personal care, and telecommunications industries, has responded by spending millions of dollars

advertising in Hispanic media. Companies like Procter and Gamble (P&G), Unilever, and Shell launched expensive advertising and sales promotion campaigns to exploit the lucrative Hispanic market. P&G increased the smell factor of its Tide Tropical Clean detergent because of the Hispanic predilection for strong scents. Unilever aimed advertising of Ragu, its pasta sauce brand, specifically at Hispanic consumers. The language used in the advertisement is Spanish while the setting is Argentina.

*the US authorities define Hispanics as persons of Mexican, Puerto Rican, Cuban, Central or South American, or other Spanish Culture (US Census Bureau)

Source: *Financial Times*, 25 March 2004; US Census Bureau, National Population; Retail Merchandiser, Mar/April 2009; Convenience Store News, 25 August 2003

Learning Task

Examine the bar chart in Figure 6.6 that shows fertility rates (number of births per woman) in several countries in 2010. Bear in mind that 2.1 is the replacement rate—the rate required to keep populations stable. In other words each woman needs on average to produce 2.1 children to prevent the population from falling.

1. In which countries would the population increase were the birth rate to continue at its 2010 level?

2. Discuss the implications of low birth rates on demand for the following sectors:
   - Retailers specializing in clothing and toys for babies and young children
   - Universities training school teachers
   - Amusement parks

3. What are the implications of an increase in the number of older people on demand for:
   - Pharmaceuticals
   - Travel companies specializing in cruises
   - Providers of nursing homes for the old

Figure 6.6 Fertility rate 2010

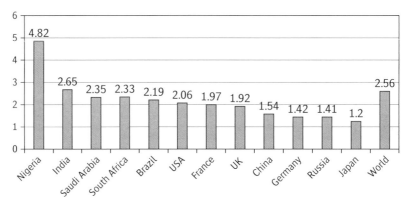

Source: CIA Factbook 2010

The OECD reckons that the ageing population could lead to shortages of labour, wage inflation, increased pressures on taxation and public expenditures, and a fall in the rate of economic growth. Unless something is done to alleviate the problem, taxes will have to rise to meet the increasing cost of pensions and health care, or public expenditure and benefits will have to be cut. Global growth could fall to less than 2% per year, which is almost one third less than for the period from 1970 to 2000. One response would be to encourage older people to work longer. This could be accompanied by a rise in the age of retirement, as has occurred in the public services in the UK. However, employers would need to change their negative attitudes to the employment of older workers. There would need to be more opportunities for flexible working and training for older people to help them develop new skills.

Urbanization

Another long-term trend in demography is the move by people from rural areas into towns and cities. This process is called urbanization. The developed world is already highly urbanized with three quarters of the population living in towns and cities, the corresponding figure for other areas of the world being less than half. According to the UN (2007), numbers living in urban areas are projected to increase to 5 billion or 60% of the world's population by 2030 (see Figure 6.7).

The pace of urbanization is particularly fast in Africa, Asia, and Latin America. Currently the proportion of people living in urban areas is 42% in China and 29% in India. The UN (2008) estimates that by 2030 the number of urban dwellers in Africa and Asia will double adding 1.7 billion, more than the combined populations of China and the USA and by 200 million in Latin America and the Caribbean.

At present, in the USA more than four out of every five people live in urban areas while the proportion is even greater in the UK, Australia, Argentina, Brazil, and South Korea. The process results in an increasing geographical concentration of people in cities. Tokyo has a population of around 33 million, New York 22 million, Seoul in South Korea 23 million, and London has 12 million. The great wave of urbanization, occurring in the last 50 years has affected poorer countries disproportionately. Large cities like Sao Paulo in Brazil, and Mumbai and Delhi in India have more than 20 million inhabitants (UNFPA 2008).

The implications of this process are manifold. It raises concerns in urban areas about increasing crime rates, lack of clean water and sanitation, sprawling ghettos of slums, and the ability of the infrastructure, for example road, rail, and energy networks to cope with such a large influx of people. Urbanization can also have repercussions on firms employing workers who have moved into cities from rural areas because people bring their rural ways with them. An executive of a UK firm producing soap in Accra the capital of Ghana, told one of the authors that their workers would not come to work when it rained because that was what they did on the farm. Furthermore, the firm had to provide transport to bring their employees to work because they were only used to walking to the farm from the village.

Figure 6.7 Percentage of population in urban areas

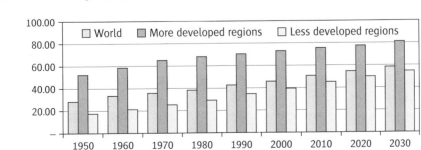

Source: UN

Mini Case Rapid Urbanization in Africa

The UN reports that Africa has joined India and China as the third region of the world to reach a population of 1 billion people, and it is expected to double its numbers by 2050. By then, Africa could have more than 60% of its population, that is over 1 billion people, living in cities compared with 500,000 in 1950 which makes it the world's fastest urbanizing continent.

The rate of growth of some cities defies belief. Cairo is now Africa's largest urban area, with 11 million people, but the UN says that by 2025 it will have been overtaken by Lagos, with around 15.8 million inhabitants and Kinshasa with 15 million. Luanda will be the continent's fourth largest city (see Figure 6.8).

The rapid increase in urban population will push up demand exponentially for shelter, food, water, and jobs and put pressure on cities already virtually overwhelmed by slums. The report says providing food and water for the billion extra people on the continent by 2050 will be a huge problem, especially because Africa expects to be hit hard by climate change.

The UN (2010) is extremely concerned by this and is urging African countries to plan their cities better, to avoid mega-slums and vast areas of deprivation developing across the

Figure 6.8 Africa's biggest cities (population millions)

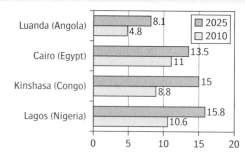

Source: UNEP 2010

continent. The pattern, according to the UN, is one of, 'inequality and human suffering, with oceans of poverty containing islands of wealth. Socio-economic conditions in African cities are now the most unequal in the world' (p 2). The situation is so serious that the stability and continuity of cities and also entire nations is under threat.

Source: www.istockphoto.com

● CHAPTER SUMMARY

We can see from our analysis that the international social and cultural environment offers major opportunities but also poses many threats and challenges to business.

One conclusion to be drawn is that business ignores cultural differences at its peril. As we have seen, in China, and in other countries with large Chinese speaking communities, a knowledge and understanding of guanxi in China is imperative. Hofstede has pointed out that, for companies, culture more often leads to conflict than synergy and that cultural differences can be a nuisance at best and are frequently a disaster. Firms need, as a matter of course, to take into account the varying national attitudes to such factors as hierarchy and power distance when considering entry to foreign markets through exports, joint ventures, takeover or when setting up completely new production facilities. To be successful abroad, firms need to be aware of the impact of culture on the conduct of business meetings, how negotiations are carried out, and on attitudes to contracts. Different national cultures may require business to respond to the local culture by changing their approach to the management of personnel, to the products they produce, and to the methods used to market their products. Failure to do so can lead to higher costs, lower levels of productivity, and poor sales and profits.

Our examination of the social environment demonstrated how social models vary from one country to another, from the less generous liberal approach in the USA to the more generous Swedish social democratic model. The debate continues to rage between the supporters of these models as to which model provides the best environment for business and which promotes economic performance and social cohesion. We have seen how changes in the social environment can be of importance for business. Demographic changes, for example, population growth in Asia and Africa but decline in Europe along with an ageing population, the process of urbanization, and different national levels of health and education all have implications for the quantity and quality of the labour supply as well as for the economic growth rate and the pattern of demand for goods and services.

● REVIEW QUESTIONS

1. The table below (Table 6.5) shows social spending as a percentage of GDP from 1990 to 2005.

   a. What is the trend in social spending over the period from 1990 to 2005? To answer this, look first at the OECD average. Do any countries buck the trend?

   b. Which countries were the highest spenders in 2005 and which the lowest?

   c. How would you explain Sweden's high levels of expenditures compared to those of the US?

   d. Some commentators have argued that globalization is leading to a 'race to the bottom' with regard to welfare spending. Do the figures lend support to that argument?

Table 6.5 Public social expenditure (as a percentage of GDP)

	1990	1995	2000	2003	2004	2005
Australia	13.6	16.6	17.8	17.8	17.7	17.1
Austria	23.9	26.5	26.4	27.5	27.3	27.2
Belgium	24.9	26.2	25.3	26.5	26.6	26.4
Canada	18.1	18.9	16.5	17.2	16.6	16.5
Czech Republic	16.0	18.2	19.8	20.7	19.7	19.5
Denmark	25.1	28.9	25.8	27.8	27.7	27.1
Finland	24.2	30.9	24.3	25.8	26.0	26.1
France	25.1	28.6	27.9	29.0	29.1	29.2
Germany	22.3	26.5	26.2	27.3	26.7	26.7
Greece	16.5	17.3	19.2	19.9	19.9	20.5
Hungary	..	..	20.0	22.2	21.7	22.5
Iceland	13.7	15.2	15.3	18.2	17.9	16.9
Ireland	14.9	15.7	13.6	15.8	16.2	16.7
Italy	19.9	19.9	23.3	24.4	24.7	25.0
Japan	11.4	14.3	16.5	18.1	18.2	18.6
Korea	2.9	3.3	5.0	5.6	6.3	6.9
Luxembourg	19.1	20.8	19.7	23.4	23.9	23.2
Mexico	3.6	4.7	5.8	7.3	7.2	7.4
Netherlands	25.6	23.8	19.8	21.2	21.1	20.9
New Zealand	21.8	18.9	19.4	18.2	18.0	18.5
Norway	22.3	23.3	21.3	24.5	23.2	21.6
Poland	14.9	22.6	20.5	22.3	21.4	21.0
Portugal	12.9	17.0	19.6	22.9	23.1	..
Slovak Republic	..	18.6	17.9	17.1	16.5	16.6
Spain	19.9	21.4	20.3	21.0	21.2	21.2
Sweden	30.2	32.1	28.5	30.4	29.9	29.4
Switzerland	13.4	17.5	17.9	20.3	20.3	20.3
Turkey	7.6	7.5	13.3	13.5	13.6	13.7
United Kingdom	17.0	20.2	19.2	20.5	21.1	21.3
United States	13.4	15.3	14.5	16.2	16.1	15.9
OECD total	18.1	19.9	19.3	20.8	20.6	20.6
Chile	..	..	10.7	10.3	9.4	9.2
Estonia	..	..	13.9	12.5	13.0	12.6
Israel	..	16.6	17.2	18.3	17.2	16.5
Slovenia	..		24.2	23.7	23.4	23.0

Source: OECD Factbook 2010: Economic, Environmental and Social Statistics

2. You are an engineering company struggling to survive in a fiercely competitive environment. Intense competition compels you to hold down costs by keeping stock levels of materials and components at a minimum, and to deliver to customers on time. Consequently, you are looking for ways to cut costs. One possibility is to set up in a cheaper location abroad.

   Your research indicates that the cheapest locations by far are found in countries with a culture that operates on event time rather than clock time. Explain what is meant by event time and clock time. Explore some of the implications for the company of setting up in an event time environment.

3. It is often claimed that UK business loses out abroad because of the inability of British managers to communicate in languages other than English. Discuss.

   To help answer this question, have a look at the CILT publication, 'Talking World Class: The impact of language skills on the UK economy' available at www.cilt.org.uk.

4. Chinese multinationals have been active investors in resource rich countries of Latin America such as Brazil. Go to Hofstede's website at www.geert-hofstede.com to discover how China and Brazil compare on the cultural dimensions.

   Explain how Hofstede's cultural dimensions could help international business manage its operations more effectively.

5. Which countries are particularly affected by the an ageing population? Tease out some of the implications of the ageing population in these countries for:

   • car manufacturers such as Ferrari and GM;

   • financial institutions such as pension funds;

   • medical schools; and

   • companies running holidays for 18–30-year-olds.

Case Study Culture and a Failed Joint Venture

Fons Trompenaars and Charles Hampden-Turner developed a model of organizational culture, similar to that of Hofstede. Elenkov and Fileva used elements of the model to analyse the reasons for the failure of a joint venture between Rover, a UK-based car maker, and Daru Car, a Bulgarian company, to manufacture cars in Bulgaria.

The first dimension they looked at was Universalism/ Particularism. Universalist cultures believe in following stand- ardized rules and sticking to agreements, with little space for relationships or friendships in business affairs. Particular- ists value the ability to respond flexibly to changes in their environment. For them, rules can be modified or bent. The UK executives, being universalists, saw business agreements, or pledges as obligations that should be respected and kept, no matter how the situation had changed and expected the same attitudes from their Bulgarian counterparts. They did not see any need to make an effort to develop relationships. The Bulgarians, however, exhibited a more particularistic

orientation, seeing the initial agreement as more of a starting point in a relationship that would evolve over time. Their focus was more on relationships and they consequently viewed personal contact as of vital importance for the success of the deal.

The second cultural dimension to cause problems for the venture was the Specific/Diffuse element reflecting the extent to which people in different cultures keep their private and working lives separate. Specific cultures maintain a high degree of separation as opposed to diffuse cultures. In specific cultures, people feel able to go directly to the point of a discussion and to state their expectations and intentions explicitly without knowing a great deal about the person with whom they are dealing. This was the Rover approach. The Bulgarians, coming from a diffuse culture, spent time trying to build up relation- ships in ways that appeared aimless to Rover executives, did not address issues directly, or clearly express their expectations of the deal.

➔

Source: Digital Vision

The third dimension, Achievement-Ascription pertains to status in the organization and whether it is acquired on merit (achievement) or on other factors such as age, family background, or social connections (ascription). Tension arose because the Rover managers believed in status being gained through merit while the Bulgarians were more attuned to the norms and values of an ascription culture. As a result, conflicts occurred when appointments were made to senior positions at the joint venture.

Elenkov and Fileva conclude that these cultural differences were 'fatal' for the joint venture. The case supports Trompenaars'

view that the vital task for international managers is not simply to be aware of cultural differences but to reconcile and take advantage of cultural diversity.

Sources: Elenkov 2006; Trompenaars 1995 and 1997; Bickerstaffe 2002

Questions

1. Explain the various cultural dimensions applied by Elenkov and Fileva:

- Universalism/Particularism
- Specific/Diffuse
- Achievement/Ascription

2. Compare and contrast the similarities and differences between the models of Trompenaars and Hofstede.

3. Discuss how cultural differences caused problems in the Rover joint venture.

4. Trompenaars identifies the USA, Canada, Australia and Switzerland as having a universalist culture. What issues might companies from these countries encounter when considering setting up operations in a particularist culture?

5. Trompenaars identifies China and Venezuela as espousing ascription norms and values. What issues might companies from these countries encounter when considering setting up operations in an achievement culture?

 Online Resource Centre
www.oxfordtextbooks.co.uk/orc/hamilton_webster2e/

Visit the supporting online resource centre for additional material which will help you with your assignments, essays, and research, or you may find these extra resources helpful when revising for exams.

● FURTHER READING

Hofstede and McCrae carried out further research correlating personality traits with cultural dimensions in 33 countries. See:

● Hofstede, G. and McCrae, R. R. (2004) 'Personality and Culture Revisited: Linking Traits and Dimensions of Culture'. *Cross-Cultural Research*, Vol 38, February

For results of a survey of business culture in 13 countries in Europe, Asia, and the Americas see:

● Ardichvili, A., Jondle, D., and Kowske, B. (2010) 'Dimensions of Ethical Business Cultures: Comparing Data from 13 Countries of Europe, Asia, and the Americas'. *Human Resource Development International*, Vol 13 Issue 3

For material on health expenditures and outcomes in Africa see:

● Anyanwu, J. C. and Erhijakpor, A. E. O. (2009) 'Health Expenditures and Health Outcomes in Africa'. *African Development Review*, Vol 21 Issue 2

The following article looks at global trends in demography:

● Walker, M. (2008) 'The New Demography of the 21st Century: Part 1—The Birthrate Surprise'. *Strategy & Leadership*, Vol 36, Issue 6

The following book is a comprehensive examination of important aspects of globalization and has a section devoted to culture:

● Goldblatt, D., Perraton, J., Held, D., and McGrew, A. (1999) *Global Transformations: Politics, Economics, Culture*. Stanford: Stanford University Press.

● REFERENCES

d'Addio, A. C. and d'Ercole, M. M. (2005) 'Trends and Determinants of Fertility Rates in OECD Countries: The Role of Policies'. OECD Social, Employment and Migration Working Papers 27, November

Adherents available at www.adherents.com

An, D. and Kim, S. (2007) 'Relating Hofstede's Masculinity Dimension to Gender Role Portrayals in Advertising: A Cross-Cultural Comparison of Web Advertisements'. *International Marketing Review*, Vol 24, No 2

Asian Development Bank (2008) Social Protection Index for Committed Poverty Reduction, Vol 2 Asia-Pacific Edition

Bates, D. and Plog, F. (1990) *Cultural Anthropology*. Maidenhead: McGraw-Hill

Better Health Channel available at www.betterhealth.vic.gov.au

Bickerstaffe, G. (2002) 'Culture Club: An Interview with Fons Trompenaars'. *Business Strategy Review*, Vol 13, Issue 1

Bond, M. H. (2002) 'Reclaiming the Individual From Hofstede's Ecological Analysis—A 20-Year Odyssey: Comment on Oyserman et al'. *Psychological Bulletin*, 128(1)

Brandolini, A. and Smeeding, T. M. (2007) 'Inequality Patterns in Western-Type Democracies: Cross-Country Differences and Time Changes'. Luxembourg Income Study, Working Paper Series, Working Paper No 458, April

Brislin, R. W. and Eugene, K. (2003) 'Cultural Diversity and People's Understanding in the Uses of Time'. *Applied Psychology: An International Review*, 52(3)

Busch, K. (2010) World Economic Crisis and the Welfare State, International Policy Analysis, February 2010

Child, J. (2002) 'Theorizing About Organization Cross-Nationally: Part 1—An Introduction' in M. Warner and P. Joynt, *Managing Across Cultures. Issues and Perspectives*, 2nd edn., 26–39. London: Thomson Learning

Central Intelligence Agency (2007) *World Factbook*. Available at www.cia.org

Chattopadhyay, A. and Sinha, K. C. (2010) 'Spatial and Gender Scenario of Literate Life Expectancy at Birth in India'. *Asia Pac J Public Health*, 22: 477

Chow, P. C. Y. (2001) Social Expenditures in Taiwan (China). World Bank Institute, January

Crystal, D. (2003) *The Cambridge Encyclopedia of Language*. Cambridge: Cambridge University Press

Eby, L. T., Adams, D. M., Russell, J. E. A., and Gaby, S. H. (2000) 'Perceptions of Organizational Readiness for Change Factors Related to Employees' Reactions to the Implementation of Team-Based Selling'. *Human Relations*, 53(1)

Elenkov, D. and Fileva, T. (2006) 'Anatomy of a Business Failure: Accepting the "Bad Luck" Explanation vs Proactively Learning in International Business' *Cross Cultural Management: An International Journal*, Vol 13, No 2

EU Commission (2005) Europe's Changing Population Structure and its Impact on Relations between the Generations, memo/05/96, Brussels, 17 March

Eric Digests available at www.ericdigests.org

Falk, R. (2006) 'The Christian Resurgence and World Order'. *The Brown Journal of World Affairs*, winter/spring, Vol xii, Issue 2

Fisher, T. F. and Ranasinghe, M. (2001) 'Culture and Foreign Companies' Choice of Entry Mode: The Case of the Singapore Building and Construction Industry'. *Construction Management and Economics*, 19(4)

Frazier, M. W. (2006) Welfare State Building: China in Comparative Perspective, Paper presented at the Annual Meeting of the American Political Science Association, August 31–September 3

Gordon G. R. (ed.) (2005) *Ethnologue: Languages of the World*, 15th edn. Dallas, Tex.: SIL International. Available at www.ethnologue.com

Green, D. G. (1999) *Benefit Dependency: How Welfare Undermines Independence*. London: Civitas

Gu, F. F., Hung, K., and Tse, D. K. (2008) 'When Does Guanxi Matter? Issues of Capitalization and Its Dark Sides'. *Journal of Marketing*, Vol 72, July 2008

Guthrie, D. (1998) 'The Declining Significance of Guanxi in China's Economic Transition'. *The China Quarterly*, No 154, June

Hemerijck, A. (2002) 'The Self-Transformation of the European Social Model'. Available at www.fas.umontreal.ca

Hewett, K., Money, R. B., and Sharma, S. (2006) 'National Culture and Industrial Buyer-Seller Relationships in the United States and Latin America'. *Journal of the Academy of Marketing Science*, Vol 34, No 3, Summer 2006

Hickson, D. J. and Pugh, D. S. (2001) *Management Worldwide: Distinctive Styles Amid Globalization*. London: Penguin Books

Ho Park, S. and Luo, Y. (2001) 'Guanxi and Organizational Dynamics: Organizational Networking in Chinese Firms'. *Strategic Management Journal*, Vol 22, Issue 5, April

Hofstede, G. (1991) *Cultures and Organizations: Software of the Mind*. New York: McGraw-Hill

Hofstede, G. (1994) UNESCO Courier. April, Vol 47, Issue 4

Hofstede, G. (2001) *Culture's Consequences: Comparing Values, Behaviors, Institutions and Organizations Across Nations*. Thousand Oaks, Calif.: Sage

Hofstede, G. (2003) Culture's *Consequences. Comparing Values, Behaviors, Institutions*. London: Sage

Hofstede, G. (2007) 'A European in Asia'. *Asian Journal of Social Psychology*, 10

Hofstede, G. and Bond, M. H. (1988) 'The Confucius Connection: From Cultural Roots to Economic Growth'. *Organizational Dynamics*, 16(4)

Holliday, I. (2000) 'Productivist Welfare Capitalism: Social Policy in East Asia'. *Political Studies*, Vol 48, September

Jayal, N. G. (1999) *Democracy and the State: Welfare, Secularism and Development in Contemporary India*. New Delhi: OUP, 1999

Jones, R. S. (2007) 'Income Inequality, Poverty and Social Spending in Japan'. OECD Economics Department Working Paper No 556, June

Kerr, C., Dunlop, J. T., Harbison, F. H., and Myers, C. A. (1960) *Industrialism and Industrial Man*. Cambridge: Harvard University Press

Lang, K. (2007) *Poverty and Discrimination*. Princeton and Oxford: Princeton University Press

Lee, H.-S. (2004) 'Outstanding Issues in Bilateral Economic Relations between Australia and South

Korea'. *Australian Journal of International Affairs*, Vol 58, Issue March

Li, H. and Zhang, Y. (2007) 'The Role of Managers' Political Networking and Functional Experience in New Venture Performance: Evidence from China's Transition Economy'. *Strategic Management Journal*, Vol 28, Issue 8, August

Ma, S. (2008) Sustainability of India's Welfare System in the Context of Globalization, MPSA Paper, 3–6 April

Martin, J. P. (2008) 'Migration and the Global Economy: Some Stylised Facts'. OECD, 29 February

McFaul, T. (2006) 'Religion in the Future Global Civilization: Globalization is Intensifying Religious Conflicts. What will Happen in the Years Ahead?'. *The Futurist*, 1 September 2006

McSweeney, B. (2002) 'Hofstede's Model of National Cultural Differences and their Consequences: A Triumph of Faith—A Failure of Analysis'. *Human Relations*, Vol 55

McSweeney, B. (2002a), 'The Essentials of Scholarship: A Reply to Geert Hofstede'. *Human Relations*, Vol 55:11

Navarro, V. and Schmitt, J. (2005) 'Economic Efficiency versus Social Equality? The U.S. Liberal Model versus the European Social Model'. *International Journal of Health Services*, Vol 35, No 4

Nisbett, R. E. (2005) *The Geography of Thought: How Asians and Westerners Think Differently—and Why*. London: Nicholas Brealey

OECD (2009) Society at a Glance—India, OECD/Korea Policy Centre (2009)—Asia/Pacific Edition

Ordóñez de Pablos, P. (undated) '"Guanxi" and Relational Capital: Eastern and Western Approaches to Manage Strategic Intangible Resources'. Available at www.iacmr.org

Pew (2010) Men's Lives Often Seen as Better: Gender Equality Universally Embraced, but Inequalities Acknowledged, Pew Global Attitudes Project, a project of the Pew Research Center

Pierson, C. and Castles, F. (eds) (2006) *The Welfare State Reader*, 2nd edn. Cambridge: Polity

Ramamoorthy, N. and Carroll, S. J. (1998) 'Individualism/Collectivism Orientations and Reactions Toward Alternative Human Resource Management Practices'. *Human Relations*, Vol 51(5)

Redpath, L. (1997) 'A Comparison of Native Culture, Non-Native Culture and New Management Ideology'. *Revue Canadienne des Sciences de l'Administration*, Vol 14(3)

Sahoo, A. J. (2006) 'Issues of Identity in the Indian Diaspora: A Transnational Perspective'. *Perspectives on Global Development and Technology*, Vol 5, Issue 1–2

Shimoni, B. with Bergmann, H. (2006) 'Managing in a Changing World: From Multiculturalism to Hybridization—The Production of Hybrid Management Cultures in Israel, Thailand, and Mexico'. *Academy of Management Perspectives*, August

Speulda, N. and McIntosh, M. (2004) 'Pew Global Attitudes Project: Global Gender Gaps'. Available at http://pewglobal.org

Swatos, W. H. Jr (ed.) (1998) *Encyclopedia of Religion and Society*. Available at http://hirr.hartsem.edu

Trompenaars, F. and Hampden-Turner, C. (1993) *The Seven Cultures of Capitalism: Value Systems for Creating Wealth in Britain, the United States, Germany, France, Japan, Sweden and the Netherlands*. London: Piatkus

Trompenaars, F. and Hampden-Turner, C. (1997) *Riding The Waves of Culture: Understanding Diversity in Global Business*, 2nd edn. London: Nicholas Brealey

UN (2007) Speed, Scale of Urban Growth Will Require 'Revolution in Thinking', June

UN (2008) World Population Prospects: The 2008 Revision

UN (2009) World Population Prospects: The 2009 Revision

UNEP (2010) The State of African Cities 2010: Governance, Inequality and Urban Land Markets, Nairobi, November

UNESCO (2010) Adult and Youth Literacy: Global Trends in Gender Parity, UIS Fact Sheet, September 2010, No 3

UNFPA (2008) State of the World Population 2007: Unleashing the Potential of Urban Growth

UNHCR (2010) 2009 Global Trends: Refugees, Asylum-Seekers, Returnees, Internally Displaced and Stateless Persons, 15 June

UNICEF (2005) 'Child Poverty in Rich Countries, 2005'. *Innocenti Report Card*, No 6

University of Maine (2001) 'The US Healthcare System: The Best in the World, or Just the Most Expensive?'. Available at http://dll.umaine.edu

Watson, J. L. (2000) 'China's Big Mac Attack'. *Foreign Affairs*, Vol 79, Issue 3, May/June

World Health Organization (2007) 'Health Status: Mortality'. Available at www.who.int

Xin, K. R. and Pearce, J. L. (1996) 'Guanxi: Connections as Substitutes for Formal Institutional Support'. *The Academy of Management Journal*, Vol 39, No 6, December

CHAPTER SEVEN

The Technological Framework

LEARNING OUTCOMES

This chapter will enable you to:

- Explain the meaning of technology and concepts associated with it

- Identify and explain the sources of technology and how firms go about innovating

- Explain why the intensity of technological activity varies by firm size, sector, and country base

- Analyse the importance of the technological environment, both domestic and foreign, for business decisions and performance

- Explain how the external environment allows business to protect its technology in an international context

Case Study Samsung

The case illustrates the importance of technology as a competitive tool. It shows how one company, Samsung, used technology to turn itself from a relatively small company, with products imitating those of its rivals, into one of the world's innovative leaders in consumer electronics.

Samsung is a multinational conglomerate based in South Korea with a total sales revenue of US$117 billion and employing around 157,000 (2009 figures). It is the world's largest consumer electronics company with sales of US$92 billion. Samsung is best known around the world as a consumer electronics brand. It is the largest producer of 3D TVs and it also makes smartphones, e-readers, notebook computers, printers, cameras, and camcorders. It is also the world's largest producer of two of the main components used in digital devices—liquid crystal displays (LCDs) and memory chips. Like other major TV makers such as Sony, Samsung is incorporating Wi-Fi into HDTVs and Blu-Ray players. Lagging a good way behind in the consumer electronics market, but offering fierce competition, are main rivals HP, Sony, LG, Toshiba, Nokia, Panasonic, Apple, Microsoft, and Dell.

Samsung's aim is to be ahead of its competitors in manufacturing technology, costs, and new product development. The company has done this by investing in technically advanced state-of-the-art plants making chips, flat screens, mobile phones, and other digital devices. Company management decided that it would no longer compete on price at the low end of the market but would improve its brand, design, and technology so it set up creative design centres in London, Tokyo, San Francisco, and Seoul.

As a result, the company has emerged over the past few years as one of the world's most powerful and fastest-growing technology companies. Its consumer electronics products, once dismissed as cheap imitations of more sophisticated Japanese products and produced with second-hand Japanese technology, have come to be regarded as some of the most innovative and desirable on the market. The company has consistently won awards for its product designs. Helped by the growing popularity of its stylish smartphones, Galaxy and Wave, it achieved, in 2010, a 22% market share and was the world's second largest maker of mobile phones after Nokia. Interbrand, in its 2010 brand survey, ranked Samsung 19th in the world putting a US$19 billion valuation on the brand.

Samsung like its rivals is subject to the main technological drivers in the sector. Convergence is driving the consumer electronics industry in technologies, products, services, and markets. Digitalization, miniaturization, and mobility and convergence—the tendency for different products to evolve towards performing similar tasks—are the main technological drivers. Intense competition is leading to commoditization of industry products, putting pressure on prices and margins, and firms are increasingly looking to technology and to emerging markets for growth. In order to mitigate competition, firms have entered into joint ventures. Samsung is no exception having established a joint venture with Sony. The company also plans to set up an advanced LCD panel plant in China, the largest market for LCD TVs.

Sources: Samsung Q3 Report 2010; Datamonitor, The Top 10 Consumer Electronics Manufacturers, September 2010; *Business Week* 18 September 2010; *Financial Times*, 25 April 2008; www.commercialwireless.ie; www.interbrand.com; www.mysolutioninfo.com; *Financial Times* 3 December 2010

Introduction

New technology is most visible in personal computers, smartphones, portable digital audio players like the iPod, digital cameras, and high definition flat panel TVs produced by the information and communications industry. It can also be seen in the products of other high-tech industries such as pharmaceuticals and biotechnology. Technology has become internationalized. Thus, consumer goods like smartphones, iPads, and BMWs can be seen on the streets of Mumbai as well as those of Berlin and Tokyo. Multinational companies, such as Microsoft, General Motors, and Sony, transfer production technologies from their domestic base to foreign operations and many like Nokia and Alcatel-Lucent take opportunities offered by the international environment to develop global research strategies, carrying out research and development both at home and abroad.

Technology is a double-edged sword for business offering many opportunities but also challenges. On the one hand, it opens up a variety of opportunities for business in terms of new products, processes, and markets. On the other, it leaves firms more open to a range of competitive threats such as takeover, increased competition, and even to the theft of their technologies. The rapid internationalization of technology means that firms need to monitor both their domestic and their foreign technological environments. For many industries, technology is of the utmost importance and can determine whether firms prosper or fall by the wayside.

What is Technology?

In simple terms, technology refers to the know-how or pool of ideas or knowledge available to society. Some is codifiable, meaning it can be written down and transferred easily to others but there is also tacit knowledge which is carried about in the heads of a firm's employees and therefore not easy to transfer.

Technological advance comprises new knowledge or additions to the pool of knowledge and can lead to changes in how businesses behave: for example changes in how goods and services are produced, how production processes are managed, the characteristics of the good or service, and how products are distributed and marketed. Technical change can refer to both groundbreaking advances in knowledge or simply to minor modifications of products and processes.

There are a number of terms associated with technology and it is useful to have an understanding of these. Research and Development (R&D) refers to the discovery of new knowledge (research) about products, processes, and services, and the application of that knowledge to create new and improved products, processes, and services that fill market needs (development).

Basic research is the pursuit of knowledge for the sake of it. In other words, it is carried out to push back the frontiers of knowledge with no thought of its commercial application. Such research is commonly funded by governments and is most often undertaken in universities or research institutes. It can be very expensive, take an inordinate length of time to yield results, and may produce no results at all.

An example of basic research was that carried out by Crick and Watson at Cambridge University. In 1953 they announced the most important biological discovery of the 20th century, the structure of deoxyribonucleic acid, DNA, the chemical of life. Crick and Watson's discovery of DNA spawned the biotechnology industry producing new treatments for genetic diseases such as cancer, multiple sclerosis, and cystic fibrosis. It led to numerous scientific discoveries that have changed our lives, from the food we eat to the seeds that farmers use in their fields and to the DNA testing used by the police to help identify criminals.

While there are businesses, for example in the electronics and pharmaceuticals industries, helping to fund basic research in the hope that some commercially exploitable ideas will be generated, firms, as a rule, do not usually get involved.

Companies are normally more interested in applied research, that is, activities intended to lead to new or improved products and processes with clear and more immediate commercial uses. Even in applied research, there is no guarantee that results will be exploitable commercially. Scientists at General Electric (GE), one of the biggest companies in the world with interests ranging from jet engines to nuclear power stations to financial services, estimate that around 20% of the company research projects are scrapped each year.

Innovation is the commercial exploitation of new knowledge, in other words, developing new ideas into products and production processes and selling them on to customers. It is often measured by R&D spending or by the number of patents—a **patent** gives its owner the exclusive right to exploit the idea and gives it the legal right to stop others from using it. But innovation can also arise through investment in new machinery and equipment, market development, skills, brands, new ways of working, new business processes, and linkages with other organizations. It can involve the implementation of major advances in technical knowledge such as the digitization of electronic equipment, or small incremental changes such as a minor improvement in a production process. When firms come up with new ideas for products, processes, brands, and so on these become part of their **intellectual property**.

The spread of innovation from one firm and industry to another, nationally and internationally is known as **technological diffusion**. Diffusion has been growing at a rapid pace as is shown by the growth of high-technology exports, foreign licensing agreements, and the foreign ownership of patents. After 1990, high-technology exports worldwide grew very rapidly with Chinese manufacturing industries performing particularly well. In 2006, with a share of 17%, China overtook the USA, EU, and Japan (Eurostat, Statistics in Focus 25/2009).

Although the intensity of cross-border technological diffusion has been increasing, it has not affected all countries equally. Taking patent ownership as a measure, countries such as Luxembourg, Russia, Hungary, Singapore, and China show high levels of foreign ownership, with more than half of domestic inventions being wholly or partly owned by foreigners. Even in the USA foreigners accounted for more than half the patents granted in 2009 (US Patent Office). On the other hand, less than 5% of patents in Japan and South Korea are foreign-owned. The foreign owners, predominantly MNCs based in the triad of the USA, the EU, or Japan, have a tendency to own patents in countries with close historical and cultural links as well as geographical proximity to their home country (OECD Science, Technology and Industry Scoreboard 2009).

The degree of internationalization varies across different technologies. R&D in pharmaceuticals, motor vehicles, chemicals and the manufacturing of information and communication technologies are more internationalized than other sectors. Furthermore, some countries are dependent on foreign companies for their R&D capabilities. Foreign MNCs account for a significant proportion of R&D spending in Ireland, Sweden, Spain, Canada, and the UK as compared with the USA and Japan. The R&D activities of US MNCs are much more internationalized than Japanese companies (OECD 2008). Figure 7.1 shows R&D by foreign MNCs in the USA and by US MNCs abroad.

Globalization in general, and multinational companies in particular, are important vehicles for the international diffusion of new knowledge through their trading, investment, and

Learning Task

Examine Figure 7.1 and answer the questions below.

1. Which regions abroad are most favoured by US MNCs for investment in R&D?
2. Which regions' MNCs like to invest in R&D in the USA?
3. Advance explanations for your answers to both questions.

Figure 7.1 R&D by foreign MNCs in USA and by US MNCs abroad 2006 (US$ billion)

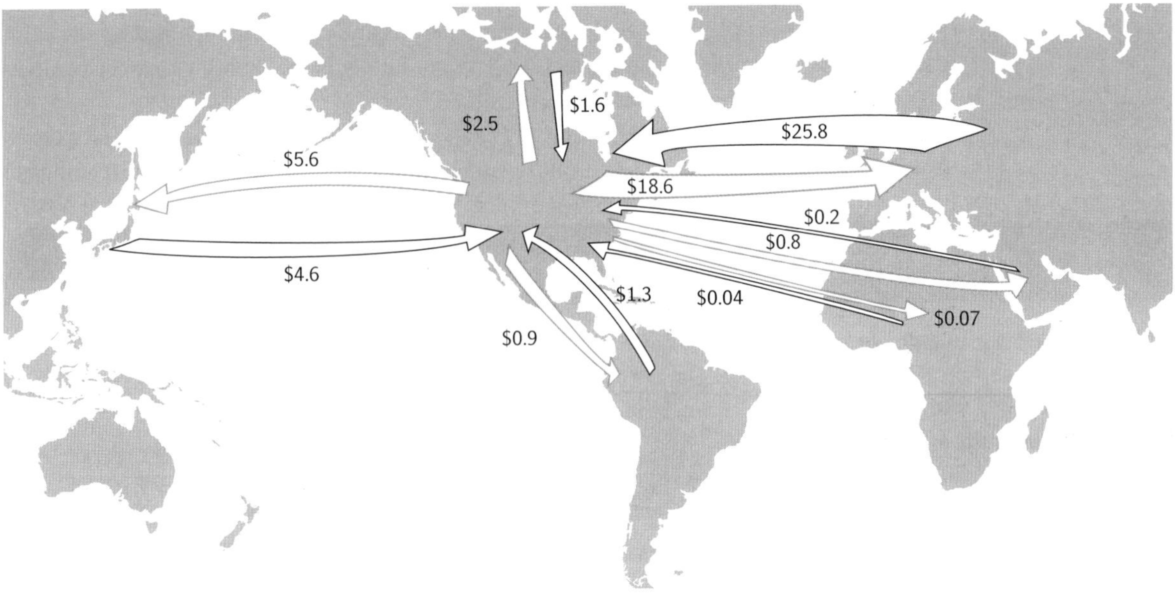

Source: National Science Foundation, Science and Engineering Indicators 2010

competitive strategies. Their influence is illustrated by the international spread of lean manufacturing in the car industry. This sets out to eliminate waste and to decrease the time between
receipt of a customer order and delivery. It was pioneered by car makers in Japan and subsequently adopted by western companies such as GM, Ford, and VW as a result of the fierce
competition they faced from their more efficient Japanese rivals.

Waves of Innovation

History has seen waves of major innovations:

- The Industrial Revolution, starting in Britain in the second half of the 18th century, involving machines such as water-driven spinning jennies and looms.
- The next wave saw steam power being used to drive the machines used in the production
  of manufactured goods in the second half of the 19th century particularly in Britain.
- The third wave occurred at the end of the 19th century with enormous expansion in chemical
  industries with the introduction of products such as synthetic dyestuffs and high explosives.
  An important advance in communications occurred with the invention of the telephone.
- In the first half of the 20th century we moved into the age of oil and the application of
  electricity to industrial processes.

The second half of the 20th century saw rapid developments in electronics, communications,
computers, aerospace, pharmaceuticals, biotechnology, petrochemicals, and synthetic materials.
There have been major advances in body imaging technology embodied in scanners using ultra-
sound, gamma rays, or X-rays. These permit scientists to obtain detailed pictures of areas inside

the body, the pictures being created by a computer linked to the imaging machine. Surgeons can identify potential tumours, the damage following a stroke, and signs of incipient dementia. Firms such as Coca Cola and BMW have used this new technology to examine areas of the brain that are used when confronted with new designs or brands or when choosing between competing products on supermarket shelves.

Some commentators, like Wonglimpiyarat (2005), suggest that another wave could be sparked by nanotechnology, the science of the ultra-small. Nanotechnology is the ability to manipulate

Mini Case Nanotechnology

This case looks at developments in nanotechnology and the product opportunities that it is creating for a range of industries.

According to the Woodrow Wilson Centre in Washington, more than US$30 billion in products incorporating nanotechnology were sold globally in 2005. By 2014, this figure could grow to US$2.6 trillion. More than 2,500 applications for patents in the technology were made in 2007. The technology has attracted the interests of 3,000 businesses worldwide. Research is being undertaken in 65 countries, 37 of which are developing countries. Up to now most research effort has been geared to the needs of rich countries. However, nanotechnology offers great opportunities to confront some major problems faced by poor countries such as providing clean drinking water or combating tropical diseases.

In 2011 there were 1,000+ products based on nanotechnology, a fivefold rise compared with 2006. These included cosmetics, clothing, health and dietary supplements, bedding, and sporting goods being produced in 24 countries. Adidas, Chanel, Gap, General Motors, and Black & Decker were all using the technology.

Source: www.nanotechproject.org; *WIPO 2010*; *Financial Times*, 18 May 2007

Source: David Hawxhurst

and manufacture things using individual particles of materials when the dimensions of the particles are 100 nanometres or less. The width of a human hair is about 100,000 nanometres (Woodrow Wilson Centre, www.nanotechproject.org; see video at www.chicagobusiness.com/ section). This is already having a big impact on firms producing computer chips, integrated circuit boards, flat displays in products like computers, televisions, and mobile phones and in textiles and biotechnology.

Information and Communications Technology

Information and communications technology (ICT) has become increasingly important in the business world. ICT is a term that encompasses all forms of technology used to create, store, exchange, and use information in its various forms whether that be business data, voice conversations, still images, motion pictures, or multimedia presentations. It involves the use of machines such as computers, telephone exchanges, robots, satellites, automatic cash dispensers, cable TV along with the software installed in them. ICT is all-pervasive affecting the home, the office, the factory and it has major implications for business both large and small from the small corner shop with its computerized accounts to supermarket chains such as Wal-Mart and Tesco which use electronic links with their suppliers to ensure that their shelves are always stocked with sufficient quantities of the appropriate goods.

The pace of change in ICT has been extraordinary due to a variety of factors. The needs of the military have been a major impetus for developing computers to solve problems related to encryption, decoding, and missile trajectory. The development of microelectronic technologies owes much to the space race between the USA and the USSR. US rockets were smaller than Soviet rockets so they could not carry as much computer equipment. Miniaturization provided the solution and led to the computer chip.

With the power and speed of computer chips doubling every 18 months and their cost falling by 50%, many new products have emerged from laptop computers to mobile phones to global positioning systems and satellite TV. An important development has been the internet which is an enormous international computer network initially developed in the US defence sector. It links a vast number of pages of information on the worldwide web which is expanding at an exponential rate. It has led to the emergence of auction companies like eBay, search engines such as Google, and social networking sites like Facebook. In 2002, it was estimated that about 10% of the world population was using the internet. By 2010, at nearly two billion people, this had risen to around 30%. The highest number of users was in Asia, with well over 800 million followed by Europe with 475 million, North America with 250+ million, Latin America with just over 200 million and Africa with 111 million (www.internetworldstats.com).

Web 2.0

There has been a number of important technological developments on the worldwide web known as Web 2.0 (see O'Reilly 2005; also see video on this topic by visiting the link on the **Online Resource Centre** for this book). These rely on user collaboration and include peer-to- peer networking, blogs, podcasts, wikis, video-sharing and social platforms like Facebook, MySpace, YouTube, Flickr, and Twitter. Web 2.0 is creating global systems that make it much easier for business-to-business and business-to-customer interaction. One place to see the application of these advances in action is in the mobile phone market, where manufacturers and service providers are creating 'apps' which users can download to their smartphones. They allow users to play games, locate nearby restaurants or friends, listen to music, find the best deals online, and access countless sources of specific information. Apple claims that more than 5 billion downloads have been made from its store of 200,000 apps. In 2010, Facebook had more than 500 million users while more than 4 billion people around the world were using mobile phones, and for 450 million of those people the web was a fully mobile experience (*McKinsey Quarterly* August 2010). Nielsen, in 2010, found that more than 60% of active internet users in Italy, Australia, the USA, and UK visited Facebook whereas the figure for Brazil was 26% and Japan 3% (http://blog.nielsen.com).

Many companies use Web 2.0 to invite their customers to rate products and recommend improvements. The data give companies powerful new insights on how to position products, create new ones, and decide on pricing strategies (*McKinsey Quarterly* 6 August 2009).

However, Andriole (2010) in a study of the impact of Web 2.0 in five US firms, in areas such as knowledge management, customer relationship management, innovation, and training found that despite the hype, firms were adopting Web 2.0 technologies slowly and deliberately. Applications were being introduced where their costs were low, and where they could be integrated with existing applications and IT infrastructures. The greatest impact was on collaboration and communication with wikis, blogs, social networks, and RSS filters having the greatest impact both internally and externally. Firms were cautious and sceptical about the new technologies and particularly concerned about the implications for intellectual property, security, and control.

The Cloud

Cloud computing offers business the possibility of using software from the internet. This means that firms do not need to have software such as Windows installed on their own computers. Company data can also be stored in the cloud. Cloud services are provided by companies like Google, Amazon, Microsoft, HP, and Tata. Cloud computing reduces the amount of money firms need to spend on IT personnel and infrastructure such as air-conditioned rooms to store servers and upgrades on software and hardware. This makes it easier for small and medium sized firms to compete because they only need to pay for the IT services they need when they need them and they can access the same IT services as their larger competitors. It is argued by commentators such as Kotler (2009) that cloud computing could make it easier for developing countries to compete with richer economies.

A potential drawback is that firms could become dependent on the cloud company to hold their confidential data and for the provision of IT services. Problems could arise were the service provider to have a breakdown (as happened with Google and Amazon—*The Observer*, 1 March 2009), leak confidential information, or go out of business.

Theorists, like Schumpeter (1976), have attempted to explain why technological innovation occurs in cycles. He built on the work of the Russian economist Kondratieff who had noted a tendency for economies to go through cycles of expansion and then contraction, each cycle or wave lasting around 50 years. Schumpeter argued that the growth phase of the cycle arose from a bunching of innovations that brought about a technological revolution and led to the creation of completely new markets and industries through the invention of new products, production processes, or the discovery of new sources of raw materials or energy.

Mini Case China and the Internet

Between 2000 and 2010 the number of internet users in China increased 20-fold to 420 million. The Chinese have embraced internet shopping with a passion with sales forecast to double to US$75 billion between 2009 and 2010. However, market potential is enormous and too huge to ignore. Western MNCs like Armani, Adidas, and Uniqlo, the Japanese clothing retailer have responded by setting up e-commerce sites with Wal-Mart planning to follow suit in 2011. Chinese companies, Geely the car maker and Danddang the bookseller have done the same.

Shopping using mobile phones has also surged following large sales of the smartphones needed to access shopping services. In China, there are nearly 900 million mobile phone users of whom an increasing number, 47 million in 2010, had smartphones. This has led to a rise in the use of phones to shop online. Estimates of market size put it at around US$1.8 billion. China's largest online retailer, Taobao.com, has been one of the main drivers behind the growth through its mobile apps.

Foreign MNCs have not all found it plain sailing in China. In 2009, Google came under increasing pressure from the Chinese authorities to censor its China site. As a result, Google moved its China web search facility to its Hong Kong site. Following its confrontation with the Chinese authorities, Google's market share of online search revenues fell from more than one third to just over one fifth. A major beneficiary of Google's problems was Baidu, the Chinese search company, whose market share grew to over 70%.

Sources: www.internetworldstats.com; *Financial Times*, 3 September 2010, 7 and 9 December 2010; *PCWorld*, 28 January 2011; www.bbc.co.uk, 23 March 2010

Source: www.istockphoto.com

Counterpoint Box 7.1 The internet—how revolutionary?

Some commentators argue that the internet is an earth-shaking innovation compared with previous examples of technological advance, such as railways or telephone networks. None can match the impact of the internet and the speed of its penetration in society. It has led to the emergence of new industries, business models, organizational structures and new companies such as Amazon, Google, Apple, eBay, YouTube, Wikipedia, Skype, and Vodafone and has revolutionized interaction through social networks like Facebook and Bebo. Internet companies have put intense competitive pressure on firms operating in sectors like book and music retailing, telecommunications, civil aviation, and holiday travel.

Sceptics like Samuelson (2000) contend that the internet did not spread faster than other innovations, that it is a work in progress, and that many other innovations have outstripped it in terms of impact, for example indoor plumbing and electricity. Critics also claim that the internet has not had much impact on productivity. Chang (2010) maintains that it has not been as important as domestic appliances that have cut the amount of time taken for housework, allowed women to enter the labour market, and abolished domestic service as an occupation.

Sources: Samuelson, R. J., *Newsweek*, 24 January 2000; Hof, R. D., 'A New Era of Bright Hopes and Terrible Fears'. *BusinessWeek*, 4 October 1999; www.youtube.com/watch?v=nDJYJsn_WzY&feature=related; Chang 2010

For the waves to occur, there have to be people willing to take the risks of exploiting the new ideas commercially. Schumpeter saw the entrepreneur as playing this vital role. Nowadays, we look to firms to carry out that function.

Who Innovates?

Research shows that the rate of innovation varies from sector to sector, industry to industry, by size of firm, and by geographical location. The European Commission (2010) found that a larger proportion of manufacturing firms than service sector firms were technological innovators, but these proportions varied widely between countries. Innovation activity seems to be relatively high in countries such as Ireland, Denmark, and Germany but low in Belgium and Spain.

In terms of firm size, the larger the firm, the more likely it is to be an innovator even in low tech industries. Big manufacturing firms spend a much larger proportion of their turnover on innovation activities than small firms. Table 7.2. shows the top ten innovators as measured by patent applications.

However, using measures of innovation other than R&D and patents shows that small and medium sized firms can also be important innovators. Historically manufacturing firms have carried out most R&D. However, research activity in the service sector is on the increase particularly in telecommunications, information technology, networking, and consultancy.

However, industries are not all equally affected by the competition arising from technological change and the opportunities and threats that it poses. Firms operating in industries where technology evolves and diffuses rapidly need to stay very aware of their technological environment. Such high technology industries include aerospace, computers and office equipment, radio, TV, and communications equipment, and pharmaceuticals. A firm in these industries failing to respond effectively to its technological environment runs the risk of falling sales,

Table 7.1 Innovation activity

High intensity R&D sectors:	Medium–high R&D intensity sectors:
• pharmaceuticals and biotechnology • health care equipment and services • technology hardware and equipment • software and computer services	• electronics and electrical equipment • cars • aerospace and defence • industrial engineering and machinery, • chemicals • household goods
Medium–low R&D intensity sectors:	**Low R&D intensity sectors:**
• food and beverages • travel and leisure, media • oil equipment • electricity • fixed line telecommunications	• oil and gas producers • industrial metals • construction • food and drug retailers • transportation • mining • tobacco

Source: WIPO 2010

Table 7.2 Top ten innovators by patent applications (PCT) 2008

Rank	Applicant's Name	Country of Origin	Number of PCT Applications	Change from 2008
1	PANASONIC CORPORATION	Japan	1,891	162
2	HUAWEI TECHNOLOGIES CO., LTD.	China	1,847	110
3	ROBERT BOSCH GMBH	Germany	1,587	314
4	KONINKLUKE PHILIPS ELECTRONICS N.V.	Netherlands	1,295	−256
5	QUALCOMM INCORPORATED	United States of America	1,280	373
6	TELEFONAKTIEBOLAGET LM ERICSSON (PUBL)	Sweden	1,240	256
7	LG ELECTRONICS INC.	Republic of Korea	1,090	98
8	NEC CORPORATION	Japan	1,069	244
9	TOYOTA JIDOSHA KABUSHIKI KAISHA	Japan	1,068	−296
10	SHARP KABUSHIKI KAISHA	Japan	997	183

Source: Document originally produced by the World Intellectual Property Organization (WIPO), the owner of the copyright

market share, and profits and even takeover or bankruptcy. This is particularly so in markets where, due to customer preference, only the latest product sells. There are some industries that are less sensitive to technological change. These are classified as medium technology industries and include motor vehicles, electrical (other than communications equipment), and non-electrical machines, chemicals excluding drugs, cars, rubber and plastics products, and shipbuilding and repairing.

Finally, there are the low-tech industries that are relatively unaffected by competition in the area of technology such as paper products, textiles, non-fashion clothes and leather goods, food, beverages and tobacco, wood products, and furniture.

The high and medium-high tech sectors together usually account for most R&D and contribute a disproportionately large share of sales of new and improved products (see Table 7.1).

Learning Task

Globally, it is the largest companies, in the richest countries, in a limited number of sectors that account for the vast majority of the money spent on R&D. Examine Table 7.3 and answer the questions below to test the validity of this claim.

1. Are the 25 companies amongst the biggest multinationals in the world? To answer this go to the latest World Investment Report at www.unctad.org

2. In which countries are these companies based? Are they all rich countries?

3. How would you explain the presence of Samsung in the list? Referring back to the case study at the start of the chapter would be a good idea at this point.

4. Examine the sectors in which these firms operate. Why should R&D spending be high in these sectors?

Table 7.3 Top 25 global companies by R&D expenditure

Rank 2010	Company	Sector	Country	R&D (£m)	Growth in R&D over last year (%)	Rank 2009
1	Toyota Motor #	Automobiles & parts	Japan	6,014	−6	1
2	Roche, Switzerland	Pharmaceuticals & biotechnology	Switzerland	5,688	9	4
3	Microsoft#	Software & computer services	USA	5,396	−3	2
4	Volkswagen	Automobiles & parts	Germany	5,144	−2	3
5	Pfizer #	Pharmaceuticals & biotechnology	USA	4,802	−2	6
6	Novartis	Pharmaceuticals & biotechnology	Switzerland	4,581	2	10
7	Nokia	Technology hardware & equipment	Finland	4,440	−6	8
8	Johnson & Johnson #	Pharmaceuticals & biotechnology	USA	4,326	−8	7
9	Sanofi-Aventis	Pharmaceuticals & biotechnology	France	4,060	0	12
10	Samsung Electronics #	Electronic & electrical equipment	South Korea	4,007	8	18
11	Siemens	Electronic & electrical equipment	Germany	3,805	2	20
12	General Motors USA #	Automobiles & parts	USA	3,758	−24	5
13	Honda Motor #	Automobiles & parts	Japan	3,746	−4	11
14	Daimler	Automobiles & parts	Germany	3,700	−6	13
15	GlaxoSmithKline	Pharmaceuticals & biotechnology	UK	3,629	10	21
16	Merck #	Pharmaceuticals & biotechnology	USA	3,619	22	25
17	Intel #	Technology hardware & equipment	USA	3,501	−1	17
18	Panasonic	Leisure goods	Japan	3,445	−7	14
19	Sony #	Leisure goods	Japan	3,308	−4	16
20	Cisco Systems #	Technology hardware & equipment	USA	3,225	1	22
21	Robert Bosch	Automobiles & parts	Germany	3,179	−9	19
22	IBM #	Software & computer services	USA	3,061	−10	15
23	Ford Motor #	Automobiles & parts	USA	3,034	−33	9
24	Nissan Motor #	Automobiles & parts	Japan	3,030	0	23
25	Takeda Pharmaceutical #	Pharmaceuticals & biotechnology	Japan	3,014	64	n/a

accounts not prepared using IFRS
Source: Department for Business Innovation and Skills, The 2010 R&D Scoreboard

Geographical Location of R&D

R&D expenditure is geographically concentrated. In 2002, almost 83% of research and development was carried out in developed countries, the USA, Japan, and in the EU. By 2007 this share had dropped to 76%. Led mainly by China, India, and the Republic of Korea, Asia overtook Europe increasing its share from 27% to 32% between 2002 and 2007.

Latin America and Africa together account for only a tiny share (UNESCO 2010; Figure 7.2).

Figure 7. 2 Location of estimated worldwide R&D expenditures: 1996 and 2007 (%)

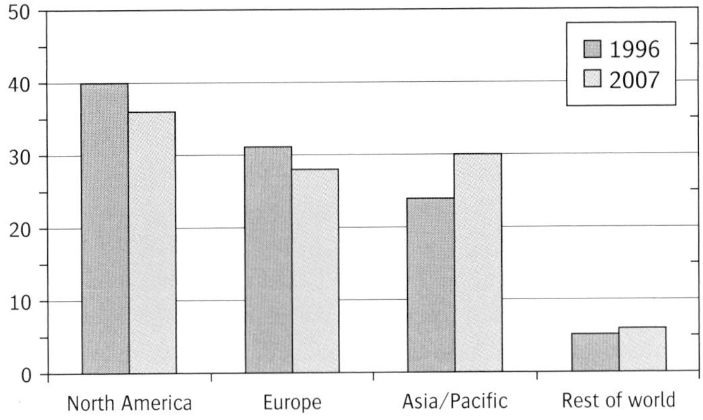

Source: National Science Foundation, Science and Engineering Indicators 2010

Sources of Technological Advance

Technological advances can come from a variety of sources both inside and outside the organization. New ideas for commercial exploitation may be generated in the wider environment by scientists and technologists working in universities or research centres, or from individual inventors. Scientists at Bristol University invented and developed a new and simpler form of dental implant and set up a company to exploit the idea commercially. The new product is simpler to use and easier and cheaper to transport. This development had significant implications for the dominant firms, Nobel Biocare of Sweden and Straumann of Switzerland in this fast growing market estimated to be worth around £1 billion. Novartis, the Swiss multinational pharmaceutical firm, bought out NeuTec Pharma a biotech company set up by Manchester University. NeuTec had developed new treatments for a number of life-threatening infections such as the superbug MRSA. Technologists at Oxford University invented a direct-drive engine allowing car manufacturers to reduce weight and improve the range of electric and hybrid vehicles by removing heavy gearbox components from the transmission (www.isis-innovation. com). Sometimes businesses establish research links with universities to give them first call on new ideas generated by the university (Fontana 2006; see video at http://mitworld.mit.edu/video/816). Haier of China, the fourth largest global producer of white goods such as fridges, freezers, and washing machines has entered into R&D contracts with several US universities.

Big firms in industries such as pharmaceuticals and electronics have their own R&D facilities which generate ideas for new goods and services. GE spends billions of dollars annually on R&D in the US, India, China, and Germany (www.ge.com/research). As part of its research effort, it runs a Global Research Centre employing thousands of researchers in the USA, India, China, Germany, and Brazil. The centre pioneered very successful breakthroughs in lasers, optical lenses, and digital X-rays which allowed doctors a more accurate view of organs and bones and did away with the need for film and light boxes (www.ge.globalresearch.com).

Business can also look to the more immediate environment as a way of facilitating the innovation process. For example, firms may cooperate with domestic or foreign rivals where the costs of innovation are high or to improve their ability to innovate. Collaboration can help lower the costs and risks of innovation as well as facilitating the commercialization of new scientific and technical knowledge and can therefore be an attractive strategy for small and medium-sized firms. The Italian furniture and textile industries, comprising mainly small firms, have formed networks of producers allowing them to cooperate on technology and ensuring that they maintain their competitive edge in the market place. Examples of cross-border collaboration can be seen in the car industry where even financially powerful big car producers feel obliged to cooperate to develop costly new models and components, for example GM's joint venture with DaimlerChrysler to develop new transmission systems and Peugeot's joint venture with BMW to develop parts for electric cars. Technology, particularly the internet, facilitates the process of collaboration—it is easy, speedy, and cheap for R&D units based in different countries to exchange information in the form of text, graphics, design drawings, video images, and so on.

Firms often try to involve suppliers, distributors, and customers (the supply chain in other words) in the innovation process to develop and share innovative ideas or to share in the development of new products or processes. In the aerospace sector, Supply Chain Relationships in Aerospace (Scria) is an example of such networking (also see Teixeira 2008).

Some companies, particularly Japanese firms such as Nissan and Toyota, look to stakeholders such as the employees to come up with ideas for improving products and processes. Every year Toyota, a Japanese car company that has outdone its western rivals for years, receives literally thousands of suggestions from assembly line workers about how it could do things even better. Workers are encouraged to find ways of shaving as little as one tenth of a second off routine tasks. Most suggestions involve tiny modifications to existing practices, for example performing a particular task while standing up rather than sitting down. If the modifications work, they are adopted throughout Toyota's factories.

Learning Task

Advance reasons why firms involved in expensive, risky, or complex research projects such as those in the pharmaceutical industry would seek cooperation in R&D with other organizations.

 Visit the **Online Resource Centre** for a useful link to Hagedorn's; paper to help with this task.

Finally, the acquisition of new machinery and equipment can be an important source of product or process innovation for small and medium-sized enterprises. The new equipment may require the business to change the way it produces the product or to produce new or improved products.

What Motivates Business to Innovate?

Technical advance is driven by a complex combination of factors in the firm's external environment: the intensity of competition, relationships with customers and suppliers, and government policies.

The Intensity of Competition

Since the mid 1980s the pace of globalization in the world economy has accelerated. The reduction in the barriers to the movement of goods, services, and capital across borders has meant that markets have become increasingly integrated, innovation has diffused much more quickly, and technological competition has grown more intense. Increasing competition from emerging economies such as China and India has also contributed to the process. Competition means that when one firm innovates, competitors may be forced to react, often in creative ways. This could involve major ground-breaking advances or, more likely, improvements and innovations around the first innovator's design, for example, 'me-too' drugs in the pharmaceutical industry. Technological competition may drive firms to launch new products and at a faster rate, add features, enter, or even create new markets. In this way technological competition begets more innovation and more competition. The increase in technological competition makes life more risky for business because one of the persistent characteristics of innovation is that most attempts to innovate fail in the marketplace. When the rate of innovation accelerates it has the effect of shortening the length of the product life cycle. The period of time from conception to the death of the product is reduced and this increases pressure on business to innovate to stay ahead of the competition.

Customers and Suppliers

Some industries may find that the pressure to innovate comes from customers or suppliers. Car components producers, hoping for contracts with big manufacturers like Nissan, get business on condition that they change their mode of operation to meet Nissan's cost and quality requirements. Nissan advises suppliers on how to go about changing their production processes in order to increase efficiency. In the North East of England, where Nissan manufactures cars, it has set up a high-tech learning centre which suppliers use to develop their skills and to improve their productivity. For example, through the centre, suppliers can find out about Kaizen, a Japanese management technique embracing the concept of continuous improvement.

On the other hand, suppliers can be the instigators of innovation. Taking health care as an example, we can see that advances in body imaging has led to new and much more sophisticated scanning techniques being used in hospitals which has implications for the treatments offered but also for the training of staff.

Government Policy

Increasingly governments have become aware of the importance of technical progress to the performance of their economies. To this end they can pursue policies which remove or mitigate the effects of some of the barriers or give a positive impetus to innovation. Some innovations never get started or suffer serious delays because of their cost, or the inability to secure finance for what financial institutions view as too risky projects. This is a particular problem for small firms who may also suffer because they are often unaware of the information that is being generated elsewhere, for example in universities and research institutes that could be commercially exploited. Lack of qualified scientific and technical personnel can be another barrier to the development and exploitation of new ideas as can the high cost of protecting intellectual property rights (IPRs) or where the degree of protection awarded to intellectual property is low. On the other hand, the regulatory framework can also be a positive influence. For example, stringent environmental and consumer regulation as found in several EU countries, can force firms to raise their game regarding innovation. Labour laws making it difficult to fire employees may cause firms to innovate by forcing them to search for less labour intensive production methods.

In 2000, the EU embarked on its **Lisbon strategy**, a ten-year plan to improve competitiveness, with innovation and the knowledge economy as two of its central planks. Member states agreed to pursue policies that would help reduce some of the important barriers to innovation with the aim of making the EU the most competitive economy in the world. To that end, the EU agreed to aim for an increase in R&D spending to 3% of GDP per year, with two thirds of that coming from private sector firms, and to coordinate R&D programmes across the members of the union. The Strategy also saw education and training as crucial in providing a workforce capable of creating knowledge-intensive industries and services. However, a review in 2010 found that its main targets had not been reached. In particular, it had failed to reach the 3% target for R&D as a percentage of GDP or to close the productivity gap with its main competitors (EU Commission 2010a).

Businesses operating in developed economies are likely to be at an advantage because of the well-developed school, and higher education and training systems which mean that a high proportion of the population is literate and numerate. Conversely, firms operating in poor countries will be at a disadvantage, although countries like China and India, focusing on closing the innovation gap with richer economies, are producing increasing numbers of highly skilled and technically qualified graduates. China, in 2007, counted almost as many researchers as the USA and more than the EU. Russia and India lag far behind China (National Science Foundation 2010; for more discussion on education see Chapters Six and Eleven).

Governments, following the prescriptions of Michael Porter (1998) for improved competitiveness, promote the emergence of industrial clusters of associated firms including suppliers, customers, competitors, and other related institutions to which rivals in other locations do not have access. Clusters allow firms to boost their competitiveness by taking advantage of the intimate knowledge of, and interaction with, other businesses located in the cluster. These are visible in countries like Italy where a textile cluster comprises not merely fabric and garment manufacture but also supporting industries like textile machinery and design, all located within a compact 200–300 square km. In Andhra Pradesh in India, the state has, through public-private partnerships, encouraged the creation of clusters in the IT, biotechnology, pharmaceutical, and textile sectors. Similar attempts to develop clusters have occurred in Latin America and in the Basque country in Spain.

Governments can pursue tax, subsidy, and **equity support regimes** that make finance more easily available, and cut the costs and risks associated with innovation. Almost all rich countries provide tax incentives and subsidies for innovation, although the focus is usually on promoting research which tends to favour big business and to discriminate against SMEs.

Why Technology is Important for Business

Technology opens up all sorts of domestic and foreign opportunities for businesses who are ready to take advantage of them. On the other hand, it can also pose many threats to firms who are unaware of, and unprepared for, technical change. It can, as we will see from the example of the internet, erode boundaries between markets and industries.

Technology can be a principal factor determining the size and growth of firms, the structure of industry on a global scale, its location and ownership and the organization of production. According to Held (1999), technology has played a part in the global restructuring of production. It has helped MNCs slice up the value chain by facilitating the location of segments of the production process to lower cost countries or to subcontract production activities to cheaper suppliers in Asia or Latin America.

Competitive advantage regarding productivity, costs, and products can all be heavily influenced by new ideas and knowledge. Those ideas and knowledge can result in new inventions, designs, trade marks, literary, and artistic works. These are the firm's intellectual property. In reality not many companies invent wholly new products; most of them adapt and extend ideas that others have already tried. Apple's iPod was not the first MP3 player, but the company added enough to make its version innovative. Similarly, drugs companies often build on each other's breakthroughs to produce 'me-too' drugs.

Opportunities

New goods and services—firms can create new and improved goods and services, revive tired products and consequently penetrate new markets, and, as a result, can end up with powerful market shares and controlling valuable processes, products, designs, and brand names. Danish firm Lego is a good example of a firm using technology to revive a flagging product, the toy building brick. The brick is now sold with electronic technology allowing customers to build a range of moving robots.

Global organization—technology makes it increasingly easy to extend globally and to integrate economic activity in many widely separated locations. Technology has thus facilitated the rapid growth of the multinational corporation with subsidiaries in many countries but with business strategies, production, and distribution still being determined and controlled by head office in a single nation. So MNCs like Unilever are able to employ more than 160,000 people and sell its products in 170 countries (www.unilever.co.uk).

Learning Task

This task requires you to examine links between R&D expenditure and company performance.

Improved performance arising from technology can enhance a company's share performance. The R&D Scoreboard suggests that share prices (and sales growth) in companies with the highest R&D intensity perform better than the average. The table below taken from the 2010 Scoreboard shows R&D expenditure as a % of sales revenue.

• GlaxoSmithKline	12.8%	• Royal Bank of Scotland	1.4%
• AstraZeneca	13.5%	• HSBC	1%
• BT	4.9%	• Rolls Royce	4.5%
• Unilever	2.2%	• Airbus	14.7%
• Royal Dutch Shell	0.4%	• BP	0.2%

1. Choose a high spending and a low spending company from the table. Construct a graph of changes in their share prices over the last five years.

2. Comment on the relative share performance of the two companies. Identify a range of technological and other factors that could have influenced their share price.

Small firms—technology can make it easier for small firms to compete with large. The internet, for example, enables all firms to communicate with customers both at national and at international level and to sell goods and services at relatively low cost. Small companies can design their own websites for as little as a few thousand pounds. Firms, producing for niche markets, can use the web to reach customers who are of little interest to conventional distributors such as Wal-Mart. The Abebooks website, for example, brings together around 14,000 independent booksellers worldwide holding over 80 million new, used, rare, and out-of-print books. In the USA the biggest music retailer is Wal-Mart. Given the need to make a return on its shelf space, it is only interested in carrying the biggest hits and cannot afford to carry a CD or DVD that sells only a handful of copies a year. The web offers firms the opportunity to tap into customers interested in the 'non-hits'. And in some areas non-hits can often be a bigger market than the best sellers.

Freezing out competitors—exclusive control of technology can give firms the ability to freeze out their rivals by excluding them from using the same knowledge or techniques. That is why in industries such as pharmaceuticals, IT hardware and software firms readily apply for patents which, if granted, will give them control of a technology. Microsoft, by 2005, was applying for around 3,000 patents when in 1990 it received a mere five, while IBM took out more patents than any other US company between 1999 and 2003. Companies may deliberately set out to hoard patents purely to frustrate rivals by preventing them from getting access to new technology. This can be a very powerful competitive tool in certain sectors such as IT software and hardware where there has got to be technical compatibility, sometimes called interoperability, between programs and equipment. In the telecommunications industry, compatibility is vital for a firm to be able to connect to the network.

Apple was particularly effective in freezing out competition when it set up iTunes. The company made it technically impossible for songs bought on iTunes to be played on competitor's equipment. Shortly after Apple launched its service in Europe it announced that it had sold 800,000 songs in the first week of operation. Both iTunes and the iPod won a market share of about 80% in the USA and the UK, as well as a substantial market share in many European countries. The iPod's strong market position gave Apple the bargaining power to strike a deal with the four biggest record companies to sell songs through iTunes for around 54p each. The agreement was widely seen as a defeat for record companies.

Another tactic used by firms to exclude rivals is to get their technical standards accepted as the norm. Microsoft has done this very successfully by managing to get Windows accepted as the standard computer operating system, and then bundling in additional software such as Internet Explorer which makes it very difficult for rival browsers to get a foothold in the market. And success breeds success. People buy Microsoft Office because they know they can take their knowledge anywhere, and because they want to be able to share their work with other users. Microsoft's dominance in operating systems has been subject to intense scrutiny by regulatory bodies particularly in the EU and the USA.

Licensing—can be used to control the diffusion of a firm's technology and also to generate significant additional income streams. In America alone, technology licensing revenue accounts for an estimated US$45 billion annually; worldwide, the figure is around US$100 billion and growing fast. IBM earned over US$1 billion annually from its intellectual-property portfolio (on the other hand, IBM also earns a lot of money by providing open-source services, that is free-to-use-and-adapt software, but then makes money by designing and tailor-making that software into commercial packages for customers who are unable or unwilling to do that for themselves) whilst HP's revenue from licensing quadrupled in less than three years, to over US$200 million

(*The Economist*, 20 October 2005). Microsoft went in for extensive licensing of its patented technology when growth in its core products started to slow down. This move by Microsoft also allowed the company to counter charges of abusing its monopoly by claiming that it was making its technology available to competitors.

Related products—a firm with a powerful technological position in one product may be able to oblige purchasers of that product to buy related products thus generating additional income. For example, a manufacturer of photocopying machines could require the customer to take its own brand of ink or toner, or a computer maker could ensure that its own peripheral equipment was used with its machines. Microsoft consumers can only use Microsoft games in their Microsoft Xbox but these games cannot be used in a Sony PlayStation (such behaviour could be seen as anti-competitive and attract the interest of the regulatory authorities—see the section on Competition Law in Chapter Nine).

Mini Case HD–DVD The Battle Between Sony and Toshiba

This case illustrates the importance to firms of getting their technical standards accepted by their customers as the industry norm if they are to capitalize on their innovations.

Source: Photodisc

Establishing one's standards as the industry norm can provoke fierce struggles such as occurred in the high definition DVD sector where Sony with its Blu-ray format and Toshiba with its HD-DVD were competing to become the high-definition replacement for DVD. Initially both companies attempted unsuccessfully to agree on a unified set of standards. Sony was particularly mindful of the last great format war in the 1980s, when its Betamax videotape lost out to VHS, even though it was widely considered a superior technology. It lost that battle and, as a result, its Betamax technology was made redundant. One reason for the defeat was that Sony failed to build a base of potential customers.

Sony and Toshiba embarked on a ferocious struggle to get their standards accepted by major customers such as Hollywood studios, TV, PC, and video console manufacturers. Toshiba managed to recruit Microsoft and Intel to its camp and intended to steal a march on Sony by being first to the market place with its new player.

However, Sony persuaded Dell and the big US film studios Walt Disney and 20th Century Fox to back Blu-ray helped by the fact that Sony Pictures is one of the main players in Hollywood. Giant US retailers Wal-Mart and Best Buy decided not to stock HD-DVD.

This was the final nail in the coffin for HD-DVD. In 2008, Toshiba announced that it was stopping production of HD-DVD Players.

Source: *Financial Times*, 9 April 2007, 7 and 8 January 2008; http://news.bbc.co.uk, 19 February 2008

Increased productivity—there is empirical evidence indicating that those countries and companies more rapidly adopting information and communication technologies tend to show higher levels of growth in productivity. For example, US companies have invested more in ICT than their European counterparts and consequently have experienced particularly strong productivity growth in sectors that make intensive use of ICT.

Reducing costs—telecommunication operators such as BT or France Telecom have also been major beneficiaries of technology. Automation of the exchanges permitted reductions in the workforce whilst the miniaturization of computer equipment created savings in the amount of floor space required. The replacement of mechanical by electronic parts in the equipment economized on maintenance because electronic parts are more reliable than mechanical components and also because electronic machinery is now constructed in modules—any problems can be diagnosed electronically, the faulty module identified, removed, and replaced by another. As regards new products, technology enabled telecoms firms to offer a plethora of new services to their customers, such as, ring back, answering services, and the ability to use wireless-free telephones and computers.

One can also see this in the driverless metros in cities such as Hong Kong, and in airport trains like those in Stansted airport in the UK. Another advantage is that technology could help firms deal with labour shortages. John Smedley, a medium-sized British manufacturer of luxury knitwear, had a costly labour intensive production process and faced a shortage of skilled textile workers. The company could have cut costs and dealt with its labour shortage by getting its sweaters made in South East Asia. But it was reluctant to do this because this would mean sacrificing the Made in England label, the hallmark of John Smedley knitwear and the reason why the company could demand high margins on its products. The company solution was to invest in new technologically advanced knitting machinery that did away with the labour needed for panel stitchers. It enabled more of its workers to focus on the design and hand finishing of its products and, additionally, allowed the company to manufacture patterned designs which permitted it to tap into new markets. The previous technology only allowed it to produce single colour items (*Financial Times*, 24 September 2005).

Job design—technology can facilitate the redesign of jobs and change the pattern of skills required by business. ICT, in the newspaper industry, has led to a disappearance of the traditional skills of the printer and a reduction in wage costs. Printing was a job traditionally done by a highly unionized workforce with skills being built up over a period of five or more years. These days news information is keyed in by the journalist via the computer whilst photographs and advertisements are input by less highly unionized and lower paid workers with computer skills which can be learned much more quickly. In this way, technology can reduce the skill levels required which means that employers do not have to pay the same levels of wages and salaries.

Monitoring and control—ICT also enhances the ability of business to monitor and control what is going on in the workplace. In call centres, employers can monitor the number of calls workers take, how long it takes to deal with customers, what is said in the conversation with clients, and the outcomes, for example, how successfully staff exploit sales opportunities, and the length of time staff are logged off on breaks. They can use the data to evaluate the performance of individual employees, or teams, and also for the call centre as a whole. Additional information can be gathered on the average length of time a caller has to wait before he or she is put through and the number of callers who ring off before they are put through. Similarly, such technology can make it easier for firms to monitor employees who are working from home or workers whose job entails them moving from one location to another such as salesmen or lorry drivers.

Internal communications—ICT can be used to improve internal communications. E-mail, wikis, and blogs (a blog is an online diary or journal) can be used cheaply and easily to reach thousands of employees simultaneously. Investment banks like Dresdner Kleinwort and law firms such as Allen & Overy introduced blogging to facilitate communication and to allow online collaboration. Some firms, such as Motorola and Apple, use their technology as a tool to improve competitiveness. Workers are encouraged to use computers to exchange information. As a result the workforce becomes more knowledgeable and more willing to accept and adapt to new ideas and change. Businesses who are successful with this approach are called learning organizations (for more on the learning organization see Senge 2006).

Threats and Challenges

While technology offers many opportunities for business to meet the objectives of generating sales and profits, it can also pose many threats and challenges.

Business organizations have to prepare for, and learn to cope with, new technology and to take advantage of the opportunities offered by technology to devise new consumers' goods and new methods of production and distribution, to create new markets, and to take advantage of new forms of industrial organization. Innovation involves change in products or processes and it can be risky especially for firms who are not good at managing change effectively because new products may not catch on in the market place and new production processes may not deliver the expected benefits. Most product innovations fail as do a significant proportion of process innovations. In IT projects, the failure rate in the UK has been estimated by Standish, the reputable analysts of project success, at more than 80% and that rate has not changed much since the mid 1990s.

If firms are not properly prepared then new technology can cause them to go out of business. Schumpeter called this the process of **creative destruction**. He argued that innovation over a period of time, by bringing in new products, new sources of supply, and new types of organization could create a form of competition that strikes not simply at profits and market shares but at their very existence. Schumpeter's notion of creative destruction is neatly encapsulated by the chief executive of Procter & Gamble who said, 'People ask me what I lose sleep over. If somebody announced an alternative to solution chemistry (i.e. washing powder) for laundry, all of a sudden I've got an US$11 billion business that's at risk' (*Financial Times,* 22 December 2005). HMV, the UK music retailer, underestimated the threat from online competition both in terms of physical CDs and in music downloading. Its sales fell sharply and its share price was undermined.

Even firms sitting on comfortable monopoly positions can find such positions threatened by new technology. The telecommunications industry is a case in point where national monopolists such as BT, Deutsche Telekom, and France Telecom who owned networks of telephone lines, found themselves under severe attack from mobile phone companies and from firms using satellite systems.

As in telecommunications, such competition may not arise from within the existing boundaries of an industry. Companies like Amazon, using the web as a new business model, have made

Mini Case Creative Destruction—The Kodak Case

The case is a good illustration of Schumpeter's concept of creative destruction. It shows how Kodak was severely punished for its slow reaction to important advances in photographic technology.

Kodak, in the 1990s, was a leading producer in the world of traditional cameras, film, and photographic paper. It was one of a handful of manufacturers operating in a capital-intensive multi-million pound industry and enjoying very high profit margins. In the early years of the new century, disruptive digital technology began to wreak havoc on Kodak's business threatening its very existence. Demand for its products took a nose dive as it began to lose customers at twice the expected rate to new digital cameras. At first, Kodak management saw falling sales as part of a slowdown in the economy. However, by 2003, the company had realized its mistake and belatedly embarked on its own digital strategy. It announced tens of thousands of job cuts at its film factories and started to produce a range of digital equipment.

Following this near disaster, the company did go on to make some successful innovations. It was one of the first to identify one of the biggest flaws of the new technology. Customers were frustrated with digital pictures that could not easily be printed out at an acceptable quality or price. Self-service kiosks were installed in thousands of shops. An online printing service was set up offering cheap prints to those with broadband internet connections. The company also pioneered easy-to-use home printers which can be linked with cameras by even the most technologically-challenged.

Source: *Financial Times*, 29 November 2006; *Forbes*, 21 August 2000; *Fortune*, 12 January 2004

Source: www.istockphoto.com

a significant impact on traditional book retailers like Waterstones. Not only does Amazon provide a greater choice of books in its 800,000 titles, it also uses digital technology that permits customers to read excerpts from 33 million pages of 120,000 volumes. In the travel business, one of the most successful forms of e-commerce, the internet has pitted travel agents and established airlines against online providers in an intense battle to win customers. Online agents such as Expedia and Travelocity have shaken up the travel booking business while low cost airlines like Ryanair and easyJet have used the internet to cut the costs of their reservation systems. This has made them even more price competitive, and has forced their established rivals, such as BA, Air France, and KLM, to extend their online reservation service. As a consequence, more and more flights and trips are being booked over the internet rather than through call centres or high-street travel agents.

The increasing use of ICT has made business more vulnerable to cybercrime which has been growing exponentially. Electronic crime takes various forms such as fraud, commercial espionage, blackmail, money laundering, and the rigging of gambling on online sites. It can be used to swamp a company's website with external communications. The website either fails completely or slows down to such an extent that service is denied to legitimate customers (see Verizon 2010 and the section on The Internet in Chapter Nine).

R&D—A Guarantee of Success?

Conventional wisdom assumes that company spending on R&D is a good thing, with the implied assumption that it will lead to innovative success. According to this view, the more a company spends on research the better the result is. But Burton Malkiel, an economics professor at Princeton and a company director in the biotechnology industry, described the risks rather colourfully, calling biotechnology a 'crapshoot' and going on to say that, 'Even biotech companies themselves don't know which one is going to make it' (*Financial Times*, 3 July 2007).

However, R&D is an input and its impact, like any other input such as labour and machinery, depends on how efficiently it is deployed. The productivity of R&D expenditure in terms of new products and processes is determined by the quality of the inputs, and those who are managing it. Consequently, there is no automatic correlation between high R&D spending and company performance.

A survey of the world's top 1,000 R&D companies by consultants Booz Allen failed to find any significant relationship between R&D spending and business success as measured by growth in sales, profit, the value of the firm on the stock market, or total shareholder return. The top 10% of R&D spenders enjoyed no consistent performance advantage over companies that spend less on R&D. Firms such as Reckitt Benckiser, the leading Anglo-Dutch producer of consumer cleaning products, spends a very low proportion of its turnover on R&D but enjoys a reputation both for innovation and for relatively high margins. Apple Computer, a very successful innovator with the AppleMac, iPod, iTunes, and iBook also challenges the conventional wisdom because it spends less on R&D than the computer industry average, and much smaller amounts than competitors such as Microsoft or Sony. However the survey did find that companies spending relatively little on R&D significantly underperformed their competitors (*Financial Times*, 8 November 2005). By contrast, Ehie and Olibe (2010) in a study of nearly 70,000 US firms found that R&D expenditures had a persistently positive effect on market value for both manufacturing and service firms, with a more pronounced effect on manufacturing.

Protecting Technology

Bill Gates reflects the importance of technology when he claims that, '. . . it has become imperative for chief executives to have not just a general understanding of the intellectual property issues facing their business and their industry, but to have quite a refined expertise relating to those issues' (*Financial Times*, 12 November 2004). The globalization of markets means that firms have to look for protection not just at home but also abroad.

Technology can be so important to company performance that business often spends much time and effort in ensuring that its intellectual property is protected and in pursuing those who infringe it. The external environment offers organizations the possibility of protecting their codifiable technology.

Methods of Protection

In richer countries the owners of intellectual property rights are normally accorded the protection of the law. Legally, the intellectual property system covers five areas and aims to provide legal protection against counterfeiters and copiers and is vital in many fields, such as music, film, biotechnology, nanotechnology, and in consumer goods where branding is important in gaining and retaining competitive advantage.

Patents—a patent can be taken out on inventions—when firms come up with a commercially exploitable idea for a new product such as the iPod, they will often apply for a patent. Patents can be granted on new inventions for a period of up to 20 years in the UK, Germany, Japan, and the USA.

Designs—designs comprise the characteristics of the product such as the shape, pattern, and colour and the law allows companies to prevent others using their designs.

Trade marks—brand names like Perrier or Persil, or logos such as the Nike swish can also be protected. Trade marks comprise any signs capable of being represented graphically particularly words, designs, letters, numerals, the shape of goods, or of their packaging provided that such signs are capable of distinguishing the goods or services of one firm from those of other businesses.

Copyright—book publishers, film, television, and music companies can take out a copyright on original literary, dramatic, musical, artistic works, sound recordings, films, and television broadcasts that they have produced and, more controversially, firms can also copyright information on genetic data. So music by Shakira or Coldplay, and television programmes such as Friends and X-Factor can be protected, as can cartoon characters such as Disney's Buzz Lightyear and Mickey Mouse.

Industrial espionage—this involves the theft of a firm's secret information which is normally protected by the law. A striking example of attempted espionage concerned Coca-Cola which treats its product formulae as closely guarded secrets. An employee at its headquarters tried to steal a sample of a secret new product with the intention of selling it to Coke's bitter rival, Pepsi. Pepsi, refusing to take advantage of this, reported the approach to Coke who called in the police. The employee was charged with unlawfully stealing and selling trade secrets (*The Guardian*, 7 July 2006).

WIPO (2010) reports a steady growth in patenting activity particularly in the areas of computer technology, digital communications, IT methods for management, electrical machinery and energy, and nanotechnology.

Counterpoint Box 7.2 Patents—a help or hindrance to innovation?

At issue here is the role which patents play in innovation. Those who argue for strong patent protection claim that such protection of intellectual property is essential to promote innovation and investment in new technologies. The monopoly conferred by a patent allows innovators to cover the costs of R&D and obtain an economic return on their investment which, in turn, provides incentives for more innovation and its commercialization. The result is new and better products and new and more efficient production processes which help boost productivity, economic growth, and consumer welfare.

On the other hand, it is claimed that patents by conferring a monopoly on the holder lead to higher prices, stifle competition and, consequently, innovation. Stiglitz, in evidence to the Federal Trade Commission hearings on innovation, argued that overly broad patents will deter other firms from pursuing follow-on innovations, thereby making new entry more difficult and stifling competition. In the same hearings, Heckman stated that most innovations are not new but build on work done by others, citing the famous quote from Newton that we stand on the shoulders of our predecessors. He felt that firms wanting to improve on the original ideas contained in the patent, rightly saw it as ridiculous to be forced to start from scratch. Opponents of the patent system often raise the argument that inventions would be developed even without a patent system, because there is still a significant competitive advantage from being first-to-market with a new product. Finally, critics also see the system as loaded against developing countries since they, primarily users rather than generators of innovation, pay the higher prices. The TRIPS (Trade-Related Agreement on Intellectual Property Rights) agreed that the WTO exacerbated the problem by strengthening patent protection. The World Bank calculated that the increase in technology licensing payments alone would cost poor countries US$45 billion a year.

Sources: Dumont and Holmes 2002; FTC 1996; Chang 2008

Problems in Protecting Technology

Even though rich countries usually provide a degree of legal protection for technology, firms, particularly small and medium-sized enterprises, may still encounter problems in protecting their IPRs.

Cost—the cost of filing a patent can be high and can vary considerably from one country to another. It is, for example, much more expensive to obtain patent protection across Europe than in the USA. One reason for this is that business can not yet take out a single patent valid in all member states of the EU. The Commission calculates that a patent validated in 13 EU countries costs as much as €20,000 which makes a European Patent more than ten times as expensive as an American patent which costs about €1,850 (IP/10/870 July 2010).

Multiple applications—these must be made in different countries to get legal protection. Patent applications usually have to be translated into the language of the country where the patent is to be registered. Getting highly technical application documents translated into various languages such as Chinese, Portuguese, Hungarian, and so on could be a very costly exercise.

Differing protection periods—in Japan designs are protected for 15 years but in Germany the period is 20 years. In the USA owners of copyright are given 95 years, while the period in the EU is 70 years. The situation is further complicated by the situation in some countries, including Australia and Germany, where firms can be granted minor patents which allow them to apply for protection for a shorter time than a full patent.

Application time: the entire procedure from application to grant will generally take over 12, and in many cases over 18 months and that time period may be further extended where the law provides for other parties to oppose the granting of the patent.

Enforcement problems—firms may have to pursue infringements through various national courts which could also be time-consuming and expensive. Once again the cost can vary country by country. In the US, enforcing a patent through the courts can cost millions of dollars whereas it is much cheaper in Europe and in countries like China and India. In some countries the level of legal protection is either low, or non-existent, or the authorities do not enforce the law. China is a particular source of concern in this regard being seen as the counterfeiting capital of the world and berated regularly by the US authorities for its lax enforcement of IPRs.

While the issues outlined above can pose challenges for big firms, it can make it virtually impossible for poorer small and medium-sized firms to protect their technology. The consequence of all these issues is that the system excludes small businesses because they cannot afford to defend their intellectual property in court.

● CHAPTER SUMMARY

In the chapter we have shown how technology refers to ideas and knowledge that business can exploit commercially. The sources of new ideas on which companies can call are many and varied, ranging from universities and research institutes to competitors, customers and suppliers, and to employees.

Globalization and technology make foreign sources of new ideas more accessible and have made it easier for business to tap in to foreign sources through, for example, cross-border R&D partnerships.

Innovations tend to be concentrated in big firms operating in the high-tech manufacturing sector. The rate of innovation varies from firm to firm, sector by sector and country to country. Firms are motivated to innovate by increasingly fierce competition from rivals, both domestic and foreign, other elements in the supply chain, developments in the ICT sector, and the policies pursued by governments.

Technology offers opportunities to business organizations to increase their profits and growth through the introduction of new and improved goods and services and through changes to their production processes. Technology also helps firms to restructure their global patterns of production through investment in low cost locations or by sub-contracting to cheaper suppliers. However, as we have seen with Kodak, technology can also pose threats and challenges for firms particularly if they allow themselves to fall behind their competitors. Technological advance, because it involves change in products or production processes, is a risky business particularly for firms that do not manage change well.

Finally the external environment offers business the means to protect its intellectual property although the degree and cost of protection can vary significantly from one country to another. In countries like China and some other South East Asian countries, where the level of protection is low, there are significant problems with the theft of IPRs, the counterfeiting of goods and the piracy of films, music, and books. Attempts to provide protection internationally haven been slow to progress and are relatively underdeveloped. Industries and firms differ to the extent to which they protect their intellectual property with companies in the IT and electronic sectors having a high propensity to protect their technology compared with firms in the car industry.

● REVIEW QUESTIONS

1. Review your understanding of the following terms:
   - technological advance;
   - applied research;

- innovation;
- technological diffusion;
- intellectual property.

2. Discuss how multinational companies could contribute to the international diffusion of technology. Illustrate your answer with examples.

3. Explain why innovation is important for big firms in the consumer electronics/pharmaceutical industry.

4. According to the R&D Scoreboard, car firms do not take out many patents compared to other industries. Give some explanations for this.

5. What problems does business encounter when trying to protect its IPRs? Use examples from China to help you answer this question.

Case Study Web 2.0

Nielsen (2010) reports that hits to social network and blog sites are growing exponentially, being visited by three quarters of global consumers who go online. Figures show that visitors spent increasing amounts of time on the sites—six hours on average in April 2010.

The rapid growth of online networks facilitated by Web 2.0 gives business great opportunities, particularly for firms selling consumer goods and services, to interact with existing and potential customers. Glenny puts it thus:

> Advertisers and companies salivate at . . . social networking sites (because they) can predict exactly what we like to do, how we like to spend our money, and with whom we like to associate . . . Nothing is secret any more—not our shopping preferences, our blood group, our sexual desires or peccadillos, our phone numbers, our political sympathies, . . . our genetic disposition to certain diseases. (*Financial Times Weekend Magazine*, 29/30 January 2011)

Asian internet users are the most active users of blogs, particularly in China and South Korea. The next most active users are in Latin America, while the established web markets of the USA and Europe have slightly lower levels of adoption, and a more passive approach to creating and sharing content (Cooke 2008).

Web 2.0 offers new ways of carrying out market research. People shopping online automatically generate large databases which business can use to analyse consumer behaviour. Companies like Amazon and Ebay 'learn' something about customers every time their sites are used. Amazon records buying

choices and then mines and sifts this data to help provide targeted recommendations to customers. Asur and Huberman (2010) found, by analysing millions of tweets that Twitter could be used to forecast box-offce revenues for films.

The rapid growth of online social networks gives firms the opportunity to observe social interactions and to increase their understanding of how advertising and marketing can be used in the age of Web 2.0.

Market research firms use social networks to target particular types of customer, conduct interviews, and build participatory research communities for their clients. Cooke (2008) reports that almost one third of survey research is carried out online and its share is still growing. In Australia, the USA and Japan, it exceeds 40% of all survey research while in the UK the figure is 21%.

Source: www.istockphoto.com   →

→ To thrive in the online world, business needs to monitor and analyse systematically what its existing and potential customers are saying about it online on platforms like Facebook, YouTube, and Twitter. Firms should listen to customers and think constantly about ways to engage with them actively using the tools provided by Web 2.0. Kimberly-Clark, for instance, used its Huggies 'Baby Countdown' widget to engage its customers on their computer desktops (widgets include dialogue boxes and icons that invite the user to act in a number of ways). Smirnoff used the viral-video marketing vehicle Tea Partay to promote its Raw Tea product. The campaign was a hit on YouTube. Similarly, Cadbury's drum-playing gorilla advertisement promoting its Dairy Milk chocolate bar, received 500,000 hits in the week after the launch when the video was uploaded on to YouTube.

Some companies have set up a blog giving customers a place to offer feedback about products and services. McKinsey (2009) advises companies to engage in cocreation with customers through collaborative efforts that can come up with product ideas and advertising campaigns, as Frito Lay, owned by PepsiCo, did with its innovative customer-created ads campaigns 'Crash the Super Bowl', 'Fight for the Flavor', and 'The Quest'.

Companies can come a cropper with their use of Web 2.0. General Motors, to promote its Tahoe model, offered prizes to internet surfers to make their own advertisements by selecting backgrounds, video shots, and text. The results generated much negative comment on the company to which it was slow to respond. One lesson from this is that companies need to be cybervigilant, that is monitor the web constantly and be prepared to respond instantly because events can unfold very rapidly on the web with disastrous results for the company image.

Sources: http://blog.nielsen.com/nielsenwire/global/social-media-accounts-for-22-percent-of-time-online; Asur and Huberman 2010; *McKinsey Quarterly*, July 2009, June 2010; Cooke 2008; www.autoblog.com; http://danzarrella.com

Questions:

1. What is Web 2.0?

2. Analyse the opportunities opened up by Web 2.0 technologies for firms:

   • carrying out market research; and

   • promoting their products.

3. What are the potential pitfalls for firms wishing to use Web 2.0 technologies. How could business try to avoid such pitfalls?

4. What do you think McKinsey means by cocreation? Explore the possible implications of this for business wishing to protect its intellectual property rights.

5. Discuss the implications for business of the greater use of blogs in the emerging markets of China and South Korea.

 Online Resource Centre

www.oxfordtextbooks.co.uk/orc/hamilton_webster2e/

Visit the supporting online resource centre for additional material which will help you with your assignments, essays, and research, or you may find these extra resources helpful when revising for exams.

● FURTHER READING

Anderson shows how the internet helps products, that in previous eras would have failed because of low demand, survive and prosper.

● Anderson, C. (2006) *The Long Tail: Why the Future of Business is Selling Less of More*. New York: Hyperion Books

Chesbrough argues that for firms to be successful innovators they should call on both the internal and external resources available to the business.

- Chesbrough, H., Vanhaverbeke, W., and West, J. (2008) *Open Innovation: Researching a New Paradigm*. New York: Oxford University Press

Edgerton analyses the importance of technology to 20th century society at the global level.

- Edgerton, D. (2007) *The Shock of the Old: Technology in Global History Since 1900*. London: Profile Books

The book by Rogers is now in its fifth edition and is a classic text in the field of the diffusion of innovation.

- Rogers, E. M. (2003) *Diffusion of Innovations*. New York: The Free Press

● REFERENCES

Andriole, S. J. (2010) 'Business Impact of Web 2.0 Technologies'. *Communication of the ACM*, December, Vol 53, No 12

Asur, S. and Huberman, B. A. (2010) 'Predicting the Future with Social Media'. March, available at: http://arxiv.org/abs/1003.5699v1

Chang, H.-J. (2008) *The Myth of Free Trade and the Secret History of Capitalism*. London: Bloomsbury Press

Chang, H.-J. (2010) *23 Things They Don't Tell You About Capitalism*. London: Allen Lane

Cooke, M. (2008) 'The New World of Web 2.0 Research'. *International Journal of Market Research*, Vol 50, Issue 5

Dumont, B. and Holmes, P. (2002) 'The Scope of Intellectual Property Rights and their Interface with Competition Law: Divergent Paths to the Same Goal?' *Economics of Innovation and New Technology*, Vol 11(2)

Ehie, I. and Olibe, K. (2010) 'The Effect of R&D Investment on Firm Value: An Examination of US Manufacturing and Service Industries'. *International Journal of Production Economics*, Vol 128, Issue 1, November

EU Commission (2010a) Lisbon Strategy Evaluation Document SEC (2010) 114 final

Fontana, R., Geunab, A., and Mat, M. (2006) 'Factors Affecting University—Industry R&D Projects: The Importance of Searching, Screening and Signaling'. *Research Policy*, Vol 35

FTC (1996) Selected Themes from the FTC'S Hearings on Global and Innovation-Based Competition, the 1996 Antitrust Conference: Antitrust Issues in Today's Economy, 7 March

Held, D. *et al.* (1999) *Global Transformations: Politics, Economics and Culture*. Stanford: Stanford University Press

Kotler, P. and Caslione, J. A. (2009) *Chaotics: The Business of Managing and Marketing in the Age of Turbulence*. New York: Amacom

National Science Foundation (2010) Science and Engineering Indicators 2010

OECD (2008) Recent Trends in the Internationalisation of R&D in the Enterprise Sector: Special Session on Globalization, 13 March

O'Reilly, T. (2005) 'What is Web 2.0: Design Patterns and Business Models for the Next Generation of Software', 30 September, available at: http://oreilly.com/web2/archive/what-is-web-20.html

Porter, M. E. (1998) *The Competitive Advantage of Nations*. Basingstoke: Palgrave MacMillan

Schumpeter, J. A. (1976) *Capitalism, Socialism & Democracy*. London: Routledge

Senge, P. M. (2006) *The Fifth Discipline: The Art and Practice of the Learning Organization*. London: Random House

Teixeira, A. A. C., Santos, P., and Brochado, A. O. (2008) 'International R&D Cooperation Between Low-tech SMEs: The Role of Cultural and Geographical

Proximity'. *European Planning Studies*, Vol 16, No 6, July

UNESCO (2010) UNESCO Science Report 2010

Verizon (2010) 2010 Data Breach Investigations Report

WIPO (2010) World Intellectual Property Indicators, 2010 edition

Wonglimpiyarat, J. (2005) 'The Nano-Revolution of Schumpeter's Kondratieff Cycle'. *Technovation*, Vol 25, Issue 11, November

CHAPTER EIGHT

The Political Environment

LEARNING OUTCOMES

This chapter will enable you to:

- Explain what is meant by the terms, political system and the state

- Analyse the characteristics of different political systems and understand their importance for business

- Identify and explain the functions performed by the institutions of the state

- Evaluate the arguments regarding the demise of the nation state

- Assess the importance of the state for business

- Analyse how business can influence the state

Case Study Politics and BlackBerry

In 2010, India ordered the country's 15 telecoms operators, including Bharti Airtel and Vodafone Essar to make BlackBerry corporate e-mail and messenger services accessible to interception by security agencies or risk suspension of their licences. It was concerned that the services could be used by terrorists. Research in Motion (RIM), the maker of the BlackBerry, is the fifth largest handset maker in the world with a market share of around 4%. It was given the choice of opening its messaging service to monitoring by the Indian intelligence agencies or face being shut down. The BlackBerry Enterprise Server system allowed business customers to channel encrypted information through RIM's routers to servers based in Canada. RIM claimed that the servers were outside its control because customers held the codes.

India took the action following similar moves against RIM by the United Arab Emirates (UAE) and Saudi Arabia. The middle eastern states were not only concerned about terrorism but also the use of the services to break laws and customs relating to personal behaviour such as talking to a member of the opposite sex. In 2009, the UAE government tried to get access to information by offering a software upgrade to BlackBerry users through Etisalat, a state-controlled mobile-phone firm. According to RIM, the software was a piece of spyware that could pass on messages sent from their BlackBerrys.

RIM is concerned about losing access to the Indian market, where it has 1 million high-spending subscribers. India is the world's fastest growing mobile phone market with about 800 million users and 20 million new customers being added every month. The company also feels that conceding to the Indian authorities would encourage other governments to interfere in its services and would undermine the confidence of its 46m users worldwide.

India also announced its intention to take similar action against Skype and Google. The Indian authorities wanted these companies to establish servers within the country so that they could exercise jurisdiction over them and monitor and control the information passing through them more easily.

Sources: *Guardian*, 3 August 2010; *Financial Times*, 13, 28, 31 August, 2 September 2010; www.economist.com/node, 5 August 2010; www.economist.com/blogs; *India Telecom News*, 13 April 2011

Source: www.istockphoto.com

Introduction

> Few relationships are as critical to the business enterprise itself as the relationship to government. The manager has responsibility for this relationship as part of his responsibility to the enterprise itself. (Drucker 1999, p 283)

This quote from Drucker, seen by some as the inventor of modern management, indicates the importance of the political environment to business. It is no surprise, in the light of Drucker's comment that firms spend so much time and money trying to influence governments and politicians like Barack Obama, David Cameron, Angela Merkel, Wen Jiabao, Vladimir Putin, and Manmohan Singh. They are major decision-makers in a powerful entity called the state. Knowledge of where decision-making power lies in the state is very important for business whether that be a firm wishing to influence the process of formulating laws or regulations, or to get permission to drill for oil, or a contract for building roads and airports.

The political environment has major implications for both the macro- and microenvironments of business. State institutions establish and enforce the legal and regulatory framework within which business operates. They can have a significant influence on a whole range of business decisions. They can stop firms doing what they want to do or force them to do things they do not want to do. For example, they can give or deny permission for one firm to take over another. The EU Commission did not allow General Electric to take over its rival Honeywell, nor Ryanair's bid for Aer Lingus. An EU recycling **directive** will increase car manufacturers' costs by forcing them to take responsibility for disposal of their products when they come to the end of their useful life. The political environment is significant for business because the decisions emanating from it can generate important opportunities for firms and also pose significant threats, not only domestically but also abroad. The ability of the state to wage wars, pursue diplomacy, agree treaties and alliances, establish policies as regards migration, taxation, interest rates, the exchange rate, the balance of payments, inflation, education, health, the environment, maintaining law and order, and guaranteeing the right to buy and sell private property all have important implications for business.

As globalization proceeds, business increasingly finds itself affected by political events outside its home base. It is important that firms build up an understanding of the diverse nature of different political systems and how they operate. This knowledge will make it easier for business better to grasp the opportunities the systems provide as well as coping with the challenges they pose.

In this chapter we examine the different types of political system, the size of the state, and how it has grown. We also consider the impact the political environment can have on business and, in the final section, we look at how firms go about influencing their political environment.

What is the Political Environment?

An important entity in the political environment is the nation state where political parties fight elections, form governments and make laws and enforce them. National governments are indeed an important part of the political environment but they are only one element of a much broader concept called the state. As you will see later, the state comprises institutions such as the civil service and the judiciary as well as governments. Governments come and go but the other elements of the state tend to be more permanent. Basically the political environment is made up of those institutions which make political decisions and implement them. The political environment not only comprises institutions operating at the national level but also, as we will see, bodies at local, regional, and supranational (above the nation state) levels.

The Institutions of the State

The core of the state can be seen as a set of institutions having the legal power, ultimately backed up by coercion (the power to make people do or stop doing things), to make decisions in matters of government over a specific geographical area and over the population living there. The state comprises the following institutions:

- the legislative branch which includes those institutions which make the laws, e.g. Parliament in the UK, Congress in the USA, the Diet in Japan. An important role in such bodies is played by the leading politician, the President in the USA, France and Russia, the Prime Minister in the UK, Japan, Italy, and Spain and the Chancellor in Germany, along with cabinet members, ministers, and senior civil servants because they determine and direct government policy.

Mini Case EU Institutions and Decision-Making

The case identifies and explains the decision-making power of institutions in the EU. Various institutions participate in EU decision-making. The most important are:

- the European Commission: this is the civil service of the EU with powers that are wide and varied. It is the only institution having the power to initiate laws and is responsible for enforcing them. It negotiates international treaties on behalf of the EU as well as the entry of new members. It is headed by a President and a number of Commissioners each with responsibility for a particular area such as the internal market, trade, and transport. While the Commission proposes new legislation, it is up to the Council of the European Union and the Parliament whether those proposals become law. The Commission seeks to uphold the interest of the EU as a whole.

- the Council of the European Union: this represents individual member states and comprises ministers from national governments. It meets on a regular basis and is arguably the most important decision-making institution. It plays a vital role in the development of EU law. It has to approve all laws and budget proposals but cannot make new laws on its own. It must get the agreement of the Parliament. The Council has the power to sign international agreements with non-EU countries.

Each country's voting power in the Council is based on its population size with the smaller less populous countries, like Malta and Cyprus, being given more votes than their population would warrant. In some areas such as common foreign and security policy, taxation, asylum and immigration policy, Council decisions have to be unanimous. In other words, each member state has the power to veto any new proposals in these areas. On most issues, however, the Council takes decisions by qualified majority voting (QMV). QMV requires around three quarters of the votes to be cast in favour of a proposal. In addition, a member state may ask for confirmation that the votes in favour represent at least 62% of the total population of the Union. If this is found not to be the case, the decision will not be adopted.

- the European Parliament (EP): this is made up of representatives elected by the citizens of each member state. Each member state has a number of seats allocated on the basis of the size of its population. The EP does not have the same powers as national parliaments. For example, it cannot propose new laws nor has it the power to legislate on matters of taxation, agricultural policy, or industrial policy. Instead, it can only discuss and vote on laws proposed by the Commission. In order for a new EU law to pass, it has to have the support of both the Parliament and the Council of the European Union. The EP also has the power to accept or reject Commissioners and to sack the entire Commission through a vote of censure.

There are two other important institutions. The first is the European Council. This brings together the heads of government and the Commission President four times a year. They map out the overall direction of the Union, for example as regards enlargement and deal with issues that have not been resolved because of their contentious nature such as the size of the budget and how it is to be spent. It decides who will be President of the Commission. Like the Commission, the Council also has a President. Under the Lisbon Treaty, a politician will be chosen to be President of the European Council for 2.5 years.

The second institution is the European Court of Justice (ECJ). The Court upholds EU law and, in EU matters, is the highest court in all of the member states. It arbitrates between member states, institutions, and individuals in cases relating to EU law. There is no right of appeal against ECJ judgments.

Sources: Europa, European institutions, and other bodies. Available at http://europa.eu; Civitas, www.civitas.org.uk

Parliaments pass policies, laws, and regulations which are then implemented by the **executive branch**. The EU Parliament is an example of a legislative body but at the supranational level (see Mini Case):

- the executive branch puts the laws into effect and ensures the desired outcomes. It gives policy advice to government ministers. This branch includes administrative bodies, such as the civil service in the UK and the European Commission in the EU—uniquely the Commission has the power to initiate policy. Regulatory agencies, which operate, to an extent, separately from central government also form part of the executive branch. Examples include the Federal Communications Commission in the USA, and the Office of the Communications Regulator (OFCOM), the water regulator (OFWAT), the energy regulator (OFGEM) in the UK. In Britain, they are known as Quasi Autonomous Non-Governmental Organizations, often referred to as Quangos. In developed countries the executive branch is usually large, running to thousands of people. Heads of government, such as the US President or the British Prime Minister, are commonly the chief executive of this branch.

- the **judicial branch** interprets and applies the laws—this branch comprises the judiciary, the police, and the armed forces which give the state its capacity to enforce the laws that it makes. Businesses operating in the geographical area are required to accept that the state has the authority to make decisions and to maintain order. If they are not prepared to accept this authority then the state can try to compel them to do so through the judicial system of police, courts, and prisons. At the EU level the Court of First Instance and the European Court of Justice interpret and apply the laws of the Union (for more discussion of EU law see the section on the EU in Chapter Nine).

Learning Task

This task lets you review your understanding of the different branches of the state. Allocate the following people to the appropriate branch of the state.

	Legislative	Executive	Judicial
Prime Minister of China			
The Cabinet Secretary (UK)			
President of the EU Commission			
The chief of police			
Vice President of Microsoft			
Supreme Court judge in the USA			
Governor of the Punjab			
Commander of the armed forces			
The Queen of Britain			

Different Political Systems

We start off by considering the political environment at the level of the nation state. If we take membership of the United Nations as an indicator of the number of independent countries in the world then there are 192. These nations operate under a variety of political systems but in each of them a national government exercises the right to make laws and to ensure that they are enforced in society. In some countries, power is concentrated in the hands of one or a few people while, in others, power is spread over a large number of different groups.

No two countries have identical political regimes.

We examine four different types of political system, **liberal democracy**, **authoritarian** and absolutist, communist, and theocratic. You will see that in the real world these regimes sometimes do not exist in their pure form. Subsequently, we go on to look at the differences between unitary states and federal states.

Liberal Democracy

There are two main characteristics of liberal democracies. The first is the right of citizens to elect governments to represent their interests. The second is the right to individual freedom. More specifically, such societies comprise:

- Governmental institutions based on majority rule with members drawn from a variety of political parties winning their positions through free elections. This occurs, for example, in the countries of Western Europe, North America, Latin American countries such as Argentina and Brazil, and Asian countries like India and Japan where voters have the choice of candidates from several political parties. The party that wins the majority of votes or seats usually becomes the party of government.

- State institutions which are constrained in their powers by other institutions. In the USA this is reflected in the separation of powers amongst different bodies. Power and responsibility is divided between the President, the Congress, the executive, and the judges. Each acts as a check and a balance on the others in the exercise of power. So the President may wish the USA to implement measures to deal with climate change—for example President Barack Obama, in 2010, wanted to pass a bill to control emissions of carbon dioxide but he had to get the approval of Congress to do so.

- Governments that are accountable to the electorate. This means that citizens can vote governments out of office if they do not like what they are doing. In the UK, India, and Japan, the electorate have the opportunity to do this in national elections that are held every four or five years.

- The right to personal freedom and to express views freely. In liberal democracies, television, radio, and the press are not under the sole control of the state so a range of views can be expressed. There is also the right to assembly which means that people can gather peacefully and demonstrate to make their views known. According to McHenry (2007) this right is exercised in India every day. These rights are guaranteed by an independent judiciary.

- A permanent, skilled, and impartial public service, for example, the civil service, responsible to the government and through it to the electorate.

- Most liberal democracies operate a mixed economy. That is true whether one looks at the countries of North America, Europe, and nations such as Argentina, India, South Africa, and Japan. In these nations, the majority of economic activity is carried out in the private sector with business and the consumer having the freedom to buy and sell goods and services. However, the state can also play an important economic role through taxation and public expenditure and ownership of, or significant shareholdings in, certain industries. It can also limit the freedom of business to trade and to make profit through the laws and regulations that it passes.

Of the 192 nations in the UN it seems that less than half are full liberal democracies. Liberal democracy is more likely to be found in rich, politically stable countries such as those in North America and in Northern and Western Europe and in Japan. This is obviously of interest to business because stability and prosperity make liberal democratic economies and their markets very attractive for business. It is therefore no surprise to find that the vast bulk of trade and foreign investment takes place among liberal democracies. Liberal democracy is found less often in countries with a low level of income per head of population. Such countries frequently experience political instability and this can be a deterrent to business getting involved in their economies. While there are countries that are clearly liberal democracies, there are others like Egypt that are moving, sometimes rather unsteadily, towards it.

There is a debate as to whether prosperity leads to the creation of liberal democratic systems or whether countries are rich because they are liberal democracies. Commentators such as Fukuyama (1993) take the former view arguing that when a country gets past a certain level of economic development the citizens will increasingly demand democratic participation and democratic political institutions. Others, such as Wright (2006), disagree, for she has found that public demands for democracy in China have fallen as the economy has prospered.

Authoritarian and Absolutist Systems

A relatively small number of countries operate under authoritarian or absolutist regimes. These are forms of government in which one person or a group of people exercise power unrestrained by laws or opposition. These countries are usually characterized by:

- Restrictions on the activities of political parties. It may be that only one political party is allowed to operate which gives total support to the ruler. Iraq, under Saddam Hussein, was a good example of this.

- The state is headed by one or several people who have unbridled power to make decisions. Myanmar (formerly known as Burma) is run by a small number of military officers.

- An absence of checks and balances on the power of the ruler. In Saudi Arabia, the royal family holds power with little constraint from parliament or the judiciary.

- A system where support for the ruler is based on **patronage**. Patronage, or **clientelism**, as it is sometimes called, occurs where favours are doled out in return for political support. Such favours can take a variety of forms such as money, jobs in government offices, or public contracts. Alternatively, the system could be based on inheritance where power and privilege is passed on from one member of the ruling family to another—once again Saudi Arabia is a good example of this. Saudi law declares the country to be a monarchy ruled by the sons and grandsons of King Abd Al Aziz Al Saud. So when King Fahd died in 2005, his crown passed to his half-brother, Abdullah.

Of course patronage is not confined to authoritarian and absolutist regimes. It also occurs in some liberal democracies. In the USA the slang expression, 'pork barrel politics' is often used to describe members of Congress lobbying to get publicly funded projects that bring money and jobs to their own districts.

In Italy, there has been a history of Christian Democrat governments distributing state jobs, tax relief, and preferential pensions treatment to blocs of reliable supporters. Fiat was a particular beneficiary because, after the Second World War, it enjoyed a privileged relationship with the Christian Democrats who built motorways, kept the price of petrol low, minimized investment in public transport, and protected the domestic car market from foreign competition (see Hopkin 2006 for discussion of clientelism in Western Europe; Ayokunle 2010 for Nigeria).

So some characteristics of authoritarian regimes may also be present in liberal democracies.

Countries operating under authoritarian or absolutist regimes only constitute a small proportion of the world's population and income. Thus, as far as business is concerned, their markets are not that important. However, firms may be interested in producing goods and services in these countries because resources like labour are often cheap. And for some primary sector industries a number of these countries are vital because they are rich in natural resources. For example, several countries in the Middle East are sitting on vast reserves of oil. Saudi Arabia is the world's single largest oil producer and has, by far, the biggest oil reserves. This makes it attractive to the big multinational oil companies such as Exxon, Shell, and BP. Oil companies need to be aware of the identity of those exercising power in these nations. Such knowledge is invaluable for these companies because it indicates where they need to apply influence when, for example, they are trying to obtain permission to drill for oil (for more on the oil industry and its political environment see the section on the political and legal environment in Chapter Four).

Communist Regimes

Communist regimes tend to have the following characteristics:

- the production of most goods and services is owned and controlled by the state. In China, even though companies such as VW and General Motors, have been allowed to invest there, the state continues to exercise a very significant degree of economic control over what is produced, how much is produced, where it is produced, and who will produce it; the system is dominated by one political party. Vietnam is another example of a one-party state where the Communist Party has tight control of the political system.

- in addition to controlling the economy, the Party controls the legislative, executive, and judicial branches of the state as well as trade unions and the media. In North Korea, for example, the Communist Party controls television and the press. (Chapter Seven discusses some of the difficulties confronted by firms like Google in dealings with the Chinese political and legal system.)

Unlike liberal democracies, communist regimes do not value so highly the right to personal freedoms. They put more emphasis on meeting the needs of society as a whole.

The political system operating in China does not apply in Hong Kong. When Britain handed the colony over to China in 1997, the Chinese authorities agreed to an arrangement under which the territory was granted more freedoms and democracy than the mainland. That is why China is described as being 'one-nation, two-systems'. While the mainland is communist, Hong Kong is seen by some as a glittering showpiece of capitalism.

Theocratic Regimes

In theocratic regimes:

- religion or faith plays a dominant role in the government;
- the rulers in government are normally the same people who lead the dominant religion;
- policies pursued by government are either identical with, or strongly influenced by, the principles of the majority religion, and typically, the government claims to rule on behalf of God or a higher power, as specified by the local religion.

There are no more than a handful of theocratic states. Iran is one example of a theocratic regime where the political process is heavily influenced by Islam. The policies of the Islamic political parties are founded on the Koran and the ayatollahs and mullahs, the religious leaders, are very influential in the formulation of policies. They, along with Islamic lawyers, sit on a council that has the power of veto over laws proposed by parliament. A priority in Iran is to resist what is seen as the corruption inherent in western materialism which makes it difficult for big western MNCs to operate there given that they are seen as the agents of the materialist culture.

Mini Case Equatorial Guinea

This case looks at a country that, in 1991, declared itself to be democratic. However, it fails to qualify as a liberal democracy on a number of grounds.

The Republic of Equatorial Guinea is a former Spanish colony located on the West coast of Africa. Since it gained independence in 1968, it has been ruled by two men from the same family.

Large oil and gas deposits were discovered offshore in the mid 1990s, and Equatorial Guinea is now one of Sub-Saharan Africa's biggest oil producers. But few ordinary people benefit from the oil revenues. Little of the oil money is spent on health, education, or on improving the infrastructure. Opponents of the regime complain that President Obiang Nguema and his supporters use the money for their own enrichment. It was reported that the President's family had amassed US$800 million in a US bank. Despite international calls for greater financial transparency in the sector, President Obiang has said oil revenue figures are a state secret. In terms of corruption it ranks 168 out of 178 countries in the Transparency International Corruption Perceptions Index (see Chapter Eleven for more on corruption and the Corruption Perceptions Index).

In 1996 Equatorial Guinea's first multi-party presidential election was held amid reports of widespread fraud and irregularities, returning the President with 99% of the vote. He won again in 2009 with 95% of the vote. The President exercises almost total control over the political system and suppresses political opposition. There are only two members of parliament who openly oppose the regime.

His government has been accused of widespread human rights abuses. The main broadcasters are state-controlled and there are only a few private newspapers. Mild criticism of public institutions is allowed but criticism of the leadership is not tolerated and self-censorship is widespread.

Source: CIA World Factbook; Transparency International 2010; www.globalwitness.org; www.bbc.co.uk; *El Pais*, 7 August 2005

Source: www.istockphoto.com

The Vatican City is another example of theocracy. It is an independent sovereign state with the Pope as its elected head. Its policies are based on the teachings of the Bible. Power is concentrated in the hands of the Pope who holds supreme legislative, executive, and judicial power. The Vatican describes itself as an 'absolute monarchy' meaning that the Pope can not be sued or prosecuted. It has 'non-member state' status at the UN. It has no permanent population, no jurisdiction over crimes committed in its territory, and depends on Italy for essential services (Robertson 2010).

Unitary and Federal Systems

Political regimes may also be classified according to the distribution of power at different levels. The regime may be unitary where most decision-making power is held by the institutions of central government and where the regions and localities have little or no autonomy. In unitary states the institutions of central government normally are responsible for important policy decisions, for the majority of public expenditure, and for the raising of taxes with the regions having fewer powers in this regard. The great majority of countries in the world have a **unitary system**. France, Italy, Japan, and China are examples of unitary states.

On the other hand the system may be federal where power is shared between the centre and the component regions. In such systems regions may have significant decision-making powers in relation to areas such as spending and taxation. Friction between the centre and the regions in federations is not unusual. Hardgrave (2008) reports that states in India compete with each other in their demands on the centre to give them more financial resources and more autonomy in administration and planning matters. More than 2 billion people live in federal states and they comprise half the world's land area. Examples of federations are the USA, Germany, Brazil, and India. In **unitary systems**, those who award contracts for goods and services and decide rates and levels of tax are located at the centre of the regime. Thus, firms wishing to be given government contracts or to influence taxation decisions have to be in a position to affect the decision-making process at the centre. In **federal systems** businesses may find themselves dealing with decision-makers at both the centre and in the various regions of the federation.

Learning Task

Table 8.1 below shows public expenditure on investment by different levels of government as a percentage of GDP. It shows that, in some countries, central government accounts for a greater share of expenditure while in others regional and local spending is more important.

1. Explain why spending in the UK and France appears to be much more centralized than either Canada or Argentina. (Hint: call up the CIA World Factbook on the web to discover the system of government in these countries.)

2. What are the implications for business wishing to sell investment goods to the public sector in:

   a. the UK?

   b. Argentina?

Table 8.1 Public investment by government level as % of GDP

	Public Investment by Government Level as % of GDP averages since 1995		
	Central	Regional	Local
Argentina	19.5	11	2.4
France	45.5	NA	10.4
Canada	18.7	21.4	7.4
UK	38.9	NA	12.1

NA Not Applicable
Source: de Mello 2010

The Size of the State

In this section we examine the size of the state relative to the economy. This is most commonly done by looking at the amount of money the state is spending and what it takes in tax as a proportion of the total income generated in the country i.e. gross domestic product. As we will see, the size and importance of the state varies from one country to another.

Public Expenditure

The three decades after the end of the Second World War in 1945 saw the biggest increase historically in public spending. This mainly reflected the fact of governments taking on responsibility for maintaining high levels of employment and adequate living standards. One result of this was a major expansion of the welfare state. Spending also increased significantly on defence arising from the cold war between the West and the Communist bloc of countries. By 1980, the state's average slice of the economy had leapt to 43% (in America the percentage topped 30%; in many small European countries it breached 50%). During the 1980s and despite the anti-government rhetoric of some countries, it continued to grow. Public spending as a percentage of GDP fell in the majority of countries in the chart after 1996 (see Figure 8.1). Towards the end of the first decade of the 21st century, OECD countries were spending the equivalent of 40% of GDP. The ratio was lower for countries like the USA, Japan, and Brazil, but still significant, at more than a third. Countries such as France, Sweden, and Denmark with highly developed welfare states top the list with Chile, South Korea, Switzerland, and Australia at the bottom.

Where does the Money Go?

The largest amounts of public spending go on subsidies and transfers, for example, pensions, social security, and unemployment benefits. This is followed by spending on defence, law and order, education and health, often referred to as public or government consumption.

Figure 8.1 General government expenditures as % of GDP

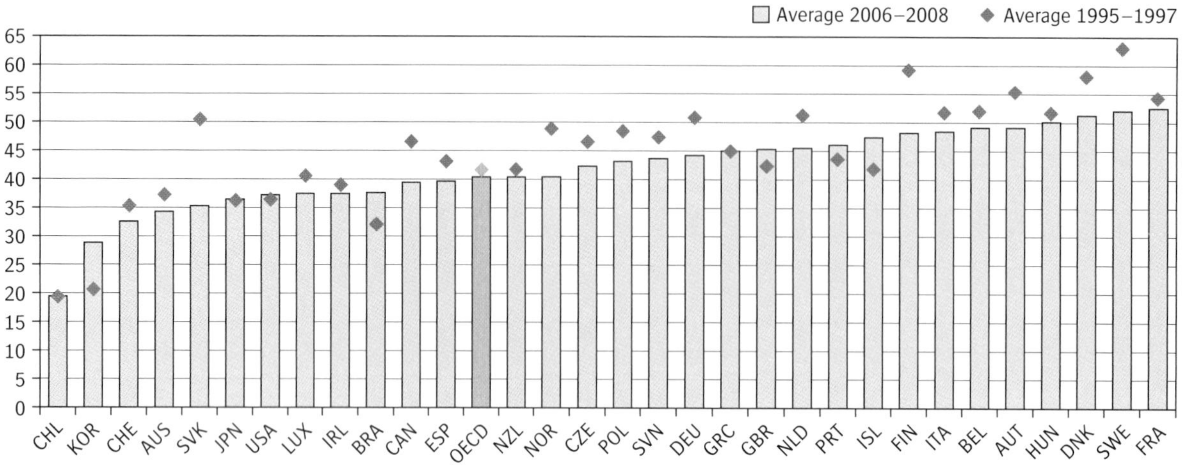

Source: OECD Factbook 2010

How the Money is Raised—Taxation and Borrowing

A clear trend since the mid 1970s was a steady increase in the proportion of total income taken by taxes. The tax-to-GDP ratio across most of the developed economies rose despite many countries cutting tax rates on personal and company income. This reflected the effects of stronger economic growth which generated higher company profits. Some countries have also tried to offset the effects of cuts in tax rates by drawing more sectors and people into the tax net and reducing the degree of **tax evasion** and **avoidance** (www.oecd.org). The tax take tends to be higher in Western European countries. In Norway, Denmark, and Sweden it is greater than half of GDP while it exceeds 40% of GDP, for example in Germany, Italy, Austria, France, Finland, and Belgium. Chile has the lowest tax ratio at around 27% followed by countries like South Korea, the USA, Japan, and Brazil ranging from 33–36%. From the 1990s, the tax take stayed the same or increased in more than half the countries in the chart (Figure 8.2).

More than 90% of the tax revenues raised in the developed economies come from three main sources: direct taxes on the income of individuals and business, indirect taxes on goods and services such as VAT and excise duties on the likes of tobacco and alcohol, and another form of direct tax, social security contributions.

Businesses pay tax on their net income i.e. their profits. There has been a widespread tendency for tax rates on profits to drop in the advanced economies. Devereux and Sørenson (2005) describe the reduction in the tax rate on profits as remarkable. In 1982, they reported that 15 countries had tax rates in excess of 40%. In Germany, Sweden, Finland, and Austria the rate was around 60%. By 2010, rates had fallen significantly across many countries (Figure 8.3). Only Japan and the USA had rates of around 40%. This trend may be due to the spread of globalization and the wish by countries to attract and retain foreign direct investment. A further reason is that host countries want to encourage those businesses to retain their earnings in the host country.

Figure 8.2 General government revenues as % of GDP

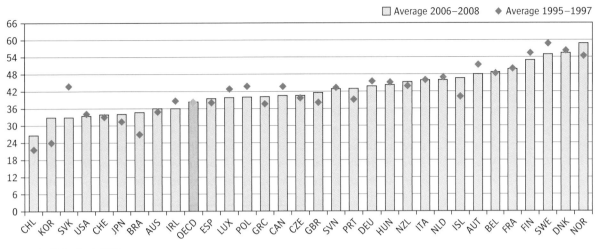

Source: OECD Factbook 2010

Figure 8.3 Profit tax rates %

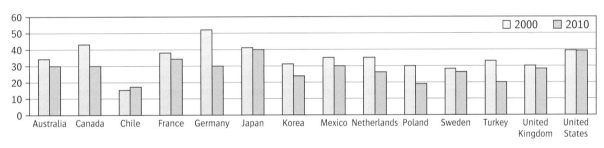

Source: OECD Factbook 2010

When spending is greater than the taxes raised, governments usually borrow to cover the deficit. The USA has, for a number of years, been running large budget deficits. In 2010, in the aftermath of the financial crisis, it was US$1.5 trillion or over 10% of GDP while the figure for the UK was around £60 billion (www.usgovernmentspending.com; www.ons.gov.uk). On the other hand, India and China were running significant budget surpluses showing that tax receipts were higher than public expenditure.

The Global Crisis and Government Finances

The global financial crisis and economic downturn caused a dramatic increase in developed country government deficits as tax revenues fell and expenditure on bailing out the banks and on unemployment benefits rose. Most developed countries tried to stimulate their economies through tax and spending policies. Finland, Korea, and the United States cut taxes significantly while Australia, Denmark, Japan, Korea, and Turkey planned for large increases in spending. China gave a massive fiscal stimulus to its economy to the tune of 2.5% of GDP by increasing investment in infrastructure and social welfare. By contrast, the UK, Hungary, Iceland, and Ireland took demand out of their economies by raising taxes and cutting spending (OECD Factbook 2010; IMF 2010).

The Demise of the Nation State?

Commentators including Ohmae (2005) and, to some extent Held (2007), argue that the state has become increasingly powerless in the face of globalization. They contend that the increasing and all-pervasive interconnectedness of national economies is fatal to the effective power of individual states. National governments can no longer manage their domestic economies because they are subject to the forces that shape the international economy. So if an individual government set profit tax on business at a much higher level than other countries then firms would relocate or ensure that their profits were earned in countries with a lower profits tax. Tax revenues would fall and the government would be obliged to revert to a lower level of profit tax. Similarly, if a government wanted to have a relatively low rate of interest then this would be undermined by investors moving their money out of the country to take advantage of higher rates elsewhere. This would reduce the supply of money available for borrowers and put upward pressure on interest rates. A government wanting to prohibit dangerous or undesirable working practices might find the affected industries moving abroad or shutting down, because the new regulation would put domestic firms at a disadvantage in competition with foreign producers. Some commentators supported their arguments with the case of Germany where welfare benefits were high relative to other countries. Generous benefits meant that, for each worker, employers had to pay a high level of social security tax on top of wages. This pushed up labour costs and made the German economy less competitive internationally. As a result Germany suffered from slow growth and high levels of unemployment. It was thus no surprise to the commentators that Germany cut back on the welfare benefit system. They saw the reforms as an indication that countries cannot buck global market forces and that the market will enforce a convergence of taxation and public expenditure among countries; in other words, there will be a race to the bottom.

Learning Task

Examine Figures 8.1 to 8.3 and answer the following questions:

1. Give some evidence of the change in the size of the state in industrialized countries in the period after 1945.

2. Come up with explanations for the change in the size of the state.

3. Advance reasons for France and Sweden being the largest public spenders and the USA and Japan among the lowest?

4. Explain why governments wish to attract and retain foreign direct investment. Why might globalization cause them to reduce company taxation?

Counterpoint Box 8.1 The nation state—dead or alive?

Critics of Ohmae's view, such as Hirst and Thompson (2005) and Scholte (2005), argue that the demise of the nation state is much exaggerated. Hirst and Thompson point out that the actual net flows between major economies are considerably less than a century ago. They contend that the main test of globalization is whether world economic trends confirm the existence of a single global economy. In this respect, they suggest, the evidence falls far short of any such claim. Others argue that globalization has not weakened the most powerful states such as the USA, Japan, and those in Western Europe who are the parent states and political voices of most of the major multinational corporations. These countries, powerful in their own right and even more so when they coordinate their policies, exercise influence through their continued domination of decision-making in the international financial institutions and forums such as the IMF, World Bank, and G20. Countries like China, Brazil, and India are also increasingly making their weight felt in the international arena. Scholte says that the most one can argue is that globalization has severely constrained the bargaining positions of smaller and weaker states, mainly in the underdeveloped world. This is hardly a new situation since small and poorer states have always had to consider the potential responses of more powerful states to the policies they adopt.

Sources: Ohmae 2005; Hirst 2005; Scholte 2005; Held 2007; Paczynska 2009

Functions of the State and their Importance for Business

Earlier on we looked at the different branches of the state. However, the boundaries of the state are not always clear-cut and, as we now discover, they can extend much further than the narrow description given above. Modern governments perform many functions besides the traditional ones of maintaining law and order and protecting the country from external attack.

A crucial role for the state is the preservation of the economic and financial system. A striking example of this occurred during the global credit crunch in 2008/09 when the US and European banking systems were in turmoil. Financial institutions, unable to borrow money, went bust or, like Northern Rock in the UK, were taken into public ownership (see Mini Case in Chapter Ten). In the USA, JP Morgan Chase took over the about-to-fail Bear Stearns bank at a bargain basement price but only after the US central bank, the Federal Reserve, had extended credit of US$30 billion to Bear Stearns. Stock markets gyrated wildly and the dollar plunged against other currencies. Governments could not allow the global financial system to crash because the money and credit provided by banks is a vital lubricant for business in a modern economy. Central banks in the USA, the UK, and the Eurozone intervened to prevent a collapse by making hundreds of billions of dollars of loans available to financial institutions (see the section on the global financial crisis in Chapter Ten).

We are now going to look in more detail at other functions that can have a significant impact on the external environment of business. By carrying out these functions state institutions can make decisions that constrain the ability of business to meet its objectives such as making profits and increasing sales or market share. On the other hand they can also provide opportunities which firms are able to exploit for commercial gain.

Law of Contract

The state has a major part to play in establishing the wider environment within which business operates. It passes laws and adopts regulations that set the legal framework or rules of the game for business, some of which are especially important. For example, in liberal democracies the state usually guarantees the right to own and to buy and sell capital assets and goods and services, the lifeblood of all commercial businesses. One particularly important aspect is the law of contract, where the state lays down and enforces rules and obligations relating to transactions around the buying and selling of goods and services. The law of contract ensures that if a business sells goods or services, it will be able to use the law to pursue the customer for payment, were that to be necessary. Similarly, a firm contracting to buy a certain quantity and quality of goods wants to be sure that it is able to use the law to remedy any shortfalls or deficiencies on the part of the supplier. Business will be reluctant to operate in countries where it is not able to enforce the terms of its contract. A good example of such a country is the Congo in Africa, which the big oil multinational, Shell, classifies as a country where state institutions are ineffective. The absence of an effective judicial system makes it virtually impossible for firms to enforce the law of contract (for more on contract law see Chapter Nine).

Law and Order and External Attack

Another function of the state is to protect its geographical area from both external and internal threats. It usually has the army, navy, and air force to deal with external threats, for example military threats from other countries, and the police, courts, and prisons for helping maintain law and order within the geographical frontiers of the state. States that can effectively protect themselves from external threat and maintain law and order internally are seen by business as providing a more stable and attractive operating environment.

Spending and Taxation

Economically, the state is the largest and most important single player in developed countries. This is reflected in the amount of money governments spend and take in tax in relation to the whole economy. Governments spend money on buying goods and services, paying the wages of state employees, and providing welfare benefits. Taxation takes the form of direct taxes, those on incomes, and indirect taxes which are levied on expenditure.

The state can use its spending on goods and services and welfare benefits and taxing along with other policies towards interest rates and the exchange rate to influence the level of total demand for the goods and services produced by business. When the economy is going into recession, the state can increase demand by raising its own spending on goods and services, or it can cut taxes or lower interest rates to encourage consumers and business to increase their spending. Alternatively, when the economy is booming and there is a danger of inflation going out of control, the state can cut spending, or raise taxes and interest rates to reduce spending and relieve inflationary pressures.

Such decisions can have major implications for business. For example a decision to raise interest rates increases the cost of borrowing for firms and is often greeted by them with dismay. The higher cost of borrowing may also cause consumers to cut back on spending on goods such as consumer durables which they would normally buy on credit. On the other hand, organizations

Mini Case Minimizing the Tax Burden

This case shows how firms go about minimizing the amount of money they hand over to governments in taxes. One approach is to evade paying taxes, which is illegal.

Tax Evasion

Globalization makes it easier for companies, especially big MNCs, to minimize their global tax burden. They can do this in several ways. One of the most commonly used is transfer pricing which involves the mispricing of cross-border trade. Firms may, for example, sell goods from subsidiaries in high-tax countries to other group companies in low-tax territories at below market prices. The goods can then be re-sold at market rates, thereby ensuring that the profit attracts less tax. Another method for reducing profits is for subsidiaries in tax havens to overcharge for services such as consultancy advice or insurance.

In 2010, Dolce and Gabbana the famous fashion designers, were charged by the Italian authorities with evading tax on €1 billion of income by channelling the money through a Luxemburg company. GlaxoSmithKline (GSK), the giant pharmaceuticals company, was presented with a US$5.2 billion bill for extra taxes and interest by the US government over revenues dating back to the late 1980s. The US Senate estimates that annual revenue losses from tax evasion total some US$100 billion while the cost to the UK taxpayer is over £15 billion. There have been moves coordinated by the OECD to clamp down on tax evasion.

Source: Gravelle 2009; www.evb.ch; http://guardian.co.uk, 26 November 2010; www.oecd.org; www.attorneygeneral.gov.uk

such as the retail banks may welcome such an increase in rates because it allows them to charge their customers more for loans. Rising interest rates often mean that banks can widen the gap between the interest they pay their customers on their current accounts and the income they can earn on their depositors' money.

Counterpoint Box 8.2 Tax avoidance

Tax avoidance is commonplace in the world of business. Bloomberg reported that companies like Google, Microsoft, Apple, and Facebook legally avoid billions of dollars of taxes every year through the use of tax havens (Visit the **Online Resource Centre** for this book to access some video links related to this topic.) Ikea also avoids paying large amounts of tax by funnelling profits through a Dutch charity.

Diageo, the drinks firm and two big drugs firms GSK and AstraZeneca, transferred the ownership of brands worth millions to low tax locations. Big retailers in the UK, including Tesco and Amazon avoid VAT by setting up subsidiaries in the Channel Islands of Jersey and Guernsey to sell products online.

Supporters of tax avoidance argue that the practice is legal and that firms are under no obligation to pay more tax than the law requires. They claim that business has a duty to shareholders to minimize the tax burden.

Critics affirm that the cost of tax avoidance by firms can be substantial. It has been estimated that the taxman loses $60 billion every year in the USA and up to £13 billion in the UK. Avoidance undermines the ability of governments to finance vital services such as health and education and to provide infrastructure, all of which are particularly important in poor countries. And the facility with which big MNCs can avoid tax places smaller domestic firms at an unfair competitive disadvantage. To be competitive with tax havens, higher tax countries may feel obliged to lower their tax rates with adverse effects on their revenues and their ability to spend. Finally, domestic taxpayers may become more reluctant to pay taxes if they see that big business can get away with not stumping up.

Source: Gravelle 2009, Tibocha 2007; www.bloomberg.com; www.taxresearch.org; guardian.co.uk 2 February 2009, 9 December 2010; *The Guardian* 12 May 2008

Negotiator

The state acts as a negotiator with other states. Negotiations can be bilateral where two countries are involved, or multilateral where more than two participate. The WTO is a multilateral body where important negotiations take place on reductions in barriers to trade and to the movement of capital across borders. Such negotiations can be very good for business particularly when they open up new markets. On the other hand, they can remove barriers that protect domestic firms from foreign competition (see section in Chapter Two on the WTO).

Regulator

Regulation can affect a very wide range of business activities. For instance, regulations could constrain the ability of the firm to take out patents, or set its own prices e.g. in the telecommunications and water industries in the UK. It could also affect the level of competition, and market entry. For example, in both the EU and the USA the authorities liberalized entry into the civil aviation market which led to new entry and a much fiercer degree of competition.

India controls entry into the retail sector. Foreign companies can not be majority shareholders in operations there and that has made companies like Tesco and Wal-Mart reluctant to invest.

Regulations could increase a firm's costs by stipulating requirements relating to consumer health and safety, to employment contracts, and to the natural environment or by requiring companies to fill in certain forms and to meet certain administrative formalities i.e. red tape (for more discussion of the impact of regulations on business see Chapter Nine).

In its role as a regulator the state can take the power to grant or refuse a firm a licence to operate or to guarantee it a monopoly. In the developed world, banks and other financial institutions usually need to get a licence to sell financial services. Tighter regulation, following the global financial crisis, means that compliance costs for banks will increase. Regulations can also determine whether or not firms can merge—the US Federal Trade Commission blocked a merger between Staples and Office Depot, the big office supplies companies.

Firms may also find that regulations lay down the technical specifications to which their products must conform. There are examples of drugs regulators, concerned about safety, demanding more rigorous testing, prohibiting the launch of a new drug or ordering pharmaceutical companies to withdraw products from the market place. The main forms of regulation are at the national level but supranational regulation is becoming increasingly important through bodies such as the World Trade Organization and the EU.

Deregulator

Just as the state can regulate so can it deregulate, or liberalize. The USA and EU liberalized their civil aviation sectors. Now EU airlines have the freedom to set their own prices, to fly over the territory of member states, to operate flights within those countries, and to set up routes between them. As a result, numerous low cost airlines emerged, such as easyJet and Ryanair, that caused all sorts of competitive problems to the established national carriers like British Airways and Lufthansa.

At the global level, western governments and the WTO through measures like the General Agreement on Trade in Services (GATS), have encouraged developing countries to open up their markets in services such as telecommunications and banking.

Arbitrator

The state also acts as an arbitrator or referee between firms who are in dispute with each other. Thus business may look to state institutions, such as the courts, or other regulatory agencies, to resolve disputes with other firms or to take action against them.

Such disputes could relate to a whole range of issues such as breach of contract, abuse of market power, and patent infringement.

Microsoft's competitors have complained on numerous occasions to the competition authorities in both the USA and the EU about Microsoft abusing its market power making it very difficult for them to compete in the software market. In the ten years up to 2009, the software giant paid fines to the EU of £1.5 billion (www.bbc.co.uk, 16 December 2009).

Customer for Goods and Services

The state can also play a vital role as a customer for business. The OECD (2009a) reports that developed countries spend, on average, 25% to 35% of GDP on individual goods and services.

In the UK, the public sector spends some £220 billion on the purchase of goods and services from 44,000 suppliers. Some firms are heavily dependent on such contracts, for example, they account for around 90% of revenue for companies like the Tribal Group and Mouchel (*Financial Times*, 8 November 2010). For some industries, such as pharmaceuticals and armaments, the single most important customer is the state and the purchasing policies pursued by the state towards those industries is of paramount importance. This can be seen in those countries with ageing populations where the state is trying to control public expenditure through pressure on pharmaceutical firms to lower prices and by turning to lower priced generic drugs. Governments are major customers for firms in the IT sector and for consultancies such as PwC and McKinsey.

The state can also be an important client for the financial sector. When governments run budget deficits they borrow money from financial institutions in exchange for financial instruments such as bonds and Treasury Bills. This can make governments major customers for lending institutions—in 2010, the US government was servicing a massive US$9 trillion in loans while the UK was paying out £42 billion in interest (www.telegraph.co.uk, 11 December 2010).

The purchasing strategies pursued by the state can have important implications for suppliers. For example, there are claims in the UK that government procurement policies favour large companies at the expense of small and medium sized enterprises. There is also much evidence that many states pursue nationalistic purchasing policies, favouring domestic producers over their foreign counterparts even when the foreign firms offer better value.

Supplier of Goods and Services

In many countries the state takes on the job of producing and selling goods and services. Sectors where the state often carries out these activities are energy, water, sanitation, transport, postal services, and telecommunications. The organizations responsible for producing in these sectors are frequently publicly owned and controlled. In times of emergency, governments sometimes take businesses into public ownership because the economic and social impact of them going out of business would be very serious. The global financial meltdown and the subsequent economic crisis gave a good illustration of this. Banks were nationalized in the USA, the UK, the Benelux countries, Iceland, and Ireland (see discussion on the global financial crisis in Chapter Ten). In the summer of 2009, General Motors the giant car maker went bankrupt and was nationalized by the US government which, in the process, spent nearly US$60 billion of taxpayers' money.

Other areas of production where the state is usually heavily involved is in the provision of welfare services with health and education services being two prime examples. In developed economies the state often exercises a high degree of control over the finances and policies pursued by schools, universities, and hospitals. The policies pursued by governments in those areas could be important for business since they could have implications for the quality of the labour force in terms of health and education levels.

As we have seen, the state supplies some goods and services essential for private sector production. For business to operate effectively, there has got to be a transport infrastructure in the form of road and rail networks, ports, and airports. Usually the state is involved in providing these and also some of the services associated with them such as rail or air travel. Similarly, state agencies can be suppliers of such vital elements as energy and telecommunications as well as basic research and development, and economic statistics. The Indian government exercises control over the railways, postal services and has large stakes in the banking and electricity industries (OECD 2009b).

Financial services may also be provided by state agencies. In the UK the Export Credit Guarantee Department (ECGD) insures exporters against the risk of not getting paid by their overseas buyer for reasons such as insolvency, war, or lack of foreign exchange.

The policies pursued by these state-owned suppliers as regards pricing and investment can have a significant impact on the performance of their customers in the private sector. For example, big energy consuming firms in the steel and chemicals industries in France will be very sensitive to the prices charged by the state monopoly suppliers, Electricité de France (EDF), or Gaz de France (GDF), because energy counts for a large proportion of their costs.

Competitor

State organizations may be important competitors for private sector firms in, for example, energy, transport, and telecommunications and in areas such as health and education. Often private sector firms complain that they face unfair competition from their state rivals. This can take several forms. State firms may be subsidized allowing them to charge artificially low prices. Most of France's electricity is produced by nuclear power which receives great dollops of subsidy from the French government. State firms may be able to raise finance at much lower rates of interest than private sector rivals simply because they are state agencies and regarded as less risky by the financial markets. Foreign private sector energy companies wishing to enter the French market could face formidable competition from their state-owned rivals, EDF, one of the world's largest electricity companies and GDF. EDF has entered markets in both Western and Eastern Europe, but foreign energy firms trying to penetrate the French market have run up against barriers to entry put up by the French state despite EU efforts to liberalize the energy market.

Figure 8.4 State aid to industry EU 2009 US$billion

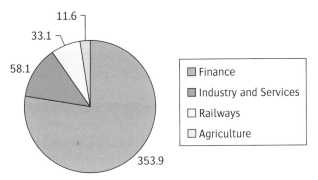

Source: EU Commission, State Aid Scoreboard, Autumn 2010

Subsidizer

The state often subsidizes business in the form of grants, tax reliefs, and cheap loans to maintain or generate employment or to maintain the production of goods and services regarded as important to the national economy (see Figure 8.4). In 2005, EuroDisney, operator of two theme parks outside Paris was experiencing financial problems. The French government came to its aid with US$500 million in investments and cheap loans through a state-owned bank.

According to the European Commission, Boeing from the mid 1980s had received subsidies worth around US$28 billion. In 2009, EU states subsidized finance, industry, services, and agriculture to the tune of more than €427 billion. The breakdown by sector is shown in Figure 8.4.

Subsidies are not confined to rich countries but are also often given by poorer countries to domestic producers. For example, Ghana's energy sector is dominated by subsidized state-owned enterprises (WTO 2007). China, in 2010, announced that it would subsidize exports of technology services and software.

Following the onset of the global financial crisis in 2007, EU member states made some €4.6 trillion available to banks mainly in the form of loan guarantees to keep the sector afloat (European Commission 2010).

In summary we can see that the exercise of the functions outlined above can have an impact on industry structure, ownership and control, for example, through the control of mergers and acquisitions or through policies to remove barriers to entry in industries such as airlines and telecommunications. It can also have a significant influence on the decisions organizations make in areas like pricing, product, and investment. Such influences may then have important implications for the performance of a company in areas such as profit performance, market share, and growth rate.

How Organizations Influence the State

As trade, overseas investment, and foreign competition have grown in importance, so firms, particularly those with international operations, have perceived the increasing importance of their relationships with state institutions. While decades of international negotiations may have made trade and the movement of capital freer, companies in many sectors confront increasing competition in their domestic markets and still face barriers in foreign markets. To protect themselves against foreign competition, to get the barriers removed, or to keep them in place for that matter, companies often appeal to forces in their political environment that could help. As the chief executive of BP said 'We've always got to be in a position to turn to the government in power' (*Financial Times*, 2 August 2002).

Because the state can have such an important impact, firms often make big efforts to influence the decisions it makes and are often prepared to devote very large amounts of resources to ensure a successful outcome to their attempts to do so. Big firms like Ford and Microsoft, have a global political strategy overseen by a senior executive with a substantial budget usually reporting directly to the chief executive. Where very important public policy issues arise the chief executive often intervenes to represent and advocate the company's interests to the state. For example, both Bill Gates and the chief executive officer of Microsoft lobbied the European Commission intensively in the run up to the decision on whether the company was abusing its Windows monopoly.

Big firms are in the best position to exercise an influence on the state. One reason for this is the possible reluctance of the state to cause hostility in businesses whose decisions on pricing, production, investment, employment, imports and exports can have a major influence on the ability of the state to achieve its goals of economic prosperity, high levels of investment and employment, low inflation, and a healthy balance of payments. Some industries, by their nature, are also well positioned to influence the state. For example, governments may be averse to taking decisions that will provoke a critical reaction in the press or on television. This gives the people who run the media the power to influence politicians especially in the run-up to national elections. The authorities may be reluctant to incur the wrath of firms operating in high technology, high growth industries for fear of losing their contribution to jobs and to economic growth. Such sensitivities may cause governments to consult business before embarking on new policies. As a lobbyist for Enron the large American MNC put it, 'We have many friends in (the UK) government. They like to run things past us some days in advance to get our view' (*Financial Times*, 29 January 2002). He could also have made a similar claim for Enron's network of contacts and influence with the administration in the USA.

The pharmaceutical industry is a good example of an industry that is often treated with care by state institutions such as the UK Medicines and Healthcare Products Regulatory Authority (MHRA). Pharmaceutical firms are major suppliers to the National Health Service (NHS). The NHS depends on the industry as providers of existing and new medicines that are important in the provision and quality of health care. The UK government is very keen to promote innovation by encouraging firms to invest in research and development. The pharmaceutical industry is a major source of R&D and innovation within the UK. It invests about £3.5 billion per year in R&D in the UK which is about a quarter of the total R&D carried out by manufacturing industry. The industry is a major exporter with export sales of around £11.8 billion per year, with a £3.1 billion trade surplus. Finally, pharmaceutical firms directly employ some 83,000 people in the UK (www.abpi.org.uk).

Methods of Influencing the State

Business employs a variety of methods to influence decision-makers in the institutions of the state to protect and promote their interests. We will now examine some of these methods.

Lobbying

Businesses try to exert influence over the state by **lobbying** individually or collectively with other firms (see Nownes 2006). To do this they set up offices or employ professional lobbyists in the cities where state institutions make their decisions. A good example is Washington in the USA, where the institutions of the federal government are located. The pharmaceutical industry has more than twice as many lobbyists in Washington as the number of elected representatives in Congress. It wields considerable power over its regulator, the Food and Drugs Administration, and donates millions of dollars each year to members of Congress sitting on important safety committees. So effective has it been that the close links between the industry, its regulator, and the Congress has been called the iron triangle. In the first six months of 2009 the industry spent more than US$110 million to influence lawmakers on President Obama's health care reforms (*Time International*, 2 November 2009).

Where businesses succeed in getting regulatory agencies to serve their interests rather than that of the wider society they are said to have captured the regulator. According to some commentators, the pharmaceutical industry has been one of the more effective in this regard with the regulatory agencies appearing to identify their interests very closely with the industries they are supposed to regulate.

Mini Case Lobbying—Banks and Basel III

The *Financial Times* reported that the Basel III plans by global regulators to compel banks to set aside billions of dollars in extra capital to create financial institutions that could withstand another global financial crisis like 2008–09, were to be pared back after intense lobbying by the industry (see the section on regulation in Chapter Ten, The Financial Framework). Bankers claimed that their proposed amendments to the new regulations would prevent an excessive rise in funding costs and in borrowing charges for customers. Some banks had argued that the original measures could cost the industry up to €5 trillion in additional costs. It was also claimed that the Basel III reforms, along with new proposed taxes on banks around the world, could cut a typical bank's return on equity from 20% to 5%.

The banks spent millions fiercely resisting the introduction of tighter regulations. Walter Mattli, Professor of International Political Economy at Oxford University, asserted that banks set out, very successfully, to water down reform proposals and to postpone compliance deadlines for as long as possible. He claimed that the banks supported their case against tighter regulation by producing studies based on highly questionable assumptions and grossly exaggerating the cost to the industry and society of proper reforms. He cited three such studies by, JP Morgan Chase, six major British banks, and the influential Institute of International Finance. By the time more valid and reliable research had been done, it was too late to rectify the damaging effects of the bankers' lobbying. Another tactic pursued by the banks, he said, was to devise ways of circumventing the new regulations. According to Mattli, 'The Goldman Sachs and JP Morgans of this world are true champions in this game'.

Sources: *Financial Times*, 25 June, 20 August, 8 November 2010; *Money Marketing*, 10 July, 28 October 2010; http://blogs.news.sky.com/kleinman; http://guardian.co.uk, 20 July 2010

Source: Stockbyte

Learning Task

Read the Mini Case, Lobbying—The Banks and Basel III

Explain the powerful influence of the banking industry on regulatory agencies. Assess whether the success of the banks in watering down regulations is good for the financial stability of the global economy.

Brussels, as the location for many EU institutions, is another major lobbying focus for business. Hundreds of trade associations have offices there, ranging from the International Federation of Industrial Energy Consumers, to the Liaison Committee of European Bicycle Manufacturers, to the International Confederation of European Beet Growers, to the Union of European Railway Industries.

Companies such as Microsoft, Intel, Procter & Gamble, General Electric, and General Motors have offices in Brussels to lobby the Commission, the European Parliament, and the Council of Ministers—the three important decision-making institutions in the EU capital. Their desire to influence the political and regulatory process in Brussels has swelled the ranks of the professional lobbyists in the city. It is estimated that around 15,000 lobbyists compete for the attention of the EU institutions, with the vast majority of them representing business. (www.europarl. europa.eu).

When deciding how to lobby, businesses have to take a number of factors into account. They must choose whether to act alone or in alliance with others in the industry, the state institutions to be influenced, the nature and amount of pressure to be exerted on the agencies and the degree of publicity that is advisable.

Big firms are usually powerful enough to lobby on their own account. Boeing is an example of this, being the world's largest manufacturer of aircraft. It spends a lot of time and resources on lobbying. For example, it lobbied the US government to take action to protect it from its main European competitor, Airbus. At its urging the US government went to the WTO arguing that Airbus had been unfairly subsidized by European countries. In response, Airbus, contending that Boeing received large subsidies from the US taxpayer, persuaded the EU authorities to lodge a counter case at the WTO.

Small and medium-sized firms, on the other hand, often find it more effective to lobby along with other firms in the same industry through, for example, trade associations operating either at national or supranational levels. At the national level in Britain, for example, the trade association for the consumer electronics industry is the British Radio and Electronic Equipment Manufacturers' Association (BREMA). BREMA is also associated with the European Association of Consumer Electronics Manufacturers (EACEM) which represents the industry in the EU.

In addition to lobbying on an industry basis, firms can also lobby through national bodies which represent business more generally, like the Confederation of British Industry (CBI) in Britain or the Bundesvereinigung der Deutschen Arbeitgebervebaende (BDA) in Germany when trying to influence the state at the country level. Or they may subscribe to supranational associations, such as the Union of Industrial and Employers Confederation of Europe (UNICE) or the European Round Table (ERT), at the European level.

State Consultation with Business

Frequently business does not need to spend time and money lobbying because it expects the state to seek its views on proposed policies, regulations, and laws. In the UK, government departments, as a matter of course, consult bodies representing the construction and vehicle industries on draft regulations. The obligation to consult business is written into the EC Treaty. It requires the Commission to consult firms when preparing proposals particularly in the areas of social policy such as employment rights, working conditions, and equal opportunities, and in public health legislation relating to fields like biotechnology. The intention in the EU is for business to play a substantial role both in drafting and in implementing new measures (see the europa website for examples of business being consulted by the EU).

Promises or Threats

Occasionally, firms try to influence the state by using promises or threats. Big MNCs are able to offer countries the attractive prospect of large investment projects generating much income and many jobs. It is no surprise that governments fall over themselves in their attempts to attract such MNC investment especially in times of high unemployment.

When energy companies offer to exploit large oil and gas reserves in poor countries like Equatorial Guinea or Nigeria they hold out the promise of vast income from gas and oil revenues which gives them a deal of bargaining power in negotiations with government.

On the other hand, if business does not like the current or proposed policies of a particular country, it can threaten to cut down investment or relocate production, thereby reducing the number of jobs. For example, the chairman of Ford Europe issued such a warning stating that his company would not hesitate to close down major assembly operations in countries wishing to give workers longer holidays or a shorter working week. Another possibility is for the firm to refuse to supply goods and services. Insurers in the USA threatened to withdraw from certain areas of health insurance if President Obama did not modify his reforms to the US health care system (www.consumerwatchdog.org).

Direct Access to Government Ministers and Civil Servants

Firms, especially large ones, are often able to get representation on government advisory committees where the concerns of business can be aired with the other committee members, civil servants, and government ministers. In the EU, business has representation on the European Economic and Social Committee which is consulted by the various institutions of the union, the Commission, Council, and the Parliament. Over and above these formal structures, big business is also in a good position to get informal access to civil servants and ministers. A refusal would be highly unlikely were Microsoft or Shell to ask for a meeting with a government minister or high-ranking civil servant.

Employment and Exchange of Personnel

Commentators often refer to the revolving door between industry and the state in terms of personnel. Some companies see major benefits in offering jobs to ex-members of the legislative or executive branches of the state such as former government ministers and high ranking civil servants. The reason given is that such people bring invaluable knowledge of how the state operates and therefore could be very useful when companies are trying to win contracts or influence policy. Others suspect that the jobs may be pay-offs for past favours to the company or that the new employees will be able to exploit their links with the state to gain improper advantage for the firm.

Etzion and Davis (2008) did a study of the comings and goings of senior personnel between US government and business during the reign of Presidents Clinton and Bush. They found that employment in government could serve as a way of joining the corporate elite. All but one head of the US armed forces ended up serving on the boards of defence companies like Boeing and Northrop Grumman. Their research also showed a flow of people from business to high level positions in government service.

Mini Case Influencing the State in China

Just as in other countries, business tries to influence the state in China. This activity is even more important there because of the desire and ability of the Communist authorities to regulate and control economic activities. While national laws are often written in broad terms, their implementation is left to regional and local governments who, therefore, have a great degree of influence over economic activities in their areas. Business, both domestic and foreign therefore needs to influence both central and provincial governments.

Holtbrugge and Berg (2004) stated that the most important methods used by business in China were lobbying, bribery, codes of conduct, public relations, and sponsorship. Guosheng and Kennedy (2009), in a survey of large domestic and foreign firms, found that guanxi was widely recognized as important by companies especially in dealings with local authorities (see opening case Chapter Six). They also discovered that firms recruited ex government officials for their knowledge of how the political system worked.

Yongqiang (2007) compared and contrasted the successful attempts by Motorola with those of Microsoft to influence the authorities. Before the company entered China, the President of Motorola visited government officials to sound out their opinions on the firm's entry. It made a very good impression by donating mobile phones to officials in the Great Hall of the People in Beijing in the presence of the Chinese Premier. When company executives visit, they always meet up with high ranking officials. Motorola even set up branches of the Communist Party and gave priority to Party members when hiring workers.

In contrast, Bill Gates did not visit China until a year after Microsoft's entry. The Chinese thought that he looked down on their domestic market and found him overbearing. Motorola also made a good impression by offering to train thousands of technicians and managers for state-owned enterprises, committing to the purchase of billions of dollars worth of parts and services from domestic suppliers, and to reaching targets on investment and output. Microsoft, in comparison, did not make any initial commitments only wishing to sell goods and services and to earn profits.

Government officials would not support the company and it got a bad name with the public. Eventually the firm did enter into joint ventures with Chinese companies and agreed to help promote the software industry and train professionals. Motorola sponsored schools and sports, helped China join the WTO and publicized itself as a Chinese company. Unlike Microsoft, Motorola was happy to adapt its codes of conduct to Chinese social and business culture.

Sources: Holtbrugge and Berg 2004; Yongqiang 2007; Guosheng and Kennedy 2009

Source: www.fotolia.com

Learning Task

1. Why should defence companies, in particular, be among the largest hirers of ex-civil servants and former government officials?

2. Discuss the pros and cons for companies of employing civil servants and government officials previously involved in negotiations with them.

In some countries, the UK for example, there is a well-developed arrangement for the temporary exchange of managers and civil servants. Here, managers give up their jobs to work for a time in the civil service while senior civil servants move in the opposite direction. The benefits for business are that managers can learn how the civil service operates, shape policy advice to ministers, make useful network of contacts in the administrative branch, while civil servants who have transferred to private firms can be persuaded of the values and methods of the business community which they take back to the civil service.

Giving Money or Gifts

Companies donate money openly to political parties particularly in the run up to elections. Firms often justify this support by insisting that they are helping those parties who will create a better environment for the effective functioning of the **market economy**. Historically, in the USA the party traditionally favoured by business has been the Republicans, in the UK the Conservatives, and in Japan the dominant LDP.

During the 2008 American presidential election the oil and gas industry donated US$36 million to political parties with the major share going to the Republican party. This was dwarfed by the law and real estate sectors who gave a total of US$370 million (www.opensecrets.org).

Firms may also give money illegally to political parties or state officials. The Christian Democratic Party in Germany was forced to admit that the party had taken US$6.1 million in undeclared contributions between 1989 and 1998 in violation of Germany's strict political funding laws. International arrest warrants were issued for two former officials of the giant French oil company Elf Aquitaine on suspicion that the money had been paid to facilitate Elf's purchase of an oil refinery and a chain of petrol stations, assets of the former East Germany that the Kohl government sold to the French company in 1992. Pei (2007) claims that Chinese political officials could be receiving in total up to US$86 billion each year. (Chapter Eleven examines the issue of corruption in more depth.)

BAE, the Britain's biggest arms manufacturer, has regularly been accused of paying bribes. A BBC investigation revealed that the company had a 'slush fund' which made £60 million of corrupt payments to Saudi officials, including providing prostitutes, Rolls-Royces, and Californian holidays. Saudi Arabia is a major purchaser of defence equipment. The *Guardian* reported that BAE had been identified as secretly paying more than £1 million through American banks to General Pinochet, the former Chilean dictator in return for defence contracts.

● CHAPTER SUMMARY

In this chapter we examined the characteristics of various political systems, the liberal democracies of Europe and North America, Communism in China, the authoritarian regime in Saudi Arabia, and the theocratic system in Iran. We saw how the political organization of countries into unitary or federal systems can have significant implications for business as regards the locus of important political decisions, for instance regarding taxing and spending. We identified and explained the different functions carried out by the state and showed how important they can be, for example, in preventing the collapse of the economic and financial system and in setting the legal and regulatory rules of the game for business. We also considered the arguments for and against the thesis that globalization had led to the demise of the nation state. Finally, we considered the variety of methods, from lobbying to the donation of money that firms use to influence their political environment.

While relationships between business and the state can be difficult there is a great degree of interdependence between the two. On the one hand, governments depend on business to deliver economic growth, low inflation, a healthy balance of payments, and to create jobs. On the other hand, business depends on the state to create and maintain an environment that provides opportunities to produce and sell goods and services and to make profits.

● REVIEW QUESTIONS

1. What is the state? Why is it important for the pharmaceutical industry? Explain with examples.

2. Compare and contrast the characteristics of liberal democratic and communist states. Which of these types of state would be more attractive for a Western MNC?

3. Why do businesses prefer to operate in countries that are politically stable? Discuss how businesses might feel about producing in countries where there is political stability but also a dictatorship.

4. To what extent do you agree that globalization has undermined the power of the nation state? Give evidence to support your arguments.

5. Find an example of a firm or industry that has tried to influence government policy. Identify the methods used and try to evaluate how effective they have been.

Case Study Shell in Nigeria

Nigeria is a federal republic comprising 36 states. Rotimi and Adesoj (2010) report that politicians engage in intense struggles, fair or foul, to retain power. They say that enormous influence in the states is exercised by political godfathers abetted by the police.

Oil is the mainstay of the Nigerian economy. It accounts for over 95% of export earnings and about 65% of government revenues. Nigeria is Africa's leading oil producer and the eighth biggest exporter in the world, accounting for 8% of US oil imports.

Shell, Exxon, and Chevron all operate in Nigeria. It has the largest natural gas reserves in Africa and that, combined with its oil, makes it attractive not only to Western MNCs but also to Russia and China. However the industry operates in an unstable environment. Local groups seeking a share of the oil wealth often attack the oil industry infrastructure and staff, forcing companies to declare force majeure on oil shipments (force majeure clauses exempts a company from fulfilling its contract for events that could not be anticipated or were beyond their ➡

→ control). At the same time, oil theft, leads to pipeline damage that is often severe, causing loss of production, pollution, and forcing companies to shut-in production (i.e. capping production below capacity). The industry has been blamed for pollution that has damaged air, soil, and water leading to losses in arable land and decreasing fish stocks. There is widespread political corruption. Nigeria ranks 134 out of 178 countries in the Transparency International Corruption Perceptions Index.

In 2009, Ann Pickard, the company's top executive in Nigeria told US diplomats that Shell had seconded employees to every relevant government department and so knew everything that was going on in those ministries. She claimed that the Nigerian government had forgotten about the extent of Shell's infiltration and was unaware of how much the company knew about its deliberations. Shell learned from the British government

Source: Photodisc

details of Gazprom's ambitions to enter the Nigerian market and was worried that the Nigerian government would hand over some of Shell's concessions to its giant Russian competitor. Shell asked the US consulate for potentially sensitive intelligence about Gazprom. Shell's concerns were justified because Gazprom did sign a deal with the Nigerian National Petroleum Corporation to build refineries, pipelines, and gas power stations. Shell was also concerned that the company would lose a significant number of their exploration and production blocks as a result of the Petroleum Industry Bill proposed by the Nigerian government.

Sources: CIA Factbook 2010; Rotimi and Adesoj 2010; Transparency International 2010; US Energy Information Administration; Political Risk Services 2009; Wheary 2009; *New York Times*, 8 June 2009; *Guardian*, 9 December 2010

Questions

1. Describe the political and social environment in Nigeria.

2. Analyse the Nigerian environment in terms of opportunities and threats for foreign energy firms like Shell.

3. Why might a company like Shell be interested in finding out what was being done in government ministries in Nigeria?

4. What are the implications of Shell's infiltration of the Nigerian government for rivals in the oil and gas industry?

5. How would you explain the links between Shell and the US embassy in Nigeria?

 Online Resource Centre
www.oxfordtextbooks.co.uk/orc/hamilton_webster2e/

Visit the supporting online resource centre for additional material which will help you with your assignments, essays, and research, or you may find these extra resources helpful when revising for exams.

● FURTHER READING

These two textbooks examine a variety of different political systems and concepts:

● Caramani, D. (2008) *Comparative Politics*. Oxford: Oxford University Press

● Hague, R. and Harrop, M. (2010) *Comparative Government and Politics: An Introduction*, 8th edn. Basingstoke: Palgrave MacMillan

For a treatment of important changes and trends see:

- Mansbach, R. W. and Rafferty, K. L. (2007) *Introduction To Global Politics: A Journey From Yesterday To Tomorrow*. London: Taylor & Francis

For a useful overview of different political regimes see:

The Georgetown University website focuses on the politics of the 35 nations comprising North and South America:

- Georgetown University. 'Political Database of the Americas'. Available at http://pdba.georgetown.edu

The Keele guide is more wide-ranging covering the Americas, Europe, Asia, Africa, and Oceania:

- Keele University. 'The Keele Guide to Latin American Government and Politics on the Internet'. Available at www.keele.ac.uk

● REFERENCES

Ayokunle, O. O. (2010) 'Political Clientelism and Rural Development in South-Western Nigeria' *Africa*, Vol 80, Issue 3

Devereux, M. P. and Sørensen, P. B. (2005) 'The Corporate Income Tax: International Trends and Options for Fundamental Reform'. October. Available at www.sbs.ox.ac.uk

Drucker, P. (1999) *Management: Tasks, Responsibilities, Practices*. Oxford: Butterworth-Heinemann

Etzion, D. and Davis, G. F. (2008) 'Revolving Doors: A Network Analysis of Corporate Officers and US Government Officials'. *Journal of Management Inquiry*, Vol 17, No 3, September

EU Commission (2010) State Aid Scoreboard, Autumn

Fukuyama, F. (1993) *The End of History and the Last Man*. London: Penguin

Gravelle, J. G. (2009) 'Tax Havens: International Tax Avoidance and Evasion'. Congressional Research Service, July 9

Guosheng, D. and Kennedy, S. (2009) Big Business and Industry Association Lobbying in China: The Paradox of Contrasting Styles, paper presented at the conference, 'US-China Business Cooperation in the 21st Century: Opportunities and Challenges for Entrepreneurs', Indiana University, 15–17 April

Hardgrave, R. L. and Kochanek, S. A. (1993) *India: Government and Politics in a Developing Nation*, 5th edn. Boston: Thompson Higher Education

Held, D. and McGrew, A.G. (2007) *Globalisation Theories: Approaches and Controversies*. Cambridge: Polity Press

Hirst, P. and Thompson, G. (2005) *Globalization in Question: The International Economy and the Possibilities of Governance*, 3rd edn. London: Polity Press

Holtbrugge, D. and Berg, N. (2004) 'How Multinational Corporations Deal with Their Socio-Political Stakeholders: An Empirical Study in Asia, Europe, and the US'. *Asian Business & Management*, (3)

Hopkin, J. (2006) Conceptualizing Political Clientelism: Political Exchange and Democratic Theory, APSA annual meeting, Philadelphia, 31 August–3 September

IMF (2010) Regional Economic Outlook: Asia and Pacific, April

McHenry, D. E. (2007) Why Don't They Use Just Words? Accounting for Indian Political Protest on the Streets and in Parliament, Association for Asian Studies Annual Meeting, Boston, 22–25 March

De Mello, L. (2010) Fiscal Decentralisation and Public Investment: The Experience of Latin America, OECD Economics Department, Working Papers No 824

Nownes, A. J. (2006) *Total Lobbying: What Lobbyists Want (and How They Try to Get It)*. Cambridge: Cambridge University Press

OECD (2009a) Government at a Glance 2009

OECD (2009b) State Owned Enterprises in India: Reviewing the Evidence, Occasional Paper, 26 January

Ohmae, K. (2005) *The Next Global Stage: The Challenges and Opportunities in Our Borderless World*. New Jersey: Wharton School Publishing

Paczynska, A. (2009) Globalisation and Globality (IPS) Conference Papers—International Studies Association, 2009 Annual Meeting

Pei, M. (2007) 'Corruption Threatens China's Future'. Carnegie Endowment, Policy Brief No 55, October

Political Risk Services (2009) Nigeria: Country Report, 1 September

Robertson, G. (2010) *The Case of the Pope: Vatican Accountability for Human Rights Abuses*. London: Penguin

Rotimi, E. O. and Adesoj, A. O. (2010) 'Mediating an Intra-Elite Struggle for Power and Privilege in Nigeria: The Police and the Oyo State Political Crisis, 2005–2007'. *International Journal of Police Science & Management*, Winter, Vol 12

Scholte, J. A. (2005) *Globalization: A Critical Introduction*. London: Palgrave MacMillan

Tibocha, J. S. and López Murcia, J. D. (2007) 'La Problemática Actual De Los Paraísos Fiscales, Revista Colombiana'. *Derecho Internacional*, No 10: 311–338, November

Transparency International (2010) Corruption Perceptions Index 2010

Wheary, J. (2009) 'One Step Forward Two Steps Back'. *World Policy Journal*, Winter, Vol 26, Issue 4

WTO (2007) Trade Policy Review: Ghana, WT/TPR/S/194, 17 December

Wright, T. (2006) 'Why Hasn't Economic Development Brought Democracy to China?' Available at www.eastwestcenter.org

Yongqiang, G. (2007) 'Dealing with Non-Market Stakeholders in the International Market: Case Studies of US-Based Multinational Enterprises in China'. *Singapore Management Review*, Vol 29, No 2

CHAPTER NINE

The Legal Environment

LEARNING OUTCOMES

This chapter will enable you to:

- Explain the importance of the legal environment for business

- Compare and contrast the different systems of law and their implications for international business

- Assess the importance of contract, tort, and criminal law for business behaviour

- Demonstrate the significance of international law for firms involved in international trade and investment

- Recognize the lack of development of the law around the internet and the difficulties this raises for firms involved in e-commerce

Case Study The 'Phoney Wars'

Makers of mobile phones have shown themselves to be very litigious. Major manufacturers have been suing each other in an increasing number of tit for tat cases in various national courts. The struggle between these telecoms companies has been called the 'Phoney Wars'.

In 2009, Nokia sued Apple in the District Court of Delaware in the US claiming that Apple had infringed patents relating to 3G networking and Wi Fi technology. It also filed a suit at the International Trade Commission (ITC), the US government trade body, asking for the blocking of iPhone, iPod and Apple computer imports into the USA, alleging that virtually all these products infringed at least one of seven Nokia patents. According to Nokia, 'Apple is attempting to get a free ride on the back of Nokia's innovation' (www.nokia.com). Apple responded by filing against Nokia in the ITC claiming anti-competitive practices and violation of patents and seeking a ban on Nokia imports into the USA. Apple argued that, 'Other companies must compete with us by inventing their own technologies, not just by stealing ours' (www.eWeek.com, 27 January 2010).

In 2010, Nokia filed another complaint in Wisconsin alleging that Apple's iPhone and iPad 3G products infringed five important Nokia patents whilst Apple took legal action against Nokia in the UK courts.

A lot of money is at stake. Less than 30% of Europeans and US users have a smartphone that can access the web, use e-mail, and run applications. This means that the potential market could be worth billions of dollars to successful handset manufacturers.

Up to now, telecoms firms have licensed technology patents to each other to ensure the interoperability of their products,

meaning, for example, that Apple and Nokia products work on Orange or O2 networks. In 2008, Sony Ericsson and Nokia proposed that royalties payable should be limited to less than 10% of the handset price. However, with no agreement being reached on how the royalties should be divided up, and faced with the enormous R&D costs of new technology, manufacturers resorted to the law, despite the high costs of litigation.

The ITC backed Nokia in its fight against Apple, saying that the courts should rule that Nokia did not infringe Apple's patents. The court cases were to be concluded in 2011.

Sources: http://guardian.co.uk, 9 November 2010; *International Business Times*, 3 November 2010; Reuters, 7 May 2010; www.nokia.com; *PC Advisor*, 1 October 2010

Source: www.fotolia.com

Introduction

In this chapter we examine the legal environment within which international business operates. We show the importance of the legal framework and how its rules and regulations can impinge on business literally from the cradle to the grave. The law can have a major influence on business behaviour, for instance when it wishes to form a company or to negotiate a contract. It can require firms to compensate those whom they injure and it can forbid business, under the threat of penalty, from undertaking certain types of behaviour such as mergers and acquisitions, colluding with competitors, and polluting the environment. We go on to consider the major systems of law prevailing across the globe and we conclude by outlining some important aspects and institutions in international law and their implications for the business community.

Changes in the legal environment can provide business opportunities but can also generate risk. The firm may find itself the subject of a claim by, for instance, a rival, a customer, or a supplier which could result in loss. This could take the form of a financial loss and could also result in damage to the company reputation. Companies may feel that they are protected by the law only to find that judges put a different interpretation on the law, or it may be that the law is not rigorously enforced. Finally, changes in the law could leave the company exposed to legal action for actions previously regarded as permissible.

Knowledge of different legal and regulatory systems operating at national and international levels is invaluable for business in a world where foreign trade, investment and outsourcing, and international e-commerce are growing rapidly.

The Importance of Law for Business

The legal environment forms a vital element of the external environment of business. Firms producing everything from laptop computers, mobile phones, air flights, toys, cosmetics, financial products, drugs, fertilizers, food, and drink are all subject to requirements laid down by the law. The legal environment sets the rules of the game within which business operates. It can influence a business from its inception, by laying down certain legal steps which must be undertaken to set the business up, to its death with rules relating to the winding up of the company. When the firm is up and running, the law cannot only tell it what to do but also what not to do. The law is a double-edged sword for business because it offers both threats and opportunities. On the one hand, it can leave firms open to legal action but, on the other, it also gives them the possibility of pursuing others to protect and promote their interests. Business is also subject to regulations. These are not laws as such but rules that take their authority from **statutes** and are usually issued by governmental agencies at all levels, national, regional, local. In most developed countries, utilities companies in the energy sector and in telecoms and water are regulated. In the UK, for example, OFWAT regulates the water industry and OFGEM the energy sector, whilst in the USA the Federal Aviation Administration (FAA) deals with aviation and the Federal Trade Commission (FTC) is responsible for protecting the consumer and dealing with monopolies.

The legal environment can influence the whole process of production and sale as regards:

- Production techniques: how firms produce goods and services can be influenced by laws and regulations. For example the EU specifies production practices which producers and processors of organic food, such as Green & Black's the chocolate firm owned by Kraft, must follow (www.defra.gov.uk).

  Firms using heavily polluting production techniques like the steel industry or coal fired power stations, emitting gases and other chemical pollutants that cause environmental damage, can find their activities being controlled by the law. While their production benefits them, it also creates externalities in the form of pollution of the environment and imposes costs not only on people living next to the plants but on the world as a whole. Long-standing laws to control emissions exist in Western Europe and North America. In the EU, the Clean Air for Europe programme fixes targets for the emission of polluting gases such as sulphur dioxide and nitrous oxide. China and India are both moving towards the adoption of EU standards for vehicle emissions. By limiting emissions, the law attempts to force the polluters to carry the cost, that is to ensure the costs previously borne by parties outside the firm are internalized.

- The characteristics of the product: the law can determine product characteristics from the materials used to the product specifications—many developed countries like the USA and the UK along with some emerging economies such as Saudi Arabia have banned asbestos since it was found to cause lung cancer and other respiratory diseases. Its use is allowed in countries like China, India, and most African countries.

- The nature of the packaging and the contents of the labels: most major economies like the USA, EU, Japan, and China have rules relating to the packaging and labelling of products such as food and hazardous chemicals.

- The content and placement of advertising and sales promotion: tobacco and alcohol are two industries that are heavily regulated in this regard. Tobacco advertising is banned on radio and television in the USA and EU with the EU ban extending to print media and the internet. It is not allowed at all in Canada and New Zealand. Tobacco firms like British American Tobacco and Philip Morris, in order to counter the effects of the advertising bans on sales, have had to find other ways of promoting their products. They have made more use of billboards and direct mailing, got their products placed in films, and sponsored music-oriented events particularly attractive to young people, for example discos, 'raves', and concerts. Squeezed in rich world markets by advertising restrictions and bans on smoking in public places, tobacco firms have also looked to markets in poorer countries from China and India to Africa and Latin America. In 2011, China also banned smoking in public places.

- How firms treat their workers: many countries, the USA, the UK, China, Japan, Brazil, South Africa, and Russia prescribe a minimum wage. The EU has a longstanding commitment to equal pay for equal work and lays down the maximum number of hours that can be worked. Both Japan and the EU have laws protecting the security of employment of older people.

- The terms and conditions of trade with customers and suppliers: these cover issues such as delivery dates, terms of payment, return policies for defective products, warranties, and so on. Most countries have statutes relating to the sale of goods and services. Usually the law requires the terms of sale to be clear, consistent, and reasonable.

- The tools of competition: this relates to how firms compete with rivals and treat customers. Many developed economies have competition laws regulating business behaviour. In the USA and the EU, for example, the law is hostile to powerful firms exploiting their monopoly power by charging customers high prices or tying them in through the imposition of exclusive contracts which force them to buy all their requirements from the same supplier. EU and US law also disapproves of firms squeezing rivals through, for example, artificially low prices. Companies wishing to go in for takeovers can also be affected by the legal environment. Both the USA and EU also prohibit cartels where firms come to an agreement to avoid competition by agreeing a common price or by sharing the market out geographically. Emerging economies tend not to have competition laws, India and China being two exceptions.

The law may also protect firms from competition from the **grey market**. The grey market refers to trade in goods through distribution channels that have not been authorized by the manufacturer. This often occurs when the price of the product varies from country to country. The good is bought in the country where it is cheap and sold at below market price in the country where price is high (http://wordiQ.com). It is sometimes called parallel importing. The practice is particularly prevalent in cigarettes, pharmaceuticals, cars, music and films, satellite television, and in electronic goods such as cameras and games consoles. The grey market can also arise when a good is in short supply in one area but plentiful in another. When Sony first introduced its PlayStation Portable in Japan, it quickly found the console being imported into Europe. The law requires that grey importers have to get the manufacturer's permission where the good is brought in from outside the EU. Sony pursued this through the British courts, stating that no permission had been given and claiming that its trade mark was being infringed (*Guardian*, 23 June 2005).

• Ownership of assets: legal systems usually confer and protect rights of ownership and possession of company assets, both physical like buildings and machinery and intellectual assets. For example, the law will often protect intellectual property by giving the holder exclusive rights to exploit the asset for a certain period of time. Protection may also be accorded to holders of copyright covering creative and artistic works including books, films, music, paintings, photographs, and software, on trade marks which are signs distinguishing the products or services of firms, and on product designs. Trade secrets may also be protected by the law.

• Financial reporting: many countries lay down rules and regulations regarding the reporting of the financial state of the company and its performance. There are also moves afoot to establish international reporting standards. Around 100 countries require, are moving towards, or allow the use of the International Financial Reporting Standards (IFRS) which establishes a framework for the preparation and presentation of financial statements so that financial information provided by companies is transparent and comparable. This harmonization of reporting standards has become more important for companies as they increasingly look overseas not only for market and investment opportunities but also to raise finance. Harmonized reporting allows firms more easily to evaluate potential distributors and candidates for joint ventures and takeovers. While the EU and many other countries around the world now subscribe to international financial reporting standards, the USA stands alone with its own generally accepted accounting principles (GAAP) (the International Accounting Standards Board is responsible for establishing the IFRS, see www.iasb.org).

In 2002, after several major accounting scandals including those at Enron and Worldcom, the USA passed the **Sarbanes-Oxley Act**. This required firms to provide more financial information and to introduce rigorous internal procedures to ensure the accuracy of that information.

The purpose of these legal requirements is usually the protection of life or health, the protection of the environment, the prevention of deceptive practices, or to ensure the quality of products, the preservation of competition, and the promotion of technological advance.

Counterpoint Box 9.1 How big a role for law?

Neoliberals argue that the law should play a minimalist role in society. It should act as the guarantor of private property. Property in this sense refers to assets such as land, housing, company shares, works of art, intellectual property, and so on. The law should protect the rights to property, in other words, the right to own, sell, lend, give away, or bequeath assets and should enforce contractual agreements. Friedman (2002), referring to the privatization programme in Russia said:

> Privatization is meaningless if you don't have the rule of law. What does it mean to privatize if you do not have security of property, if you can't use your property as you want to?

Neoliberals argue that this is vital for the operation of the market by, for example, reducing the costs of transactions between buyers and sellers. These views draw heavily on the ideas of Hayek, Von Mises, Schumpeter, and Friedman.

Critics of the neoliberal position argue that the law has got to do much more than guarantee private property. According to this school of thought, markets can lead to undesirable outcomes which domestic and international law should try to prevent, for example the behaviour of financial institutions that led to the global financial crisis, the creation of monopolies, or damage to the environment. Ownership of an asset should not give the right to do as one pleases. The law should stop the owner of a coal-fired power station from polluting the air. Furthermore, the law needs to respond to major disparities in income and wealth and gender inequalities and to ensure the human right to health and education.

Sources: Glinavos 2008; Friedman 2002; Stiglitz 2010; Patel 2009

Learning Task

Countries such as Brazil, China, and India are introducing IFRS. This will force firms in these countries to disclose more information on their operations. It also changes how they treat certain costs and revenues in their accounts which could have an impact on reported profits. For some companies profits will rise but for others they will fall. It could also have the effect of increasing the amount of debt a company has on its balance sheet. (For a discussion of the impact on the India power sector see the link on the accompanying **Online Resource Centre** for the book.)

1. Advance reasons why firms might be unhappy about their government adopting the IFRS framework.

2. In 2010, China announced new accounting standards largely in line with IFRS. Discuss the implications of this for foreign firms looking for takeover opportunities there.

Go to the website set up by the consultants Deloitte at www.iasplus.com for more information on IFRS and to see which countries have signed up to IFRS.

Systems and Sources of Law

Contrary to a widespread misapprehension, laws are not simply the product of decisions made by governments and parliaments. There are four major legal systems in the world which are drawn, in large degree, from different sources. They comprise civil law, common law, customary law, and **religious law**. Civil law and **common law systems** are predominant in the world and, for that reason, are of most importance to business.

The particular systems operating in countries or regions are the result of the interaction of many historical forces, socio-cultural, political, economic, and technological. One particularly important influence in many countries is the historical legacy of empire. Thus, countries in Africa which were part of the French empire are likely to have a law based on the French system (see end of chapter Case Study) while former British colonies tend to have systems based on English law. Furthermore, the boundaries between the different systems can break down as the systems evolve over time. Globalization contributes to this blurring of the boundaries because one country's legal system can end up incorporating elements from others. Thus, the system in Japan has been heavily influenced by the German legal code and has also been subject to English and American influences. Similarly, the Chinese system reflects, to a degree, Soviet and Continental legal principles.

Business can find that the various legal systems create very different legal environments within which to operate. Laws, regulations, procedures, and outcomes may vary enormously from one system to another.

Civil Law Systems

Most legal systems in the world have their basis in civil law (see Figure 9.1), the primary source of which is legislation. Civil law is a body of laws and legal concepts which have their basis in the legal codes of the Roman Empire. **Civil law systems** give precedence to written law, sometimes called codified law. Judges apply and interpret the law which is drawn from legal codes and statutes—statutes are written laws passed by legislative bodies such as national or regional parliaments.

The legal systems in Continental Europe and in Central and South America are largely codified and set out in legislation. In the USA, Louisiana is the sole state having a legal structure based on civil law with Quebec being in a similar position in Canada. Scottish law is heavily influenced by Roman law but has not gone in for the extensive codification so prevalent on the continent. Other countries, for example in Scandinavia, while not so influenced by Roman law, have systems akin to civil law because of their heavy dependence on the laws written into statutes.

The procedure in civil law systems is inquisitorial where judges collect evidence and question witnesses to discover the truth. Rather than orally presenting their case, each side must provide written statements of it to the judge. A consequence of this emphasis on the written word is that lawyers act as advisors rather than as oral advocates of their client's case to the judge. Judges then decide, on the basis of the evidence, whether the case should go to trial but trials are relatively rare. Should a trial occur, panels of judges or lay assessors review the written evidence gathered by the judge and come to a decision. Juries are used in some criminal trials. In civil systems, court decisions applying the law may influence subsequent decisions but do not become binding.

One advantage to business of civil law systems is that because the law is codified in written form, it is easier to find and to articulate clearly (www.duhaime.org). On the other hand, the emphasis on written evidence means that there must be effective document storage and retrieval systems to handle all the paperwork generated by the system if the law is to be properly applied.

Figure 9.1 Legal systems across the world

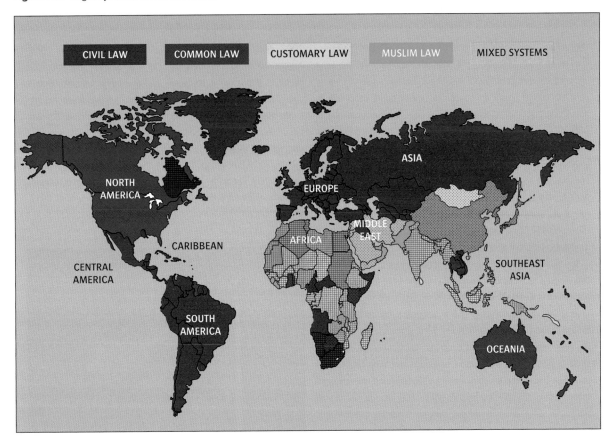

Source: University of Ottawa. Available at www.droitcivil.uottawa.ca

While this may be the case in Continental Europe, many poorer countries say in Africa or Latin America do not have efficient bureaucratic systems and, as a result, are not in a good position to apply the law effectively.

To avoid confusion it is useful to note that the term civil law is also used to refer to law dealing with the rights and duties of one individual to another, for instance, in relation to the law of contract.

Common Law Systems

Common law is a legal system based on English law which accords greater importance to judgments in court cases than to written codes and statutes. Common law is also known as case law or judge-made law inasmuch as legal principles are determined by judgments in court cases (Mayson 2005).

Courts, by interpreting and applying the law, determine its meaning and, through their judgments, fill in gaps in the legislative code. Court judgments can set precedents which are binding on themselves and on lower courts when judging similar cases—in other words it becomes the

Mini Case **Argentina**

The Argentinian legal system combines civil and common law. Heavily influenced by the Spanish legal system, the laws are contained in detailed Codes. The judiciary is seen as weak, politicized and prone to corruption while court proceedings are slow and inefficient (Transparency International 2010; PRS 2010; Heritage Foundation 2010). Although Argentina has signed up to international treaties on intellectual property, the enforcement of intellectual property rights is unsatisfactory. For example, patent protection is a problem area particularly with regard to pharmaceutical products. These factors reduce the appeal of the country to foreign business. To avoid using the domestic legal system, many foreign investors resort to international arbitration.

Argentina's foreign investment regime appears to be one of the world's most liberal. Foreign and domestic investors have equal rights to establish and own businesses. However, foreign investment is restricted in a few sectors such as electricity, finance, and telecommunications. Foreign exchange and capital flows are also subject to controls. Foreign companies may send profits abroad but export revenues must be repatriated to Argentina. Some sectors remain vulnerable to government intervention. Companies in the utility and energy sectors in particular have been in serious dispute with the government over its decision to freeze prices. Several foreign mining companies pursued legal action to challenge the government's

2007 decision to impose a tax on their exports. In 2009, Argentina introduced new minimum prices on 800 imported products, claiming it to be an anti-dumping measure. Brazil, one of its major trading partners, saw the move as protectionist.

The Heritage Foundation sums up the situation thus 'Corruption, weak institutions, and uncertain creditor, contract, and property rights are serious deterrents to investment.'

Sources: CIA Factbook 2010; Heritage Foundation 2010 Index of Economic Freedom; PRS, Country Report: Argentina, April 2010; Transparency International, Global Corruption Barometer 2010

Source: EyeWire

law for everyone to follow. Binding **precedents** are usually made by courts at the higher levels. Judges in lower level courts cannot usually issue binding precedents.

Precedent has a very important role in the common law. From the perspective of business it has the advantage of ensuring certainty and consistent application of the law. Unlike civil law, precedent allows the law to develop and to respond to changes in society. At the same time it may be very difficult to find or to state as it is spread across many cases. It may also give rise to laws based on court decisions in extreme, unusual, or unevenly argued cases—to put it another way, a case may be decided not on the relative merits of the evidence but because a lawyer has made an effective presentation of the case in court.

Common law systems are found in countries that have had close ties with Britain such as the USA, Canada, India, and Australia. In some of these countries the common law system may sit alongside codes and statutes but it remains the fundamental basis of the legal system.

Where there is a clash between legislative statutes and common law, statutes take precedence. So statutes generally have the power to change the established common law, but the common law cannot overrule or change statues (www.leeds.ac.uk/law).

Learning Task

Look at the map in Figure 9.2 below indicating the legal systems in place in Europe.

- Which is the dominant legal system in Europe?
- What are the main characteristics of the dominant system?
- What legal issues might be encountered by a Hungarian firm wishing to do business in Scotland (both of which form part of the EU)?

Figure 9.2 Legal systems across Europe

Source: University of Ottawa. Available at www.droitcivil.uottawa.ca

Common law, in contrast to civil law systems, is adversarial in nature. Thus, both sides are in competition to persuade judge and jury of the legitimacy of their case. In proceedings, lawyers act as the principal advocate of their client's case and witnesses are called to give oral testimony. Oral argument plays a more important role in common law. In court cases the judge plays the role of impartial arbiter.

Mini Case India

As a former British colony, it is no surprise that the Indian legal system is based on English common law. While the system is regarded by commentators like the Economist Intelligence Unit (EIU) as relatively impartial, free and fair, Chakrabarti sees it as being riddled by significant levels of corruption. Both, however, argue that it is notoriously slow due to factors such as over-burdened courts and antiquated systems of criminal evidence.

Foreign investment is prohibited in many areas or subsectors of real estate, retailing, legal services, security services, nuclear energy, and railways and there are controls on capital trans-actions and transfers of foreign exchange. The Indian authorities aim to create an environment for foreign investors that is trans-parent, predictable, simple, and clear and reduces the regula-tory burden. On paper, the country's legal system provides some of the best investor protection in the world. However, the EIU reports that regulatory policy can be overturned as a result of pressure from vested interests and of conflicts between gov-ernment departments. Enforcement is a major problem and disputes can take decades to resolve (for example the Union Carbide/Bhopal incident in 1984 took 26 years to be resolved). That is why many foreign MNCs include clauses in their con-tracts allowing for the resolution of disputes through inter-national arbitration rather than the local courts.

The legal environment varies from city to city. The World Bank reports that, from a legal and regulatory viewpoint, it is easiest to do business in cities such as Ludhiana in the Punjab and Hyderabad in Andhra Pradesh compared with cities like Kochi in Kerala and Kolkata in West Bengal.

Rupert Murdoch, the head of News Corporation, when asked his preferred choice of investment location among Mexico, India, the USA and China responded, 'Oh, number one would be India. As against China, it has a rule of law, it's an infinitely complic-ated country, but it has a huge advantage over other developing countries, in that there is a rule of law, and it does work . . . China . . . is remarkable . . . But you never know . . . if someone

doesn't like you . . . your partner is in jail on Monday morning or something and you've got no business. For safety, every time [I would choose] India.' (cited in Silverstein 2010, p 796).

Sources: Chakrabarti 2008; Economist Intelligence Unit 2010; Government of India 2010; World Bank 2009; Political Risk Services 2010; Heritage Foundation Freedom Index 2010

Source: Fuse

Customary Law Systems

There is no single agreed definition of customary law. It can be seen as a body of rules, values, and traditions based on knowledge gained from life experiences or on religious or philosophical principles. It establishes standards or procedures to be followed when dealing with social rela-tionships such as marriage, adultery, and divorce but can also play a part in the ownership and use of land and issues around fishing rights. Customary law, like common law, is often not written into statutes and can be fluid and evolutionary. While hardly any countries operate under a legal system which is wholly customary there are a large number of countries where it plays an important role. This is true in a number of African countries in some of which it operates in combination with either civil or common law systems depending on whether the area was colonized by France or Britain (see end case on Trafigura and the Ivory Coast). It also plays a part in the legal systems of China and India as well as islands in the South Pacific (Care 2000).

Muslim Law Systems

Muslim law systems are codes of law mainly based on Sharia law which is derived from the religious principles contained in the Koran and in the teachings and example of Mohammed. In some Muslim countries the law is limited to regulating personal behaviour while, in others, its impact is much more wide-ranging. Examples of the latter include countries such as Iran, Saudi Arabia, Sudan, and Libya, and parts of Nigeria. This regulates all aspects of life, both public and private. The law forbids consumption of alcohol and pork as well as gambling, fraud, slander, the making of images, and usury (that is lending money and charging the borrower interest), especially at an exorbitant or illegally high rate, (Britannica Concise Encyclopaedia). Townsend (2010) nevertheless reports that Islamic banks in places like Bahrain, Dubai, Malaysia, and Singapore, untouched by the global financial crisis, have been growing at 20% per year and hold some US$1 trillion in assets.

Mini Case Sharia Law and the Financial Sector

This case shows how financial institutions have responded to clients who demand financial products that conform with Sharia law. The high price of oil has meant that investors in Muslim countries in the Middle East have billions of dollars available for investment and thus constitute a potentially lucrative market for the financial sector.

London is a leading centre for Islamic finance. Between 2006 and 2010 it issued Sharia-compliant bonds called sukuks to the value of US$17.7 billion. Société Générale, the French bank, set up the first Sharia-compliant hedge funds in London. Hedge funds often sell shares short. Selling short means that you agree to sell a security that you do not own at its current price, in anticipation of a fall in its price. Once the price falls you buy the share and then transfer it to your customer at a profit. Selling short is not compliant with Sharia law. Consequently the bank

put in place systems to replicate the effects of selling shares short without breaking Islamic law. The bank did this by offering investors sukuks.

Another example concerned the buy-out of the company that makes James Bond's favourite car, the Aston Martin. The finance associated with this had to be Sharia-compliant because the key financiers behind the deal were two Kuwaiti groups that only invested in accordance with Islamic principles. West LB, the German bank, was given the task of arranging £225 million of finance in a way that accorded with the Koran's opposition to interest and speculation. It was expected that the finance would be raised by the issue of sukuks.

Sources: www.zamya.com; *Financial Times*, 22 December 2006 and 17 March 2007

Important Aspects of the Law for Business

There is a wide range of laws applicable to business such as the law of contract, tort, criminal law, and international law. Contract law and the law of tort deal with disputes between business and the firms and individuals it deals with. Both give rise to actions by the concerned/ aggrieved parties through the civil courts. Criminal liability on the other hand, involves a business committing a crime against the state. Cases are initiated by state bodies such as the Crown Prosecution Service in the UK or the Department of Justice in the USA and are heard in the criminal courts.

Contract Law

When firms do business they are constantly entering into contracts which can either be written or oral. Essentially contracts are struck when a firm buys or sells goods or services from a supplier or a customer, or takes on employees. The contract is a legally binding agreement between the parties concerned and may be formal, informal, written, or oral. The contract is likely to cover such elements as price, payment terms, contract duration, the consequences of breaching the contract, the process for resolving disputes between the parties, and what will happen if there are unforeseen events such as wars or revolutions (see Hagedoorn and Hesen 2007 for a discussion of contract issues in technology partnerships between firms). The contract obliges those involved to fulfil their side of the agreement. If they fail to do so then they are in breach of contract and may be pursued by the aggrieved party through the courts.

Mini Case Contract Law—Ecuador and Occidental Oil

In 2006, the Ecuadorian government declared its intention to take over oilfields in the Amazonian jungle operated by Occidental. The US company was responsible for producing 20% of the country's oil. The government accused the company of breaking its contract by selling 40% of its stake in the oilfield to a Canadian company without government permission. The contract was cancelled and PetroEcuador, the state-owned oil company, took over the operation of the field. Occidental claimed that it had stuck to its legal obligation, that its assets had been expropriated, and that the decision violated a US/ Ecuador bilateral investment treaty. After trying unsuccessfully to negotiate a settlement, the company filed a US$1 billion lawsuit against the government at the arbitration body, the International Centre for the Settlement of Investment Disputes (ICSID) based in the World Bank (see section below on International Arbitration).

The Ecuadorian move followed: a previous dispute with Occidental over tax which resulted in Ecuador being found liable to Occidental for more than US$75 million in damages; a decision by Ecuador to increase taxes on oil companies to 50% when prices exceeded the levels stipulated in contracts; and a growing nationwide resentment of foreign oil companies. In 2005, protestors in the Amazonian region, demanding a more equitable distribution of the income from oil, had seized two airports, set up road blocks, blew up an oil pipeline, and took control of more than 250 oil wells.

Sources: ICSID 2008; Economist Intelligence Unit 2006; Emerging Markets Monitor, 22 May 2006; *The Economist* 20 May 2006; Political Risk Services 2007

Tort Law

Tort is an area of the law concerned with injuries to people or damage to their assets. The law obliges firms to ensure that their activities do not cause damage, intentional or accidental, to others and is in addition to any contractual arrangement that may exist. Business activities, therefore, that involve, for example, negligence leading to injury to a customer, selling defective goods or counterfeiting another company's product is a tort (The Stationery Office, *Business Law*).

A very famous tort case was the McDonald's coffee case in the USA. A customer called Liebeck won millions of dollars of damages against McDonald's when she claimed that the company's negligence had caused her to get burned with coffee that was far too hot. A more recent tort case was brought by Alcatel-Lucent, a French-based multinational communications company employing around 80,000 people and operating in 130 countries. Alcatel took Microsoft to court claiming an infringement of two of its MP3 technology patents which allowed for digital encoding and compression of music which could then be sent over the internet. The US court found in favour of Alcatel and ordered the software giant to pay US$1.5 billion in damages (*Financial Times*, 23 February 2007).

Learning Task

A case of tort occurred in the UK when a drugs trial by a US company, Parexel, went wrong. Six men ended up fighting for their lives after suffering severe reactions on taking the drug. Their bodies swelled up to enormous proportions and one of the six ended up losing fingers and toes. TeGenero, the German company that had developed the drug, went out of business as a result of the botched drugs trial. Four of the victims started legal action against Parexel after it had failed to discuss the possibility of compensation.

1. What would you expect to be the basis of the victims' case under the law of the tort?

2. What was the effect of the case on the companies involved? (Google the result of the legal action against Parexel.)

Criminal Law

Criminal law applies across many business activities and has become increasingly important in areas such as financial reporting, the proper description and pricing of goods and services, and the safety of goods and services, particularly food. In the USA, after several business scandals involving the likes of Enron and WorldCom, both of whom were involved in fraudulent accounting (WorldCom artificially inflated its profits by billions of dollars), Congress introduced more criminal legislation. This tightened the rules in areas such as financial reporting, tax crimes, foreign currency violations, health and safety in the workplace, and crimes against the environment.

Siemens, the giant German multinational, came under the spotlight of the criminal law when state prosecutors in Germany carried out a criminal investigation. The case concerned an alleged €420 million bribery scandal at the telecommunications division of the company. Siemens conceded that something had gone awry and admitted that there were important weaknesses in its financial controls.

The case had an undesirable knock-on effect for Siemens' management because it raised questions among banks, financial analysts, and Siemens' big shareholders on whether Siemens was too big or too complicated to be managed properly and whether it would be better broken up into smaller units.

The bribery allegations reinforced their concerns because it followed Siemens' failures with its mobile phone, semiconductor and telecoms equipment, and personal computer operations. The bribery case also raised concerns in other German companies including MAN, Continental, and Linde about tightening their anti-corruption systems (*Financial Times*, 14 and 22 December 2006, 15 March 2007).

International Law

Usually when operating in foreign countries, business has to follow the law of the land. However, international law is playing an increasingly important role in the world of international business. As business has become more globalized, so has the law, developing in ways aimed at facilitating international trade and investment. Another development is that international contracts are increasingly being written in English (Jennings 2006).

International law can reduce the uncertainty, costs, and the disputes associated with international commerce when there are doubts about which country's laws apply. In such situations firms, unsure of their rights, could be less willing to go in for foreign trade and investment. There are a variety of organizations, conventions, codes, and treaties which play a role in international commerce. We now look at some of the most important.

Codes and Conventions

Some national laws have ended up being used by firms involved in international business. One example is the Uniform Commercial Code in the USA. It sets down standard rules governing the sale of goods, is in force in many US states, and has been adopted by other countries (www.ilpf.org).

Another element of international contract law is the United Nations Convention on Contracts for the International Sale of Goods (CISG) of 1980. It is very similar in content to the Uniform Commercial Code. It aims to make international trade as convenient and economical as trading across state borders in the USA. By 2010, 76 states, accounting for around two thirds of world trade had signed up to this convention. The CISG establishes a set of rules governing sales of goods between professional sellers and buyers who have their places of business in different countries. By adopting it, a country undertakes to treat the Convention's rules as part of its law. The Convention aims to reduce the uncertainty and the disagreements that arise when the sales law of one country differs from that of another (http://law.pace.edu).

Given that so many countries have signed up to it, the CISG might seem like a significant advance in the law relating to international trade. However, the reality is that many firms deliberately do not use the convention. In the EU, this is true of producers of oils, seeds, fats, and grain and of most large Dutch companies. This unwillingness to use the agreement appears due to some of the terms used in the convention being open to differing interpretations. Also it may be that firms are ignorant of various elements of the CISG and are not prepared to invest time and money to find out. Another deterrent factor is that the convention only covers some aspects of the relationship between the buyer and seller so that in other areas national laws apply. Finally, countries such as the UK, India, Indonesia, and Portugal are not party to the convention (Smits 2005; www.cisg.law.pace.edu).

An organization trying to facilitate the legal processes around international commerce is the International Institute for the Unification of Private Law (Unidroit) which lays down principles for international commercial contracts. It is an independent, intergovernmental organization whose purpose is to help modernize, harmonize, and coordinate commercial law between states. In 1964, a convention was signed relating to the Law on the International Sale of Goods. However, the agreement did not apply to the sale of all products. For example, it did not cover sales of financial products such as stocks and shares, or sales of electricity. In 2002, a law relating to franchises was agreed (see www.unidroit.org).

Learning Task

The World Bank carries out research on the problems associated with doing business in different countries. It researches legal issues around the setting up of a business and with the enforcement of contracts in different countries. It found that enforcing a contract in Australia took 395 days whilst in India it took 1,420, in Brazil 661, China 406, and Russia 281. It also found very large variations between countries in terms of the efficiency of the judicial system in resolving a commercial dispute. The Bank collects information on two indicators:

- time in calendar days to resolve a dispute and the cost in court fees; and
- attorney fees, where the use of attorneys is mandatory or common, expressed as a percentage of the value of the claim.

Go to Doing Business on the World Bank website and carry out the tasks below.

1. In which country does it take most/least time to enforce a contract through the local courts?

2. Which countries are most/least expensive?

3. How might MNCs deal with problems of enforcing contracts in countries where it takes a lot of time and costs a lot of money?

International Arbitration

Sometimes disputes arise between firms based in one country and firms or governments of other countries. For example, there can be disagreement between the firms as to which national law should apply. That such disputes arise is hardly surprising given the rapid growth of international trade and investment. In such situations, international arbitration has become increasingly popular for businesses. There are a number of international agencies who will arbitrate between the warring parties. For example, firms can use commercial arbitration under the **New York Convention** set up in 1958 under the aegis of the United Nations and called Uncitral (see United Nations Commission on International Trade Law at www.uncitral.org). Uncitral was used in a dispute between BP and its Russian partners in the TNK BP joint venture over BP's agreement to swap shares with Rosneft, the Russian energy giant (BP Group Results 1st Quarter 2011).

Another international body helping to resolve disputes between governments and foreign business around investment, is the **International Centre for the Settlement of Investment Disputes (ICSID)** which is based at the World Bank in Washington. It deals with cases such as that involving three Italian mining companies who filed a complaint against South Africa, saying that the Pretoria government's positive racial discrimination laws violated investment treaties with other countries. The companies complained that their granite mining operations had been expropriated because they were not conforming to South Africa's black economic empowerment policy and that this violated treaties that South Africa had signed with Italy and Luxembourg (*Financial Times*, 9 March 2007; for other cases and information about ICSID go to the website at www.worldbank.org/icsid).

The World Trade Organization, where its rules have been broken, also arbitrates in disputes on matters of foreign trade, investment, and intellectual property rights. Firms can not take a complaint direct to the WTO, for the disputes procedures can only be activated at the request of a member government. This is illustrated by the dispute between the USA and the EU over subsidies being given to Boeing and Airbus. Both sides, at the behest of the two companies, complained

---

Mini Case Dispute at the World Trade Organization

This case traces the outcome of a dispute lodged by the tiny Caribbean country, Antigua and Barbuda against the USA at the WTO.

The dispute arose because, in 2006, the USA enforced the law which declared it illegal for American banks and credit card companies to process payments to online gambling businesses outside its borders. However, banks could continue to process payments for gaming firms operating WITHIN the USA. Antigua argued that this was discriminatory, broke WTO rules, and was effectively stifling Antigua's thriving gaming industry.

European gaming firms were also unhappy with the USA and had been urging the EU to take the case to the WTO. Internet gambling in the USA, in the run-up to 2006, had been booming to the benefit of a small group of companies like BetonSports, PartyGaming, SportingBet, Empire Online, and 888. Some internet gaming companies were making up to 80% of their revenue and profits on bets from the USA.

The Organization ruled that the USA had broken WTO rules by discriminating against offshore gambling firms through not applying the same rules to American operators. It allowed Antigua to impose an annual US$21 million of trade sanctions against America. In response to the ruling, Washington announced its intention to remove internet gambling from its WTO treaty obligations (see video at www.youtube.com/watch?v=TyuAi1mn7Ys). The USA avoided further disputes on the issue being lodged with the WTO by conceding trade concessions in postal services and warehousing to the EU (see video at www.youtube.com/watch?v=4yHLugvdKbc). Deals were also struck with other aggrieved parties, Canada and Japan, as compensation for the USA breaching WTO rules. Meanwhile, share prices in gaming companies collapsed and the industry underwent significant restructuring through mergers and acquisitions.

Sources: WTO 2007; *Financial Times*, 22 December 2007

that the billions of dollars of subsidies were in breach of the WTO rules (for information on disputes at the WTO, see www.wto.org).

When companies agree to insert an international arbitration clause into a contract it means that disputes between them are dealt with by an independent arbitrator rather than a court. This has a number of advantages over litigation through national courts. The first advantage is neutrality because arbitrators have to meet strict independence tests and can be drawn from countries other than those of the firms concerned. The second is confidentiality. Proceedings, unlike court cases, are normally private so that there is no public washing of dirty linen. Thirdly, the procedures are flexible and lastly, awards made, for instance under the New York Convention, can be widely enforced in almost all trading countries unlike national court decisions. The disadvantages are that it can be more costly than court litigation, there is normally no right of appeal, it does not work so well when there are more than two companies involved and, finally, there is no possibility of a quick decision even when there is no justifiable defence.

International Law and IPRs

Globalization has put an onus on firms to find ways of protecting intellectual property rights abroad. This has become particularly important in certain sectors such as film, music, and software where the growth of the internet and digitization makes copying much easier. Such protection is relatively well developed in the rich economies of North America and Europe but much less so in poorer countries such as China and India—a further deterrent in pursuing cases in China is the corruption of the judiciary, and in India, the time it takes for the wheels of justice to turn. It is therefore hardly surprising that companies prefer to pursue infringements of their IPRs in countries with well-developed systems of protection where cases are dealt with in a timely fashion and where the judiciary is not tainted by corruption. Thus, 3M, the US technology multinational chose to file an IPR lawsuit with a federal court in Minnesota and the US International Trade Commission against other producers of laptops including Sony, Matsushita, and Hitachi of Japan and Lenovo of China. 3M complained that the laptop makers had infringed the technology it used in its lithium-ion batteries (www.techworld.com).

As pointed out in the section on protecting technology in Chapter Seven the costs of taking out protection can vary significantly from one country to another as can the time taken to get protection, the level of protection given, and the ease with which firms can pursue violators of their property rights.

So intellectual property laws can vary from country to country—even in the EU there is still no single system of granting patents. Usually an application in one country for protection of a firm's IPRs only results in the granting of protection in that country. In the past, firms seeking protection in other countries had to make separate applications in each which could be very costly in terms of money and time.

However, the situation is changing. Two systems now exist that reduce the need for separate national applications. The Patent Cooperation Treaty allows firms to file a single application indicating in which countries it is seeking protection. The European Patent Convention allows for an application to be filed at the European Patents Office in Munich. The Office can

Learning Task

There have been a variety of alternative explanations put forward to explain the differences in degrees and level of protection accorded to IPRs by countries. One explanation suggests that differences have their roots in legal traditions. It is argued that two of the major traditions, the British common law and the French civil law, differ in terms of the priority they attach to protecting the rights of private investors as against those of the state. Historically British common law gave priority to the protection of private property owners against the crown while the French civil law was more concerned to support and consolidate the power of the state. This led French civil law to focus on the rights of the state and less on the rights of the individual investors when compared to British common law. These different traditions spread as France and Britain expanded their empires. The theory predicts that the legal tradition will be a major determinant of property rights protection (Ayyagari 2006).

Some results of Ayyagari's research are shown in Table 9.1. Examine it and the map (Figure 9.1) and consider to what extent the predictions of the theory are accurate.

Scores go from 1 with higher numbers indicating better government enforcement of the law protecting IPRs.

Table 9.1 Protection of IPRs

Country	Score
Australia	5
Zimbabwe	2
Mauritius	4
France	4
UK	5

Source: Ayyagari, Demirguc-Kunt, and Maksimovic 2006

grant separate national patents for specified countries. There have also been some moves towards harmonization of laws as a result of international treaties including the Agreement on Trade-Related Aspects of Intellectual Property Rights (TRIPS) agreed through the WTO. It aims to establish minimum levels of protection that each government has to give to the intellectual property of other WTO members. Member governments have to ensure that their intellectual property rights systems do not discriminate against foreigners, that they can be enforced in law, and that the penalties for infringement are tough enough to deter further violations. The procedures must not be unnecessarily complicated, costly, or time-consuming (www.wto.org).

European Union

The European Union (EU) comprises 27 members all of whom are bound by the EU laws. The primary source of EU law is the Treaties such as the Treaty of Rome as modified by the Single European Act, the Treaties of Maastricht, Amsterdam, Nice, and Lisbon. The secondary source of EU law consists of directives which are binding on the member states but whose implementation is their responsibility, regulations which are binding and implemented consistently across the EU and finally, decisions which are made by European institutions like the Commission, the Council of Ministers, and the European Parliament dealing with specific issues, countries, institutions, or individuals. European law develops through a combination of case law setting precedents and statutory law. In any clash with national law, EU law takes precedence.

Mini Case An EU Decision—Genetically Modified Foods

From the 1990s there have been fears in the EU about the effects of genetically modified (GM) foods on human and animal health and on the environment. GM foods are grown from seeds whose genes have been modified to increase the yield or quality of the crops of products such as wheat, rice, cotton, and potatoes. They were being promoted by big multi-nationals such as Monsanto from the USA and the German company Bayer who had been involved in developing the GM seeds.

In 2003 the EU Parliament and Council made a decision that GM food could only be sold in the EU subject to certain conditions. It had to be proved that: it did not adversely affect human or animal health or the environment; the consumer was not being misled about the fact that the food had been genetically modified; its nutritional value would not be less for humans or animals than the foods it was replacing.

The EU decision was bad news for GM companies, cutting them off from a very lucrative market. The USA, Canada, and Brazil complained to the World Trade Organization that the EU was breaking WTO rules. The WTO found in favour of the complainants.

Sources: Council Directive 90/220/EEC of 23 April 1990 and Regulation (EC) No 1829/2003 of the European Parliament and of the Council of 22 September 2003 available at http://eur-lex. europa.eu; www.wto.org

Source: www.istockphoto.com

Single Market Programme

An essential element of the EU project is the Single Market programme. The programme, by removing internal barriers such as frontier checks, different technical standards for goods and services, and obliging members to recognize academic or vocational qualifications gained in another member state, tries to ensure that goods, services, capital, and people can move freely across borders. The Single Market requires that laws of the various member states do not favour domestic firms over those of other members in areas such as trade, investment, the establishment of businesses on their territory, or the movement of workers.

The EU has seen that different national contract laws can constitute a barrier to the movement of goods and services so it has passed several directives, at least 12 according to Smits (2005), to deal with this. However, they do not replace national laws by laying down a general law of contract but only apply to certain types of contract and to specific areas of contract law such as that relating to the sale of tour packages and timeshares, on combating late payment in commercial transactions, or in the distance marketing of financial services.

For example, the Consumer Sales Directive does not attempt to harmonize different national laws nor does it require firms to offer the same product guarantee throughout the EU. It does however require firms to provide specific information on product guarantees. The information has to be written in plain and intelligible language regarding the consumer's legal rights under the national legislation and has to make clear that these rights are unaffected by the product guarantee. The guarantee also needs to indicate the duration and territorial scope of the guarantee and how to make a claim (Schulte-Nölke 2006). The EU is trying to enable consumers to pursue EU-wide claims against firms providing faulty goods or services. As the Commissioner responsible for consumer affairs put it, 'I want a citizen in Birmingham to feel as comfortable shopping for a digital camera from a website in Berlin or Budapest as they would in their high street' (*Financial Times*, 14 March 2007). The Commission wants to encourage consumers to buy more abroad.

Smits (2005) points out that EU directives in the field of contract law allow member states to create more stringent rules in the area covered by the directive. In particular in the area of consumer protection, some member states tend to enact rules that are tougher than the directives prescribe. This means that business still has to deal with differences in national legislation among the member states which may make it less convenient and more costly to do business abroad.

The result is that there remain significant differences in contract law within the EU with each country in the EU having its own contract law. These can be classified in three main groups. First, England, Ireland, and Cyprus have common law systems which emphasize judge-made law. The second type is the civil law system which holds sway in France, Belgium, Luxemburg, Spain, Portugal, Italy, Malta, Germany, Austria, Greece, and the Netherlands. The civil law is in place in nearly all of the former Communist countries of Eastern Europe that entered the EU in 2004 such as Poland, the Czech Republic, Slovakia, Hungary, Estonia, Lithuania, Latvia, and Slovenia (see Smits who sees the new entrants as somewhat distinct from the other members operating civil law systems). Finally, the Scandinavian countries of Denmark, Sweden, and Finland form the third group which has a number of common statutes relating to contract.

Competition Law

Business operating in the EU is also subject to the competition laws which are important in helping to maintain a barrier-free single market. These laws which are policed by the Commission cover four main areas.

Firstly, cartels that prevent or distort competition in the EU are strictly forbidden by Article 101 (ex Article 81) of the Treaty. Cartels are often popular with firms because it allows them to avoid competition by agreeing to set the same price for their products or by sharing the market out between them (see Table 9.2). Firms are tempted to set up price-fixing cartels by the significant hike they can make in their prices. It has been calculated that international cartels overcharge their customers by an extra 30–33% on average (*Financial Times*, 9 May 2006). In 2010, ten producers of computer chips including Infineon (Germany), Samsung (South Korea), and the Japanese firms Hitachi, Mitsubishi, and Toshiba were fined a total of €331 million for operating a price-fixing cartel (the Commission has the power to fine companies up to a maximum of 10% of their annual turnover) (IP/10/586). Similarly, 11 air cargo firms were fined €799 million—they were Air Canada, Air France-KLM, British Airways, Cathay Pacific, Cargolux, Japan Airlines, LAN Chile, Martinair, SAS, Singapore Airlines, and Qantas (IP/10/1487).

Secondly, Article 102 (ex Article 82) prohibits firms with a strong market position from abusing their dominant position by, for instance exploiting customers through high prices or squeezing their rivals through artificially low prices. The Commission imposed a fine of over

Table 9.2 Ten highest cartel fines by company

Year	Undertaking**	Case	Amount in €*
2008	Saint Gobain	Car glass	896.000.000
2009	E.ON	Gas	553.000.000
2009	GDF Suez	Gas	553.000.000
2007	ThyssenKrupp	Elevators and escalators	479.669.850
2001	F. Hoffmann-La Roche AG	Vitamins	462.000.000
2007	Siemens AG	Gas insulated switchgear	396.562.500
2008	Pilkington	Car glass	370.000.000
2010	Ideal Standard	Bathroom fittings	326.091.196

Source: http://ec.europa.eu

€1 billion on Intel for abuse of its dominant position in the market for a certain type of computer chip, the x86 CPU, for which Intel held a 70% share of the €22 billion world market. The fine was levied on two grounds: for giving illegal rebates to customers if they bought all their requirements of a particular chip from Intel; and paying customers like Dell, Acer, HP, and Lenovo to stop or delay the launch of competitors' products—in this case the main rival to Intel was AMD (IP/09/745).

The third area of the law covers mergers. Under the EC Merger Regulation, the Commission has the power to regulate big mergers. Firms have to notify the Commission of proposed mergers. The Commission can wave the merger through as it did with the takeover of Scottish Power by the Spanish firm Iberdrola or it can approve the merger subject to certain conditions. When Nestlé wanted to take over Perrier it had to agree to sell off some of its brands before the Commission would give its approval. The EU, fearful that a merger would lead to reduced competition and increased prices, allowed Unilever to acquire the household and body care products divisions of Sara Lee on condition that it sell off a number of body care brands (Speech 10/658). Finally, permission can be refused where the acquisition would reduce competition in the market place. Thus, the merger between Tetra Laval the dominant producer of packaging for carton drinks, and Sidel, a market leader in the production of machines used for making PET plastic bottles was turned down (see http://ec.europa.eu and www.freshfields.com).

Finally, Article 107 (ex Article 87) of the Treaty frowns on assistance given by governments to firms that distort or threaten competition and impedes the smooth functioning of the single market programme. It wants to avoid governments giving aid to domestic firms to the detriment of their foreign rivals. In 2005, Olympic, the struggling Greek airline, was forced to repay up to €540 million in illegal state aid it had received from the Greek government. The Commission ruled that the payouts gave the airline an advantage not available to competitors (www.bbc.co.uk). To ensure no breach of Article 107, the Commission monitored closely the many government financial support schemes, amounting to a massive €4 trillion, that were put in place across the EU to help the banking sector face up to the damage wreaked by the global financial crisis (IP/10/623).

The Internet

There has been a massive growth of e-commerce. However, no single code of law applies to the internet alone. Hedley (2006) sees the laws that apply as 'a bewildering mix of the specific, the general and the metaphorical' (p 1). Some legal commentators see internet law as incomprehensible.

Legislation, either national or international, makes very few specific references to the internet but many areas of law can be applied to it, for example legislation on communications in the areas of trade, defamation, and pornography. Contract law is also problematic since the extent to which it applies to the internet is a matter of debate. For example, traditionally contracts require a signature to be legally valid but there is, as yet, no agreed definition on what constitutes a legally valid electronic signature. The rise of the internet has been accompanied by the increased use of standard electronic contracts. Some academics like Friedman (2004) are concerned that these are slanted against the consumer because the internet, much more than paper contracts, allows retailers to hide pro-seller clauses. However, a survey of 55 internet retailers found that less than 10% had sites where contracts were even enforceable and that relatively few included terms detrimental to the consumer (Mann 2008).

While it is widely accepted that certain activities on the Net breach criminal law, there can be great obstacles to enforcing it. For instance, the victim of someone hacking into their computer systems may be based in one country, say the USA, and the perpetrator thousands of miles away in another, say China. In 2009, the overall cost of cybercrime was estimated to be as much as US$1 trillion on a global basis (Hartley 2010; www.techrepublic.com, 14 September 2010).

Moreover, there is no obvious means for any one government to control the Net. Individual states find it difficult to control the activities of internet users when the activity is taking place outside their territory and Hedley (2006) questions their ability even when the activity occurs within their national frontiers. He goes on to argue that effective legal control can only be exercised at the international level. To that end, an International Convention on Cybercrime came into effect in 2004. By 2010, it had 46 signatories and had been ratified by 26, that is, approved in accordance with domestic law and thus rendered enforceable. The majority of signatories are European but other countries like the USA, Canada, Japan, and South Africa have signed up (Council of Europe). The Convention required countries to include a range of internet-related activities in their domestic laws, for example relating to computer hacking, child pornography, computer-related fraud, and infringements of copyright (Council of Europe).

Up to now, Internet Service Providers (ISPs) like China Telecom, Telefonica, TalkTalk, Comcast, and MSN have borne the main burden of regulation and control. They have been obliged by national police and intelligence services to spy on customers and to provide data such as telephone conversations, e-mail records, and web pages viewed to the authorities.

Counterpoint Box 9.2 Regulating the internet

Wikileaks is an organization publishing information on governments and business given to it by whistle-blowers. In 2010, it published around 250,000 cables on the internet from 250 US embassies around the world. Many cables included information classified as secret, others were simply embarrassing, for example some of the cables gave very uncomplimentary opinions on world leaders. The information got extensive coverage in newspapers like the *Guardian, Le Monde, El País*, and the *New York Times*.

Critics of Wikileaks argued that that publication of the documents betrayed the USA, gave succour to terrorist organizations such as Al Qaeda and was a threat to international security. The US administration claimed that the leaks could expose those cooperating with the USA in Afghanistan to retaliation from the Taliban. Wikileaks' supporters claimed that no crime had been committed because the US Constitution protects those publishing classified documents given to them by others.

Massive attacks occurred on servers used by Wikileaks to close them down and governments tried to stop server companies dealing with Wikileaks. Wikileaks simply transferred to service providers in other jurisdictions. Under intense pressure from the US government, companies including Visa, Mastercard, Amazon, PayPal, and Google cut ties to Wikileaks. Supporters of Wikileaks, echoing Friedman's concerns regarding electronic contracts, argued that the terms of service agreements allowed internet companies to do as they wish with customers. Naughton described government attempts to stop Wikileaks thus, 'It has been comical watching them and their agencies stomp about the Net like maddened, half-blind giants trying to whack a mole' (*Guardian*, 7 December 2010). He predicted that the leaks would continue as there were thousands of copies of the cables. Hackers, globally, supported Wikileaks by sending mountains of requests to Amazon, Visa, Mastercard, and PayPal's websites trying to knock them out of commission (see a video on this topic via the link on the supporting **Online Resource Centre**).

Sources: http://guardian.co.uk; *Bloomberg Opinion*, 28 July 2010; www.wired.com; http://thelastword.msnbc.msn.com; www.upi.com/Top_News/US/2010/11/29

● CHAPTER SUMMARY

As we have seen the law constitutes a very important element of the environment within which firms must operate. Every aspect of a business operation can be affected by the law from its inception to its demise. The law can have a major influence on what firms produce, the production processes used, the prices they charge, where they sell, and how they go about advertising and promoting their goods and services. The strategies and policies that firms pursue to boost revenues, cut costs, and increase profits are shaped by the legal environments within which they operate. However, the law should not be seen solely as a constraint on business activities. It acts as a protection to firms and offers opportunities as we saw with the issue of Sharia-compliant sukuk bonds.

Companies wishing to get involved in international trade and investment find very different legal environments across the world. The principles on which the systems are based, and the procedures under which they operate, can vary widely depending on the prevailing legal system. Business can find that what is acceptable in common or civil law systems may not be permissible in countries where the system of Sharia law prevails. Even where countries have a similar legal tradition, firms may encounter very different experiences in each. For example, Germany, Italy, and Colombia all have civil law systems but the time taken to enforce a contract through the local courts varies enormously.

Some of the problems of dealing with different national legal frameworks is being eased by the development of international laws and arbitration procedures under the auspices of institutions such as the WTO, EU, and the World Bank.

The law relating to the internet is seriously underdeveloped at both national and international level. There is no code of generally accepted internationally agreed laws to which business can have recourse and the mixture of laws which do seem to apply are complex. As a result, firms involved in e-commerce face much risk and uncertainty when wishing to have recourse to the law or when they themselves are being pursued through the courts.

Business operating internationally whether through trade or investment has to be aware of the national and international systems of law. It needs to monitor how the law is changing and must be prepared to deal effectively with the constraints and opportunities generated by the legal environment.

● REVIEW QUESTIONS

1. Why is the legal environment important for business?

2. Explain why knowledge of different legal systems would be useful for firms involved in international trade and investment.

3. Explain why firms involved in international trade might use international arbitration bodies to settle disputes.

4. In 2005, an EU regulation (Regulation (EC) No 261/2004) came into force requiring airlines to compensate passengers for flight delays and cancellations by providing accommodation, refreshments, means of communication, or financial reimbursement, and to inform passengers of their rights to these.

   a) What are the implications of the regulation for airlines?

   b) Go to Europa, the official EU website, to find out how the industry has responded to the regulation. See the Report at http://ec.europa.eu.

   c) In 2010, a volcano in Iceland erupted. The ash from the volcano disrupted flights particularly in Europe. Some travel insurance firms argued that the volcanic ash was an act of God and that, consequently, they did not need to compensate customers whose flights had been cancelled. Find out if that argument applied to airlines (see http://europa.eu/rapid/pressReleasesAction.do?reference=MEMO/10/131&format=HTML).

5. In 2007, Tate & Lyle, the UK based sugar refiner and corn miller accused three Chinese manufacturers and 18 USA and Chinese distributors of violating patents on Splenda its artificial sweetener. Its USA subsidiary filed the complaint with the US International Trade Commission.

   • Why would the company choose to pursue the case in the USA?

   • Find out the result of the case and the reasoning behind the Commission's decision.

6. In 2010 the European Commission launched an antitrust investigation into Google.

   a) Find out:

      • under which article of the EU Treaty Google was being investigated; and

      • the reasons why the EU Commission initiated the case.

   b) Check Europa, the official EU website to find out what has happened in the case (see http://europa.eu/rapid/pressReleasesAction.do?reference=IP/10/1624).

Case Study Trafigura and the Ivory Coast

Trafigura is a diversified Swiss-based multinational company with a turnover of US$47 billion, employing around 2,000 people in 44 countries. It trades in commodities including oil, biofuels, and metals, owns and operates mines in Peru, and has storage and warehousing facilities in the Americas, Africa, Asia, and Europe. It is the world's second largest trader of non-ferrous metals and third largest independent trader in oil. It also runs offshore hedge funds.

The case began in 2006 when a ship leased by Trafigura arrived in port in Amsterdam wishing to get rid of waste which it claimed to be routine slops from the cleaning out of its tanks. When the Dutch disposal company received protests from residents about the foul smell, it demanded a much higher price for specialist disposal. Unwilling to meet this bill, Trafigura pumped the waste back aboard and left. It ended up dumping its 500 tons of untreated cargo cheaply in the Ivory Coast in West Africa. Allegedly as a result, large numbers of people living near the dumps fell ill and needed medical treatment— estimates range from 30,000 to 100,000 including a number of deaths. The Dutch authorities laid criminal charges, accusing Trafigura of trying to get rid of waste cheaply in the Netherlands, and illegally exporting hazardous waste from Europe to Africa. The Dutch court fined the company €1 million.

In 2009, Trafigura paid out of court compensation totalling £30m to the thousands of Africans who needed medical treatment. Two years previously, the company had paid £100m to the Ivorian government to release two of its executives from prison and to help clean up the waste. The payments did not represent any admission of liability.

The company consistently denied the charges arguing that the waste could not have caused serious illness and said that it was considering an appeal against the Dutch court decision. In 2009, it took out a super injunction in the UK, a legal mechanism that prevented the media discussing the Minton Report, a scientific study commissioned by Trafigura about its own waste dumping in West Africa that had been leaked to the *Guardian* newspaper. However, the super injunction was lifted when the report was published by Wikileaks and on the website of the Norwegian Broadcasting Corporation. Trafigura also took out a libel action against the BBC which led to the Corporation accepting that the evidence did not establish that the waste had caused illness or death.

Sources: Trafigura Corporate Brochure; *The Guardian* 17 December 2009, 1 June and 23 July 2010; *Reuters* 14 February 2007; www.trafigura.com; see videos: for Trafigura's view on the case:

Source: www.istockphoto.com

www.youtube.com/watch?v=51kQPGAEqOM; for BBC reports: www.youtube.com/watch?v=x04vIFmsJec&feature=related; www. youtube.com/watch?v=0ww8y4GBMXg&feature=related; and from Al Jazeera:www.youtube.com/watch?v=AxiwQyBT_GE&feature=fvw

Questions

1. Which system of law would Trafigura have faced in the Dutch courts? What would be the major differences had the case been heard in English courts?

2. Discuss the arguments for and against the company paying compensation to those needing medical treatment and to the Ivorian government while continuing to deny that the waste caused any medical harm. To help you answer this, have a look at: www.nrk.no/contentfile/file/1.6286804!trafigura.doc

3. What legal mechanisms did the company use to protect its position? In the light of globalization, assess the success of these mechanisms for Trafigura.

4. The legal system in the Ivory Coast is based on the French civil law model and on customary law. There is political and social instability and the president is seen by some commentators as a despot. What issues do these raise for Trafigura dealing with political and legal authorities in the Ivory Coast?

5. The EU has adopted the 1989 Basel Convention which bans the export of hazardous waste to developing countries (EEC Regulation 259/93). In the light of the Trafigura case, how effective is the law? For information see the European Environment Agency website: www.eea.europa.eu/articles/international-shipments-of-waste-and-the-environment; and the BBC website: www.bbc.co.uk/news/world-europe-10846395.

Online Resource Centre
www.oxfordtextbooks.co.uk/orc/hamilton_webster2e/

Visit the supporting online resource centre for additional material which will help you with your assignments, essays, and research, or you may find these extra resources helpful when revising for exams.

● FURTHER READING

For sources of EU law see Europa, the official website of the EU and the Cornell University site at http://library.lawschool.cornell.edu.

The book by Carr covers the main legal aspects of overseas sales. It includes an examination of the developments in e-commerce.

● Carr, I. (2010) *International Trade Law*. 4th edn. Abingdon: Routledge-Cavendish

The book by Glenn gives a global view of the traditions of various legal systems, for example Islamic and Jewish. It examines national laws in the wider context of legal traditions.

● Glenn, H. P. (2007) *Legal Traditions of the World: Sustainable Diversity in Law*, 3rd edn. Oxford: Oxford University Press

The following reference is a standard text on international commercial law. It examines the legal framework and its application to commercial cases.

● Goode, R. (2007) *Transnational Commercial Law: Text, Cases and Materials*. Oxford: Oxford University Press

The book by Matsushita takes a comprehensive look at the history of the World Trade Organization, the law under which it operates, and its policies and practices.

● Matsushita, M., Schoenbaum, T. J., and Mavroidis, P. C. (2006) *The World Trade Organization: Law, Practice, and Policy*, 2nd edn. Oxford: Oxford University Press

● REFERENCES

Ayyagari, M., Demirguc-Kunt, A., and Maksimovic, V. (2006) 'What Determines Protection of Property Rights? An Analysis of Direct and Indirect Effects'. Robert H. Smith School Research Paper No RHS 06-032

Britannica Concise Encyclopaedia. Available at www.britannica.com

Care, J. C. (2000) 'The Status of Customary Law in Fiji Islands after the Constitutional Amendment Act 1997'. *Journal of South Pacific Law*, Vol 4

Chakrabarti, R., Megginson, W., and Yadav, P. K. (2008) 'Corporate Governance in India'. *Journal of Applied Corporate Finance*, Winter, Vol 20, Issue 1

Council of Europe. Convention on Cybercrime. Available at http://conventions.coe.int/Treaty/EN/Treaties/html/185.htm

Economist Intelligence Unit (2006) Risk Briefing, Business Latin America, 10 July

Economist Intelligence Unit (2010) India: Risk Overview, Business Asia, 19 April

Friedman, M. (2002) *Preface* to Economic Freedom of the World Report: 2002 Annual Report, Cato Institute

Friedman, S. E. (2004) 'Text and Circumstance: Warranty Disclaimers in a World of Rolling Contracts'. *Arizona Law Review*, Vol 46, p 677

Glinavos, I. (2008) 'Neoliberal Law: Unintended Consequences of Market-Friendly Law Reforms'. *Third World Quarterly*, Sep, Vol 29, Issue 6

Government of India (2010) Ministry of Commerce & Industry, Consolidated FDI Policy, Circular 1

Hagedoorn, J. and Hesen, G. (2007) 'Contract Law and the Governance of Inter-Firm Technology Partnerships: An Analysis of Different Modes of Partnering and Their Contractual Implications'. *Journal of Management Studies*, 44:3

Hartley, B. (2010) 'A Global Convention on Cybercrime?' *The Columbia Science and Technology Law Review*, 23 March

Hedley, S. (2006) *The Law of Electronic Commerce and the Internet in the UK and Ireland*. London: Cavendish Publishing

ICSID, Occidental Petroleum Corp. v. Ecuador (Occidental), Decision on Jurisdiction, ICISD Case No. ARB/06/11 (Sept. 9, 2008)

Jennings, M. M. (2006) *Business: Its Legal, Ethical, and Global Environment*, 7th edn. Ohio: Thomson West

Mann, R. J. and Siebeneicher, T. (2008) 'Just One Click: The Reality of Internet Retail Contracting'. *Columbia Law Review*, Vol 108, No 4

Mayson, S., French, D., and Ryan, C. (2005) *Mayson, French and Ryan on Company Law*, 22nd edn. Oxford: Oxford University Press

Patel, R. (2009) *The Value of Nothing*. London: Portobello Books

Political Risk Services (2007) Political Risk Yearbook: Ecuador Country Report, 2007

Political Risk Services (2010) Political Risk Yearbook, Argentina: Country Report, 2010

Political Risk Services (2010) Political Risk Yearbook, India: Country Report 2010

Schulte-Nölke, H. (ed.) (2006) 'EC Consumer Law Compendium—Comparative Analysis.' December. Available at http://ec.europa.eu

Silverstein, D. and Hohler, D. C. (2010) 'A Rule-of-Law Metric for Quantifying and Assessing the Changing Legal Environment of Business'. *American Business Law Journal*, Vol 47, Issue 4, 795, Winter

Smits, J. M. (2005) 'Diversity of Contract Law and the European Internal Market'. Maastricht Faculty of Law Working Paper 2005/9. Available at www.unimaas.nl

Stiglitz, J. (2010) *Freefall: Free Markets and the Sinking of the Global Economy*. London: Penguin

Townsend, M. (2010) 'The Battle over Islamic Finance'. *Institutional Investor*, Jul/Aug, Vol 44, Issue 6

World Bank (2009) Doing Business in India 2009

WTO (2007) United States—Measures Affecting the Cross-Border Supply of Gambling and Betting Services, WT/DS285/ARB, 21 December 2007

CHAPTER TEN

The Financial Framework

LEARNING OUTCOMES

This chapter will enable you to

- Explain what money is and its importance for business

- Assess the significance of inflation and interest rates for the business environment

- Analyse the role and importance of international financial institutions and markets

- Explain the restructuring and the increasing integration of the international financial system

- Explain the characteristics and impact of the global financial crisis

- Assess the challenges faced by financial regulators

Case Study The Global Financial Crisis and the BRIC Economies

The global financial meltdown which erupted in the USA in 2007 did not leave the BRIC economies of Brazil, Russia, India, and China unscathed. Foreign investors fled and stock exchanges tumbled. Russia's decline was the most dramatic with its share index falling by over three-quarters. China's fell by almost two thirds, India's more than halved, while Brazil's lost around a third of its value. However, unlike the developed world which went into deep recession, in India and China economic growth simply slowed down while the Brazilian economy stagnated. In contrast the Russian economy experienced a sharp contraction of 7.9% (see Table 10.1).

Table 10.1 Growth in output %

	Growth in Output %		
	2008	2009	2010 (forecast)
Brazil	5.1	−0.2	7.5
Russia	5.2	−7.9	4
India	6.4	5.7	9.7
China	9.6	9.1	10.5
USA	0.0	−2.6	2.6
Germany	1.0	−4.7	3.3
Japan	−1.2	−5.2	2.8
UK	−0.1	−4.9	1.7

Source: International Monetary Fund, World Economic Outlook Database, October 2010

A combination of factors helped Brazil, India, and China weather the storm of the credit crunch. Large foreign exchange reserves (2007 figures: US$1,528 billion in China, US$266 billion in India, and US$179 billion in Brazil) helped reassure foreign investors that there was a cushion against external shocks, increases in public spending on infrastructure projects gave a boost to demand, growing domestic consumer demand and reductions in interest rates allowed Brazil, India, and China to withstand the crisis and continue to grow.

In previous crises the flight of foreign capital from emerging markets generally forced them to increase interest rates to maintain financial stability thereby reducing demand for goods and services in their economies, thus aggravating the crisis. The fact that, with the exception of Russia, the BRICs managed to avoid a major banking crisis helped them weather the financial meltdown. Banks in most emerging market economies had not engaged in the financial engineering undertaken by financial institutions in the developed world. Their balance sheets typically did not contain the toxic assets such as mortgage-backed securities, credit default swaps, and collateralized debt obligations that increasingly dominated those of banks in the rich countries (for discussion of toxic assets see video at: www.youtube.com/watch?v=06PwMyJY1vA). Emerging country banks were reluctant to take on such assets or were prevented by regulators from doing so. The result was that Brazil, India and China increased their contribution to growth in world output during the crisis. During 2007 and 2008, the BRIC economies contributed 45% of global growth up from 24% in the first six years of the decade. The IMF forecasts for 2010 showed the BRIC countries growing faster than rich countries (see Table 10.1).

Sources: BIS Annual Report 2009/10; Boorman, 2009; Eichengreen 2009; Goldman Sachs, 2009

Source: iQoncept

Introduction

In this chapter we are going to look at the international financial environment, that part of the international economy concerned with money, interest rates, and financial assets such as deposits, company shares, bonds, derivatives, and foreign currencies. We examine the major private financial institutions and the markets where they operate and the extraordinarily fast rate at which these institutions and markets have grown both at home and abroad. We also look at the operation of organizations such as the Bank for International Settlements, the International Monetary Fund, the World Bank, the European Central Bank.

We go on to examine the characteristics of the 2007 global financial crisis that shook the international monetary system. Finally, we consider how the financial system is regulated and the effectiveness of regulation in maintaining stability in the international financial system.

Money

Money is an essential element of the international financial environment, playing as it does, a number of vitally important roles for business:

- A medium of exchange—money allows businesses to receive payment from customers both at home and abroad and to pay their suppliers.
- A common measure of value—money enables firms to place a value on the goods and services that they buy and sell.
- Divisibility—money can be broken down into different units of value, cents and dollars or pence and pounds, facilitating the process of exchange.
- A store of wealth-money gives business the ability to store wealth. Businesses can build up reserves of money now which can then be used later to buy goods and services or to invest.

The Importance of Confidence

Underpinning the idea of money is an agreement to accept something that, in itself, may have no fundamental use to us.

Normally, we have confidence that it can be exchanged in the market for something that does have use, goods and services. Were that confidence to melt away, the whole financial and economic system would be under threat. In such a situation, neither individuals nor businesses would be prepared to accept money in exchange for goods and services and the system of monetary exchange would collapse with drastic consequences for the economy in general, and business in particular.

Money takes various forms moving from the more to the less liquid. Liquidity refers to how quickly and cheaply an asset can be converted into cash. Thus paper money or cash is the most liquid asset because it can be exchanged very easily for goods and services. Current bank accounts are another example of high liquidity insofar as the money in them is quickly and easily accessible and also because it can be easily transferred by cheque or electronic means. Less liquid are savings accounts and deposits which need notice before money can be withdrawn. Even less liquid are a variety of financial assets such as stocks and bonds which are less easily turned into cash.

Inflation and Interest Rates

Inflation

Inflation can be defined as an increase in the overall price level of goods and services in an economy over a particular period of time or as a reduction in the value of money. It is usually measured by collecting price information on a representative sample of goods and services and using the information to calculate a Price Index that shows the change in the general price level. Businesses operating in countries with relatively high rates of inflation can find their international competitiveness undermined as the rising costs of goods and services feed higher costs of production. And this process may be exacerbated when workers respond to rising prices by demanding higher wages. On the other hand this could open up selling opportunities for firms operating out of low inflation economies. They are likely to find it easier to compete with firms operating in countries suffering from high inflation.

The rate of inflation in rich countries started to pick up after 2004 with vigorous growth in the global economy. Rapid growth, particularly in countries like China, led to increases in demand for commodities such as oil and other raw materials which pushed up their prices. Up to then low import prices had helped to hold down rich country inflation rates. The Federal Reserve estimated that falling import prices had reduced US inflation by between 0.5 and 1 percentage point a year from the mid 1990s. Rising inflation was viewed with concern in most countries with the major exception of Japan where economic growth had been stalled for many years. The rise in inflation above zero was seen as finally signalling the end of that country's 15 years of stagnation.

The onset of the global financial crisis in 2007 led to a slowdown in inflation globally to the point where, in 2009, price levels were deflating i.e. dropping, in the USA, UK, Japan, and Switzerland, and commodity prices, with the exception of oil, dropped by around one fifth over 2008. Subsequently, commodity prices, including food prices, picked up, good news for producers of natural resources such as mining companies like Rio Tinto and Billiton, not so good news for large consumers of materials like steel such as Volkswagen or domestic appliance producers like Electrolux (World Bank, Global Economic Prospects, Summer 2010).

Inflation generally runs at a higher rate in emerging economies and this is reflected in the 2009 figures (see Figure 10.1). African countries, Ghana and Egypt, with a rate of almost 20% and 12% per year respectively, contrast markedly with price falls in the USA and Japan.

Interest Rates

An interest rate is the price paid for the temporary use of someone else's money. Interest is a cost to borrowers but income to lenders. When interest rates rise in a country then this increases the cost of borrowing to business. Business could, given the removal of barriers to the movement of capital, shop around in other countries for cheaper rates. A hike in interest rates may also depress demand for goods and services as consumers find it more expensive to borrow to buy consumer durables such as cars, computers, plasma TVs, and so forth. On the other hand rising

Figure 10.1 Inflation rates %

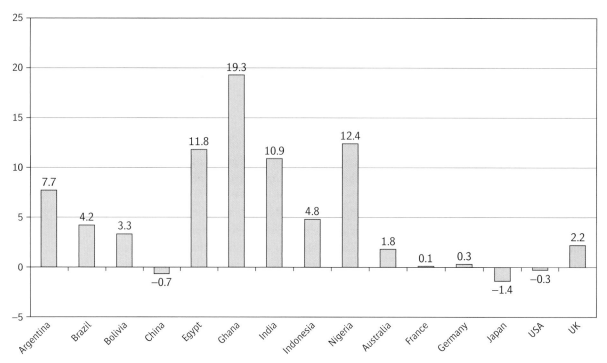

Source: CIA Factbook 2010

interest rates could benefit financial institutions who lend money because they can charge more for their loans.

Neumeyer (2005) found that real interest rates in emerging economies such as Argentina and Korea helped dampen down fluctuations in economic activity but found no such link between interest rates and the business cycle in developed economies (to get the real rate of interest, subtract inflation rate from the interest rate: when the interest rate is 12% and inflation 5%, the real interest rate is 7%).

All the world's leading central banks, concerned about rising inflation after 2004, increased interest rates. However, the global financial crisis caused them to reverse the policy. By 2010, central banks in the Eurozone, the USA, the UK, and Japan all had interest rates at 1% or less (www.fxstreet.com).

Financial Institutions—Who Are They and What Do They Do?

The functioning of the international economy and the production and the trading and investment activities of the organizations and individuals within it, are dependent on the effective operation of a variety of financial institutions, both public and private. We first of all look at several international financial institutions and their functions and then we examine an array of other organizations in the financial sector.

International Financial Institutions

There are several international financial institutions whose main aim is to facilitate the effective operation of the international payments mechanism and to ensure stability in the international financial system.

The Bank for International Settlements (BIS) has 56 members, 55 of which are countries represented at the BIS by their central banks, the other being the European Central Bank. The BIS fosters international monetary and financial cooperation and stability. It serves as an international central bank for national central banks such as the Federal Reserve, the European Central Bank, and the Bank of China. It acts as a forum to promote discussion and policy analysis among central banks and in the international financial community.

The BIS deals with the central banks on a daily basis and, by buying and selling foreign currencies and gold, helps them manage their foreign currency and gold reserves. It also advises the central banks and other international institutions on how to prevent financial fraud. In 2010 the BIS held currency deposits representing around 3% of world currency reserves (BIS Annual Report 2009/10). In times of financial crisis, the BIS offers short-term credits to central banks and may also coordinate emergency short-term lending to countries.

The Bank played a key role in establishing BASEL I, II, and III which recommended levels of capital banks need to guard against the risk of collapse. The BIS hosts the Financial Stability Board (FSB), set up in 2009 in the aftermath of the global financial crisis. The FSB promotes international financial stability by monitoring the world financial system and advising on effective regulation (BIS Annual Report 2009/10; www.financialstabilityboard.org).

The International Monetary Fund (IMF) which has 187 members was established to preserve international financial stability, in other words, to avoid financial crises that could threaten the international financial system. Up to the early 1970s that meant sustaining the system of fixed currency exchange rates set up by the Bretton Woods Agreement. Member countries contribute funds to a pool from which they can borrow on a temporary basis when running balance of payments deficits. Applicants for loans may face IMF demands for changes in government policy such as cutting public expenditures on social programmes, reducing subsidies on basic necessities, increasing taxes, eliminating import tariffs, and the privatization of publicly owned assets (Leonard 2006).

The move in the 1970s away from fixed exchange rates seemed to remove one of the main reasons for the IMF's existence. However, its services are still required e.g. in the mid 1990s when the stability of the international financial system came under threat due to a wave of financial crises in Mexico, South East Asia, Russia, Brazil, Turkey, and Argentina. In the cases of Brazil, Russia, and Argentina, the IMF intervened massively in the currency markets by pumping in millions of dollars to support their exchange rates.

It has some very ambitious aims: to promote global monetary cooperation, secure financial stability, facilitate international trade, promote high employment and sustainable economic growth, and reduce poverty. The IMF differs from the BIS insofar as it can provide temporary financial assistance to members to enable them to correct international payment imbalances. The idea is that such assistance discourages countries from trying to rectify their balance of payments deficits by resorting to policies such as competitive currency **devaluations** that could have disruptive effects on the international trading and financial systems, exchange controls, or trade protection.

During the latest global financial crisis, the IMF came to the rescue of countries with large amounts of financial assistance. For example, Greece was given a loan of US$30 billion, Hungary and Ukraine each got support of around US$16 billion, while Latvia secured an IMF stand-by arrangement worth more than US$2.3 billion (www.imf.org). These loans came with conditions forcing countries to implement austerity measures. The deal forced Latvia to: cut local government employees' wages by an immediate 15%; agree a 30% cut in nominal spending on wages from 2008 to 2009, reduce government spending by the equivalent of 4.5% of GDP; impose a pension freeze and a rise in value-added tax (www.brettonwoodsproject.org). In 2009, in the aftermath of the crisis, IMF members agreed to double the resources available to the IMF to US$1 trillion. While this represented a significant increase in resources, they remained minuscule compared with the cost to banks of the financial crisis. The Fund estimated that for the USA alone, banks had to write down loans and make provisions for losses to the sum of US$588 billion as a result of the financial crisis. The figure for Eurozone banks was US$442 billion (IMF 2010).

While the ability of the IMF to deal with global financial crises has been strengthened, it is difficult to envisage it making a significant difference were there to be another full-blown financial crisis of global dimensions such as that starting in autumn 2007.

The World Bank, with 187 member countries, was set up to reduce global poverty and to improve standards of living. It provides low cost loans and interest-free credit to developing countries for education, health, and for the development of infrastructure projects in water supply, transport, and communications. World Bank projects can be a source of lucrative contracts for businesses such as water, energy, and telecommunications utilities as well as construction companies.

It provides over US$24 billion of assistance to developing countries each year (www.bicusa.org). Like the IMF, the Bank may have the capacity to bring about change in individual countries but its budget does not equip it to have a major impact on the billions of people who continue to live in poverty.

The European Central Bank (ECB) is the central bank for countries that are members of the Eurozone (17 in 2011). Its main job is the control of inflation. It uses the tools of **monetary policy**, in other words the **money supply** and interest rates to achieve price stability. The ECB

Counterpoint Box 10.1 The IMF and World Bank

The World Bank, along with the IMF, has come in for criticism. The critics claim that neither institution works in the best interest of poor countries but on behalf of the rich economies. They provide assistance to debt-ridden or near-bankrupt developing countries that are powerless to resist their demands for the introduction of reforms that remove barriers to business in advanced economies wishing to export goods or services to those poor countries, import raw materials from them, or to invest there. In addition, poor countries are pressurized to cut public expenditure, remove state monopolies, and prioritize repayment of debt to foreign banks and investors. This hits the poor in those countries as jobs are cut, health and education

budgets reduced, price supports removed, and food and natural resources exported abroad.

Supporters argue that the removal of barriers to trade, public monopolies, and subsidies increases competition leading to a more efficient allocation of resources and economic growth. Countries would be in an even worse state were they not forced to adopt responsible budgetary policies. The IMF has made efforts to protect the vulnerable during the latest crisis by inclusion of a commitment to strengthen the provision of social safety nets.

Sources: Stiglitz 2002; Harrigan 2010; Muuka 1998; www.imf.org; www.brettonwoodsproject.org

conducts foreign exchange operations on behalf of member states, manages their foreign reserves, and promotes the smooth operation of payments systems within the zone. It carries out the tasks typically associated with national central banks.

Private Financial Institutions

There is a whole range of other financial institutions carrying out a range of functions invaluable for business. Banks, insurance companies, pension funds, investment trusts, unit trusts, all act as intermediaries between those who wish to borrow money and those who wish to lend. Retail banks take deposits from private individuals, firms, and other bodies. Insurance companies, pension funds, and unit trusts collect longer-term savings which they then invest in a variety of stocks and shares. By not being dependent on the shares of a single company, they offer savers the possibility of spreading risk. Investment banks (also called merchant banks) provide a range of financial services to business. They give advice in areas such as mergers and acquisitions, the disposal of businesses, and arranging issues of new shares.

Private equity funds including venture capital companies, are another source of funding for business. These firms gather funds from private and public pension funds, charitable foundations, business, and wealthy individuals and often use them to finance smaller, sometimes start-up, companies. They usually do this in return for a share in the ownership of the company (see Deloitte 2010 for information on the global outlook for venture capital).

Functions of Financial Institutions

We now look in more detail at some of the important functions performed by financial institutions for business.

Mini Case Microfinance and Developing Countries

While credit is usually easily obtainable in rich countries, business and populations in developing countries have great difficulty in accessing finance from mainstream financial institutions because they are regarded as high risk.

To remedy this difficulty, the concept of microfinance has been developed. This provides loans often of US$100 or less in poor countries with a particular emphasis on rural areas. It is seen as an effective way of assisting local business. It creates employment, and reduces poverty. In 2008, up to 25,000 microfinance institutions were serving around 70 million clients in over 100 countries in Asia, Africa, and Latin America. Grameen Bank was a pioneer in the field.

Borrowers are trusted to pay back the loan so they are not required to provide any security (collateral). Neither do they need to pay high rates of interest, nor do they come under legal and other pressures to pay back loans.

Sources: Sengupta and Aubuchon 2008; and for a critical assessment of microfinance see, Beck and Ogden 2007

Source: Brett Matthews

Mobilizing Savings and Providing Credit

The mobilization and pooling of savings is one of the most obvious and important functions of the financial sector. Savings facilities such as bank accounts, enable businesses and households to store their money in a secure place. In countries, where secure facilities for savings are lacking, or where there is a lack of confidence in the stability of the financial sector, for example in some developing economies, people often opt to save in physical assets such as gold or jewellery, or store their savings at home. In such situations business can find it difficult to raise finance and may have to rely on internally generated profits. By offering such facilities, the financial sector pools savings and channels them to businesses to be used productively in the economy. Interest paid on savings may increase the amount saved, giving a boost to the funds available for businesses to invest.

Financial intermediaries, by pooling the savings of firms and individuals and lending them on to business, can make it easier and cheaper for business to export and import and to finance investment for expansion or for the introduction of new technology. Thus the sector can help business service new foreign markets and sources of supply and can also make it easier for firms to improve competitiveness by increasing productivity or by introducing new products. The global financial crisis led to a freezing of credit making it more difficult for non-financial businesses to finance their operations.

Payment Facilities

Financial intermediaries facilitate the exchange of goods and services both in terms of domestic and cross-border transactions by providing mechanisms to make and receive payments. To be effective, payments systems need to be readily available for both domestic and foreign buyers and sellers through bank branches or electronically and they also need to be affordable, fast, and safe from fraud.

Good payments mechanisms free up firms to concentrate on what they do best, make goods and services, and this ability to specialize makes it easier for them to innovate and to increase productivity. Anything that reduces transactions costs and better facilitates the exchange of goods and services—whether that be faster payments systems, more bank branches, or improved remittance services—will help to promote business growth.

Normally payments systems are more highly developed in the advanced economies than in poorer countries but systems can vary from one rich country to another. The existence of multiple payments systems can raise problems of **inter-operability**, that is the ability of the various systems to accept payments from others. Inter-operability may be made more difficult when systems are using incompatible hardware or software systems. While this may not be such an important issue for big multinational companies whose subsidiaries are trading with each other and where payments systems are internal to the company, it does have major implications for firms dependent on making or receiving cross-border payments from third parties.

There are various systems which operate internationally and facilitate cross-border payment:

- SWIFT, the Society for Worldwide Interbank Financial Telecommunication, was set up to increase the automation of financial transaction processes. In 2009, SWIFT had nearly 14,000 members in 209 countries processing some 4 billion transactions (SWIFT Annual Review 2009). Its services are used by banks, central banks, and other financial institutions such as securities brokers and dealers, investment management institutions, money brokers along with big MNCs such as Microsoft, GE, and DuPont.

- Continuous Linked Settlement (CLS) has 71 of the world's largest banks and more than 9,000 other institutions using the system to settle more than half of global foreign exchange transactions. It deals in the 17 main currencies used in global trade. Average daily transactions exceed US$5 trillion (www.cls-group.com).

- Visa International and MasterCard are other international organizations offering a range of cashless payment services. Visa has nearly 16,000 financial institution customers worldwide and handles some 66 billion transactions annually to the value of US$4.8 trillion. Membership is limited to deposit-taking financial institutions and to bank-owned organizations operating in the bank card sector, such as Carte Bleue in France and Servizi Interbancari in Italy. MasterCard transactions total US$2.5 trillion in value and it and Visa each have around 2 billion cards circulating worldwide (http://corporate.visa.com; www.mastercard.com).

- PayPal and Alibaba are two online payments companies offering secure methods of payment for goods and services on the web on sites such as eBay. They are not registered

Learning Task

Table 10.2 shows the extent to which payments are made by cheque and electronically in a number of countries. Examine the table and carry out the following tasks.

1. Comment on the change in importance of cheques and E-money as a means of payment.
2. Compare and contrast the use of E-money as a means of payment in Germany and Singapore.
3. What are the implications of your answer to question 2 for a German firm wishing to do business in Singapore?

Table 10.2 Payment method

	Cheque		E-money payments	
	2004	2008	2004	2008
Belgium	1.1	0.4	5.9	3.7
Canada	18.9	13.0	nav	nav
France	29.7	22.1	0.1	0.2
Germany	0.8	0.4	0.3	0.3
Hong Kong SAR	nav	nav	nav	nav
Italy	15.7	11.1	0.3	2.1
Japan	3.5	nav	nav	nav
Netherlands	nap	nap	3.4	3.7
Singapore	4.6	3.8	85.3	84.3
Sweden	0.1	0.0	nap	nap
Switzerland	0.3	0.1	1.9	1.4
United Kingdom	15.9	9.2	nav	nav
United States	41.3	26.0	nav	nav
CPSS	28.7	18.8	1.3	1.9

nav – not available   nap – not applicable

Source: BIS, Committee on Payment and Settlement Systems (2009)

as banks and therefore need the support of existing financial institutions to offer their services. PayPal operates in multiple currencies in nearly 200 countries with millions of account holders (www.paypal-media.com).

Electronic payments systems have become more widely available internationally and this has enabled firms to move their business-to-business (B2B) and business-to-consumer (B2C) activities on to the web. Electronic payments across the European Union are now fast and cheap, and are generally more efficient than payments within the USA. In Japan, cash is used extensively compared with other industrial countries. However, Japanese businesses and consumers do also use direct debits, credit transfers, credit cards, debit cards, and bills and cheques. Electronic payments have been increasing partly reflecting the development of a variety of access channels such as Automatic Teller Machines (ATMs), the internet, and mobile phones. In China, online business is growing rapidly. One Chinese bank has nearly 40 million online personal banking customers and 700,000 online business clients (Datamonitor 2010).

By contrast, in Russia, the population continues to prefer payment in cash. This is the major payment means used for retail payments for goods and services. Cash is also used for paying salaries, pensions, welfare allowances, and grants. However, the use of ATMs is growing very rapidly as is the use of 'plastic' as a means of payment with Visa and MasterCard the main players. Compared to richer countries the Russian payments system is underdeveloped.

Although the majority of Sub-Saharan African countries, including Nigeria, Sierra Leone, and Tanzania, still have largely cash and cheque-based economies, significant progress is being made in the regional development of electronic payment systems. Africa has seen an explosive growth in the use of mobile phones. East African countries, like Kenya have moved rapidly to develop the use of mobiles for money transfers. While Latin American countries do have electronic payments systems, in many more than half of the population have no bank accounts so payments are made in cash. However, the use of debit and credit cards there is increasing quickly (www.gtnews.com).

Reconciling Liquidity and Long-Term Finance Needs

Business investment projects often require a medium to long-term commitment of capital whereas many savers prefer to have ready access to their savings. In other words, they like their savings to be 'liquid'. Banks and other financial intermediaries can offer finance to business for medium and long-term investment because they combine the savings of many households and businesses. Experience shows that savers do not usually all want to withdraw their money at the same time. As a result, financial institutions need only keep a proportion of their assets in a liquid form to meet the demands of those savers wishing to withdraw money whilst, at the same time, being able to provide medium to long-term capital for business investment.

Spreading the Risk

Savers are usually averse to risk and generally reluctant to invest all their money in a single project. They much prefer to spread the risk by investing in a range of projects. Financial intermediaries such as banks, stock exchanges, and hedge funds facilitate the spreading of risk by aggregating savings and then spreading them among both low and high risk investment projects. This can enable business to get finance for high risk projects such as those involving ground-breaking technology.

Industry Restructuring and Diversification

Financial institutions have similar objectives to other private sector commercial organizations: at the most basic level they wish to survive, but they also aim to make profits and grow. Profits are made from the commissions, charges, and interest rates levied on the financial services offered, both domestically and increasingly abroad. They also benefit from arbitrage which involves taking advantage of price differences between markets when a financial product can be bought cheaply in, say, Tokyo and sold for a higher price in Amsterdam.

Domestic Consolidation and International Expansion

In pursuit of their objectives, financial institutions have been getting bigger through mergers and acquisitions, and also through organic growth—in other words increasing their own output and sales. This has led to industry restructuring. The global banking system now comprises a small number of large banks operating in highly concentrated markets with relatively low rates of entry and exit. The financial crisis accelerated these trends. In 1998, the five largest global banks had around 8% of global banking assets. By 2008, the figure had doubled to around 16% (Alessandri 2009; see Figure 10.2). Market concentration is even higher in some countries. In 2008, the five biggest US banks controlled about 50% of the country's banking assets whereas the corresponding figure for 2001 was 32% (Stella 2009).

Fifty years ago, banks and other financial institutions tended to confine their operations to their domestic markets. Increasingly, they have expanded their operations abroad—the big German bank, Deutsche Bank offers a wide range of financial services to private and business clients in over 70 countries (www.db.com).

US banks, such as Citigroup, and European banks, like Royal Bank of Scotland (RBS), have also gone in for mergers, both at home and abroad, to get round the problem of slow-growing domestic markets. Both have made moves into China. RBS paid almost £2 billion for a 10% stake in the Bank of China while Citigroup was prepared to pay over US$3 billion for a controlling

Figure 10.2 Global concentration—banks and hedge funds

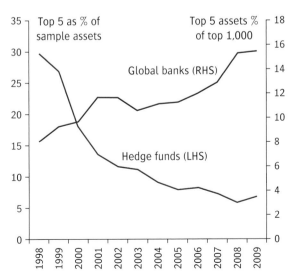

Source: The Banker; Alessandri 2009

Table 10.3 Global daily foreign exchange turnover

Size and structure of banks' foreign operations Positions at end-2007	BE	CA	CH	DE	ES	FR	IT	JP	NL	UK	US
Number of banks[1]	18	17	23	1,801	96	135	724	106	49	17	33
Total assets ($bn)[2]	2,218	2,437	3,810	10,585	4,541	8,359	4,180	9,845	4,649	10,008	9,904
Foreign claims ($bn)[3]	1,608	912	3,390	5,177	1,416	4,456	1,543	2,571	2,962	4,378	2,285
Over total assets (%)	72	37	89	49	31	53	37	26	64	44	23
US dollar share (%)	23	70	60	33	36	31	10	48	31	42	52

[1] Number of banking groups (headquartered in the country shown in the columns) that report in the BIS consolidated banking statistics.   [2] Total assets (including 'strictly domestic assets') aggregated across BIS reporting banks. For reporting jurisdictions which do not provide this aggregate (DE, ES, FR, IT, JP), total assets are estimated by aggregating the worldwide consolidated balance sheets for a similar set of large banks headquartered in the country, using Bank Scope.   [3] Foreign claims as reported in the BIS consolidated banking statistics (IB basis) plus foreign currency claims vis-à-vis residents of the home country booked by home offices; BE Belgium; CA Canada; CH Switzerland; DE Germany; ES Spain; FR France; IT Italy; JP Japan; NL Netherlands; UK United Kingdom; US United States

Source: McCauley 2010

stake in the Guangdong Development Bank (*Financial Times*, 19 August 2005 and 15 November 2006; Lo 2009).

The strategies pursued by financial institutions have led to a restructuring of the sector and have resulted in the creation of large financial conglomerates selling a range of products in a variety of countries.

Learning Task

Examine Table 10.3.

1. Which country's banks are most/least internationalized?
2. Advance possible explanations for your answer to question 1.

Product Diversification

Financial institutions have also grown by expanding their product range. Traditionally banks borrowed and lent money but did not sell insurance or trade in shares. Building societies made long-term loans on the security of private houses but did not provide banking services such as current accounts. In their quest for profits and growth, they have diversified and consequently have become less specialized. Big retail banks, for example, have increasingly seen their future as financial supermarkets selling a range of financial products and services. As a result the various institutions now compete with each other over a wider product range.

Product Innovation

The financial sector has been very inventive in devising new financial products. A major development has been the growth of the hedge fund. Hedging implies action to reduce risk. While hedge funds do attempt to reduce risk they also trade in a range of financial assets from equities to bonds to commodities and strive to take advantage of arbitrage opportunities. So, for example, if a currency or commodity is selling for one price in London and a higher price in New York then hedge funds will buy in London and sell in New York. Hedge funds often use complex mathematical models to make predictions of future price movements of financial assets to determine their trading strategies. Their aim is to produce good performance regardless of the underlying trends in the financial markets.

Derivatives, Swaps, and Options

In financial markets, stock prices, bond prices, currency rates, interest rates, and dividends go up and down, creating risk. Derivatives are financial products derived from other existing products like shares, bonds, currencies, and commodities such as cocoa and zinc. Derivatives give the right to buy or sell these existing products in the future at an agreed price. Firms such as airlines use them to insulate themselves against increases in fuel prices. Others use them to gamble on future price changes. **Swaps** are derivatives which firms can use to cover themselves against adverse movements in interest rates, inflation, exchange rates, and the possibility of borrowers defaulting on their loans. Thus, pension funds can use inflation swaps to protect the value of their assets against increases in inflation while lenders, concerned about defaulting loans, can use credit default swaps. These work like this: two banks, one of whom has lent to General Motors and one to VW, can diversify their risk by agreeing to swap part of their liabilities. Both would then be less exposed to a default by their original borrower. This ability to spread risks may make financial institutions more willing to lend consequently making it easier for non-financial firms to borrow. The market in credit derivative products grew to such an extent that in 2009 US$615 trillion was outstanding (www.bis.org). Much of the trade in derivative products does not take place through financial markets but between individual institutions. Such trade is called over-the-counter (OTC) trading. According to the BIS (2010), turnover in foreign exchange OTC derivatives in 2009 reached US$8 trillion. In 2010, activity in interest rate derivatives was worth US$2.1 trillion an increase of almost 25% over the previous year and the equivalent of UK GDP.

Another derivative is the **option** to buy or sell a specific amount of an existing product derivative at a specified price over a certain period of time. The buyer pays an amount of money for the option and the potential loss is limited to the price paid. When an option is not exercised, the money spent to purchase the option is lost. So a firm could take out an option to borrow money at a specific rate of interest of say 8% over a certain time, for example six months. If the interest rate rises above 8%, the firm can exercise its option. If the interest rate falls below 8%, then the firm borrows at the lower rate and loses the price it paid for the option.

Motives for Industry Restructuring and Diversification

Economies of scale—financial organizations hope to gain scale economies in the purchasing of supplies and savings from getting rid of duplication (a merged bank does not need more than one HQ building, one marketing department, and so on). This proclivity to merge has continued despite research literature showing that economies of scale can be exhausted by the time a bank reaches a relatively modest size. A study of European banks in the 1990s, published by the European Investment Bank, put the figure for savings banks as low as €600 million (US$760 million) in assets. More recent studies suggest far higher thresholds, up to US$25 billion (*The Economist*, 18 May 2006).

Economies of scope—the idea here is that the extra costs of selling additional products alongside the old ones are small compared to the increase in revenues. So a bank can diversify into credit cards or insurance and apply its traditional skills of selling loans to the marketing of these products. The logic is that selling extra financial products through established branch networks to existing customers, offers a low cost, high productivity method of distribution.

Market share—when a bank takes over a competitor this increases its market share, reduces competition and may, because the takeover makes it bigger, reduce the vulnerability to takeover.

Restructuring was also a response to the external environment:

- Global financial crisis—this caused banks to merge. For example, a number of Spanish savings banks were forced to merge by the government. In the USA, Bank of America merged with Merrill Lynch and, in the UK, Lloyds TSB, and HBOS. It was also expected that the crisis would lead to increased regulatory costs and stronger capital requirements which could force a new round of bank mergers.

- To finance the increase in international trade and investment which grew at unprecedented rates in the period after the Second World War.

- Economic expansion in developing nations in South East Asia led to an increased demand for financial services.

- To avoid regulation by the monetary authorities. Financial institutions have been very clever in developing business outside regulated areas where there are profits to be made. Austrian banks, for example, faced lighter regulation than their German counterparts regarding the amount of information they had to provide on their borrowers. The Austrians attracted German clients by advertising their lax rules leading to complaints of unfair competition by German banks (*The Economist*, 19 May 2005).

- The large increase in the price of oil in the 1970s led to oil-producing countries having very big trade surpluses. International syndicates of banks were formed to channel the enormous sums of money from those countries to borrowers in other nations.

- Opportunities offered by the progressive deregulation of financial markets which has been occurring since the early 1970s. Deregulation involves the removal or reduction of certain governmental controls on financial institutions allowing them to move into other product areas and also into other countries.

Learning Task

Table 10.4 shows the assets of ten of the biggest banks. Examine the table and carry out the tasks below.

1. Comment on the rate of growth in the value of total assets between:
   - 1995 and 2007
   - 2007 and 2009
2. Advance possible explanations for your answers to question 1.   →

➜

3. The Royal Bank of Scotland (RBS) was not one of the big banks in 1995 but joined them in the first decade of the new century.

   • Suggest reasons for the growth of RBS.

   • Comment on and explain the change in asset value of the Royal Bank of Scotland between 2007 and 2009.

4. How would explain the appearance of Chinese banks in the table?

Table 10.4 World's top ten banks by assets (US$ billion)

Big Banks by Value of Assets $ (figures are rounded up)

Bank	Assets 1995 $bn	Bank	Assets 2007 $tn	Bank	Assets 2009 $tn
HSBC Holdings	352	HSBC Holdings	2,4	Bank of America Corp	2,2
Crédit Agricole Groupe	386	Citigroup	2,2	JP Morgan Chase & Co	2,0
Union Bank of Switzerland	336	Royal Bank of Scotland	3,8	Citigroup	1,9
Citicorp	257	JP Morgan Chase & Co	1,6	Royal Bank of Scotland	2,7
Dai-Ichi Kangyo Bank	499	Bank of America Corp	1,7	HSBC Holdings	2,4
Deutsche Bank	503	Mitsubishi Group	1,8	Wells Fargo & Co Industrial	1,2
Sumitomo Bank	500	Crédit Agricole Group	2,3	Commercial Bank of China	1,7
Sanwa Bank	501	Industrial and Commercial Bank of China	1,2	BNP Paribas	3.0
Mitsubishi Bank	475	Banco Santander	1,3	Banco Santander	1,6
Sakura Bank	478	Bank of China	.8	Barclays	2,2
Total assets	$4.3 tn		$19.1 tn		$21.0 tn

Source: The Banker

The product and geographical diversification strategies followed by the financial sector have increased the international integration of financial institutions and markets. This has been facilitated by the falling cost and the cross-border diffusion of information and communications technologies. Institutions can move funds around the world to markets in different time zones easily, cheaply, and quickly. New technology has helped financial institutions, 'by-pass international frontiers and create a global whirligig of money and securities' (*The Economist*, 3 October 1992).

Financial Markets

Financial institutions usually operate through markets. Markets are mechanisms for bringing together borrowers and lenders. For example, capital markets, such as the bond and stock markets, bring together organizations, both public and private, wishing to borrow and lend long-term funds in exchange for shares and bonds. The issue of new bonds and shares to raise money takes place in the **primary market**. Stock exchanges also enable shareholders to buy and sell existing shares in the **secondary market**. Non-financial organizations also purchase bonds or shares in the secondary market. Money markets, on the other hand, enable organizations to borrow and lend short term for anything up to, or just over, a year trading in such instruments as derivatives and certificate of deposits (CDs). Companies with surplus cash that is not needed for a short period of time can earn a return on that cash by lending it into the money market.

Other financial markets include the foreign exchange market which facilitates trading between those who wish to trade in currencies such as importers and exporters and speculators. A variety of institutions trade in foreign currencies, non-financial companies wishing to buy goods and services abroad, central banks trying to influence the exchange rate, commercial banks trading on their own account, financial institutions wishing to buy foreign securities and bonds, hedge funds, governments financing their military bases abroad, and so on. In fact, importers and exporters account for only a very small proportion of this trading as foreign currencies have increasingly been seen as assets in their own right. The amount of foreign exchange traded is enormous. BIS (2010) figures show that daily turnover doubled from almost US$2 trillion in 2004 to US$4 trillion in 2010, 70 times the value of international trade in goods and services (Figure 10.3). The major currencies traded are the US dollar, the euro, and the yen. BIS (2007) suggested that the massive growth in foreign currency turnover up to 2007 was due, in part, to trends in exchange rates and interest rate differentials. Investors could borrow in low interest rate currencies, such as the US dollar, and move the money into a higher interest rate currency with an appreciating exchange rate such as the Australian dollar. In 2010, growth was mainly attributed to the activities of hedge funds, insurance companies, and central banks (BIS 2010).

International banking activity has grown very rapidly since the 1960s when banks in London were permitted to accept foreign currency deposits. These banks were able to attract US dollar deposits, or eurodollars, because they faced a lighter system of regulation than banks in the USA. The eurodollar market became so large that it was described as a 'vast, integrated global money and capital system, almost totally outside all government regulation, that can send billions of "stateless" currencies hurtling around the world 24 hours a day' (Martin 1994).

Figure 10.3 Global daily foreign exchange turnover

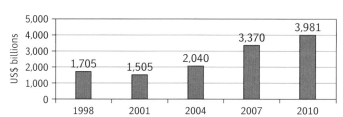

Source: BIS 2010

The Major Markets

Modern communications and information technology allow financial institutions to operate from virtually anywhere nowadays, yet the financial sector prefers to cluster in certain locations. London and New York are the two leading global financial centres and appear to act as a magnet for finance companies. London is pre-eminent in international bond trading and leads the way in OTC derivatives, marine insurance, and trading in foreign equities. It is also the most popular place for foreign banks to locate, with 249 foreign banks operating there, compared to 120 in New York (www.cityoflondon.gov.uk; www.citidex.com). Tokyo, Chicago, Frankfurt, Singapore, and Hong Kong are other important centres.

Financial Crises

There is no generally accepted theory to explain the causes of financial crises but one thing is sure, they are a recurring phenomenon. They involve bouts of speculation when assets are bought, in the hope that the price will rise, or sold, in the expectation of a fall in price. If the price rises, those who purchased the asset can sell and make a profit. If the price falls, sellers can profit by buying the asset back at a lower price. The objects of speculation can be financial assets such as shares, bonds, or currencies, or physical assets such as land, property, or works of art. Crises occur when the speculation destabilizes the market causing prices to rise or fall dramatically.

Galbraith (1990) and Stiglitz (2002) examine how destabilizing speculative episodes, so-called bubbles, develop. When an asset is increasing in price it attracts new buyers who assume that prices will continue to rise. This boosts demand for the asset and its price goes up. With prices soaring, investors charge in to take advantage of the easy profits to be made. Speculative euphoria develops as market participants come to believe that the upward movement in prices will go on indefinitely. As the value of the asset rises, investors are able to use it as security to borrow money from the banks to buy more of the asset. However, inevitably, there comes a tipping point, the causes of which are much debated, where some participants decide to withdraw from the market perhaps due to an external shock, bad news, or even a rumour. The resulting fall in price sparks off panic in the market with investors rushing to off-load their assets leading to a market collapse. Stiglitz (2002) makes the point that the excessive optimism or euphoria generated by bubbles is often followed by periods of excessive pessimism. Financial crises are contagious domestically and internationally. For example, a banking crisis can make borrowing more difficult and costly for firms and consumers. This could cause them to reduce their demand for goods and services leading to spare capacity, bankruptcies, and increasing unemployment. In an increasingly interconnected world, a financial crisis in one country can very quickly spread to others as happened during the South East Asian crisis of the late 1990s and the credit crunch of 2007.

In summary, financial crises are characterized by:

- bouts of speculative activity, market euphoria, and rapidly rising prices;

- a tipping point which leads to panic selling, excessive pessimism, and plummeting prices;

- contagion of domestic and foreign economies.

Research by Reinhart and Rogoff (2008) shows that full-blown financial crises are deep and prolonged. House prices in real terms decline by an average of 35% and share prices by 55%. Output drops by over 9% from the peak to the trough of the bubble, unemployment increases by over 9% while the real value of government debt explodes by 86%. And problems remain after the crisis subsides. Reinhart found that growth in real incomes tended to be much lower during the decade following crises and that unemployment rates were higher with the most extreme increases occurring in the richest advanced economies (*Financial Times*, 31 August 2010).

Reinhart and Rogoff (2008a) show that financial crises have been regular occurrences in world history. In the 20 years up to 2007, many countries experienced such crises, including Sweden, Turkey, the Czech Republic, Argentina, Mexico, South Korea, Indonesia, Russia, and Japan. Reinhart and Rogoff, claim that financial crises have repeatedly been the result of high international capital mobility and often follow when countries experience large inflows of capital.

Anatomy of the Financial Crisis 2007 Onwards

Easy Credit and Bad Loans

The main elements of the crisis can be summarized as follows. Low interest rates drove bankers to engage in a ferocious search for higher returns and the resulting higher bonuses (FSA 2009). More than a trillion dollars was channelled into the US mortgage market, lent to the poorest, high-risk borrowers with low or uncertain incomes, high ratios of debt to income, and poor credit histories (Reinhart and Rogoff 2008). Borrowers took the loans to cash in on the boom in US house prices. These became known as subprime loans. Borrowers were led into taking loans by what Feldstein (2007) called 'teaser rates', unrealistically low rates at the start of the loan which, when they subsequently rose, became too expensive for customers to pay. They were only obliged to pay back a minimum amount each month which neither covered the interest nor paid back any of the capital sum. The result, in many cases, was that the size of the debt increased. This was not a great problem when interest rates were low and house prices rising. In the five years up to 2005, house prices rose by more than half in the USA. In addition, large amounts of savings from trade surplus countries like China were being recycled into US finance markets.

Superstructure of Complex Financial Products on Subprime Foundations

The boom in subprime loans was accompanied by explosive growth and complexity in financial products such as derivatives, credit default swaps and collateralized debt obligations, many based on subprime mortgages. Lenders repackaged poor quality mortgages with more traditional and less risky financial products like bonds and sold them on to US and foreign financial institutions, a process called securitization. Buyers then used the securities as collateral to borrow more money. Financiers seeking higher returns on their investments, and driven by the prospect of massive bonuses, were misled by mathematical models indicating that the new products would diversify risk and reduce the possibility of a collapse in the financial system. Because risk was reduced, banks needed to hold less capital (Financial Services Authority 2009). Finance companies did not need to show these securities on their balance sheets leading to a lack of information and transparency on levels of risk and on which institutions were carrying most risk. Lax regulatory systems and weak supervision of complex financial products allowed this dangerous process to occur (Naudé 2009).

Tipping Point, Impact, and Government Response

By the summer of 2007, house prices in the USA were falling and teaser rates began to expire. The rate of default on loans by subprime borrowers ballooned and the value of the assets held by the institutions plummeted. There was widespread panic and a flight from risk. This led to a credit crunch with institutions refusing to lend money to other finance firms fearing that they were carrying large amounts of subprime assets off the balance sheet. Facing a severe shortage of liquidity, institutions started a mass sell-off of their financial assets which was difficult given the lack of credibility and trust in the finance industry.

In the USA, bad subprime debts and the drying up of liquidity led to the shock collapse of the giant investment multinational investment bank, Lehman Brothers (see end of chapter Case Study). The government forced a fire sale of Bear Stearns to JP Morgan and a takeover of Wachovia by Wells Fargo. The government bailed out institutions such as AIG, Goldman Sachs, and Morgan Stanley to the tune of US$700 billion through its Troubled Asset Relief Programme (TARP) and nationalized Fanny Mae and Freddie Mac, two of the biggest operators in the mortgage market.

The crisis was not confined to the USA. The interconnectedness of financial markets, especially amongst the developed countries meant that panic was contagious, spreading rapidly across borders. Acharya (2010) found that the main foreign traders of subprime securities were based in the UK, Germany, the Netherlands, and Japan. Banks had to be taken into public ownership not only in the USA but also in the UK, the Netherlands, France, Iceland, and Portugal. The Irish and Icelandic economies went into meltdown with the former, along with Greece and Portugal, forced to accept a bail-out by the IMF and the EU and the latter to go cap in hand to the IMF. The EU set up the €750 billion European Financial Stability Fund to secure financial stability by providing assistance to struggling Eurozone members (www.efsf.europa.eu).

There was a run on institutions, even those with no direct connection to the US subprime market. Northern Rock, the fifth largest British bank, unable to borrow on the money markets because of the credit crunch, had to be taken into public ownership (see Mini Case on page 301). Although banks in developing countries were relatively unscathed by the crisis, the Bank of China was left holding nearly £5 billion of securities backed by US subprime mortgages.

Share prices on stock markets in New York, London, Paris, Frankfurt, and Tokyo plunged and financial markets became extremely volatile with share prices and currencies fluctuating violently.

The crisis meant that the value of bank assets had to be written down by US$2.3 trillion. It helped create the deepest recession in developed economies since the 1930s, led to an increase in unemployment of 30 million, and to a massive increase in government deficits (IMF Global 2010a; www.imf.org). Stiglitz (2010) sums up the crisis:

> A deregulated market awash in liquidity and low interest rates, a global real estate bubble, and skyrocketing subprime lending were a toxic combination. (p 1)

Central banks in the USA, Europe, and Japan went on the offensive pumping massive amounts of financial assistance credit into the financial system. Alessandri (2009) estimates total assistance at US$14 trillion or one quarter of global GDP. They also reduced interest rates on fears of sharp falls in consumption and investment in their economies as a result of the crisis. Anxious to avoid a collapse in the global economy, the G20 met in 2009 and agreed to a significant increase in resources for the IMF, and committed themselves to a US$5 trillion fiscal expansion promoting growth and jobs (Visit the supporting **Online Resource Centre** for this book to access videos of G20 leaders commenting on the outcome of the summit.) Subsequently, while the USA continued its expansionary economic policies, the UK, Spain, Greece, and Ireland introduced measures making significant cuts in public expenditure and raising taxes.

Learning Task

Go to www.imf.org and call up the October 2010 edition of the World Economic Outlook. In Chapter Two, you will find a discussion of the performance of the world economy. Drawing on the map in Figure 2.2 and the figures in Table 2.1, answer the questions below.

1. Which performed best and worst in terms of GDP growth, developed or emerging economies?

2. Which particular countries have performed best and worst in growth of GDP? What are the implications for markets for goods and services in those countries?

3. How would an understanding of the global financial crisis help explain your answers to questions 1 and 2?

Counterpoint Box 10.2 The financial meltdown and the free market

Alan Greenspan, head of the Federal Reserve for 18 years up to 2006, was a great advocate of the free market. Even with the onset of the global financial crisis in 2007, he stuck to his position, 'free, competitive markets are by far the unrivaled way to organize economies' (2008a). Leaving financial markets free from government intervention enabled them to gather resources from savers and allocate them swiftly and efficiently to borrowers. Countries letting financial markets operate freely could grasp market opportunities more quickly and benefit from higher levels of competitiveness and growth. New financial products such as pricing options and derivatives helped to spread risks and to create 'a far more flexible, efficient, and hence resilient financial system' (Greenspan 2005). Therefore, governments should not regulate financial markets tightly because those markets are best able to withstand and recover from shocks when provided with maximum flexibility. Greenspan's critics assert that his free market ideology led to excessive risk-taking in the finance industry, creating an enormous bubble and ultimately resulting in a devastating financial crisis and recession.

In the USA, by March 2009, the stock market had fallen by 40% in seven months and over 4 million jobs had disappeared. World output was falling for the first time since the Second World War and global unemployment had increased by 30 million between 2007 and 2009, three quarters of which had occurred in the advanced economies. New financial products, rather than spread risk, had made economies and the global financial system much more unstable. Long before the onset of the crisis, credit derivatives were described by Warren Buffet, one of the world's most influential investors, as 'time bombs' and 'financial weapons of mass destruction' (Berkshire Hathaway annual report 2002), while the head of the UK Financial Services Authority referred to an 'explosion of exotic product development' and described many activities of the finance industry as 'socially useless' (*Prospect Magazine*, 27 August 2009; *Guardian*, 22 September 2010).

Critics, like Johnson (2010), argue that the finance industry in the USA is far too powerful—a financial oligarchy that has captured the institutions of US government by convincing them that, 'more finance is good, more unfettered finance is better, and completely unregulated finance is best' (p 160). Supporters of tighter regulation of the finance industry point out that Greenspan, in an appearance before a Congressional committee in 2008, accepted that, in the face of 'a once-in-a-century credit tsunami', his belief in the self-correcting powers of the free market had been misplaced (Visit the accompanying **Online Resource Centre** for a video link on this topic.) Critics argue that much tighter regulation of the finance industry is required if a repeat of the latest global financial crisis is to be avoided.

Sources: Greenspan (2005), (2008), and (2008a); Johnson and Kwak (2010); Johnson (2010); IMF/ILO (2010)

Learning Task

Compare and contrast the arguments advanced by Greenspan and his critics. Decide which side is most convincing and explain why.

Mini Case Northern Rock—A Credit Crunch Casualty

Northern Rock, one of the biggest mortgage lenders in the UK, financed most of its lending by borrowing from other financial institutions and relatively little from individual savers. In the summer of 2007, liquidity in credit markets started to dry up due to the subprime mortgage crisis in the USA. As a result, Northern Rock found it increasingly difficult to raise money by selling its securitized or bundled mortgages to other financial institutions, or borrow on the money markets. It was forced to go cap in hand to the Bank of England. When this became public, worried depositors flocked to Northern Rock bank branches to withdraw their savings, in other words there was a 'run on the bank'. The value of Northern Rock shares plummeted. The Bank of England bailed out Northern Rock to the tune of £25 billion and the government guaranteed the deposits of all the company's savers. After unsuccessfully trying to sell Northern Rock to a private buyer, the British government took the company into public ownership. Subsequently the company shrank with between 2,000 and 3,000 Northern Rock employees losing their jobs. The case raised questions about the failure of the regulatory system to address the issue of bank liquidity and about the lack of coordination between the three responsible bodies, the Bank of England, the Financial Services Authority, and the Treasury.

Sources: *The Observer*, 16 September 2007; www.telegraph.co.uk, 23 January 2008; www.ft.com, 17 and 20 February 2008; *Guardian*, 8 June 2010

Source: Alex Gunningham

Financial Regulation

Regulation plays an important role at both a domestic and an international level. It is a big element in the financial sector's external environment because of the effect it can have on their sales turnover, costs, and profits.

Effective regulation is also important for non-financial firms. Businesses and individuals dealing with financial institutions have an interest in those institutions being effectively regulated and supervised. Regulation can avoid hiccups in payments systems, protect customers against financial fraud, ensure financial institutions are prudent in weighing up risks and that they have enough cash and other liquid assets on hand so that they do not go bankrupt when things go wrong.

Another major reason for regulation is the failure of countries and financiers to learn the lessons of history. Reinhart and Rogoff (2008a) see this in a widespread view that 'this time it is different', because countries and financiers have learned from the mistakes made in previous crises (p 53). Major crises are unlikely to occur, so it is argued, thanks to wiser macroeconomic policies, sophisticated mathematical models, and more discriminating lending practices. In response, Reinhart and Rogoff comment, 'the ability of governments and investors to delude themselves, giving rise to periodic bouts of euphoria that usually end in tears, seems to have remained a constant' (p 53). Galbraith (1990) talks about 'the extreme brevity of the financial memory [which means that] financial disaster is quickly forgotten' (p13).

So regulation is necessary, not simply to protect the interest of customers, but also to ensure the stability of the whole financial system. Evidence also shows that effective regulation can have a positive effect on a country's economic income and output, which could be good news for business seeking expanding markets (Levine, Loayza and Beck 2000; OECD 2006).

Different Systems of Regulation

Regulatory systems can vary quite considerably from one country to another. The authorities face a number of dilemmas regarding regulation. Tight regulation could reduce the attractiveness of their financial centres, while too little regulation could frighten customers away.

Mini Case The Crisis and Sub-Saharan Africa

Sub-Saharan Africa (SSA) comprises all those countries south of the Sahara desert. The SSA countries while bearing no responsibility for the global financial crisis suffered from the recession caused in large part by the crisis. In the four years up to 2008 SSA economies had managed real growth of more than 6%. The growth rate fell to just over 2% in 2009 (see Figure 10.4). The impact of the global financial crisis on countries in the region was quite varied. Growth in oil-exporting countries like Nigeria and Angola, decelerated sharply, reflecting the drop in oil and other commodity prices. Output levels in most middle-income countries including South Africa and Botswana, were dragged down by the sharp fall in export volumes in early 2009 as world demand collapsed. In contrast, many low-income countries, such as Kenya and Tanzania, escaped fairly lightly and some fragile economies like Liberia and Congo actually experienced a small increase in output growth in 2009.

The 2007/08 meltdown in advanced economy financial markets also produced an abrupt stop in capital flows to emerging markets and developing countries. Furthermore, remittances declined from Africans abroad who found they had lower incomes as a result of the crisis. The slowdown in growth led to a reduction in tax revenues in many countries. In the virtually complete absence of any government financed social safety nets, the slowdown in growth caused much suffering in terms of poverty and unemployment. It was estimated that South Africa lost 1 million jobs in 2009.

However, according to the IMF, the effects were not as serious as they had been in previous crises because many African countries had undertaken policies before the crisis of strengthening budget positions, reducing debt burdens, holding down inflation, and building comfortable reserve cushions. This allowed countries to use public spending to counteract the crisis, including maintaining social spending where it existed. Most SSA countries also reduced interest rates. (See IMF video via the link on the supporting **Online Resource Centre**.)

Sources: IMF, Regional Economic Outlook: Sub-Saharan Africa, April 2010; www.imf.org/external/np/sec/pr/2010/pr1073.htm; www.imf.org/external/np/speeches/2010/021710.htm; www.imf.org/external/np/sec/pr/2010/pr10164.htm ➜

➜

Figure 10.4 Sub-Saharan Africa: real GDP growth %

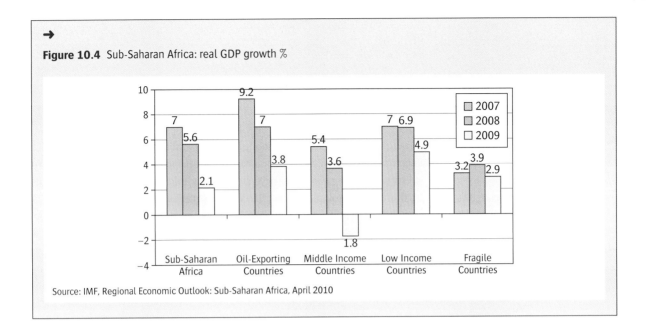

Source: IMF, Regional Economic Outlook: Sub-Saharan Africa, April 2010

At one extreme is a state-owned banking system in which banks are an arm of government and are never allowed to go bust; at the other is a lightly regulated system of private banks without an explicit safety-net in which bank failures are common. Either extreme faces certain dangers. Banking systems, where no bank can be allowed to fail, and depositors face no risk of loss, may breed management and depositor recklessness. At the other extreme, systems which rely only on market discipline run the risk of unnecessary bank and possibly, systemic failure and great loss to depositors.

In many countries, the state has a major presence in the financial sector. State intervention plays an important role in both the developing and the developed world, taking various forms of intervention from explicit intervention in the banking system in China and Germany to implicit government-sponsored enterprises in the USA. Intervention is particularly prevalent in banking, where public sector banks still account for an estimated 40% of total banking sector assets. A large swathe of the German, French, and Austrian banks is publicly owned while the banking system is in private hands in many countries, including Canada, Japan, New Zealand, the UK, and the USA, at least they were up to the financial meltdown in 2008. Up to 1991 Indian banks were nationalized, and used as a source of finance for public sector spending and investment by big companies. Liberalization has since taken place only very slowly but India, like Italy, continues to restrict foreign ownership. State intervention can also extend to insurance schemes and pension funds, but generally these are subject to less systematic regulation than the banks (*The Economist*, 19 October 2006; IMF Survey, Vol 33, No 10, 31 May 2004).

In the Eurozone, the European Central Bank carries out a supervisory function in cooperation with the national central banks and regulatory bodies. The UK has a tradition of 'light-touch' regulation and the regulatory and supervisory structure is much simpler, the functions being mainly carried out by the Bank of England. Some developing countries do have regulators but, as in the case of India, often seem to find it difficult to strike an appropriate balance between regulating the sector effectively and providing a good enabling environment for financial sector development.

The Regulatory Challenge

In the run up to the global crisis, financial markets were being transformed by a remarkable wave of cross-border growth and innovation in the form of new products such as derivatives. The tendency of financial institutions towards conglomeracy and the increasing cross-border integration of the sector meant that a shock in one part of the sector, or of the world, could very quickly spread and turn into a big threat to the system as a whole, as illustrated by the credit crunch of 2007. Furthermore, regulatory systems in some countries were very loose (see OECD 2006). There was also a danger that some regulators had been captured by the financial institutions they were supposed to regulate. This was reflected in their willingness to take on trust what the financial institutions told them rather than subjecting them to intensive scrutiny. Furthermore, many countries lacked any real regulation to speak of—the British Virgin Islands and the Cayman Islands being two examples. But it was not just small obscure islands. The big international financial markets, London, New York, and Tokyo all had a thriving offshore business operating safely away from the eyes of the regulator (www.bbc.co.uk). A final issue was that regulation was not applied uniformly across the range of financial products with some financial products being tightly regulated whilst others faced hardly any regulation at all.

The financial meltdown demonstrated the inability of regulation both at national and international levels to prevent crises. This was widely recognized during the crisis but enthusiasm for much tighter regulation began to wane with the recovery of the financial system and the ferocious resistance from the finance sector.

As a result of the crisis, the Basel Committee on Banking Supervision, comprising regulators from the major industrialized countries, agreed a package of measures called Basel III. This nearly trebled to 7% the minimum amount of equity capital banks had to hold against losses, $2^1/_2$% of which was to be held as buffer. Banks straying into the buffer zone would be subject to restrictions on share dividends and discretionary bonuses if regulators felt that they were extending credit too freely. The new rules were to be phased in from 2013 to 2019.

An official US inquiry into the crisis found that there had been dramatic failures in the corporate governance and risk management in banks (National Commission 2011). The USA, in order to avert future financial crises, imposed tighter regulations on financial firms that would have the effect of reducing their profits. It boosted consumer protection, forced banks to be more transparent and to reduce risky trading and investing activities. The transparency around derivatives was increased by obliging them to be traded on exchanges rather than over the counter. A new, more orderly process for liquidating troubled financial firms was established (Schoenholtz 2010). Critics however argued that the regulations had been watered down due to intense lobbying by the financial sector and that another financial crisis could occur before the regulations took full effect (Helleiner 2010; *Financial Times*, 20 August 2010).

The EU established three new financial supervisory bodies for the banking, securities markets, and insurance and occupational pensions sectors and set up the European Systemic Risk Board (ESRB). The Commission proposed: new capital requirements for the financial sector; rules governing banker pay and bonuses; stronger rules on disclosure of financial information. It is also looking for ways to regulate credit rating agencies and auditing firms. While responsibility for financial supervision remains at national level, a new body, the European Supervisory Authorities will act as coordinator. Measures such as the Markets in Financial Instruments Directive (MiFID) and the Market Abuse Directive (MAD) were brought forward to promote efficiency, stability, and transparency in financial markets (EU Commission 2011; *Financial Times*, 13 September 2010).

The head of the IMF, in the autumn of 2010, fearing that banks were getting back to 'business as usual', expressed concern about the slow progress in improving financial regulation (see how banks resisted tighter regulation in the Mini Case, The Banks and Basel III in Chapter Eight). He argued that much more needed to be done to make financial sectors safer around the world. He called for more international cooperation and coordination of regulation particularly in relation to cross-border finance (www.imf.org).

● CHAPTER SUMMARY

In this chapter we have examined the importance of the financial environment for business, whether that be in the provision of money and credit, the operation of systems of payment, or providing protection against risk by the financial sector or the impact of monetary phenomena such as inflation, interest rates, or exchange rates. We have also seen how the big financial institutions and the increasingly integrated financial markets of London, New York, and Tokyo are vital for the effective functioning of business and the economies in which it operates.

In the advanced economies business has relatively easy access to finance through a variety of financial institutions offering a wide range of financial products. As we have seen, access to finance in developing countries is much more difficult, making it harder for businesses to start up and grow.

The financial sector has grown rapidly in terms of output and employment and has become highly internationalized. The industry has come to be dominated by a small number of very large and diversified companies operating across the globe. These big financial institutions have become very powerful actors on the world stage.

Because of their size, the extent of their diversification and internationalization, and their ability to invent new financial products, they continue to pose great challenges to the regulatory authorities. The regulation of the financial sector is fragmented within and between different countries and can vary considerably from one state to another. Financial crises occur regularly in the system, affecting not only the country where they started but moving at terrifying speed across continents and markets and threatening major parts of the global economy as we saw with the global crisis of 2007. While improvements in regulation have occurred, many critics argue that they remain inadequate and that the stability of the international finance system cannot be taken for granted.

● REVIEW QUESTIONS

1. Discuss why the level of interest rates and inflation are important for international business.

2. Why is it vital for business to have confidence in the international payments system?

3. Explain the increasing internationalization of the banking system. What factors have made it easier for banks to internationalize their operations?

4. Why do financial institutions like to cluster in places like London given the obvious disadvantages of traffic congestion, overcrowded and unreliable public transport, and high office prices by international standards? (A useful source of information is the Global Financial Centres Index produced by the City of London and available on its website. See also www.bankofengland.co.uk/publications/events/ccbs_cew2008/presentation_sukudhew.pdf)

5. In the 2007 global financial crisis:

   • in which country did the crisis have its origins?

   • which asset was at the root of the bubble?

   • what role did securitization play in the crisis?

   • what was the tipping point of the crisis?

   • what were the effects of the crisis on non-US banks?

6. Analyse the need for effective regulation of the financial system. Explain why bankers resist the tightening of regulation.

Case Study Lehman Goes Bankrupt

In March 2008, Bear Stearns, the failing investment bank was purchased by JP Morgan in a US$240 million deal backed by the federal government. Financial markets were shaken by Bear's demise, and Lehman, a giant investment bank with offices worldwide, was widely considered to be the next bank that might fail. There was a strong suspicion in the marketplace that many of the US$700 billion of Lehman's assets were securities related to mortgages on property and not worth the value stated in the balance sheet. As the market for these securities deteriorated in 2008, confidence in the bank eroded and panic set in. Lehman began to suffer huge losses and a plunging stock price. Citibank, which had been extending billions of dollars of credit daily to Lehman in the United States, Europe and Asia, requested a deposit of US$3–5 billion from Lehman to help cover its risk exposure. Confidence in Lehman nose-dived and other institutions like JP Morgan and Bank of America, trying to protect their interests, also demanded more collateral on loans making it harder for Lehman to borrow. Fearing the worst, HSBC ceased doing business with Lehman. Ratings firms such as Standard and Poor downgraded many of the Lehman assets. The firm filed for bankruptcy in September 2008.

Prior to the bankruptcy, Lehman worked hard to make its financial condition look better than it was. An official investigation into the Lehman collapse found that the company had deliberately misrepresented its financial position by removing US$50 billion of subprime assets from its balance sheet to conceal its heavy borrowing, or leverage. The report was heavily critical of the Lehman auditors, Ernst & Young who were aware of, but did not question, Lehman's manipulation of the balance sheet. The author of the report also revealed that the regulatory authorities in the USA were aware that Lehman had broken its own risk management rules. The investigation found that Lehman's assets were mainly long term while its liabilities were short term. Lehman therefore had to fund itself by borrowing billions of dollars each day to be able to open for business. Confidence was critical. Were lenders to lose confidence and refuse loans, then Lehman would be unable to fund itself and continue to operate—precisely what happened. The business model used by Lehman was used by all major investment banks. Like other banks, Lehman paid out enormous bonuses which encouraged managers to take excessive risks.

The collapse of Lehman spread panic through the international system and brought lending between financial institutions to a virtual halt. European banks had bought large amounts of subprime financial assets from US institutions like Lehman which the rating agencies, S&P, Moody's, and Fitch had given a triple A, the highest rating. Wholesale money markets in Europe dried up and banks such as Northern Rock that were heavily dependent on borrowing from other financial firms found themselves with big liquidity problems. Within days of Lehman ➜

Source: Jakub Krechowicz

imploding, the insurer AIG and savings bank Washington Mutual were in trouble and the US government scrambled to put together a US$700 billion banking bailout package.

Barclays of the UK ended up buying some of Lehman's North American assets while Nomura, the Japanese bank, purchased its Asian division at bargain prices.

Sources: Valukas 2010; in Knowledge@Wharton 2010; *The Economist* online, 10 March 2010; www.bloomberg.com

(Visit the links located on the book's **Online Resource Centre** for videos re Lehman Bankruptcy.)

Questions

1. Advance reasons for Lehman going bankrupt.

2. Why is confidence so important in financial markets? Illustrate by reference to the Lehman case.

3. How would you assess the role played by:

- the ratings agencies;
- Lehman's auditors; and
- the regulatory authorities?

4. Analyse the spillover effects of the Lehman collapse to other financial institutions and other countries.

Online Resource Centre

www.oxfordtextbooks.co.uk/orc/hamilton_webster2e/

Visit the supporting online resource centre for additional material which will help you with your assignments, essays, and research, or you may find these extra resources helpful when revising for exams.

● FURTHER READING

For more on the international monetary system see:

- World Economic Forum (2007) *The International Monetary System, the IMF and the G20: A Great Transformation in the Making?*. London: Palgrave Macmillan

For an analysis of financial crises refer to:

- Kindelberger, C. P. and Aliber, R. (2005) *Manias, Panics and Crashes: A History of Financial Crises*, 5th edn. Hoboken: John Wiley & Sons
- Reinhart, C. and Rogoff, K. (2008a) This Time is Different: A Panoramic View of Eight Centuries of Financial Crises, March, available at www.nber.org/papers/w13882

For the 2007 crisis:

- Stiglitz, J. E. (2010) *Freefall: Free Markets and the Sinking of the Global Economy*. London: Allen Lane

- Tett, G. (2010) *Fool's Gold: How Unrestrained Greed Corrupted a Dream*. London: Abacus

For a critical examination of policies pursued by the IMF and the World Bank:

- Stiglitz, J. E. (2002) *Globalization and its Discontents*. London: Penguin

● REFERENCES

Acharya, V. and Schnabl, P. (2010) 'Do Global Banks Spread Global Imbalances? Asset-Backed Commercial Paper during the Financial Crisis of 2007–09'. *IMF Economic Review*, Vol 58, Issue 1, August

Alessandri, P. and Haldane, A. G. (2009) *Banking On the State*, Bank of England, November

BIS (2010) Triennial Central Bank Survey of Foreign Exchange and Derivatives Market Activity in April 2010—Preliminary Global Results—Turnover

Beck, S. and Ogden, T. (2007) 'Beware of Bad Microcredit'. *Harvard Business Review*, Vol 85, Issue 9, September

Boorman, J. (2009) The Impact of the Financial Crisis on Emerging Market Economies: The Transmission Mechanism, Policy Response and Lessons, Global Meeting of the Emerging Markets Forum 2009, Mumbai, India, 23 June

Committee on Payment and Settlement Systems (2009) Statistics on Payment and Settlement Systems in Selected Countries, December

Datamonitor (2010) China Construction Bank Corporation: Company Profile, 22 July

Deloitte (2010) Global Trends in Venture Capital: Outlook for the Future, 28 July, available at: http://admin.bvca.co.uk/library/documents/2010GTVC_slidepack.pdf

DFID (2004) 'The Importance of Financial Sector Development for Growth and Poverty Reduction'. Policy Division Working Paper. Available at www.dfid.gov.uk

Eichengreen, B. (2009) Lessons of the Crisis for Emerging Markets, Asian Development Bank Institute Working Paper No 179, 15 December

EU Commission (2011) Regulating Financial Services for Sustainable Growth, February

Feldstein, M. (2007) Housing, Housing Finance and Monetary Policy, 1 September, available at www.kc.frb.org

Financial Services Authority (2009) The Turner Review: A Regulatory Response to the Global Banking Crisis, March

Galbraith, J. K. (1990) *A Short History of Financial Euphoria*. London: Pelican

Goldman Sachs (2009) The Long-Term Outlook for the BRICs and N-11 Post Crisis, Global Economics Paper No 192, 4 December

Greenspan, A. (2005) Economic Flexibility, Remarks to the National Association for Business Economics Annual Meeting, Chicago, Illinois, 27 September

Greenspan, A. (2008a) 'A Response to My Critics'. The Economists' Forum, FT.com, 6 April

Greenspan, A. (2008) *The Age of Turbulence: Adventures in a New World*. London: Penguin Books

Harrigan, J. (2010) *Globalisation, Democratisation and Radicalisation in the Arab World*. Basingstoke: Palgrave MacMillan

Helleiner, E. (2010) 'Filling a Hole in Global Financial Governance? The Politics of Regulating Sovereign Debt Restructuring' in Mattli, W. and Woods, N. (eds), *The Politics of Global Regulation*. Princeton: Princeton University Press

IMF (2010a) Global Financial Stability Report: Meeting New Challenges to Stability and Building a Safer System, April 2010

IMF (2010) World Economic Outlook, October

IMF (2010a) IMF Conditionality, 9 April

IMF/ILO (2010) The Challenges of Growth, Employment and Social Cohesion, Discussion Document, www.osloconference2010.org/discussionpaper.pdf

Johnson, S. (2009) 'Financial Oligarchy and the Crisis'. *Brown Journal of World Affairs*, Spring/Summer 2010, Vol XVI, Issue II and *The Atlantic*, May 2009

Johnson, S. and Kwak, J. (2010) *13 Bankers: The Wall Street Takeover and the Next Financial Meltdown*. New York: Pantheon Books

Knowledge@Wharton (2010) Lehman's Demise and Repo 105: No Accounting for Deception

Leonard, T. M. (2006) *Encyclopaedia of the Developing World*. London: Taylor & Francis

Levine, R., Loayza, N., and Beck, T. (2000) 'Financial Intermediation and Growth: Causality and Causes'. *Journal of Monetary Economics*, Vol 46, Issue 1, August

Lo, W.-C., Ng, M. C. M. (2009) 'Banking Reform and Corporate Governance'. *The Chinese Economy*, Vol 42, No 5, September–October 2009

Martin, R. (1994) 'Stateless Monies, Global Financial Integration and National Economic Autonomy: The End of Geography' in Stuart Corbridge *et al.* (eds), *Money, Power and Space*. Oxford: Blackwell

McCauley, R., McGuire, P., and Von Goetz, P. (2010) 'The Architecture of Global Banking: From International to Multinational?' *BIS Quarterly Review*, March

Muuka, G. N. (1998) 'In Defense of World Bank and IMF Conditionality in Structural Adjustment Programs'. *Journal of Business in Developing Nations*, Vol 2

National Commission (2011) Financial Crisis Inquiry Report, January

Naudé, W. (2009) The Financial Crisis of 2008 and the Developing Countries, Discussion Paper No 2009/01, United Nations University, January

Neumeyer, P. A. and Perri, F. (2005) 'Business Cycles in Emerging Economies: The Role of Interest Rates'. *Journal of Monetary Economics*, Vol 52(2)

OECD (2006) Regulation of Financial Systems and Economic Growth, Working Paper 34

Reinhart, C. and Rogoff, K. (2008) The Aftermath of Financial Crises, paper presented at the American Economic Association meeting, 3 January 2009

Reinhart, C. and Rogoff, K. (2008a) This Time is Different: A Panoramic View of Eight Centuries of Financial Crises, March, available at www.nber.org/papers/w13882

Requena-Silvente, F. and Walkjer, J. (2007) 'The Impact of Exchange Rate Fluctuations on Profit Margins: The UK Car Market, 1971–2002'. *Journal of Applied Economics*, Vol X, No 1, May

Schoenholtz, K. and Wachtel, P. (2010) *The Architecture of Financial Regulation: July 2010 Archives: Dodd-Frank and the Fed*, available at w4.stern.nyu.edu

Sengupta, R. and Aubuchon, C. P. (2008) 'The Microfinance Revolution: An Overview'. *Federal Reserve Bank of St. Louis Review*, Vol 90(1), January/February

Stella, P. (2009) The Federal Reserve System Balance Sheet: What Happened and Why It Matters, IMF WP/09/120, May

Stiglitz, J. E. (2002) *Globalization and its Discontents*. London: Penguin

Stiglitz, J. E. (2010) *Freefall: Free Markets and the Sinking of the Global Economy*. London: Allen Lane

Valukas, A. R. (2010) Lehman Brothers Holdings in United States Bankruptcy Court Southern District of New York, Chapter 11, Case No 08,13555 (JMP) 11 March 2010

CHAPTER ELEVEN

Corporate Social Responsibility

LEARNING OUTCOMES:

At the end of this chapter you will be able to:

- Define corporate social responsibility

- Assess the free market case against corporate social responsibility

- Explain the business and moral cases for corporate social responsibility

- Identify corporate social responsibility issues in the global economy

- Discuss the implications of corporate social responsibility for business

Case Study Giant Banks and Auditors

In Chapter One we defined globalization as a process in which barriers separating different regions of the world are reduced or removed, thereby stimulating greater exchange and linkages between nations. As globalization progresses business is confronted by important new challenges. Some of these challenges relate to the way business is done. This case looks at the actions of banks and their auditors and brings into question whether organizations have an ethical obligation to meet more than the minimum standards required.

The collapse of Lehman Brothers, the enormous US investment bank in 2008, which helped bring about a near meltdown in the global financial system, brought the management of giant banks and the auditing profession sector under scrutiny. An official report on the biggest bankruptcy in US history heavily criticized Lehman's management and its auditor Ernst & Young (E&Y), one of the Big Four consultancy firms. It claimed that Lehman management had manipulated its balance sheet in a way that could result in legal proceedings and concluded that there was credible evidence that E&Y did not meet professional standards.

The report alleged that E&Y took no steps to question or challenge the non-disclosure by Lehman executives of their use of US$50 billion of temporary, off-balance sheet transactions, that flattered the bank's financial position. Lehman had excluded its principal investments in real estate, its private equity investments and its leveraged loans backing buyout deals, thereby leaving out its most risky assets from the balance sheet. Lehman's practices meant that neither investors nor regulators had a true picture of just how vulnerable it was to swings in the markets for the illiquid assets in which it had invested.

Others noted that the Big Four firms PwC, KPMG, Deloitte, and E&Y, signed off successful audits of other banks at the centre of

the crisis and also made huge fees in the process. E&Y was paid US$27.8 million for auditing Lehman, Deloitte earned £17m for auditing RBS, and KPMG received US$9 million for auditing HBOS. PwC earned £1.8m for the last year of its audit of Northern Rock. There was no suggestion, however, that these firms failed to meet required professional standards in these cases.

E&Y responded to the allegations by saying that Lehman's collapse resulted from unprecedented events in the markets and that financial statements were presented in accordance with generally accepted accounting principles (GAAP) in the USA. Critics claim that conforming to the principles does not always result in a clear picture of a company's financial health. They saw the steps taken by Lehman as a way of window dressing the state of the firm's finances.

Concerns were also raised about the Big Four also acting as management consultants to banks they were auditing on the ground that they would be reluctant to challenge the banks on their financial manoeuvrings for fear of losing lucrative consultancy contracts. Critics argued that, to avoid this conflict of interest, auditors should be banned from taking fees for other work.

Steven Thomas, a US trial attorney, said that confidence in the profession was being eroded 'and leaves us asking why do we have auditors?' (*Financial Times*, 15 March 2010). Professor Sikka argued that accountancy firms appear, like the Woody Allen character Zelig, at every major corporate crash, only to fade from view when difficult questions are asked.

Sources: Valukas, A. R. (2010) Lehman Brothers Holdings Inc., *et al*. Chapter 11, Case No 08-13555 (JMP), United States Bankruptcy Court Southern District of New York; *Financial Times*, 13 and 15 March 2010; *Guardian*, 16 March 2010

Introduction

Multinational corporations are often accused of a number of abuses related to their business activities. Many have appeared in the press accused of, inter alia, bribery and corruption, abusing human rights, sanction busting, dumping, undermining governments, exploiting uneducated consumers, using forced labour, low wages, poor health and safety standards, exploiting natural resources, using child labour, and corruption. One of the many problems for business operating internationally is that standards and 'the way of doing things' differ from country to country. That is not to say this is a justification for the type of abuses listed above but it does bring into question the very fundamental question of the role of business in society and to what extent business has any responsibility for some of the problems of society. This chapter explores the concept of **Corporate Social Responsibility** (CSR), discusses some examples related to the concept, and looks at the implications for business.

CSR can be defined as the notion that corporations have an obligation to society to take into account not just their economic impact but also their social and environmental impact. The European Commission's definition of CSR is:

> A concept whereby companies integrate social and environmental concerns in their business operations and in their interaction with their stakeholders on a voluntary basis (http://ec.europa.eu/enterprise/policies/sustainable-business/corporate-social-responsibility/index_en.htm).

Gap Inc. describes a socially responsible company thus:

> We believe it means going beyond the basics of ethical business practices to embrace a broader, deeper responsibility to people and the planet. We also believe the choices we make say a lot about our company. We're not perfect, but we're committed to following a simple principle: Do what's right (www2.gapinc.com/GapIncSubSites/csr/EmbracingOurResponsibility/ER_Overview.shtml).

We use the term corporate social responsibility throughout this chapter but it appears that business is not very keen on this term. Marks and Spencer refers to its CSR activities as 'Plan A', because there is no 'Plan B'. In other words this is how we do business and we do not need to give it any special label. Others have dropped the 'social' which some object to as too narrow, or 'outside our remit' or as a label imposed from outside. Other labels used are 'triple-bottom-line reporting' (i.e. economic social and environmental), '**sustainable development**', and the most recent 'corporate citizenship'. Although there are different interpretations of these (different) terms they are all essentially about the obligation to society in its widest sense.

Debates about CSR

CSR is not new and whether business has any social responsibility has been the subject of endless debate.

For some there is only one social responsibility of business and that is, in the words of Milton Friedman (1970) 'to use its resources and engage in activities designed to increase its profits so long as it stays within the rules of the game, which is to say, engages in open and free competition without deception or fraud'. This reflects the view that a free market society is made up of diverse entities each with a specialist role within society. The role of business is economic and the people who run businesses are expert in that field. Their role is to combine resources to produce some product or service for sale at a profit. They compete with other firms by keeping costs as low as possible and supplying consumers with the goods and services they want at the lowest possible price. Those who are effective at doing this survive and make a profit. Those who fail go out of business. It is the drive to supply consumers with the goods and services they want and at the same time to make as much profit as possible by driving costs down and selling as much as possible which makes for a dynamic and efficient economy. If there are social and environmental problems then this shouldn't be for business people to solve because it would divert them from the role for which they are best equipped and the result would be a less efficient economy. These problems are best left to governments who can employ experts in those fields.

In this debate and particularly in the field of international business we are talking about a particular form of business organization and that is the 'corporation'. To become a corporation a business has to go through a legal process which creates a body which has a separate legal existence from its owners and from those who work in or manage it. Gap Inc., BP, Motorola, exist quite separately from the people who work in or manage the organization and from those who own a share in the assets of the business, the shareholders. Shareholders change as shares are bought and sold through various stock exchanges. Managers and other workers change but the corporation continues in existence. It is said to have perpetual succession.

In Friedman's view the corporation should act no differently from the single owner business. Managers are employed as the agents of the principals (the owners) and should work in their interest and that, in his view, is to make as much profit as possible. In that way both dividends and share value increase. Managers are not experts in social welfare or dealing with environmental problems so how would they know how to deploy resources to deal with these problems. Nor, unlike politicians, have they been elected so the use of funds for some purpose other than profit maximization would not only be wasteful it would be undemocratic, particularly as

Counterpoint Box 11.1 Executive responsibility—to whom?

The rise in executive pay has been the subject of much public criticism in both the USA and in Western Europe. This intensified following the global financial crisis of 2007/08.

Hutton (2011) reported that the median pay for the chief executives of the 100 largest companies on the London Stock Exchange had risen to 88 times UK median earnings and 202 times the national minimum wage, up from 47 times and 124 times respectively in 2000. Bebchuk *et al.* (2009) estimate that the top executive teams of US investment banks Bear Stearns and Lehman Brothers received about US$1.4 billion and US$1 billion respectively from cash bonuses and equity sales during 2000–08 and suggested that this might have encouraged managers to take excessive risks, an important cause of the meltdown in the global financial system. A study by the Hay group (2011) found no correlation between CEO pay in the UK and business performance.

Bebchuk and Fried (2006) argue that managers use their power to influence their compensation packages. As a result they end up being paid excessive sums that do not lead to improved company performance and therefore do not serve shareholders' interests. They contend that executive pay is significantly decoupled from company performance. They argue that executives owe their primary duty to shareholders but that corporate governance in the USA disenfranchises the true owners, the shareholders.

Lipton and Savitt (2007) defend multi-million dollar executive pay packages, arguing that highly paid executives have built great firms. They challenge Bebchuk's idea that corporations are the private property of shareholders. They insist that shareholders are merely owners of shares, not of the firm. Their right to exercise control over the company should be limited but they have the right to share in the profits generated by it. They contend that it is management's prerogative to do what is in the best interest of all the corporation's stakeholders by balancing the interests of shareholders as well as other stakeholders such as management and employees, creditors, regulators, suppliers, and consumers.

Sources: Hutton, W. (2011) Hutton Review of Fair Pay in the Public Sector, HM Treasury, March; Hay Group (2011) Getting the Balance Right: The Ratio of CEO to Average Employee Pay and What It Means for Company Performance; Bebchuk, L. A. and Fried, J. M. (2006) 'Pay without Performance: Overview of the Issues'. *Academy of Management Perspectives*, Feb, Vol 20, Issue 1; Bebchuk, L. A., Cohen, A., and Holger, S. (2010) 'The Wages of Failure: Executive Compensation at Bear Stearns and Lehman 2000–2008'. *Yale Journal on Regulation*, Summer, Vol 27, Issue 2; Lipton, M. and Savitt, W. (2007) 'The Many Myths of Lucian Bebclink'. *Virginia Law Review*, May, Vol 93, Issue 3

managers as a group do not tend to be representative of the population at large, usually being more conservative than the general population.

Friedman's criticisms of CSR were not that business did not have a social role but that its role and its obligation to society was to supply goods and services at the lowest price possible. His view was founded in a fundamental belief in the virtues of a free market economy in which each player contributed, without knowing it, to the greater good of society.

A further criticism by Friedman was the notion of a corporation, a legal creation, assuming moral responsibilities. In his words, 'What does it mean to say that "business" has responsibilities? Only people can have responsibilities. A corporation is an artificial person and in this sense may have artificial responsibilities, but business as a whole cannot be said to have responsibilities, even in this vague sense' (Friedman 1970). There is no argument that the corporation exists as a separate legal entity with legal rights and duties. It is capable of owning and disposing of assets, employing people, entering into contracts, incurring and being owed debts, inflicting and suffering damage, suing and being sued. If it (the corporation) is held responsible for these actions why then can it not be morally responsible for its actions? As Goodpaster and Mathews (1982) point out 'if a group can act like a person in some ways, then we can expect it to behave like a person in other ways'. We have no problem referring to a company's business strategy or its marketing plan. We would not think or refer to these examples as an individual's strategy or plan. This is because corporations have complex internal decision-making structures which arrive at decisions in line with corporate goals (French 1979). The outcome is rarely attributable to any one person but is usually the result of a series of discussions between directors, managers, and staff. In other words the corporation acts just like an individual. Examples from legal cases support the difficulty in identifying individuals responsible for corporate decisions. In *P & O European Ferries (Dover) Ltd* ((1991) 93 Cr App R 72) Mr Justice Turner ruled that a company may be properly indicted for manslaughter. That case however, ended in the acquittal of the defendant company because the Crown could not show that a 'controlling mind' had been grossly negligent. The 'controlling mind' of a company is somebody who can be shown to be in control of the operations of a company and not responsible to another person. In large companies the 'controlling mind' has proved difficult to identify but the smaller the company the easier it is to identify. In *R v Kite and OLL Ltd*, the 'Lyme Bay' disaster, several school children, who were canoeing across Lyme Bay, died because of the poor safety standards of the company. In this case it was possible to identify the Managing Director, Peter Kite, as the 'controlling mind' and he was successfully prosecuted for corporate manslaughter. It was because of the difficulty of identifying the 'controlling mind' that the UK strengthened legislation in this area with the introduction of The Corporate Manslaughter and Corporate Homicide Act 2007 (CMA) which came into force throughout the UK on 6 April 2008.

Another argument supporting the case for assigning moral responsibility to a company is the existence not just of a decision-making structure but also of a set of beliefs and values which guide individual decision-making. This is commonly known as the 'culture' of the organization. Nowadays this is more often than not enshrined in a written statement such as the one below for the HSBC group. Note that its values include 'ethical and sustainable business practice'.

Group Values

The HSBC Group Values describe how employees should interact with each other internally, with customers and with the wider community. All employees are expected to have and reflect Group Values.

Open to different ideas and cultures

- Having a diverse and inclusive culture underpinned by a meritocratic approach to recruitment, selection, and promotion
- Putting the team's interests ahead of the individual's
- Being a fair and objective employer

Connected with our customers, community, and each other

- Proactive and hands-on management at all levels
- Appropriate delegation of authority with accountability
- Ethical and sustainable business practice, taking responsibility for the social and environmental impacts of decisions, especially in relation to lending and investment. Commitment to the welfare of communities and the environment

Dependable and doing the right thing

- Openly esteemed commitment to quality, competence, truth, and fair dealing
- Commitment to complying with the spirit and letter of all laws and regulations wherever the Group conducts its business
- Having and displaying highest personal standards of integrity at all levels

Source: www.hsbc.com/1/2/about/values-principles

Learning task

Give examples where HSBC's values, and particularly CSR, might conflict with the quest for profit maximization.

Some find Friedman's view of the modern corporation at odds with reality and particularly the view that modern capitalism is at all like the classical capitalism of economics textbooks where firms have no economic or political power because they are subject to market forces. As we saw in Chapter Three most modern markets are oligopolistic in nature with a few very large and powerful firms dominating many markets. We also saw in Chapter One that these players are active politically using their power to influence policy in their favour, for example, in removing barriers to trade and investment. The idea that the modern corporation is a passive player in the economy is far from the truth. They are powerful players in the world economy whose actions will have an impact both economically and socially so the modern argument about CSR is not whether corporations should engage in CSR but how they do it and why they do it. In terms of how, as we shall see, there is no universal agreement about what constitutes good CSR.

The Moral Case for Corporate Social Responsibility

The moral case for CSR is that it is the right thing to do, not because it yields greater financial return, but as a good corporate citizen with the same social and environmental obligations of any other citizen, i.e. you and me.

The first stage in this argument attributes the status of 'personhood' to the corporation so that they could be considered 'moral agents' and held accountable for their actions. See the argument above (Goodpaster and Mathews, French) which likens the corporation to an individual.

The second strand of the argument emphasizes the social nature of the corporation, i.e. that it is a creation of society and should therefore serve the needs of society. Writers (Donaldson 1982, Anshen 1983) draw on social contract theory (the view that individuals' moral and/or political obligations are dependent upon an agreement between them to form society) to support these arguments. Anshen (op cit) argues that the agreement is one that changes as society evolves. In the 1950s when living conditions were much worse in the west than they are now society's expectation of business (and so their obligation to society) was to produce the goods required by society. Indeed it is as well to remember that, from society's point of view, the basic purpose of business is to be the efficient provider of goods and services. Environmental damage, poor working conditions, and inequalities were seen as a fair price to pay for the improving standard of living. As western societies grew richer then the trade off between material well-being and the quality of life changed and the expectations of business to provide safe places to work, not to damage the environment, to respect human rights etc. have become the expectation confronting business.

Stakeholder theory is an offshoot of this theory which says that business corporations are part of the wider society in which they develop relationships with groups or constituencies (to include biodiversity). These groups are said to have a 'stake' in the organization because the activities of the organization will have an effect on them and, in turn, they can impact on the organization. They are part of a social system and dependent on each other as opposed to the Friedman view which sees them as separate entities operating at arm's length.

Other writers, such as De George (2010), reinforce this view of corporations as social institutions by emphasizing that they are indeed creations of society. They are legal creations permitted by the state. They have to go though a process of application to receive their 'charter of incorporation' which brings them into existence and as such society can then expect these institutions to act for society as a whole. It is the corporations 'licence to operate' which can of course be withdrawn if those expectations are not met. This also underpins the 'corporate citizen' view of the corporations in which the corporation is regarded as an institutional citizen with rights and obligations like any other citizen.

Other arguments put forward include the following:

- Large corporations have enormous economic power and are endowed with substantial resources which they should use responsibly for the good of society.

- Business decisions will have social and environmental consequences so corporations must take responsibility for those decisions.

- Business has been instrumental in causing many of today's problems, such as global warming and resource depletion, and therefore has a responsibility to solve these problems and avoid creating further problems.

The Business Case

The view of the corporation as a private body with an agent(s) acting for a principal(s) is peculiar to the UK and North America. In continental Europe and Japan corporations are viewed much more as public bodies with obligations to a wider set of groups, investors, employees, suppliers, and customers. These countries regard corporations as social institutions with a strong public interest agenda. In these companies managers are charged with pursuing the interests of all stakeholders whereas in the UK and North America the maximization of shareholder value is the goal. In the UK, the Companies Act 1985 extended the duties of directors to act not just in the interest of its members (shareholders) but also employees. This has been extended in the Companies Act 2006 which includes the following section:

172 Duty to promote the success of the company

(1) A director of a company must act in the way he considers, in good faith, would be most likely to promote the success of the company for the benefit of its members as a whole, and in doing so have regard (amongst other matters) to—

(a) the likely consequences of any decision in the long term,

(b) the interests of the company's employees,

(c) the need to foster the company's business relationships with suppliers, customers and others,

(d) the impact of the company's operations on the community and the environment,

(e) the desirability of the company maintaining a reputation for high standards of business conduct, and

(f) the need to act fairly as between members of the company

Note that this is to 'promote the success of the company'. Rather than driving a new agenda, this is legislation catching up with reality as most large corporations have already realized that to be successful, or at least not to court disaster, then they must, as a minimum, take into account all of their stakeholders. In the words of the UK government 'It enshrines in statute the concept of Enlightened Shareholder Value which recognises that directors will be more likely to achieve long term sustainable success for the benefit of their shareholders if their companies pay appropriate regard to wider matters such as the environment and their employees.'

According to the UK government 'CSR is essentially about companies moving beyond a base of legal compliance to integrating socially responsible behaviour into their core values, in recognition of the sound business benefits in doing so' (www.csr.gov.uk).

For the UK government then the reason for business to undertake CSR is because it makes good business sense although it would be difficult to sell to business in any other way. In many cases business has come to accept CSR not because of the positive benefits it might bring but because they have awakened to the risks of ignoring it. Scandals such as those at Enron and Worldcom undermined public trust in big business. Shell's failure to consult with or to take into account the reaction of Greenpeace to their proposed sinking of a North Sea oil platform led to international protests and a damaged reputation. Nike, Gap, Big Pharma, Yahoo, BP, and many others have suffered damage to their reputations from well publicized CSR failures. Reputation management is a critical component of corporate success and one of the reasons that, according to Porter and Kramer (2006) 'of the 250 largest multinational corporations, 64% published CSR reports in 2005'. The authors go on to say that much of this was about demonstrating the company's social sensitivity rather than a coherent framework for CSR activities. Very often this activity is lodged in the public relations departments of these companies and is a defensive reaction focused on avoiding the disasters that have struck others.

From the corporation's point of view there is good reason for this as modern consumers are better and more instantly informed than ever. An oil spill in Alaska, a chemical explosion in

India, violation of tribal rights in Nigeria, an explosion on an oil rig in the Gulf, the revelation of child labour in a garment factory all make headline news in the western media. Consumers want to know where the products they consume come from, under what conditions they were produced and, more recently, what size the carbon footprint is. Body Shop built its marketing strategy around being aware of these concerns and responding to them.

Non-governmental organizations (NGOs) such as Greenpeace, Friends of the Earth, Christian Aid, Oxfam, WWF, and Amnesty International are also watching (see for example, www. ethicalcorp.com). There are literally hundreds of thousands, if not millions, of these organizations operating across the world, many of them exceedingly well resourced. (See Crane and Matten (2010) Chapter 10 for a discussion of civil society.) Greenpeace operates across more than 40 countries and has 2.8 million supporters actively financing its activities as well as receiving money from charitable foundations. Oxfam works in over 70 countries with an income, in the 11 months to March 2010, of £318 million.

Another reason that many large corporations have increased the size of their CSR departments is to deal with NGOs. NGOs of course differ in their view of business. Some, such as the Business Council for Sustainable Business have a membership made up of some of the world's leading companies. The council has as part of its vision 'to support the business license to operate' by being a 'leading business advocate on sustainable development' (www.wbcsd.org). So not all NGOs are critical of business but many are and some, such as Oxfam, have a quite different view of the world and a different set of priorities especially in the international arena. Sensible companies try to build relationships with relevant NGOs either through dialogue or in some cases through partnership. The World Food programme, managed by the UN, has a number of corporate partners including TNT, Caterpillar, LG, Unilever, and Vodafone. TNT is a global mail, express, and logistics company and supports WWF by organizing airlift services in emergencies such as the Asian tsunami in 2004 and the Haiti earthquake in 2010. It also gives money and supplies and has an active volunteering programme with staff seconded to WFP around the world (http://www.movingtheworld.org/our_partnership_with_wfp) (www.wfp.org).

Mini Case Proctor and Gamble Unilever and Sustainability

Proctor and Gamble and Unilever are two of the world's largest consumer products companies competing head on. Both claim to recognize their responsibility to society. P & G, echoing one of the earlier arguments for CSR, explain their purpose as:

> Companies like P&G are a force in the world. Our market capitalization is greater than the GDP of many countries, and we serve consumers in more than 180 countries. With this stature comes both responsibility and opportunity. Our responsibility is to be an ethical corporate citizen . . .

And for Unilever: Our corporate purpose states that to succeed requires 'the highest standards of corporate behaviour towards everyone we work with, the communities we touch, and the environment on which we have an impact'.

Both have announced new sustainability initiatives. Unilever aims by 2020 to:

- halve the environmental impact of their footprint;
- help more than 1 billion people take action to improve their health and well-being; and
- source 100% of their agricultural raw material sustainably.

While P & G aim to:

- power their plants with 100% renewable energy;
- use 100% renewable or recycled materials for all products and packaging;
- power their plants with 100% renewable energy;

➜

- use 100% renewable or recycled materials for all products and packaging; and
- design products to maximize the conservation of resources.

This is not entirely altruistic as both recognize the business benefits of this type of action. As Unilever's CEO Paul Polman put it 'consumers want more. They see food shortages, malnutrition and climate change, and governments are not addressing those problems. Companies that do this will get a competitive advantage. Those that do not will put themselves at risk.'

Sources: www.pg.com/en_UK/company.shtml; www.unilever.co.uk; *Guardian*, 15 November 2010, Unilever unveil sustainability vision

Source: Cultura

As we have seen CSR is definitely on the corporate agenda but whether business sees this as a duty to society, in the sense implied here, is open to great doubt. The evidence presented earlier paints a picture of business reluctantly taking up CSR as a defensive reaction to protect reputation possibly leading to a recognition that CSR activities may well improve business performance. Many commentators would contend that the argument is a distraction. In the words of David Grayson (Doughty Chair of Corporate Responsibility, Cranfield School of Management):

> In my experience, business leaders committed to Corporate Responsibility do it for a mixture of 'it just makes business sense and it's the right thing to do'. In practice, those percentages may vary for the same business leader depending on the topic; and certainly will vary even within a business and between businesses. I think we should stop searching for the Holy Grail of precise motivation. We would be much more sensibly employed on improving the practice of management so that whatever the particular motivation, the performance can be commercially viable. (Sense and Sustainability: Inaugural lecture 2007)

So what are those 'sound business benefits'?

Leading companies have now moved from the defensive stances of early CSR efforts to explore new ways of engaging with a range of external stakeholders. From their research Sustainability Ltd in their report, 'Buried Treasure, Uncovering the Case for Corporate Sustainability' (available at www.sustainability.co.uk), identify ten benefits which make up the business case. The first four of these are financial performance measures while the remaining six are the financial drivers of that performance.

- Shareholder value—seen by many as the best way to measure performance especially over the long term. CSR activities were found at worst to be neutral and in some instances added considerable value.
- Revenue—there is strong evidence of a positive impact on revenues.
- Operational efficiency—more efficient environmental processes can lead to operational efficiency as can reducing waste. Better motivated staff (see below) can also help companies reduce their operating costs.

- Access to capital—CSR activity has limited impact on availability to capital as investors have traditionally looked only at the financial indicators of performance but as companies improve their CSR strategies and financial performance improves as a result of this, then greater access to capital should follow. There are an increasing number of investment funds which screen out companies that do not meet certain CSR performance criteria, e.g. anything to do with the arms trade. This is commonly known as socially responsible investing (SRI).

- Customer attraction—many surveys show that customers are concerned about the environmental impact of the products they consume, about who made them, and under what conditions they were made. Some are prepared to pay a premium price for goods which they consider meet high CSR standards.

- Brand value and reputation is strongly influenced by CSR activities. The market value of a company is largely dependent upon its reputation and the value of its brands. According to Interbrand (www.interbrand.com/en/best-global-brands/Best-Global-Brands-2010.aspx). Coca Cola is the most valuable brand in the world at US$70.5 billion with IBM second at US$64.7 billion. Harley-Davidson having suffered some negative press was the biggest faller in value in 2010 (–24%) with Toyota (–16%) the second biggest faller after a product recall and seeming reluctance to acknowledge the problem.

- Human and intellectual capital—just as prospective employees are put off from what are seen as bad employers then those seen as leaders in the field of CSR will more easily attract and retain staff. Moreover they are likely to have a more highly motivated workforce.

- Risk profile—i.e. the extent to which a company is at risk of losing reputation. In November 2007 one of Gap's suppliers was found to be using child labour. Gap, a member of the Business Leaders Initiative on Human Rights, a group of companies wishing to incorporate human rights in global business, was quick to respond having the policies and infrastructure already in place.

- Innovation—the incentive to design and deliver new products, services, or processes can come from the drive to undertake CSR activities. Water is vital to Coca Cola so they are involved in a number of projects (see www.thecoca-colacompany.com/citizenship/environment.html), one of which is plant performance in which they have been able to improve water use efficiency by more than 13% since 2004.

- Licence to operate—this is the level of acceptance by customers, local communities, NGOs, and other stakeholders of the companies' right to operate. A poor reputation can lead to constant criticism from activist groups and a loss of reputation. Conversely those with a good reputation can often more easily recover when things go wrong. Monsanto is the world's leading producer of genetically modified seed and also adopts fairly aggressive marketing methods. It does not seem to be particularly concerned about its 'licence to operate' and as a result tends to be more targeted by activists than do similar companies.

Learning Task

Look up TNT's website at www.tnt.com and focusing on the Corporate Responsibility and Partnerships sections identify the CSR activities of TNT. Using the list above explain how these activities will benefit TNT.

Global CSR

Is global CSR any different from domestic CSR? Not in principle but the implementation is far more complex. Take the argument above that modern CSR reflects the changed expectations of society and that the trade off between growth and the negative impacts of that growth is no longer acceptable. China could justifiably argue that they are at that stage in their growth where the cost of their improved living standards, in terms of damage to the environment, is acceptable. They are of course growing in entirely different conditions in which global warming is a threat to everybody but what does this mean for the global corporations operating in China? Should they be able to operate under the less stringent environmental legislation that exists in that country or should they be working to the same standards that they work to in their home economy? Is there an obligation on the West to share new technologies with developing countries as much of the growth of companies in the West took place in an era of less stringent environmental controls?

Countries differ not just in their environmental legislation but also in the institutions that govern the countries that in some cases are not very effective. They also differ in their customs and their culture (see Chapter Six). Setting up operations overseas because it is cheaper might be very attractive but why is it cheaper? Wages are lower, working hours longer, health and safety regulations are lax and not policed very well. Is this acceptable? Child labour is illegal but quite common. Would you tolerate this if these were your factories or if it was happening in your supplier's factories? If the answer is no and an undercover investigator discovers this and reports it to the western media, how would you react? Would you instantly close down the factory? What effect would this have on the children working there? These are the types of issues facing global companies in their everyday operations and it isn't that there is one domestic set of circumstances and one overseas set of circumstances, every country will have some differences. Shell, for example, is a global group of companies working in more than 130 countries and territories and employing 108,000 people worldwide.

Whose standards?

Global companies have the problem of doing business in many countries in which the 'ways of doing things' differ. They therefore have the difficult task of deciding which standards to adopt. Should they take a principled stand and adopt a universal set of values wherever they operate or take a different approach in each country and operate according to the appropriate standards of that country? The first approach appears morally attractive in that we have a tendency to assume that our own standards are the 'right' or 'best' standards and we therefore tend to judge others by those standards but this can result in an ethnocentric (believing that the customs and traditions of your own nationality are better than those of others) morality which opens multinational companies to the charge of cultural imperialism. It would satisfy those critics who accuse MNCs of exploiting cultural differences for their own benefit but it may offend those host cultures whose accepted practices may be very different or it may well be impossible to operate without adopting host country practices. For example, when Google entered China it agreed to some censorship of search results to comply with the Chinese government. This offended many in the West used to freedom of expression but Google argued that it would be more damaging to pull out of China altogether. Google moved its operation to Hong Kong in March 2011 in an attempt to bypass Chinese censorship but it is possible that the service will be completely blocked (see Mini Case in Chapter Seven).

Learning Task

Consider the claim put forward by Google that it would be more damaging to pull out of China alto-gether. Why would it be more damaging? Draw up a map of stakeholders and assess the impact of withdrawal on each of them. Do you think Google was right to stay in China and how will the move to Hong Kong affect its stakeholders?

 You might want to access the website of the pressure group Reporters without Borders (www.rsf.org) or visit the **Online Resource Centre** for the book to access related BBC news items and an article from the *Guardian* newspaper.

The other extreme is termed **cultural relativism** and put simply says 'when in Rome do as the Romans do'. This approach recognizes that countries and cultures are different and that MNCs in operating in different countries should recognize and accommodate those differences. This is often used as a reason by MNCs to adopt practices that enhance their profits, such as the employ-ment of child labour or lax health and safety standards, which would be questionable in their home country.

These extreme ethical approaches are useful to business decision-makers to the extent that they do serve to highlight the problems. Donaldson (1989) has suggested that there are some universal principles that companies and nations could agree to work towards. This entails respect for and promotion of some minimal rights:

- freedom of physical movement;
- ownership of property;
- freedom from torture;
- fair trial;
- freedom from discrimination;
- physical security;
- free speech and association;
- education;
- political participation; and
- subsistence.

One might argue about which rights should be included and this may appear as a peculiarly western set of rights but this approach to prescribing minimum standards is the approach that has been developed albeit in a fragmented fashion. Many companies have responded to the CSR debate by developing their own codes of conduct for their global operations and many interna-tional organizations have developed principles which seek to guide companies to best practice in CSR. The United Nations (UN) Global Compact is one such initiative in which the UN and several campaigning organizations such as Oxfam and Amnesty International came together to agree a set of principles for CSR. There were originally nine principles in the areas of human rights, labour, the environment and a tenth concerning anti-corruption was added in 2004. This initiative was launched in 2000 and now has about 8,000 participants (of which 6,066, are businesses (www.unglobalcompact.org/news/95-01-20-2011) in 130 countries.

The Ten Principles

The principles are derived from:

- The Universal Declaration of Human Rights
- The International Labour Organization's Declaration on Fundamental Principles and Rights at Work
- The Rio Declaration on Environment and Development
- The United Nations Convention Against Corruption

The Global Compact asks companies to embrace, support, and enact, within their sphere of influence, a set of core values in the areas of human rights, labour standards, the environment, and anti-corruption:

Table 11.1 UN Global Compact Principles

Human Rights	Principle 1: businesses should support and respect the protection of internationally proclaimed human rights.
	Principle 2: make sure that they are not complicit in human rights abuses.
Labour Standards	Principle 3: businesses should uphold the freedom of association and the effective recognition of the right to collective bargaining.
	Principle 4: the elimination of all forms of forced and compulsory labour.
	Principle 5: the effective abolition of child labour.
	Principle 6: the elimination of discrimination in respect of employment and occupation.
Environment	Principle 7: businesses should support a precautionary approach to environmental challenges.
	Principle 8: undertake initiatives to promote greater environmental responsibility.
	Principle 9: encourage the development and diffusion of environmentally friendly technologies.
Anti-Corruption	Principle 10: businesses should work against corruption in all its forms, including extortion and bribery.

Source: www.unglobalcompact.org

Learning task

Use the UN's website on the Global Compact to explain why adherence to these principles is in the best interest of business.

Four of the major weaknesses of these codes are:

1. Not many of the world's MNCs are members. 6,066 sounds like a lot but is actually only a small proportion of the world's tens of thousands of MNCs. However, many of those who have joined are important in terms of size and reputation.

2. The codes are voluntary and the UN cannot afford to be too selective about who joins the initiative.

3. It is difficult to monitor the impact the Compact is making.

4. No effective sanctions for breaches of the code exist although over 2,000 companies have been expelled from the Compact for failing to report progress for two consecutive years.

Companies that join are simply required to work towards implementation of the principles. They do have to report annually on their activities through what the Compact refers to as 'Communication on Progress'. This entails a statement of continuing support, a description of practical actions, and a measurement of outcomes. In measuring outcomes participants are encouraged to use the Global Reporting Initiative (GRI). The GRI is an attempt to produce standard sustainability reporting guidelines and make it as routine for companies as financial reporting. The GRI produces a standard format for companies to report on their economic, environmental, and social performance. Over 1,000 organizations, ranging from companies, public bodies, NGOs, and industry groups, use the guidelines which makes it the most common framework in use.

For an article critical of the Global Compact see UN Global Compact: *Ten years of greenwashing* by John Entine in *Ethical Corporate Magazine* at www.jonentine.com/ethical_corporation/2010_11_United_Nations_Global_Compact.pdf and for a response see http://unglobalcompact.wordpress.com and http://globalcompactcritics.blogspot.com for a critical blog.

The picture then is of a complex global system in which the ability of the state to look after the public interest, even in relatively developed economies, is diminished. Global companies operate in many states which are weak and often corrupt. There are major world issues such as climate change, poverty, health issues, human rights, corruption, and ecosystem problems which are also beyond the powers of national governments and internationally there is a lack of effective governance. There is also a growing number of very active NGOs, often campaigning on a single issue, who are demanding action from companies. In turn the health of companies will in the long term depend on the health of the global economic, social and political, and environmental systems. The case for CSR rests on a recognition by companies of this scenario and that they are in a unique position to address these issues. Many have responded, perhaps for defensive reasons, by engaging with their stakeholders and developing codes of conduct for their global activities. International organizations have also added to the drive for CSR by developing their own codes or sets of principles to which they encourage companies to adhere.

Having examined the case for CSR we now turn to examine in more detail some of the specific issues facing global companies.

Corruption

Corruption is a major issue for international business. Corruption occurs when organizations or individuals profit improperly through their position. According to the World Bank,

'It involves behaviour on the part of officials in the public and private sectors, in which they improperly and unlawfully enrich themselves and/or those close to them, or induce others to do so, by misusing the position in which they are placed.' It occurs in both the public and the private sectors, for example, when private businesses want public contracts or licences or when private firms wish to do business with others. Bribery is only one example of corruption. It can also include **extortion**, that is where threats and violence are used to get someone to act or not act in a certain way, **favouritism**, **nepotism**, **embezzlement**, fraud, and illegal monetary contributions to political parties (SIDA, see www.sida.se). In some cultures corruption is accepted as the norm and many commentators, and sometimes the law, make a distinction between bribes and so called 'facilitation payments' which are everyday small payments made to officials to 'ease the wheels of business'. International pressure groups such as Transparency International make no such distinction.

What's Wrong with Bribery and Corruption?

According to Transparency International it is impossible to gauge the cost of corruption although they present a number of informed estimates (see www.transparency.org.uk/corruption-data). Sue Hawley (2000) estimated that western businesses pay massive amounts of money to gain contracts or concessions they would not otherwise have won. She estimates that something in the order of US$80 billion a year is paid and that this is about the amount that the UN believes would be needed to eradicate world poverty. The BBC reported in December 2010 (www.bbc.co.uk/news/world-africa-11913876) that the Kenyan government had said that it could be losing up to one third of its national budget to corruption. This of course only reflects the direct financial costs and takes no account of the additional social cost when funds do not reach the intended recipients. The cost of these bribes falls mainly on the poor whether it is through the diversion of aid money into corrupt officials' pockets or the hiking of prices when the cost of a bribe is passed on in raised prices to consumers.

- Bribery and corruption undermine the proper workings of a market economy which can seriously reduce GDP in the poorest countries. It distorts price and cost considerations so that resources are not necessarily used in the most efficient way. Decisions are based on 'who pays the biggest bribes' rather than price, quality, service, and innovation. This raises prices for everyone which has the greatest impact on the poor.

- Resources are often diverted away from public service projects such as schools and hospitals towards more high profile projects such as dams and power stations where there is more scope for improper payments. This again impacts most on the poor who are denied vital public services.

- Corruption is ethically wrong. It is an abuse of power which undermines the integrity of all concerned.

- Corruption undermines the democratic process and the rule of law. Just as business has to earn its licence to operate so does government. Politicians, government officers, and institutions all lose their legitimacy in a climate of corruption. Again the poor are likely to be the biggest losers in such a situation.

- The environment is also likely to suffer in such a regime through the lack of environmental legislation or its non-enforcement as corrupt officials fill their pockets in return for turning a blind eye.

- For business there are several risks:
  - the risk that accusations of corruption, whether proved or not, can lead to loss of reputation;
  - a legal risk. Bribery and corruption is generally illegal wherever it occurs but even if not, because of international pressure (the UN convention against corruption), it is becoming increasingly illegal at home to engage in these practices elsewhere;
  - in paying bribes there is no certainty you get what you want and no recourse to any retribution or compensation if you do not;
  - if you are known as a bribe payer then repeat demands are likely to be made;
  - it adds substantially to the cost of doing business;
  - if you cheat so will your competitors. It makes doing business much more difficult; and
  - employees and other stakeholders will lose trust in the business.

Transparency International was founded in 1993 to fight corruption. Each year Transparency International produces the **Corruption Perceptions Index**. This index ranks 178 countries according to the level of corruption perceived to exist among public officials and politicians. A score of zero indicates highly corrupt and a score of ten very clean.

On the map (Figure 11.1), the darker the colour the higher the perceived incidence of corruption which is generally low in North America, Western Europe, and Australasia and high in Central and South America, Africa, Asia, and Eastern Europe.

Figure 11.1 Corruption Perceptions Index 2010

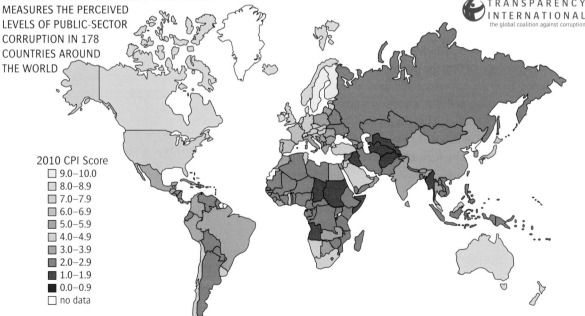

Learning Task

Access the website of Transparency International at www.transparency.org and access the Corruption Perceptions Index on which the map above is based.

1. Explain what the Corruption Perceptions Index measures.

2. Look up Table 2.1 in Chapter Two. For each of the countries plot on a graph their rank and CPI score against their GDP. What conclusions can you draw from your graph?

Mini Case Alcatel-Lucent

Alcatel-Lucent is a French global communications company. According to their CSR website 'Alcatel-Lucent is committed to ethical business conduct. As a company, we understand that only by upholding the highest level of business ethics and personal integrity can we achieve and sustain long-term business excellence. For this reason, integrity is a core value for Alcatel-Lucent from its inception' (www.alcatel-lucent.com/csr/htm/en/aResponsibleBehavior.html).

In 2010 Alcatel-Lucent agreed to a settlement of US$137 million in penalties and fines and a three-year French anti-corruption compliance monitor to evaluate the effectiveness of their internal controls, record-keeping, and financial reporting policies and procedures. Alcatel-Lucent had been accused of bribing government officials to win business.

Source: www.istockphoto.com

Much of Alcatel's business was done through subsidiaries who used consultants to pay more than US$8 million in bribes to government officials in Costa Rica, Malaysia, Honduras, and Taiwan between 2001 and 2006. These bribes were either not documented or recorded as 'consulting fees'.

'Alcatel and its subsidiaries failed to detect or investigate numerous red flags suggesting their employees were directing sham consultants to provide gifts and payments to foreign government officials to illegally win business,' said Robert Khuzami, director of The Securities and Exchange Commission's division of enforcement.

In an earlier prosecution by the Department of Justice two Alcatel employees had been indicted on charges of corruption, money laundering, and conspiracy. One is still at large and the other pleaded guilty. Interestingly Costa Rican law recognizes the concept of 'social damage' implying that a financial

retribution should be made by those found guilty of a corruption crime to repair the damage caused to a society. Alcatel paid US$10 million to the Costa Rican authorities in social damages.

Steve Reynolds, Alcatel-Lucent General Counsel made the following statement following the US$137 million settlement:

> We take responsibility for and regret what happened and have implemented policies and procedures to prevent these violations from happening again. The violations largely occurred prior to the merger of Alcatel and Lucent Technologies and involved improper activities in several countries. Alcatel-Lucent, created as a result of the merger of Alcatel and Lucent Technologies at the end of 2006, is a radically different company today.

Source: US Securities and Exchange Commission at www.sec.gov/news/press/2010/2010-258.htm; Transparency International; www.alcatel-lucent.com/wps/portal/pressroom

Counterpoint Box 11.2 Corruption—is it always a bad thing?

Corruption occurs on a large scale and is growing. Transparency International (2009) estimates that, corrupt politicians and government officials in developing countries receive bribes believed to total some US$20 to 40 billion annually.

In 2006, Paul Wolfowitz the head of the World Bank said:

> corruption is often at the very root of why governments do not work. Today one of the biggest threats to development in many countries . . . is corruption. It weakens fundamental systems, it distorts markets, and it encourages people to apply their skills and energies in nonproductive ways. In the end, governments and citizens will pay a price, in lower incomes, in lower investment, and in more volatile economic fluctuations . . . where corruption is rampant, contracts are unenforceable, competition is skewed, and the costs of doing business becomes stifling (web.worldbank.org).

However, corruption is not always seen as a bad thing. Chang (2008) argues that bribery does not inevitably slow down economic development. For example, where a public servant takes a bribe from a firm and invests that money in a project as productive as the firm would have done, then the act of bribery may have little or no adverse effect on efficiency or growth. He also asserts that a company getting a contract through bribery may be the most efficient contender for the contract. In fact, it is likely that the most efficient firms can afford to pay the highest bribes. Some economists see corruption as rectifying market failure. A government may set a price for a good or service which does not reflect market pressures of supply and demand. A bribe could result in the authorities turning a blind eye to illegal trading on the black market which could move the price closer to an equilibrium level thereby bringing about a more efficient allocation of resources.

Sources: Chang, H.-J. (2008) *Bad Samaritans: The Myth of Free Trade and the Secret History of Capitalism*. New York: Bloomsbury Press; Underkuffler, L. S. (2009) 'Defining Corruption: Implications for Action' in Rotberg, R. I. (ed), *Corruption, Global Security, and World Order*. Cambridge: Brookings Institution; Transparency International, Global Corruption Report 2009

Child Labour

Trying to arrive at a clear picture of child work is a difficult task. We are all familiar with the horror pictures of child mine workers, soldiers, and prostitutes but most child work takes place within the family in agriculture and domestic work and in societies where this is often seen as culturally acceptable. The International Labour Office (ILO) divides child work into three different categories:

- Economically active: a very wide category which refers to any form of productive work, paid or unpaid.
- Child labour: work that is done by a child under the specified age for work which either deprives them of schooling, causes them to leave school early, or requires a combination of schooling and long hours of work.
- Hazardous work: the worst form of child labour exposing children to conditions which are damaging to their mental, physical, and emotional development and which the international community has agreed to try to end.

In 2008 there were 306 million children aged between 5 and 17 who were economically active with 215 million involved in child labour and more than 115 million (74 million boys and 41 million girls) undertaking hazardous work. They do it because their survival and that of their families depend on it (ILO 2010).

Not all work done by children is considered harmful and therefore in policy terms it is not just a case of eliminating all child work. Work that does not damage health or interfere with schooling may be considered positive in contributing to personal development by developing skills and experience and preparing children for adult life, so called 'child work'. The ILO has two conventions relating to child labour. Convention 138 allows 'child work' but aims at the abolition of child labour and stipulates that the minimum age for entry into the workforce should not be less than the minimum age for finishing school. Convention 182 calls for elimination of the worst forms of child labour for all under 18s. This includes slavery, forced recruitment for use in armed conflict, prostitution, any illicit activity, and work which is likely to harm the health, safety, and morals of children. These conventions lay down the basic principles to be implemented by ratifying countries and are tools for governments to use, in consultation with employers and workers, to draft legislation to conform with internationally acceptable standards. Nearly 87% of ILO members covering 77% of the world's children have ratified convention 182 and 79%, covering less than 63% have ratified convention 138. This still leaves a large number of children in countries that have made no commitment to either convention.

Child labour is not simply a problem of the developing world although most takes place there. The Asian Pacific region has the highest number of child workers with 96.4 million representing nearly 14.8% of the age group. This figure had declined by 26 million from 2004. Sub-Saharan Africa has the highest incidence of child labour at 28.4% and unlike all the other areas the numbers had increased since 2004 from 49.3 million to 58.2 million.

Mini Case Cocoa Production in West Africa

The global chocolate market is worth more than US$5 billion per year. Most of that chocolate starts life in West Africa where 75% of the world's cocoa production is grown. The Ivory Coast is the largest producer with 40% of world production. Here some 650,000 small, family-run farms of less than 4 hectares grow cocoa as a cash crop alongside crops grown for food. Farms are often remote and as mechanization is not appropriate production is labour intensive.

The global supply chain is quite complex with many intermediaries before the chocolate reaches the final consumer. Cocoa growers generally sell to a middleman for cash once or twice a year and have to take whatever price they can get. The middleman sells on to processors or exporters. Prices are ultimately determined on the London Cocoa Terminal Market and the New York Cocoa Exchange but like many cash crops the farmer receives a fraction of the world price.

There is therefore great pressure on the farmer to keep costs down and one way of achieving this is to employ child labour. Most of the children are under 14, kept from schooling, work 12 hour days, apply pesticides, and use machetes to clear fields and split harvested cocoa pods to extract the beans. All of this falls into the ILO convention 182 of 'the worst form of child labour'.

In 2000 a British TV documentary was broadcast claiming that many children were working as slaves in the Ivory Coast. Because the demand for child labour outstrips the supply children were purchased from the neighbouring states of Burkino Faso, Mali, and Togo. Impoverished parents would receive between £70 and £100 for each child, depending on the age. These children, some as young as six, were forced to endure the harsh working conditions, long hours, and many also faced physical abuse by their masters.

An industry protocol (the Harkin-Engel protocol) was signed on 19 September 2001 which acknowledged that there were problems of forced child labour in West Africa and made a commitment to eliminate the problem. The protocol also established the International Cocoa Initiative made up of chocolate companies, confectionery trade associations, NGOs, and trade unions to work with governments to end the worst forms of child labour. The University of Tulane, under contract to the US Department of Labor, oversees the protocol and reports on activities in the Chocolate industry. Its fourth report found ➜

➜ that there were 820,000 children working in cocoa in the Ivory Coast, only 40% were enrolled in school and only 5% were paid for their work. 8,243 (about 1%) children had been reached as a result of interventions by public and private stakeholders and Tulane concluded that this was not sufficient in light of commitments under the protocol.

Sources: www.bbc.co.uk; Anti-Slavery International, The Cocoa Industry in West Africa: A History of Exploitation; Schrage, E. and Ewing, A. (2005) 'The Cocoa Industry and Child Labour'. *The Journal of Corporate Citizenship*; University of Tulane report is available at http://childlabor-payson.org

Also interesting is the International Labor Rights Global Exchange, Green America, and Oasis USA, 'Time to Raise the Bar: The Real Corporate Social Responsibility Report for the Hershey Company'. Available online: www.laborrights.org/stop-childforced-labor/cocoa-campaign/resources/12395

Source: www.istockphoto.com

Why do Children Work?

Reasons for child work can be divided into push and pull, or supply and demand, factors.

On the supply side or what pushes children into work:

- Poverty—poverty remains the most important factor which pushes children into work.
- Lack of educational opportunities—poor educational facilities or expensive facilities can exacerbate the problem.
- Family breakdown—divorce, death, or illness can leave the family unit short on income. This has become a major problem in Africa because of the HIV/AIDS epidemic.
- Cultural practices—in many countries it is the practice for young children to help the family by looking after younger brothers and sisters or helping out on the land, by collecting firewood, or tending chickens for example.

On the demand side or what pulls children into work:

- Cheap labour—employers tend to pay children less than their adult counterparts. Some, especially domestic workers, work unpaid.
- Obedience—even where children are paid the same rate as adults employers often prefer to employ children as they are much easier to control.
- Skills—the so-called 'nimble fingers' argument especially in industries such as carpet weaving. Probably a mythical argument but one which is used to justify the employment of children.
- Inadequate laws—or poorly understood and policed laws enable employers to continue employing children.
- Poor infrastructure—establishing the age of children in some countries can be difficult.

What's wrong with child labour?

- Child labour is a denial of fundamental human rights. The United Nations has adopted the Convention on the Rights of the Child. Article 32 says that children should not be engaged in work which is hazardous, interferes with education, or is harmful to health.
- It steals their childhood from them.
- It prevents their education.
- Children are exploited by paying them low wages or no wages at all.
- Children often work in poor conditions which can cause long-term health problems.
- It perpetuates poverty because lack of education limits earning potential.
- It can mean lower wages for everybody as they swell the labour supply and are usually paid lower wages than adults.
- They replace adult labour because they are cheaper to employ and easier to control.
- It is a long-term cost to society as children are not allowed to fulfil their potential as productive human beings.

Millennium Development Goals

In 2000 the 189 members of the United Nations adopted the **Millennium Development Goals**. Eight goals with associated targets were established for the alleviation of world poverty and general development goals. These goals had been developed at a number of conferences that had taken place in the 1990s so although they were announced in 2000 the baseline for assessing progress towards them is 1990. The target date for achieving most of these is 2015. The goals and targets are:

Table 11.2 Millennium Development Goals

	Goal		Target
1	Eradicate extreme poverty and hunger	1	Halve, between 1990 and 2015, the proportion of people whose income is less the US$1 a day
		2	Halve, between 1990 and 2015, the proportion of people who suffer from hunger
2	Achieve universal primary education	3	Ensure that, by 2015, children everywhere, boys and girls alike, will be able to complete a full course of primary schooling
3	Promote gender equality and empower women	4	Eliminate gender disparity in primary and secondary education, preferably by 2005, and to all levels of education no later than 2015
4	Reduce child mortality rate	5	Reduce by two thirds, between 1990 and 2015, the under-five mortality rate
5	Improve maternal health	6	Reduce by three quarters, between 1990 and 2015, the maternal mortality ratio

Table 11.2 (*Cont'd*)

	Goal		Target
6	Combat HIV/AIDS and other diseases	7	Have halted by 2015 and begun to reverse the spreads of HIV/AIDS
		8	Have halted by 2015 and begun to reverse the incidence of malaria and other major diseases
7	Ensure environmental sustainability	9	Integrate the principles of sustainable development into country policies and programmes and reverse the loss of environmental resources
		10	Halve, by 2015, the proportion of people without sustainable access to safe drinking water and basic sanitation
		11	By 2020, to have achieved a significant improvement in the lives of at least 100 million slum dwellers
8	Develop a global partnership for development	12	Develop further an open, rule based, predictable, non-discriminatory trading and financial system
		13	Address the special needs of the least developed countries
		14	Address the special needs of landlocked countries and small island developing states
		15	Deal comprehensively with the debt problems of developing countries through national and international measures in order to make debt sustainable in the long term
		16	In cooperation with developing countries, develop and implement strategies for decent and productive work for youth
		17	In cooperation with pharmaceutical companies, provide access to affordable essential drugs in developing countries
		18	In cooperation with the private sector, make available the benefits of new technologies, especially information and communications

Source: The Millennium Development Goals Report Statistical Annex 2006 http://undp.org

The goals are not without their critics. See, for example, Clemens and Moss (2005) who argue that:

> Many poor countries, especially those in Africa, will miss the MDGs by a large margin. But neither African inaction nor a lack of aid will necessarily be the reason. Instead responsibility for near-certain failure lies with the overly-ambitious goals themselves and unrealistic expectation placed on aid.

Others, such as Easterly (2008) criticize the MDGs because they are unfair to Africa whose low starting point made it almost a certainty they would miss the goals. Leo and Barmeier (2010) of the Center for Global Development say that the targets were global and not supposed to be applied to regions or an individual country. Regional reporting tends to mask the fact that some countries are doing well and others not so well. China's good performance for example, masks some poor records and large African countries such as Nigeria, not doing so well, pulls down the regional performance and masks some who have done very well. Many of those not doing well, they note, have been devastated by conflict. What all seem to be agreed on is that the targets have focused the world's attention, generated discussion, and gained public support for aid programmes.

How close is the world to reaching these targets? According to Gordon Brown (the then UK Prime Minister) in a speech to the United Nations (in New York) (31 July 2007) 'we are a million miles away from success'. According to him at current rates of progress the goal of reducing **infant mortality** rates by two-thirds would not be met until 2050, and of providing primary education for every child not until 2100.

For the world as a whole the first target of halving the proportion of people living on less than US$1 a day in developing countries should be met but this has been threatened by the recent food crisis with prices of food soaring and it also depends on achieving a fairly rapid, by historical standards, growth rate in developing countries averaging 3.6% per year. How this affects each area is dependent on the rate of economic growth in that area. Projections are that over 700 million people will be earning less than US$1 per day in 2015 and because of projected low growth rates in Sub-Saharan Africa the number of poor will actually increase to 345 million, nearly half of the world's poor.

The *Guardian* newspaper has set up a section of their website dedicated to development and aid and progress and commentary on the MDGs can be found at (www.guardian.co.uk/global-development).

Mini Case European Cooperative for Rural Development

The European Cooperative for Rural Development (EUCORD) is a Brussels based not-for-profit organization which was registered in 2003. EUCORD specializes in bringing together public and private sector partners to undertake rural development projects. It works with local NGOs to implement these projects and takes responsibility for the overall management of the project and especially the financial reporting and accountability. Its slogan is 'Bringing Market Led Solutions to the Rural Poor'.

Eucord current projects are:

- the West African Potato Value Chain Development Project in Sierra Leone, Guinea, and Senegal to enhance the income of potato farmers, mostly women;

- Dutch funded smallholder rice and sorghum projects in DR Congo and Burundi;

- USAID funded project for vulnerable rural families in Nigeria; and

- two projects in Mali funded by the Alliance for a Green Revolution in Africa.

One of its most successful projects was the West African Sorghum Supply Chain project in Ghana and Sierra Leone. The aim of the project was to develop a reliable supply of sorghum. This five-year scheme received US$2.8 million in funds from the Common Fund for Commodities (a branch of the United Nations) and two private sector drinks companies, Diageo of the UK and Heineken of the Netherlands. Both companies brewed beer in many African countries but used traditional ingredients and imported barley produced elsewhere because conditions for growing barley are not ideal in Africa. Although they brewed beer with sorghum in Nigeria they did not in Ghana and Sierra Leone because they could not be sure of the reliability and quality of the supplies from local producers. But such has been the success of the project that when strong global demand led to rocketing prices for barley they were able to switch to using sorghum as their main ingredient. They are both now looking to brew beer from sorghum in as many African countries as possible. What has started as a socially responsible project in the end turned out to be a sustainable business enterprise.

Sources: www.eucord.org; *Financial Times*, 10 January 2008

Nelson and Prescott (2003) in an article for the United Nations Development Programme point out why it is increasingly in the interests of business for the MDGs to succeed. They point out three business benefits:

- Investing in a sound business environment—a healthy and competent workforce, prosperous consumers, productive companies, and a well governed economy.
- Managing direct costs and risks—environmental degradation, climate change, HIV/AIDS, poor health education systems can add to the cost and risks of doing business.
- Harnessing new business opportunities—innovative companies are finding that the MDGs are not just a matter of responsibility but that they provide long-term business opportunities.

Social entrepreneurship

As in the above case, solving social and environmental problems can be seen as opportunities for business development. In their book, *The Power of Unreasonable People: How Social Entrepreneurs Create Markets and Change the World*, John Elkington and Pamela Hartigan argue that our future depends on what they refer to as 'social entrepreneurs'. Social entrepreneurs are people who look to establish social enterprises to deliver goods and services not yet met by existing market arrangements. The term entrepreneur is not new and these people are no different from the entrepreneurs of old in one sense but the difference is that they are looking for solutions to some of the world's pressing problems. Profits are generated but the aim is to benefit those who are the worst off and grow the business. These are not the major multinational companies but in the main small and medium enterprises who are challenging the accepted ways of doing things. A good example is the UK's Belu Water, a bottled water company that donates all of it profits to global clean water projects. This company has changed the practices of the bottled drinks industry by using carbon-neutral packaging. It uses a compostable bottle made from corn and is challenging others to use similar packaging. With its profits it has installed hand pumps and wells for 20,000 people in India and Mali.

Similarly Bill Gates, founder of Microsoft, has made a case for leading businesses to 'do right by doing good' in what he calls 'creative capitalism'. In this he urged firms to turn their attention to solve the world's big problems, and particularly the world's inequalities. It is possible to make profits in these markets but where they couldn't he hoped recognition would be an incentive. Recognizing that this may not do the trick he also called on governments to favour those companies adopting 'creative capitalism' and pointed out the business benefits discussed earlier in this chapter such as attracting increasingly values-driven young workers.

One aspect of company help to the world's poor has come from an increase in International volunteering. According to Hills and Mahmud (2007) ten years ago there hardly was any international corporate volunteering but now 40% of major American corporations send volunteers around the world to work on development projects.

One example they give is of Pfizer (one of the world's leading pharmaceutical companies) which developed the Global Health Fellow programme in 2002 to send skilled employees to provide technical assistance to partners for 3–6 months in Africa, Latin America, or Asia. 128 fellows had been deployed in 31 countries by September 2007. This provides much improved healthcare to these countries, increases the skill level of local staff, and improves the morale and leadership skills of Pfizer employees. It also helps Pfizer's image and subsequent relationships with global health providers to be seen actively providing solutions on a voluntary basis.

● CHAPTER SUMMARY

In this chapter we defined corporate social responsibility as the economic, social, and environmental obligations firms have to society. Some have a view that the only obligation that business owes to society is to maximize profit but many point out that CSR is not necessarily at odds with profit maximization as there is a strong business argument for pursuing CSR. Others argue that companies have a moral duty to pursue a wider set of objectives.

Firms operating in the international business environment face a more complex set of circumstances than those operating only in their own domestic economy not just because of the different economic and legal context but because of very different cultural norms. Firms must be wary of what might be seen as cultural imperialism. The United Nations has established the Global Compact which seeks to guide companies to best practice in CSR.

Two areas were highlighted to be of particular concern, child labour and corruption both still common in much of the world. The Global Compact has standards to guide companies in both of these areas. The United Nations announced in 2000 the Millennium Development Goals, a set of targets for the alleviation of poverty and other development goals. They recognize the interdependence between growth, poverty reduction, and sustainable development. Some progress has been made but this has been far from uniform across the world or the goals. Their achievement will only be possible if business with government makes it their business in what Bill Gates calls 'creative capitalism'. Social entrepreneurs will also contribute to these major world challenges.

● REVIEW QUESTIONS

1. Explain what commentators mean when they claim that there is only one responsibility of business and that is to make as much money as possible for their owners.

2. Social responsibility is just good PR. Discuss.

3. Explain, using examples, what is meant by cultural relativism.

4. You are working for a large multinational drinks company wanting to set up a bottling plant overseas. In order to obtain planning permission you need to make a facilitation payment (bribe) to a local politician but your company has a strict no bribes policy. The building of the plant will be subcontracted to a domestic construction company and one way round this would be to inflate the payment to this company so that they could make the facilitation payment. What would you do? Justify your decision.

5. Explain what is meant by child labour. What might the consequences be for a major western firm caught employing young children in overseas factories.

6. Define what is meant by social entrepreneurship. Explain, giving examples, how social entrepreneurs might contribute to the achievement of the Millennium Development Goals.

Case Study The Bangladesh Garment Industry

On 12 December 2010 the BBC reported 'At least three people were killed and dozens more injured when police in Bangladesh clashed with garment factory workers demanding better pay, police have said' (www.bbc.co.uk/news/world-south-asia-11978254).

The garment industry is Bangladesh's leading exporter accounting for some 80% of exports. According to the Apparels Bulletin of Bangladesh (www.apparel.com.bd) retail giants including Wal-Mart, JC Penny, Zara, Tesco, IKEA, and Marks and Spencer have all increased orders from Bangladesh. Between July and September of 2010 apparel exports grew by more than 30%. Bangladesh is one of the cheapest places in the world to make clothes and is taking over from China as a cheap source of garments. More than 3 million workers, most of them women, work long hours, often in dangerous conditions for a minimum wage of 3,000 taka per month (about US$43). This has just been increased from 1,662 taka per month (about US$24). That was the rate set in 2006 by the government following serious labour disputes. Workers have been demanding a rate of 5,000 taka (about US$72) per month, far more than the US$30 employers want to pay. The protests in December were over claims by workers that some employers were not paying the new rate or were reclassifying workers to avoid paying the higher rate.

War on Want reported on the Bangladeshi garment industry in 2006, Fashion Victims 1 and followed this up with another report two years later to see if there had been any changes. They focused on six factories producing clothes for Primark, Tesco, and Asda. In 2008 they found little had changed from 2006 when they found people working up to 80 hours per week, sometimes to 3am (Bangladeshi law limits the working week to 60 hours including overtime). They found low pay, late payment of wages, poor working conditions, physical and verbal abuse which was often of a sexual nature, and a complete lack of trade union representation.

Source: www.istockphoto.com   ➜

→ The garment industry has also been the victim of a number of catastrophes because of lax health and safety. In 2005 the Spectrum/Shahriyar Sweater factory collapsed killing 64 workers and injuring 80. In February 2010 a fire at the Garib & Garib Sweater Ltd factory killed 21 workers and injured 50. According to the Clean Clothes Campaign between 2005 and 2010 at least 172 workers have been killed.

In another fire in December 2010 another 28 more workers were killed and at least 100 injured. The fire was on the 9th and 10th floors of a factory owned by the Hameem Group making clothes for western companies such as Gap. This factory was typical of many Bangladeshi garment factories housed in multi-storey buildings not originally intended for this use. The machinery often overloads the electrical circuitry, often the cause of the fires. Some of the fire exits were locked, allegedly to prevent theft, so some suffocated, some jumped to their deaths, and others were trampled in the rush to the few open exits.

Sources: Fashion Victims II, How Clothing Retailers are Keeping Workers in Poverty; War on Want, December 2008; *Financial Times*, 20 December 2010; www.labourbehindthelabel.org/news/item911-thatsitfire

Questions

1. Do western companies have any responsibility for the conditions in Bangladeshi garment factories? Explain your answer.

2. War on Want claim that the aggressive buying practices of retailers undermine voluntary initiatives such as the Ethical Trading Initiative. Some of these companies, including Gap, are members of the Ethical Trading Initiative. What does this say about voluntary initiatives such as the ETI? (You can find information on the ETI and Bangladesh by visiting the links on the supporting **Online Resource Centre** for the book.)

3. How can western companies improve working conditions in these factories?

4. Do western consumers share any responsibility? Is there anything they can do or should governments intervene?

5. How far is Bangladesh from achieving the MDGs?

Online Resource Centre
www.oxfordtextbooks.co.uk/orc/hamilton_webster2e/

Visit the supporting online resource centre for additional material which will help you with your assignments, essays, and research, or you may find these extra resources helpful when revising for exams.

● FURTHER READING

For a textbook exploring ethics and the CSR agenda within the context of globalization read:

● Crane, A. and Matten, D. (2010) *Business Ethics—A European Perspective: Managing Corporate Citizenship and Sustainability in the Age of Globalisation*, 3rd edn. Oxford: Oxford University Press

They also have a blog at:

● http://craneandmatten.blogspot.com/2010/12/top-10-corporate-responsibility-stories.html

For a more recent view of the case against CSR see an article by:

● Aneel Karnani in the Wall Street Journal, http://online.wsj.com/article/SB10001424052748703338004575230112664504890.html?mod=WSJ_hpp_editorsPicks_2

For a book advocating a strategic approach to CSR taking into account global stakeholders see:

● Werther, B. and Chandler, D. (2006) *Strategic Corporate Social Responsibility*. London: Sage Publications

To read more about social entrepreneurship see:

● Elkington, J. and Hartigan, P. (2008) *The Power of Unreasonable People: How Social Entrepreneurs Create Markets and Change the World*. Boston, MA: Harvard Business Press

● REFERENCES

Anshen, M., (1970) 'Changing the Social Contract: A Roll for Business'. Reprinted in Beauchamp, T. and Bowie, N. (eds) (1983) *Ethical Theory and Business*, 2nd edn. London: Prentice Hall

Clemens, M. and Moss, T. (2005) What's Wrong with the Millennium Development Goals, Centre for Global Development

De George, R. (2010) *Business Ethics*, 7th edn. London: Pearson

Donaldson, T. (1982) *Corporations and Morality*. London: Prentice Hall

Donaldson, T. (1989) *The Ethics of International Business*. New York: Oxford University Press

Easterly, W. (2008) 'How the Millennium Goals are Unfair to Africa'. *World Development*, Vol 37, No 1, p 26

French, P. (1979) 'The Corporation as a Moral Person'. *American Philosophical Quarterly*, reprinted in Donaldson, T. and Werhane, P. (eds) (1983) *Ethical Issues in Business*. London: Prentice Hall

Friedman, M. (1970) 'The Social Responsibility of Business Is to Increase it Profits'. Reprinted in Donaldson, T. and Werhane, P. (eds) (1983) *Ethical Issues in Business*. London: Prentice Hall

Goodpaster, K. and Mathews, J. (1982) 'Can a Corporation have a Conscience?' *Harvard Business Review*, reprinted in Beauchamp, T. L. and Bowie, N. E. (1983) *Ethical Theory and Business*, 2nd edn. London: Prentice Hall

Grayson, D. (2007) Sense and Sustainability. Inaugural lecture available at www.som.cranfield.ac.uk/som/research/centres/ccr/downloads/LectureText.pdf

Hawley, S. (2000) Exporting Corruption Privatisation, Multinationals and Bribery, Corner House Briefing 19

Hills, G. and Mahmud, A. (2007) Volunteering for Impact. Best Practices in Individual and Corporate Volunteering

International Labour Office (2010) Global Child Labour Developments: Measuring Trends from 2004 to 2008

Leo, B. and Barmeier, J. (2010) Who are the MDG Trailblazers? A New MDG Progress Index, Center for Global Development, Working Paper 222

Nelson, J. and Prescott, D. (2003) Business and the Millennium Development Goals, A Framework for Action. UNDP and the International Business Leaders Forum

Porter, M. E. and Kramer, M. R. (2006) 'Strategy and Society: The Link Between Competitive Advantage and Corporate Social Responsibility'. *Harvard Business Review*, Vol 84(12)

CHAPTER TWELVE

The Ecological Environment

Dorron Otter

LEARNING OUTCOMES

This chapter will enable you to:

- **Examine the ecological impacts of business activity**

- **Describe the range of global initiatives designed to address ecological problems**

- **Engage in the debates as to the role of business in causing, preventing, and curing ecological damage**

- **Analyse the problems posed by global climate change**

Case Study BP: From British to Beyond Petroleum (and back again!)

In 1997 BP (British Petroleum) officially recognized the potential dangers of man-made climate change and rebranded itself as being 'Beyond Petroleum'. Its attempts to be seen as a 'green' company transcending national boundaries appeared to be working as there was clear market evidence that people were reacting favourably to this new image, however, this was undermined by an explosion at the Texas City refinery which killed 15 people followed by an oil spill that closed the Prudhoe Bay oilfield in Alaska.

On April 2010 an explosion ripped through an offshore oil drilling well, the 'Deepwater Horizon', owned by the company Transocean but leased to BP, killing 11 people and injuring another 18. The location of the well was in the Gulf of Mexico 40 miles off the Louisiana coastline of the United States. The Deepwater Horizon had been designed to operate at very low depths as increasing demand for oil pushes exploration companies to seek new sources in increasingly inaccessible places.

Trying to cap the leak proved to be an enormous technological challenge costing billions of dollars. However, on top of this cost was the cost in terms of human life and injury to the marine environment itself as well as the damage to the economic and social lives of the fishing and tourism businesses that depended on the eco-system of the Gulf of Mexico. The estimated total cost has been put at US$40 billion.

By the time the leak was blocked in September 2010, it is estimated that 4.9 million barrels of oil had leaked into the ocean making this the biggest accidental marine spill in history.

In the immediate furore after the accident President Obama voiced his anger at BP's perceived mismanagement of its operations. His reference to BP as 'British Petroleum' caused a temporary media frenzy as British newspapers attempted to portray this as an attack on British business but Obama was quick to point out that this was not his intention. He was determined

Source: www.istockphoto.com

→ that BP would pay all the costs of the accident itself and the substantial cleanup operation as well as all the compensation to those whose livelihoods would be affected by the oil spill. While Obama was clear that BP should indeed be held wholly responsible for the effects of the accident he also placed the accident in the wider context of our over reliance on fossil fuels and the technical challenges facing oil companies in seeking to develop increasingly inaccessible reserves.

Sources: Wearden, G. (2010) 'BP Oil Spill Costs to Hit £40 Billion' at www.guardian.co.uk/business/2010/nov/02/bp-oil-spill-costs-40-billion-dollars?INTCMP=SRCHt (accessed 14/03/2011); BBC News Excerpts: BP Oil Spill Report at www.bbc.co.uk/news/world-us-canada-12125559 (accessed 16/03/11); BP Deepwater Horizon Accident at www.bp.com/sectiongenericarticle800.do?categoryId=9036575&contentId=7067541 (accessed 16/04/11)

Introduction

This chapter examines the relationship between business activity and the global ecological environment and the debates as to the responsibility of business in terms of its contribution to global ecological problems and the possible responses to dealing with these challenges.

The Ecological Problem

It is simple to outline the basic ecological problem in the context of business. We need to extract the resources that we need for production from the ecological environment. If we exploit the sources of these materials without replacing what we have taken then we face a long-term certain problem of resource depletion. Not all resources can be replaced, especially the fossil fuels on which so much of the world's energy supplies currently depend. It is also clear that the nature of much of our productive processes results in pollution or other forms of ecological damage. Nature itself can provide ways of neutralizing these harmful by-products in the form of 'sinks' such as the oceans, forests, and plants that can absorb the pollutants but the rising acidification of seas, deforestation, and loss of biodiversity are all undermining this. As we will see the debate provoked by attempts to quantify the 'state of the world' in terms of the rate of resource depletion and its effects on food supplies, water availability, and energy or the 'carrying capacity' of the planet is hotly contested.

The Economic Approach to Explaining the Ecological Problem

Economic analysis has been very influential in explaining why there is a conflict between our rational desire to increase our incomes and our ability to increase our quality of life.

While free markets in theory bring about consumer satisfaction and profits for producers, there are dangers of market failure. In relation to the external ecological environment it may well be the case that while markets ensure that private benefits accrue to consumers and producers, there may well be social costs that are incurred. Social costs or **negative externalities** occur as the result of the production or consumption of goods and services but for which no individual or organization pays. They will therefore need to be identified and mechanisms devised to either reduce or eradicate them or at least allow them to be paid for.

Consider the external environmental problems caused by motor transport. Drivers and their passengers or the customers for whom they are driving, derive enormous benefit from this activity and are prepared to pay for the initial costs of the vehicle itself and the substantial running costs including the cost of the (fossil) fuels needed to power the vehicles.

These private costs are not the only costs as there are substantial external environmental costs. Motor vehicles produce pollutants damaging to the environment not least of which is the production of greenhouse gases (GHGs). This is especially the case when cars are on congested roads. The costs of lost output through time delays to people and goods are also considerable. It is argued that it is only fair that motorists sitting inside the relative comfort of their vehicles should pay for the external costs that they are imposing on society through higher road taxes, petrol duties, or even paying to use the road through 'road pricing' schemes such as the congestion charge in London. Of course it might well be that the better environmental solution would be to switch away from car use to greener forms of transport such as buses, trains, cycles and yes, even walking.

This market based analysis of the externalities of production and consumption can point the way to 'correct' the environmental market failures. The simplest way might be to simply devise a way whereby the agents who are responsible for the pollution pay for this. This process of 'internalizing the externality' ensures that the 'polluter pays principle' is implemented and this can be seen as being fair in terms of forcing those responsible for environmental damage to at least pay for it and of course the revenue raised could be used to invest in measures to clean up the environment or 'compensate' those affected. It might also have the effect of discouraging the amount of environmentally damaging behaviour that occurs. Along the same lines regulation could be put in place to 'permit' pollution to take place but only in return for compensation payments.

However, critics of this approach argue that levying of environmental charges may encourage the belief that the problem is solved even though the environmentally damaging behaviour still continues. Robert Goodin sees this as the 'selling of environmental indulgences' and argues that we should just simply not cause the pollution in the first place (Goodin 2007).

Furthermore there are equity implications. Is it 'fair' to charge green taxes if more prosperous members of society or businesses can afford to pay while the poorer ones are unfairly penalized? On a global level, there is an inherent inequity in resource use, and a potential one in the solutions being designed to deal with environmental problems. The developed world got rich by being able to industrialize in a world where the environment was effectively ignored. Now that policies are being implemented to deal with these it would not be fair if the developing world was being asked to adhere to the same levels of environmental protection. It is argued that the richer countries can afford to pay for the cost of the environmental harm they have mostly caused, and developing countries should not be asked to adopt environmental regulations at their early stage in the development process.

The analysis of ecological problems as the negative externalities of market failure has become commonly accepted, but what is contested is where the responsibility for such externalities should fall, and the range of policy measures we should adopt to address these.

Business as Usual

One of the biggest fears for those concerned about the environmental impact of businesses is that, even where they recognize potential problems, all too often they continue with 'business as usual' behaviour (BAU). Indeed, some argue that businesses will actively seek to resist pressure to change to preserve their profits. Others argue that, given the right incentives, businesses will choose to 'go green' and that there is very often a 'business case' to be made for sustainable business practices as this will boost profitability either through the enhanced reputation that being seen to be green brings or through the reduction in costs that better use of resources brings. In 2006, to the irritation of many people who had been espousing the case for the need for business to embrace the CSR agenda for many years, the attention of many leading CEOs was grabbed by an article by Porter and Kramer that argued that there is a clear connection between corporately responsible behaviour and successful performance. They have subsequently developed their ideas into what they now refer to as the need for the companies of the future to develop 'Shared Value' and you can see what they mean by visiting the **Online Resource Centre** for the book, where you can access a link to a related podcast.

There is a range of pressure groups across the business, environmental, and academic communities that seek to promote and profile such responsible behaviour such as the World Business Council for Sustainable Development, Forum for the Future, Net Impact, The Ethical Corporation, and the Globally Responsible Leadership Initiative (see www.wbcsd.org, www.forumforthefuture.org, www.netimpact.org, www.ethcialcorp.com, and www.grli.org). Visiting these sites will give you a good idea of the range of initiatives that are being undertaken in relation to sustainable business practices.

Learning Task

Look at cases which are profiled as examples of responsible business practice in relation to the ecological environment (see, for example, www.bitc.org.uk or www.wbcsd.org).

What are the problems that businesses face in addressing environmentally responsible business practice, and how convincing do you think the case for this is?

Perspectives on the Role of Business

Business activity is essentially the conversion of natural resources into goods and services to satisfy the needs, wants, and desires of human beings but this generation of economic growth creates environmental problems. Industries such as steel, cement, oil, power generation, chemicals, and transport are heavy polluters in a range of ways. There are competing perspectives about ways in which businesses will respond to the environmental challenges.

Views from the Right

For free market exponents it is the ability of private businesses to operate in markets free from government regulation that will drive economic progress. While the indirect cost of growth might be environmental damage there is a trade off to be made between this and growth in living standards and business plays a vital role in developing 'environmentally friendly' technologies —given the right incentives. Where this isn't realistic then the negative costs can be measured and businesses can be charged for the environmental damage according to the 'polluter pays principle'.

Views from the Left

There are however, objections to this version of the secret for economic success.

Critics of business see it as being primarily interested in maximizing profits and in cutting costs will treat the environment as a free 'sink' for pollution.

Businesses have a vested interest in encouraging consumers to buy more and more and so are indirectly responsible for rampant consumerism. While it could be argued that businesses are simply responding to the wishes of consumers it is the business in pursuit of profit that has every interest in fuelling consumer demand. Sheehan questions the notion of scarcity as being the basis of the economic problem. For Sheehan while this may be the case in poorer, less developed countries and for the poor in the developed world, what drives consumption are the demands of the rich who live in relative abundance. Why do people who have everything still want more? Why do consumers with no room left in their wardrobes still want more clothes? Sheehan argues that the 'institution of marketing' fuels this culture of consumption and helps businesses slake their thirst for ever more sales (Sheehan 2010). In similar vein Annie Leonard has produced a video entitled *The Story of Stuff* in which she questions why American people, who have what could be seen as enough, still want more stuff (www.storyofstuff.com). While directed mainly at schoolchildren this short video does illustrate the views that consumer capitalism is the cause of environmental degradation.

Learning Task

Watch the video *The Story of Stuff* and think about how you react to this?

- Is it telling you anything you already know?
- Is there anything that you agree with?
- Is there anything you don't agree with?
- What is your overall reaction to this video?

A major source of disquiet is the belief that the distribution of income and wealth that results from free markets is highly unequal and that the immediate problem facing the world is not that there is not enough to go around, but that the fruits of economic growth are enjoyed by the richer members of society whilst the poor lose out. The biggest global problem is the gap between the living standards of the 'Global North' as opposed to the 'Global South' and that those consumers in the former are responsible for far more global environmental damage than those in the latter.

Governments need to ensure that businesses do not develop positions of monopoly power but all too often struggle to enforce environmental control over the power of 'Big Business' especially when increasingly globalization means that corporations operate across national boundaries and, therefore, different regulatory regimes.

Green Views

The development of the modern 'green' movement can be traced to the publication of *The Silent Spring* by Rachel Carson in 1962. A biologist, Carson became very concerned about the use of pesticides in agriculture and their effects on human beings through links with cancers, and on wildlife—hence the emotive title of the book, looking into a future where birdsong was not heard. Her books and articles had a huge influence on the grass roots environmental movement in the USA and resulted in the eventual ban of the pesticide, DDT (Dichlorodiphenyltrichloroethane), in the USA. It also attracted a large volume of criticism from the chemical industry (Carson 1962). This theme of environmental claim and business counterclaim will be seen again in this chapter.

 Counterpoint Box 12.1 Tragedy of the Commons

In 1968 Garrett Hardin provided a critique of what he saw as an essential problem for the future of humanity. 'The Tragedy of the Commons' published in the journal *Science*, argued that when human beings have access to commonly owned resources for which they do not have to pay we each, as an individual, seek to get as much as we can from this shared resource but collectively the result of this action will be that we will all soon exhaust the resource and so all lose out (Hardin 1968).

Hardin used the example of feudal agricultural societies where farmers/peasants worked mostly on land owned by land-lords but where there might be some limited commons land available for grazing livestock. A rational farmer would seek not to overgraze land if s/he had private ownership of it but would see the benefit in having fallow periods to allow the land to recover from potential overgrazing. The 'Tragedy of the Commons' is where, if land is not privately owned, or in economic terms, property rights are not clearly defined, then each farmer will end up overusing the land in the fear that if they keep their animals off the land others will not.

Source: Hardin 1968

At the heart of 'green thinking' is the belief that we need to move away from an **anthropocentric** view of the world which sees human beings as the driving force of nature and the sole beneficiaries of the resources that are there to be exploited, to an **ecocentric** view of the world that recognizes our interdependence with nature. Whilst there is an enormous range of opinion within the green movement it is commonly accepted that our lives would be improved by not abusing nature and recognizing that we need to alter the prevailing economic model of growth by accounting for environmental costs.

The Limits to Growth focused on the key areas of population: food production, industrialization, pollution, and consumption of non-renewable resources and predicted growth trends would, within the next one hundred years, cause sudden falls in population and industrial production unless action was taken to create ecological and economic stability based on a more equitable sharing out of the products of economic prosperity (Meadows 1972).

Other influential books include *The Costs of Economic Growth* (Mishan 1969) and *Small is Beautiful* (Schumacher 1973). The former was one of the first economics books to outline the costs of economic growth and the methods of cost-benefit analysis that are needed when judging economic decisions and the latter's focus is clear in its subtitle: *Economics as if People Mattered*.

Environmental Regulation

There have always been voices raised to challenge the view that economic growth represented human progress. Even at the beginning of the industrial revolution in Europe a range of people from poets to social activists and politicians were anxious about the costs of economic growth. These criticisms were often centred on what they saw as the destruction of the natural environment and the effect on traditional ways of life as a result of industrialization. A fierce condemnation of the effect of the new capitalist expansion on the social environment of the poor urban working class was produced by Friedrich Engels in his *The Condition of the Working Class in England* (Engels 1844). (This book can be reviewed at www.gutenberg.org/wiki/Main_Page.) The dramatic success of the industrial revolution clearly had a severely damaging impact on a range of environmental factors such as public health, pollution, and sanitation and it was clear that there was an urgent need for governments, both local and national, to clean up the mess that was the by-product of economic growth.

In the 20th century it became accepted that business activity needed to be regulated in order to protect the natural environment, and that the government would have to take direct control over a range of environmental areas to deal with these externalities. Environmental legislation was seen as the responsibility of national governments although as global trade increased and with the rise of the multinational corporation it is clear that not all countries have the same levels of governance and ability or willingness to enforce environmental regulations.

It has been increasingly acknowledged that if trade was to be free and fair between nations then it was important that all countries played by the same rules in terms of environmental protection to stop certain countries gaining from cheaper costs because of looser environmental compliance. Within formally agreed custom unions such as the European Union there is an insistence that all member states adhere to the same environmental rules so environmental legislation is determined at the EU level. However, in the absence of the political and legal structures which bind the members of the union together and form the basis of the common market it is difficult sometimes to reconcile the rush to liberalize trade and investment across borders with the need to have commonly agreed environmental standards. Trying to develop common international environmental standards that are legally binding and enforceable is very difficult.

The World Trade Organization claims that:

> Sustainable development and the protection and preservation of the environment are fundamental goals of the WTO (www.wto.org/english/tratop_e/envir_e.htm).

Lack of international environmental rules can lead to trade disputes and claims of double standards. Developing countries will point to the developed world's hypocrisy in insisting on levels of environmental protection that they themselves did not have to implement as they were developing and claim that this is simply being used as an artificial restraint on trade. Developed countries cry foul of what they perceive to be relatively poorer environmental standards in developing countries' exports with the developing countries so gaining an unfair advantage in relation to trade. Equally there are accusations that multinational businesses are able to exploit their ability to work across boundaries by being able to avoid paying attention to the environment in the same way as they would if operating in more tightly regulated developed markets. But this is contentious territory as the Trafigura case in Chapter Nine illustrated. Did Trafigura, as critics allege, deliberately seek to avoid paying the high costs of ensuring that waste products from one of its ships were disposed of safely by offloading this waste in a country with less stringent environmental protection laws or ability to ensure environmental compliance. Trafigura argues that this was not the case and that it cannot be blamed if the Ivorian waste disposal firm it contracted to deal with the waste acted in an irresponsible manner and that it had sought to use a country which had signed up to the recognized international standards for disposal of hazardous ship waste.

The impact of business on the ecological environment is explicitly recognized in the environmental regulations with which businesses have to comply. In the UK you can explore the range of such legislation by visiting www.envirowise.gov.uk. At the global level as a result of the 1992 Rio declaration (discussed below) the international standard, ISO 14001, was developed to provide a framework for the development of an environmental management system and the supporting audit programme (see www.iso-14001.org.uk for the details of how businesses can seek accreditation for this).

Binding environmental legislation is only possible at the international level if nation states agree to pool sovereignty in order to participate in custom unions such as the EU. Various attempts have been made to enforce international environmental standards through measures such as ISO 14001 and through initiatives such as the UN Global Compact which is an attempt to provide an enabling framework in which businesses can address issues concerning human rights, labour standards, the environment, and measures to combat corruption. (See Chapter Eleven for a fuller examination of this.)

ISO 14001 sets out the steps that a business can take to establish an environmental management system. Successful implementation of this means that businesses that undertake an audit of the targets that they set can apply for ISO certification. To be eligible for the standard businesses must show that they not only comply with legislation but that they have all looked at all areas where there is an environmental impact. The underlying philosophy of the standard is that there is a clear 'business case' through a systematic ISO 14001 approach. According to the ISO this can encompass benefits such as:

- reduced cost of waste management;
- savings in consumption of energy and materials;
- lower distribution costs;
- improved corporate image among regulators, customers, and the public; and
- a framework for continual improvement of environmental performance (www.iso.org).

In relation to the three principles that relate to the environment, the UN Global Compact is keen to impress on businesses that there need not be a conflict between preserving the environment and business success.

This could be best seen in terms of a continuum in that if businesses do not take action now to reduce their environmental impact their profits will suffer in the future. This short-term action is seen as an investment to prevent longer term costs and is referred to as mitigation. It is argued that some changes as a result of ecological damage are already upon us and so businesses will need to play their part in adapting to these changes now to save the need for greater adaptation changes in the future.

Principle 7 emphasizes the need to operationalize the precautionary principle. The basis of this principle is that we should never introduce technological change without having a full risk assessment of the effects of this change.

In Principle 8 the UN Global Compact is clear that there is a compelling case for 'environmentally responsible business practice' and outlines the following advantages to such an approach:

- cleaner production and eco-efficiency leads to improved resource productivity and lower costs;
- new economic instruments (taxes, charges, trade permits) and tougher environmental regulations will reward those companies who seek to improve eco-efficiency;
- insurance companies prefer to cover a cleaner, lower risk company and banks are more willing to lend to a company whose operations will not burden the bank with environmental lawsuits or large clean-up bills;
- being seen to be green helps a company's brand image and employees tend to prefer to work for an environmentally responsible company;
- environmental pollution threatens human health; and
- customers are demanding cleaner products.

Source: www.unglobalcompact.org/AboutTheGC/TheTenPrinciples/principle8.html

Finally, Principle 9 asserts the important role that business can play in both developing and adopting the technologies that will enable the environment to be safeguarded.

Mini Case Plan A or Plan B?

Marks and Spencer launched its Plan A in 2007 which mapped out a five-year programme of environmental change with 100 commitments. In March 2010 it reported that it had achieved 62 of these commitments and in recognition of this extended its commitments to 180 targets (www.marksandspencer.com).

Marks and Spencer aim to support this plan with what they call the five pillars of: Climate Change, Waste, Sustainable Raw Materials, Health, and being a Fair Partner.

Each pillar has its own goal, and the aim was that by 2012 Marks and Spencer would:

- become **carbon neutral**;
- send no waste to landfill;
- extend sustainable sourcing;
- help improve the lives of people in our supply chain; and
- help customers and employees live a healthier life-style.

Reporting in 2010 Marks and Spencer were still aiming to become the world's most sustainable company by 2015 but were acknowledging that there were challenges to overcome especially in regards to developing reliable indicators and measurements to report progress. (See http://plana.marksandspencer.com/media/pdf/planA-2010.pdf.)

We have seen that some environmental activists are cynical about the genuine commitment of businesses to move beyond 'green washing' and even where such cynicism does not exist environmentalists such as Lester Brown argue that in order for real change to occur it is not businesses alone that can effect such change. Since 1974, when he founded the Worldwatch Institute, Brown has been an influential figure in the world environment movement. In 2001 Brown established the Earth Policy Institute to act as a more direct campaigning organization which translates research into policy proposals. For Brown there has to be an alternative to what he terms 'Plan A' (not related to the Plan A of M and S) or the belief that despite this range of problems there is no alternative than to follow the 'Business as Usual' model (Brown 2009).

The latest version of this is Plan B 4.0, 'Mobilising to Save Civilisation' (this can be downloaded in full at www.earth-policy.org/index.php?/books/pb4/pb4_table_of_contents).

In this, Brown both charts what he sees as the fundamental challenges facing us, as well as the policies that need to be developed to combat these.

The central question that needs to be posed is the extent to which the response of businesses is such as to fully address the ecological challenges.

Businesses are now urged to show their commitment to change through moving away from simply reporting their financial bottom line. It is argued that they should also report on their 'social' and 'environmental' impacts and this has in turn produced a variety of systems to account for the environment. In 1994, John Elkington developed the concept of 'triple bottom line accounting' as a way of highlighting the responsibility of businesses in relation to social and environmental performance as well as financial performance and this is commonly referred to as the trio of 'People, Planet and Profit' (Elkington 1994).

However, there is no commonly agreed set of procedures for doing this and instead there is a hotchpotch of approaches developed by some businesses eager to publicize their social credentials. Whilst many leading businesses have been undertaking a range of environmental initiatives, there remains an unwillingness to be subject to government regulation to enforce compliance. Critics question the ability of self regulation to achieve real benefits and see this desire to be 'seen to be green' as sitting uneasily with the temptation to trumpet this as a way of securing competitive advantage through 'green washing' (see Chapter Eleven).

Learning Task

1. In what ways do businesses potentially have a negative impact on the ecological environment?

2. To what extent do you think that strategies such as Marks and Spencer's Plan A are an adequate response by business to the ecological challenge?

3. In what sense do ecological problems represent a 'global tragedy of the commons'?

Global Cooperation—Establishing Effective Environmental Regimes

There is a growing recognition of the global nature of environmental problems.

What is the point of one country or area having stringent environmental safeguards if others do not, since ecological systems overlap? In other words environmental problems are often 'trans-boundary'. National policies alone are not sufficient and put businesses at a severe competitive disadvantage if such policies are not universally applied. In the field of international relations this is a recurrent theme, namely, how can international cooperation be achieved in a world of 'anarchy' or, in other words, one in which there is no overall global authority to which all countries must obey.

There are a number of global commons issues that require international cooperation if they are to be addressed. The following are examples that have been the focus of attempts to develop a global response:

- desertification;
- deforestation;
- loss of biodiversity;

- whaling;
- protection of fisheries and the marine environment;
- acid rain;
- protection of the ozone layer; and
- climate change.

In 1972 the Stockholm conference explored the causes of 'acid rain' and its effects on lakes and forests in Northern Europe and this led to the formation of the United Nations Environment Programme. The notion that pollution does not respect national borders was given direct expression when the radioactivity from the Chernobyl nuclear explosion in 1984 covered most of Western Europe and in the recognition of the effect of chloro-fluoro carbons (CFC) gases on the ozone layer.

For effective action to be undertaken it is important to devise a system of international cooperation and this is referred to in international relations literature as a 'regime'. To establish such regimes multilateral treaties are required and these may either be regulated through a committee of organization or through what is referred to as the convention/protocol process or a combination of both. The International Convention for the Regulation of Whaling makes annual schedules of catch regulations and the Convention on International Trade in Endangered Species of Wild Fauna and Flora regulates which species are to be controlled.

In the convention/protocol process, initially states come together and agree an initial 'framework convention' to identify the problems and ways of dealing with these but which initially may not contain specific obligations. Once agreement is made for the convention this is then followed by a series of meetings at which 'protocols' are negotiated which then do require

Mini Case Ozone Depletion

Ozone in the upper atmosphere is important as it acts as a barrier to prevent ultraviolet radiation getting through to the earth. If there is a depletion of the ozone layer then this can lead to increases in skin cancers, immune disorders for humans, and other species as well as crop damage. In the 1970s it became clear that the release of CFCs into the atmosphere was indeed causing depletion of the ozone layer. CFCs were primarily used for refrigeration and air conditioning and were also commonly found in aerosols and fire extinguishers.

What has been remarkable is the speed with which action was taken to curb the use of CFCs and other ozone depleting substances. Initially the industries involved in the manufacture of CFCs, such as DuPont, were resistant to changing their behaviour, arguing that it was not feasible to develop substitutes for CFCs. However, a combination of consumer pressure

and US government determination to take a lead in regulating against their use, once the scientific evidence became clear, was vital. At the global level the signing of the Montreal Protocol in 1987 established a very effective international regime for cooperation to phase out CFCs. Since customers would now be obliged to use substitutes to CFC producing goods, even if these were more expensive, and once it became clear that the market for these was now a global one there was a real incentive for the chemical companies such as DuPont and others to spend the required research and development funds in developing substitutes.

Sources: De Sombre, E. (2007) Global Environment and World Politics, www.undp.org/ozone

member states to sign up to specific actions. The Montreal Protocol (1987) was the first global agreement to phase out those chemicals held responsible for ozone depletion. The Kyoto Protocol (1997) was the first step in developing a regime to tackle climate change.

In 1987, *Our Common Future*, a report from the United Nations World Commission on the Environment and Development (WCED) was published. This built on the work of the Stockholm conference which also looked at environmental concerns more widely. The publication of *Our Common Future* and the work of the WCED led to the 1992 Conference at Rio de Janeiro and the adoption of Agenda 21, the Rio Declaration, and to the establishment of the Commission of Sustainable Development.

The fact that states have the right to exert their own sovereignty over their own resources makes the process of environmental regime creation a complex and at times very slow process with conflicts between the interests of states and of course differences in their respective power and influence.

As well as the problems of establishing such global cooperation there are also specific problems that relate to the nature of environmental issues.

Risk and Uncertainty

The main obstacle when examining environmental problems is that often these problems are not immediately obvious.

Environmental policy requires people and organizations to change their behaviour in relation to resource use so that we recognize that the ecological environment is not a free good and that we are made fully aware of the social costs of environmental damage. It is clear that across many parts of the world there has been an increase in environmental awareness and in areas such as recycling this has changed behaviour. However, a major barrier to effecting more widespread environmental improvements lies in our lack of knowledge of exactly what our ecological impact is and indeed the measures we should take to minimize this.

Environmental policies involve a 'trade-off' in that there is a conflict between short-term production and the immediate gratification of consumption and longer term well-being. While people may well be more aware of the costs of motoring and air travel the predicted rises in the uses of these modes of transport shows that people are not prepared to alter their behaviour voluntarily.

For both consumers and producers the costs of adapting to ecological change may appear to be too great and the task for environmental policy lies both in how to deal with this resistance and in persuading us all that the long term benefits of preventing ecological damage are greater than the costs of taking action now to minimize it.

The Role of Science

In order for risks to be quantified, we need careful research and analysis and this entails further problems. Scientific surveys are often very complex and contradictory and most people lack the understanding to unravel the findings. Faced with this lack of understanding it is easy for people to simply ignore the debates and carry on as usual.

The Notion of Sustainable Development

At the heart of the debate about the nature of the ecological environment lies the concept of sustainable development. The commonly accepted definition of this was outlined in the Brundtland Report (1987):

> Sustainable Development is development that meets the needs of the present without compromising the ability of future generations to meet their own needs.

This part of the statement is the bit which is most quoted and clearly shows the commitment that is made here to ensuring **intra-generational equity** in other words that our actions today should not undermine the standards of living of the future. However, what is often left out is the full version which goes on to say:

> it contains within it two key concepts: the concept of 'needs', in particular the essential needs of the world's poor, to which overriding priority should be given; and the idea of limitations imposed by the state of technology and social organization on the environment's ability to meet present and future needs (WCED 1987, 43).

This second statement directly argues that growth is needed if it is to help the poor and that is important as 'inter-generational' equity or the need to ensure that people living today are able to benefit from growth.

The 1992 Earth Summit held in Rio de Janeiro, Brazil was pivotal in that it formulated Agenda 21, a comprehensive programme to be adopted globally, nationally, and locally to promote sustainable development in the 21st century. The Rio declaration outlined 27 key principles concerning the actions that states should take in order to safeguard the environment and these were adopted by the 178 countries that took part in the Earth Summit. It established the United Nations Framework Convention on Climate Change (UNFCCC), an international environmental treaty to deal with climate change. Every year there is a Conference of the Parties to the Convention (COP) to monitor progress on actions to combat climate change.

While the Brundtland definition has become the widely accepted definition of **sustainability** there is still wide disagreement as to the implications of this statement.

How exactly do we define the 'needs of the present'? President George W Bush made it clear that he would not take any environmental action if it was against the 'economic interests' of the USA. In the UK, the then Director General of the Confederation of Business Industry, Digby Jones, criticized the government for *'risking the sacrifice of UK jobs on the altar of green credentials'* (Jarman 2007). In the USA and indeed specifically across the globe in relation to climate change, the election of President Obama in 2009 raised the prospect of a new leadership role for the USA regarding global environmental agreements. However, after the midterm US elections in 2011 the increased majority of the Republican Party Congress meant that there was real pressure to rein back on environmental promises.

Global Climate Change

There is a clear consensus that the most pressing ecological problem of our age is that of global climate change. The Intergovernmental Panel on Climate Change was established in 1989 by the World Meteorological Office and the United Nations Environment Programme to provide an objective source of information about climate change. In its Fourth Assessment Report published in November 2007 it clearly states that global climate change is occurring, that 'anthropogenic' activity is a contributing factor and that there is a need to reduce the **GHGs** that are the cause of global warming:

> Warming of the climate system is unequivocal, as is now evident from observations of increases in global average air and ocean temperatures, widespread melting of snow and ice, and rising global average sea level.

> Most of the observed increase in globally averaged temperatures since the mid-20th century is very likely due to the observed increase in anthropogenic greenhouse gas concentrations (IPCC 2007 Fourth Assessment Report, www.ipcc.ch).

This report is important as it represents the views of a multinational and comprehensive range of experts assembled by UNEP about the precise role of human beings in increasing the threats posed by climate change. Work is now underway to prepare the Fifth Assessment Report which is due to be published in 2013.

GHG emissions are problematic because once emitted into the atmosphere they stay there for many, many years. They help create the 'greenhouse effect' in that they prevent the solar rays that penetrate the earth's atmosphere from going back out again so leading to a gradual warming of the planet's surface.

Meyer illustrates the problem by using a 'bath-tap' analogy (Meyer 2007). The dominant green house gas from anthropogenic sources is carbon dioxide (CO_2) and business is responsible for around 40% of these emissions. Just as a bath will fill if the tap is left running, so the atmosphere fills up as emissions flow from sources such as the burning of fossil fuels for energy use. If there is no outflow from the bath over time the constant flow will mean that the stock of water will rise. If there is a plug hole with no plug then this stock need not rise so fast as some of the water is drained away. In relation to our CO_2 emissions this means that if we have 'sinks' to absorb the carbon such as forests or the oceans then not all the carbon will be added to the total stock. If, for example, the flow of water is twice the rate at which it drains away then the net increase in the stock of water will be 50% of the flow.

Meyer reports that in recent years this has been the case with the 50% of carbon emissions being retained in the atmosphere and the remaining 50% being re-absorbed. It has been on that basis that future projections of the rise in global temperatures have been made. Ice core sampling allows CO_2 atmospheric concentration to be measured for half a million years. This has fluctuated in the band of 180 to 280 parts per million by volume (ppmv) and there is a very close correlation with these fluctuations and the changes in global temperature.

During the last 200 years there has been a rise in CO_2 concentration from 280 ppmv to a level 391 ppmv as of January 2011. Figure 12.1 below shows the trend in CO_2 emissions (see http://climate.nasa.gov/evidence).

Up until recently the annual increase of atmospheric CO_2 has been 1.5 ppmv. Since each additional ppmv adds 2.13 billion tonnes (gigatonnes expressed as GTC) of carbon to the atmosphere this means that the addition to the stock of carbon in weight terms has been 3.3 GTC. In total the annual emissions of carbon however have been around 6.5 GTC as the sinks have absorbed around 50% of all emissions. However, in recent years the rate of atmospheric increase rose to nearer 3 ppmv meaning that we are approaching the point at which 100% of emissions were retained in the atmosphere. This 'aggravated accumulation' will mean that the level of the

Figure 12.1 Rising CO_2 levels

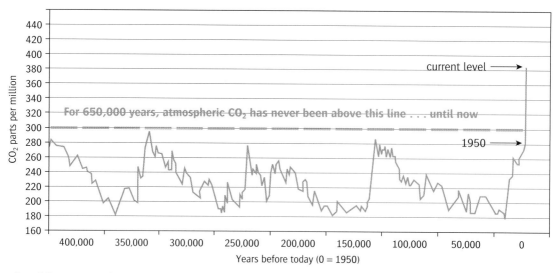

Source: http://climate.nasa.gov/evidence (Courtesy NASA/JPL-Caltech)

Figure 12.2 Global air temperature

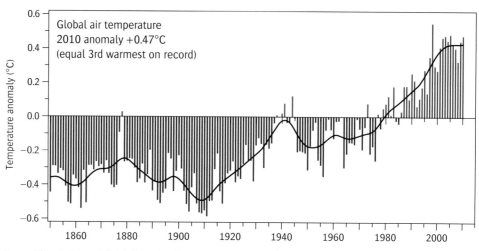

Source: Climatic Research Unit Information Sheet, www.cru.uea.ac.uk/cru/info/warming

bathwater will rise more quickly and is in serious danger of overflowing. Emissions are increasing and the sinks' ability to absorb these are decreasing as the oceans warm and acidification occurs and forests are burned to increase land availability.

Figure 12.2 shows the evidence about temperature rises on the basis of the methodology used by the Climatic Research Unit at the University of East Anglia in the UK whose work directly informs the Intergovernmental Panel on Climate Change (IPCC).

This chart is drawn by taking the average global and marine temperatures in the period 1961–1990 and then, using time series analysis from a variety of temperature monitoring methods, shows the variation (or anomaly) from this norm from 1850–2010.

Commenting on this data the CRU states:

> The period 2001–2010 (0.44°C above 1961–90 mean) was 0.20°C warmer than the 1991–2000 decade (0.24°C above 1961–90 mean). The warmest year of the entire series has been 1998, with a temperature of 0.55°C above the 1961–90 mean. After 1998, the next nine warmest years in the series are all in the decade 2001–2010. During this decade, only 2008 is not in the ten warmest years. Even though 2008 was the coldest year of the 21st century it was still the 12th warmest year of the whole record.

Under the Kyoto Protocol (see below) countries agreed to identify and quantify the sources of GHG emissions. Tables 12.1 and 12.2 below show the data for the UK in 2008.

The Kyoto Protocol identified a basket of six GHGs that countries should seek to reduce and uses a base year of 1990 for CO_2, CH_4, and NO_2 and 1995 for fluorinated compounds. The UK agreed to reduce its GHGs to 12.5% below the base year in the period 2008–2012.

However to illustrate the speed with which the science has begun to alter official policy responses, The UK Climate Change Act, passed in 2008, includes legally binding targets to reduce GHGs by at least 80% by 2050, and by at least 34% by 2020, both below base year levels. This will be achieved by setting five-year carbon budgets.

Table 12.1 Total emissions by sector (*excluding LULUCF)

Energy Supply	34.9%
Transport	21.0%
Business	15.2%
Residential	13.4%
Agriculture	7.7%
Waste Management	3.6%
Industrial Process	2.6%
Public	1.6%

Table 12.2 Total emissions by gas (*excluding LULUCF)

Carbon Dioxide CO_2	85%
Methane CH_4	7.7%
Nitrous Oxide NO_2	5.4%
Hydro fluorocarbons	1.8%
Sulfur hexafluoride	0.1%

* Excluding land use, land use change, and forestry (LULUCF)
Source of Data UK GHG Inventory (UNFCCC coverage) (AEA 2010) adapted from chart at www.decc.gov.uk/assets/decc/Statistics/climate_change/1217-ghg-inventory-summary-factsheet-overview.pdf. Permission to use data from www.nationalarchives.gov.uk/doc/open-government-licence

At the heart of the UNFCCC and Kyoto Protocol are three mechanisms which are designed to reduce global GHGs:

- Developed countries are set assigned amounts of GHGs in any time period and through International Emissions trading can trade any unused amounts with other countries (see Counterpoint Box below).
- The Clean Development Mechanism allows developed countries to fund carbon reducing projects in less developed countries in return for carbon credits.
- Joint implementation allows cooperation between developed countries where one country can help another by investing in emissions reduction projects and earn credits.

Counterpoint Box 12.2 European emissions trading system

This is a *cap and trade* system which was first established in 2005. Having agreed to the national target of emissions each country then allocates individual targets across businesses which are responsible for high levels of GHGs. (At the moment this covers the energy, iron, steel, mineral, wood pulp, board, and paper industries.) These allowances must then be adhered to and if a firm exceeds these then they either pay a fine or else they seek to purchase allowances from a firm that has not used all its allowances.

In principle if the cap is set at progressively lower levels then this should see reductions in GHGs. As market prices are set for carbon then there will be an incentive for firms to cut

back on emissions and invest in non-polluting technologies. Even if initially they cannot, revenues raised from the scheme can be used to develop renewables, act against deforestation, undertake forest plantation as well as researching into and developing carbon capture and storage facilities and undertake extensive energy efficiency programmes.

Businesses will be obliged to declare their emissions and submit to certificated verification procedures. The first phase was not so successful as it is now acknowledged that initial caps were far too generous and so prices collapsed but phase II has worked better.

Carbon reductions are occurring in many countries but for many critics the current targets are too little and too late. It must be remembered that reductions in GHG emissions are not cuts in the amount of emissions but simply slow the rate of flow but the overall stock of GHGs in the atmosphere rises inexorably.

For environmentalists such as Meyer the implication is clear and that is that we need urgent cuts in emissions ppmv and that the current targets to stabilize emissions at 550 ppmv are simply too high and will result in runaway climate change (Meyer 2007).

This echoes the views of James Lovelock. Lovelock published *The Gaia Hypothesis* in 1972. For Lovelock the **biosphere**, or the relatively thin layer of land and water between the molten interior of the Earth and the exterior upper atmosphere supports all life. The Earth can be seen as a single system which is self-regulating. This system ensures that interactions and feedbacks between all the physical, chemical, biological, and human components of the Earth make life on the planet possible. To this Lovelock ascribed the name 'Gaia' (after a Greek Goddess) as a metaphor for the Earth as a living system. However, Gaia is now under threat as a result of a rise in the levels of carbon dioxide in the atmosphere. It is these levels that control the temperature of the Earth (Lovelock 1979). In the past 'Gaia' has been able to ensure that life on Earth was not only possible but was also comfortable, however, Lovelock now argues that there is clear scientific evidence that we are approaching 'the tipping point' at which levels of carbon dioxide (CO_2) will not only lead to rises in global warming and the severe consequences for human life that these will entail, but also that once this tipping point is reached the feedback mechanisms that have led to rises in these temperatures will lead to even faster increases.

In his most recent exposition of his ideas, *The Revenge of Gaia*, Lovelock writes:

> We are now approaching one of these tipping points and our future is like that of the passengers on a small pleasure boat sailing quietly above the Niagara falls, not knowing that the engines are about to fail. (Lovelock 2007)

The Effects of Climate Change

The Fourth Assessment Report reaffirmed the five areas of concern that had been highlighted in the Third Assessment Report. These areas of concern are as follows:

Risks to Unique and Threatened Systems

If global temperatures were to exceed 1980–1999 levels by 1.5 to 2.5°C then there is medium confidence that 20–30% of plant and animal species are likely to be at increased risk of extinction. It warns also of increases risk of coral reef damage and increased vulnerability of indigenous peoples in the Arctic and small island communities.

Risk of Extreme Weather Events

The report has 'higher confidence' in the projected increases in droughts, heatwaves, and floods as well as their adverse consequences.

Distribution of Impacts and Vulnerabilities

The most vulnerable people will be people in the weakest economic position, especially the poor and the elderly in both developing and developed countries alike. It is estimated that 32,000 people died in Western Europe as a result of the heatwave in 2003.

Aggregate Impacts

The report attempts to counter an often expressed view that while global warming may well cause problems for some it will also equally bring benefits to others. It is easy to see how people living in cold northern climates might welcome warmer conditions! However, if global warming were to increase, the report argues that the net costs will increase over time whilst any possible benefits will decrease.

Risk of Large Scale Singularities

There is high confidence that the melting of the Greenland and Antarctic ice sheets will give a greater rise to sea levels then current models predict, but that will be a centuries long process.

The IPCC emphasizes that adaptation and mitigation measures are unlikely to stop all climate change effects but (that combined) they can significantly reduce the risks. Conversely delays in reducing emissions will significantly constrain the opportunities to lower stabilization levels and increase the risk of severe climate change impacts.

Technology, both that which is presently available and that which is likely to become commercially available, is seen as offering a realistic hope that stabilization levels can be achieved.

In 2007 the UK government asked the respected economist Nicholas Stern to look at the economics of climate change. For Stern:

> Climate change presents a unique challenge for economics; it is the greatest and widest ranging market failure ever seen. (p i)

Stern is clear that the costs of climate change in terms of Gross National Product and quality of life will be much greater than the costs of taking action to mitigate against these now. With business as usual (BAU) there is a very high chance that the rise in global temperatures will exceed 2°C and indeed there is some evidence that they may rise even as high as 5–6°C in the next century which would:

> take us into territory unknown to human experience and involve radical changes in the world around us. (Stern Review p ix)

If this were to be the case over the next two centuries there could be a reduction in global GNP in the range of 5–20%. This is a high range of uncertainty but this is inevitable given the difficulty of estimating such costs in general and so far into the future.

In order to stabilize the climate Stern estimated this would require an 80% reduction in carbon in the long run compared to current levels. As was shown above, this figure was subsequently adopted by the UK government in its Climate Change Act of 2008.

This is not going to be an easy task. At present levels are continuing to rise, so adding to the stock of carbon and the longer this goes on the greater the difficulty in reducing this. Stern is optimistic that it will be possible to stabilize the climate at 550ppmv by allowing annual emissions to peak in the next 10 to 20 years and then gradually cutting emissions by 1–3% each year until 2050. However, since it is the richer developed countries that are currently the main producers of carbon this will require them to make severe cuts in their carbon.

The Stern Review highlights four main policy areas that need to be addressed if we are to be able to mitigate against the worst effects of climate change and adapt to those that will occur:

- reducing demand for emissions intensive goods and services;
- increase resource efficiency;
- action on non-energy emissions such as avoiding deforestation; and
- switching to low carbon technologies for power, heat, and transport.

Stern is keen to emphasize that while this may be seen to be a threat to BAU behaviour, in practice these changes may well provide opportunities to create markets for low-carbon energy products and to reduce costs through developing new low energy systems.

The Sceptical Environmentalists

Bjorn Lomborg in his book *The Skeptical Environmentalist*, argues that both the risks of global warming are overestimated and also that even where such risks can be proven, it is important for us not to prevent the present generations from reaping the fruits of economic growth for the uncertain prediction that unspecified groups in the future might suffer as a result of environmental damage (Lomborg 2001). In similar vein the Nobel Prize winning economist Solow has argued:

> those who are so urgent about not inflicting poverty on the future have to explain why they do not attach even higher priority to reducing poverty today. (Solow in Rao 2000, p 86)

Lomborg is by no means the only critic to dispute the scientific evidence. (See Booker 2009, Lawson 2008, Singer and Avery 2007.)

This academic debate can often be clouded by mutual accusations of 'dirty tricks' across the spectrum of the debate. Climate change campaigners argue that there is a 'business of climate denial' with powerful business groups spending large amounts of money to lobby hard against legislation and spread disinformation to undermine the strength of the climate change evidence and as the case below illustrates these accusations are met by counter-accusations from those who dispute the evidence.

Mini Case Climategate

There is a small but highly vocal minority of critics who argue that the earth has been subject to variations in temperature before and that this is the result of natural factors such as solar and volcanic activity. Some go further and dispute the accuracy of the data arguing that there is now too much of a vested interest in the scientific community to prove the existence of anthropogenic climate change which sometimes leads them to misrepresent the data. This dispute was clearly shown in 2009.

The Climate Research Unit (CRU) at the University of East Anglia is renowned for its work on providing the evidence for climate change. It was inundated by Freedom of Information requests made by what appeared to be a concerted campaign from climate sceptics. In the event, as a result of an illegal hacking of the University's servers, thousands of CRU documents including e-mails were made public. In amongst this mass of e-mails there was reference by the Head of the Unit, Dr Phil Jones to 'Mike's Nature Trick'. In a previous study of the data Michael Mann writing in the journal *Nature* first brought to the world's attention the so-called 'hockey stick' graph of climate change which showed average world temperatures being relatively stable for thousands of years until rising rapidly in the last 150 years. There was one problem though with this interpretation of the data in that in amongst the enormous amount of data from a variety of ways of measuring average temperatures there was one set of data from a particular sample of tree rings that showed that there have been unexplained rises above the average in previous periods. As this was such a minor exception to the mass of the other evidence it had been decided to exclude this data and other researchers had sought to show that this would be a highly reasonable thing to do. However, the way in which this was reported in the media was to allege that climate change scientists were trying to mislead the public and suppress information that cast doubt on the existence of anthropogenic climate change.

As a result of the furore caused by what was dubbed the 'Climategate' scandal three separate enquiries were held into the work of the CRU and no evidence was found of attempting to suppress data or misrepresenting the evidence. Within the climate change research community there remains the belief that this was an orchestrated attempt by climate sceptics to undermine the strength of the evidence in the run up to the Copenhagen conference.

Sources: Booker, C. (2009) 'Climate Change: This is the Worst Scientific Scandal of our Generation' at www.telegraph.co.uk/comment/columnists/christopherbooker/6679082/Climate-change-this-is-the-worst-scientific-scandal-of-our-generation.html (accessed 10/03/2011); Carrington, D. (2010) Q and A: 'Climategate' at www.guardian.co.uk/environment/2010/jul/07/climate-emails-question-answer (accessed 10/03/2011); Somaiya, R. (2010) 'Third Inquiry Clears Climate Change Scientists of Serious Doing' at www.newsweek.com/2010/07/07/third-enquiry-clears-climategate-scientists-of-serious-wrongdoing.html (accessed 10/03/11) ➜

Source: Photodisc

The Progress on Climate Change Action

The Kyoto Protocol set binding agreements only up to 2012 so it was always acknowledged that further agreements would be needed. While it was seen as a start in framing the global response to climate change there was a consensus that this framework needed to be strengthened. This was partly as a result of the increasing scientific evidence and its impact on public opinion as well as the growing influence of environmental pressure groups. At the global political level, the change in attitudes towards the acceptance of climate change as being real and anthropogenic in its causes by countries such as Australia and the USA gave rise to the real hope that at the Copenhagen Climate Conference in December 2009 (COP 15), there would be a common agreement as to how to achieve the big reductions in GHGs now needed and a framework in which there could be mutual cooperation between the developed and the developing world.

In a speech in August 2009 Ban Ki Moon, the General Secretary of the UN who had championed the need for global agreements to deal with climate change argued that climate change is:

> simply the greatest collective challenge we face as a human family (as reported in the *Daily Telegraph*, 10 August 2009, www.telegraph.co.uk/earth/environment/climatechange/6004553/Ban-Ki-moon-warns-of-catastrophe-without-world-deal-on-climate-change.html#)

Ban had urged world leaders to make real progress at COP 15. It is widely agreed that these talks ended not only in failure but also brought into stark highlight the divergences in the perceived responsibility for taking action between the developed world and the developing world. The Copenhagen accord was eventually drawn up and signed by only the USA, China, Brazil, India, and South Africa. While it acknowledged that climate change was one of the greatest challenges faced by humanity and that actions should be taken to stabilize world average temperatures to at or below a 2% rise, no specific legally binding targets were given for reducing CO_2.

COP 16 held in Cancun Mexico appeared to be more successful with some important commitments being made in terms of pledges by developed nations to put pledges for reducing GHGs by 2012 into the Copenhagen accord but these are not legally binding. Countries also agreed in principle to inspections to verify GHG emissions. Developing countries agreed to look at ways of cutting GHGs and there was agreement to establish a global climate aid fund to transfer money to developing countries to allow them to deal with climate change effects. There was also the establishment of a green technology fund to foster green technologies in the developing world as well as proposals to tackle deforestation. The decision as to whether to develop a new set of Kyoto protocols after they expire in 2012 was postponed until the next COP in Durban in 2011 (www.guardian.co.uk/environment/2010/dec/13/cancun-climate-agreement and http://unfccc.int/2860.php).

In January 2011 Ban Ki Moon announced that he would no longer be taking a direct hands-on approach to climate change. This could either be seen as his being confident that the COP process would now begin to deliver on the promises made or that his assessment was that the prospect of getting binding 'top-down' agreements was unlikely.

Instead Ban has promised to put his efforts into developing new approaches to sustainable development at the grass roots level in individual developing countries and this will form the centrepiece of the 2012 Earth Summit to be held in Rio to mark the 20th anniversary of the first Earth Summit in 1992.

Learning Task

1. How aware are you about the science behind the debate about global warming?

2. What changes have you made, if any, to minimize your own 'ecological footprint'?

3. Have a go at measuring your own ecological footprint (see, for example, www.footprint.wwf.org.uk). What reaction do you have to such a footprint exercise?

● CHAPTER SUMMARY

The nature of many environmental problems is that they are trans-boundary, and if we are to avoid potential tragedies of the (global) commons then there needs to be concerted action at the global level, which is then translated into national and local environmental action.

It is clear businesses have a big role to play. As converters of resources into products attention has to be focused on their roles as sustainable businesses not just in relation to the 'bottom' line of profit but also in relation to their impact on people and profit. The Rio Declaration and Agenda 21 established a comprehensive set of ambitious principles for states to promote in relation to environmental policy. The UN Global Compact then translated these principles into the principles for responsible business behaviour.

It is evident there are obstacles to environmental policies. Businesses have to balance the risks of incurring the costs of environmental compliance with the risks of not doing anything. Here there is a clear role for science and economics to specify these risks. For businesses with the short-term goal of maximizing shareholder value it is all too easy to maintain 'business as usual' but the increasing recognition of the range of global environmental problems means that this is not a realistic possibility. Across the spectrum of business there are many examples of how individual businesses are seeking to address these concerns but, especially, in relation to climate change it is argued that the response has not been enough. It is clear that unless businesses rise to the challenge there will be calls for tougher environmental regulation. It is also equally clear that in order to make these changes businesses do need help and advice from outside of the company, and there is a need to then embed global responsibility into the overall business strategy.

● REVIEW QUESTIONS

1. What is the meaning of the term 'the tragedy of the commons' and how does this relate to ecological damage?

2. Explain how it is argued that market based measures such as the 'polluter pays principle' address ecological problems.

3. Why do 'green' thinkers and activists argue that such market based measures are not adequate to tackle the ecological problem?

4. What is the range of measures that businesses themselves can make in response to ecological problems?

5. How can governments ensure businesses adhere to their ecological responsibilities?

Case Study The Downsides of Rapid Economic Growth

While across the world levels of absolute poverty are falling and incomes are rising there are serious social and environmental problems associated with rapid economic growth. In countries such as China, India, and Brazil the pace of change has been extremely fast with rates of growth ranging from 8–11% for the three countries in 2010 and a major feature of this has been the speed of urbanization. China's urban population is predicted to rise from 430 million in 2001 to 850 million in 2015 and all are struggling to cope with the environmental consequences of such rapid change such as pressure on housing, transport, water quality and quantity, and airborne pollution. While attention is often focused on the very large cities often it is in the smaller towns of between 5,000–10,000 that the problems are worst as they lack the resources to deal with the problems.

However, average income per capita in these countries is low and especially in the case of Brazil and India a major feature of this urbanization has been the creation of vast slums. The Millennium Development Goals of the United Nations explicitly recognizes that it is the poor who often suffer the most from the environmental degradation brought about through rapid economic growth and explicitly targets the need for sustainable development to be central to growth strategies, as well as focusing attention on the need to improve the lives of slum dwellers and improve sustainable access to water.

These problems are not confined to the urban environment. In Brazil, there is the constant threat of deforestation in the Amazon which is a concern for the world community as a whole given its vital function in terms of absorbing GHGs as well as ➡

→ preserving biodiversity. There is growing evidence too that climate change is impacting more precisely in agricultural areas which are less fertile (www.worldbank.org; www.undp.org).

As countries develop it is argued that entrepreneurs need to be allowed to pursue their own interests and that their pursuit of profits will encourage them to be responsive to market needs. Simon Kuznets argued that as countries develop it is inevitable that the gap between high income earners will grow relative to the poor but that as countries mature this gap will close. If you plotted the relationship between inequality and income on a diagram, as incomes rise at first so does the level of inequality but over time this gap begins to fall. This is referred to as the 'Kuznets Curve' As economic growth increases more and more people will be employed and governments will be able to use greater tax revenues from the higher incomes to engage in education and health programmes raising general well-being. The 'Kuznets' hypothesis is the basis of what has come to be called 'trickle down' economics. In similar vein it is argued that there is an environmental Kuznets Curve in that as countries develop rapidly it is inevitable that the environmental

costs will increase but as they become richer they can afford higher levels of protection and/or invest in the new environmentally friendly technologies.

However, the pace of change in the developing countries coupled with the realization that global environmental problems impact more on the most vulnerable in the developing world has led many to question this belief in the infallibility of the market.

There is much that developing countries themselves can do to improve their own local environments ranging from proper pricing policies for natural resources through to more clearly defined property rights, programmes to improve the economic livelihoods of both the rural and urban poor, and regulations to enforce industrial emissions.

However, it is argued that the developed world itself has a big responsibility in helping the developing world. In relation to climate change we have seen that a major feature in negotiations is in accepting differential commitments to reduce emissions for the developed as opposed to the developing world. Furthermore, it is argued that the richer countries should help

Source: Photodisc

→ the poorer countries by supporting them in terms of green technology transfer and also through direct aid both to help reduce poverty and also help countries adapt to and mitigate against the worst effects of global environmental change.

Questions

1. In what ways might there be a conflict between the goals of economic growth and the concept of sustainable development.

2. What are the difficulties faced by developing countries in adopting the same levels of environmental protection as implemented in the developed world?

3. What are the main challenges that face developed countries in dealing with environmental problems both nationally and globally?

4. To what extent should developed countries seek to help developing countries in dealing with environmental problems and how might this be achieved?

Online Resource Centre
www.oxfordtextbooks.co.uk/orc/hamilton_webster2e/

Visit the supporting online resource centre for additional material which will help you with your assignments, essays, and research, or you may find these extra resources helpful when revising for exams.

● FURTHER READING

● IPPC (2007) Fourth Assessment Report (available at www.ipcc.ch/publications_and_data/publications_ipcc_fourth_assessment_report_synthesis_report.htm, accessed 10/03/11)

This is the synthesis report of the UN Intergovernmental Panel on Climate Change and contains all the established academic evidence regarding climate change and its effects:

● Stern, N. (2007) *The Economics of Climate Change—The Stern Review*. Cambridge: Cambridge University Press

This report identifies the causes of global climate change and proposes policies to combat it:

● Brown, L. R. (2009) *Plan B 4.0 Mobilizing to Save Civilization*. New York: W.W. Norton (available at www.earth-policy.org/images/uploads/book_files/pb4book.pdf, accessed 10/03/11)

This book gives an accessible overview of the Earth Policy Institute's view of the major global environmental challenges and future policies needed:

● Judge, E. (2011) 'Global Warming, Pollution, Resource Depletion and Sustainable Development: Is Business the Problem and Can It Be Part of the Solution?' in Wetherly, P. and Otter, D., *The Business Environment—Themes and Issues*. Oxford: Oxford University Press

This chapter provides a good introduction to the issues surrounding the relationship between business and sustainable development.

● Booker, C. (2009) *The Real Global Warming Disaster. Is the Obsession With Climate Change Turning Out To Be The Most Costly Scientific Blunder In History?* London: Continuum.

This book presents the views of a climate change sceptic.

● REFERENCES

Brown, L. (2008) *Plan 3.0—Mobilizing to Save Civilization*. Washington: Earth Policy Institute

Carson, R. (1962) *The Silent Spring*. Boston: Houghton Mifflin

De Sombre, E. (2007) *The Global Environment and World Politics*. London: Continuum

Elkington, J. (1994) 'Towards the Sustainable Corporation—Win-Win-Win Business Strategies for Sustainable Development'. *California Management Review*, Vol 36(2)

Forum for the Future (2008) 'Leader Business 2.0—Hallmarks of Sustainable Performance'. Available at www.forumforthefuture.org.uk

Goodin, R. (2007) 'Selling Environmental Indulgences' in Dryzek, J. S. and Schlosberg, D. *Debating the Earth—The Environmental Politics Reader*. Oxford: Oxford University Press

Hardin, G. (1968) 'The Tragedy of the Commons'. *Science*, 162, 13 December, American Association for the Advancement of Science

IPCC (2007) Fourth Assessment Report—Synthesis Report. Available at www.ipcc.ch

Jarman, M. (2007) 'First They Blocked, Now Do They Bluff? Corporations Respond to Climate Change' in D. Cromwell and M. Levene (eds), *Surviving Climate Change—The Struggle to Avert Climate Catastrophe*. London: Pluto Press

Lawson, N. (2008) *An Appeal To Reason: A Cool Look At Global Warming*. London: Duckworth

Lomborg, B. (2001) *The Skeptical Environmentalist*. Cambridge: Cambridge University Press

Lovelock, J. (1979) *A New Look at Life on Earth*. Oxford: Oxford University Press

Lovelock, J. (2007) *The Revenge of Gaia*. London: Penguin

Meadows, D. H. *et al.* (1972) *The Limits to Growth*. New York: Universe Books

Meyer, A. (2007) 'The Case for Contraction and Convergence' in D. Cromwell and M. Levene (eds), *Surviving Climate Change—The Struggle to Avert Climate Catastrophe*. London: Pluto Press

Mishan, E. (1969) *The Costs of Economic Growth*. London: Penguin

Porter, M. E. and Kramer, M. R. (2006) 'Strategy and Society—The Link Between Competitive Advantage and Corporate Social Responsibility'. *The Harvard Business Review*, December

Rao, P. K. (2000) *Sustainable Development—Economics and Policy*. Oxford: Blackwell

Schumacher, E. F. (1973) *Small is Beautiful—Economics as if People Mattered*. New York: Harper and Row

Sheehan, B. (2010) *The Economics of Abundance: Affluent Consumption and the Global Economy*. Cheltenham: Edward Elgar

Singer, S. F. and Avery, D. T. (2007) *Unstoppable Global Warming Every 1,500 years*. Plymouth: Rowman and Littlefield

Stern, N. (2007) The Stern Review, Executive Summary—the Economics of Climate Change, HM Treasury. Available at www.hm-treasury.gov.uk

WCED (1987) *Our Common Future*. Oxford: Oxford University Press (commonly known as Brundtland Report)

Glossary

Absolute cost barriers obstacles deterring entry of new firms because the capital costs of entering are huge or where the existing firms control a vital resource, e.g. oil reserves—the company Aramco controls 98% of Saudi Arabian oil reserves

Accountability the idea that organizations and people should take responsibility for their actions and their outcomes

Acquisition one firm takes over or merges with another; some authors use this term when a deal is contested

Advanced economy a country whose per capita income is high by world standards

Ageing population an increase in the average age of the population

Anthropocentric a view of the world that sees humans as being the most important species on earth

Applied research research specifically seeking knowledge that can be exploited commercially

Arbitration a process to resolve disputes that avoids using the courts

Authoritarian system one person or a group of people exercise power unrestrained by laws or opposition

Barriers to entry obstacles that prevent new firms from entering an industry and competing with existing firms on an equal basis

Basic research the pursuit of knowledge for the sake of it with no explicit aim to exploit the results commercially

Biodiversity the variety of life forms which exist on Earth. There is clear evidence that ecological changes can lead to a reduction in this

Biofuels fuel made from renewable sources of energy such as plants

Biosphere the regions of the Earth, both above and below the Earth's crust, that support life. This includes the atmosphere, air, and all water

Biotechnology the use of biological systems or living organisms to make or modify products or processes

Born global refers to firms who get involved in international activities immediately after their birth

Bribery the offer of inducements in return for illegal favours

BRIC economy refers to Brazil, Russia, India, and China. Countries whose economies have been growing relatively rapidly in the first years of the 21st century and are seen as becoming major economic powers in the future

Brownfield investment where a firm expands by taking over existing production or service assets—most FDI is brownfield investment

Capital intensive where production of a good or service relies more heavily on capital, in the form of plant and equipment, than labour

Capital markets physical and electronic markets that bring together savers and investors, e.g. the stock market

Carbon neutral a production process or product that does not add to the carbon dioxide in the atmosphere

Cartel firms come together to agree on a common price or to divide the market between them

Cash crops crops grown to be sold in the market for money rather than for the consumption of the producer

Centrally planned economy major economic decisions, e.g. on production, prices, and investment are made directly by government rather than being left to market forces

Civil law system based on statutes and written codes

Clientelism politicians confer favours on members of the electorate in order to obtain votes—sometimes referred to as patronage

Collectivized where the means of production are owned by the people collectively or by the state on their behalf

Common law system accords more importance to court judgments than to written codes and statutes

Communist system usually a one-party system where the party controls the institutions of the state and owns and controls most of the production of goods and services

Comparative advantage the ability of a country to produce a good at lower cost, relative to other goods, compared to another country; even if a country is not the most efficient at producing the good, it can still benefit from specializing in producing and exporting that good

Competitive advantage strategies, skills, knowledge, or resources that allow firms to compete more effectively

Complementary product a product that is manufactured or used with another product, e.g. computers and computer software

Concentration ratio (CR) a way of measuring market concentration that takes the proportion of industry sales or output accounted for by the largest firms. A CR 5 shows the share of the 5 largest firms in the market

Contract a legally binding agreement between a buyer and a seller

Convention on Contracts for the International Sale of Goods (CISG) UN rules governing the sale of goods between professional buyers and sellers in different countries

Convertibility means that one currency can be legally exchanged for another

Copyright the holder has the exclusive right to publish and sell literary, musical, or artistic works

Corporate Social Responsibility (CSR) organizations take responsibility for the impact of their activities on society including customers, suppliers, employees, shareholders, communities as well as the environment.

Corporatist social model welfare system offering relatively generous benefits and where work is seen as very important—found in countries such as Germany and Japan

Corruption where people misuse their power to enrich themselves

Corruption Perceptions Index a ranking of countries by level of corruption carried out by Transparency International

Creative capitalism the notion that business needs to generate profits and to solve the world's problems, e.g. use market forces to better address global poverty

Creative destruction the process by which radical new products, processes, transportation systems, and markets transforms industry by destroying the old ways of doing things

Cross elasticity of demand a measure of the extent to which customers change their purchasing patterns when one firm changes its price

Cross-border merger when a firm based in one country merges with a firm based in another

Cultural imperialism the imposition of one country's culture on another country

Cultural relativism understanding other cultures and not judging them according to one's own cultural norms and values

Culture shared beliefs, values, customs, and behaviours prevalent in a society that are transmitted from generation to generation

Customary law body of rules, values, and traditions based on knowledge gained from life experiences or on religious or philosophical principles

Customs union a free trade area but with the addition that members agree to levy a common tariff on imports of goods from non-members

Cybercrime crime committed using computers and the internet

Deforestation the destruction of forests either as a result of logging for timber or as people seek to clear forests so that they can farm the land

Demography the study of population in its various aspects—size, age, gender, ethnic group, and so on

Derivative in financial markets an asset whose value derives from some other asset. Buying an equity derivative does not mean buying shares but involves taking out a contract linked to the level of share price. The contract can offer protection against adverse movements in the price of the share

Desertification the process by which once fertile areas of land become deserts. This is seen as a consequence of ecological damage

Devaluation a fall in the value of one currency against others

Developed Countries see Advanced economy

Developing Countries countries whose incomes are low by world standards

Directive (EU) laws that bind member states but are their responsibility to implement

Disposable income income remaining net of taxes and benefit payments available for spending or saving

Distribution of income the division of income among social groups in an economy or among countries

Diversified firm a business that operates in more than one industry or one market

Divestment where a firm disposes of part of the business

DDT Dichloro-Diphenyl-Trichloroethane, a pesticide that was widely used in agriculture in the 1950s

Dumping selling goods in a foreign market at below their costs of production or below the price in the domestic market

Ecocentric a view of the world that stresses that all species are important and that the health of the planet depends on our recognition of the mutual inter-dependence between all species

Economic growth the rate of change in GDP

Economic nationalism the state protects domestic business firms from foreign competition. They become richer and more powerful and this, in turn, increases the power of the state; same as mercantilism

Economies of scale reduction in unit costs associated with large scale production

Economies of scope cost savings resulting from increasing the number of different goods or services produced

Embezzlement refers to the stealing of money or other assets

Emerging economy an economy with low-to-middle per capita income; originally it referred to economies emerging from communism

Equity support regime government support for innovation by buying shares and taking a stake in the ownership

Ethnocentric a belief that the values of your own race or nation are better than others

Eurozone members of the EU having the euro as their currency

Excess capacity where demand is not sufficient to keep all resources in a firm or industry fully occupied

Exchange rates the price of one currency expressed in terms of another, e.g. £1 = US$2

Executive branch implements laws, regulations, and policies and gives policy advice to government ministers

Export credits loans offered by countries, often at low cost, to buyers of exports

Export guarantees where exporters are guaranteed by governments that they will receive payment for their goods or services

Export processing zone (epz) an area where MNCs can invest, produce, and trade under favourable conditions such as being allowed to import and produce without paying tax

External factors components of the micro- and macro-environments of business

Extortion obtaining money or other benefits by the use of violence or the threat of violence

Factors of production inputs combined by organizations to produce goods and services: the main categories are land, labour, and capital

Favouritism where a person is favoured unfairly over others, e.g. in the award of contracts

Federal system there is a sharing of significant decision-making powers between central and regional governments

Feminine society one which values highly the quality of life and human relationships

Financial markets these are mechanisms for bringing together buyers and sellers of financial assets—they can be located in one place or be dispersed

Fixed costs costs that do not vary with the level of output and are incurred whether output is produced or not

Fixed exchange rate when the exchange rate of a currency is fixed against others—in reality a completely fixed rate is difficult to achieve

Floating exchange rate when the exchange is allowed to float freely against other currencies

Foreign direct investment (FDI) the establishment, acquisition, or increase in production facilities in a foreign country.

Foreign indirect investment (FII) the purchase of financial assets in a foreign country.

Franchising granting the right to an individual or firm to market a company's goods or services within a certain territory or location; McDonald's, Subway, and Domino's are examples of companies granting franchises to others.

Fraud deception by those aiming to make an illegal gain

Free trade goods and services are completely free to move across frontiers—i.e. there are no tariffs or non-tariff barriers

Free trade area member states agree to remove tariffs and quotas on goods from other members of the area. Members have the freedom to set the level of tariff imposed on imports of goods from non-members of the area

GATT an international organization set up to remove barriers, particularly tariffs and quotas, to international trade; was subsumed into the WTO

GHGs Green House Gases of which the most serious for climate change are carbon dioxide, methane, and nitrous oxide

Global income the total value of world income generated by the production of goods and services

Global integration the interconnections between countries which increase with the reduction in barriers to the movement of goods, services, capital, and people

Global North this is not a geographically precise term but refers to those areas of the world which are regarded as being economically advanced or developed

Global South in comparison to the Global North this refers to all countries which are developing as opposed to being already developed countries

Global supply chain the sequence of steps that a good goes through to get from the producer of the raw materials to the final product

Globalization the creation of linkages or interconnections between nations. It is usually understood as a process in which barriers (physical, political, economic, cultural) separating different regions of the world are reduced or removed, thereby stimulating exchanges in goods, services, money, and people

Governance the structures and procedures countries and companies use to manage their affairs

Greenfield investment where a firm sets up completely new production or service facilities

Greenhouse gases gases in the atmosphere helping to bring about climate change: the most important are water vapour, carbon dioxide, methane, nitrous oxide, and ozone

Grey market goods sold at a lower price than that intended by the maker; the goods are often bought cheaply in one national market, exported and sold at a higher price in another

Gross Domestic Product the value of all goods and service produced within the geographical boundaries of a country

Guanxi the reciprocal exchange of favours and mutual obligations among participants in a social network in China

HDI (Human Development Indicators) used by the UN to measure human development: they include life expectancy, adult literacy rates, and GDP per capita

Hedge funds financial institutions selling financial products that allow clients to reduce financial risk or to speculate in equities, commodities, interest rates, and exchange rates; they also operate on their own account

Herfindahl-Hirschmann Index gives a measure of market concentration that includes all firms in the market. The more competitive the market the closer the value of the index is to zero. The value of the index for pure monopoly is 10,000

Horizontal merger where a firm takes over a competitor, i.e. the merging firms are operating at the same stage of production

ICSID agency based at the World Bank that resolves international commercial disputes between business

Impact analysis the process of identifying the impact on business of a change in its external environment

Income inelastic when the quantity demanded of a good or services changes proportionately less than national income, i.e. the value of income elasticity is less than one

Industrial revolution a transformation from an agricultural economy to an industrialized economy with large-scale mass production carried out in factories in towns

Industry comprises all those firms who are competing directly with each other

Industry based view an organization's performance is determined by its position in relation to the external environment

Infant mortality the death rate of children in the first year of life, expressed as the number of deaths per 1,000 live births

Inflation a rise in the general price level or an increase in the average of all prices of goods and services over a period of time

Information and Communications Technology (ICT) technology that is relevant to communications, the internet, satellite communications, mobile telephony, digital television

Information revolution the increasing importance of information and the increasing ease with which information can be accessed

Innovation the commercial exploitation of new knowledge

Intellectual property rights (IPRs) legal protection of ideas and knowledge embodied in new goods, services, and production processes

Interest rate the price paid to borrow someone else's money, sometimes called the price of money

Internal factors the internal strengths and weaknesses of the organization

International arbitration companies in different countries who are in dispute can ask that their case be resolved under the New York Convention or by referring it to ICSID at the World Bank

International Comparison Programme the world bank's programme which is developing ways of comparing relative standards of living

International Labour Organization (ILO) a UN agency promoting social justice in the workplace

International Monetary Fund (IMF) an international agency promoting monetary cooperation and stability

Inter-operability the ability of systems such as IT systems to work together

ISIC the UN industrial classification system

Judicial branch institutions such as the police, courts, prison system, and armed forces responsible for enforcing the law

Labour intensive where production of a good or service relies more heavily on labour than on capital, i.e. plant and equipment

Lean manufacturing a process aimed at eliminating waste and reducing the time between receipt of a customer order and delivery

Legislative branch political institutions like parliaments with the power to make laws, regulations, and policies

Liberal democracy a system in which citizens have the right to elect their government and to individual freedom

Liberal social model a form of welfare system offering relatively low welfare benefits and distinguishing between those deserving welfare support and those who do not—found in North America and Australia

Liberalization the reduction of barriers to trade or of entry into a market

Licensing where a firm grants permission for another to use its assets, e.g. to produce its product, use its production processes, or its brand name

Life expectancy the average number of years that a person can expect to live from birth which varies significantly between countries

Liquidity the ease with which assets can be turned into cash

Lisbon strategy EU ten-year plan to improve competitiveness

Lobbying attempt to influence the decisions taken by others, e.g. state institutions

Macroenvironment comprises all the political, economic and financial, socio-cultural, technological, and ecological elements in the wider environment of business

Maquiladora a factory set up in Mexico close to the US border as a result of the establishment of NAFTA

Market comprises competing goods and services, the firms producing those goods/services, and the geographical area where the firms compete

Market concentration measures the distribution of market power by market share

Market deregulation the reduction of barriers of entry into a market

Market economy an economy where prices and output are determined by the decisions of consumers and private firms interacting through markets

Market growth the change over time in the demand for a good or service

Market ideology a set of beliefs asserting that all economic decisions are best left to private individuals and firms through the market; government intervention in the market is abhorred

Market size measured by the sales turnover of a good or service in a market: the relative size of the overall economy

Masculine society one where money, incomes, promotion, and status are highly valued

Mature market a market characterized by low growth

Mercantilism the idea that international trade should primarily serve to increase a country's financial wealth, especially of gold and foreign currency—in this view exports are good and imports bad

Merger occurs where two or more companies combine their assets into a single company; some authors use the term merger only when all parties are happy to conclude the deal

Microenvironment the components of the firm's immediate environment: rivals; customers; suppliers; potential competitors; and substitutes

Microfinance makes finance accessible to poor people in developing countries; seen as a way of relieving poverty

Migrant the UN defines migrants as people currently residing for more than a year in a country other than where they were born

Migration the movement of people across national borders from one country to another

Millennium Development Goals Eight Goals adopted by the United Nations concerning world poverty and general development

Monarchical refers to country where the monarch is the head of state

Monetary policy attempts by the authorities to influence monetary variables such as money supply, interest rates, exchange rates

Money an accepted medium of exchange for goods and services

Money laundering making illegally acquired money appear to come from a legitimate source

Money supply there are various definitions—all include the quantity of currency in circulation and then add various other financial assets such as bank current and deposit accounts

Monopolistic competition a market structure where there are many sellers producing differentiated products

Monopoly a market structure where there is only one seller

Multinational Corporations (MNCs) companies who own and control operations in more than one country

NACE the EU system of industrial classification

NAFTA a free trade area comprising the USA, Canada, and Mexico

NAICS the system of industrial classification used by members of NAFTA, the USA, Canada, and Mexico

Nanotechnology the science of the ultra-small

National income income generated by a country's production of goods and services—the same as GDP

Natural monopoly occurs where the market can be supplied more cheaply by a single firm rather than by a number of competitors, e.g. in the supply of water where it would not be economical to build more than one supply network

Negative externalities these are the costs of either the production or consumption of goods and services that are not borne by the direct producers or consumers but which affect society in general, e.g. exhaust fumes from vehicles pollute the air that we all have to breathe

Neo-mercantilism government policies to encourage exports, discourage imports, control outflows of money with the aim of building up reserves of foreign exchange

Nepotism conferring favours on the members of one's family

New trade theory models of trade that incorporate market imperfections such as monopoly elements and product differentiation into their analysis

New York Convention a commercial body set up under the aegis of the UN to resolve international commercial disputes between companies

Non-governmental Organization (NGO) not for profit organizations who try to persuade government and business on a variety of issues such as human rights, the environment, and global poverty

Norms rules in a culture indicating what is acceptable and unacceptable in terms of peoples' behaviour

OECD international organization comprising 30 member countries, mostly advanced: tries to promote sustainable economic development, financial stability, and world trade

Offshoring transfer of jobs abroad

Oligopoly a market structure with few sellers where the decision of one seller can affect and provoke a response from the others

Open economy a completely open economy is one where there are no restrictions on foreign trade, investment, and migration

Opportunities occur where the external environment offers business the possibility of meeting or exceeding its targets

Opportunity cost the sacrifice made by choosing to follow one course of action: the opportunity cost to a country deciding to use resources to manufacture more of a product is the benefit it gives up by not using those resources to make another good

Option the right to buy or sell an asset at an agreed price

Organizational culture comprises the values and assumptions underpinning the operation of the business; for example, regarding how authority is exercised and distributed in the firm and how employees are rewarded and controlled

Patent a patent gives the holder the exclusive right to exploit the invention commercially for a fixed period of time

Patronage see Clientelism

Per capita per head

Perfect competition a market structure with many sellers, homogeneous products, free entry and exit, and where buyers and sellers have perfect knowledge of market conditions

PESTLE a model facilitating analysis of the macro-environment, the acronym standing for Political; Economic and Financial; Socio-cultural; Technological; Legal; Ecological

Piracy the unauthorized duplication of goods such as software or films protected by patent or copyright;

robbery committed at sea usually through the illegal capture of a ship

Planned economy a system where the means of production are owned by the state on behalf of the people and where the state plans and controls the economy

Poverty occurs where people do not have enough resources to meet their needs in absolute terms and relative to others; the World Bank uses income of US$1/US$2 a day to measure global poverty

Power difference the extent to which a society accepts hierarchical differences, e.g. inequality in the workplace

Precedent when the decision of a court binds others in subsequent cases when similar questions of law are addressed

Price leadership a situation where prices and price changes are determined by the dominant firm or a firm accepted by others as a price leader

Primary market a market where the first trading in new issues of stocks and shares occurs

Product differentiation where firms try to convince consumers that their products are different from those of their competitors through activities such as product design, branding, packaging, and advertising

Product life cycle stages of development through which a product typically moves: introduction; growth; maturity; decline

Productivity the amount of output per unit of resource input, e.g. productivity per worker; used as a measure of efficiency

Public procurement the purchase of goods and services by government departments, nationalized industries, and public utilities in telecommunications, gas, water

Purchasing power parity where the value of, e.g. GDP is adjusted to take account of the buying power of income in each economy. It takes account of the relative cost of living

Qualified Majority Voting (QMV) EU system where any proposal must receive three quarters of the votes to be approved

Quota limitation imposed by governments on the total amount of a good to be imported; the amount of money IMF member countries are required to subscribe to the Fund

Recession a significant decline in the rate of economic growth; technically it can be defined as a fall in GDP over two successive three-month periods

Regional Trade Area (RTA) barriers to movement such as tariffs and quotas are abolished among the members

Regulation rules that take their authority from statutes

Regulation (EU) laws which must be applied consistently in all member states

Religious law based on religious principles, e.g. Sharia law or Muslim law is based on the religious principles contained in the Koran

Resource based view an organization's performance is determined by its resources and capabilities

Revenue the income firms generate from their production of goods and services

Risk analysis systematic attempt to assess the likelihood of the occurrence of certain events

Rules of origin laws and regulations determining the origin of a good—this can be an issue in free trade areas where the origin of the good determines whether a tariff is imposed

Sarbanes-Oxley Act a US law laying down tougher rules for publicly quoted companies regarding the reporting of financial information

Scanning the process of identifying issues in the macroenvironment which have an impact on the organization

Scenario planning using views of the future to help organizations to plan

Screening a technique to assess whether countries are attractive as a market or as a production location

Secondary market where stocks and shares are traded after their initial offering on the primary market

Secularism a doctrine opposing the influence of religion in politics, education, and social issues such as divorce and abortion

Security refers to a share, bond, or other tradable financial asset

Shadow economy goods and services produced (legally and illegally) but not recorded in official figures—no tax is paid and laws and regulations are ignored

Share option a right to acquire shares in the future at a fixed price; often given to founders or senior managers

Social democratic model welfare benefits are generous and available to all; the system is committed to maintaining high employment and low unemployment

Social entrepreneurs where entrepreneurial/business approaches are used to deal with social problems, e.g. providing microfinance to help reduce rural poverty in developing countries

Soviet bloc the Soviet Union and its allies in Eastern Europe such as Poland, East Germany, Hungary, and Romania; the bloc started to collapse in the late 1980s

Special Drawing Right (SDR) artificial currency created by the IMF to ease world liquidity problems

Specialization concentration on certain activities, e.g. the law of comparative advantage suggests that countries should specialize in producing those goods at which they are relatively most efficient/least inefficient

Spot price/rate the current price or rate

Stakeholder individuals or groups who have an interest in an organization and who can affect or be affected by the activities of the organization

Stakeholder mapping a way of prioritizing stakeholders by comparing their power against their interest

State a set of institutions having the legal power to make decisions in matters of government over a specific geographical area and over the population living there

Statute a law passed by a legislative body such as a national or regional parliament

Strategy deciding the long-term direction of an organization

Subsidies financial assistance from governments to business often to protect it from foreign competition

Sukuk a bond that is compliant with Sharia law

Supply chain the systems and agencies involved in getting a good from the raw material supplier to the final consumer

Sustainability the ability of productive activities to continue without harm to the ecological system

Sustainable development economic development that does not endanger the incomes, resources, and environment of future generations

Swap a means of hedging or reducing the risk of adverse price or rate changes

SWOT comprises four factors, Strengths, Weaknesses, Opportunities, and Threats arising from a structured analysis of their internal operations (SW) and their external environment (OT)

Tariff a tax levied by countries on imports or exports

Tax avoidance exploiting legal loopholes to avoid paying tax

Tax evasion illegally avoiding paying tax

Technological advance new knowledge or additions to the pool of knowledge

Technological diffusion the spreading of new technologies within and between economies

Technology the know-how or pool of ideas or knowledge available to society

Theocratic regime religious principles play a dominant role in government and those holding political power also lead the dominant religion

Threats occur when the external environment threatens the ability of business to meet its targets

Tied aid countries receiving financial aid are required to buy goods and services produced by firms in the donor country

Tort an area of law concerned with injuries to people or damage to their assets

Trade gap when imports of merchandise exceed exports of merchandise over a particular time period

Trade surplus when the value of goods exceeds the value of imported goods

Trans-boundary processes which occur across national frontiers. Pollution in one country can often cross over into other countries. Carbon emissions are a prime example of trans-boundary pollution

Transnational Corporation synonym for MNC—a company with operations in more than one country; also used to refer to MNCs who see themselves as a global company and thus not tied to any particular country

Triad comprises NAFTA, the EU, and Japan

Trillion one thousand billion, i.e. a trillion has nine zeros

UNCTAD a UN agency aimed at promoting trade and investment opportunities for developing countries and helping them integrate equitably into the world economy

Unidroit an organization trying to harmonize commercial law between countries

Uniform Commercial Code rules in force in many US states governing the sale of goods

Unitary system major decisions on policy, public expenditure, and tax rest with central government with regions having little power in these areas

Urbanization the increase in the proportion of a population living in towns and cities areas

Vertical merger a merger of firms at different stages of production of a product from raw materials to finished products to distribution. An example would be a steel manufacturer taking over a mining company producing iron ore

Vertically integrated firm a business operating at more than one stage of the production process of a good

World Bank international institution providing financial and technical help to developing countries

World Economic Forum (WEF) a think tank bringing together technical experts, and business and political leaders who try to find solutions to major global economic, political, and social problems. It holds an annual meeting in Davos, Switzerland

World system the global system whose countries and regions are interconnected through a network of trade, investment, and migration linkages

World Trade Organization (WTO) international organization aimed at liberalizing world trade and investment; the successor to GATT

Index

A

absolute cost barriers 80–1
abuse of dominant position 272–3
  Microsoft 242
abuse of power
  corruption as 325
accountability
  government to electorate 226
Accra
  population of 181
achievement motivation theory 160
acquisitions
  cross-border 15, 77
Adebooks website 208
advertising 71
  competition 76
  global 88–9
  legal environment affecting 255
  spending on 88
Aer Lingus
  European Commission intervenes in
    bid by Ryanair for 223
aerospace
  development of 195
Afghanistan War 117
Africa
  asbestos 255
  corruption 26
  customary law 263
  FDI 124
  individualism 162
  intra- and inter-regional trade 50
  investing in 144
  market fragmentation 69
  masculinity 162
  migration 16
  possibility of joining BRIC economies
    47
  power distance 163
  slave labour from 44
  to miss Millennium Development
    Goals 332
  tobacco product promotion in 255
  uncertainty avoidance 162
  urbanization 181–2
Africa Progress Panel 47
age 172
ageing 179–80
Agenda 21
  adoption of 351–2
Agreement on Trade-Related Aspects of
  Intellectual Property Rights (TRIPS)
  270

agricultural products
  tariffs 24
agricultural subsidies 58
  OECD 25
agriculture 48
  decline in China 36
  emissions by industry 355
  Uganda 51
AIG 299, 307
Air France
  merger with KLM 77
air temperature
  changes in 354
air transport 141
Airbus
  effect of exchange rate on 60
airline industry
  impact of internet on 213
  liberalization 94–5
airports 240
Alaska
  oil spills in 106
Alcatel-Lucent
  bribery paid by subsidiaries 327
Alcatel-Lucent v Microsoft 265
alcohol
  regulation of advertising and
    promotion 255
Alibaba 289
Alliance for a Green Revolution in Africa
  333
aluminium industry
  cost cutting in 23
Amazon 198, 211, 213
  deforestation 362
  tax avoidance 237
American Council for Capital Formation
  115
American Enterprise Institute 115
Amnesty International 318, 322
Andreessen Horowitz 114
Anglicanism 19
Angola 47
  GDP 39
Anheuser-Busch Inbev 14
animals
  threat from climate change 357
Annecy Round
  GATT 57
Antarctic
  melting of ice sheets 357
anti-globalization protests 58
Antigua
  tourism 16

Apple Inc 208
  attempts to block imports into US 253
  profile of 67
Arabian Sea
  piracy 146
arbitrator
  state as 239
ArcelorMittal 14, 126
Arctic National Wildlife Refuge
  oil drilling in 96
Arenius, Pia 122
Argentina
  attitude to women in the workplace 165
  financial crisis 285, 298
  GDP 39
  inflation 284
  legal system 260
  liberal democracy 226
  mixed economy 227
  urbanization 181
armaments
  importance of state as customer for
    239
armed forces 225
asbestos
  banned in Saudi Arabia 255
Asia
  AXA operations in 116
  Dell's operations in 4
  FDI 124
  individualism 162
  intra- and inter-regional trade 50
  languages 167
  liberal democracy 226
  migration 16
  perceived incidence of corruption 326
  R&D 203
  social expenditure as percentage of
    GDP 176–7
  terrorist attacks on US businesses in 97
  urbanization 181
Asia-Pacific region 4
  child labour 329
asset price collapse 147
assets
  protection of ownership 256
Association of Southeast Asian Nations
  (ASEAN) 21
AstraZeneca 83
  tax avoidance 237
attitudes 111
Auchan 96
auction companies
  emergence of online 197

auditors
  concerns over 311
Australasia
  perceived incidence of corruption 326
Australia
  bushfires 117
  common law system 260
  cultural attitudes towards time 170
  economic growth 42
  exports 51
  floods 117
  GDP 38–9
  HDI ranking 41
  increased public spending 233
  inflation 284
  intellectual property rights 270
  migration 16, 179
  negotiations 164
  PPP 40
  profit tax rates 233
  projected economic development 46
  public expenditure 231
  public social expenditure as
    percentage of GDP 184
  ranking on Economic Freedom Index
    140
  social expenditure as percentage of
    GDP 174
  universities 18
  urbanization 181
Austria
  business tax 232
  contract law 272
  corporatist model 173
  public social expenditure as
    percentage of GDP 184
  state intervention in banking system
    303
  tax-to-GDP ratio 232
Austrian School of Economics 74
authoritarian/absolutists systems 227–8
Automatic Teller Machines (ATMs)
  development of 290
Avatar 17
avian flu pandemic 19
AXA
  global business environment and
    116–8

B

B&Q 96
bad loans
  financial crisis (2007/08) 298
BAE
  political donations 247
Bahamas
  tourism 16

Bahrain 263
  ranking on Economic Freedom Index
    140
balance of payments 105
Bali
  terrorist incident in 117
Balkans
  political unrest 16
Baltic states 44
Ban Ki Moon 360–1
Banco Santander
  assets of 295
Bangladesh 44
  garment industry 336–7
  perceived as low cost country 6
  piracy 146
  population 178
  social expenditure as percentage of
    GDP 176
bank accounts 290
Bank of America Corp 306
  assets of 295
  merger with Merrill Lynch 294
bank assets
  written down 299
Bank of China 285, 299
  assets of 295
  RBS takes stake in 291
Bank of England
  regulatory role 303
Bank for International Settlements (BIS)
    282
  role of 285
banking system 28, 143
  crisis in 235
  developing countries encourage to
    open markets in 238
  Indian control over 240
banks
  assets of ten largest 295
  as example of private financial
    institution 287
  global concentration 291
  lobbying by in opposition to Basel III
    243
  nationalization 240, 299
  risk management 304
Barbuda
  tourism 16
Barclays 307
  assets of 295
barriers
  removal of to facilitate globalization 5
Basel Committee on Banking
  Supervision 304
Basel III 304
  lobbying by financial institutions in
    opposition to 243

Bear Stearns 235, 299, 306
beer
  market for 73–4
Belgium
  contract law 272
  exports 49
  imports 49
  innovation activity 200
  payment method 289
  public social expenditure as
    percentage of GDP 184
  tax-to-GDP ratio 232
beliefs 111
Belu Water 334
benefits 111, 174
  Germany 234
Benelux
  migration 179
  nationalization of banks 240
Benin
  GDP 39
Bharti Airtel 93
Big Pharma 317
bilateral trade 58
biodiversity
  attempt to develop global response to
    349
  preserving 363
biopharmaceutical companies
  challenges from 83
biotechnology industry
  development of 195
  rise of 193
bird flu 97
birth rate
  declining 112, 178
black economic empowerment policy
  South Africa 268
BlackBerry
  India attempts to exercise jurisdiction
    over 222
blogging 218
  to facilitate communication 211
Blu-ray 209
BMW
  joint venture with Peugeot 204
BNP Paribas
  assets of 295
body imaging technology 195–6
Boeing 96, 128
Bofors 55
Bolivia
  energy reserves 106
  GDP 39
  inflation 284
  nationalization of natural gas
    production 29
  shadow economy 40

Bombay
    population of 181
bond issues 296
bond trading 297
Booz Allen 213
border controls
    as barrier to globalization 25
borders
    abolition of 21
'born global' companies 123
Botswana
    effects of financial crisis on 302
    GDP 39
BP 13–4, 106, 313, 317
    dispute between Russian partners in
        joint venture 268
    Gulf of Mexico oil spill 340–1
brand value 320
    enhanced by CSR 320
Brazil 4, 23
    attitude to women in the workplace 165
    capital controls 25
    deforestation 362
    economic development 42, 63–4
    effect of financial crisis on 281
    as example of federal system 230
    expanding market 5
    FDI 128
    fertility rates 180
    floods 117
    football 30
    GDP 39, 110
    growth in output 281
    inflation 284
    liberal democracy 226
    market access 58
    minimum wage 255
    MNC investment in 14
    population 178
    potential of 44
    projected economic development 46
    signatory to Copenhagen accord 361
    tariffs 24
    tax-to-GDP ratio 232
    urbanization 181
Brent Oil and Gas Field
    decommissioning 102–3
Brent Spar Oil
    disposal of storage terminal 102–3
Bretton Woods Agreement (1944) 285
bribery 247, 266, 325–8
    example of corruption 325
    MNCs accused of 311
    repeated demands likely to be made 326
BRIC (Brazil, Russia and China)
        economies 43–7
    effects of financial crisis on 281
    possibility of Africa joining 47

British American Tobacco 255
British Radio and Electronic Equipment
        Manufacturers' Association
        (BREMA) 244
British Virgin Islands
    lack of financial regulation 304
Brown, Gordon 333
Brown, Lester Russel 348
brownfield investment 15
Brundtland Report (1987) 352
BT 28
Buddhism 166
budget deficits
    reducing 107
building societies 292
Bulgaria 185
    banking 28
    GDP 39
Bundesvereiningung der Deutschen
        Arbeitgeberverbaende (DBA) 244
Burger King 17
Buried Treasure: Uncovering the Case for
        Corporate Sustainability 319
Burkino Faso
    child labour 329
Burundi
    smallholder rice and sorghum projects
        in 333
Bush, President George Walker 96, 352
bushfires
    Australia 117
business
    effect of bribery and corruption on 326
    emissions by industry 355
    importance of relationship to
        government 222–3
    important aspects of law for 264–9
    practices 26
    registration 143
    responding to environmental
        challenges 343–5
    role in society 100
business taxes 232
'business as usual' behaviour 342–3, 358

C

cable television 17
Cadbury
    advertising on YouTube 218
Café Jubilee 151
Cairo
    population of 182
Californiazation 23
call centres
    factors influencing location 4
Cambridge Antibody Technology Group
        83

cameras
    grey market 256
Cameron, David 222
Canada 44
    banking in private hands 303
    common law system 260
    controls on tobacco and alcohol
        advertising 255
    GDP 110
    global competitiveness ranking 133
    Indians in 169
    migrants 16
    payment method 289
    profit tax rates 233
    projected economic development 46
    public social expenditure as
        percentage of GDP 184
    ranking on Economic Freedom Index
        140
    social expenditure as percentage of
        GDP 174
Canada Pension Plan Investment Board
        114
Cancun Climate Change Conference
        (2010) 361
capital
    CSR affecting 320
capital controls
    as barrier to globalization 25
capital markets 296
capitalism 44
car industry 69
    China 28, 82
    implication of Council Directive
        2000/53 on end-of-life vehicles 223
    industry rivalry 79
    Russia 79
    South East Asia 28
carbon dioxide 353
    emissions 355
    rising levels 354
carbon neutrality
    Marks and Spencer plan for 348
Caribbean
    piracy 146
    shadow economy 40
Carrefour 96
    process of internationalization 122
cars
    grey market 256
    variation in prices 69
Carson, Rachel Louise [1907–64] 345
Carte Bleue 289
cartels 71, 78–9
    fines imposed for operating 273
    forbidden in EU 272
    legislation against 255
case law 259

cash
  preference over electronic payments 290
caste 172
Caterpillar 318
Catholicism 19, 168, 178–9
Cayman Islands
  lack of financial regulation 304
cellular technology
  development of 22
censorship
  China 321
Central America
  intra- and inter-regional trade 50
  perceived incidence of corruption 326
central banks 285
  financial assistance given by 299
Central Europe 44
  AXA operations in 116
  free market ideology 20
Central Intelligence Agency's World
    Factbook
  as source of data on markets 135
certificate of deposits (CDs) 296
Chad 47
change
  drivers of 100
Channel Islands
  used for tax avoidance 237
cheap labour
  advantages of 125
  as reason for child labour 330
checks and balances
  lack of in authoritarian/absolutists
    systems 227
Chelsea FC
  owned by Russian businessman 19
chemical industry
  development of 195
Cheney, Vice President Dick 96
cheques 289
Chernobyl nuclear disaster 350
Chevron Corp 14
Chicago
  as major financial centre 297
child labour 321–2, 328–31
  categories of 328
  cocoa production 329–30
  MNCs accused of using 311
  reasons for 330–1
child mortality
  eradication as Millennium
    Development Goal 331Chile
  bribes 247
  global competitiveness ranking 133
  profit tax rates 233
  public expenditure 231
  public social expenditure as
    percentage of GDP 184

risk associated with 147
  tax-to-GDP ratio 232
China 4, 15, 44, 332
  asbestos 255
  attitude to women in the workplace 165
  car industry 82
  car production 28
  censorship 321
  cheap labour 125
  communism 228
  competition law 255
  CSR 321
  currency manipulation 95
  economic development 41–2, 95, 106,
    110
  effect of financial crisis on 281
  effects of 2008 earthquake 97
  emissions control 254–5
  EPZs in 22
  as example of unitary system 230
  exchange rate 61
  expanding market 5
  exports 8–9, 49, 51, 95
  favoured by foreign MNCs 12
  FDI 124, 128
  fertility rates 180
  fierce competition for natural
    resources from 127
  free market ideology 20
  GDP 36, 38–9, 110
  growth of e-commerce 290
  growth in output 281
  health indicators 175
  importance of guanxi 158
  imports 49
  increased public spending 233
  inflation 284
  influencing state in 246
  intellectual property rights 26, 269
  internet 22, 199
  joins WTO 22, 36
  liberalization 96, 105
  major FDI recipient 12
  market access 58
  minimum wage 255
  MNC investment in 14
  moves towards market economy 44
  perceived as low cost country 6
  population 178
  problems of Google in 321
  projected economic development 46
  quotas on car manufacture 124
  religion 166
  signatory to Copenhagen accord 361
  social expenditure as percentage of
    GDP 176
  state intervention in banking system 303
  subsidies 241

sustainability of growth 110
  tax policy used to restrict imports of
    car parts 107
  Tesco expands into 45
  tobacco product promotion in 255
  trade surplus 95
  uncertainty avoidance 162
  US ban on export of satellites to 55
  welfare policy 177
  world economy and 36–7
chloro-fluoro carbon (CFC) gases 350
chocolate industry 329–30
Chowla, Pert 43
Christian Aid 318
Christian Democratic Party
  political donations in Germany 247
Christianity 166
church
  influential role on corporatist model
    173
Church of England 20
churches
  effects of globalization on 19–20
cigarettes
  grey market 256
Cisco Systems
  R&D expenditure 202
Citibank 306
Citicorp
  assets of 295
Citigroup 291–2
  assets of 295
civil aviation
  deregulation 238
  EU and US opens market 238
  liberalization of market 29
civil law 258–9
  common law contrasted 261
civil servants
  access to 245
civil unrest 16
  ethnic groups 145
Clean Air for Europe programme 254
Clean Clothes Campaign 337
Clean Development Mechanisms 356
clean water projects 334
clientelism 227
  Italy 228
climate change 103, 324
  attempt to develop global response to
    350–1
  costs of 358
  denial 359
  effects of 357–8
  global 352–7
  impact on languages 167
  Marks and Spencer plan for 348
  progress on action 360–1

Climate Change Act (2008) 355
Climate Research Unit, University of East
    Anglia 354–5
'Climategate' 359
cloud computing 198–200
cloud technology 103
Coca-Cola
    brand value 320
    market domination 72
    rank and value as international brand
        81
cocaine
    production in Columbia 19
cocoa industry
    political instability and 108
cocoa production
    West Africa 329–30
codes
    international law 266–7
coffee
    consumption in India 151
Coffee Club 151
Coffee Republic 151
Cold War
    defence spending due to 231
collaboration
    in innovation 203–4
colonies
    legal systems of former 258
colonization 43–4, 50
Columbia
    cocaine production 19
Commercial Bank of China
    assets of 295
Commission on Sustainable
    Development 351
Committee on Payment and Settlement
    Systems (CPSS) 289
commodity prices
    rising 283
common currency 21
common law 259–62
    civil law contrasted 261
    role of precedents in 259–60
common market 21
common policies 21
Commonwealth of Independent States
    (CIS)
    intra- and inter-regional trade 50
communication
    as driver of globalization 20
Communication on Progress 324
communications
    development of 195
    ICT enhancing internal 211
    improvements in 22
communism 44, 106
    fall of 17, 21, 28, 124–5

communist regimes
    characteristics of 228
companies
    attribution of 'personhood' to 316
    'controlling mind' 314
    diversification 69
    economic power 316
    interdependence 68
    legal position of 313–4
    moral responsibility 315
    perception of 316–7
    political donations 96, 247
    social nature of 316
Companies Act (1985) 317
Companies Act (2006) 317
competition 6, 20, 23, 71, 142–3
    analysing 75–86
    areas of 76–7
    as driver of globalization 20
    effect of technology on 208
    Five Forces model of 75–86
    foreign exchange and 59
    intensity 77–8
    internationalization of 52
    Lisbon strategy 205–6
    motive for innovation 204–5
    new entrants 80–2
    telecommunications 211–2
competition law 143, 255
    EU 272–3
competitive advantage 53–4
    determinants of 54
competitive indices
    usefulness of 133–4
competitiveness 52–3
    WEF's 12 pillars of 131–2
competitors
    states as 240
complementary products 85
computer hacking 97–8
computers
    development of 195
    increasing speed of 197
concentration ration (CR)
    markets 73
Condition of the Working Class in England,
    The 346
Confederation of British Industry (CBI)
    244, 352
Conference on the Human
    Environment, Stockholm (1972)
    350
confidence
    importance of 282–3
confiscation
    assets 145
congestion charge
    London 342

Congo
    effects of financial crisis on 302
    impossibility of enforcing contract law
        in 236
    smallholder rice and sorghum projects
        in 333
Conocophillips 14
construction companies 6
consultancy
    importance of state as customer for
        239
consultation
    obligation on state 245
consumer capitalism
    cause of environmental degradation
        344
consumer empowerment 103
Consumer Sales Directive (Council
    Directive 1999/44 on certain
    aspects of the sale of consumer
    goods and associated guarantees)
    271
consumerism 344
contain trips 97
continuous linked settlement (CLS) 289
contraception 179
contract law 236, 264
    differences in 272
    EU 272
contract for sale of goods 271
control
    ICT enhancing 210–1
'controlling mind'
    corporations 314
Convention on Cybercrime (2001) 274
Convention on International Trade in
    Endangered Species of Wild Fauna
    and Flora (1972) 350
Convention on the Recognition and
    Enforcement of Foreign Arbitral
    Awards 1958 (New York
    Convention) 268
Convention relating to a Uniform Law
    on the Formation of Contracts for
    the International Sale of Goods
    (1964) 267
conventions
    international law 266–7
Copenhagen Climate Conference (2009)
    360
copyright
    laws protecting 214
coral reefs
    threat from climate change 357
corporate governance
    failures of 304
corporate image
    improved 347

corporate manslaughter 314
Corporate Manslaughter and Corporate
    Homicide Act (2007) 314
corporate scandals 100
corporate social responsibility (CSR) 100,
    311–35
    benefits of 319–20
    business case for 316–20
    criticism by Friedman of 314
    debates on 312–5
    definition 312
    ethical approaches to 322
    global 321–35
    moral case for 315–6
    ten principles for 323–4
    whose standards to apply 321–3
corporate tax
    factors influencing location 4
corporations *see* companies
corporatist model
    society 173, 177
corruption 26–7, 145, 147, 323–8
    acceptability in some cultures 325
    costs of 325
    cultural attitudes towards 159
    major issue for international business
        324–8
    MNCs accused of 311
    not always perceived as bad thing
        328
    principles of Global Compact 323
Corus 127
Costa Rica 4
costs
    effect of technology on 207
    ICT reducing 210
    protecting technology 215–6
Costs of Economic Growth, The 345
Council of the European Union 224
Council of Ministers
    focus for lobbying 244
country risk 145
country similarity theory 52
Court of First Instance
    role of 225
Crédit Agricole Groupe
    assets of 295
'creative capitalism' 334
creative destruction
    notion of 211–2
credit 288
    financial crisis (2007/08) 298
credit card theft 98
credit crunch (2007/8) 11, 111, 299
crime
    effects of globalization on 19
    risk of 144
criminal law 265–6

Croatia
    banking 28
cross elasticity 68, 72
cross-border crime 19
cross-border mergers and acquisitions
    15, 77
cross-border money flows 11
cross-border payments 288–90
Crown Prosecution Service 264
Cuba
    US trade embargo on 55
cultural differences 111
    as barrier to globalization 26–8
    research into 161
cultural factors
    local 143
cultural imperialism
    resisting 56
cultural practices
    as reason for child labour 330
cultural relativism 322
culture
    definition 159
    importance of 158–86
    national 161–2
    purchasing and 163–4
currency 143
    difficulties arising in comparison 135
    fluctuations in 62
currency manipulation
    China 95
currency trading 11
currency volatility 147
current accounts 292
customary law systems 262–3
customer attraction
    enhanced by CSR 320
customer costs 84
customer integration 84
customers
    as instigators of innovation 205
    relations with 83–4
    states as 239
customs unions 21, 346
CVRD 126
cyber security 148
cybercrime
    businesses vulnerable to 213
    increased risk of 98
Cyprus
    contract law 272
    global competitiveness ranking 133
Czech Republic
    banking 28
    contract law 272
    financial crisis 298
    public social expenditure as
        percentage of GDP 184

D

Dai-Ichi Kangyo Bank
    assets of 295
Daimler 14
    joint venture with General Motors 204
    R&D expenditure 202
Daru Car
    failed joint venture with Rover 185–6
data
    collecting on markets 130–6
    problems with collecting international
        135
data centres
    factors influencing location 4
Datamonitor 142
DDT
    banning of 345
de Castries, Henri 117
death rate
    declining 178
decision-making
    international strategy 128
decisions
    EU 270
Declaration on Fundamental Principles
    and Rights at Work (ILO) 323
default
    loans 299
defence
    public expenditure 231
deforestation
    attempt to develop global response to
        349
    Brazil 362
Dell 52
    globalization 4–5
Dell Notebook
    globalization of production 4
Deloitte 84, 311
demand conditions
    competitive advantage of nations 53
democracy
    corruption undermining 325
Democratic Republic of the Congo 47
demographic challenges 148
demography 177–82
    Japan 112–3
Denmark
    contract law 272
    increased public spending 233
    innovation activity 200
    public expenditure 231
    public social expenditure as
        percentage of GDP 184
    ranking on Economic Freedom Index 140
    tax-to-GDP ratio 232
    welfare spending 173

deoxyribonucleic acid (DNA)
  discovery of structure of 193
deregulation
  financial markets 294
  state 238
derivatives 296
  development of 293
  over-the-counter 297
desertification
  attempt to develop global resonse to
    349
designs
  laws protecting 214
Deutsche Bank 291
  assets of 295
Deutsche Telekom 14
developing countries
  competition from MNCs in 126–7
  cultural attitudes towards time 171
  economic growth 42
  environmental protection 363
  green technology 364
  innovation 206
  little FDI involvement 12
  microfinance 287
  population growth 44
  WTO assistance for 57
development
  global partnership for 332
  income thresholds for establishing
    stages of 132
Devyani International Ltd 151
Diageo
  tax avoidance 237
diet 111
  globalization of 17–8
  influence of migrants on 17
dietary rules
  religious 166
diffusion
  cross-border technological 194
  using licensing to control technology
    208–9
Dillon Round
  GATT 57
direct taxes 232
directives
  EU 270
discrimination
  freedom from 322
Disney
  rank and value as international brand
    81
disposable income
  inequalities in 172
dispute resolution 143
  India 262
  international arbitration 267–9

disruptive technologies 103
distribution
  competition 76
  lowering cost of 347
  networks 143
diversification
  companies 69
  motives for financial institutions
    293–4
divisibility
  money 282
Doha Development Agenda 58
Doha Round
  GATT 57–8
Dolce and Gabbana
  tax evasion 237
dollar
  currencies pegged to 61
  exchange rate 60
domestic appliance manufacture 69
domestic rivalry 53
dominant position
  abuse of 272–3
  Microsoft 96
Domino's Pizza
  coping with cultural differences 27
dotcom crash (2000) 111
downloading
  illegal 98
driverless transport 210
drugs 19
Dubai 263
dumping
  MNCs accused of 311
  trade 56

E

e-commerce 213
  China 290
  growth of 274
e-money payments 289–90
EADS
  effect of exchange rate on 60
Earth Policy Institute 348
Earth Summit (2012) 361
earthquakes 117
  risk of 144
East Africa
  mobile phone use 290
East Asia
  cultural attitudes towards time 170
  financial crises 11, 111
  rise of newly industrialized economies
    44
  social environment 161
Easterlin paradox 41
Easterlin, Richard A. 41

Eastern Europe 21, 44
  AXA operations in 116
  contract law 272
  free market ideology 20
  little FDI involvement 12
  perceived incidence of corruption 326
eBay 197
ebookers 28
ecological environment 115
  ecological problem 341–3
  importance to business 340–62
  market assessment 141
  role of science 351
ecological problem
  economic approach to explaining
    341–2
ecological stability 345
economic blocs
  triad of 7
economic development 108
  Brazil 63–4
  China 36, 95, 110
  downside of rapid 362–4
  estimated annual growth rate 109
  projected 46
economic environment 108–11
  importance in assessing markets
    139–40
Economic Freedom Index (2008) 140
economic growth 40–3
  background to 43–4
  equated with human progress 346
economic integration 21
economic nationalism 50
economic risk 145
Economic and Social Data Service (ESDS)
    International
  as source of data on markets 135
economic stability 131, 345
economies of scale 81–2, 293
economies of scope 294
Economist Intelligence Unit (EIU)
  as source of date on markets 130
economy
  role of state in preservation of 235
ecosystem problems 324
Ecuador
  dispute with Occidental Oil 264
education 111, 322
  effect of globalization on 18
  inequalities in 172
  lack of opportunities as reason for
    child labour 330
  state involvement in provision of 240
Egypt 44, 47
  attitude to women in the workplace
    165
  GDP 39

inflation 284
  risk associated with 147
elderly
  threat from climate change 357
elections
  free 226
electric cars
  development of 203
Électricité de France 14
electricity
  development of 195
electricity industry
  Indian control over 240
electricity production and supply 141
electronic signature 274
electronics
  development of 195
  grey market 256
Elf Aquitaine
  political donations 247
Elkington, John 334, 349
embargos
  trade 55
embezzlement 325
emerging economies
  inflation 283
  lack of competition law 255
emerging markets
  AXA operations in 117
  FDI 124
emissions
  by sector 355
  carbon dioxide 353
emissions control 254–5
emissions trading 356
employee protection 255
employment security
  older people 255
employment 111
  companies employing former
    government ministers 245–6
empowerment of women
  achievement as Millennium
    Development Goal 331
End-of-life Vehicles Directive (Council
  Directive 2000/53 on end-of-life
  vehicles)
  implications for car producers 223
energy 240
  emissions by industry 355
  EU dependence on foreign countries
    for 5–6
  saving cost of 347
energy market
  concentration of 76
energy sector
  Ghana 241
  regulation of 254

enforcement
  patent infringement 216
Engels, Frierich [1820–95] 346
England
  contract law 272
Eni Group 14
Enron 100, 117, 242, 317
environment 58, 323
  effect of bribery and corruption on
    325
  external 94–104
  impact of business on 100
  principles of Global Compact 323
  scanning 99–104
  static 94–5
  turbulent 94–6
environmental charges 342
environmental costs 351
  globalization 29
environmental damage
  price for improving standard of living
    316
environmental degradation 40
  consumer capitalism as cause of 344
environmental impact
  reducing 318
environmental legislation
  differences in 321
environmental management systems 347
environmental policy
  risk and uncertainty 351
environmental protection 103
  legal environment affecting 254–5
  legislation on 347
environmental regimes
  establishing global through
    cooperation 349–51
environmental regulation 346–9
  avoiding 125–6
environmental sustainability
  improvement of as Millennium
    Development Goal 332
'environmentally friendly' technologies
    115
  developing 343–4
E.On 14
equal pay 255
Equatorial Guinea
  MNCs' negotiations in 245
  profile of 229
Erasmus programme 18
ergonomically active
  child labour 328
Ernst & Young 84, 306
  auditor of Lehman Bros 311
Estonia
  contract law 272
  development of Skype in 114

natural gas market 76
  public social expenditure as
    percentage of GDP 184
Ethical Corporation 343
Ethiopia 47
ethnic groups 172
  civil unrest 145
euro 21
  currencies pegged to 61
EuroDisney
  subsidized by French government 241
Euromoney 147
Europe
  debt crisis 42
  Dell's operations in 4
  immigration 16
  intra- and inter-regional trade 50
  legal systems 261
  migration 16
  mixed economy 227
  perception of companies in 316
  R&D 203
European Association of Consumer
    Electronics Manufacturers (EACEM)
    244
European Central Bank (ECB) 282, 285
  role of 286–7
  supervisory function in Eurozone 303
European Commission
  definition of CSR 312
  focus for lobbying 244
  role of 224
European Cooperative for Rural
    Development (EUCORD) 333
European Council
  role of 224
European Court of Justice (ECJ)
  role of 224–5
European Financial Stability Fund 299
European Investment Bank 293
European Monetary System
  crisis in (1992) 110
European Parliament (EP)
  focus for lobbying 244
  role of 224
European Patents Office 269
European Round Table (ERT) 20, 244
European Supervisory Authorities 305
European Systemic Risk Board (ESRB)
    305
European Union (EU) 21, 107
  agricultural subsidies 25
  capital controls 25
  cartels 255
  competition law 255, 272–3
  contract law 272
  controls on tobacco and alcohol
    advertising 255

European Union (EU) (cont'd)
  decision on genetically modified foods
    271
  decision-making by 224
  dependence on foreign countries for
    energy 5
  economic growth 42
  electronic payments 290
  financial supervision by 304–5
  focus for lobbying 244
  former communist countries join
    22
  free trade 346
  influence on business 223
  legal framework 270
  liberalization of civil aviation market
    238
  Lisbon strategy 205–6
  market access 58
  merger control 273
  presidency 224
  public procurement 25
  quotas 124
  regulation by 238
  reporting standards 256
  secondary legislation 270
  sets up European Financial Stability
    Fund 299
  Single Market programme 271–2
  subsidies 241
  tariffs 24
  voting power 224
Eurozone 62, 99
  assistance for 299
  supervisory function of ECB 303
exchange
  money as medium of 282
exchange rate 58–62, 107–8, 296
  dollar 60
  financial risk 98
  fixed 61
  floating 62
  fluctuations 99
  impact on business strategy 60
  manipulation of 55
excise duties 232
executive branch
  parliaments 225
executive pay 313
executive responsibility 313
expatriate employees 143
expectancy theory 160
Expedia 213
exploitation
  MNCs accused of 311
Export Credit Guarantee Department
  (ECGD) 240
export credits 54

export guarantees 55
export processing zones (EPZ) 22, 55
export promotion agencies 55
exports 7–8, 48, 143
  Australia 51
  China 36, 95
  compared with GDP 9
  as part of internationalization process
    123
  South East Asia 49
  subsidies 54
expropriation
  assets 145
extended enterprise 100–1
external environment 94–104
external threats
  protection from 235
extortion 325
ExxonMobil 13–4
  plan to stall action on global warming
    115

F

Facebook 197, 218
'facilitation payments' 325
factor conditions
  competitive advantage of nations 53
factor proportions theory 51
fair trial 322
family breakdown
  as reason for child labour 330
Fanny Mae
  nationalization of 299
farming
  subsidies 25
fast food 17
favouritism 325
Federal Aviation Administration (FAA)
  254
Federal Communications Commission
  225
Federal Reserve 285
federal systems 230
Federal Trade Commission (FTC) 238,
  254
fertility rates 180
Fiat
  move into Eastern Europe 124–5
Fiji
  Indians in 169
films 18
  grey market 256
finance
  risk assessment 147
financial assistance
  exports 54–5
  from central banks 299

financial crises 285, 297–301
  characteristics of 297
  East Asia 11
financial crisis (2007/08) 8, 179, 241,
  298–301
  BRIC economies 281
  effect on inflation 283
  free market and 300
  government revenue affected by
    233–4
financial environment 108–11
  importance in assessing markets
    139–40
financial flows 9–15
  as indicator of globalization 7
financial framework 281–307
financial incentives
  FDI 139
financial institutions 11
  domestic consolidation 291–2
  expansion 291–2
  functions of 284–95
  international 285–7
  lobbying by in opposition to Basel III
    243
  private 287
  product diversification 292
  product innovation 292–3
  restructuring and diversification
    291–5
financial intermediaries 288
financial market sophistication
  as one of WEF's 12 pillars of
    competitiveness 131
financial markets 296–7
  effects on financial institutions of
    deregulation 294
  financial risk 98
  increased integration 11
  integration 22
  interconnectedness 299
  liberalization 303
  state intervention 303
financial regulation 301–5
financial reporting 143
  regulations for 256
financial risks
  globalization 97
  increasing importance of 98
financial sector
  Sharia law and 263
  state as client of 239
financial services
  avoidance of regulation 294
  provision by state agencies 240
  South East Asia 294
Financial Services Authority (FSA)
  regulatory role 303

financial system 143
   role of state in preservation of 235
Financial Times 47
Finland
   business tax 232
   contract law 272
   inequalities 172
   natural gas market 76
   public social expenditure as
      percentage of GDP 184
   tax cuts 233
   tax-to-GDP ratio 232
firm strategy, structure and rivalry
   competitive advantage of nations 53
fiscal crises 147
fiscal incentives
   FDI 139
fisheries
   attempt to develop global response to
      350
fishing rights
   customary law 263
Five Forces model of competition 75–86
floods 16, 117
Florida
   hurricane (2005) 98
flu pandemics 117
food
   packaging and labelling 255
   religious rules concerning 166
Food and Drugs Administration
   pharmaceutical industry's power over
      243
food production 345
football
   effects of globalization on 19
   globalization and 30
footwear industry 23
forced labour
   MNCs accused of using 311
forced migration 16
Ford Europe 245
Ford Motor Co 14, 19, 28
   new car factory near St Petersburg 15
   R&D expenditure 202
forecasting
   unreliability of 104
foreign aid
   as barrier to globalization 25
foreign banks
   operating in London 297
   operating in New York 297
foreign currency
   trade in 296
   turnover 296
foreign direct investment (FDI) 9, 11–5,
      107
   barriers to 138

definition 11–2
football 19
foreign indirect investment
   distinguished 12
growth during 1990s 12
incentives for 139
inflows 12–3
major recipients 12
outflows 13
reasons for 124–8
foreign equities 297
foreign exchange 55
   competition and 59
   controls on 50, 143
   daily turnover 292, 296
   market activity 11
   spot rate 61
   trading 296
foreign exchange markets 296
foreign exchange privileges
   FDI 139
foreign indirect investment 9–11
   foreign direct investment
      distinguished 12
foreign investment
   controls on 50
foreign markets
   globalization raising dependence on
      29
   screening and evaluating 128–44
foreign ownership 143
foreign trade
   risk assessment 146
   daily turnover 292
Forum for the Future 343
Foxconn 4
France 44
   attitude to women in the workplace
      165
   banks taken into public ownership
      299
   contract law 272
   corporatist model 173
   dominates UK outward investment
      activity 124
   as example of unitary system 230
   exports 9, 49
   fast food consumption 17
   fertility rates 180
   GDP 39, 110
   imports 49
   individualism 162
   inflation 284
   intellectual property rights 270
   major FDI recipient 12
   migration 16, 179
   natural gas market 76
   payment method 289

profit tax rates 233
   projected economic development 46
   public expenditure 231
   public social expenditure as
      percentage of GDP 184
   state intervention in banking system
      303
   tax-to-GDP ratio 232
   uncertainty avoidance 162
   unemployment 175
France Telecom 14, 29
franchising
   as part of internationalization process
      123
Frankfurt
   as major financial centre 297
   stock market fall 299
fraud 325
Freddie Mac
   nationalization of 299
free market
   effects of financial crisis (2007/08) on
      300
   environment and 343–4
   globalization 24
   inequalities of 344
free market ideology 20
free movement of people 21
free speech 322
free trade 50, 55, 346
   WTO principle 57
free trade areas 21
freedom of association 322
freedom of expression 226
Friedman, Milton [1912–2006] 312–3,
      315
Friends of the Earth 318
Friis, Janus 114
frontiers
   protection 235
funds
   freezing of 145

G

G7
   economic growth 42
Gaia Hypothesis, The 356
games consoles
   grey market 256
Gap Inc 313, 317
   definition of CSR 312
garment industry
   Bangladesh 336–7
Gates, Bill 242, 334
Gazprom 249
GDF Suez 14
gender 172

gender equality
  achievement as Millennium
    Development Goal 331
General Agreement on Tariffs and Trade
  (GATT) 21, 44, 56–7
  rounds of 57
  WTO compared 58
General Agreement on Trade in Services
  (GATS) 238
General Electric (GE) 14, 193
  European Commission intervenes in
    takeover of Honeywell 223
  office in Brussels for lobbying
    purposes 244
  operates Global Research Centre 203
  rank and value as international brand
    81
General Motors 19, 28
  affected by Japanese earthquake 6
  joint venture with DaimlerChrysler
    204
  office in Brussels for lobbying
    purposes 244
  R&D expenditure 202
generally accepted accounting principles
  (GAAP) 256
genetically modified foods
  EU decision on 271
Geneva Round
  GATT 57
geographical distance
  as barrier to globalization 26–8
Georgia
  shadow economy 40
Germany 4, 44
  attitude to women in the workplace
    165
  benefits 234
  business tax 232
  contract law 272
  corporatist model 173
  economic growth 42
  economy shrinkage 42
  as example of federal system 230
  exports 8–9, 49
  fertility rates 180
  GDP 39, 110
  global competitiveness ranking 133
  growth in output 281
  imports 49
  individualism 162
  inflation 284
  innovation activity 200
  main traders of subprime securities
    based in 299
  major FDI recipient 12
  migrants 16
  natural gas market 76

old age dependency 113
  payment method 289
  political donations 247
  profit tax rates 233
  projected economic development 46
  public social expenditure as
    percentage of GDP 184
  ranking on Economic Freedom Index
    140
  skills shortages 16
  social expenditure as percentage of
    GDP 174
  social security 234
  state intervention in banking system
    303
  tax-to-GDP ratio 232
  uncertainty avoidance 162
  unemployment 175
Ghana 47, 181
  energy sector 241
  GDP 39
  inflation 284
GlaxoSmithKline 83
  R&D expenditure 202
Glencore 127
Global Climate Science Data Centre
  proposal for 115
Global Competitive Index
  2010 rankings 133
Global Economic Prospects Report 42
global economy
  measuring 37
global grid 104, 114
Global Health Fellow programme 334
global income 109
global macroeconomic imbalances 147
global organization
  effect of technology on 207–8
global partnership for development
  achievement as Millennium
    Development Goal 332
Global Reporting Initiative (GRI) 324
Global Research Centre
  operated by GE 203
Global Scenario 104
global warming 96, 115, 354–6
  expected to cause large waves of
    migration 16
  GHGs as cause of 353
GlobalEDGE
  as source of date on markets 130–1
globalization
  all-pervasiveness of 17–20
  barriers to 24–8
  benefits of 28–9
  costs for business 29
  Dell 4–5
  drivers of 20–4

environmental costs 29
  examples of 5
  football and 30
  free market 24
  indicators of 7
  misnomer of 7
  opportunities and threats 96–9
  process of 5–7
  raising dependence on foreign markets
    29
  threats posed by 6
Globally Responsible Leadership
  Initiative 343
Goldman Sachs 43, 47, 299
Goodin, Robert 342
goods
  state as customer for 239
  state as supplier of 239–40
goods market efficiency
  as one of WEF's 12 pillars of
    competitiveness 131
Google 198
  bypasses Chinese censorship in Hong
    Kong 321–2
  India attempts to exercise jurisdiction
    over 222
  problems in China 321
  rank and value as international brand
    81
government effectiveness
  risk assessment 146
government incentives
  factors influencing location 4
government ministers
  access to 245
governments
  importance of business relationship
    with 222–3
  as instigators of innovation 205–6
  protection of business by 106
  removal of trade barriers by 21–2
Grayson, David 319
'great rebalancing' 103
Greece
  contract law 272
  economic problems 299
  old age dependency 113
  public social expenditure as
    percentage of GDP 184
  shadow economy 40
  terrorism 97
green movement
  development of 345
green technology
  developing countries 364
greenfield investment 15
greenhouse gases (GHGs) 115, 342, 353
  absorbing 362

mechanisms to reduce 356
targets for reduction of 355
Greenland
melting of ice sheets 357
Greenpeace 317–8
Greenspan, Alan 300
grey market 256
gross domestic product (GDP) 110
by country 39
exports compared with 9
growth of 40–3
as indicator of standard of living 38–40
measuring 37–8
public expenditure as percentage of 231
shrinking 108
group values 314–5
Growth Isn't Possible 43
GSK
tax avoidance 237
Guangdong Development Bank
Citigroup takes stake in 292
guanxi
importance in China 158
guarantees 272
Guernsey
used for tax avoidance 237
Guinea
potato farming 333
Gulf of Mexico
hurricanes 98
oil spill (2010) 144, 340–1
Guyana
Indians in 169

H

hacktivism 98
Haier 203
Haiti
GDP 39
Hardin, Garrett James [1915–2003] 345
Harley-Davidson
brand value 320
Hartigan, Pamela 334
hazardous chemicals
packaging and labelling 255
hazardous waste
illegal exporting of 277
hazardous work
child labour 328
HBOS
merger with Lloyds TSB 294
HD-DVD 209
heads of government 225
health 111, 324
effects of globalization on 19
inequalities in 172

Marks and Spencer plan for 348
as one of WEF's 12 pillars of competitiveness 131
health care 111, 173
health care reforms (US) 243
insurers' opposition to 245
health and safety 322
lack of in Bangladeshi garment industry 337
MNCs accused of low standards of 311
health services
state involvement in provision of 240
heatwave
Europe (2003) 117, 357
Heckser, Eli Filip [1879–1952] 51
Heckser-Ohlin theory 51
hedge funds
global concentration 291
growth of 292–3
Herfindahl-Hirschmann Index (HHI) 73
Hewlett-Packard
rank and value as international brand 81
higher education
as one of WEF's 12 pillars of competitiveness 131
Hindus 166
Hispanic population
spending power in US 179
HIV/AIDS 97
combating as Millennium Development Goals 332
Hofstede, Geert 161
Home Depot 96
home workers
advantages of Skype 114
Honda Motor 14
R&D expenditure 202
Honduras
EPZs in 22
Honeywell
European Commission intervenes in takeover by GE 223
Hong Kong 44, 228
Google bypasses Chinese censorship by 321–2
imports 49
major FDI recipient 12
as major financial centre 297
payment method 289
ranking on Economic Freedom Index 140
risk associated with 147
Hong Kong Ministerial Council meeting (2005) 58
horizontal mergers 77
hours of work 255
Bangladeshi garment industry 336

House
as example of media globalization 17
house prices
affected by financial crises 298
fall in US 299
rise in US 298
housing market
downturn in US 11
HP 198
HSBC 28
assets of 295
Huawei Technologies Co Ltd
patent applications 201
human capital
enhanced by CSR 320
Human Development Index (HDI) 41
human progress
equated with economic growth 346
human rights 322–4
MNCs accused of abuses of 311
principles of Global Compact 323
violations of 16
Hungary
contract law 272
public social expenditure as percentage of GDP 184
tax rises 234
hunger
eradication as Millennium Development Goal 331
Hurricane Katrina 117
hurricanes 16, 98
risk of 144
Hussein, Saddam [1937–2006] 227
Hutchison Whampoa 14
hybrid cars
development of 203
hydro fluorocarbons
emissions 355
hyper-competition 103

I

Iberdrota 14
IBM
brand value 320
Leonovo acquires IBM's personal computer business 127
R&D expenditure 202
rank and value as international brand 81
Iceland
banks taken into public ownership 299
economic problems 299
nationalization of banks 240
public social expenditure as percentage of GDP 184
tax rises 234

identity theft 98
IKEA 23, 96
    import of garments from Bangladesh
        336
illegal economy 147
illegal immigration
    United States 16
illicit trade 147
ILO Convention No.138 329
ILO Convention No.182 329
IMD World Competitiveness Yearbook
    as source of data on markets 130
immigration
    Europe 16
immigration controls
    as barrier to globalization 25
imports 7–8, 49, 143
    capital intensive 51
    China using tax policy to restrict 107
    national defence and 55–6
    prevention of undesirable products 56
improvements in goods and services
    competition 76
incentives 143
Inception 17
Inco 126
income
    inequalities in 172
income distribution 111
income thresholds
    for establishing stages of development
        132
incomes
    affected by financial crises 298
India 15, 17, 44
    asbestos 255
    attempts to exercise jurisdiction over
        BlackBerry 222
    attitude to women in the workplace
        165
    capital controls 25
    cheap labour 125
    clean water projects 334
    common law system 260
    competition law 255
    control over industry 240
    earthquake 117
    economic growth 42
    effect of financial crisis on 281
    emissions control 254–5
    as example of federal system 230
    expanding market 5
    exports 51
    fertility rates 180
    free market ideology 20
    GDP 38–9
    growth in output 281
    health indicators 175

inflation 284
intellectual property rights 269
internet use 22
legal system 93, 262
liberal democracy 226
liberalization 105
market access 58
mixed economy 227
MNC investment in 14
nationalization of banks 303
outsourcing to 28
population 178
PPP 40
profile 150–1
projected economic development 46
signatory to Copenhagen accord 361
social expenditure as percentage of
    GDP 176
social programme 177
state control of entry to retail sector
    238
tariffs 24
tobacco product promotion in 255
Indian Ocean
    piracy 146
    tsunami (2004) 117
Indians
    diaspora 169
indigenous peoples
    threat from climate change 357
indirect taxes 232
individualism
    as dimension of culture 162
Indonesia 44
    attitude to women in the workplace
        165
    AXA operations in 117
    economic growth 42
    financial crisis 298
    GDP 39
    inflation 284
    piracy 146
    population 178
    potential of 44
    profile of 141
    projected economic development 46
    quotas on car manufacture 124
    social expenditure as percentage of
        GDP 176
    as source of cheap labour 125
industrial clusters
    emergence of 206
Industrial and Commercial Bank of
    China
    assets of 295
industrial espionage 214
industrial process
    emissions by industry 355

Industrial Revolution 195, 346
industrialization 345
    effect on natural environment 346
industry
    analysing 86
    analysing competitive environment
        75–86
    China 36
    markets and 68–70
industry based view (IBV) 100
industry rivalry 76–80
    car industry 79
inequalities 172
    free market 344
    living standards 344
inequality
    price for improving standard of living
        316
infections
    new treatments for 203
Infineon 4
inflation 108, 283
information and communications
    technology (ICT) 197
information revolution 103
information technology
    importance of state as customer for 239
infrastructure 140–1
    inadequacies as reason for child labour
        330
    key elements 141
    as one of WEF's 12 pillars of
        competitiveness 131
    reliability of 145
    risk assessment 147
infringement
    patent 216, 253
innovation 194
    activity 200–2
    collaboration in 203–4
    cross-border collaboration 204
    enhanced by CSR 320
    historical waves of 195–7
    motives for 204–6
    as one of WEF's 12 pillars of
        competitiveness 131
institutions
    as one of WEF's 12 pillars of
        competitiveness 131
insurance 143
    bills for hurricanes 144
    effects of terrorism on 97
    rising cost of 144
insurance companies
    as example of private financial
        institution 287
    opposition to health reforms in US
        245

Intel
office in Brussels for lobbying
purposes 244
R&D expenditure 202
rank and value as international brand
81
intellectual capital
enhanced by CSR 320
intellectual property rights
as barrier to globalization 26
international law affecting 269–70
protection 143
interconnections
facilitating globalization 5
interdependence
companies 68
interest rates 108, 283–4, 296
giving up control of 107
Intergovernmental Panel on Climate
Change (IPCC) 354, 358
establishment of 352
internal communications
ICT enhancing internal 211
International Accounting Standards
Board 107, 256
international arbitration 267–9
international banking
growth of 296
international brands
rank and value of 81
International Centre for the Settlement
of Investment Disputes (ICSID) 268
International Cocoa Initiative 329
International Comparison Program 38
International Confederation of European
Beet Growers 244
International Convention for the
Regulation of Whaling (1946) 350
international environmental standards 347
International Federation of Industrial
Energy Consumers 244
international financial institutions 285–7
International Financial Reporting
Standards (IFRS) 256
International Institute for the Unification
of Private Law (Unidroit) 267
international institutions
increasing importance of 107
international joint ventures 80
International Labour Office (ILO) 328
international law 266–9
International Monetary Fund (IMF) 38,
40, 44, 107–8, 282
intervention in financial crises 285
role of 285
as source of data on markets 134
International Organisation for Migration
16

International Product Life Cycle model
51–2
international strategy
decision-making 128
international trade 7–8, 48–62, 89
codes and conventions affecting 266
growth of 48
as indicator of globalization 7
pattern of 48–50
restructuring to facilitate 294
International Trade Commission (ITC) 253
International Trade Organization
proposal for 56
internationalization
process of 122–4
technology 192, 194
traditional model of 123
internet 22
China 199
development of 199
legal issues associated with 274
payments by 290
regulation 275
internet capacity 141
Internet Service Providers (ISPs) 274
interpreters 169
Interpublic 88
intra-firm trade flows 9
intra-industry trade 52
Investing Across Borders 138
investment guarantees 143
investment trusts
as example of private financial
institution 287
iPhone
attempts to block imports into US 253
iPod
attempts to block imports into US 253
Iran
earthquake 117
Muslim law in 263
nationalization of BP 106
Iraq
authoritarian/absolutist regime under
Saddam Hussein 227
nationalization of BP 106
Iraq War (2003) 117
Ireland 4
contract law 272
economic problems 299
innovation activity 200
migration 179
nationalization of banks 240
public social expenditure as
percentage of GDP 184
ranking on Economic Freedom Index
140
tax rises 234

Islam 166
political process influenced by 229
Islamic banks 263
ISO 14001 347
Israel 4
public social expenditure as
percentage of GDP 184
terrorism 97
Istanbul
terrorist incident in 117
Italy 44
clientelism 228
contract law 272
corporatist model 173
declining birth rate 178
economic growth 41
as example of unitary system 230
exports 49
GDP 39, 110
imports 49
migration 179
natural gas market 76
old age dependency 113
payment method 289
projected economic development 46
public social expenditure as
percentage of GDP 184
shadow economy 40
shoe industry 53
tax-to-GDP ratio 232
Ivory Coast
child labour 329
political instability 108
waste dumping by Trafigura in 277

J

Japan 4, 44
agricultural subsidies 25
attitude to women in the workplace
165
banking in private hands 303
business tax 232
capital controls 25
consequences of earthquake in 144
demographic time bomb 112–3
economic growth 42
economy shrinkage 42
emergence of as economic power 44
as example of unitary system 230
exports 8, 49
fertility rates 180
financial crisis 298
foreign aid 25
GDP 38–9, 110
growth in output 281
imports 49
increased public spending 233

Japan (cont'd)
  inequalities 172
  inflation 284
  liberal democracy 226
  main traders of subprime securities based in 299
  major FDI recipient 12
  market access 58
  masculinity 162
  meeting structure 164
  minimum wage 255
  mixed economy 227
  payment method 289
  perception of companies in 316
  population 178
  PPP 40
  profit tax rates 233
  projected economic development 46
  protection of infant industries in 55
  protectionism 50
  public social expenditure as percentage of GDP 184
  social environment 161
  social expenditure as percentage of GDP 174
  tariffs 24
  tax-to-GDP ratio 232
  Tesco expands into 45
  uncertainty avoidance 162
Japanese earthquake (2011)
  global effects of 6
JC Penny
  import of garments from Bangladesh 336
Jersey
  used for tax avoidance 237
Jews 166
Jiaboa, Wen 222
job design
  technology helping with 210
John Smedley 210
Johnson & Johnson
  R&D expenditure 202
Johnson, Victoria 43
joint ventures
  cultural factors in failure 185–6
  international 80
  as part of internationalization process 123
Joltid 114
Jones, Digby 352
Jones, Philip D. 359
Jordan
  attitude to women in the workplace 165
JP Morgan 299, 306
  assets of 295
Judaism 19

judge-made law 259
judicial branch
  parliaments 225
judicial system
  necessity for 236
judiciary 225
jurisdiction
  problems associated with internet 274
Just-in-Time supply 18–9

K

Keating, Michaels 47
Kennedy Round
  GATT 57
Kenya 47
  attitude to women in the workplace 165
  corruption 325
  economic growth 42
  effects of financial crisis on 302
  EPZs in 22
  mobile phone use 290
  political risk 145
Key Note 142
kidnapping
  risk of 145
Kimberley-Clark
  Huggies 'Baby Countdown' widget 218
Kinshasa
  population of 182
Kite, Peter 314
KLM
  merger with Air France 77
knowledge
  difussion of new 194–5
Kodak 127
  creative destruction 212
Koninkluke Philips Electronics
  patent applications 201
KPMG 83, 311
Kuwait
  global competitiveness ranking 133
Kuznets Curve 363
Kuznets, Simon [1901–85] 363
Kyoto Protocol see Protocol to the 1992 Framework Convention on Climate Change

L

labelling 255
labour 323
  sources of cheap 28
labour costs 23
  reducing 125
labour flows 16–7

labour force
  feminization of 172
  migration and 179
labour market
  efficiency as one of WEF's 12 pillars of competitiveness 131
  risk assessment 147
labour regulations 143
labour shortages
  technology helping with 210
labour standards 58
  principles of Global Compact 323
labour unrest 146
Lagos
  population of 182
Lakshmi Mittal 126
land
  customary law 263
  inequalities in 172
landfill
  Marks and Spencer plans to send no waste to 348
language 111
  countries speaking the same 169–70
  cultural importance of 167–70
  differences 26
language skills 170
Latin America
  electronic payments 290
  free market ideology 20
  individualism 162
  liberal democracy 226
  migration 16
  power distance 163
  shadow economy 40
  terrorism 97
  tobacco product promotion in 255
  uncertainty avoidance 162
  urbanization 181
Latvia
  contract law 272
  natural gas market 76
law
  aspects of for business 264–9
  codification in civil law systems 258
  importance for business 254–7
  inadequacies as reason for child labour 330
  interpretation by courts 259–60
  role in society 257
law of comparative advantage 55
law enforcement 106, 225
  India 262
law and order 236
Lebanon
  attitude to women in the workplace 165
  importance of remittances from abroad to economy 11

legal barriers
  competition 81
legal environment 106–8, 253–75
legal risk
  bribery and corruption 326
legal systems 257–62
  Argentina 260
  effects of globalization on 258
  Europe 261
  India 93, 262
  risk assessment 146
Lehman Bros
  collapse of 299, 306–7, 311
Lenovo
  acquisition of IBM's personal
    computer business by 127
Leonard, Annie 344
Leontieff paradox 51
Leontieff, Wassily Wassilyovich
    [1905–99] 51
Lesotho
  importance of remittances from
    abroad to economy 11
lesser developed countries
  tariff protection 107
Levitt, Theodore [1925–2006] 20
LG Display 4
LG Electronics 318
  patent applications 201
Liaison Committee of European Bicycle
    Manufacturers 244
liberal democracy 106, 226–7
liberal social model
  society 173
liberalization 5, 58
  airline industry 94–5
  China 96
  civil aviation by EU and US 238
  financial markets 303
  MNCs and 20
Liberia
  effects of financial crisis on 302
Libya 47
  Muslim law in 263
licensing
  as part of internationalization process 123
  to control diffusion of technology 208–9
Liebeck v McDonald's Restaurants 265
Life Sciences 83
lifestyles 111
  inequalities in 172
Limits to Growth, The 43, 345
linguistic insularity 169
linkages
  facilitating globalization 5
liquidity 306
  effect of financial crisis on 299
  long-term financial needs 290

Lisbon strategy
  competitiveness 205–6
literacy
  definitional problems 135
Lithuania
  contract law 272
  natural gas market 76
Liverpool FC
  foreign ownership 19
living conditions 111
living standards
  inequalities 344
Lloyds TSB
  merger with HBSO 294
loans
  rate of default 299
lobbying 243–4
  EU as focus for 244
locations
  Dell's selection of 4–5
Lomborg, Bjorn 358–9
London
  congestion charge 342
  as major financial centre 297
  population of 181
  stock market fall 299
  terrorist incident in 117
London Cocoa Terminal Market 329
Long Term Capital Management
  collapse of 110
Louisiana
  hurricane (2005) 98
  legal system 258
Lovelock, James 356
low cost airlines 69
low interest loans 54
low pay
  Bangladeshi garment industry 336
  MNCs accused of paying 311
Luanda
  population of 182
Lufthansa 29
Luxembourg
  contract law 272
  global competitiveness ranking 133
  migrants 16
  public social expenditure as
    percentage of GDP 184
  risk associated with 147
  shadow economy 40
Lyme Bay tragedy (1993) 314

M

McDonaldization 23
McDonald's 17
  coping with cultural differences
    158–9

  rank and value as international brand 81
  sets up in Moscow 19
macroeconomy
  as one of WEF's 12 pillars of
    competitiveness 131
  risk assessment 146
macroenvironment 104–6
  definition 93
Madrid
  terrorist incident in 117
majority rule
  as indicator of liberal democracy 226
Makro 96
Malaysia 4, 44, 263
  AXA operations in 117
  GDP 39
  Indians in 169
  intellectual property rights 26
  ranking on Economic Freedom Index
    140
  social expenditure as percentage of
    GDP 176
  Tesco expands into 45
Mali 47
  child labour 329
  clean water projects 334
Malkiel, Burton 213
Malta
  contract law 272
malware 98
management
  homogenization of 160
managers
  role of 313
Manchester United FC
  foreign ownership 19
Manchester University 203
Mann, Michael E. 359
manufactured goods 48
manufacturing
  labour intensive 51
  tariffs 24
maquiladoras 29
marine environment
  attempt to develop global response to
    350
marine insurance 297
Market Abuse Directive (Council
    Directive 2003/6 on insider dealing
    and market abuse) 305
market concentration
  natural gas 76
market disruption 146
market economy
  bribery and corruption undermining
    325
market privileges
  FDI 139

market share 142, 294
market size
    as one of WEF's 12 pillars of
        competitiveness 131
marketing 71, 143
markets
    access 58
    assessing potential 136–8
    attractiveness 129, 149
    collecting data on 130–6
    concentration 72
    defining 68
    domination 72
    fragmentation 69
    general business environment 138–41
    geographical boundaries 69–70
    growth 137, 142
    industry and 68–70
    initial screening 136
    location 129
    measuring concentration 73–4
    new entrants 80–2
    opening of 28
    power 72–4
    quality of demand 137
    selection 148–9
    site potential 137
    size 136–7, 142
    structures 70–2
    volatility 111
Markets in Financial Instruments
        Directive (Council Directive
        2004/39 on markets in financial
        instruments) 305
Marks and Spencer
    import of garments from Bangladesh
        336
    programme for environmental change
        348
Marsh Report: Terrorism Risk Insurance
        (2010) 97
masculinity
    as dimension of culture 162
MasterCard 289–90
materials
    saving cost of 347
maternal health
    improvement of as Millennium
        Development Goal 331
Mattli, Walter 243
maturing product stage
    production 52
Mauritius
    Indians in 169
    intellectual property rights 270
media
    globalization of 17
Medimmune 83

Mediterranean
    cultural attitudes towards time 170
meeting
    cultural differences 164
mercantalism 50
Merck 83
    R&D expenditure 202
Mercosur 21
Merger Regulation (Regulation 139/2004
        on the control of concentrations
        between undertakings) 273
mergers
    cross-border 15, 77
    EU controls on 273
Merkel, Angela 222
Merrill Lynch
    merger with Bank of America 294
Messi, Lionel 19
methane
    emissions 355
Metro 96
Mexico 4, 23, 29, 44
    attitude to women in the workplace
        165
    AXA operations in 117
    financial crisis 285, 298
    health indicators 175
    inequalities 172
    potential of 44
    profit tax rates 233
    projected economic development 46
    public social expenditure as
        percentage of GDP 184
    source of swine flu pandemic 19
microelectronics
    emergence of 113–4
microenvironment 105
microfinance 287
Microsoft 198, 208, 239
    abuse of dominant position 242
    dominant position 96
    market power 72
    office in Brussels for lobbying
        purposes 244
    R&D expenditure 202
    rank and value as international brand
        81
    related products 209
Microsoft Office 208
middle class
    definition 138
    growth of 140
Middle East
    corruption 26
    Indians in 169
    intra- and inter-regional trade 50
    terrorist attacks on US businesses in 97
    uprisings in 144

migrant remittances 11
migration 16–7
    effect on population size 179
    global warming expected to cause 16
    as indicator of globalization 7
    reasons for 16
    short term 16
military dictatorship 106
military equipment
    US ban on export of to Venezuela 55
military threats
    protection from 235
Millennium Development Goals (MDGs)
        331–4, 362
    criticism of 332–3
    reasons why they should succeed 334
minimum wage 143, 255
mining 48, 77, 126
Mintel 142
Mishan, Edward 43
Mitsubishi Bank
    assets of 295
Mitsubishi Group
    assets of 295
Mittal Steel 126
mixed economy
    liberal democracy 227
mobile phones 197–8
    increased demand for 22
    litigiousness between manufacturers
        253
    money transfer by 290
    payments by 290
Moldova
    importance of remittances from
        abroad to economy 11
money
    electronic movement 19, 22
    importance of in international
        financial environment 282
money laundering 19
money markets 296
monitoring
    ICT enhancing 210
monopolies 254
    market structure 70–1
    national 211
monopolistic competition
    market structure 70–1
monopoly 73
Montreal Protocol on Substances that
        Deplete the Stratospheric Ozone
        Layer (1987) 351
Moody's 306
moral responsibility
    companies 314
Morgan Stanley 299
Mormons 166

Morocco 47
mortgage-related securities 11
mortgages 298
most favoured nation status 56–7
motor transport
  environmental costs of 342
motor vehicle
  pollution caused by 342
Motorola 313
movement
  freedom of physical 322
Mozambique
  risk associated with 147
multinational companies (MNCs) 7, 9, 14
  abuses by 311–2
  competition from developing countries' 126–7
  FDI involvement 12
  international joint ventures 80
  involvement in R&D 194
  liberalization and 20
  promises and threats by 245
  table of top 25 14
  technology assisting growth of 207
  use of technology 206
Mumbai
  terrorist incident in 117
Murdoch, Rupert 262
music
  grey market 256
Muslim law systems 263
Muslims 19
Myanmar (Burma)
  as example of authoritarian/absolutist regime 227

N

nanotechnology 196–7
nation state
  viability of 235
National Association of Manufacturers 20
national defence 55–6
National Health Service (NHS) 173
  pharmaceutical industry and 242
National Intelligence Council of the USA 104
national monopolies 211
national taste 26
nationalization 145
  gas production in Bolivia 29
natural disasters 144
  forcing migration 16
  globalization 97
natural environment
  effect of industrialization on 346

natural gas
  market concentration 76
  nationalization in Bolivia 29
natural resources 12
  depletion 40
  fierce competition from China for 127
  internationalization to obtain 126
  MNCs accused of exploiting 311
NEC Corp
  patent applications 201
negligence 265
negotiations
  cultural differences 164
negotiator
  state as 238
neo-mercantilism (economic nationalism) 50
Nepal
  uprising by Maoist rebels 144
nepotism 325
Net Impact 343
Netherlands
  banks taken into public ownership 299
  contract law 272
  exports 49
  imports 49
  individualism 162
  inequalities 172
  main traders of subprime securities based in 299
  migrants 16
  payment method 289
  profit tax rates 233
  public social expenditure as percentage of GDP 184
  welfare spending 173
networking 197
networks
  growth of online 217
NeuTec Pharma 203
New Delhi
  population of 181
New Orleans
  evacuation of after hurricane 98
new product stage
  production 52
new trade theory 52
New York
  as major financial centre 297
  population of 181
  stock market fall 299
New York Convention (Convention on the Recognition and Enforcement of Foreign Arbitral Awards 1958) 268
New Zealand
  banking in private hands 303
  controls on tobacco and alcohol advertising 255

cultural attitudes towards time 170
HDI ranking 41
migrants 16
public social expenditure as percentage of GDP 184
ranking on Economic Freedom Index 140
Nguema, Oblang 229
Nigeria 44, 47, 332
  attitude to women in the workplace 165
  cash and cheque-based economy 290
  economic growth 42
  fertility rates 180
  funding for vulnerable rural families in 333
  inflation 284
  MNCs' negotiations in 245
  Muslim law in 263
  nationalization of BP 106
  piracy 146
  population 178
  Shell's operations in 247–8
Nigeria Shell 102
Nike 317
NimbleGen 83
Nissan Motor 19
  R&D expenditure 202
nitrous oxide
  emissions 355
Nobel Biocare 203
Nokia 31–2, 253
  R&D expenditure 202
  rank and value as international brand 81
non-discrimination
  WTO principle 56–7
non-governmental organizations (NGOs)
  influence on CSR 318
non-renewable resources
  consumption of 345
non-tariff barriers 54
North Africa
  political unrest 16
  uprisings in 144
North America
  cultural attitudes towards time 170–1
  Dell's operations in 4
  internet use 22
  intra- and inter-regional trade 50
  liberal democracy 226
  migration 16
  mixed economy 227
  perceived incidence of corruption 326
  perception of companies in 316
  R&D 203
  social environment 161

North Atlantic Free Trade Area (NAFTA) 21, 29
North Atlantic Treaty Organization (NATO)
  former communist countries join 22
North Western Europe
  internet use 22
Northern Rock 235, 306
  crisis at 299, 301
Norway
  agricultural subsidies 25
  HDI ranking 41
  public social expenditure as percentage of GDP 184
  ranking on Economic Freedom Index 140
  risk associated with 147
  tariffs 24
  tax-to-GDP ratio 232
Novartis 203
  R&D expenditure 202
nuclear industry
  affected by Japanese earthquake 6

O

Obama, President Barak 222, 226, 243, 245, 340, 352
obedience
  as reason for child labour 330
Occidental Oil
  dispute with Ecuador 264
Office of the Communications Regulator (OFCOM) 225
Office Depot
  merger with Staples blocked 238
offshore financial centres 304
offshore gambling
  US dispute over 268
offshoring 9
OFGEM 225, 254
OFWAT 225, 254
Ohlin, Bertil Gotthard [1899–1979] 51
oil
  Chinese demand for 36
  depletion of reserves 40
  drilling in Arctic National Wildlife Refuge 96
oil companies
  effects of hurricanes on 98
oil industry 69
  competition 77
  development of 195
oil prices
  effect on financial institutions 294
oil reserves
  Saudi Arabia 228

oil spill
  Gulf of Mexico 340–1
old age dependency 112
older people
  security of employment 255
oligopoly 78
  market structure 70–1
Oman
  GDP 39
Omnicom 88
O'Neill, Jim 47
operational efficiency
  enhanced by CSR 319
opportunities
  effect of technology on 207–11
  globalization 96–9
options
  development of 293
Organization for Economic Co-operation and Development (OECD)
  agricultural subsidies 25
  shadow economy 40
  as source of data on markets 135
organizations
  change 100
organized crime 145, 147
Our Common Future 351
output
  growth in 281
outsourcing 28
over-the-counter (OTC) trading 293, 297
ownership
  property 322
  protection of rights 256
  restrictions 138
Oxfam 318, 322
Oxford University 203
ozone depletion 115, 350
ozone layer
  attempt to develop global response to 350
  damage to 115

P

package tours 271
packaging 255
Pakistan 17
  attitude to women in the workplace 165
  GDP 39
  perceived as low cost country 6
  population 178
  social expenditure as percentage of GDP 176
Panasonic Corp
  patent applications 201
  R&D expenditure 202

pandemics 97
Paris
  stock market fall 299
parliaments
  role of 225
Patent Cooperation Treaty 269
patents
  enforcement problems 216
  infringement 253
  as method of protecting technology 214
  multiple applications 215
  ownership 194
  role in innovation 215
  top applicants for 201
patronage 227–8
payments 288–90
  method by country 289
  risk assessment 146
PayPal 289–90
pension funds
  as example of private financial institution 287
pensions 111
perfect competition
  market structure 70–1
personal freedom
  not valued in communist regimes 228
'personhood'
  attributed to companies 316
personnel
  exchange of 245–7
PESTLE model 75, 105–6
petrochemicals
  development of 195
petrol duties 342
Peugeot
  joint venture with BMW 204
Pfizer 83
  develops Global Health Fellow programme 334
  R&D expenditure 202
pharmaceutical industry
  development of 195
  grey market 256
  importance of state as customer for 239
  lobbying 243
  relations with state institutions 242
  threat from substitutes 83
Pharmacia
  merger with Upjohn 158
Philip Morris 255
Philippines 4, 44
  social expenditure as percentage of GDP 176
  as source of cheap labour 125

PHP Billiton 77, 126
physical movement
    freedom of 322
physical security 322
Pickard, Ann 249
Pinochet, Augusto [1915–2006] 247
piracy 145
    Somalia 146
plants
    threat from climate change 357
PlayStation Portable
    victim of grey market 256
Poland 4
    attitude to women in the workplace
        165
    contract law 272
    declining birth rate 178
    GDP 39
    natural gas market 76
    profit tax rates 233
    public social expenditure as
        percentage of GDP 184
police 225
political change
    globalization and 21
political donations
    company 96
    illegal 325
    as means of influencing decision-
        making 247
political environment 106–8
    definition 223
    effect on business 222–47
    importance in assessing markets
        138–9
political instability 16, 147
    cocoa industry and 108
political integration 21
political leadership
    change in 145
political participation 322
political parties
    restrictions on 227
political regimes 106
political risks
    globalization 97
political stability
    risk assessment 146
political systems
    types of 226–30
polluter pays principle 342
pollution 345
    avoiding controls on 126
    effect of Industrial Revolution on 346
    resulting from production 254
    taxation 115
pollution control 115
Pope 230

population 345
    ageing 179–80
    changes in size 178–81
    characteristics 111
    China 37
    growth forecast 44
    world 177
'pork barrel politics' 228
pornography 19
port security 97
Porter, Michael Eugene 52–3, 75
Porter's Five Forces 100, 143
ports 141, 240
Portugal
    banks taken into public ownership
        299
    contract law 272
    economic problems 299
    public social expenditure as
        percentage of GDP 184
postal services
    Indian control over 240
poverty 44, 47, 173, 324
    cultural attitudes towards 159
    definitional problems 135
    eradication as Millennium
        Development Goal 331
    as reason for child labour 330
    Sweden 174
    threat from climate change 357
    United Kingdom 174
    United States 175
power distance
    as dimension of culture 162
Power of Unreasonable People, The: How Social
    Entrepreneurs Create Markets and
    Change the World 334
precautionary principle 347
precedents
    role in common law 259–60
predatory pricing 255
predictability
    WTO principle 57
prediction
    unreliability of 104
premier football league
    FDI in 19
Presidency
    EU 224
pressure groups
    environmental 343
price
    competition 76
    discrimination 69
price fixing 78
    BP 106
prices 143
    variations in 69

PricewaterhouseCoopers 83, 311
pricing the planet 104
pricing policy 71
Primark
    import of garments from Bangladesh
        336
primary education
    achievement as Millennium
        Development Goal 331
    as one of WEF's 12 pillars of
        competitiveness 131
private equity funds 287
private financial institutions 287
privatization 107
    Russia 257
Proctor & Gamble
    office in Brussels for lobbying
        purposes 244
    sustainability and 318–9
product characteristics
    legal environment affecting 255
product differentiation 81, 84
product diversification
    financial institutions 292
product innovation
    competition 77
    failures 211–2
product market
    assessing 142–3
production
    internationalization to reduce costs
        125–6
    legal environment affecting 254
    site assessment 143
    stages of 51–2
productivity
    effect of technology on 207
    ICT increasing 210
productivity imperative 103
products
    effect of technology on 207
profits
    businesses having vested interest in
        maximizing 344
    taxes on 232
promise
    MNCs 245
promotion 143
property
    destruction 145
    inequalities in 172
    ownership 322
    seizure 145
prostitution 19
protection periods
    differing 215
protectionism 24, 50, 95, 124
Protestantism 166

Protocol to the 1992 United Nations Framework Convention on Climate Change (1997) (Kyoto) 96, 115, 351, 355–6
public borrowing 233
public expenditure 231–4, 236–7
  raising funds for 232–3
  reducing 107
  welfare provision 173
  where the money goes 231
public health
  effect of Industrial Revolution on 346
public procurement
  as barrier to globalization 25
public sector
  spending by 239
public service
  bribery and corruption diverting resources from projects 325
  liberal democracy 226
public transport 141, 342
Publicis 88
purchasing
  culture and 163–4
purchasing power 109
purchasing power parity (PPP) 38, 40
Puritanism 20
Putin
  Vladimir 222

Q

Qatar
  HDI ranking 41
  migrants 16
Qualcomm Inc
  patent applications 201
quality circles 19
quality standards 97
Quangos (Quasi Autonomous Non-Governmental Organizations) 225
Quebec
  legal system 258
quotas 50
  EU 124

R

R. v Kite and OLL Ltd 314
R. v P & O European Ferries (Dover) Ltd 314
race 26
racketeering 146
rail networks 240
  Indian control over 240
rating agencies 306
raw materials 50
  increasing demand for 126

Marks and Spencer plan for sustainable 348
recession
  decline in world trade caused by 8
reciprocity
  WTO principle 57
recycling 318–9
refugees
  effect on language 169
regional taste 26
regional trade areas (RTAs) 21
regional trading blocs
  establishment of 107
regulation
  avoidance by financial institutions 294
  as barrier to globalization 24–6
  challenges posed by financial crisis 304–5
  environmental 345–9
  financial markets 301–5
  lax contributing to financial crisis (2007/08) 298
  risk assessment 146
  supranational 238
  systems of 302–3
regulations
  EU 270
regulator
  state as 238
regulatory agencies 225
regulatory incentives
  FDI 139
reinsurance
  rising cost of 144
related products
  Microsoft 209
  using technology to force purchase of 209
related and supporting industries
  competitive advantage of nations 53
religion 111
  cultural importance of 166
  effects of globalization on 19–20
  food rules in 166
  geographical distribution 167
religious belief 26
remote workers
  advantages of Skype 114
remuneration
  executive 313
Renault
  affected by Japanese earthquake 6
renewable energy 6, 318
renminbi 61
  Chinese ambitions for 95
reporting standards
  harmonization of 256
Republican party
  political donations 247

reputation
  effect of bribery and corruption on 326
  enhanced by CSR 320
reputation management 317
research
  abortive 193–4
  funding 193
research and development (R&D) 80, 213
  definition 193
  foreign MNCs involvement 194
  geographical location of 202–3
  global companies by expenditure 202
  state involvement in 240
Research in Motion (RIM) 222
residential
  emissions by industry 355
residential mortgages 11
resource security 148
resources
  states' right to exert sovereignty over own 351
  struggle for 77
resources based view (RBV) 100
restructuring
  motives for financial institutions 293–4
  as response to global financial crisis 294
retail sector
  Indian state control of entry into 238
retaliation
  dumping 56
retirement age
  changing 180
retrenchment 148
revenue
  impact of CSR on 319
Ricardo, David [1772–1823] 51
rights
  respect for minimal 322
Rio Declaration on Environment and Development (1992) 323, 351
Rio Earth Summit (1992) 352, 361
Rio Tinto 126
'rise of the rest' 103
risk
  environmental policy 351
  spreading 290
risk assessment 144–8
risk management
  banks 304
risk profile
  CSR and 320
rivalry 53
road congestion
  costs of 342
road network 141

road pricing 342
road taxes 342
roads 240
Robert Bosch GmbH
    patent applications 201
    R&D expenditure 202
Roche 83
    R&D expenditure 202
Roman law
    Scottish law influenced by 258
Ronaldo, Cristiano 19
Rosneft 268
Rover
    failed joint venture with Daru Car
        185–6
Royal Bank of Scotland (RBS) 291
    assets of 295
Royal Dutch Shell
    business principles 102
Rubber
    process of internationalization 123
rule of law
    India 262
Rusal 126
Russia 15, 44
    attitude to women in the workplace 165
    AXA operations in 116
    car industry 79
    death rate 178
    default on debt repayments 110
    dispute with Ukraine 6
    economic growth 42
    effect of financial crisis on 281
    electronic payments 290
    energy 5
    energy reserves 106
    expanding market 5
    fertility rates 180
    financial crisis 285, 298
    GDP 39
    growth in output 281
    inequalities 172
    major FDI recipient 12
    minimum wage 255
    population 178
    potential of 44
    privatization 257
    projected economic development 46
Russian mafia 19
Ryanair
    European Commission intervenes in
        bid for Aer Lingus 223

S

Saab 55
St Lucia
    tourism 16

Sakura Bank
    assets of 295
sale of goods 271
sales promotion 71
    competition 76
    legal environment affecting 255
Samsung Electronics
    R&D expenditure 202
Samsung Group 4
    use of technology 192
sanction busing
    MNCs accused of 311
sanitation
    effect of Industrial Revolution on 346
Sanofi-Aventis
    R&D expenditure 202
Sanwa Bank
    assets of 295
Sao Paulo
    population of 181
Sarbanes-Oxley Act (2002) (United
        States) 256
Sarkozy, Nicholas 41
SARS 117
satellite television 17
    grey market 256
satellites
    US ban on export of to China 55
Saudi Arabia
    attempts to exercise jurisdiction over
        BlackBerry 222
    ban on asbestos 255
    bribes 247
    cultural attitudes towards time 171
    as example of authoritarian/absolutist
        regime 227
    fertility rates 180
    Muslim law in 263
    oil reserves 228
    regime based on patronage 227
savings 288
Scandinavia
    contract law 272
    inequalities 172
    legal system 258
    masculinity 162
    power distance 163
    social democratic model 174
    welfare spending 172
Schering Plough 83
Schumpter, Joseph Alois [1883–1950]
        211–2
science
    role in environmental environment
        351
science and technology infrastructure 141
Scottish law
    influenced by Roman law 258

sea levels
    rising 115
Seattle Ministerial Council meeting
        (1999) 58
secondary markets 296
secularism 168
security
    risk assessment 146
    Skype 114
Senegal
    potato farming 333
Seoul
    population of 181
separation of powers
    liberal democracy 226
service market
    assessing 142–3
services
    China 36
    state as customer for 239
    state as supplier of 239–40
Servizi Interbancari 289
Seventh Day Adventists 166
sexuality
    cultural attitudes towards 159
shadow economy 40
share issues 296
share prices
    affected by financial crises 298
    falling 299
shareholder value 317
    enhanced by CSR 319
    maximizing 100
shareholders 313
shares
    inequalities in 172
Sharia law 263
Sharp Kabushiki Kaisha
    patent applications 201
Shell Group 13–4
    failure to consult on sinking of North
        Sea oil platform 317
    operations in Nigeria 247–8
shoe industry
    Italy 53
shortages 147
Siemens 13–4
    alleged bribery 266
    R&D expenditure 202
Sierra Leone 47
    cash and cheque-based economy 290
    potato farming 333
Silent Spring, The 345
Silver Lake Partners 114
Simms, Andrew 43
Simpsons, The
    as example of media globalization
        17

Singapore 4, 44, 263
  global competitiveness ranking 133
  as major financial centre 297
  payment method 289
  ranking on Economic Freedom Index
    140
  risk associated with 147
Singh, Manmohan 222
Single European Act (1986) 270
Single Market Programme
  EU 26, 271–2
Skeptical Environmentalist, The 358
skill levels 51
skills
  as reason for child labour 330
skills shortages 16
Skype 114
  India attempts to exercise jurisdiction
    over 222
  problems associated with 114
slave trade 44
Slovakia
  contract law 272
  natural gas market 76
  public social expenditure as
    percentage of GDP 184
Slovenia
  contract law 272
  global competitiveness ranking 133
  public social expenditure as
    percentage of GDP 184
small firms
  technology assisting growth of 207–8
Small is Beautiful 345
small island communities
  threat from climate change 357
Smirnoff
  advertising on YouTube 218
Smith, Adam [1723–90] 50
smoking
  restrictions on 255
social class 172
social contract theory 316
social costs
  ecological problem 341–2
social democratic model
  society 174–5
social entrepreneurship 334–5
social environment
  effect on business 172–82
social expenditure
  by country as percentage of GDP 174,
    184
social media
  keeping in touch with stakeholders by
    103
social models 172–7
  clash of 175–6

social networks
  growth of online 217
social norms 26
social organization 111
social relationships 111
social security
  Germany 234
social security contributions 232
society
  Chinese 158
  divisions within 172
  evolution of 316
  role of law in 257
Society for Worldwide Interbank
    Financial Telecommuniation
    (SWIFT) 288
socio-cultural environment 111–3
  assessing markets 140
  importance of 158–78, 180–6
Socrates programme 18
Solow, Robert Merton 359
Somalia
  piracy 146
Sony 77, 256
  R&D expenditure 202
  technology battle with Toshiba 209
Sony/Ericsson
  affected by Japanese earthquake 6
South Africa 47
  black economic empowerment policy
    268
  effects of financial crisis on 302
  fertility rates 180
  GDP 39
  Indians in 169
  market access 58
  minimum wage 255
  mixed economy 227
  signatory to Copenhagen accord 361
South America
  cultural attitudes towards time 170
  Dell's operations in 4
  intra- and inter-regional trade 50
  perceived incidence of corruption 326
  piracy 146
  terrorist attacks on US businesses in 97
South Asia
  cultural attitudes towards time 170
South East Asia 23
  car production 28
  economic expansion leading to
    increased demand for financial
    services 294
  exports 49
  financial crisis 285
  free market ideology 20
  market fragmentation 69
  tobacco firms 28

South Korea 4, 44
  attitude to women in the workplace 165
  AXA operations in 116
  exports 49
  financial crisis 298
  increased public spending 233
  market access 58
  negotiations 164
  profit tax rates 233
  projected economic development 46
  protection of infant industries in 55
  public expenditure 231
  public social expenditure as
    percentage of GDP 184
  social expenditure as percentage of
    GDP 176
  tax cuts 233
  tax-to-GDP ratio 232
  Tesco expands into 45
  urbanization 181
sovereign wealth funds 103
sovereignty
  states' right to exert over own
    resources 351
Soviet bloc 44
Soviet Union
  collapse of 44, 106
Spain
  attitude to women in the workplace 165
  contract law 272
  declining birth rate 178
  GDP 110
  innovation activity 200
  natural gas market 76
  old age dependency 113
  projected economic development 46
  public social expenditure as
    percentage of GDP 184
  terrorism 97
special assistance
  WTO principle for developing
    countries 57
Spectrum/Shahriyar Sweater factory
  collapse of 337
spending power
  Hispanic population in US 179
sport
  effects of globalization on 19
spot rate
  foreign exchange 61
Sri Lanka
  floods 117
  Indians in 169
  social expenditure as percentage of
    GDP 176
stability
  WTO principle 57
stakeholder empowerment 103

stakeholder theory 316
stakeholders
  definition 100–1
  importance of 101
  keeping in touch with 103
  mapping 102
  notion of 100
  role in innovation 204
standard of living
  GDP as indicator of 38–40
  price for improving 316
Standard and Poor's 306
standardized stage
  production 52
standards
  CSR 321–3
Staples
  merger with Office Depot blocked 238
Starbucks 151
state
  arbitration role 239
  as competitor for private sector firms
    240
  customer for goods and services 239
  deregulation by 238
  effect of globalization on 234
  fragility 147
  functions affecting business 235–41
  influence on by organizations 241–7
  institutions of 223–5
  intervention in financial markets 303
  methods of influencing 242–7
  negotiator role 238
  obligation to consult 245
  regulator role 238
  relationship with business 222–3
  role of 104
  size of 231–4
  spending and taxation by 236–7
  subsidies provided by 241
  supplier of goods and services 239–40
statutes
  precedence over common law 260
steam power
  development of 195
  as driver of economic growth 43
steel
  US levy on imports of 124
Stern, Nicholas 358
Stern Review on the Economics of
    Climate Change 358
Stiglitz, Joseph 41
stock exchanges 11, 143, 296
stock markets
  risk of crashes 144
  share prices falling 299
Stockholm Conference (1972) 350
Story of Stuff, The 344

strategic management 100
Straumann 203
Stuxnet worm 98
SUAL 127
sub-Saharan Africa 47, 51
  cash and cheque-based economies 290
  child labour 329
  economic growth 42
  effects of financial crisis on 302–3
  growth in GDP 303
  shadow economy 40
  to miss Millennium Development
    Goals 333
subprime loans
  rise in 298
subprime mortgages 299
subprime securities
  main traders of 299
subsidiaries
  for tax avoidance 237
subsidies
  agricultural 58
  as barrier to globalization 24–5
  China 241
  environmental 115
  exports 54
  farming 25
  state provision of 241
  types of 54–5
subsidized services
  FDI 139
subsistence 322
substitutes
  competition from 82
  pharmaceutical industry 83
Subway 17
Sudan
  Muslim law in 263
suicide
  cultural attitudes towards 159
sulfur hexafluoride
  emissions 355
Sumitomo Bank
  assets of 295
supervision
  lax contributing to financial crisis
    (2007/08) 298
suppliers 84–5
  as instigators of innovation 205
supply chain
  disruption 145
  globalization 97
  Marks and Spencer plan for 348
Supply Chain Relationships 204
supply shortages 146
Surinam
  Indians in 169
sustainability 318–9

sustainable development 346
  notion of 352
swaps
  development of 293
Sweden
  business tax 232
  contract law 272
  financial crisis 298
  GDP 39
  global competitiveness ranking 133
  health indicators 175
  migrants 16
  payment method 289
  poverty 174
  profit tax rates 233
  public expenditure 231
  social expenditure as percentage of
    GDP 174, 184
  tax-to-GDP ratio 232
swine flu pandemic 19
Switzerland
  agricultural subsidies 25
  global competitiveness ranking 133
  migrants 16
  payment method 289
  public expenditure 231
  ranking on Economic Freedom Index
    140
  risk associated with 147
  shadow economy 40
  social expenditure as percentage of
    GDP 184
SWOT analysis 105
synthetic materials
  development of 195

T

Taipei
  social expenditure as percentage of
    GDP 176
Taiwan 44
  effects of 1999 earthquake 97
  inequalities 172
  protection of infant industries in 55
  ranking on Economic Freedom Index
    140
Tajikistan
  importance of remittances from
    abroad to economy 11
Takeda Pharmaceutical
  R&D expenditure 202
takeovers
  effects of legal environment on 255
Tanzania 47
  cash and cheque-based economy 290
  economic growth 42
  effects of financial crisis on 302

tariff barriers 54
tariffs 50, 143
    as barrier to globalization 24–5
    definition 54
    GATT/WTO role in reducing 58
    lesser developed countires 107
Tata 127, 198
Tata Coffee 151
Tata Motors
    global environment of 10–1
tax avoidance 237
tax breaks 54
tax evasion 237
tax policy
    China using to restrict imports of car
        parts 107
    risk assessment 147
tax-to-GDP ratio 232
taxation 143, 232–3, 236–7
    commitment to low 173
    effect of global downturn on 233–4
    raising 107
technical assistance 334
technical standards 208
    as barrier to globalization 25–6
technological environment 113–4
    importance in assessing markets
        140–1
technological framework
    effect on business 192–217
technological readiness
    as one of WEF's 12 pillars of
        competitiveness 131
technology
    cycles of innovation 198–200
    definition 193–5
    as driver of globalization 20
    globalization and 22–3
    importance for business 206–13
    internationalization 192, 194
    problems in protecting 215–6
    protecting 214–6
    sources of advance 203–4
    threats and challenges from 211–3
telecommunications 240
    competition 211–2
    developing countries encourage to
        open markets in 238
    increased demand for 22
    liberalization of market 29
    mobile and fixed-line telephone
        competition 82
    regulation of 254
telecommunications infrastructure
    influencing company location 4
teleconferencing 114
Telefonaktiebolaget LM Ericsson
    patent applications 201

Telefonica 14
TeleGeography 114
telephony
    network 141
    reduction in cost of 22
temperature
    increase in 353
terrorism 97, 117, 145
    effects on insurance 97
    risk of 144
terrorist attacks of 9/11
    effects of 97, 111
Tesco 28, 124, 238
    expansion into Asia 45
    expansion into US 121
    import of garments from Bangladesh
        336
    tax avoidance 237
Thailand 4, 44
    avian flue 19
    AXA operations in 117
    power distance 163
    as source of cheap labour 125
    Tesco expands into 45
theocratic regimes 229–30
threats 325
    globalization 96–9
    MNCs 245
time
    cultural attitudes towards 159,
        170–1
    length of in patent application 215
timeshare 271
TNT 318
tobacco
    regulation of advertising and
        promotion 255
tobacco firms
    South East Asia 28
Togo
    child labour 329
Tokyo
    as major financial centre 297
    population of 181
    stock market fall 299
Tokyo Round
    GATT 57
Torquay Round
    GATT 57
tort law 265
torture
    freedom from 322
Toshiba 4
    technology battle with Sony 209
Total 13–4
tourism 16
Toyota Jidosha Kabushiki Kaisha
    patent applications 201

Toyota Motor Co 14, 28
    brand value 320
    involving stakeholders in innovation
        204
    R&D expenditure 202
trade
    control of 56–8
    dumping 56
    globalization 20
    interventions 54–62
    legislation governing 255
    reasons for 50–4
    types of 48
trade associations
    focus for lobbying 244
trade barriers 124
    factors influencing location 4
    governments removal of 21–2
    reducing 107
    removal 20, 28–9
trade concessions
    WTO principle for developing
        countries 57
trade embargos 55
trade marks
    laws protecting 214
trade regulations 143
trade secrets
    protection of 256
trade in services
    growth of 8
trade statistics
    importance in assessing markets 137
trade surplus 50
    China 95
trade union representation
    lack of in Bangladeshi garment
        industry 336
Trafigura
    waste dumping in Ivory Coast by 277,
        346–7
Tragedy of the Commons, The 345
training
    as one of WEF's 12 pillars of
        competitiveness 131
translators 169
transparency
    WTO principle 57
Transparency International Corruption
    Perception Index 93, 229, 249,
        325–6
transport
    as driver of globalization 20
    emissions by industry 355
    reduction in cost of 22
transport infrastructure 69, 240
    influencing company location 4
transportation costs 28

travel
    as driver of globalization 20
travel agents
    impact of internet on 213
travel industry
    impact of internet on 213
Travelocity 213
Treaty of Amsterdam (1997) 270
Treaty on the Functioning of the
        European Union
    Art.101 272
    Art.107 273
Treaty of Maastricht (1992) 270
Treaty of Nice (2001) 270
Treaty of Rome (1957) 270
triad
    economic blocks 7
Trinidad
    Indians in 169
'triple bottom line accounting' 349
trojans 98
Troubled Asset Relief Programme
        (TARP) 299
Tunisia 47
    risk associated with 147
Turkey 44
    attitude to women in the workplace 165
    financial crisis 285, 298
    GDP 39
    profit tax rates 233
    projected economic development 46
    public social expenditure as
        percentage of GDP 184
Twilight
    as example of media globalization 17
Twitter 218

U

Uganda
    Indians in 169
    reliance on agriculture 51
UK Trade and Investment
    as source of data on markets 135
Ukraine
    AXA operations in 116
    death rate 178
    dispute with Russia 6
uncertainty
    environmental policy 351
uncertainty avoidance
    as dimension of culture 162
UNCTAD 13
    as source of data on markets 135
unemployment 111, 174
    affected by financial crises 298
    definitional problems 135
    increase in 299

Uniform Commercial Code (United
        States) 266
Unilever 318
    sustainability and 318–9
    technology assisting growth of 207
Union Bank of Switzerland
    assets of 295
Union of European Railway Industries
        244
Union of Industrial and Employers
        Confederation of Europe (UNICE)
        244
unit trusts
    as example of private financial
        institution 287
unitary systems 230
United Arab Emirates (UAE)
    attempts to exercise jurisdiction over
        BlackBerry 222
United Kingdom 23, 44
    attitude to women in the workplace
        165
    banking in private hands 303
    banks taken into public ownership 299
    economic growth 42
    economy shrinkage 42
    exchange of personnel 247
    exports 9, 49
    favoured location for Japanese car
        companies 18
    FDI 124
    fertility rates 180
    GDP 39, 110
    growth in output 281
    imports 49
    Indians in 169
    industrial power of 44
    inflation 284
    intellectual property rights 270
    main traders of subprime securities
        based in 299
    migration 16, 179
    minimum wage 255
    nationalization of banks 240
    natural gas market 76
    payment method 289
    perception of companies in 316
    poverty 174
    profit tax rates 233
    projected economic development 46
    public social expenditure as
        percentage of GDP 184
    ranking on Economic Freedom Index
        140
    risk associated with 147
    skills shortages 16
    social expenditure as percentage of
        GDP 174

tax rises 234
    uncertainty avoidance 162
    urbanization 181
    welfare spending 173
United Nations Commission on
        International Trade (Unictral) 268
United Nations Convention Against
        Corruption (2003) 323
United Nations Convention on Contracts
        for the International Sale of Goods
        (1980) 266–7
United Nations Development
        Programme (UNDP) 41, 334
United Nations Environment
        Programme (UNEP) 350, 352–3
United Nations Framework Convention
        on Climate Change (UNFCCC) 352,
        356
United Nations Global Compact 322,
        347–8
    annual report 324
    principles 323
    weaknesses 324
United Nations International Trade
        Statistics Yearbook 137
United Nations (UN)
    membership as indicator of
        independence 226
United Nations World Commission on
        the Environment and Development
        (WCED) 351
United States 23, 44
    attitude to women in the workplace
        165
    ban on export of military equipment
        to Venezuela 55
    ban on export of satellites to China
        55
    banking in private hands 303
    banks taken into public ownership
        299
    business tax 232
    capital controls 25
    cartels 255
    common law system 260
    competition law 255
    controls on tobacco and alcohol
        advertising 255
    dispute over offshore gambling 268
    downturn in housing market 11
    economic growth 42
    economy shrinkage 42
    electronic payments 290
    embargo on trade with Cuba 55
    evolution of firms 52
    as example of federal system 230
    exports 8–9, 49, 51
    failure to ratify Kyoto Protocol 115

United States (*cont'd*)
favoured location for Japanese car companies 18
fertility rates 180
foreign aid 25
GDP 39, 110
global competitiveness ranking 133
growth in output 281
health care reforms 243
health indicators 175
illegal immigration 16
imports 49
Indians in 169
individualism 162
industrial power of 44
inequalities 172
inflation 284
insurers' opposition to health care reforms 245
liberalization of civil aviation market 238
losing position as dominant world power 106
major FDI recipient 12
market access 58
market maturity 5
masculinity 162
migration 179
minimum wage 255
nationalization of banks 240
payment method 289
political donations 96, 247
population 178
poverty 174
power distance 163
profit tax rates 233
projected economic development 46
public expenditure 231
public social expenditure as percentage of GDP 184
ranking on Economic Freedom Index 140
reporting standards 256
risk associated with 147
shadow economy 40
signatory to Copenhagen accord 361
skills shortages 16
social democratic model 174
social expenditure as percentage of GDP 174
spending power of Hispanic population 179
state intervention in banking system 303
stock market crash (1987) 110
tax cuts 233
tax-to-GDP ratio 232
Tesco expands into 121

uncertainty avoidance 162
Uniform Commercial Code 266
universities 18
welfare spending 173
Universal Declaration of Human Rights (1948) 323
universities
involvement in R&D 203
partnerships with foreign colleges 18
recruitment of students from abroad 18
Upjohn
merger with Pharmacia 158
Uppsala model 122–3
uprisings
risk of 144
urbanization 111, 181–2
Uruguay Round
GATT 57
US International Trade Commission 269
utilities
regulation of 254

V

value
money as measure of 282
values 26, 111
VAT 232
Vatican City
as example of theocratic regime 230
vehicle emissions 255
Venezuela
energy reserves 106
GDP 39
masculinity 162
US ban on export of military equipment to 55
venture capital companies 287
Vernon, Raymond [1913–99] 51–2
vertical mergers 77
video conferencing 114
Vietnam 44, 228
avian flu 19
economic growth 42
first case to WTO 56
GDP 39
joins WTO 56, 59
perceived as low cost country 6
social expenditure as percentage of GDP 176
violence 325
cultural attitudes towards 159
viruses 98
Visa International 289–90
visas 143

Vodafone Group 13–4, 93, 318
VOIP (voice over internet protocol) system 114
Volkswagen Group 14, 28
affected by Japanese earthquake 6
move into Eastern Europe 124–5
price discrimination by 69
R&D expenditure 202
volunteering
increase in 334
voting power
EU 224

W

Wachovia
takeover by Wells Fargo 299
Wal-Mart 14, 96, 124, 208, 238
brownfield investment by 15
import of garments from Bangladesh 336
War on Want
report on Bangladeshi garment industry 336
wars 145
risk of 144
Washington Mutual 307
waste
Marks and Spencer plan for 348
waste disposal 346–7
waste management
cost of 347
emissions by industry 355
water
regulation of 254
water supply 141
water-food-energy nexus 147
Waterstones
impact of Amazon on 213
wealth
creation 50
distribution 111
inequalities in 172
storage of 282
weapons of mass destruction 148
weather
risk of extreme events 357
Web 2.0 197–8, 217–8
welfare provision 111
welfare services
state involvement in provision of 240
welfare states 172–3
Wells Fargo & Co Industrial
assets of 295
takes over Wachovia 299
West Africa
cocoa production 329–30

West African Potato Value Chain
    Development Project 333
Western Europe 51
    cultural attitudes towards time 170
    liberal democracy 226
    perceived incidence of corruption 326
    universities 18
whaling
    attempt to develop global response to
    350
wholly owned subsidiaries
    as part of internationalization process
    123
Wikileaks 275
Windows Phone
    Nokia's adoption of 31–2
women
    attitudes to in workplace 165
    cultural attitudes towards 159
    empowerment of 331
women trafficking 19
work permits 143
working conditions 111
    Bangladeshi garment industry 336
    standard of living and 316

World Bank 38, 42–4, 47, 107, 138, 147,
    282, 324
    role of 286
    as source of data on markets 134
World Business Council for Sustainable
    Development 318, 343
World Economic Forum
    as source of data on markets 131–3
World Economic Outlook database 38
World Food programme 318
World Intellectual Property
    Organization (WIPO) 214
World Meteorological Office 352
world population 177
World Trade Organization (WTO) 9,
    20–1, 107, 270, 346
    background to 56
    China joins 22, 36
    first case brought by Vietnam 56
    GATT compared 58
    international arbitration by 268–9
    negotiator role 238
    regulation by 238
    as source of data on markets 135
    Vietnam joins 56, 59

World War II
    effects of 44
Worldcom 317
Worldwatch Institute 348
worms 98
WPP 88
WWF 318

Y

Yahoo 317
YouTube 218

Z

Zara
    import of garments from Bangladesh
    336
Zenithoptimedia 88
Zennstrom, Niklas 114
Zero sum game 51
Zimbabwe 16
    intellectual property rights 270
    risk associated with 147
    shadow economy 40